Afrikaner Political Thought: Analysis and Documents

Volume One: 1780–1850

PERSPECTIVES ON SOUTHERN AFRICA

1 The Autobiography of an Unknown South African, by Naboth Mokgatle (1971)

2 Modernizing Racial Domination: *South Africa's Political Dynamics,* by Heribert Adam (1971)

3 The Rise of African Nationalism in South Africa: *The African National Congress, 1912–1952,* by Peter Walshe (1971)

4 Tales from Southern Africa, by A.C. Jordan (1973)

5 Lesotho 1970: *An African Coup Under the Microscope,* by B.M. Khaketla (1972)

6 Towards an African Literature: *The Emergence of Literary Form in Xhosa,* by A.C. Jordan (1972)

7 Law, Order, and Liberty in South Africa, by A.S. Mathews (1972)

8 Swaziland: *The Dynamics of Political Modernization,* by Christian P. Potholm (1972)

9 The South West Africa/Namibia Dispute: *Documents and Scholarly Writings on the Controversy Between South Africa and the United Nations,* by John Dugard (1973)

10 Confrontation and Accommodation in Southern Africa: *The Limits of Independence,* by Kenneth W. Grundy (1973)

11 The Rise of Afrikanerdom: *Power, Apartheid, and the Afrikaner Civil Religion,* by T. Dunbar Moodie (1975)

12 Justice in South Africa, by Albie Sachs (1973)

13 Afrikaner Politics in South Africa, 1934–1948, by Newell M. Stultz (1974)

14 Crown and Charter: *The Early Years of the British South Africa Company,* by John S. Galbraith (1975)

15 Politics of Zambia, edited by William Tordoff (1975)

16 Corporate Power in an African State: *The Political Impact of Multinational Mining Companies in Zambia,* by Richard Sklar (1975)

17 Change in Contemporary South Africa, edited by Leonard Thompson and Jeffrey Butler (1975)

18 The Tradition of Resistance in Mozambique: *The Zambesi Valley, 1850–1921,* by Allen F. Isaacman (1976)

19 Black Power in South Africa: *The Evolution of an Ideology,* by Gail Gerhart (1978)

20 Black Heart: *Gore-Brown and the Politics of Multiracial Zambia,* by Robert I. Rotberg (1977)

21 The Black Homelands of South Africa: *The Political and Economic Development of Bophuthatswana and KwaZulu,* by Jeffrey Butler, Robert I. Rotberg, and John Adams (1977)

22 Afrikaner Political Thought: *Analysis and Documents* (3 vols.), by André du Toit and Hermann Giliomee (*Volume 1: 1780–1850,* 1983)

23 Angola Under the Portuguese: *The Myth and the Reality,* by Gerald Bender (1978)

24 Land and Racial Domination in Rhodesia, by Robin Palmer (1977)

25 The Roots of Rural Poverty in Central and Southern Africa, edited by Robin Palmer and Neil Parsons (1977)

26 The Soul of Mbira: *Music and Traditions of the Shona People of Zimbabwe,* by Paul Berliner (1978)

27 The Darker Reaches of Government: *Access to Information About Public Administration in England, the United States, and South Africa,* by Anthony S. Mathews (1979)

28 The Rise and Fall of the South African Peasantry, by Colin Bundy (1979)

29 South Africa: *Time Running Out.* The Report of the Study Commission on U.S. Policy Toward Southern Africa (1981)

30 The Revolt of the Hereros, by Jon M. Bridgman (1981)

31 The White Tribe of Africa: *South Africa in Perspective,* by David Harrison (1982)

32 The House of Phalo: *A History of the Xhosa People in the Days of Their Independence,* by J.B. Peires (1982)

33 Soldiers Without Politics: *Blacks in the South African Armed Forces,* by Kenneth W. Grundy (1983)

34 Education, Race, and Social Change in South Africa, by John A. Marcum (1982)

Afrikaner Political Thought

Analysis and Documents

VOLUME ONE: 1780–1850

ANDRÉ DU TOIT AND HERMANN GILIOMEE

Perspectives on Southern Africa, 22

UNIVERSITY OF CALIFORNIA PRESS
BERKELEY · LOS ANGELES · LONDON

University of California Press, Berkeley and Los Angeles

University of California Press, Ltd., London, England

First published in 1983 by David Philip, Publisher (Pty) Ltd., Cape Town, South Africa

Library of Congress Cataloging in Publication Data

Du Toit, André.
Afrikaner political thought.
(Perspectives on Southern Africa; 22)
Bibliography: p.
Includes index.
Contents: vol. 1. 1780–1850.
1. Afrikaners–Politics and government. 2. South Africa–Politics and government. 3. Afrikaners–Ethnic identity. I. Giliomee, Hermann Buhr, 1938– . II. Title. III. Series.
DT888.D8 1983 968 82-40090
ISBN 0-520-04319-7

Printed in South Africa

Contents

Preface

This book has been a considerable time in the making. The idea of a short volume on Afrikaner political thinking from its beginning to the present day was first mooted in the autumn of 1973 by William McClung of the University of California Press. A proper source-book and authoritative survey of themes and trends was clearly needed, but it would also necessitate a new departure in the settled ways of South African historiography. The initial idea thus resulted in a collaborative effort between historian and political philosopher, Hermann Giliomee and André du Toit. To start with we bravely made short lists of the twenty or thirty major documents covering the period 1775 to 1975. But the project soon became an historical education for the political philosopher, and the historian too found that he had to revise many of his earlier views and methodological habits. We both found that we had gravely underestimated the wealth and variety of source material, and we soon became convinced of the need to make this available to a wider public in an accessible form. In this way the proposed short volume expanded into a substantial three-volume project, and the initial deadline of 1975 had to be extended to 1979 for this first volume covering the period 1775 to 1850. As a result of several delays publication was held up until the second half of 1982, but in the mean time we have been making good progress on the second volume covering the period 1850 to 1910. If all goes well this should be published in somewhat less than the almost ten-year time-span required for the first volume.

The nature of the book has required a rather complicated working procedure and sharing of responsibilities. Though we could draw on Hermann Giliomee's archival researches in the particular periods and areas where he had done specialized work, it was clearly beyond the bounds of possibility to review *all* the potentially relevant primary documents over the period as a whole. We did make a number of special sorties into particularly promising or important areas, but on the whole we have had to rely on the existing secondary literature (and on published sources of various kinds). Our usual procedure was to identify promising leads in historical monographs and then to trace the primary documents in archival holdings (or in contemporary publications). We did not stick to a fixed set of preconceived ideas about the themes or categories to be dealt with, but allowed ourselves to be guided by the internal coherence and articulation of the material itself. In this way the present volume has come to be organized around five major thematic areas. In some cases an emergent theme stretched beyond the chronological boundary of this volume. Thus the chapters 'Language and nationality 1820–75' and 'Church, religion and equality 1825–90', which in part belong to the period covered by this volume, will be included in volume two. The theme 'Obligation, rights and resistance' will be dealt with in a single chapter covering the period 1775 to 1915, and will also appear in the next volume.

Once the documents for publication had been selected they had to be edited and, in many cases, translated. Wherever translations were extant we made use of these, and in such cases retained the linguistic usages of the originals (allowing ourselves only some minor modernizations of spelling and punctuation). In other cases we had to provide the translations ourselves. In this we were ably assisted by Andrew Nash, as research assistant, who did sterling work in translating documents that in the original eighteenth-century Dutch officialese or in the barely literate scrawls of Afrikaner frontiersmen were sometimes hardly intelligible. In some cases we found that only *after* the major effort of translation did we ourselves fully understand the original text!

We had the opportunity to discuss these themes and documents at a series of interdisciplinary and graduate seminars at Stellenbosch University from 1975 on, and benefited from the comments of Johan Degenaar, Dian Joubert, John Shingler, Johan Graaff, Jan Visagie, Andrew Nash and others. At the beginning of 1978 André du Toit presented a course of lectures on aspects of this material at the Summer School of the University of Cape Town, and received very helpful comments from Ken Hughes and Christopher Saunders, amongst others. When it came to the preparation of the final drafts our rough division of labour was that Hermann Giliomee took the major responsibility for the historical introduction and André du Toit for the theoretical and philosophical aspects. The first drafts for the interpretative introductions to each of the five thematic chapters were written by André du Toit, but we constantly exchanged ideas and criticized each other's drafts, so that the final product is indeed a book for which we can both assume full responsibility.

During the ten years of working on the book we have accumulated many intellectual debts. Apart from those already mentioned it is also a pleasure to extend our thanks to some of those who helped us in various ways. There were several historians who did not consider as secret possessions the prizes they had discovered in the salt mines of the archives and who were happy to share them with us or to show us the road to elusive documents. In particular we wish to thank Gerrit Schutte of the Vrije Universiteit in Amsterdam for his help with the Swellengrebel documents, Chris Venter of the University of Stellenbosch for the Gideon Joubert documents, Robert Ross in Leiden, and Ben Liebenberg of the University of South Africa. More generally Johan Degenaar in Stellenbosch and Leonard Thompson of Yale University always provided encouragement and inspiration.

The final draft of this first volume took shape at Yale University in the first half of 1978 when we were both associated with the Southern African Research Program. We wish to thank the National Endowment for the Humanities and the Ford Foundation, which funded SARP, as it became affectionately known. Hermann Giliomee was awarded a fellowship with SARP in 1977–8 and André du Toit in 1981. At the beginning of 1978 a special grant from the Ford Foundation, resulting from the personal interest of Bill Carmichael and Sheila Avrin MacLean in this project, made it possible for André du Toit to join SARP as an associate fellow. Some of the draft chapters were discussed during the SARP weekly seminars or on a Thursday evening working session. Both these occasions were attended in 1977–8 by the SARP directors Leonard Thompson, William Foltz and Stanley Greenberg (Jeffrey Butler was absent on study leave in South Africa) and SARP fellows Heribert Adam, Newell Stultz and Richard Ralston, as well as Anthony Delius, an associate fellow. We wish to thank the SARP directors and fellows for many stimulating discussions and memorable evenings. In September and October 1978 André du Toit had the opportunity to do research in the Netherlands as a guest of the Vrije Universiteit of Amsterdam and to clarify various aspects of the eighteenth-century background to the Cape

Patriot movement. On this occasion Harry Brinkman, Gerrit Schutte and Bob Goudzwaard provided valuable guidance and comment.

We also wish to thank the University of Stellenbosch for providing funding for research assistance to this project in 1976 and 1977, and for granting leave of absence to Hermann Giliomee in 1977–8 and to André du Toit in 1981.

Our wives Maretha and Annette could share in only some of the incidental insights and discoveries of this project, but wittingly or unwittingly had to carry many of the burdens. Sometimes they rightly had little faith that the book would ever see the light of day, but without them it certainly would never have done so.

This volume is dedicated to the memory of André Hugo, who before his early and untimely death did so much to give our generation a sense of the possible integrity of Afrikaner political thinking.

André du Toit, Hermann Giliomee
Stellenbosch, September 1982

Introduction

The political hegemony of Afrikaner nationalism is a central product of South African history; it is also fraught with consequences for the future. Afrikaner ascendancy in South Africa may have come about only in the recent past, and it may increasingly be challenged from within the country as well as from without, but, for the time being, it is a fact, and Afrikaner political thinking a matter of consequence. At the very least, the racial policies and ideologies of the Nationalist regime are liable to be major focal points in the evolving pattern of conflict as long as the regime remains in power. Thus a central issue in recent literature on South Africa has been whether this ruling group is swayed by rigid ideological considerations and a 'laager mentality', or guided by a more pragmatic perception of class and ethnic interests. Usually such discussions are conducted within too narrow a framework and with too limited a time span. There is a great temptation to take the short view and to concentrate only on the current situation and its immediate antecedents. Thus the many studies which have dealt with the current scene or have focused on the policies and ideologies of the past three decades have been able to shed only a limited amount of light.

A broader perspective should also take account of the material contribution of capitalist development to the growth and entrenchment of the racial and class order of the apartheid society. Still, the importance of the ideology, belief system and policies of the ruling group can hardly be overestimated. Here again it is only by taking the longer view that a reliable perspective can be gained. As in other societies, the intellectual origins of current modes of political thinking, like the historical origins of the social and political structures themselves, go back far and deep. A number of specific historical factors have contributed to the formation of Afrikaner political thinking: the conditions of colonial settlement, the heritage of a labour and social order resulting from a slave society, the lack of institutional controls on a shifting frontier that endured for generations, the lessons of more than a century's political and military struggles against imperial rule, the traumatic transformation of a traditional farming community through urbanization and industrialization. Without regard to the significance of such historical factors underlying the intellectual structure of Afrikaner political thinking, the nuances and import of more recent shifts of policy and opinion can hardly be assessed either accurately or reliably. Yet there are almost no serious and systematic studies in this field. Various conceptions of 'Afrikaner political thinking' and its history frequently figure in the literature; but more often than not these are stereotypes deriving from a very restricted range of sources and showing little regard for the actual historical context. It is the purpose of the present work to fill this important gap both by making available the primary material itself and by carefully analyzing and interpreting the main themes, issues and trends in the history of Afrikaner political thinking.

Our concern with the long view of Afrikaner political thinking is also inspired by our own interest in the future of the Afrikaners, as distinct from the fate of Afrikaner nationalism. For the present Afrikaner nationalism is in the ascendant and Nationalist policies and racial ideologies have become closely identified with the very conception of 'the Afrikaner'. But not all Afrikaners are, or were, nationalists. In fact, the emergence and rise of Afrikaner nationalism is relatively recent; it is not identical with, but only a stage of, Afrikaner political history. Current Afrikaner thinking itself is varied, and some Afrikaners are increasingly concerned with the moral and political consequences of Afrikaner nationalism in a divided and unequal society. Merely to raise questions concerning the position of the Afrikaners in a South Africa where they no longer have a monopoly of political power is, to many Afrikaners, fraught with the threats of loss of culture and identity. To some extent the possibility of a non-nationalist Afrikaner future is tied up with a recovery of the chequered career of earlier Afrikaner political history, with its varied forms, different modes, and complex and interlocking traditions of thought. Thus, a rigorous and critical history of Afrikaner political thinking from its origins is necessary if the recent Afrikaner nationalist phase is to appear to Afrikaners themselves in its proper historical context and dimensions.

Given the hold of nationalist models on recent Afrikaner thinking, it follows that the project of tracing the roots, scope and major trends of Afrikaner political thought may serve two different, though related, ends.

First there is the enterprise of showing the growth of the nationalist strand in Afrikaner thinking in its historical context and through its main stages since the awakening of an Afrikaner nationalist consciousness around 1880. With all the attention given to its more recent manifestations, it remains a remarkable fact that the intellectual history of this particular tradition of Afrikaner political thinking is an almost unknown quantity, to current exponents of Afrikaner nationalism themselves as much as to outside observers. There are, of course, numerous works dealing with the general political history of Afrikaner nationalism, including biographies of the major leaders and spokesmen as well as a number of institutional histories.[1] But the intellectual history of Afrikaner nationalist thinking and its relation to other traditions of Afrikaner thinking remains to be charted. Afrikaner nationalist thinkers have tended to be so much involved in the vanguard of their cultural and political movement that they have concerned themselves with the past only in so far as it served their nationalist concerns, and have shown little interest in a critical investigation of the genesis and function of Afrikaner nationalist thinking itself. To outside observers the early stage of Afrikaner nationalist thinking is a rather obscure and relatively inaccessible phenomenon. In recent years some important research has been done on certain specific aspects and stages, such as Dunbar Moodie's work on the civil religion of Afrikaner nationalism in the 1930s[2] and Irving Hexham's study of the origins of 'Christian Nationalism' in the early decades of the present century.[3] However, other and equally important aspects and stages of the history of Afrikaner nationalist thinking have not yet been dealt with adequately or critically at all. Many gaps thus remain to be filled before any reliable survey of the growth of even the nationalist strand in Afrikaner thinking will be possible. This will, in part, be the task of the later volumes of the present work, but it falls outside the scope of this first volume, which deals with the history of Afrikaner political thinking until the middle of the nineteenth century, and ends well before the first serious stirrings of Afrikaner nationalist thinking.

The present volume is primarily concerned with the second and related end of a general history of Afrikaner political thinking, namely the recovery, and the placing in its historical context, of the (pre-nationalist) origins and formation of Afrikaner political thinking. This enterprise is faced with two sets of difficulties.

First there are the difficulties inherent in any pioneering venture in intellectual history. Little or nothing has been done about the history of political thinking in South Africa, nor indeed about any kind of intellectual history. This does not mean that there is no intellectual history, or that historians have ignored the relevant documents: they have dealt with them in other terms. History is one of the oldest-established academic disciplines in South Africa, and in the last hundred years historians have done much primary research and have also produced a considerable body of general analyses and interpretations. From the general historian's point of view, however, political thinking is just one aspect of the history of earlier periods. South African historians have accordingly utilized the recorded evidence of the political thinking of earlier periods along with whatever other kinds of historical data they could find. But little or no attempt has been made to investigate these texts as intellectual constructions in their own right. Of course, every such intellectual construction is itself an historical phenomenon embedded in the concerns of a particular time and place. It is precisely the task of a history of political thinking to trace the growth and transformation of different political viewpoints in interaction with changing historical contexts. In the present case of early Afrikaner political thinking this involves the dual task of establishing and making available the primary documents themselves, and of providing the necessary critical analyses and interpretations of the main themes, issues and traditions.

The second set of difficulties concerns the many stereotypes, political myths, and unhistorical images which abound in the absence of any adequate and critical intellectual history. In particular, early Afrikaner history has to be recovered from the nationalist interpretation which later generations have imposed on it. One of the main ingredients of nationalism is a strong consciousness of the nation's history. In the case of Afrikaner nationalism the growth of national consciousness has proceeded in tandem with the origins and growth of Afrikaner historiography, which, especially in its early stages, was aimed more at furthering a popular historical consciousness than at disinterested research.[4] Though the nationalist movement itself only dated from the 1870s, it soon, in terms of the logic of nationalist thinking, laid claim to the history of other and different epochs as well. Typically, Afrikaner nationalism views the entire history of the Afrikaners in its own image with earlier events becoming simply the proto-history of the Afrikaner 'nation'. This leads to a double distortion of Afrikaner history. On the one hand, everything that does not fit the nationalist paradigm is excised from Afrikaner history as such. Since Afrikaner history is defined in nationalist terms, that which does not fit the latter does not belong to the former. On the other hand, the meaning of earlier events and thinking in Afrikaner history ante-dating the rise of nationalism is systematically recast in nationalist vein. In this way a comprehensive version of Afrikaner history has gained currency, in which an undocumented popular mythology is combined with essentially unhistorical interpretations of specific data by historians, to fashion the meaning of Afrikaner history in nationalist terms. It is no easy task to recover the political thinking of pre-nationalist Afrikaners in their own terms, particularly if, like the Trekker leaders, they have become part of the nationalist pantheon or, like Stockenström, are mainly known as a foil for nationalist constructions.

The difficulty is increased by the paradox that many of these myths and stereotypes concerning Afrikaner history are reinforced by the orthodoxies of liberal historiography in South Africa. Much the same uncritical assumptions, though often with negative rather than positive evaluations, tend to be shared by both schools of thought. Thus latterday Afrikaner nationalist notions of being a chosen people, with a proud Calvinist lineage, are mirrored in the pervasive use in liberal historiography of 'primitive Calvinism' as an explanatory concept for the origin of distinctively Afrikaner political and racial ideas and ideologies.[5] In neither case is the attempt adequately made to spell out the characteristic features and contents of such a 'Calvinistic' tradition in Afrikaner political thinking, or to provide the necessary detailed documentary evidence for its existence before the late nineteenth century. Similarly, the Afrikaner nationalist focus on the trekboer and the Trekker as the archetypal figures of Afrikaner history, the preoccupation with the Great Trek as its central event, and the assumption that the northern republics with their wars of independence are its political centre of gravity, have been reinforced in liberal historiography by the concern with the 'frontier tradition' as the source of traditional race attitudes, stereotypes and policies.[6] In important respects these liberal orthodoxies have recently been challenged by a new generation of revisionist historians, but they remain influential when it comes to the assessment of early Afrikaner political thinking. Both liberal and nationalist historians continue to focus on the frontiersman and the Trekker as the typical Afrikaners, but have trouble in considering Afrikaner officials, such as Stockenström, or lawyers, such as Truter, or townsmen, as Afrikaners at all.

Though to some extent the historian will, at least conceptually and politically, always remain a child of his own time and not of the historical period that he is studying, he can become increasingly self-conscious about the differences between conceptual frameworks then and now, and deliberately set out to test the interpretation of earlier thinking for retrospective distortions. The present work will not primarily be concerned with a systematic critique of these received orthodoxies, but will rather seek to develop substantive interpretations of major themes closely based on the material provided in the primary texts themselves. Therefore we shall not, for example, set out to provide a deliberate dismantling of the myth of 'primitive Calvinism' as a seminal source of early Afrikaner political thinking. By implication, however, the absence of such a theme from the primary material as well as from our own analyses should be taken as serious and deliberate. The onus is on those who wish to reinstate this and similar received stereotypes to provide the necessary primary documentation and analysis.

In the rest of this introduction we shall deal with the following problems relevant to a history of Afrikaner political thinking in general, and to this first volume in particular:

1 The need for such a history, given the state of the existing literature, to take the form of an extensive *source publication* of relevant primary documents, as well as an analysis and interpretation of major themes. (Arising from this some account must be given of the principles and criteria governing such a source publication for the purposes of a history of political thinking.)

2 The conception of, and the criteria for, *political thinking* which govern the selection of documents and thus the specific focus of the entire project. (In this connection some account must be given of the way in which the investigation of political thinking is related to its historical context.)

3 The difference between a history of the *political thinking* of a group and a history of its *social attitudes*, particularly in the case of a group like the Afrikaners who did not constitute a complete and differentiated society but only a segment of a plural society under alien rule.

4 The question of who is, or is not, to count as *an Afrikaner* for the purposes of a

history of Afrikaner political thinking during the eighteenth and nineteenth centuries, and which criteria might best be used to decide this.

5 The *emergence* of Afrikaner political thinking and the historical period from which its history might justifiably be said to commence.

Principles and criteria for a source publication

Perhaps the major impediment in the way of a reinterpretation of the history of Afrikaner political thinking, and even simply of an adequate knowledge of its central ideas and traditions, is the relative unavailability of the primary sources and seminal texts. The core of Afrikaner political thinking is not to be found in a small number of well-known works of eminent thinkers. It has to be traced through and collated from a wide variety of incidental publications, speeches, pamphlets, essays, articles in newspapers and journals, many of which have long since been out of print, and, of course, archival material, particularly for the earlier periods. The few attempts which have been made to remedy this situation mostly deal with more recent periods and have either been inadequate and unrepresentative, e.g. Brookes's 'documentary study' *Apartheid*,[7] or they have had a different focus from that of the history of Afrikaner political ideas as such. Thus the otherwise very useful source book provided by Krüger's *South African Parties and Policies 1910–1960*[8] is primarily concerned with party-political policies, and also casts its net wider than Afrikaner politics only.

For earlier periods a wide range of general source books, archival publications and official records exists. Scattered through these many volumes is much important and relevant material for a history of Afrikaner political thinking, but by and large it is accessible only to the specialist and professional historian. Where attempts have been made to gather material more specifically relevant to general *political* history, these, such as Eybers's *Select Constitutional Documents Illustrating South African History 1795–1910*,[9] tend to have a very narrow focus on constitutional issues and official records. As far as the history of Afrikaner political thinking itself is concerned, Scholtz's ambitious ten-volume survey, published under the title of *The Development of the Political Thought of the Afrikaner*,[10] should have more than filled the gaps, but unfortunately the work suffers from a number of serious defects. In the first place the work is not, despite its title, a history of Afrikaner political thinking, but a general history of the Afrikaners with particular emphasis on selected cultural and political aspects. Rather than attempting a proper intellectual history, Scholtz has assimilated this to general political and cultural history. Whatever the merits or shortcomings of this wide-ranging project may be, it has to be judged according to the regular standards and criteria of the historian's craft. From the point of view of the history of political thinking, its main importance lies in the extent to which it reproduces or paraphrases a fair amount of relevant primary documents. Even so, Scholtz does not allow the primary texts to speak for themselves, but weaves them into a narrative designed to prove and illustrate a few (remarkably unhistorical) theses of his own concerning the central themes of Afrikaner political history.

The basic enterprise of making available an adequate range of relevant primary documents—which must of necessity precede any attempt at analysis and interpretation—thus still has to be done. The historian of Afrikaner political thinking cannot even start from an established canon of classic texts which need only to be made available. A few exceptional documents, such as Retief's *Manifesto*, have of course gained generally recognized 'classic' status. But the greater part of the primary material must first be rescued from its relative historical obscurity: an extensive source publication of the key primary documents is necessary.

Such a source publication of primary documents for the purposes of a history of political thinking must differ from standard historical source publications in at least two important ways. First, it is a basic aim of historical source publications to publish the full and unadulterated text of the original primary documents. Though various kinds of practical considerations might influence the actual selection of the general area or range of documents to be published, a source publication will lose its value for historians if the printed documents cannot be relied on to provide a full and faithful rendering of the original. It is on this principle that editorial scope and responsibility are based. Obviously this cannot apply in the same way to a source publication providing material for the history of political thinking. Here it is a primary editorial task to edit *selectively*, to reproduce those parts of the primary text that would bring out the author's political concepts, opinions and arguments clearly and coherently, and to remove all irrelevant and extraneous matter if that is necessary. The task of editing extends to that of translation, in the widest sense, from the often impenetrable style of eighteenth-century Dutch officialese to the ungrammatical formulations of semi-literate frontiersmen. Even apart from considerations of space and cost, it would defeat the purposes of such an enterprise to publish primary documents *in toto* if the actual political thought contained therein were to remain buried or obscured. Often the political thinking in the primary texts can only be salvaged by careful editing and translation. Nevertheless, the selective editing of the texts inevitable in this kind of source publication cannot involve any omission or suppression of their intellectual content to suit the preferences, interpretations or theories of the historian himself. There is of course an inevitable risk that controversial historical interpretations will unconsciously be projected through the very process of selecting and editing the primary source material. However, the publication of selections from historical documents illustrating a particular thesis or providing support for a certain interpretation of the history of Afrikaner political thinking would be self-defeating as an attempt to provide a reliable basis for the history of political thinking. The criterion for such a source publication must be faithfulness to the intellectual constructions contained in the historical material itself. Only if all aspects of the political concepts, opinions and arguments in the primary documents are reproduced, and only if a wide and representative range of primary documents is provided, would there be an adequate basis for subsequent analysis and interpretation. It is thus a test of adequacy for such a source publication whether it can provide the material in terms of which rival analyses and interpretations can be constructed, contested and refuted.

Secondly, a standard historical source publication is normally organized on strictly chronological principles. For purposes of analysis and interpretation the historian might select data relevant to a particular theme or hypothesis, but that is not the task of a source publication. In the case of a history of political thinking, however, a strictly chronological presentation of primary documents has disadvantages as well as advantages. Chronological juxtaposition will sometimes help to bring out the substantive links between such diverse political concerns as the agitation for representative government, the implementation of imperial slave ordinances, the outcry about vagrancy, Afrikaans–English ethnic animosities and some minor cases of civil disobedience in the Cape around 1830. More often it will serve to confuse and obscure the intellectual continuities, the patterns persisting over considerable periods of time, or to soften the contrasts between different views on similar issues when these reemerge after some appreciable time, as the Cape franchise question did in the 1880s after being dormant since the early 1850s. Individual texts form part of larger discussions; they address themselves to a common range of topics or problems; and they utilize shared conceptual resources or intellectual paradigms. An adequate source publication for the purposes of a history of political thinking should bring out this internal thematic articulation of the historical material. Obviously such a thematic structure may not be imposed through an arbitrary manipulation of selected texts according to some preconceived set of categories on the part of the historian. Once again the criterion must be fidelity to the intellectual structure of the historical material itself. It will be clear that such a labour of intellectual and historical reconstruction can never lay claim to either complete objectivity or total exhaustiveness. However, scrupulous attention to the actual topics and issues to which men addressed their political thinking in the specific historical contexts, and a critical investigation of the kind of views and arguments which they *could* advance in terms of the available intellectual resources and within the prevailing conceptual frameworks,[11] should ensure a degree of overall historical veracity.

A source publication structured in this way will, we hope, be better suited to serve the aim of the historian of ideas, which must be to deal not with mere snippets of thought taken out of context but to uncover the pervasive and embracing conceptual frameworks of earlier thinking. This can be done only by analyzing comprehensive intellectual constructions, and here the ways of the historian of ideas and the 'regular' historian often tend to part. The latter generally does not feel obliged to deal with earlier political thinking in its own terms as an intellectual construction. Of course he might make good use of expressions of the political thinking of the time, particularly if it can help to explain certain political developments or actions. But normally he is not interested in it for its own sake. Typically he will use a specific quote or remark, often only a single sentence or phrase, in support of or as illustration to some particular point he is making.

In this connection it is instructive, for example, to refer to the work of F. A. van Jaarsveld, who, perhaps more than any other historian of the Afrikaner, did so much to broaden the range of historical investigation to include intellectual themes as well. In his important work on the awakening of Afrikaner nationalism[12] Van Jaarsveld builds his case throughout by means of judicious quotes from contemporary documents. Almost without exception, however, these consist of fragments of sentences, or mere phrases, at most one or two sentences. Because they are drawn from such a wide range of documents Van Jaarsveld can construct a powerful case in support of his theses. On the other hand, this method inevitably runs the risk of taking historical contents out of their original intellectual contexts, and it allows considerable scope for manipulation of such material in terms of preconceived ideas, thus furthering the perpetuation of historical myths and stereotypes. This work of Van Jaarsveld probably suffers less in this respect than do other similar works, but the point remains that nowhere does he attempt an extended analysis of the intellectual structure of a substantive historical document or series of documents in order to interpret its main statements or concepts in terms of the contemporary intellectual context. He probably, and quite rightly, does not see this as his task. But this is the proper task of the historian of ideas.

The task of the historian of ideas extends beyond source publication to analysis and interpretation. The primary documents may often speak for themselves, but in many cases they do so in foreign or forgotten conceptual accents and idioms, which create considerable problems of communication. Often the main concepts and arguments are largely implicit, or relate to aspects and features of the historical context in ways that are not immediately apparent from the texts themselves. It may sometimes happen that certain basic political views remain unstated and that certain crucial assumptions are not articulated, for the simple reason that in the prevailing intellectual climate they went quite unchallenged and did not need to be asserted. For all these reasons each of the sections of primary documents on a particular thematic topic in this volume is accompanied by an analytic essay, which is to serve both as an introduction to the texts themselves and as a critical and constructive interpretation based on them. Together these various thematic essays will constitute the first steps towards an adequate critical history of Afrikaner political thinking.

What counts as political thinking?

The historian doing primary research for a history of political thinking over a period of some two hundred years is confronted with an enormous amount of material: in archives and collections of private papers, in newspapers, pamphlets, books. How does one decide what counts as relevant instances of *Afrikaner political thinking*? This must be done in terms of some criterion of what counts, in general, as historically significant political thinking. This is a complex matter involving notions of 'thinking' and 'the political', each of which must briefly be dealt with.

Many documents of great historical significance obviously do not directly express or reflect any kind of systematic thinking. Conversely, some documents that might have been of little or dubious value to regular historians are of great interest to the historian of ideas. A history of political thinking need not be confined to academic writing in the grand manner of the classics of the history of political theory. There were no Afrikaner political philosophers who could remotely be compared with a Locke or a Rousseau, but this does not mean that there was no political thinking of consequence. What, then, might qualify as political thinking in the relevant sense? In taking their stands on the issues of the day ordinary men may make use of generalized arguments; they may invoke certain shared moral principles; and they may develop their views in terms of a more or less coherent set of general concepts. In so far as this happens we are dealing with instances of political *thinking*. Such thinking is often closely connected with immediate practical concerns, for example with advocacy of a certain course of public action or with the defence of particular rights and interests. At the same time it may also involve some more general mode of justification or legitimation. Even if it does not begin to approach the explicit and systematic rationality of abstract political theory, political thinking at this practical level exhibits a mode of intelligibility that can be investigated in its own right. What key concepts are used? What moral principles are invoked and for what purposes? What kind of arguments are used, and with what sort of 'logic'? In answering questions such as these we begin to sketch the intellectual lineaments of particular political viewpoints. Selecting the primary documents that would qualify for a history of political thinking thus goes hand in hand with their analysis and interpretation.

The problematic notion of what is 'political' cannot be dealt with here at any length. It must suffice to say that while we cannot narrowly restrict it to constitutional issues and 'party political' affairs only, it would also be self-defeating to extend it to include what might be termed the 'internal politics' of the family, a club, or a church. It must be taken in its main sense as relating to the 'politics' of larger and diverse societies: to the conflicts between diverse groups sharing a common territory in their competition for scarce resources, their canvassing of rival interests, their attempts to gain ascendancy, and their attempts to maintain or reform a certain labour or legal or social order. The crucial aspect of such 'political' activity, as Bernard Crick amongst others has emphasized, is therefore to be found in its *public* character.[13] Political thinking, likewise, will bear on public concerns rather than merely reflect private preoccupations. A history of political thinking will therefore be concerned with documents bearing on a range of public issues, and above all with those which are of an argumentative nature rather than of a merely illustrative character. It is with this dual criterion in mind that the selection of documents in this volume has taken place.

For a proper understanding of the political thinking contained in these primary documents, it is essential that they be viewed within the correct historical context. All political thought is closely bound up with the historical contexts which gave rise to it, though in the case of the great classics of the history of political thought this may be less apparent. The intellectual constructions of a Plato, Hobbes or Hegel are so rich and complex that they invite a purely philosophical interpretation: formalizing the relations between ideas, spelling out the systematic coherence or otherwise of a body of thought, investigating the logical connections between, or the conceptual incompatibility of, different abstract political theories. In such a rarefied philosophical atmosphere the historical context easily disappears from view: we appear to move in an autonomous dimension of the history of ideas that at best runs parallel to concrete political history. Recently the methodological credentials of this approach have been questioned by a new generation of philosophers, who have urged the case for a more rigorously *historical* treatment of the received canon of political thought.[14]

The importance of the historical context is even greater when we deal with the development of political thinking at the much less abstract and theoretical level that is characteristic of early Afrikaner political thinking. The history of Afrikaner political thought not only includes no one of the intellectual stature of a Locke or a Rousseau, there is also no canon of *minor* theorists constituting a local tradition of political theory (the Afrikaner equivalents of a John Winthrop, a Madison or a Jefferson in the history of American political thought). The simple fact is that until well into the twentieth century there simply were *no* Afrikaner political theorists of any kind—good, bad, or indifferent. Afrikaner political thinking, such as it was, was the product of ordinary men of affairs, not of philosophers or academically trained theorists. As a result there is even less of a case for a quasi-autonomous history of Afrikaner political ideas that would proceed on some abstract plane of thought. Emergent Afrikaner political thinking was embedded in the concrete historical situation of an isolated and struggling colonial society based on slavery. The Afrikaner community was a segment of an evolving plural society stratified along the (often coinciding) lines of race, legal status, ethnicity and class. The issues absorbing the political and intellectual energies of Afrikaner spokesmen were provided by the specific historical contexts of settlement, conquest and frontier conflict, of slavery and imperial reform. Their political thinking was concerned with such contextual issues, and seldom, or only by implication, with any of the central and 'perennial issues' of classical political theory. A history of Afrikaner political thinking must therefore be based squarely on a careful analysis of these specific and changing local historical contexts. Every volume of this project is accordingly provided with a general introductory chapter setting out the structural context and developments for the period concerned.

The close connection of political thinking with the structural historical context may throw further light on the criteria applicable to the selection of primary documents for a history of political thinking. It is not merely that historically significant events and issues, allied to structural changes, tend to call forth serious political thinking, and that the historian of ideas may thus use his knowledge of the historical context as a guide to the topics of contemporary political thought. There is also the question whether we can conceive of serious political thinking about events and issues that are in themselves historically insignificant or, conversely, whether historically significant developments can be of such a nature that they do not, in principle, call for political thinking at all.

A case in point is the contrast between two of the earliest incidents in Afrikaner intellectual history: the Drakenstein church conflict of the 1770s and the Cape Patriot movement of the 1780s. Both events stirred strong feelings in important sections of the community over a protracted period of time, but whereas the Cape Patriot movement was concerned with basic issues, the Drakenstein conflict dealt only with personal and parochial disputes. This contrast is reflected in the character of the *thinking* itself. If we analyse the host of Drakenstein documents with respect to the terms in which they represented the issues, and the kind of arguments which they used, then it becomes clear that, whatever personal significance the participants themselves attached to these issues, they conceived the conflict in such a way that its significance appeared only in petty and parochial terms, that it was not in any way linked with the more general concerns of a wider society, and that their concerns could not be shared by people in other places and other times. In short, their thinking was not *political* in the sense we have given to this term. The Cape Patriots, on the other hand, were also motivated by grievances against particular individuals, but they cast their complaints in terms of general notions of oppression and arbitrary rule; they linked their protests with basic policy issues regarding the East India Company's monopolistic practices and the rights of officials and burghers; and they attempted to show that their own cause could be defended in terms of the colony's very 'constitution', and was of consequence to its future development and prosperity. In all these respects their writings exhibit the essential features of *political* thinking, in pointing to public concerns rather than private preoccupations, to common interests rather than particular grievances, and to shared values and principles rather than idiosyncratic commitments.

In practice these features can be taken as defining the criteria for the historian of political thinking, in his task of selecting primary documents from the vast amount of available material. Faced with any particular set of documents, we disqualified those which contain merely random 'grumbling' or are only of private and particular interest. Consider a few examples drawn from the same general area of trekboer complaints in the early nineteenth century. The archives contain large numbers of letters, petitions and reports from individual farmers and fieldcornets relating complaints about cattle thefts, labour problems and the like. The overwhelming majority are concerned with particular claims; they express personal grievances, or are of local significance only and hence cannot be considered to contain political thinking of any kind. They can safely be left aside. Sometimes we also find, often in conjunction with some dramatic event such as a frontier war affecting the fortunes of large numbers of different people in various places, that attempts are made to aggregate these particular complaints and grievances into collective terms. A good example of this is Piet Retief's letter to Duncan Campbell, the Civil Commissioner for Albany, on 11 April 1836, following the frontier war of 1835.[15] However, this letter is still a fairly random list of collective grievances, and contains only the most rudimentary kind of political thinking. As a primary document relevant to a history of political thinking it is at best a borderline case. This becomes clear if we compare it with other documents, like, say, Retief's own *Manifesto* of a year later, J. N. Boshof's letter of 17 February 1839 published in the *Grahamstown Journal,* or the letter of the Natal Volksraad to Governor Napier of 21 February 1842.[16] Substantially the same grievances reappear in each case but they are integrated into a more coherent intellectual framework and related to more general political concepts and shared moral principles. They are clear evidence of the emergence of a fairly coherent body of political thinking among the Trekkers and must therefore be included in any collection of primary documents of this kind.

The application of these criteria cannot always be so straightforward, particularly in those early periods where the available historical documentation itself is inadequate or deficient. Thus we know, for example, that according to all accounts the 'Black Circuit' of 1812 and the outcome of the Slachtersnek Rebellion had, at the time, a momentous impact on the political thinking of frontier colonists on law, order and equality. Yet it has proved almost impossible to find any contemporary articulation of this in the primary documents that would count as political thinking according to the criteria just discussed. On reflection this is quite understandable. Before the introduction of newspapers and journals in the Cape in the 1820s and the subsequent securing of the freedom of the press, there did not exist any easily accessible forum for public discussion or any protection for the expression of dissenting views. The archival records in this regard consist almost entirely of official papers or correspondence to and from government officials, hardly the place for forthright rejections of government policy. It is alleged that a 'Book of Grievances' dating back to the time of the Slachtersnek Rebellion was among Piet Retief's private papers,[17] but short of recovering sources of this kind the historian is forced to read between the lines of the existing material for evidence of political views.

In order to fill such gaps some documents which are of an illustrative rather than an argumentative character, and very much on the borderline as instances of political thinking, have had to be included.

Political thinking and representative social attitudes

A history of Afrikaner political thinking must be differentiated from a history of Afrikaner social attitudes. This follows from the specific nature of political thinking itself, as discussed above, and it also follows from the peculiar social composition and historical circumstances of the Afrikaners as a group. There can be no doubt that an historical investigation of the origins and changing patterns of Afrikaner social attitudes would be an important undertaking. But the object and procedures of such a history would be very different from that of a history of Afrikaner political thinking. It would be directed at the discovery of the whole range and variety of attitudes and conceptions of the *average* member of the Afrikaner group at various times, and thus with that area which we have been designating as that of private rather than public concerns. The appropriate question with regard to each historical finding or generalization concerning such Afrikaner social attitudes at a given time would be one related to its representativeness. Accordingly the relevant kind of primary documents would also be those which are of an *illustrative*, rather than an argumentative nature. The guiding principle in the utilization of such historical data would be whether there are good reasons to believe that these documented expressions of particular social attitudes reflected attitudes which were widely shared. For that reason the writings of those few early Afrikaners who held official positions or who had received a better formal education (the landdrosts, ministers, lawyers, journalists and teachers) would not be considered as representative of the social attitudes of the early Afrikaner community at large. But, conversely, the observations of experienced travellers provide a major source of relevant historical data, often of greater value for such a social history than that contained in local primary documents.

The case is very different when it comes to a history of Afrikaner political thinking. It cannot and should not be assumed that there is a simple and direct relation between the set of social attitudes prevalent among a certain group at a given time and the political thinking articulated by its spokesmen and leaders. Obviously there will be some connection. But the dominant considerations determining the debate of public concerns may be very different from the realities of private or even communal life. The nature of the larger political environment, and more specifically the conceptual framework of public policy, are of crucial importance here. In a culturally homogeneous and self-contained society developing into a nation state, on the British or the French model, the connections between widely held social attitudes and the framework of public policy may be relatively straightforward. It is different where, as in a colonial situation, the ruling powers are a culturally alien group imposing their own moral values as the basis of public policy. Similarly in a plural society it is the interplay between the claims and interests of conflicting groups which constitute the main area of public concern. To any group which does not constitute a complete and differentiated society with an autonomous internal political life, this larger political environment must be as important to the articulation of its political thinking as the social attitudes prevalent within that group itself—and the connections between such social attitudes and political thinking will not be straightforward.

This is particularly true of a group like the Afrikaners who throughout their early history never constituted a 'total' community, a self-contained Afrikaner society. Their political context, at first, was that of a colony, and later their republics remained part of the sphere of interest of an imperial great power. Socially the Afrikaners were a segment of an evolving plural society, and moreover one that was, so to speak, stunted at both ends. At the one end the eighteenth-century farmers and trekboers were dependent on slaves and Khoikhoi servants for their manual labour, and even the Trekkers did not establish self-sufficient Afrikaner settlements in the interior but took along their 'Coloured' servants or employed local blacks. At the other end, and even more important for the present argument, until nearly the end of the nineteenth century the Afrikaner community in the interior lacked the institutional resources to produce their own intellectual leaders. Thus, not only were the Afrikaners as a group often governed by foreign powers and administered by culturally alien officials, but (if the rural Afrikaners in the interior are taken as the reference group) their clergymen, teachers, lawyers, journalists and merchants all had to be recruited from 'outside'. And so we have Brand and Burgers being imported as leaders of the northern republics, Scottish ministers constituting the core establishment of the Dutch Reformed Church, Dutchmen running the civil service of the South African Republic, and so on.

In these circumstances early Afrikaner political thinking cannot be expected to constitute an accurate reflection of the social attitudes prevailing among the average members of this group at that time. In the first place those exceptional individuals who had had a better formal education and a wider experience of public affairs, and who for those reasons alone were already unrepresentative, contributed a disproportionate share to the body of such political thinking. The social backgrounds and personal careers even of a Piet Retief, Gerrit Maritz or J. N. Boshof were hardly representative of the average members of the Trekker communities, and in the case of the officials and leaders based and bred in the Cape, from Van Ryneveld, Truter and Stockenström to Brand and Burgers, the distance was of course much greater still. But even more important, in the second place, those public concerns which constituted the subject matter of political thinking were not so much the internal affairs of the

Afrikaner community but rather their relations with the colonial authorities (and later the imperial powers) and with the other major groups in the evolving plural society. At the very least the colonists had to address their petitions, claims and grievances to the established authorities, and to cast these in a form that would be acceptable to them. If it is true that the political thinking of Andries Stockenström in advocating the equality of all classes before the law, embodied in Ordinance No. 50,-[18] certainly cannot be regarded as representative of Afrikaner attitudes in the 1820s, then it is equally true that the petitions on this matter of, for example, the inhabitants of Agter-Renosterberg in 1829[19] were not a direct articulation of their personal feelings and attitudes either, but an attempt to present their interests and claims in a 'diplomatic' form that would be acceptable to the colonial authorities in terms of avowed public policy. Even Retief's *Manifesto* was not a straightforward articulation of whatever moved the hearts and minds of the average frontiersman and Trekker, but a political statement, carefully calculated to anticipate official strictures, to rebut missionary and philanthropic criticisms, and to win the sympathies of a wider colonial audience.

The above is worth spelling out. Owing both to the peculiar social composition of the Afrikaners as a group and to the nature of their political environment, early Afrikaner political thinking could not be a direct expression of the set of social attitudes prevailing within this group itself. Such political thinking as there was arose in interaction with the ruling powers of a colonial world and with the contending forces of widely differing groups in an evolving plural society; it was not the expression of the internal intellectual history of a self-contained community maturing in isolation. The issues of public policy and the affairs of public concern to which it had to address itself related, on the whole, to that wider and more complex social and political world in which the Afrikaners found themselves, and very much less to the internal affairs of the Afrikaner community itself. The spokesmen and leaders who set out to deal with these matters were, typically, those relatively unrepresentative individuals who had received a better education and who had a wider and more varied experience than the average Afrikaner of the time; and the intellectual framework and conceptual idiom in which they expressed themselves were, more often than not, derived and adapted from the political attitudes and patterns of the wider world surrounding them. Thus the idea of a pure and untainted Afrikaner tradition of political thinking arising from within the Afrikaner group itself and expressing the reality of Afrikaner experience and Afrikaner social attitudes is untenable: it is a sociological impossibility, a conceptual confusion and a political mystification.

That this idea has nevertheless been so influential in much Afrikaner historiography (even if more implicitly assumed than explicitly acknowledged) is of course due to the Afrikaner nationalist ideology retrospectively imposed on all Afrikaner political history. It is central to nationalist thinking to regard the Afrikaners as a *nation*, and hence as a complete and self-contained society whose political traditions cannot have any external origins but must arise from within itself. Afrikaner political thinking must be the direct expression of Afrikaner social attitudes. In fact, the actual nature and history of early Afrikaner political thinking—the political thinking, that is, not of a nation but of a minority group and a segment of plural society in a colonial situation—is of a very different order altogether and must be reconstructed afresh in this historical and political context.

Who counts as an Afrikaner?

How do we determine who counts as an Afrikaner for the purposes of a history of

Afrikaner political thinking in the eighteenth and nineteenth centuries? This is a difficult as well as a controversial question. During the course of the eighteenth century the original Dutch, German and French settlers came to constitute the core of the early Afrikaner community, to which individuals of diverse backgrounds were readily assimilated. The boundaries of the emergent Afrikaner group remained vague and fluctuating. Though a core membership of the Afrikaner group may readily be established throughout this period, it is in many cases very difficult to know whether or not a particular individual should be counted as an Afrikaner or not. The problem becomes particularly acute when we come to the history of Afrikaner political thinking. For the reasons explained in the previous section such political thinking as there was could hardly be the product of the average member of the group. It had to be provided by those exceptional individuals who had had a better formal education and greater public experience. The Afrikaner communities in the interior, in particular, lacked the institutional resources to produce the intellectual leaders with these qualifications. Thus it often came about that clergymen, teachers, journalists and administrators had to be 'imported' from the Cape or even from Europe, and within a short time these relative strangers would appear as the main spokesmen for local views and interests.

However, there are definite limits beyond which Afrikaner membership cannot be extended. Thus even in the time of Company rule a clear division has to be made between the settled colonists, on the one hand, and the European-born or transient Company officials on the other hand. From the early nineteenth century a distinctive British community, with stronger institutional resources, also grew up, based in the Eastern Cape and Natal as well as in towns throughout the sub-continent. Even in Bloemfontein and Pretoria some of the leading citizens from the earliest days cannot be regarded as members of the Afrikaner group. To avoid arbitrary inclusion or exclusion it is clearly necessary to devise a more or less consistent set of criteria.

It is not possible to set up a simple and objective test of who is to count as an Afrikaner throughout the whole period under survey. Five different factors are relevant (which, on their own, are either inadequate or invite complications).

1 The use of Afrikaans as a home language would be central to any contemporary definition of who is an Afrikaner, but this is of course not easily applicable to earlier periods. Even apart from the long transitional period in which Dutch remained the official and public language it is, for example, well known that many Afrikaners used English for social purposes round the turn of the previous century due to their educational background at the time.

2 The facts of terminological usage and self-conception are not a sure guide.[20] The term 'Afrikaner' has been used, at various times, to refer to: certain groups of indigenous peoples; locally born (white) colonists; colonists of mainly Dutch descent to the exclusion of other groups; anyone, whether Afrikaans- or English-speaking, who identifies with South African interests. Similarly, the forebears of contemporary Afrikaners have, at various times, conceived of and referred to themselves as, *inter alia*, 'Christians', 'colonists', 'inhabitants', 'emigrants', 'Boers' and 'South Africans', as well as 'Afrikaners'. It is therefore only occasionally possible or relevant to ask whether, at the time, a particular individual considered himself literally as an 'Afrikaner' or not.

3 Questions of descent and kinship, though a main factor in determining the core membership of the Afrikaner group, are of little help in the many borderline cases. Race as such cannot be an absolute criterion. Genealogical researches have estab-

lished that blacks contributed to the composition of even the core Afrikaner ancestry by at least seven per cent.[21] Considerations of descent and kinship, in a wider sense, cannot be applied to the large number of first generation cases (and if pressed would rule out even a Dr Verwoerd!). Even for later generations they cannot be conclusive, given the phenomenon of anglicization. Thus the Cloetes, for example, one of the oldest and best-established Afrikaner families at the Cape, intermarried and associated with members of the new British regime to such an extent that the transition from the Afrikaner to the British community might be located within the careers of Henry and Josiah Cloete themselves.

4 Considerations of communal and institutional association are often, as in the above case of the Cloetes, of decisive significance. In the eighteenth century whites could be identified either as settled colonists or as temporary, European-born Company officials. Some locally-born individuals also served as officials, but their strongest ties of kinship and interest were with the colonists. Some individuals joined the ranks of the colonists by leaving Company service. Certainly by the middle of the nineteenth century, when Afrikaner and British communities existed side by side, each with its own distinctive religious and cultural organizations, its newspapers and later its separate political organizations and aspirations, it is of particular significance to our problem to know with which of these rival sets of institutions any particular individual tended to associate. Where immigrants like H. T. Bührman in the Transvaal, or Carl Borckenhagen, the outspoken editor of the Free State paper *De Express*, or Dr Changuion in the Cape, associated themselves fully with the Afrikaner community and its institutions rather than with their British counterparts, it must be difficult to deny their claims to a place in the history of Afrikaner political thinking, even if they were born, bred and educated in Europe. Church leaders constitute an especially problematic category. On the one hand, the minister of the Dutch Reformed congregation held a position of great prominence and influence in the Afrikaner community. On the other hand, until the middle of the nineteenth century he was, with very few exceptions, not born and bred as a member of that community. A Dutch clergyman coming to a South African congregation in the eighteenth century came with a different social, cultural and educational background from that of the average member of his congregation. It is well known that in the early nineteenth century many Dutch Reformed clergymen were recruited from Scotland, so much so that by the 1830s they constituted a majority in the Cape Synod. Many of them later completely assimilated with the Afrikaner community, but other cases are far from straightforward. An example here is Dr Andrew Murray, a second generation Dutch Reformed minister and easily the dominant Afrikaner church leader in the latter part of the nineteenth century. There can be no doubt of his influence on Afrikaner cultural life in general, yet in some respects he never wholly assimilated with the Afrikaner community and deliberately associated himself instead with Anglo-saxon cultural norms and institutions.

5 With this we come to political and ideological definitions of who is to count as an Afrikaner. It is characteristic of Afrikaner nationalist thinking to stress, above all, such politically charged definitions of Afrikaner membership. Those who did not subscribe to Afrikaner nationalist views and norms are defined as not really Afrikaners. It is a basic assumption of the present study that we cannot start with some preconceived notion of Afrikaner political thought and disqualify whatever does not agree with that. Rather we should, conversely, investigate whatever Afrikaners produced that might count as political thinking. Individual figures like Maynier, Stockenström, Lord De Villiers, Jan Hofmeyr (Jr) or Abraham Fischer may or may not be

counted as Afrikaners, but they cannot be included or excluded *because* they held certain political views which are not supposed to be 'Afrikaner views'. If individual Afrikaners at times held views very different from that of the majority, then it is a fact that those views were exceptional and perhaps controversial, but it does not thereby remove them from the history of Afrikaner political thinking. Particularly hard cases occur where political controversies involve some of the criteria for Afrikaner membership itself. Thus at the time of the first Afrikaans language movement around 1875 three distinct positions in cultural politics can be distinguished among Afrikaners of the time: those, like S. J. du Toit, who promoted Afrikaans as the language of the future; those, like Onze Jan Hofmeyr, who stood by Dutch as the official language; and those, like Chief Justice De Villiers, who opted for English. Each of these individuals came from impeccable Afrikaner backgrounds and they took different stands on a public issue that faced Afrikaners generally. De Villiers cannot be considered not an Afrikaner simply because of this political stand, and indeed his public choice for English at that juncture, with the reasons he gave for this choice, constitute a significant contribution to Afrikaner political thinking on the general theme of language and nationality. At the same time such a political stand carries with it consequences for a continuing association with English institutions and cultural norms, and De Villiers himself did become progressively anglicized. Perhaps a distinction might be made between anglicization as a deliberate political choice of some Afrikaners at certain times, and hence part of Afrikaner political history, as against the anglicized products of the next generation who usually cannot be considered any longer members of the Afrikaner group at all.

Some general conclusions may be derived from the above discussion. First, though it may be true that the core membership of the Afrikaner group is determined essentially in ethnic terms it should also be recognized that when it comes to political thinking some non-core members figure largely. As such this is a reflection of the nature of the Afrikaner community itself, which was not a differentiated and intellectually self-sufficient society but continually had to recruit and absorb individuals for this purpose from outside the core group. It would be an illusory exercise to attempt any isolation of the political thinking of 'core Afrikaners', such as Piet Retief and D. F. Malan, as distinct from the contribution of relative new-comers or outsiders, such as Andrew Murray and Hendrik Verwoerd. Secondly, the credentials of individuals who did not belong to the core membership must be decided mainly in terms of communal and institutional association. In effect this means that both the individual's self-conception and the ascriptive judgements of his contemporaries must be taken into account. Even so, by the nature of the case, there will be many borderline cases which must be dealt with on an *ad hoc* basis.

Our own approach, accordingly, has been to avoid hard and fast definitions, to adopt inclusive rather than exclusive criteria, and to let contemporary historical evidence rather than retrospective judgements have the last word. In the Dutch period we include all settled colonists and locally born officials, except those of the very highest rank such as Governor Swellengrebel, as Afrikaners. First generation immigrants and officials leaving Company service would generally, but not necessarily, be included as well. In the British period all colonists and officials descended from and primarily associating with the Afrikaner rather than the local British community are included as Afrikaners. Newcomers are judged on the extent of their communal and institutional association. Anglicized Afrikaners of the first generation are regarded as borderline cases but the next generation is not included. As a rule borderline cases are included as contributions to the general discussion and debate, with reservations noted should this be necessary, unless there are specific reasons why they should be positively excluded.

Thus we have had no hesitation in including and giving prominence to figures like Van Ryneveld, Truter and Stockenström in the early nineteenth century. Though their credentials as Afrikaners are regarded as controversial and dubious by some Afrikaner nationalist historians, this is on the basis of retrospective political judgements rather than on that of contemporary historical evidence. Thus Stockenström, for example, regarded himself as belonging to the Afrikaner community and was so regarded by his contemporaries, both Afrikaner and non-Afrikaner.[22] We have also included documents by individuals born and educated in Europe, such as Dr Changuion or the Reverend Huet, where these are definite participant contributions to local discussions and debates, though noting the influence of their training and cultural background. In a single exceptional case we have included a document by Hendrik Swellengrebel, who, though born in the Cape, can certainly not be regarded as an Afrikaner but whose writing has a very close connection with the political problems and thinking of the Cape Patriots at the time, in so far as it was drafted in close consultation with them and was accepted and presented by them as reflecting their own views.

The emergence of Afrikaner political thinking

Any historical survey must start somewhere, but at what date should a history of Afrikaner political thinking start? A definite answer to this question can only be arbitrary. In the course of almost 150 years between Van Riebeeck's settlement of the Cape and the end of Company rule the new Afrikaner community took shape, and the self-conceptions and political categories of erstwhile Company servants, free Dutchmen at the Cape, or French refugees began to change. But the emergence of distinctively Afrikaner political thinking did not take place in a single and dramatic qualitative leap. We will not even attempt to pinpoint the earliest stirrings of Afrikaner political thinking. For our purposes it is sufficient that by 1780 the crucial transition certainly had taken place. Already in the previous decade evidence can be found on a variety of issues of what might be termed, without begging too many questions, Afrikaner political thinking. In Chapter One some account is given of why c. 1780 constituted an important turning-point in the political affairs of the Cape. Accordingly we have included primary documents from the 1770s on, but not from earlier periods.

Should the history of Afrikaner political thinking not rather start with, for example, the conflict of Adam Tas and other Cape freeburghers with Governor Willem Adriaan van der Stel and his official clique at the outset of the eighteenth century? And beyond that, what of the first freeburghers in the time of Van Riebeeck himself? We do not want to dispute the significance of such events for Afrikaner political history. Their significance clearly appears in at least two different contexts. First, the establishment of the first freeburghers and the conflict with Van der Stel obviously had far-reaching consequences for the course of early Cape history. These events were also centrally relevant to the later emergence of the Afrikaner community itself: the freeburghers soon developed separate interests and lifestyles from that of Company officials; locally-born colonists came increasingly to differ in outlook from European-born and transient Company servants; and the dramatic conflict with Van der Stel served to highlight these differences and to fuse together disparate groups of colonists such as the French refugees and the Dutch burghers. On any account these are important events in the proto-history of the Afrikaner group. Secondly, these same events later gained additional significance as, in retrospect, the 'founding events' of the new Afrikaner group. Already at the end of the eighteenth century we find that the Cape Patriots in their political struggles appealed to 'Father Van Riebeeck' and the constitutional rights he bestowed on the first freeburghers, and elevated Tas and Van der Heijden into heroic archetypes in the historical struggle against arbitrary rule.[23] (It is incidentally of some relevance that no similar historical consciousness centred on the Cape is evident from the writings of Tas himself.) Much later still Afrikaner nationalist historiography canonized the historical and political significance of these events in the nationalist reconstruction of the rise of the Afrikaner 'nation'.

But although the early freeburghers and Adam Tas are important to the protohistory of the Afrikaner, and retrospectively gained even greater stature as important 'founding' figures, it does not follow that their political thinking, such as it was, should be included in a history of Afrikaner political thinking. First, there is not much evidence of political thinking, in any serious sense, at all. In part this is a function of the scale and primitive stage of development of the Cape settlement at the time. In 1700 the population of the settlement, not counting slaves and Khoikhoi, was still less than two thousand. The Cape was little more than a victualling station and the dispute of the freeburghers with Van der Stel and his official clique centred on the question of who was to produce the supplies. Even in the writings of Tas, the most articulate of the burghers, there is little indication that they saw their grievances other than as those of a particular interest group pitted in unfair competition against another group of suppliers who had greater access to resources and power.

Secondly, they saw the conflict within a political framework provided by the Company, rather than in terms of a local polity. In the last resort the Netherlands was still seen as the fatherland of all concerned, and there was no conception of the Cape as a separate colony with its own history and political concerns. Tas, a recent arrival from the Netherlands, acted and wrote, quite as much as the officials, as a Dutchman in a Dutch outpost, and did not view himself as someone 'from the Cape', much less an Afrikaner. Presumably the outlook of locally-born freeburghers would have differed in some ways already, and much has been made of a few scattered phrases as evidence of a burgeoning Afrikaner self-conception, but at best these can be viewed only as possible transitional phenomena.[24]

Thirdly, there are considerations of continuity. Subsequent to the brief flare-up of political activity at the Cape around 1707, the rest of the eighteenth century saw little public dispute or discussion of any kind. Whatever changes were taking place in the political consciousness of the emerging Afrikaner group did not do so in public and visible ways. There are no direct links between the efforts and aims of Tas and his fellow freeburghers at the beginning of the eighteenth century and the political activities of Afrikaners several generations later, notwithstanding Tas's revival as a founding father and heroic figure of local history. From the 1780s on, however, there is an unbroken sequence of Afrikaner political thinking on a variety of themes and issues, and it is with this development that the present work will be concerned.

1 *The historical context 1780–1850*

In this introductory survey the historical context of early Afrikaner political thinking will be outlined. Rather than providing a mere summary of events we will describe the major structural factors and changes relevant to the development of Afrikaner political thought. The thematic content of the political thinking itself will be analyzed and interpreted in the introductions to the respective sections of selected texts.

Our survey of Afrikaner political thinking starts around the year 1780, more than a century after the initial colonial settlement. This starting-point is linked to a number of important political events such as the Cape Patriot movement and the first frontier wars with the Xhosa. These events themselves are evidence of important structural changes in the colonial situation. By 1780 the settlement at the Cape had completed the transformation from its origins as a refreshment post to a colonial society. By 1780, also, a number of severe structural constraints on colonial development were becoming manifest in a pervasive 'colonial crisis'. For a proper understanding of the origins of Afrikaner political thinking in the late eighteenth century a brief outline of this structural context is necessary.

From refreshment post to colony

In a number of basic ways the colonial settlement at the Cape in the late eighteenth century had come to differ from the original settlement: in the kind and extent of settlement, in the rationale for its existence, in the structure of administration, and in the composition of its population. In 1652 the Dutch East India Company had established an outpost on the southern tip of the African continent with limited objectives. The Cape was to be an easily defensible refreshment station serving its ships plying the oceans between Europe and Asia. Administratively it was to be kept as confined as possible to save expenses. Economically it was to exist for the Company's benefit and the interest of the mother country. It was to be a European outpost which would associate amiably with the 'wild nations' of the country for the sake of the cattle trade,[1] but otherwise would keep to itself and its task of becoming self-sufficient.

In the course of little more than a century these initial objectives were superseded by a number of structural changes in a way no one had foreseen in 1652. The small outpost on the Cape peninsula grew into a settlement which, by the end of the eighteenth century, covered some 110 000 square miles from the Atlantic coastline to the Fish River and from the Indian Ocean to the Nieuwveld mountains and Koussie (Buffalo) River in the north. This radically affected the structure of administration. During the first decades of European settlement Company officials manned a city council cum port authority which could exercise control over all its subjects. Towards the end of the eighteenth century the outpost had become an unwieldy colony in which much *de facto* power had slipped into the hands of burgher officers occupying key positions in the local administration. At the same time, the composition of the outpost's population was transformed. During the initial years the population consisted almost exclusively of the one hundred or so Europeans who had founded it. By 1800 this European community had become part of an extended plural society. In 1798 the colony had a population of 21 746 'Christians' (of whom roughly 20 000 were Europeans), 25 754 slaves and 14 447 Khoikhoi ('Hottentots'). Also within the limits of the colony were unknown numbers of Xhosa, Khoikhoi resisters and aboriginal hunters.

The most important agent of the transformation of the outpost was the community of freeburghers created in 1657 when the Company decided to abandon state production of commodities needed by the refreshment station. It was the freeburghers who made the colony self-sufficient in wheat and wine; it was they who penetrated beyond the coastal mountain ranges, rapidly extending the limits of the settlement by carving out extensive cattle farms. Ultimately it was they who thwarted any plans for close settlement.

Structural constraints on colonial development

By 1780 a 'colonial crisis', the product of some severe structural constraints in the development of the colony, had become manifest.

1 There were the constraints on agricultural and commercial development: chronic overproduction, a small market that was easily glutted and the monopolistic practices of the Company. Originally the Company did not intend settling more colonists at the Cape than was absolutely necessary for supplying the provisions it needed, thus creating a balance between supply and demand. Even with limited European immigration the balance was upset by a drastic increase in the productive capacity of the colonists owing to the introduction of slave and to a lesser extent Khoikhoi labour, as well as the fertility of the colonists who in each generation more than replaced themselves. On the other hand there was no concomitant increase in the opportunities to dispose of surplus produce. As a commercial enterprise the Company refused to abandon its prior claims in favour of the colonists' interests. The colonists were compelled to continue selling most of their produce to the Company at low official prices. Trade with the Cape Town public, bakeries or passing ships was restricted while private trade between the Cape and other areas was prohibited. As a result the colonists came to depend heavily on smuggling for profit. Wars abroad also brought periods of prosperity, owing to greater numbers of ships calling at the Cape. This was followed, however, by much longer spells of depression and inertia.

2 Company policy and the economy stunted the social stratification and diversification of the community of European settlers. At the one end the Company wished to monopolize all profitable activities, and thwarted the emergence of local industry at the Cape. Consequently, the colonists had few occupational opportunities. In Cape Town, where opportunities were greatest, they could become clerks in the service of the Company, or keep boarding houses and engage in trading activities, including smuggling. None was a source of great wealth, and in the circumstances only a very small upper class emerged. At the other end the social development of the European sector of society was also constrained by the availability of slave and Khoikhoi labour. With slaves providing manual and skilled labour and the Khoikhoi serving as herdsmen on the farms in the interior, the colonists produced no working or artisan class. Beyond Cape Town, farming and the frontier careers of hunting and bartering were virtually the only occupational opportunities. The colonists in the interior did not generate labour which could be employed, only farmers who wanted to

employ labour. Underlying this attitude was the aversion to manual work in the service of someone else, which came to be considered by the colonists as something which did not befit anyone with the status of freeman.

3 The third constraint related to the pattern of settlement of the interior,[2] and first came into prominence in the 1780s. From the 1700s overproduction of wheat and wine and the lack of careers stimulated the growth of cattle farming beyond the arable lands of the southwestern Cape. It was mainly the surplus colonists—the young, the poor and the landless—who participated in the rapid expansion of the pastoralists, called *trekboers*. The trekboers colonized the vast expanses of the interior by acquiring extensive loan farms from the government. In their subsistence farming land was utilized in a most extensive way, unimproved pasture being the basic resource, and dispossessed Khoikhoi, and later also Xhosa, the labour force. When an area became relatively more densely settled they or their sons simply expanded further. The trekboers entered their period of crisis in the 1780s when further expansion was blocked in the north by the arid regions and 'Bushmen', and in the east by Xhosa. As the days of abundant land came to an end, farms had to support an increasing number of colonists and cattle, causing a sharp decline in the quality of stock and pasture. Very few saw a solution in reducing the number of cattle (and cattle-owners) on a farm, improving the pasture and establishing stronger links with the Cape Town market. Besides, capital was scarce, transportation facilities were poor, a local market did not exist and Cape Town was far away. Despite their increasing numbers, few poor young men were prepared to enter the service of richer colonists or find a career outside farming. Two factors were behind this: the social stigma attached to manual labour in the service of others, and their expectation that new land would still be opened up beyond the frontier. For the time being, however, this expectation was not to be realized.

4 There were administrative and institutional constraints. By 1780 the colony of settlement was formally administered as if it were still a refreshment station extending not far beyond Cape Town. The administrative apparatus of the central government was basically the same as it had been a century before, and it was still located only in Cape Town. Colonists were compelled to travel vast distances to appear before the Court of Justice or the Matrimonial Court, or to transact business with the Orphan Chamber which administered estates. In the interior itself there was a lack of those socializing agencies which could instil respect for law and authority. The trekboer dispersal meant tenuous ties with schools and churches—in fact with organized state and society. The central government, travellers from Europe and prominent colonists commonly expressed the fear that this would lead to increasing lawlessness, moral degeneration and ultimately to the barbarization of the colonists. Their fears were not wholly unfounded. On a material plane there were indeed resemblances between the colonists and the indigenous people in their common struggle to adapt to the environment. However, unlike the *prazeros* of Mozambique who through intermarriage became absorbed in the indigenous population and shifted their loyalties there,[3] the trekboers remained loyal to their own culture and kinship network. They did not fall away from their church and they tried to give their children the rudiments of education. They were not averse to government control but set one condition: that they were supported in their struggle to establish domination over the 'heathen peoples'. However, the government in Cape Town had neither the wish nor the resources to do this, thus further undermining its authority in the eyes of the frontier communities, who basically had to find their own ways and means of maintaining themselves.

It was when trekboer expansion was temporarily halted after 1770 that the effects of these enduring social, economic and administrative constraints came to be felt most sharply throughout the colony. In their increasing conflicts with Xhosa and 'Bushmen', the frontiersmen had greater need of the resources of government and organized society to enable them to establish and maintain control. However, the economic crisis of the colony impinged most severely on the colonists of the southwestern Cape, and it was they who first articulated their sense of it.

The political troubles which started at the Cape in 1778 were not due simply to a growing awareness of the general decline in socio-economic conditions. The trigger was, in fact, a sharp increase in the level of business activity during the preceding decade, due mainly to a substantial increase in the number of foreign ships visiting the Cape. Being irregular, these visits had a destabilizing effect on the Cape economy. Years of frequent visits, shortages of supplies and high prices were followed by a sharp decrease of visits, surpluses and low prices. Used to stagnancy for so long, the colonists found it difficult to adapt to this volatile economy.

The increased volume of trade and the fluctuating market also stimulated new economic developments holding danger for those who did not adapt successfully. Firstly there was the rise of big producers who acquired the means to mature their wine and hoard their wheat in order to sell in favourable times. Their rise was cause for grave concern to other and lesser producers.[4] Secondly there was the rise of a small entrepreneurial class. Acting independently, or in partnership with some wealthy burghers, certain top Company officials began to dominate—monopolize, the colonists would say—the supply of passing ships, which had always been one of the most important sources of revenue for the burghers.

For the colonists of the southwestern Cape the 1770s, in fact, heralded new times: rising expectations followed by increased frustration, new opportunities but also greater hazards. Thus the foreign ships brought more prosperity but also growing irritation at the low official prices at which colonists were compelled to deliver part of their produce, and at the profiteering of the officials who bought it on behalf of the Company.

It was primarily these economic frustrations and grievances of the colonists which were articulated by the Cape Patriot movement,[5] which started in 1778 in the southwestern Cape. But the Patriot movement was much more than a protest against the venality of Company officials and their private trading. The thinking of the Patriots showed a more general political awareness, extending to a reflection on and a confrontation with the underlying structural crisis of colonial society. This was further stimulated by contacts with the Patriot movement in Holland, which relayed certain Enlightenment ideas to the Cape where they were adapted to local circumstances. In short, we have here the emergence of a measure of political thinking and consciousness which can rightly be called the origins of Afrikaner political thought.

Afrikaner political consciousness and white settler society

In speaking of an emerging Afrikaner political consciousness we must be careful not to ignore the social differences and economic cleavages existing among the late eighteenth-century white population at the Cape. From the outset Afrikaner political thinking was not the unified product of an undifferentiated group consciousness, but tended to reflect the social differences and economic cleavages which existed within the settler community at large. The most obvious differences were between the settled colonists of the southwestern Cape enjoying an established community life, and the isolated cattle farmers of the interior. Politically the dominant group was the former: a small, fairly prosperous bourgeoisie, consisting of top government officials (some born at the Cape), the monopolists and entrepreneurs of Cape Town, and a few wealthy wine and wheat farmers who lived on large farms resembling feudal manors, employed white foremen and owned many slaves. Despite some political differences this group had much in common and a high incidence of marriages between members of the 'best families' connected them even more closely. This group tended to produce the leaders of the local colonial society. Some, like the Van Ryneveld and Truters, climbed as far as sons of the colony could on the ladder of government service. Others, like the Berghs, led the Patriot movement against the government. For even within this small local bourgeoisie one has to differentiate between the Orangists and Patriots. The former supported the aristocratic party in the Netherlands, desired to maintain existing monopolies, privileges and differences in rank and status, and feared the rising tide of democracy in the Western world. The Patriots drew their inspiration from the struggle of the Dutch Patriotic movement against aristocratic privileges and for popular sovereignty. Their strategy was to mobilize the colonists of the southwestern Cape behind the banner of burgher rights and greater participation in the government of the Cape Colony. As the century drew to a close and the company began to disintegrate under the weight of its financial troubles, the Orangists looked to England and the Patriots to France for outside support.

The large majority of townsmen in Cape Town and the smaller farmers in the southwestern Cape managed to live respectably, but enjoyed no great wealth and were often in debt. They also had closer affinities with the trekboers of the interior. However, the high officials, and to a lesser extent the burgher gentry, considered the trekboers to be the worst part of the population: they were degenerate, uncultured and lazy, almost less civilized than the 'Hottentots'. These trekboers, in turn, held no high opinion of the dominant colonial group, whom they considered as vain and avaricious, oppressive of the common man.

Yet for all these internal differences the vast majority had one thing in common. In contrast to European-born Company officials and other expatriates, most whites by the end of the eighteenth century no longer considered themselves Dutchmen, Germans or Frenchmen. Their conception of being rooted in Africa, their only true home, found expression in the term 'Afrikaner' which now began to come into general usage. They also used various other terms when referring to themselves, such as 'Christian', 'inhabitant' *(ingezeetene)*, and 'colonist'; but 'Afrikaner' was to become the term that epitomized the concept of a settler society which had become indigenous. The term set them off both from expatriate officials, cosmopolitan sailors and travellers, and from the slaves in their midst. It was a term worthy of esteem, of pride; it reflected the self-conception of a group beginning to articulate its sense of its own social existence and political status.

This measure of independence of spirit was a prerequisite for the emergence of any indigenous political activity and thinking. The special strains and stresses which Cape society was undergoing at this period both gave rise to the Cape Patriot movement and also provided the object of its political activities and reflections. This meant that the Patriot movement differed significantly from any previous colonial development at the Cape. The struggle of the freeburghers against W. A. van der Stel and his official clique (1705–1707), while touching on some wider issues, was basically a refreshment post dispute which revolved around the question of who was to produce the supplies. It did not entail any real constitutional demands, and it did not rest on any coherent consciousness of the place and roots of this group in the settlement. In contrast, the Cape Patriots, as a consciously indigenous group, were vitally concerned not only with a number of specific grievances but also with the unsound constitution of the colony. In effect they were faced with a crisis of a special kind: how could the colonists survive as Europeans, as civilized men and as Christians in a colony in which the means of livelihood were so limited? This gave rise to such broader questions as the nature of their citizenship, their relationship with the government and their place in the colony's plural society. These were to become some of the main themes in the early development of Afrikaner political thought.

The issue of citizenship was of particular importance to the Cape Patriots. In chapter six we will trace how their thinking was influenced on the one hand by traditional notions of their historical civil rights as Dutch citizens and on the other hand by certain new Enlightenment ideas. On the whole, however, the direct impact of such Enlightenment ideas proved to be restricted to the Cape Patriots only, and even in their case it was adapted to express sectional interests in the prevailing colonial context rather than any doctrine of natural rights. Instead the enduring themes of the thinking of Afrikaners during the next decades and well into the nineteenth century were to be their place in the colony's plural society and the relation between that society and successive colonial governments. More than by Enlightenment ideas, Afrikaner political thought in the period 1780–1850 was thus to be shaped by the structure of Cape society and the changes and reforms brought about during the early decades of British rule. We will briefly deal with the major features of (1) the social and racial order; (2) slavery and the labour order; (3) the legal and political order. Following this sketch of the structure of Cape society at the end of the eighteenth century, the influence of British rules and reforms in the opening decades of the nineteenth century will be discussed.

The social and racial order

By the end of the eighteenth century Cape society was no longer in a state of flux; social and racial divisions had lost much of their earlier ambiguity and fluidity, and the various groups had been more firmly incorporated in the segmented order of a plural society.[6]

The political thinking of the emergent Afrikaner group would in time be profoundly affected by its position in this social and racial order. It was of particular significance that though this order had distinct class features, it ultimately was that of a caste society. The dominant class comprised officials and burghers holding the key positions of power, and owners of slaves and land who monopolized the instruments of production.[7] With very few exceptions this dominant class was white. At the bottom of this order were the servile class consisting of slaves who were joined by growing numbers of Khoikhoi and free black servants. There was also a mixed middle category of people: some were white but poor, some were black but free. Although all were poor they did not form a coherent class. The poor whites tended to identify strongly with the richer whites, insisting on the protection, respect and rights due to burghers. In general they received this from both the government, which, for example, issued a proclamation that no slave might jostle a European even if he was of the meanest rank, and from the colonists who, for example, accepted them as *bijwoners* (tenant farmers). But the free blacks of Cape Town, like the baptized *Bastaards* on the frontier, remained a small and depressed group increasingly subject to discriminatory practices as the eighteenth century drew to an end. In areas such as Cape Town and Namaqualand there was considerable miscegenation. However, children born of crossracial relationships tended to gravitate towards the black community, particularly if they were illegitimate.[8]

Afrikaners thus all belonged to the dominant caste or, if poor and landless themselves, tended to identify strongly with this group. Doubtless the existence of such a distinct and 'respectable' white community next to the poor, servile and unfree classes would prove to be a powerful formative influence on emergent Afrikaner political thinking. Yet the absence of explicitly racial categories in early Afrikaner self-conceptions points to a more complex and less reductive explanation. In fact the social and racial order must itself be seen in the context of both the labour order and the legal status order.

Slavery and the labour order

The peculiar racial labour order which developed at the Cape during the course of the eighteenth century is of great significance to much of the Afrikaner's later social and political history. This labour order was characterized by three central features: (1) the basic institution of slavery; (2) the servile, subordinate position of the majority of Khoikhoi and free blacks; and (3) the dominant position of the white group which did not itself produce a labour or artisan class but depended on slave and indigenous labour while attaching a racial stigma to manual labour in the service of others.

The significance of slavery cannot be confined to the immediate characteristics of the institution itself. Tannenbaum has perceptively observed that 'it is better to speak of slave society rather than of slavery, for the effects of the labor system—slave or free—permeate the entire social structure and influence all its ways. If we are to speak of slavery, we must do it in its larger setting, as a way of life for both master and slave, for both the economy and the culture, for the family and the community.'[9] In important respects this proved to be true of slavery and society at the Cape as well as the American South. As the number of slaves increased in the eighteenth century,[10] the effects of slavery began to permeate the entire social order. The belief became entrenched that the proper role of the white inhabitants was to be a land- and slave-owning élite, and that manual or even skilled labour in the service of someone else did not befit anyone with the status of freeman. Slavery, then, came to inform the meaning of other status groups as well. Cardozo remarked that in a slave society freedom is defined by slavery; thus everyone aspired to have slaves.[11] With respect to the Cape an observer remarked in 1743: 'Having imported slaves, every common or ordinary European becomes a gentleman and prefers to be served than to serve. . . . The majority of farmers in the Cape are not farmers in the real sense of the word . . . and many of them consider it a shame to work with their hands.'[12]

Slavery impinged on the fabric of social life in a number of further ways, both directly and indirectly. In denying slaves the right to marry, and by allowing slave families to be broken up and sold separately, Christian notions of the sanctity of family life were eroded. Pass regulations to police the movements of slaves set a precedent for controlling indigenous labour. In the final analysis slavery affected the colonists' basic sense of security. For the slaveholders of the southwestern Cape the enemy was not on the border but inside: a dangerous slave community plotting to seize what every colonist knew to be man's most valuable prize—liberty. Slavery thus was not merely the foundation on which the economy rested: its effects extended far beyond the actual slaves and slaveholders themselves. In a slave society, slavery is the basis of the whole social order.

Slavery as a labour system was subject to various statutes issued by the metropolitan authorities. In contrast, neither the metropolitan nor the Cape government concerned itself much with the employment of indigenous labour. This left a clear field for the colonists to establish their own practices of labour control. On the one hand they adopted some of the institutions of slavery, such as passes, to regulate the movement of the indigenous workers under their control. Other slave-related practices were extended. For instance, the so-called indenture system, under which the children of slave men and Khoikhoi women were apprenticed for a certain period, was often informally applied as well to Khoikhoi children whose fathers were not slaves. However, in some cases the frontier evoked different responses. When frontiersmen lacked the means to establish total control they had to induce Khoikhoi to stay in their service by providing some marginal advantage. The trekboers did not control their environment to the extent that they could simply coerce people to stay in their service. Although there were risks, unwilling labourers could always run away and settle beyond the frontier. In the frontier zone labour relations thus covered the full spectrum from a master-client relationship to serfdom. In a master-client relationship, more prevalent on the open frontier, there was always some *quid pro quo*: the master provided a measure of protection for his clients in more or less fair exchange for their services. As the frontier began to close this evolved into a paternalistic order where the master had to provide for, and dispense justice to, those under his control who had begun to lose much of their status as free agents and were bound by duty to work properly and obey their master's commands. Such paternalism could shade into more extreme forms of labour-oppression in which an adequate and docile labour force was ensured through extra-economic devices such as forcibly retaining the cattle and families of labourers who might want to abscond.

The legal and political order

The significance of the racial order as well as the labour order of Cape society must also be understood in relation to the administrative structure (or rather the lack of it, especially outside the capital), and to the hierarchy of legal status groups basic to the colony's political order. The wholly inadequate administrative apparatus that was surviving almost 150 years after the initial settlement of the Cape was due to the parsimonious policies of the Dutch East India Company and its unwillingness to administer the settlement as a colony rather than a mere refreshment station. Cape Town itself was fairly well policed and administered, but, beyond, the only centres of authority were the drostdys of Stellenbosch and Swellendam and, after 1786, Graaff-Reinet. As Van Ryneveld remarked in 1802 this constituted no more than a 'nominal police'.[13] The landdrosts, as the major officials appointed to these drostdys, had very little independent means for enforcing their authority. The landdrost in charge of Graaff-Reinet, a district roughly the size of Portugal, was assisted by a secretary and only four or five mounted police *(ordonnantie ruiters)*. To ensure compliance with the law he was forced to rely on the support of the local board of *heemraden* and in particular on the *veldwachtmeesters*, later called *veldkornetten* (field-cornets), appointed to the various divisions of the district. But these *heemraden* and field-cornets were colonists themselves, sharing the interests and values of their fellow colonists, on whose support they were indeed dependent. As a result the key role in local administration was played by men who often acted as agents of the colonists rather than of the colonial government. Thus the capacity of the state to impose some kind of law and order on the turbulent frontier society was minimal.

During its early period of formation from 1652 to c. 1720 it was the Company's distinctions among different legal status groups which initially structured Cape society. In law and in practice the colonial government consistently discriminated among four primary legal categories: Company servants, freeburghers, slaves and indigenous aliens. In effect this produced an hierarchical order with the two free groups of Company servants and freeburghers in a politically dominant position as against both slaves and the indigenous Khoikhoi classed as aliens. Company servants manned the central government, the freeburghers played a key role in local government. Though the Company servants always worried about maintaining their authority over the burghers, they needed the burghers as much as the burghers needed them. The community of freeburghers was founded by the Company in 1657 in order to make the Cape self-sufficient in wheat and wine; an offshoot of this agricultural community, the trekboers, made the colony self-sufficient in meat. To facilitate production the Company accorded the burghers special privileges: only they could hold land or exercise burgher rights like practising 'a burgher craft or occupation' (in practice this meant farming) or holding office as *heemraad*, field-cornet, etc. The burghers wanted to take these rights further. They assumed that they were entitled to receive special protection from the government and to have a privileged status above those of slaves and Khoikhoi. By contrast the status of slaves was, of course, one of complete legal subordination, while that of aliens, initially at least, would tend to exclude the Khoikhoi from any of the rights and privileges of regular subjects, such as recourse to the courts.

By 1780 these distinctions had become blurred in some important respects without, however, upsetting the basic features of the hierarchical political order. First, in practice there was little to distinguish the political status of a Company servant from that of a burgher, except in the case of the few top officials. The dominant class in the community was increasingly marked by colour alone rather than a combination of colour, occupation and legal status. Secondly, the 'alien' status of the Khoikhoi was now little more than a fiction. As a result of the trekboer expansion during the course of the eighteenth century large numbers of Khoikhoi had been incorporated into the colony as farm servants. Already in the seventeenth century the Company had begun to establish its authority over Khoikhoi under Dutch law. Early in the eighteenth century there were already a few cases of Khoikhoi bringing charges against burghers before colonial courts. However, by 1780 their legal status was still far from settled: they were not independent aliens, nor were they burghers. Some contemporary observers felt that the actual status of many Khoikhoi labourers was little better than that of slaves.[14] Thirdly, the legal position of the so-called free blacks or manumitted slaves was also increasingly ambivalent. Originally their position as freemen meant that they suffered no legal discrimination. They could, and sometimes did, hold office or land under the landholding system of the colony—the two distinctive characteristics of freeburgher status. However, from the second half of the eighteenth century the position of the free blacks began to decline. Very few were still regarded as burghers, they were discriminated against by the government and colonists alike, and by 1816 they were even considered to be in danger of merging again with the slave group. Lastly, even the position of slaves was not quite clear. Technically they had no legal rights: they were property under the control of their masters, who could punish them. Yet a slave was obviously a person, and in cases of extreme cruelty slaves' complaints against their masters were sometimes upheld. Occasionally they were allowed to give evidence against their masters in courts.

In sum, then, the traditional hierarchy of legal status groups persisted, though with a growing measure of vagueness and ambiguity concerning the precise legal and civic status of the various subordinate groups. But the hierarchy tended to reinforce the economic and social order of Cape society.

The significance of the structure of the Cape plural society

It would be difficult, and indeed quite misleading, to attempt to identify any one of the racial or labour or legal status orders by itself as the primary context for early Afrikaner political thought. More important was the way in which political and economic dominance, cultural and racial exclusivism, and legal and status differences all tended to reinforce each other in a clear hierarchical order. Not all whites were rich, but virtually all the rich were white. Slaves, obviously, were not white and were almost exclusively held by whites: by the Company itself, by (white) Company servants and by (white) freeburghers. More and more Khoikhoi became an unfree labour force on farms owned or held (with a few exceptions as in areas on the northwestern frontier) by white freeburghers. Poor and landless whites did not become part of this unfree labour force, but retained their burgher status and remained part of the Afrikaner kinship system even if they lived as *bijwooners* on the land of other whites.

Culturally, the dominant group of white freeburghers and Company servants considered themselves to have a special claim to the Christian religion and literacy, two of the main attributes of what was regarded as civilization. They expected the government to provide them with churches and schools. The government did not meet these expectations, but the few clergymen in the colony (by 1790 there were still less than 10, in a total population of 60 000, of whom 20 000 were white) did concentrate their activities on the officials and the burghers. In spite of the rudimentary nature of educational and religious institutions, baptism and literacy remained extremely important as cultural symbols through which group membership was expressed.

In the absence of efficient administrative and legal machinery, the Afrikaner's earliest conception of his political and civic status in society was determined less by the statute book than by the matrix of the established order, which embraced the various and mutually reinforcing hierarchical elements of the labour and economic system, the pyramid of legal status groups, and the racial and cultural segmentation of a plural society. When they conceived of themselves as 'burghers' or 'Christians' or 'inhabitants', this was essentially a differential notion implying a hierarchical superiority as against those who were non-burghers (but slaves or servile), heathens or aliens. Though there does not seem to be any document in which this was directly and explicitly developed by Afrikaners themselves, it is clear that there was a widely held and deeply ingrained belief that slaves, Khoikhoi and Xhosa, who were all black, belonged in *a completely different—and inferior—civic and legal category* from whites. Thus when Governor Janssens visited the eastern frontier in 1803, he remarked of the whites living there, 'They call themselves people and Christians, and the Kaffirs and Hottentots heathens, and on the strength of this they consider themselves entitled to anything.'[15] Only in this way can we account for the violent objections to attempts to introduce legal equality between colonists and Khoikhoi. Indeed the later profound rejection of such *gelykstelling* is indeed the best evidence for the importance of this basic differentiation in early Afrikaner political thinking.

The impact of British rule and reforms

The advent of British rule from 1795 did not bring any radical break in this social and political order. Indeed, the Cape was administered according to the principles adopted for the newly conquered colonies of the 'Second British Empire'. Thus, in the spirit of the Quebec Act of 1774, the existing laws and institutions of colonies with culturally alien populations should be retained 'as nearly as circumstances will permit', rather than imposing a new and British order. The Cape, along with the other colonies acquired by Britain at the end of the eighteenth century, was primarily regarded not as a plantation, the produce from which would supply the mother country with raw materials for her factories, nor as a promising new colonial settlement to be developed as a British province with appropriate constitutional institutions, but as a strategic stronghold for the protection of the new maritime empire in the East. From the imperial point of view the main object of government was to establish order and tranquillity.[16]

However, even given this conciliatory and non-interfering policy, the new rulers still introduced new concepts of government which would ultimately transform the political order of the colony. Thus, in the first place, the new British rulers were from the outset determined to provide the 'smack of firm government',[17] and so brought to bear a more energetic and autocratic view of the government's role in establishing law and order. Even during the temporary occupation from 1795 to 1803 the colonial Governors showed that they would not tolerate the insubordination of burghers which had marked the last days of the Company. The new government quartered troops at the homes of disaffected colonists in the southwestern Cape and sent British and Khoikhoi troops against frontier rebels. The government itself was, unlike that of the older British colonies, a deliberate autocracy in which all civil and military power was concentrated in the hands of the Governor alone, to ensure direct and absolute imperial control, unhampered by local legislatures or advisory councils. Still, even if the Cape Governor could be said to be among the most powerful of all colonial Governors, he was dependent on the co-operation (which he got) of key Afrikaner officials for running the main legal and political institutions. At the level of local government, however, little or no administrative apparatus was available, or provided, for translating this more dynamic notion of government into regular practice. The major measure for extending law and order into the interior was the introduction of the Circuit Courts from 1811. However, though they were undoubtedly of great significance in gradually establishing the new notion that no one could any longer be a law unto himself, the basic problems of effective security and protection remained.

In the second place, at the same time as the transition to British rule a new concern with the rights and liberties of subject peoples was introduced to the Cape. Basically, this was related to a general change in the intellectual and ideological climate of the time, but it is important to differentiate the specific agents of this change in the colonial setting. The fact is that, until the last quarter of the eighteenth century, both Britain and the Netherlands were, on the whole, remarkably unconcerned with the fate meted out to the aboriginal subject peoples of their empires. The humanitarian ethos associated with the Enlightenment, which affected some officials at the Cape, produced, among other things, a new sensitivity to the plight of aboriginal subjects. The evangelical and missionary movements, so much in the forefront of the campaigns against the slave trade and later for the 'protection of aboriginal peoples', also began their activities at the Cape in this period. However, apart from Van der Kemp and Read's allegations of cruelties and atrocities suffered by the Khoikhoi which led to the 'Black Circuit' of 1812, they did not have any serious impact on the political order of the Cape until the rise to prominence of Dr Philip in the 1820s.

Of more immediate significance was the fact that from the start the new British rulers, military governors and Tories though they were, proclaimed the rights and liberties of their Khoikhoi subjects much more vigorously than the Company had ever done. In doing this they were articulating the new concept of imperial trusteeship and paternal despotism that had emerged in the speeches of the younger Pitt, Burke, Fox and Sheridan during the parliamentary debates connected with the trial of Warren Hastings and the investigations into the affairs of the East India Company in the 1780s.[18] The classic formulation of this notion of imperial trusteeship was given by the leading parliamentary spokesman and philosopher of conservatism, Edmund Burke, in 1783: 'All political power which is set over men, and . . . all privilege claimed or exercised in exclusion of them, being wholly artificial, and for so much a derogation from the natural equality of mankind at large, ought to be some way or other exercised ultimately for their benefit. If this is true with regard to every species of political dominion . . . then such rights, or privileges, or whatever else you choose to call them, are all in the strictest sense a *trust*; and it is of the very essence of every *trust* to be rendered accountable; and even totally to *cease*, when it substantially varies from the purposes for which alone it could have lawful existence.'[19] Above all, this notion of trusteeship implied an obligation on the part of colonial governors to eliminate cruel and inhumane treatment of people under their control and to extend to them the protection of law.

Thus Governors Craig and Macartney, though committed not to interfere with the existing Roman–Dutch legal system at the Cape, could no longer allow torture as an instrument of justice to coerce confession, and death by torture as an extreme form of capital punishment for slaves. When the Cape Court of Justice was not prepared to put into effect the reform suggested by Craig in 1796, it was abolished by Macartney (document 3.3). Concerning the Khoikhoi, the British Governors proclaimed their right to leave service and to have access to the courts. The ambiguous legal and civic status of the Khoikhoi could no longer be tolerated as it had been in the time of the Company. They were either subjects or not; and in 1809 Caledon firmly proclaimed that they had civic obligations as well as rights 'in the same manner as all inhabitants'.[20] These obligations, as we shall shortly see, simply spelled out the servile and subordinate position of the Khoikhoi in the colonial order, but Caledon's Code also definitely brought them 'within the law', and in this sense transformed the old political order of the eighteenth century. Through a combination of missionary pressures in England and the initiatives of local officials and Governors, the Khoikhoi's equal civic status was finally proclaimed by Ordinance 50 in 1828, nullifying the restrictions on the personal freedoms of free people of colour. In principle this meant the end of the old hierarchy of legal status, though in practice the local government by and large lacked the ability and the will to translate the intention of the ordinance into day-to-day policies.[21]

For, in the third place, concern for the protection of indigenous subjects had to be combined with the need for labour. Cape Town's demand for meat greatly increased after the coming of the British in 1795, emphasizing the importance of a docile indigenous work force. This need for labour regulation further increased after the abolition of the slave trade in 1807. Consequently the British were prepared to institutionalize some of the labour controls of the burghers such as passes and the indenture system. In the opening decades of the nineteenth century these kinds of controls did not yet meet with opposition in London. Although they opposed plantation slavery, even Britain's reformers seemed to give their approval to coercive forms of labour which did not involve the ownership of one person by another.[22] Various interests were thus combined in Caledon's Hottentot Proclamation of 1809. The Khoikhoi were thereby brought within the law, but the primary intention of the proclamation was to insist that as such they were subject to 'proper regularity in regard to their places of abode and occupations'. For the sake of liberty they should be employed by contracts; for the sake of order they should carry passes. And to meet the demands of labour they should enter the service of the burghers rather than leading an indolent life, 'by which they are rendered useless both for themselves and the community at large'.[23] While Ordinance 50 revised the restrictive conditions for the contracting of labour it did not supply the means to render effective its intention of creating a free labour force. Apart from an undoubted increase in the incidence of vagrancy, the informal processes taking place at the local level proved decisive in upholding the main features of the old order of subordination and labour repression.

There remains, of course, in the fourth place, the abolition of the basic institution of slavery. Even here the actual impact on the fabric of the social and economic order was not the total disruption that many had anticipated. The emancipation of the slaves at the Cape was achieved without a traumatic struggle. This can be attributed to various factors. Slavery was not abolished after a prolonged internal struggle during which the pressures of an indigenous abolitionist movement, a slave insurrection or a civil war polarized and transformed the social structure. It was done by the external intervention of an imperial power. Moreover, the presence of the British military detachment stationed at the Cape guaranteed that emancipation would not mean disruption and chaos, at least in the southwestern Cape, where the majority of slaves lived.

The most immediate effect of abolition on the colonial slaveholders was the loss of their capital investment in slaves. But even here the steadily declining value of slaves, from an average price of 3000 rixdollars in 1821 to only 600 rixdollars in 1834,[24] as well as the creation of local financial institutions and alternative avenues for capital investment, softened the blow. All this took place in the context of an enduring and increasing labour shortage. While the Cape economy began to expand after the British conquest, a number of factors, including the ending of the importation of slaves in 1808, the relatively slow natural increase of the slave and Khoikhoi populations taken together with their depletion due to epidemics and the settlement of many Khoikhoi outside the colony, and the limitations on employing Xhosa as labourers on farms due to the frontier situations, all combined to make the labour needs of the colonists as acute as ever. In the 1820s and 1830s the labour shortage was further increased by Ordinance 50, which protected the Khoikhoi from 'improvident' service contracts, by the refusal of the government to pass vagrancy acts, and by the establishment of several missionary stations where thousands of Khoikhoi could find a living outside employment on the farms. In these circumstances the emancipated slaves were quickly absorbed into the labour market, where the established informal processes proved sufficient to maintain the essentials of the old labour order even under the changed statutory conditions.

In sum, therefore, the impact of British rule and reform on the earlier order was more evident at the level of intent than of practice. The avowed aim of establishing more orderly and efficient government was significant in promise more than achievement; the proclamation of 'equal protection and equal justice' to all subjects was not effectively translated into practice; and the institutionalized informal processes of labour repression survived the formal repeal of restrictive statutory regulations and the abolition of slavery. However, this practical ineffectiveness did not mean that the impact of the avowed aims of such British policies was therefore to be any less on the political thinking of Afrikaners nurtured by the old order.

The changing contexts of frontier conflict

Eventually it was the Afrikaners on the eastern frontier[25] who reacted most tellingly to the new social order sought by British reforms. This reaction can best be understood through an analysis of the dynamics of the eastern frontier as it changed from the 1770s on, when trekboers and Xhosa began to settle interspersed with each other in the Zuurveld area between the Sundays and the Fish Rivers. The eastern frontier was not a boundary, demarcating an area of political control, but a frontier *zone*, where two or more ethnic communities co-existed with conflicting claims to the land, and where there was no authority strong enough to exercise undisputed control over the process of colonization.[26] The frontier processes of settlement and conflict within this zone did not conform to any single unvarying pattern, and we can distinguish three substantially different frontier contexts in the course of half a century.

1 There was the period of the *open frontier* from c. 1770 to 1793. This was a period in which Xhosa and trekboers jostled each other in the disputed Zuurveld area, but before any major frontier wars had taken place or set patterns of strategy and thinking had evolved. After the initial clashes of 1780 and 1781 the frontier had remained comparatively quiet for a decade. Towards the end of the 1780s, however, the frontier situation moved in the direction of open conflict. To the old disputes over land and water new and explosive issues were now added. Mainly as a result of political turmoil in the Xhosa hinterland there was an increased influx into the Zuurveld of Xhosa, some of whom recouped their losses suffered in intra-Xhosa battles by stealing cattle from the colonists on a small scale. At the same time some white farmers who had begun to use Xhosa labour became embroiled in disputes with their servants. There were increasing allegations of arbitrary punishment and of the withholding of wages. In the early 1790s these conflicts increased sharply. The Xhosa were apparently no longer as intimidated by the colonists' having guns as they had been in the decade immediately following the first clashes, while some frontier colonists resorted to outright force against individual Xhosa, sometimes even against chiefs. In short, it became quite clear that there was a serious and general breakdown of authority characteristic of the open frontier.

This authority crisis existed on two levels. It concerned firstly the relationship between the colonists and the Xhosa. Both spurned the claims of the other, yet neither was able to establish undisputed control. No mutually accepted procedure for resolving disputes between colonists and Xhosa existed. Secondly the colonial government experienced difficulty in asserting its authority over the frontier colonists. Prior to the 1780s the expanding trekboers had enjoyed a remarkable lack of institutional control. Moreover the Cape eastern frontier had from the beginning been characterized by a tendency towards factional strife and a 'general atmosphere of contentiousness'.[27] Woeke and Maynier, the first landdrosts of the frontier district of Graaff-Reinet, which was established in 1786, far from being able to establish general law and order, soon became involved in acrimonious disputes with colonists, especially those living close to the Xhosa. At the same time a feud existed between the boards of *heemraden* and officers of the militia, expressing the interests of the northern divisions, which wanted firmer action against the 'Bushmen', and the southeastern divisions, which in turn demanded the forcible expulsion of the Xhosa.

2 With the war of 1793 these tensions came to a head, and we can distinguish the qualitatively different context of the period of the *frontier crisis* which lasted until 1812. The dimensions of this crisis appeared in a dramatic setback to the colonists' claims to control of the land and of the indigenous peoples in the frontier zone. During the frontier wars of 1793 and 1799, bands of Xhosa and Khoikhoi repulsed the attacks

of the commandos and subsequently penetrated deep into the colony, prompting the evacuation of virtually the entire southeastern part of Graaff-Reinet by the colonists. Moreover, burgher rebellions in 1795, 1799 and 1801 against the colonial authorities, together with the uprising of the Khoikhoi servants against their masters (1799), constituted nothing less than a general breakdown of white authority structures in the frontier zone.

3 There was the period of the *closing frontier*. The permanent presence of a British military force on the frontier from 1810 changed the basic balance of power in favour of the colonial authorities, and thereby the whole context and character of daily interaction. Any disputes between the colonists and the indigenous peoples now took place within a framework in which the British army and the commandos were ultimately able to impose white control. Whereas before 1811 the frontier colonists could often maintain their position only with difficulty, the frontier war of 1811–12 resulted in the expulsion of the Xhosa from the heretofore perennially disputed Zuurveld. In a subsequent encounter in 1819 the Xhosa were driven beyond the Keiskamma River, and the area between the Fish and the Keiskamma Rivers was declared a 'Neutral Area', where Xhosa were allowed to settle only on sufferance. On their own the colonists could not have achieved such striking military successes.

The British also finally established the colonial government as the undisputed authority over the frontier colonists. With the start of the nineteenth century the eastern frontier began to close for the colonists in various ways. The government bolstered its authority not only through the stationing of troops but also by the creation of new drostdys on the frontier, Uitenhage in 1804 (by the Batavian Government), and George and Albany in 1811 and 1814 respectively. From the second decade of the century Circuit Courts brought the instruments of law and justice to the frontier itself, and slowly began to break down the arbitrary power the colonists exercised over their Khoikhoi servants. The crushing of the Slachtersnek Rebellion in 1815 firmly brought the days of open defiance of the government to an end. At the same time the nature of the commandos changed radically. In the days of the open frontier, commandos were often raised without the direct involvement, and sometimes even without the sanction, of the authorities. After the British took over, commandos were still called up but they now served essentially as auxiliary forces subservient to the British military, and acted under much more effective government control. Moreover, whereas previously the colonial authorities had only laid down general and largely ineffective guidelines, they now intervened to construct specific policies such as the 'Spoor Law'.[28]

The frontier was also closing in a much broader sense: it was gradually being integrated into the administrative compass and the norms and value system of the British Empire. Henceforth, the financial policies and humanitarian reforms conceived in the metropolitan centre would increasingly impinge on the frontier.[29] No sooner, for example, had a start been made on the construction of a series of military forts for frontier defence in 1817, than imperial retrenchment necessitated the withdrawal of most of the troops. And by the late 1820s the influence of 'Exeter Hall' and the missionaries was becoming a serious factor in frontier politics.

Through these successive phases of frontier history thus ran the common theme of the increasing political alienation of the frontier colonists from the colonial authorities. In the days of the open frontier the government in the Cape had been incapable of providing the military assistance which the frontier colonists required. At the height of the frontier crisis a series of burgher rebellions actually struck out at the local representatives of the colonial administration. But when a stronger government finally proved capable of establishing its military ascendancy and political authority on the closing frontier, it brought about a curtailment of the burghers' own habitual freedom of action and arbitrary powers, proposing policies based on alien concepts and values, while not yet affording the frontier colonists any clear benefits of greater security and protection.

The incompletely closed frontier and the origins of the Great Trek

The fact is that the frontier had not yet been effectively and finally closed, and it was precisely because of this that the new social order (rule of law, legal equality, and the emancipation of the Khoikhoi and slaves) being introduced by the British was such a traumatic experience for many frontier colonists. First, while the semi-autonomous role of the commandos had been curbed drastically, the British standing army on the frontier was still not strong enough to preclude effectively all Xhosa incursions. There was always the threat of a new attack on the frontier districts, and this was dramatically realized in the wars of 1819 and 1834–35. While the colonial government was thus increasingly limiting the frontiersman's traditional discretionary freedom of action in self-defence, it could not yet guarantee his basic security. Secondly, while frontiersmen who for so long had enjoyed a remarkable freedom from institutional controls increasingly had to reckon with the forces of law and order, they also, like Afrikaner slave-owners and employers generally, in the 1820s and 1830s faced the prospect of a social revolution based on the legal equality of all classes. However, though the law could free the slaves and enact the legal equality of the labouring classes, it was not capable of launching any systematic programme to improve their economic, social or political position. At the same time the weak administration of the frontier districts was not sufficiently strengthened to police the new labour order effectively.

The proclaimed social and legal revolution thus failed in two ways. In practice Ordinance 50 of 1828 did not succeed in substituting effective legal procedures for the informal relationships long since existing on the farms, and thus did little to give better protection to Khoikhoi remaining in service. At the same time the ordinance did release the Khoikhoi from their formal obligation to work, without, however, instituting effective government controls to prevent them from resorting to vagrancy, squatting and stock-theft as alternatives to farm labour. In the days of the open frontier the colonists would have attempted to prevent this by vigilante action; in the days of the closing frontier this option was restricted. The Khoikhoi in the meantime were trapped in a limbo between abject poverty and political equality.

For the frontier colonists the result of this attempted but incompleted closing of the frontier was a pervasive sense of insecurity, which affected them in three ways, and to which the origins of the Great Trek may be traced.

1 There was the general insecurity produced by a situation in which order (as they defined it, i.e. closely connected with control over the indigenous peoples) did not prevail. After the war of 1811–12 the frontier farmers temporarily experienced greater security, though the war of 1819 served to question the basis of that security. But it was particularly from 1828 that, in their eyes, the situation rapidly deteriorated. With the passing of Ordinance 50, in the words of J. S. Marais, 'Khoikhoi vagrancy and unauthorized squatting became endemic.'[30] The colonists experienced this as a direct threat to their property. The decision to supplement the indigenous labour force by bringing pass-bearing Xhosa into the colony (Ordinance 49) further increased the problem of vagrancy and small-scale thefts. A recent study[31] concludes that on the eve of the Great Trek the colonists were suffering heavy losses through

the 'almost incessant series of thefts' by Khoikhoi and Xhosa. Small bands of vagrants lived off the cattle they captured on farms. Insecurity of property thus became one of the central causes of the Trek. To this may be added the uncertainties of tenure brought about by new land reforms[32] which, in doing away with the traditional and popular system of landholding, were accompanied by long delays in surveying and providing title deeds.

All these enduring threats to settlement and property on the eastern frontier were brought to a head by the disastrous frontier war of 1834–35. In a letter of 1838 a once prosperous farmer tells how he was left destitute twice by raids. 'What is left to me,' he asks, with reference to the latest devastating war, 'after all my years of labour and sweat? Literally nothing.'[33] Undoubtedly the Trek would itself be fraught with insecurity, but in circumstances like these it began to appear to many frontiersmen as the more attractive alternative. If the government could not adopt adequate measures to ensure their security on the frontier, perhaps this could be attained by some concerted movement of their own. In this sense it was not just the consequences of British Government control of the frontier, but also of its relative inefficiency, that led to the Great Trek.

2 There was the psychological and status insecurity triggered off by the challenge to their racial values posed by Ordinance 50 and the emancipation of the slaves. Although in practice Ordinance 50 was to leave the class order virtually intact, it produced all the fear and suspicion that usually arise in a traditional society when structural changes are proposed that threaten the way of life and the accepted normative basis of society. The old racial order and white arbitrary rule were no longer legitimate; nothing that they could trust had yet emerged in its place. In this sense vagrancy was not only a threat to their property but also an assault on their self-esteem and social status both as whites and the dominant class. Large-scale emigration from the colony and settlement outside the area of British control held out the possibility of a trekboer society where the 'proper' relations between master and servant according to the norms of the accustomed racial social order could be reinstated.

In this context the Trek acquires significance as an implicitly political action that sets it apart from similar and quantitatively much larger population movements, as in the colonization of the American interior. At the same time the Trekkers did not (unlike the Puritans in New England) set out with the primary objective of founding new societies based on their own religious and political ideas. The Trek rather offered them the possibility of maintaining important aspects of their existing social order by moving away from the increasing pressures of the closing frontier and frustrating government controls. In this sense the Trek was an essentially conservative exercise in the politics of survival, and not a revolutionary movement or an aggressive expansion.[34] The frontier colonists lacked both the power and the inclination to stage a direct rebellion against those British policies which they perceived as threatening to their place in the established order. The Trek thus provided another way out, an alternative enabling them to avert the unwelcome effects of these reforms without having to challenge or resist them in any direct way.

3 There was an economic insecurity rooted in an agricultural crisis. For nearly a hundred years the way of life and economy of trekboer society had depended on the easy availability of free land. By the end of the eighteenth century, however, further expansion was checked by the dense settlement of the Xhosa and by firmer government controls. In reports from officials and petitions from landless colonists it is clear that there was no more free land with adequate water supplies available for subsis-

tence farming in the eastern and northeastern districts.[35] The 1820s and 1830s witnessed a sharp increase in land prices in the eastern districts. This threatened to spell the end of a way of life where people could easily subsist on their own and escape working for wages by simply moving on. The new generation faced the loss of status entailed by entering someone else's service.[36] Even landholders found it increasingly difficult to subsist, and were caught up in a vicious circle of overpopulation of land, water shortage and deterioration of pastures. If they were to survive, it was crucial that they should switch to intensive subsistence farming in order to increase the carrying capacity of the land. But technical equipment (such as windmills) and irrigation methods were still primitive. At the same time the long distance from the Cape Town market and the absence of easily marketable commodities (wool was only marketed on a large scale in the 1850s) did not yet justify a more intensive application of capital and labour. In short, with the closing of the Cape frontier, trekboer society entered a transitional period which required extremely difficult social and economic adjustments to the traditional practice of extensive farming.[37] The times were fraught with economic uncertainty, further compounded by severe droughts and disastrous frontier wars. In these circumstances the risks entailed by venturing on the Trek were more than compensated for by the attractive alternative to present economic insecurity of resuming the traditional trekboer mode of colonization by opening new frontiers in the interior.

These economic conditions alone did not cause the Trek. This becomes clear if we compare the Trek with other and less dramatic instances of trekboer expansion during the same period. Already in the 1820s, after the threat from the 'Bushmen' raiders was finally overcome, trekboers once again started moving across the colonial borders on a small scale, particularly in the northeast. This movement, which to some extent alleviated the land shortage, had predominantly economic causes, and lacked the concomitant political motivation of the Trek. The origins of the Great Trek itself, which only got under way in the mid-1830s, can best be understood by taking into account the total and cumulative nature of the political, psychological and economic insecurities described above. The effect of these different levels and kinds of insecurity was that many frontier colonists saw themselves as trapped in an impossible situation. Unable to change their external environment, they were also unable or unwilling to adjust internally to the new context of the closing frontier. The Great Trek was, so to speak, an open door allowing them to effect a wholesale change in their external environment and to regain their former freedom from institutional control without becoming involved in an inevitably futile rebellion. As a result of the Great Trek the frontier of the mid-eighteenth century, with its undiversified economy and lack of political controls, opened in the interior. It was only towards the end of the nineteenth century that this new frontier would finally close, forcing Afrikaners to face the same painful choices as those which had confronted earlier generations on the Cape eastern frontier.[38]

The context and consequences of the Great Trek

This section will not tell the story of the Great Trek and of the first fumbling attempts at state-building in Natal and Trans-orangia in the 1830s and 1840s. It is a story well known, though perhaps less well understood in its more immediate context and consequences. In retrospect the Trek has gained epic proportions as the founding act of Afrikaner nation-building and as a central episode in the making of modern South Africa. Seen within its immediate historical context, however, the significance and consequences of the Trek are less clear and more complex.

The Trek constituted a deliberate and organized migration and settlement, not in open or unoccupied land, but in an area that had long known settlement by a variety of Nguni and Sotho–Tswana peoples.[39] To some extent the route followed by the Trek across the Highveld to Natal might be seen as an instinctive 'outflanking' of the denser Xhosa settlement on the Cape eastern frontier that had checked the earlier trekboer expansion half a century before.[40] The timing of the Trek proved to be highly opportune. It took place in the aftermath of the *Difaqane,* the cataclysmic series of upheavals, following from the rise of the Zulu kingdom, which had convulsed and dispersed Nguni and Sotho–Tswana society throughout the 1820s and early 1830s. In terms of geographical range and the numbers of people involved in war, conquest, displacement and social disruption the Difaqane may well be considered as positively dwarfing the Great Trek.[41] But it certainly greatly facilitated Trekker penetration of the interior. In the Vaal–Orange area, for instance, nearly every Sotho community had been utterly disrupted during the previous decade, old settlements had been abandoned, stock destroyed and fields left uncultivated.[42] When the Trekkers moved into this area they could thus more readily start new settlements, and they probably did not realize to what extent the influx of African people in subsequent years consisted of dispersed communities attempting to return to their traditional lands. The disruption by the Difaqane of the social and political structures of these indigenous communities precluded any significant or sustained resistance to the establishment of the new Trekker settlements once the initial military offensives against the Trekker parties on the part of the Ndebele conquest state and the Zulu kingdom had failed.

Two main stages may be distinguished in the history of the Trek. The first stage was characterized by the concerted and organized migration of a number of large Trekker parties, and by the military struggles with the Ndebele and Zulu kingdoms. After initial setbacks, the Trekkers' advantages in the co-ordinated use of wagons, horses and guns proved more than adequate in beating off the challenges by the military forces of these most powerful kingdoms in the interior. By the early 1840s the immediate security of Trekker settlements in Natal and on the central Highveld had thus been ensured, and they could begin to set about establishing the most necessary social and political institutions. During the second stage, migration continued from the Cape Colony, and by 1845 a further ten thousand Afrikaners had joined the initial five to six thousand Trekkers, though this occurred in a much less organized fashion. The central political question during this period was not the conflict with the indigenous peoples, but whether or not the British colonial authorities would attempt to gain control of these new settlements and thus, as it were, capture the Trek movement from behind. Despite some minor engagements, such as that at Congella in 1843 and Boomplaats in 1848, this was not essentially a military confrontation. The Trekker communities knew that they were not strong enough to offer any direct challenge to the imperial forces, and the colonial authorities were reluctantly drawn in by strategic and humanitarian considerations to the annexation first of Natal and then of the Orange River Sovereignty.[43] Owing to changes in imperial policy and the crisis on the Cape eastern frontier, this trend was then abruptly reversed by the Sand River Convention of 1852, giving recognition to the independence of the Trekkers living north of the Vaal River, and by the Bloemfontein Convention of 1854, withdrawing British sovereignty from beyond the Orange River. The Great Trek had thus, after all, resulted in establishing a number of Trekker settlements outside British control, at least for the time being.

Although the Voortrekker settlements in the interior survived without further serious challenges from the indigenous population after the initial clashes with the

Ndebele and Zulu, there was never any question that their conquest of the interior would result in the same utter destruction of indigenous society on the pattern of that of the Khoikhoi in the Cape or the Amer-indians in North America. The decades following the Difaqane saw a gradual process of regeneration of Nguni and Sotho–Tswana society, with the rise of the Southern Sotho kingdom of Moshweshwe as a pre-eminent example. Almost everywhere on the Highveld and in Natal the numbers of the Bantu-speaking peoples and the range and density of their settlements surpassed those of the whites. By 1850 the Trekkers had settled in the interior and could maintain themselves; however, they had not yet established white hegemony.[44] The Trek rather resulted in the opening of an extended frontier zone in the interior, where for a long time neither they, nor the indigenous societies, nor, for that matter, the British colonial authorities, could establish undisputed political control.

The greatest impact of the Trek was perhaps on the Afrikaners themselves. By 1850 it had brought about a number of significant though sometimes also ambiguous changes in the social and political fortunes of the Afrikaners.

1 In the first place, the Trek had resulted in both the physical dispersal of the small Afrikaner community across an enormously extended area, as well as a considerable degree of social and political fragmentation. To some of the participants the Trek undoubtedly proved to be a crucial and formative political experience,[45] but not all Afrikaners trekked, and not all of those who did trek shared the same views about the Trek's purpose and achievements. Thus there came about a significant political cleavage between those Afrikaners who had trekked and who were to found the new independent settlements, and those who had stayed behind and who were to participate in the economic and social development of a more diverse and mature colonial society (see the next section). Even among the Afrikaners outside the Cape Colony there were significant differences in outlook between the more independent-minded Trekkers and the more loyalist trekboers who had had little political motivation for their movement into the southern Free State and who remained oriented towards colonial society.[46]

As for the Trekkers themselves, there were important internal divisions, based on the different main trek parties, and focused on their respective leaders, such as Potgieter and Pretorius. These leaders held somewhat different views about the aims of the Trek and the best way to deal with the British authorities, and became involved in personal disputes. Moreover, tensions between the patriarchal and somewhat autocratic leaders, on the one hand, and the *Volksraad-party*, on the other, threatened to bring about further conflicts of both a personal and an ideological nature. Following the British annexation of Natal, another division appeared between those who once more crossed the Drakensberg to get beyond the range of British rule, and those who for quite some time were prepared to stay behind, including such leading figures as Pretorius and Boshof. And when the British finally decided to withdraw from the Highveld, the Trekker settlements there were left divided between two republics whose mutual relations remained unresolved for quite some time to come. The Transvaal, particularly, had to cope with further internal factional conflict, based on the three main areas of relatively autonomous settlement, which repeatedly came to the verge of civil war in the ensuing decade and a half of semi-anarchy. If the Great Trek would later come to serve as a major unifying symbol in the rise of Afrikaner nationalism, its immediate historical consequence was rather to promote the dispersal and political fragmentation of the relatively homogeneous trekboer society.

2 In the second place, the Trekkers, as a result of the Trek, became involved in a

more intensive process of interaction with the indigenous peoples than heretofore, particularly the Bantu-speaking communities, under conditions in which, at least initially, white hegemony was not ensured. In the Cape Colony the trekboers had long since gained ascendancy over the Khoikhoi, and it was only on the eastern frontier itself that colonists had had direct dealings with the Xhosa. In the decades preceding the Trek the new British settlers had been partially interposed in the areas where the most intensive interaction took place, while in the last resort British military forces determined the balance of power in this frontier zone. Now the Trekkers were projected into a situation where they had to deal directly with every variety of indigenous society. Dispersed in small communities and on individual farms, they had to cope with the rapidly growing African population in their midst, while surrounded by established or expanding chiefdoms such as Moshweshwe's Sotho kingdom. In the absence of the necessary resources the Trekkers did not impose a comprehensive social or political order of their own on these peoples. Neither did they merge with them. They maintained their (Afrikaner) kinship system virtually intact, and even when they lived in interspersed settlements with indigenous communities, or rented land from them, very few Trekkers were prepared to acknowledge any other authority over themselves. On the other hand, they did expect the indigenous people to enter into service so as to satisfy their labour needs, and often considered such service to be a condition for families or communities to remain on the land claimed by the Trekker farmers, though they could not always enforce this. Thus the Great Trek did not result in the creation of a self-sufficient Trekker society, but in a complex new social pattern of interaction in which the Trekker community was just one component. In time they would develop into the dominant caste of a new plural society, but that would require the development of institutional controls that were as yet lacking.

3 In the third place, while the Great Trek had removed them from the institutional controls of colonial society, the Trekkers could only with great difficulty and to a limited extent provide their own alternatives or substitutes. For a considerable period the Trekker community hardly knew any organized religion, education or trade. Though they continued to put great stock in the value of Christianity and literacy as cultural symbols expressing their exclusive group membership, they could provide neither religious ministers nor teachers from their own numbers. Earlier links with the Cape market had largely been severed, but they did not succeed in their efforts to gain access to an independent port as a trading outlet, and continued to rely on *smousen* (itinerant traders) for trade in whatever commodities they needed. The result was an undiversified economy based on easy access to land and extensive stock-farming. What little capital they had brought with them from the colony continued to dwindle for several decades, and many Trekkers became increasingly impoverished.[47] The experiments in self-government during and after the migration allowed the Trekkers to develop their own ideas concerning the social and political order. The partially representative institutions adopted on the Trek itself and in the subsequent settlements, the pass system promulgated by the Natal Volksraad, and the principle of the inequality of white and non-white written into the earliest Transvaal constitutions thus reflect the trend of Trekker political thinking. However, the practical implementation of these institutions and principles was hamstrung by limited means and lack of resources. The Trekker governments had great difficulty in finding administrators of experience and ability, and little success in levying taxes or enforcing unpopular decisions. For a considerable time the extended patriarchal family remained the main social unit and the local veldkornet dispensed what dis-

cretionary power he could muster with little or no centralized control.[48] The consolidation of relatively stable republican states belongs, as does the gaining of white hegemony in the interior, not to the period of the Great Trek and its immediate aftermath, but to the second half of the nineteenth century.

Structural changes and colonial grievances 1806–54

Those Afrikaners who did not trek still had to adapt to a number of significant changes in the structure of colonial society during the first half of the nineteenth century. Their history was less dramatic than that of the Trekkers, and the crucial accommodations proceeded fairly smoothly, but there were also underlying tensions and grievances. In part the history of the colonial Afrikaners during this period can be described in terms of their participation in the growth of a more mature and diversified society. At the same time this was also a process through which they increasingly became more of a minority group, culturally alienated from the central institutions of that society. The implicit conflict was largely resolved by the movement towards representative selfgovernment in mid-century.

In the fifty years following the second British occupation the Cape Colony experienced a remarkable population growth, even without large-scale immigration. In 1806 the total population numbered 77 075 of which about 25 000 were whites; in 1855 there were 111 956 whites and a total population of 350 000. At the turn of the century there had been only one town and five or six villages. By 1850 a number of small towns and mission centres were spread throughout the colony, while Grahamstown and Port Elizabeth were beginning to rival Cape Town as a centre of government and as a harbour. Colonial society did not merely grow, there was also a diversification of cultures and ethnic groups. At the turn of the century the mainly farming community of Dutch descent still predominated, with Khoikhoi and slaves in subordinated positions. The British settlers of 1820, unlike their French and German predecessors of the seventeenth and eighteenth centuries, did not assimilate to this Afrikaner norm, but remained a distinct cultural group. Ordinance 50 of 1828 and the abolition of slavery in the 1830s released the subordinated groups from formal constraints and created a new class of free people of colour. Ordinance 49 of 1827 allowed Xhosa to enter the colony as labourers, and with the annexation of 1835 the Mfengu were incorporated as colonial subjects. Dutch was no longer the main language but had to give way to English and even Xhosa; the colonial Afrikaners increasingly became just one of the many and diverse groups in colonial society.

At the same time the Afrikaners participated in and benefited from the growth of a more mature and diversified society. The first half of the nineteenth century saw important developments in and extensions of the institutional structure of colonial society on a number of fronts. Education was better organized and the school system greatly extended. Of particular importance was the prestigious school established by the society *Tot Nut van't Algemeen* which trained many leading Cape Afrikaners between 1804 and 1870. Especially in the 1830s and 1840s, with Dr Changuion playing a central role, *Tot Nut van't Algemeen* became an important cultural and intellectual centre in Cape Town. Until the beginning of the nineteenth century, schools had been limited to the immediate neighbourhood of Cape Town itself. Now, following Cradock's proclamation of 1812, public education was for the first time extended to the country districts as well. By 1827 there were 26 free public schools (teaching English and Dutch) and 20 Dutch fee-paying schools in the country districts.[49] A similar rapid extension took place in organized religion. After almost 150 years the Dutch Reformed Church still had only six congregations in 1795, and these were largely left to their own devices. In 1824, when the number of congregations had grown to 14, the first Cape Synod was constituted, which by 1854 embraced 49 congregations. At the same time the extension of religious toleration had led to the spread of other denominations as well, while a large number of missionary institutions came into being. A major development for the public discussion and dissemination of ideas was the establishment of a local and independent press. Until the end of the eighteenth century the Cape had had no printing press at all. From 1800 a press was allowed to operate under strict government licence. Following the arrival of the British Settlers a brief but sharp struggle in the 1820s led to the recognition of the freedom of the press, bringing public policy within the scope of general debate. With Pringle, Dr Faure had already launched the monthly *Nederlandsch Zuid-Afrikaansche Tijdschrift* in 1824, but it was the newspaper *De Zuid-Afrikaan* under the editorship of Christoffel Brand that developed into the major forum for the Cape Afrikaner community in the 1830s and 1840s.

With the end of Company rule the Cape economy was put on a surer foundation. Already during the first British occupation monopolies and official privileges had been abolished, and the restrictions on internal trade lifted. Once the Cape Colony became a permanent British possession, it was economically incorporated into an imperial system which was much larger and more dynamic than that of the Company. This stimulated investment and agricultural production. As the result of imperial preference, wine producers and exporters engaged in a profitable trade. Colonial exports rose sharply from 180 000 rixdollars in 1807 to 1 320 000 rixdollars in 1815.[50] However, when Britain began to withdraw this preference in 1825 the wine trade slumped. It was wool which gave the Cape its first stable export product. The value of wool exports rose steadily from £16 186 in 1835 to £634 130 in 1855.[51] The importance of the wool trade required sheep farmers to switch from the traditional indigenous fat-tailed sheep to imported Spanish merinos, and to engage in more intensive and commercial farming. British rule also brought long-needed fiscal reforms. Following the rather painful process of conversion to sterling and the revaluation of the rixdollar the Cape had a stable currency from 1825. Local financial institutions began to develop, including insurance companies from the 1830s. The first commercial bank was established in 1837, and by 1863 many towns had acquired their own district banks. The infrastructure of the economy was also improved. Thus the system of roads to the interior was greatly extended, particularly in the 1840s. Formerly inaccessible and isolated districts were tied more closely to the Cape market.

There also took place the reform and extension of legal institutions and of the administrative machinery. Circuit courts were introduced in 1811, and the Charter of Justice of 1827 established an independent and professional bench.[52] Administrative officials now received regular salaries instead of the old system of perquisites and fees. Local government was extended by the creation of a number of new districts, growing from 4 in 1800 to 11 in 1826 and 22 in 1855. The replacement in 1827 of the traditional institution of the board of landdrosts and heemraden by magistrates and civil commissioners furthered the growth of more bureaucratic and centralized controls in place of the old system of local and discretionary powers.

The growth and diversification of the Cape colonial society throughout this period remained subject to important constraints and suffered significant disruptions. Though conditions did improve, the economy remained sluggish and characterized by a general scarcity of resources. The initial upturn in wine production and export was followed in the 1820s by a period of retrenchment and inflation. More disruptive were the basic changes in the labour order, caused by the amelioration and then abolition of slavery in conjunction with the ending of the legal subordination of the Khoikhoi. The regulations governing compensation for the slaves freed in 1834 resulted in direct financial losses to many owners, though the impact of emancipation on the general economy was not in fact as destructive as had been feared or claimed.[53] Farmers did have to cope with severe shortages of labour as many emancipated slaves and Khoikhoi servants moved from farms to towns or missionary institutes. Since the government refused to pass vagrancy laws other means had to be found to attract labour. In the west and the east agricultural wages rose sharply, doubling in some cases. However, farmers also began to employ other methods which in the long run tied labourers almost as tightly as before to their masters, for instance the 'hut' system and the 'dop' system.[54] In practice, older informal methods of settling disputes between masters and servants also continued to be more important than the new order of legal and contractual equality, which still lacked the administrative machinery necessary for successful enforcement.[55]

The major grievances of the largely farming community of Cape Afrikaners centred first on the various proposed regulations lessening the authority of masters over their slaves, and later on the effects of 'vagrancy'. Around 1830 there were a number of protest meetings of slave-owners in the western Cape, and even some attempts at civil disobedience against the institution of Slave Protectors. *De Zuid-Afrikaan* initially acted as spokesman and apologist for the slave-owners, and in the mid-1830s it gave especial prominence to the 'vagrancy problem', and to the pernicious influence imputed to the missionary and philanthropic lobby. Apparently the political energies of the Cape Afrikaners were absorbed by these actions. Certainly it is somewhat surprising, at least in retrospect, that they were so little concerned with the various other ways in which, culturally and ethnically, they were evidently being relegated to the position of a minority group.

The earlier part of the nineteenth century can be described in terms of the rise of British hegemony in colonial society. British rule did not just bring the growth of organized education, religion and law in general. It also meant that almost without exception control of these various social institutions was not in the hands of the local Afrikaner community. This had not been the case with the more rudimentary institutions in the time of the Dutch East India Company either. But though there may have been great differences between the educational background and social outlook of the Dutch clergymen and teachers and the Cape officials, on the one hand, and the local Afrikaner community, on the other, they did share a common cultural heritage. Now not only the Colonial Office in Cape Town and the local magistrates were British, but increasingly this applied to the courts, schools and even the church as well. Though the traditional Roman–Dutch system was largely retained in civil law, criminal process was brought into conformity with English principles and presided over by British-trained magistrates and judges. In the schools Somerset sponsored a deliberate anglicization policy, and even in the Dutch Reformed Church ministers of Scottish extraction predominated. In 1837 no less than 12 of the total of 22 ministers were Scots.

Thus the control of these crucial social institutions was now largely in culturally alien hands. At the same time the arrival of some 5 000 British settlers in 1820 meant that henceforth a significant section of the colonial population itself was English. They were people who claimed to have a superior culture and a greater measure of sophistication. Englishmen like John Fairbairn, who had been instrumental in establishing a free press, and the missionary John Philip set the tone for public debate. In addition after 1830 very few Afrikaners succeeded in attaining the high offices once held by a Van Ryneveld or a Truter, and few gained any prominence in the public life of the colony. Still, throughout this period there is little evidence of any cultural grievances or ethnic resentments resulting from this, and organized resistance is conspicuously lacking.

There were, of course, good reasons for this lack of resistance to British rule, such as the presence of a large British military force and, at the outset, the legacy of grievances against the Company. British rule also meant distinct advantages: the Cape Afrikaners profited from the growing economy, the greater number of schools and churches, and easier access to the courts. But there also soon grew attachments to British authority which went beyond that. From the outset important sections of the Afrikaner community had willingly co-operated with the new British rulers. Several prominent families in the southwestern Cape became anglicized quite early on. More significantly, *De Zuid-Afrikaan*, while showing great empathy for the Voortrekkers, deplored the Great Trek and evidently hoped that the Trekkers would again submit themselves to British authority, which was seen as synonymous with civilized progress and order.[56] In Cape Town and the larger centres there was an increasing acceptance of English as the medium for public discourse and an almost unquestioned assumption that the trend towards anglicization would be inevitable and irreversible. It was only with the language movement of the 1870s that the earlier anglicization policy would, in retrospect, become a burning grievance.[57]

The movement towards representative government

The Cape Afrikaners' share in the movement towards representative government which first emerged in the mid-1820s and gathered considerable force in the late 1840s should be seen against the background of the trends indicated in the previous section. Though it was to introduce a number of liberal reforms, British rule at first did not bring any extension of representative government to the Cape. As has been indicated earlier (p. 11), it took the form of a decided autocracy in which a succession of military governors governed by proclamation, with supreme authority over all branches of government. Initially there was strict control of the press, and a ban on unauthorized public meetings imposed in 1822 was only repealed in 1848. In fact, the opening decades of British rule saw the withering and demise of existing institutions with some representative function. The old Court of Justice with its burgher members, the Burgher Senate and the boards of landdrosts and heemraden were all abolished in 1828. The commando system lost much of its earlier autonomy on the frontier, and burghers increasingly experienced commando duty as a thankless burden. To some extent these institutions were replaced by the Council of Advice (1825) and later by the Legislative Council, which had an element of nominated representation. But these were alien bodies with little or no Afrikaner participation, a far cry from the familiar and traditional institutions, and they were not even very effective.

The delay in granting representative institutions to the Cape was also a question of priorities. When Britain reconquered the Cape in 1806 her main political objective was to establish effective control over this vital strategic link in her world empire. In addition the main priorities, for the Governors on the spot as well as the Colonial Office in London, were to reform the administrative system, to stimulate the economy and to change the labour order from bonded labour to free labour, while bringing law and order to the frontier. Political rights would have to wait for the successful implementation of these reforms. 'The British Government recognized,' as De Kiewiet said, 'that slaves without freedom, Hottentots without rights, and a Kafir frontier without peace were issues that had precedence over representative assemblies.'[58] From the colonists' point of view, on the contrary, these same issues were so many sound reasons for having self-government. Opposition to the proposed imperial reforms of slavery was the chief source of the demands for greater local control which were expressed from the mid-1820s. In 1826 the Burgher Senate refused to publish the Slave Ordinance of 1826. When the government cajoled this appointed body into compliance, several well-subscribed petitions requested that it be made an elective body. The regulations of 1830 and 1831 which aimed at the amelioration of slavery evoked an angry protest meeting of Koeberg farmers, prompting the Governor to ban contentious gatherings.[59] In the mid-1830s concern about the need for greater control of vagrancy was closely connected with arguments for the need to establish self-government. To the policymakers in Whitehall, on the other hand, this demonstrated why colonial affairs could not yet be left in local hands: the interests of the indigenous and subordinated peoples had to be protected by the imperial government.[60] A representative assembly for the Cape would have to wait until the rights of the subordinated groups had been ensured, and the more pressing social and economic problems had been solved.

By the 1840s this had to a large extent come about. The administrative system was reformed along British lines, the Khoikhoi were proclaimed legal equals of the colonists, the slaves were free and revenues were rising. In the meantime the Durham Report, recommending a greater measure of self-government for the colonies, had landed on the desk of the imperial government. Self-government followed in the 1840s for Australia, Canada and New Zealand. In South Africa Britain also wished to limit the extent of imperial responsibility, largely for economic reasons. She was prepared to grant political power to the colonists provided the liberal and humanitarian reforms of the preceding decades would not be threatened. For the time being the furthest Britain was prepared to go was the institution of a Legislative Council (in 1842), consisting of five officials and five to seven unofficial members, appointed by the Governor. It was a body which could discuss a limited number of topics, and the unofficial members were easily dominated by a strong and concerted executive.

From 1846 the movement towards representative government gained greater momentum. Even the imperial and colonial authorities agreed that the Cape was now ready to receive representative institutions at parliamentary level. Elected municipal councils had been functioning since 1836, and divisional road boards since 1843. In 1848 the Governor, Sir Harry Smith, with the support of his Executive Council, recommended the granting of representative government as suggested by Earl Grey, the Colonial Secretary. Still, this was not to come about without the most severe constitutional and political struggle in the history of the colony. Fundamentally this may be ascribed to the fact that social and economic developments had outstripped the existing political institutions. An increasingly self-confident and politically conscious colonial society was no longer prepared simply to accept the autocratic decisions of a Governor and his Executive Council on matters affecting their own interest, as they saw this, nor were they prepared to wait patiently for the transfer of representative government and leave the mechanics of transition and the details of the new constitution in the hands of the colonial authorities. Already during the frontier war of 1846 bitter rivalry emerged between the colonists called up to serve in the burgher forces and the military authorities. Many leading colonists were greatly aggrieved at the treatment they received from high officials, and in institutional terms this meant the final breakdown of the commando system as well as a serious loss of confidence in the colonial regime.

From 1848 the revolutionary currents of contemporary developments in Europe stirred similar aspirations in South Africa, and the situation became more volatile. Andries Pretorius's abortive rebellion on the other side of the Orange did not proceed without some feelers for possible support in the Cape, and rumours and scares abounded. It was the anti-convict agitation of 1848–9 which proved to be the major occasion for mobilizing colonial feeling in defence of common interests. The episode demonstrated that the colonists had become a political force to be reckoned with, that they were capable of effective organization and that they were prepared to use coercive and semi-violent means in pursuit of their aims. It also brought Cape Afrikaners and English liberals together in united opposition to the autocratic powers of local officials and imperial government. This coalition persisted during the subsequent constitutional struggle following the resignation of the unofficial elected members of the Legislative Council, when the Governor did not appoint all the five leading the list, and during the protracted disputes about the proposed new franchise qualifications. The general climate of crisis was further stimulated by the disastrous frontier war of 1850, followed by the rebellion of the 'Coloured' inhabitants of the Kat River settlement in 1851, which in turn gave rise to a near panic about a possible 'Coloured' rising in the western Cape. However, by the time the new constitution was promulgated in 1853 the political situation had become more stable and the early years of the new Cape parliament proved to be relatively uneventful, the new representative institutions proving adequate for the claims and interests of colonial society.

The Cape Afrikaners had participated in the movement towards representative government, but not as an exclusive ethnic group. The divisive issues of slavery and legal equality having been settled two decades earlier, the struggle could now focus on the autocratic and despotic nature of colonial government, with the corruption and neglect of colonial interests which that entailed. In the process it was natural to form common cause with like-minded English colonists, and the constitutional goal of a 'low' franchise favoured the numerically superior Afrikaners, as well as the 'Coloured' group. The granting of representative government thus relieved some of the Cape Afrikaners' alienation from the political institutions of colonial society, but it did not stimulate them to mobilize as an exclusive ethnic group. Afrikaner political leaders were not to play a prominent role in the new Cape parliament, and the entry of Cape Afrikaners into ethnic politics would only come about three decades later.

2 *The colonial crisis, labour and slavery 1780–1840*

Early Afrikaner thinking on problems of political economy dealt with both the general structure of the colony's economic and social 'constitution' and specific aspects and institutions of the labour order at the Cape, such as slavery. In particular, the existence of different forms of labour coercion raised grave moral and social problems. On the other hand, attempts at reform initiated by the imperial authorities disturbed vested interests, occasioned serious practical difficulties and threatened to upset the whole social order.

Tracing the way in which Afrikaner thinking at the time addressed itself to these specific issues may prove to have more than merely historical significance. Slavery, for example, has long since been abolished, and is generally regarded as belonging to a closed chapter of South African history. Yet it contributed in a number of crucial ways to the formation of a racial, labour and social order that was to endure much longer, in some respects even to the present day. Moreover, there are important similarities in the kind of problem represented by slavery then and, for example, by migrant labour in South Africa today. Both have been regarded as 'moral cancers' in the fabric of society, yet at the same time 'necessary evils', basic to the survival of the social and economic system. Again, there are close analogies in the similar tensions, then and now, between the moral imperatives for reform and emancipation as against the practical obstacles in the way of implementing social and economic change.

In analyzing and interpreting the texts collected in this section it will thus be relevant to ask questions like the following: what were the views of Afrikaners at the time about slavery as an institution? Did it pose particular moral problems for them, and, if so, did they address themselves to their solution? What kinds of considerations were decisive in their thinking about the practical possibilities of reform and emancipation? What were the reactions to the imperial measures towards reform and emancipation? The answers to these questions will begin to throw some light on basic Afrikaner moral and political approaches to problems of labour coercion and reform.

It will be seen, however, that these documents do not deal exclusively with specific institutions of the existing labour order. Particularly at the outset of this period we find some texts which attempt a general and even a theoretical analysis of the entire structure of the colony's social and economic system. In fact, documents like the petition of 1784 (document 2.1b) and the two texts by Van Ryneveld of 1797 and 1805 (2.3, 2.5) set out to diagnose nothing less than the structural crisis in the colony's 'constitution' at the end of the eighteenth century.[1] We will briefly deal with these general analyses before turning to the thinking on specific aspects of slavery and forced labour, reform and emancipation.

Analyzing the colonial crisis

The petition of 1784 and the two texts by Van Ryneveld, though far from substantial works, show a number of features that set them apart from most of the other texts in this section, and indeed in the entire volume. They set out to address the most basic and general problems raised by the colony's 'constitution', and they do so at a level of theoretical analysis that hardly recurs in the whole of the ensuing century of Afrikaner thinking. In fact, the 1784 petition turns out to have been drafted in Holland and not at the Cape, and cannot without considerable qualification be counted as a contribution to Afrikaner political thinking at all. We will mainly refer to it for comparative purposes.

What are the distinctive features of the mode of thinking employed in these texts? First, it is resolutely *secular*. The main ideas and arguments are not drawn from a religious world-view or derived from some theological doctrine. Secondly, it is *analytical* in intent rather than polemical or activistic. It is not primarily concerned with apportioning blame or establishing the merits of individuals or their actions. The writers are not directly concerned with advocating a certain course of action or a specific policy; they aim throughout at presenting their subject-matter as objectively as possible. They set out to consider the relevant facts in terms of rational norms or universal laws. In addition they attempt to distinguish between superficial symptoms and the underlying structural causes. In all of this their mode of thought is typical of the rational-empirical approach of Enlightenment thinking.

These documents should properly be viewed, then, not so much within the local context of an emerging tradition of indigenous political thought, but rather within the larger context of the intellectual world of the late eighteenth-century Enlightenment in Europe and the United States.

The 1784 petition (2.1b) was the product not of its signatories, but of Hendrik Swellengrebel, an associate of and sympathiser with the Cape colonists in Holland.[2] Swellengrebel, the son of the first and only individual born at the Cape to become Governor of the colony under the Company, had left the Cape at an early age. He had studied at the university of Utrecht, had diverse scientific interests, including botany and political economy, and moved in moderate Dutch Patriot circles. In all these respects he was a typical figure of the Dutch Enlightenment. He valued his connection with the Cape, and returned for an extended visit, which included a journey into the interior anticipating that of Governor Van Plettenberg, from 1776 to 1777. By means of an extensive correspondence with friends and relatives, such as Hendrik Cloete and J. J. Lesueur, he was kept well informed of developments at the Cape. He supported the Cape Patriots in their efforts to bring about necessary reforms in the colony, though he did not always approve of their strategy, such as the attacks on the malpractices of individual officials. When the original Burgher petition of 1779 (2.1a) was turned down by the directors of the Company at the end of 1783, he forwarded a draft petition to the Cape to be signed by a number of local burghers who had not been part of the mainstream of the Patriot movement itself. They belonged to some of the foremost Cape families, and also had family ties with some of the main Company officials.[3] The content of this petition showed a thorough knowledge of conditions at the Cape, and a sympathetic identification with its problems and prospects. Nevertheless its intellectual sources were those of the European Enlightenment, and it is instructive to compare it in style and content with the 1779 petition.

The 1779 petition played a central role in the events connected with the Patriot movement at the Cape, while the 1784 petition was historically of minor and incidental significance. In so far as intellectual stature and content are concerned, however, the roles are reversed. Broadly speaking the 1784 petition endorsed the picture already given in the 1779 petition of economic conditions at the Cape, but with two main differences. There is much less emphasis on the oppression caused by Company rule and on the illicit trading practices of various officials. And there is an attempt to provide a general theoretical analysis instead. The 1779 petition was basically concerned with the 'well-founded grievances' and 'the complaints of the burghers concerning the quite improper conduct of most Company officials'. This was illustrated by an exhaustive listing of allegations against different officials. The general description of the condition of the colony in the introductory section did give an outline of some of the more obvious features of the economy. However, this can hardly be called a thorough analysis. In so far as there was any attempt to diagnose the root cause of the malaise and not just to describe its symptoms, the petitioners clearly tended to blame everything on the malpractices of corrupt and oppressive officials. The petition accordingly concluded with various proposals for reforms of Company policies on this score.

In contrast, the 1784 petition defined the political and economic problems of the colony in different and more analytical terms. It sets out to define the nature and location of the colonial crisis, and it found these not in the actions of particular individuals, nor even in specific policies of the Company. The 'most important cause' is the very 'constitution of this colony itself', that is, its underlying economic structure. In order to describe and analyze this basic 'constitution' of the colony, the petition utilizes a quite sophisticated and purely economic model. This model is basically that of an ideal market economy, where the interplay of relative levels of production and consumption determine price-movements, applied to the local colonial situation. More specifically, the writer takes into account such factors as relative profit-margins, the generation of capital, the importance of an infra-structure, and the role of growth and diversification in the means of production for the creation of new employment. Significantly, there is no evidence of any mercantilistic argument or notion, in the strict sense of the colony's being exclusively viewed in terms of the benefit of trade for the colonizing power.

Coupled with this market-model of the political economy we find the assertion of the profit motive as some kind of universal principle of economic activity: 'It is a general rule that the farmer cannot exist unless he is able to realize the fruit of his labour and of the land in a financially rewarding way.' Both in its general assumptions and in the details of its analysis the petition is clearly inspired by the new science of economics emerging at this time in Scotland and France. But it will also be clear that, whatever the direct sources for or indirect influences on Swellengrebel's writing might be, he is simply applying these general economic theories to the situation at the Cape. There is no indication that the underlying structure of the political economy of the Cape might have any peculiar features of its own, that it might be in a special stage of development, or that it might not be entirely subject to the 'universal principles' of economic activity. In this respect there are important differences between this approach and that developed some years later by Van Ryneveld (2.3 and 2.5).

W. S. van Ryneveld, a senior government official both under Company rule and during the first and second British occupations, was undoubtedly the leading intellect of his time at the Cape. Though he addressed himself to the same basic problems of the colony's political economy, and provided a similar general and theoretical analysis, Van Ryneveld conceived the nature of the underlying colonial crisis in terms different from those of the 1784 petition. He did not use a purely economic model for his analysis, but a more embracing model of society. In this wider social perspective the problem then appeared as basically one of *development*, a process in which different stages had to be differentiated, each with their own rules or laws.

In Van Ryneveld's view the ideal or goal of all political economy is provided by what he terms 'a regular society, where diligence and industry . . . compose the foundation of the prosperity of the people' (2.3). This ideal is clearly modelled on the leading industrial societies of Europe, or what Van Ryneveld calls 'the civilized world' (2.5). But 'the civilized world' is not a universal phenomenon and, even more important, the basic principles of the political economy of these advanced societies do not apply elsewhere in the same way. Van Ryneveld therefore starts with the recognition that there are different kinds or stages of social and economic development, and that the laws of economic and social activity of one stage do not necessarily apply in another: 'the saying that "he who does not work, will also not eat" is true in the civilized world', but it is not necessarily true in other kinds of societies (2.5). This led Van Ryneveld to an important revision of the view of the profit-motive as a universal principle of economic acitivity. He pointed out that in the particular conditions of the largely subsistent farming of colonists on an open frontier, or of aboriginal nomads, there were perfectly good reasons for both the trekboer and the Khoikhoi *not* to be guided by this principle (2.3, 2.5).[4] Van Ryneveld, unlike Swellengrebel in the 1784 petition, realized that an unqualified application of the market model to the Cape was inadequate. There are modes of economic activity different from the ideal of capitalist free enterprise, and each has its own imperatives: 'There is no man in the world who works without being incited to it by some motives. These consist either in ambition or in necessity. The former generally takes place among civilized men. . . . Such kinds of motives are however not to be looked for in the peasants of this country.' (2.3)

To Van Ryneveld, therefore, the problem becomes one of development of a 'regular progress' (2.5) from the economic and social conditions obtaining at the Cape to those of a 'regular society'. It would appear that he posits certain universal laws of development as governing this process, a process conceived as basically one of continuing economic differentiation and social stratification. Economic development leads to the appearance of different social classes, which in turn create both new social and economic needs, and provide the kind of labour force required for further economic and industrial development (2.5). These structural developments would determine the present and future fate of the colony. Thus, once the frontier was closed and land no longer easily available, the colonists would be forced to work for others, social classes would develop, free labour would become available and the conditions for industry and trade would improve (2.3). After Van Ryneveld's unexpected death in 1812 at a relatively early age it would be a long time before anyone in South Africa again attempted to see its socio-economic problems within so broad a theoretical perspective.

Views on slavery and the prospects of reform

The colonial crisis, then, was rooted in the specific kind of economic development of the colony which did not provide for the emergence of a white working class, and which made the colonists totally dependent on slavery and an immobile indigenous labour force. But reform, also, was a matter for grave practical and political concern: given the peculiar labour order that had emerged by the end of the eighteenth century, and given the crucial significance of slavery for the whole fabric of society, it will be clear that the various measures for reform implemented by the British imperial authorities, from the stopping of the slave trade in 1807 to the abolition of slavery in the 1830s, held out threats to the basic structure of colonial society. How did the Afrikaners at the time think about these matters? What problems and issues did they raise concerning slavery, and how did they respond to the imperial reforms? The texts collected in this chapter begin to provide some of the answers to these questions.

It is of some significance that we do not find in these texts any attempt to justify or defend the institution of slavery as such. No doubt, given the peculiar racial cast of the labour order at the Cape, racial and other prejudices strongly coloured the slaveholders' views of slavery, but we do not find any explicit racist defence of slavery based on, for example, the supposed innate inferiority of other races. Historians have pointed out that we do not find elaborate defences or justifications of slavery itself in other slave societies either until well into the nineteenth century, presumably because earlier there had been no pressing need for them.[5] Also, at the Cape there was no prolonged struggle with a locally based abolitionist movement that could polarize views and attitudes. The local community was confronted with a series of *faits accomplis* by the imperial government, which it was in no position to contest in any serious political struggle. Still, the fact remains that all the writers who comment on slavery in these texts clearly recognize that slavery in itself is morally undesirable, an evil system. Slavery is not just hard of itself and with respect to the lot of the slaves; it also has undesirable consequences for the masters, and in fact for the whole fabric of society. In Van Ryneveld's words, 'The facility of procuring slaves renders the inhabitants of this country lazy, haughty and brutal. Every kind of vice and a perfect corruption of morals is owing to that.' (2.3) At the same time it is not really made clear what the precise basis is for this moral judgement of slavery and its consequences. That is supposed to be self-evident. Thus, in a crucial passage Van Ryneveld writes, 'It is true, slavery is hard of itself. I have at the moment that I write the present memorial a feeling of all its weight, that ought to make an impression on the mind of every reasonable being.' (2.3) He then leaves it at that.

But how much weight exactly is given to this moral judgement of slavery as a hard and evil system? It is of equal significance that, with the possible exception of Stockenström, no one in these texts comes out unambiguously in favour of abolition. Afrikaner thinking on slavery tended towards some form of practical compromise. This is again brought out well in Van Ryneveld's words, 'However injurious slavery of itself may be to the morals and industry of the inhabitants, still the keeping of slaves is now become, as it is styled, a necessary evil.' (2.3) The key concept of 'a necessary evil' (cf. also 2.7b) indicates a rejection of moral absolutism.

Quite apart from the question of whether slavery was morally wrong or not, other kinds of considerations also had to be taken into account. This throws some light on the nature of early Afrikaner political thinking in coming to grips with an important social and practical problem. From these texts it appears that four other kinds of considerations were prominent in Afrikaner thinking on slavery and reform: historical, economic, legalistic and political. Let us deal briefly with each in turn.

1 Historical considerations, supporting some kind of practical realism, are much in evidence throughout these texts. The major argument is that, however undesirable slavery might be in principle, it was now a historical reality and must be considered as such. Van Ryneveld expressed this well: 'It would have been desirable that the colony should have begun without slavery. . . . But that is something different—it would change the entire condition of the colony and of everything in the colony. . . . For 125 years the colony's course has fluctuated with that of slavery. Since then, everything has gained a certain permanence, and to change this now, to bring it back to the

condition in which one would have liked the colony to have been started after so many years, would take a miracle, and be beyond the powers of men.' (2.5) Moreover, the argument is used that historically slavery was instituted, sanctioned, and encouraged by the authorities rather than sought by the local community (2.7b, 2.8a). Presumably this must be taken to imply some relief from the full moral responsibility for slavery. Since the colonial community was not autonomous in introducing slavery in the first place, could it then be expected that they should take full moral responsibility for abolishing it?

2 Considerations of economic costs and consequences have a high priority throughout these texts whenever they deal with the prospects of reform. Asked whether abolition was at all feasible, Van Ryneveld at once spelled out the dependence of the economy on slave labour, given the shortage of manual labour, the high cost of free labour as a substitute, and the inevitable disruptions to the economy should slavery or the slave trade be abolished (2.3). Whatever the accuracy of these prognoses proved to be in fact, it is clear that in the thinking of someone like Van Ryneveld these kinds of economic considerations were given great weight. Later, when the emancipation of the slaves was imminent, the colonists constantly reiterated that they had no fundamental objection to this, provided that they were protected from general economic disruptions and compensated for their immediate losses (2.8b, 2.9a). In this connection it is also interesting to note that the supposedly better treatment of the slaves at the Cape was attributed not so much to any special moral virtues of the local community but rather to an economic interest in the relatively high value of Cape slaves as capital investment (2.3, 2.8a, 2.8b, 2.9a). Denyssen in fact argues that the owners' self-interest in their increasingly valuable property would provide a more effective protection against ill-treatment of the slaves than any legal measures or moral appeals (2.7a). In short, it appears that Afrikaner views on slavery and emancipation were more inclined towards a utilitarian calculation of costs and benefits than towards any moral absolutism or ideological rigidity of principle.

3 More problematic is the use made of another set of arguments, which would appear to be primarily legalistic in kind. Though the colonists did not want to take full responsibility for slavery since they themselves did not desire or initiate it in the first place, they did not hesitate, on the other hand, to claim that they had acquired certain rights from the government's earlier encouragement and sanctioning of slavery. Thus the Burgher Senate argued that, from the legitimacy that had formerly been accorded to slave-ownership, certain inalienable rights could be derived concerning this kind of property-ownership, to which the government could be legally and morally held (2.8a). In defending property rights in slaves, the Burgher Senate speaks of 'inviolable' and 'sacred' rights (cf. also 2.7b). However, it is not difficult to sense an element of opportunism in this appeal rather than any full-blooded endorsement of the ideology of private property. There are indeed some indications of a (cynical?) insight into the way in which the conventions of law and government may be utilized to give legitimacy to what are otherwise recognized as morally somewhat dubious interests.

4 More decisive in determining thinking on slavery and its possible abolition was a clear insight into the wider political consequences. Slavery was not viewed as a specific economic institution which could be assessed in isolation from the rest of the social and political order. It was realized that to talk about slavery was to talk about the Cape as a slave society. Van Ryneveld is quite clear about the fact that slavery, whatever its vices, had become so crucially interwoven with the very structure of

Cape society that it 'cannot be removed without sacrificing the Colony, and perhaps the poor slaves themselves, that are in it.'[6] (2.3, 2.5) Most acutely he suggests that the question of the abolition of slavery, properly understood, amounts to nothing less than proposing a new social order in which slavery *would be unnecessary* (2.5). The same point concerning the crucial significance for the whole social and political order is made in more dramatic terms when Denyssen argues that a slave rising should not be regarded as an ordinary criminal offence, but that, as an 'attack on the existing order of public affairs', it amounted to a political offence, in fact to nothing less than treason (2.7b). In this way it may also be understandable why the colonists saw the prospect of emancipation as nothing short of a total revolution, an overturning of the whole existing order which could be conceived only in terms of violence and utter ruin (cf. 2.8a, 2.8b, 3.8). Though these anticipations of revolutionary ruin were to prove far off the mark, this does not lessen their significance. Fundamentally they indicate an awareness of the central importance of slavery to the entire social and political order, and of the far-reaching implications of radical change to so basic an institution in Cape society.

What, then, are the general characteristics of early Afrikaner political thought on such vital issues as slavery and emancipation? Taken together the various kinds of considerations that are prevalent in these texts suggest an approach that is neither inclined to any kind of doctrinaire or absolutist moralism, nor at all characteristic of the political ideologies of either liberalism or Calvinism. It may perhaps best be characterized as a form of pragmatic realism in which *a priori* moral principles are not much in evidence, as against a pervasive awareness of historical realities, economic interests, and possible social and political costs. The basic premisses and assumptions of this kind of thinking were well expressed by Van Ryneveld, in terms with which most of the other Afrikaners of the time probably would have agreed. 'One must accept things as they are, and not as they ought to be. Therefore, however one might think about these things [i.e. slavery], and whatever one has to say about them, in this respect [i.e. abolition] one can do no more than wish.' (2.5) The conservative bias in favour of the existing order will be clear. However, it does not altogether exclude possible reform, though as Van Ryneveld goes on to make clear in the same passage, this will have to be of a moderate and cautious, piecemeal nature.

The thinking on slavery and emancipation as it emerges from these documents also shows another characteristic. The stands taken by the colonists were almost always *in reaction to* external initiatives. Slavery itself they saw as something that had been imposed by the government on the local community, who had had little or no say in the matter and in good faith had invested in slaves. In the same way the moves towards reform and emancipation were seen as primarily initiatives of the imperial authorities, to which they could react positively or negatively, but not as something they could do themselves. There is also a pattern to these reactions: they are clearly opportunistic.

In 1797, at a time when the practices of slavery and the slave trade were still well established, we find Van Ryneveld saying that not only the total abolition of slavery at the Cape but even the interdiction of the slave trade were practical impossibilities (2.3). In the 1820s, when it became clear that the British government was serious in its moves towards reform and emancipation, we find the Burgher Senate saying that they are very much agreed on the principles of reform and abolition, and that 'the only matter in dispute therefore is the manner in which this is to be effected'. (2.8a, 2.8b) But neither the proposed schemes for gradual emancipation by freeing the female children of slaves, nor the expressions of 'philanthropic sentiment and concern' by the Graaff-Reinet heemraden (2.9a) carry much in the way of conviction that slavery was morally wrong. It is difficult not to feel that this is little more than an attempted holding operation and that, had they been left to their own devices, little would have come of any proposals for reform or abolition. Faced, however, with the reality of a changed situation, and with the imperial authority's evident resolve, they were readily prepared to accommodate to their own best advantage, while expressing grave fears about the possible social consequences and costs. In the circumstances this is quite understandable and little else could probably have been expected. However, given the enduring relevance to the South African labour order of practical and moral problems first raised in connection with slavery, the fact that they did not develop clear ideas on where exactly they stood with respect to slavery and abolition or, in a wider context, with respect to 'the rights of man' was to prove highly significant in the later development of Afrikaner political thinking.

Forced labour and paternalism

Slavery was not the only kind of involuntary labour system extant at the Cape. During the course of the eighteenth century large numbers of Khoikhoi had become incorporated as a labouring class on the white farms. In some cases their condition was not far removed from that of slaves.[7] Specific practices associated with slavery, such as the indenture system, were extended to the indigenous labour force as well. Document 2.2, the minutes of the Stellenbosch landdrost and heemraden of 1780, illustrates how early Afrikaner thinking turned to the pass system, which had been developed for slaves, as a means to control Khoikhoi labourers as well. Particularly on the closing frontier, labour-repressive mechanisms were developed to ensure the immobility of a docile labour force. The view of a farmer in 1798 is that 'the Hottentots who have entered service should be put in leg-irons for a while when they steal or desert so that this nation can be tamed a little, as they are extremely devious'. (3.4b) Forced labour was thus a more general practice than the institution of slavery alone, and even after the abolition of slavery informal practices of labour oppression persisted. In the Cape Colony, colonists were unsuccessful in their efforts to get a vagrant law that would re-introduce the pass system subsequent to Ordinance 50. But in the Voortrekker republic in Natal they had a freer hand to devise their own labour legislation and, as the letters from landdrost Zietsman in 1840 illustrate, their thinking at once tended towards a pass system 'according to the Dutch practice'. (2.12) In the Transvaal, allegations of slavery were to persist well into the second half of the nineteenth century. Proposals for labour control were usually careful to allow for some degree of contractual freedom for labourers as between different masters (2.12, 3.13d). But they were clear that free blacks should not be allowed 'to remove themselves from society', (3.13d) and that in society they should be prohibited 'from moving about without fixed employment'. (2.12)

The prevalence of such labour compulsion raises economic, political and moral questions. What were the views of early Afrikaner thinkers on the issues connected with involuntary labour? The texts collected in this chapter begin to suggest some of the answers.

Van Ryneveld again takes the most general view, and in doing so, illuminates the basic dilemma. He readily concedes that labour should be free. However, in the conditions obtaining at the Cape—easy access to land, an expanding frontier, an indigenous population used to a nomadic and subsistent way of life—such free labour was not forthcoming. Apart from slavery, 'a necessary evil', he rejects other forms of legalized coercion. 'Now one might ask why the government does not force these and similar sorts of free men [i.e. the Khoikhoi] in the colony to work and to do the heavy farm labour. It is for this simple reason: that the government has, with respect, no right to do this.' (2.5) The result was clearly a dilemma: the conditions of the colony were such that there was an acute labour shortage that could not be met by free labour, but legalized coercion was ruled out as well. Van Ryneveld does not indicate how the dilemma was to be resolved, but others came to different conclusions. Landdrost Van der Riet, in his defence of the indenture system (2.6a), claims that the Khoikhoi 'are by nature untrustworthy, slothful and drowsy', and invokes their unwillingness to do any voluntary work, and their destitute conditions (cf. also 2.11b). Given the labour needs of the farmers, it was only right that some coercive measures should be applied, in the interests of both parties (cf. also 2.12).

The set of ideas and assumptions involved in this legitimization of coercive labour practices constitutes the pattern of thought characteristic of *paternalism.* Eugene Genovese has shown how in the slave society of the American South the intolerable strains, inherent in a system where men were compelled to become the involuntary instruments of other men's wills, were comprehended and legitimized by the paternalist conception of an organic relation involving mutual duties and responsibilities. 'Paternalism defined the involuntary labour of the slaves as a legitimate return to their masters for protection and direction. . . . It grew out of the necessity to discipline and morally justify a system of exploitation. . . . For the masters, paternalism meant reciprocal duties within which the master had a duty to provide for his people and to treat them with humanity, and the slaves had a duty to work properly and to do as they were told. Necessarily, the slaves also had, from the white point of view, incurred an obligation to be grateful.'[9] In the texts collected in this section similar paternalist views can be found, both in connection with slavery itself and concerning other types of forced labour. Thus a Graaff-Reinet heemraad, though favourably disposed to the prospect of emancipation, nevertheless insists, 'But do not deprive me of my paternal authority, under which both my children and slaves are happy, and which is necessary for their and my peace.' (2.9b) When the slave-owners speak of their 'philanthropic sentiment and concern' (2.9a) for the slaves in their care, this is properly understood in a paternalist sense. Denyssen likewise introduces an explicit paternal analogy. 'The slave is almost as safe in the protection of his master as the child is in that of his father. And this is especially the case with house-slaves . . . for whom a natural feeling of love unites itself with self-interest, so that they find true friends and protectors in their masters.' (2.7b) Similar paternalist notions appear in the memorial of the Cape Town burghers (cf. 2.8b), and in a remarkable phrase in a letter of N. T. van der Walt to Stockenström, when he writes of his Khoikhoi and 'Bushman' servants, '*We have been educated in one house*; nothing would hurt me so much as to see that peace destroyed, to establish which I have done so much.' (3.13d)

But the paternalist argument is most fully developed in Landdrost Van der Riet's apology for the indenture system applied to the Khoikhoi. It is not merely a question of the farmer requiring labour which the Khoikhoi are unwilling to provide on a voluntary basis, so that he has to resort to compulsion. Binding Khoikhoi children (and indirectly their families as well) to long periods of service is justified because their own destitute conditions require the care and protection of a master, and in exchange for this trouble and expense they can be held to have incurred the duty of protracted service (2.6a). The repeated expressions of concern for the fate of orphaned Khoikhoi children, or even for the general plight of the wandering or 'vagrant' Khoikhoi groups not yet incorporated on the white farms (cf. 2.11a), need not be seen as simply hypocritical. It often reflected a genuine expression of paternalist responsibility, which functioned at the same time to legitimize the maintenance of practices of forced labour. Paternalism is characteristic of pre-industrial labour relationships when landowners exercised far-reaching rights over their dependents in return for accepting responsibilities towards them. The claim 'He is mine' is thus likely to mean 'He is my responsibility, he is attached to me, he works for me.'[10] But this paternalistic aspect of the labour relationship should not be allowed to obscure the essentially coercive nature of slavery. Certainly Stockenström (2.9b) has few illusions about this. The absolute power of the master to ensure the complete submission of the slave to his will was central to the institution, and the evils arising from excessive power in the hands of the master were thus inseparable from slavery. They could not finally be checked by any paternal bond of mutual affection and obligation, but only by the restraints imposed by the law. Attempts at an amelioration of slavery were misconceived. By undermining the coercive basis of the institution such half-measures only invited 'the greatest calamities'; only full emancipation could provide any solution. Other officials, including Denyssen himself in 1813, also clearly spell out the necessarily coercive basis of slavery (2.7a).

But the logic of labour compulsion was not confined to slavery only. In a most acute and perceptive analysis F. R. Bresler shows how the 'despotic and barbaric treatment' to which free-born Khoikhoi labourers were often subjected was neither a matter of accidental excesses nor attributable to the moral failings of the farmers, but inherent in the nature of the forced labour system. Fear and intimidation as the basis of labour compliance meant both a pervasive feeling of insecurity on the part of the workers who were at the mercy of their masters' power, and conversely the resulting frequent desertions which deprived employers of any assurance of a stable labour force. Similarly the coercive basis of the labour relation precluded any bond of interest or loyalty, resulting in 'the faithlessness of such Hottentots towards those whom they regard not as their masters but as their executioners, and whom they serve only through hunger or fear'.[11] (2.4) Thus a vicious circle arose in which the very consequences of forced labour required further coercive measures, and the awareness of this necessity came to provide a legitimation for it.

A similar analysis is provided by Stockenström in discussing the possible implementation of the indenture system for Xhosa workers from across the frontier. There might be some basis for a stable master-client relationship, from which both parties can benefit: 'the master, because he is released from part of his own labour; the savage, because he is released from a bloody enemy, and gets once more a sufficient meal'. (2.10b) But if there is an attempt to coerce the worker into a long-term involuntary servitude while the master has less than absolute power over him, and the worker retains his own interests and inclinations, then a violent chain-reaction is set in motion. 'He will show his aversion to his fetters, become obstinate, the master resents, the apprentice deserts, is retaken and punished; all mutual kind feeling is lost . . . and the upshot is, that they try to do each other as much mischief as they can. . . .' (2.10b) Stockenström concludes that there is no alternative to free labour, and that the workers should be allowed full scope to dispose of their labour as dearly as they could, to whom they pleased. He pointed out to farmers pressing for stricter labour controls that better wages would remove the need for such harsh measures. If labourers were remunerated 'not according to the will of the master but according to the demand of the servant as is the case in respect of free labourers throughout the world, there would be no need to compel [them] to remain within [the colony]'. (3.13e)

An important assumption underlies this analysis. Throughout, both parties are assumed to be in some basic sense free agents who will pursue what they conceive to be their own interests with whatever resources happen to be available, even under the conditions of a coercive relation. This does not imply any belief in the 'natural goodness' of man. On the contrary, as appears from a letter (2.6b) by Truter (who used the 'natural freedom' axiom most consistently), the human material may in both cases be assumed to be defective. The farmers, in the absence of the effective restraints of the law or other civilizing agencies of society, are liable to give free reign to their passions and abuse their positions as masters. The Khoikhoi, in their backward stage of civilization, are inclined to lack the necessary industry, loyalty and application in their duties as workers. But despite these differences due to environmental factors, both parties are assumed to be fundamentally equal as free human agents. This assumption had to be rejected by the proponents of the paternalistic approach. Landdrost Van der Riet, in reply (2.6a) to Truter's arguments based on the principle of natural freedom, concedes that they might have some validity if applied only to 'Christians', but denies that they could be brought to bear on the Khoikhoi, being as they are 'of the most stupid sort . . . who therefore never think, nor can think, as Christians do'. In a significant passage Van der Riet proceeds to point out the full social and political implications of the issues involved here. What would be the consequences to colonial society if the indigenous inhabitants were to act on their supposed equal freedom, and go on to stake their claims as the original owners of the land? The political order of the colony in fact required that, though not slaves, the Khoikhoi should be made to have a proper sense of their subordinate position, and that any dangerous ideas of freedom should be counteracted.

Much the same line of thinking appears, though in a rather different context, in Denyssen's treatment (2.7b) of the causes of the Bokkeveld slave insurrection. In many ways Denyssen's discussion is an acute and sophisticated analysis of the dynamics of rising expectations in a revolutionary situation. But it is also squarely based on the assumptions of a paternalist order. Denyssen clearly admits the coercive nature of slavery. 'Can any greater inequality exist than that between the class of free men and that of slaves, where the latter have not freely consented to bind themselves, for their whole lives, to the service of their masters?' However unequal and coercive this relation might be, it is not inherently unstable. Denyssen points to the relative absence of slave risings in the history of the Cape as a slave society, and ascribes this to the inculcation of the necessary awareness in the slaves' minds that they were bound to serve and obey. 'This impression,' he claims, 'was essential in order to preserve this country from unrest and commotion.' But once the slaves were made aware of the possibility of any alternative to their actual condition, only then did they become conscious of that position as one of inequality, of oppression and unjust exploitation. It was these new expectations which fanned the slaves' dissatisfactions and grievances, which made their position of subjection intolerable, and which in turn gave rise to hopes of general emancipation. And when these rising expectations were frustrated or disappointed, insurrections ensued. 'This disappointed hope was the cause.' Denyssen's analysis of the 'logic' of emancipation is of considerable interest for its own sake, but for our purposes what it reveals about the fundamental assumptions of paternalist thinking is of greater importance. Basically Denyssen is arguing that if there had been no interference with slavery from outside by would-be reformers or agitators, the slaves would have remained perfectly content. 'No matter how unequal the condition of one might be from the other', this did not yet in itself constitute any grounds for discontent or uprising. Alone, slaves are incapable of conceiving of themselves as free agents. This idea has to be introduced from outside. In this sense, then, slaves and their masters are not assumed to be inherently free agents. And since this is the case, he holds that the paternalist order of slavery is justified. Later Afrikaner thinking on other forms of involuntary labour and on race would find it difficult to rid itself of these and similar assumptions, and it would long remain only a minority that was prepared to accept the premisses of free labour even in a plural society.

2.1a In the midst of an abundance of cattle, wheat and wine the inhabitants of this Colony must lead a narrowly circumscribed way of life because there is no market for their produce.

—The Burgher Petition to the Dutch Chamber of Seventeen, 9 Oct. 1779 *(Memorie gedaan aan Vergadering van Zeventienen door Kaapsche Vrijburgers)*. (Translated and edited from *Kaapsche Geschillen*, Amsterdam 1785, Cape Archives C 742.)

The first major document in the Cape Patriots' efforts to obtain redress from the supreme colonial authorities in the Netherlands was the Burgher Petition of 1779. Having refused the request of some 400 burghers of the Western Cape to be permitted to send a delegation with their complaints to the Chamber of Seventeen, the Cape government nevertheless allowed the four delegates Jacobus van Reenen, Barend Jacob Artoys, Tieleman Roos and Nicolaas Godfried Heyns to proceed to the Netherlands, ostensibly on private business. They appeared with the petition before the Chamber of Seventeen on 16 October 1779, and submitted a further memorandum in 1782. In their response, only given at the end of 1783, the directors of the Company for the most part exonerated the officials at the Cape and refused to grant any important reforms. (Further extracts from the Burger Petition are included as Document 6.1b.)

Compelled by dire need, we the undersigned, on our own behalf and on behalf of the entire citizenry of the Cape of Good Hope, humbly take the liberty of putting before Your Honours our legitimate complaints about the deteriorating condition of the citizens and freeburghers here, and the well-founded grievances which we and our fellow-citizens have about the oppressive and illegal private trade carried on by various of Your Honours' officials here. We also humbly submit some requests for measures which we, under the respectful correction of Your Honours' wiser and more enlightened judgements, consider as the best and most necessary means of redress in all these matters. With all due respect and humility we thus submit ourselves to Your Honours' fatherly care and favourable protection. . . .

In order, therefore, to be as brief as possible in putting all these matters to Your Honours, the undersigned will proceed as follows in this memorial. First they will give a truthful outline . . . of the present condition of the citizens and inhabitants at the Cape of Good Hope itself as well as in the outlying districts which fall under the jurisdiction of the government. Secondly they will describe as clearly and accurately as possible the complaints of the burghers concerning the quite improper mode of conduct of most Company officials concerning the honourable Company itself and the memorialists in particular. . . . And finally, they will take the liberty of putting forward their humble requests concerning the improvement and redress of these matters. . . .

. . . it is in general . . . sufficiently well known that, through the natural fertility of the land at the Cape, the colony here has since early times produced enough wine and wheat not only to provide sufficient refreshment for the ships of the honourable Company, but also to meet the requirements of Batavia. . . . As it was then possible

. . . to market all the wine and wheat which the farmers could produce, agriculture grew rapidly. . . . But, when later the requirements of Batavia diminished, especially as far as wine was concerned, . . . the colonists began to feel keenly the reduction in trade. . . . Thus at that time men enjoyed abundance, yet were actually poor, as they could not put this to use.

Fortunately, however, a French fleet arrived at that time, which was short of everything. This not only put prices back to earlier levels, but even increased them considerably beyond what they had been. This meant that many could put aside some money, which they are living off even now. From that time on, income has been extremely erratic, according to the arrival of foreign ships, to which the citizens and farmers have sold their produce.

The citizens of the capital have long been accustomed to making their livings by selling various products of the country to the ships, and buying in turn some European or Indian goods which they then sell to the farmers. Company officials are bound by law to allow them this source of income as a free privilege. . . . But, notwithstanding these express laws, orders and instructions, . . . various of the most prominent and powerful of the Company officials do not scruple to buy up the greatest and most profitable part of the goods from the incoming ships. In view of their influence and authority with the sailors and the convenience of having at their disposal Company servants, stores and vehicles, it costs them far less to buy up these goods. This acts to the detriment of private citizens, who in turn are obliged to buy that which they absolutely cannot do without from them [the company officials], at high prices fixed according to their discretion. . . . This defective condition has brought about a situation in which many colonists who are not able to subsist on arable farming have had to trek over the mountains and apply themselves to cattle farming. Through the increase in their numbers and because all the districts do not provide good grazing, they have had to disperse widely, so that some are now situated up to 40 days' journey from the capital. . . . All this has reduced them to such poverty that many families, not able to subsist separately on one farm, move into a single hut together, while the younger men, who have no means of establishing themselves, must remain unmarried or live among the Hottentots. In time, this miscegenation could produce a new generation which might prove even more formidable than the Bushmen are at present.

The effect which this savage way of life must have on the education of children is also easily ascertainable. The children are effectively deprived of all proper education, because poverty prevents many parents from employing a schoolmaster, and the schoolmasters who are to be found there are mostly persons who, through their incompetence or bad conduct, could not manage nearer to the capital and have to teach at a place far away from there.

So bad is the situation for the inhabitants of this colony, that in the midst of an abundance of cattle, wheat and wine, they must lead a narrowly circumscribed way of life or suffer complete poverty, because there is no adequate market for their produce. And this languishing condition of the Cape citizenry and colonists . . . is largely caused, and further aggravated, by the oppression under whose burden the entire citizenry [*Burgerstaat*] must groan, and by the unauthorized private trade conducted by several of Your Honours' officials here, against which we and our fellow-citizens direct our legitimate objections and just complaints. . . .

Thus we request that Your Honours will give favourable attention and will comply with the following special appeals for redress, with which we will conclude this petition.

In the first place then Your Honours are most earnestly requested on behalf of the citizens and inhabitants of the Cape . . . to ensure that no official discharged with a pension nor anyone who is still in service at the Cape, from the highest to the lowest, with no exceptions whatsoever, may carry on any trade or commerce, directly or indirectly, for themselves or for others. . . .

Secondly, Your Honours are respectfully requested to issue the necessary instructions so that a citizen might in future have the freedom to sell and deliver his produce, once the honourable Company has been adequately provided for, to foreign ships, without having to pay any duty on it to the fiscal. . . .

Your Honours are also requested to allow the citizens to punish their slaves, although not to tyrannize them. . . .

J. van Renen
Barend Jacob Artoys
Th. Roos
Ns. Gd. Heyns

2.1b It is in the constitution of this colony itself that the most important cause is to be found for our not being able to live in a state of peace and happiness.

—Petition from some inhabitants to the governor and Political Council of the Cape, 17 Feb. 1784. (Translated from the text published as Appendix E in C. Beyers, *Die Kaapse Patriotte*. The original draft is to be published as part of the Swellengrebel papers edited by G. Schutte for the Van Riebeeck Society.)

The Cape Patriots appealed to the States General against the decision by the Chamber of Seventeen in 1783 on the initial Burgher Petition of 1779. Further petitions were submitted and they received some aid in publicizing their grievances from Patriot circles in the Netherlands. The Petition of 1784 was initiated by Hendrik Swellengrebel, who had been born in Cape Town while his father was governor there and had again visited the colony in 1776–1777. He maintained close contacts with prominent burghers at the Cape, such as Hendrik Cloete, and assisted the Cape delegates in the Netherlands. Swellengrebel drafted the petition and sent it to Cape Town with the suggestion that it be signed by some of the most prominent Western Cape farmers who had not taken an active part in the Patriot movement, and addressed as a separate request to the Cape government.

. . . The undersigned citizens and inhabitants of the Cape of Good Hope respectfully note that, for some time, it has come to their attention that discontent has become so prevalent among a considerable number of inhabitants of this colony, that one has much ground for wondering whether public order can be maintained without disruption, as is necessary for the general welfare.

Your petitioners are of the opinion that it is in the constitution of this colony itself that the most important cause is to be found for their not being able to live in a state of peace and happiness, such as that in which their forefathers lived, but which, now more than ever before, they seem to be about to relinquish, and which, as they fear with the utmost anxiety, their children will enjoy increasingly less of as time goes by.

The undersigned, in petitioning, take the liberty of requesting Your Honours to reflect upon the manner in which, after this colony had been established in the middle of the preceding century on very fertile soil and in a favourable climate, and its inhabitants had advanced its agriculture by every appropriate means, it soon established the aims of its foundation, viz. to expand into a refreshment station for the honourable East India Company's out-going and homecoming ships, and, in many respects, to provide a pantry for various Indian offices.

Although the number of colonists increased greatly through natural growth, as a result of the settlement of various French refugees and allowing Company servants to enter the citizenry, they still had a fortunate source of existence in agriculture for as long as there was sufficient consumption, even after the prices of these products were reduced by Governor General Van Imhoff, on the gracious promise that the honourable Company would take all such produce which could be delivered.

Although later, and particularly after the death of the above-mentioned Governor General, the favourable disposition of the honourable Company ceased, the colonists were still able to support themselves for a time, in spite of the resulting reduction in consumption, through the arrival of an ever-increasing number of foreign ships. . . . The detrimental effects of inadequate consumption have made themselves felt to an even greater extent as the number of colonists has increased daily, while the means of subsistence has not increased proportionally.

Although a slight opportunity is offered from time to time by the arrival of a greater number of foreign ships than usual, and the richer colonists, who can store their products when prices are low, can get a good price for this produce (although this is nevertheless considerably diminished by the fact that their capital is profitlessly tied up in this produce), the less prosperous colonists, who must sell their grain and wine for their daily sustenance, usually cannot profit from the advantage of sporadically greater markets, and at least cannot be compensated in any way for the damage suffered from continually low prices.

The natural consequences of this must be real poverty for a considerable number of the colonists, who are therefore unable to make a living from arable farming, and who have trekked over the mountains in large numbers to seek to maintain themselves by cattle breeding there. Yet no matter how well one may fare in animal husbandry, this source of subsistence must also be reduced, as one's assets do not grow with increases in one's herds, but, on the contrary, the price must come down, as the pastoralists settle further away from the metropolis, and the herds which have been sold have to be driven over increasingly long distances. This, in turn, has a detrimental effect upon those who, having been the first to establish themselves over the mountains and being able to support themselves quite well there, are now continually obliged to lower the prices of meat, butter and soap by the great increase in competitors. These reductions in price are such that, in the present situation, prices provide only a sober return on costs at best, and they no longer allow the farmers across the mountains any real profit, except for farms belonging to prominent arable farmers, who cannot spare sufficient pastures at their wine and wheat farms for the breeding of the necessary stock, and those belonging to the contracted Company butchers.

However vast the colony might be, experience has already taught that the natural fertility of the soil is not sufficient to feed as great a number of cattle as each man is now obliged to keep in order to compensate by large quantities for the small profit-margins which are obtainable in their occupation because of low prices. At the same time, keeping so many cattle makes the proper conservation of the pastures impracticable, and is the cause of people having had to leave various divisions, which have declined altogether through the lack of proper farming practices, and of strife arising so often because of the proximity of neighbouring farms, which would otherwise be . . . situated a fair distance from each other. Apart from this, young colonists, who can find no place for themselves among the already established farms, are continually having to move further up the coast and further inland, and are even settling so far away that they have to bring in the produce of a whole year in 25, 30 or up to 40 stages in one wagon-load, and it often happens that for this they receive only 100 rixdollars. Of this slight sum, they must then still pay 48 rixdollars for two loan-farms, for which it is absolutely necessary for them to stock up enough butter for a wagon-load. Thus they are left with only 50 rixdollars, and they have to use all of that to buy their clothing and to buy all their domestic requirements which the land has not produced except milk, meat and wheat. Yet there are many who are not even able to harvest wheat, as long as that requires the expense of a plough, etc., to which their restricted financial circumstances do not extend—since apart from this, they must provide themselves with a wagon and other most necessary equipment as well, whose cost takes away the largest part of their slight profits.

All this has, in turn, as its consequence, that however miserable this sort of existence may be, many young colonists do not even have the means for this, and have to settle here or there in a miserable hut among the Hottentots, where they live off the flesh of wild buck, sometimes even rhinoceros, and even off the carcasses of the prey of carnivorous animals. One cannot sufficiently bemoan the sorry lot of the descendants of proper European parents, who, relying on favourable assurances given to them, left their fatherland and settled in a wild country, in the reasonable expectation that they and their descendants would at least enjoy the benefits of the first necessity of an orderly state. This the present colonists, in the present condition of the colony, have none but the most desperate prospect of getting, and they look with compassion to the fate of their children. At the same time they must see the approach of a complete bastardization of morals from so primitive a life-style in the veld, and this in their own beloved progeny, who might otherwise, under the favourable hand of Providence, have served as a blessing, They must see a completely degenerate nation, which might become just as dangerous for the colony as the Bushman-Hottentots now are. Thus one might be justified in asking the anxious question: 'If this country cannot even support the people with whom any civilization rests, what will it let happen to those who mix their blood with that of Hottentots and Kaffirs?'

The undersigned would not deny that there would certainly be better opportunities for employment for many young colonists if agriculture were organized in the way it is in the home country, and they entered the service of others. But the undersigned feel it worthy of constant consideration that it is hardly to be expected—while those in the original part of the colony employ slaves and those in the interior usually employ Hottentots, and while it is a completely different matter to work in one's father's house or on one's own account than to do the same work for another in the capacity of a servant—that our young men will want to enter service on an equal footing with Hottentots and slaves, at least for as long as the necessary arrangements towards this end are not knowledgeably, cautiously and only gradually implemented.

Your petitioners cannot envisage more than a very few opportunities for employment being created for young inhabitants in the military or naval service of the government, as it cannot be required of them to expose themselves to the extreme danger of being used in the Indian establishment, as it is generally known how fatal those parts are for Europeans, and particularly for us Afrikaners, who are always susceptible to that fatal child ailment. Thus it is not to be wondered at that men prefer living in a healthy country even in primitive conditions, in which one is suddenly placed beyond all constraints, to exposing themselves to such clear danger in another country.

However extraordinarily the capital has flourished in the last few years, through the presence of a great number of troops and the arrival of foreign ships, this prosperity will not continue once this unusual state of affairs ceases. This is because, apart from the usual bad effects of such sudden wealth, the means of subsistence for so great a number of citizens in one town, where there is no manufacturing, cannot be increased or changed, and thus cannot provide many good opportunities for newcomers to seek honest and rewarding employment, particularly while unwillingness to earn a living by doing the work of slaves keeps many a European from the trades.

The undersigned must indeed agree that the farmers have occasionally, also in the last few years, been able to sell their produce at advantageous prices. Yet they would still remark that, as the greater payment is also caused by the unusual needs of the warring powers, and is therefore simply a fortunate coincidence, one should realize that the profits thus acquired—just as at previous occasionally favourable opportunities when more foreign ships than usual arrived—are no more than the forerunners of a new poverty. In fact, the profits which remain after redemption of capital expenditure, through which many gained real wealth, are superfluous, and cannot be invested anywhere but in the expansion of someone's farming activities. This must of course lead to an increase in the produce brought on to the market, but, by the same token, brings a reduction in the prices of the same when consumption does not increase proportionately. In this way, the arable farmer will find himself burdened with increasingly expensive maintenance of his farm, because of increases in the numbers of his slaves, more buildings and the greater quantity of equipment which he comes to need to farm on this scale, as well as the extra trouble of ensuring that the necessary number of cattle are bred for his expanded undertakings.

Over and above all these considerations, which might be related to external consumption, the colonists themselves do not have full enjoyment of their own produce, because of the lack of facilities to communicate with one another. This occurs in the case of the wine farmers who very often have wine which they can put to no use, while a stock-farmer in the interior is very seldom able to fortify himself with a draught of wine. These former, in turn, live where vast forests extend to the sea, and have to go to great lengths to transport wood from these forests to the wine farms, where the houses are often without ceilings, for lack of timber.

At the same time, it is a general rule that the farmer cannot exist unless he is able to realize the fruit of his labour and of the land in a financially rewarding way. Thus it also appears obvious to the petitioners that this colony, consisting solely of farmers, will eventually not be able to subsist without steady consumption proportionate to the quantity of its produce, and without the means of drawing the distantly located colonists from their primitive life-style and attracting them to arable farming. Similarly, as much as possible would have to be done to facilitate internal transportation, which is presently so difficult that all other advantages are considerably reduced and agriculture is hindered.

The undersigned petitioners are of the opinion that the great degree of discontent which prevails in the colony has its principal source in the real defects of the constitution. This constitution was basically sound at the foundation of this establishment and for as long as only as much was produced as was necessary for a refreshment station, but now that the colony ordinarily produces more than can reasonably be paid for . . . it is no longer suitable. As trustworthy inhabitants, who have the welfare of the land of their residence at heart, the undersigned are of the opinion that this disturbing situation might and must be presented, respectfully, to the highly enlightened consideration of their government.

Js. Ms. Cruywagen H. O. Eksteen the elder Hendk. Cloete etc.

2.2 *Stellenbosch landdrost and heemraden on the need for pass laws 1780*

2.2 So that such order might be established among these free bastard Hottentots as would be to the greatest use and benefit of the inhabitants.

—Minutes of Landdrost O. G. de Wet and heemraden of Stellenbosch, 7 Aug. 1780. (Translated from the transcript of the original in Moodie, *Afschriften*, Vol. 6, Cape Archives.)

Pass laws as a feature of the South African labour order originated in connection with slavery. According to a proclamation first issued in 1708 slaves were expected to carry passes when sent on errands by their masters or to work in the fields as cattle-herds. This document from 1780 shows how the colonists' thinking tended towards using the same device to prevent absconding among other members of the servile class. The government did not accept the proposal of the Stellenbosch body, but in 1797 and 1798 the landdrost and heemraden of both Swellendam and Graaff-Reinet ordained that Hottentots travelling from one place to another should carry passes. A similar pass provision was incorporated in the 'Hottentot Proclamation' of 1809.

. . . The landdrost said further that it has appeared that when one of that class of slaves who is the product of the union of female slaves with Hottentots and who usually is not distinguishable from other free bastard Hottentots, succeeds in deserting from his master, he has a good opportunity of passing himself off as [a] free [black]. This he can do by pretending to be a free bastard Hottentot, particularly when he is not otherwise known. . . . Thus they can wander about, causing harm to and annoying many of the inhabitants. Moreover, it had been found that such fugitive slaves even had the temerity to enter the service of the inhabitants as free bastard Hottentots.

[The landdrost continued] that, on the other hand, it had recently occurred that certain bastard Hottentots, who were actually free, having been born of a Hottentot or bastard Hottentot mother and slave father, had inherited little of the recognizable complexion of the Hottentots, and had been suspected of being fugitive slaves. They had been apprehended as such, and brought to prison here, and after they had been fed for some time at the colony's expense and had suffered innocent incarceration, they had once again to be released. The landdrost thus suggested that, should it be generally desired that a standing order be drawn up to prevent similar inconveniences and irregularities occurring among these free bastard Hottentots, it might be advisable to bring this matter to the attention of the honourable governor and Political Council, along with any such request as might be thought practicable in this matter.

This was carefully considered, and it was also remarked upon that the number of these free bastard Hottentots who are entering the wage service of the inhabitants, particularly in the outlying districts, was increasing more and more each day. [This meant] that any such order would be of great general value and benefit, especially if the supreme authorities might see fit to legislate as follows:

Each and every one of the free bastard Hottentots residing among the inhabitants is to be obliged, within a fixed time, to request and receive a document or pass, stating his name, on whose land he lives and in whose service he is. He must always have this document or pass with him, and must be able to show it every time he leaves his place of residence.

[These passes would have to renewed regularly, and at their renewal] these bastard Hottentots, who have so far been exempted from all common taxation, would also be able to contribute a fair share from the wages which they come to enjoy. And, at the same time, a complete list of them might be made, from which the honourable governor and council could always ascertain, if they so desired, how many bastard Hottentots there are in the outlying districts among the inhabitants as well as the number of competent militia among them.

Each and every one of the inhabitants is to be forbidden, on pain of certain penalties, to provide food or shelter to any bastard Hottentot not in possession of such a document or pass. Instead these inhabitants will be obliged to detain such bastard Hottentots as are unable to show a pass or document, and to hand them over to the nearest veldwagtmeester, so that they might be taken from one veldwagtmeester to the next and eventually brought to jail. And if it is then found that such [a prisoner] is a free bastard Hottentot—for many of them are often inclined to wander about without a fixed place of residence to the inconvenience and annoyance of the inhabitants—he will then be put under the obligation of taking up and keeping to a permanent place of residence. This is not, however, to have the effect of diminishing their freedom to enter the service of other inhabitants once the period of service has expired.

Nobody will be permitted, on pain of a fixed fine, to let any free bastard Hottentot enter his service unless that Hottentot can give proof that he has completed his proper period of service, or that he has been discharged from service for some good reason and has the freedom to enter service elsewhere.

This entire proposal was unanimously approved and it was decided to address this request to the honourable Governor and Council and, for the reasons and motives given above, respectfully to request that these measures might meet with their approval . . . so that such order might be established among these free bastard Hottentots as would be, in the opinions of Your Honours, to the greatest use and benefit of the inhabitants.

2.3 It is true, slavery is hard of itself, but it has now become a necessary evil in this Colony.

—Replies of W. S. van Ryneveld to Governor Macartney's questionnaire, 29 Nov. 1797. (Edited from the translation published in the *Journal of Secondary Education*, September and December 1931. The original is in the Gubbins Collection of Africana at the University of the Witwatersrand, Johannesburg.)

Slavery at the Cape received renewed attention as a result of the British occupation in 1795. Part of the British government's instructions to the first governor, Lord Macartney, was to investigate the feasibility of abolishing the importation of slaves. Macartney directed a questionnaire to W. S. van Ryneveld (1765—1812) who was a member of the Council of Policy at the time of the British conquest and had been reappointed by the new rulers as fiscal (public prosecutor). The importation of slaves was eventually abolished during the second British occupation in 1809.

Question What material injury or inconvenience would result to the Colony, if the importation of slaves were to be prohibited?

. . . An immediate interdiction to the importation of slaves, would, of course, effectuate that the culture, especially the two principal branches thereof, viz. corn and wine, first would begin to languish, and afterwards entirely to decay.

We know very well, that here, both within and without the Colony, no sufficient number of white people can be obtained to perform in culture the labour of the slaves; and, on the other hand, experience shows us every day that the procreation of slaves, in proportion to number, is very trifling, and even not worth mentioning; and that, moreover, a very considerable number of slaves is lost by continual disorders, especially by bile and putrid fevers, to which they are very subject.

The political state of this Colony, I think, is actually of that nature that, however injurious slavery of itself may be to the morals and industry of the inhabitants, still the keeping of slaves has now become, as it is styled, a necessary evil; and, at least, a sudden interdiction to the importation of slaves would occasion a general injury, as long as such a number of hands as is requisite for the culture cannot be obtained from another part, at a rate that may be thought proportionate to the produce arising from the lands. . . . It is very true that at present there may be found some white or free persons apt for that purpose; yet apart from the number of these persons not being sufficient in any degree to supply the number of slaves wanted, the high hire and expensive maintenance of such free labourers would still render the employing of them impracticable. . . .

Question If not prohibited, . . . how may the same be regulated in order to . . . prevent the inconveniences that have been occasioned in other colonies by too great a number of slaves?

. . . The treatment of the slaves here is in general on a quite different and much milder footing than it is in the said colonies [the West Indies], owing not only to the laws properly guarding in this respect, but also to the high price of the slaves themselves being a continual incitement to care, for such masters as are influenced more by selfishness than by any principle of humanity.

The enforcement of the laws and institutes already established on the subject of granting protection to those that are oppressed, and by awarding a moderate punishment to those that deserve it, can be the only means of entirely removing every apprehension of inconveniences arising from any number of slaves.

It is true, slavery is hard of itself. I have at the moment that I write the present memorial a feeling of all its weight, that ought to make an impression on the mind of every reasonable being; yet, besides it not being my task to treat of slavery by itself, a subject on which so many books have already, particularly in the present century, been published, I cannot but observe that slavery in this Colony has now become a necessary evil, which cannot be removed without sacrificing the Colony, and perhaps the poor slaves themselves that are in it. Lucky however it is that this Colony is always ruled by a well-regulated Government which, though for the sake of good order, and for preventing inconveniences, it is obliged to make a distinction between a slave and his master, that by so doing the former may be kept in a proper bond of subordination, it will however never omit to adopt and pursue any means tending to alleviate the fate of these creatures, as much as circumstances will admit of.

In the meanwhile, every impartial man, I think, cannot but own that the slaves are generally not ill-treated here and that every act, contrary to the principles of humanity, is always duly checked.

Question Is not the climate of the Cape sufficiently moderate for the white inhabitants to be able to till the ground and to pursue the same rural labour as the peasants in Spain, Portugal, Sicily and other warm countries?

. . . There are many who are of the opinion that the white people are not able to perform the same hard rural labour as the slaves, for the reason that the principal rural labour, namely, ploughing and reaping, is always to be performed either during the winter when the cold is very severe, or in the summer when the heat is most oppressive. But as to my own opinion, I cannot find that the climate should be the cause why the natives of the country, who are accustomed from their very youth to the climate, should not be able to pursue the same rural labours as the peasants in Spain, Portugal, Sicily and other warm climates; yet I acknowledge that our present peasants are not fit, because not accustomed to it.

It is true that tillage, and especially the culture of grain, requires hard work, and is attended with many inconveniences and much troubles—the ground is hard and either hilly or clayish—so that imported utensils, viz. spades, pickaxes, ploughs, ploughshares, that are used in other countries are not strong enough for and of no use to this Colony. The peasants here are, therefore, obliged always to get a special kind of strong spade and ploughshare for tilling this country, either to be made here, or sent from Europe to them: all which evinces the rural labour here to be extremely fatiguing and toilsome.

Still, the proverb says 'Custom is second nature', and therefore I ought to reply . . . that our peasant would be able to till the ground and to pursue the same rural labour as the peasants in Spain, Portugal, Sicily and other warm climates, if they were accustomed to it from their youth and if necessity compelled them to it.

Here I state two conditions: in the first place the peasants should be accustomed to every kind of rural labour from their youth, and secondly, necessity should incite them to it. And indeed this needs no demonstration.

A peasant, who has always been accustomed to have his work done by slaves, and who has therefore done nothing but superintend it, will not always be easily brought to perform every kind of rural labour. Still, I know a few peasants who from their very youth have been obliged to work like the slaves, which shows that the climate is no obstacle for a white inhabitant to perform rural labours.

But I cannot yet see how the white inhabitants can be reduced to that necessity. It speaks for itself that there is no man in the world who works without being incited to it by some motives. These consist either in ambition or in necessity. The former generally takes place among civilized men, among whom there often appear some who, incited by ambition, devote themselves to hard labour, and from which they are not to be taken off, although not compelled to it by necessity. Such kinds of motives are however not to be looked for in the peasants of this country. The slender instruction they have received must class them among such men as do not work but from necessity.

Whence, of course, it follows that as long as there are in this country those resources to get subsistence in an easier manner, no farmer will by way of preference devote himself to such a really toilsome and hard labour as our tillage, and especially our culture of grain. This is not to be attributed to any peculiar vice in our peasants, but it resides in the nature of the case itself. When a young peasant marries and sees an opportunity of obtaining land fit for breeding cattle, by which he may get his livelihood, he would act like a fool by leaving that, and hiring himself out to his fellow peasant, in order there, along with the slaves, by a continual labour, to earn scarcely as much as only food and clothing for himself. . . .

Question If there were no slaves at the Cape, would not the white peasants become more industrious and useful to the State? Does not the facility of procuring slaves, and the general custom of making use of them, render the white inhabitants more haughty, more lazy and more brutal?

. . . There are (to return properly to my subject) two principle causes that prevent the white people here from doing rural labour, viz.:

1st. The great extent of the country, without sufficient population, so that the country is really in want of hands for carrying on the tillage;

2nd. The introduction of slavery.

I perfectly acknowledge . . . that if there were no slaves at the Cape the peasants would then be more industrious and useful to the State, and that the facility of procuring slaves renders the inhabitants of this country lazy, haughty and brutal.

Every kind of vice and a perfect corruption of morals is owing to that. But how to help it? If slavery had been interdicted at the first settling of this Colony, then the inhabitants would doubtless have become more industrious and useful to each other; they would be obliged to associate in a narrower compass of land, and the Colony would never have so exceedingly extended beyond its ability and beyond the exigence of its population.

Yet, the business is done. Slavery exists and is now even indispensible. It is absolutely necessary because there are no other hands to till this extensive country, and therefore it will be the work, not of years, but as it were of centuries to remove by attentive and proper regulation this evil established with the first settling of the Colony.

Should the slaves be now declared free, that would immediately render both the country and these poor creatures themselves miserable; not only all tillage would then be at an end, but also the number of freemen, instead of their being (as now) useful members of, would then really become a charge to, society. And should the importation of slaves be interdicted, on a sudden, without any means being provided towards supplying other hands for the tillage, then the Colony would thereby be caused to languish (the procreation of slaves being so inconsiderable in comparison with their mortality) and especially the culture of grain would thereby be reduced to decay.

In order to improve gradually the industry of this Colony, it will be absolutely necessary, on the one hand, to obviate the further enlarging of this settlement. As long as one may infringe upon the countries of the Kaffirs, Bushmen, etc., to take their lands and to live upon the breeding of cattle, then so long no person will be anxious about the state of his children, so long no sufficient number of hands will be to be obtained in the country itself to carry on the tillage, so long the inhabitants will never enter into the service of each other, and, finally, so long the importation of slaves also will be necessary for the sake of the culture of grain. While on the other hand a person will never scruple to settle himself throughout the whole country of Africa among all the nations, and, by so doing, at length to become like those wild nations.

The Government, intending to frame from this Colony a regular Society, where diligence and industry are to compose the foundation of the prosperity of the people, ought therefore, and in the first place, to take care that no person do in future settle beyond the boundaries of this Colony, and that by that regulation the young people be, of course, obliged to endeavour to earn their subsistence in the bosom of the Colony itself; from doing which, sufficient motives will then always and in proportion to the increase of population arise, to be industrious and so to promote both their own welfare and the prosperity of the community in general. . . .

2.4 Regarding their cruel treatment of the Hottentots as necessary, the inhabitants consequently also regard it as legitimate.

—Court pleading of F. R. Bresler at the trial of R. H. Brits, 28 May 1801. (Translated from the original in the Cape Archives, CJ 483, pp. 245–7.)

2.4 F. R. Bresler on the cruel treatment of Khoi labourers 1801

Even before the institution of Circuit Courts in 1811 or the controversial 'Black Circuit' of 1812, the maltreatment of Khoikhoi labourers by farmers in the interior was a cause of concern to enlightened officials. In this document from the trial of a farmer for killing a Khoikhoi woman, F. R. Bresler (1766–1825), the successor to Maynier as landdrost of Graaff-Reinet from 1796 to 1802, who was acting as public prosecutor, outlines the vicious circle of terror and resistance as colonists tried to convert once free hunters and herders into docile labourers.

. . . The numerous examples of despotic and barbaric treatment which many of the inhabitants often inflict upon those free-born Hottentots and Bastards who are in their service, though only as contracted workers, do not only have these two extreme consequences. The first of these is the overwhelming fear of the Hottentots for their masters. From this fear they frequently desert their service after what are only very trivial misdeeds and thereby become so accustomed to moving around that they eventually come to prefer a vagabondeering life. By the same token, the inhabitants are never assured of the presence of their servants. The second extreme consequence is the faithlessness of such Hottentots towards those whom they regard not as their masters but as their executioners, and whom they serve only through hunger or fear. But, apart from this, there is also a further deplorable consequence which results from this, viz. that the unlimited lust for power of the masters and the faithlessness and other vices of the Hottentots together result in many of the inhabitants regarding their cruel treatment of the Hottentots as necessary. Consequently they regard it also as legitimate and inflict it without restraint. The more civilized of our compatriots, however, view this with revulsion, call it inhuman, and to Europeans it often seems unbelievable, until they see it themselves in practice. . . .

2.5 That there is still no real class division among the true inhabitants of this Colony provides proof of the slight progress made in the welfare of the Colony.

—W. S. van Ryneveld's *A Sketch of the Condition of the Colony in 1805*. (Translated from the text published in *Het Nederduitsch Zuid-Afrikaansche Tijdschrift*, Vol. 8, 1831.)

During the Batavian administration (1803–1806) Van Ryneveld, as a senior official under both the Company and during the British occupation, was requested by the new government to draw up reports on various aspects of the economy and the administration. His 'Beschouwing over de veeteelt, landbouw, handel en finantie van de Kolonie de Kaap de Goede Hoop' (1805), from which the following excerpt is taken, was posthumously published in Het Nederduitsch Zuid-Afrikaansch Tijdschrift, *1831–1833.*

. . . Need certainly teaches one to pray, but poverty *alone* is not always the most certain incentive for work, as can be seen from thousands of examples. Barbarians do not work, and they are in want. There are whole nations, who would rather forfeit all enjoyments and satisfactions in life than devote themselves to heavy labour. The greatness, the extravagance and the wealth of the Indian princes is laboured for by thousands of their poor inhabitants, often without these wretches having anything but the first necessities of life. So different is the nature of one country and people from that of others.

The general rule that *poverty makes people work* cannot be applied at all times and in all cases. This rule has many exceptions throughout the world, according to the circumstances of countries, peoples and climate. A poor people can often be satisfied with very little. The Bushmen eat locusts, the Hottentots dig for bulbs and they neither have nor know of other luxuries. Even so they live, and they have reason to ask, why should we bother about heavy work?—we live, and that is enough.

It is true that, in the civilized world, in a country in which a high level of prosperity has been achieved, in which, therefore, there is regular progress in agriculture, in trade, in manufacturing, the poor man *must* work. He cannot do nothing; he must steal, or do something, and then he still always picks the work which is easiest for him. And why is this? Because he no longer has parents who can keep him; because he can no longer get land cheaply; because he can no longer find convenient work, e.g. as a farmer's *knecht*, as an overseer, and so on. The increase in population actually creates that economy in want, that necessary thrift among the lower classes in the world which is so useful to human society. Thus the practice of the crafts is made easier and cheaper. Anyone who wants to live among so great a number of people of all classes and occupations and who wants to eat, who, since others are clothed, wants to clothe himself as well so as not to be an exception in the society in which he lives—he must put out his hands and work. In this sense, the saying that *'he who does not work, will also not eat'* is true in the civilized world.

He who in *such a society*, does not put out his hands and work, *will truly also not eat*! . . .

Among those who are the true inhabitants of this Colony, there are still no real class divisions. This in turn provides proof of the only slight progress made in the welfare of the Colony.

At the establishment of a Colony, all its people are equal. Through enterprise and industriousness, one person is able to raise himself above the others. The more the population and prosperity increases, the more as a natural consequence the classes [*standen*] will come to be distinguished. Let the entire history of the world be considered, and one will find that, to the extent that the prosperity of a country increases, so the inhabitants spontaneously come to be divided into different classes in which they can be useful to themselves and to the country. Inhabitants of the greatest wealth and the direst poverty are to be found in the most fertile and the happiest countries. The poor are always necessarily the greatest in number and often the most useful as well. The more the population increases, the more the classes, from either side as it were, are raised towards their ultimate ends. It is in this way that regular progress is brought about in agriculture and manufacturing; in this way a supply of manual labour is ensured; in this way luxury is increased as a fair reward given more to the rich than to the poor. . . .

In fact, no society in which one wants to have industry can exist where all the inhabitants are equally poor or equally rich—that is morally impossible. If one is observant, one will already find relevant matter for consideration in this Colony. It is true that many young people do not work; yet there are also many, on the other hand, who are doing ordinary farm work for their parents. How many are not wagon-drivers? How many are overseers on their parents' farms? How many who plough the fields? And how many who help with the work that must be done with the cattle? When the population increases and the farms are all fully occupied, one will soon see just the same results as in other countries. Here, as elsewhere, necessity will then get people working, and, even if there were still to be many slaves in the Colony, these could not belong to any but the rich. Even if the heavy farm work is always done by slaves, it is my opinion that in these circumstances the idle hands of the poor inhabitants, at least, will soon be brought to work of their own accord. Then the needs of a larger, better-endowed part of the Colony will eliminate the sources of the idleness of others, and make them into the hard-working and useful members of society on which, we hope, the true prosperity of a well-populated and happy country will be firmly established. . . .

There must be labour, and indeed ordinary manual labour, for the development of agriculture. If one wants agriculture to prosper and expand in accordance with the interests of the country and its increasing needs, then the number of the manual workers must be increased. . . .

The philosopher might say that . . . labour ought to be free—and I agree that this ought to be the case, but this labour is not forthcoming nor is it possible to obtain it. . . .

Consider the ordinary free labour already here.

Hottentots, naked as they are, can indeed be employed as cattle-herds, wagon-drivers or team-leaders, also for ploughing or for work with cattle, which is easy work. Yet they will never do the ordinary farming work of digging the land and so on, which the slaves do, for any length of time. They prefer to spend their time in laziness and idleness, to suffer want and poverty, than to be employed for this work. Now one might ask why the Government does not force these and similar sorts of free men in the Colony to work and to do heavy farm labour. It is for this simple reason: that the Government has, with respect, no right to do this. The Government regulates the industry of its inhabitants only so that it does not cause society to suffer any harm, or so that industry benefits thereby. Furthermore, the Government may punish an inhabitant, or free person, when he commits a crime. When a poor man begs, or becomes a burden on society, the Government must deal with him. It keeps a watchful eye on the layabout since there exists an assumption of bad behaviour against him in society. Yet there are other incentives apart from Government coercion to get the idler to work, and these incentives are indeed found in other countries and other circumstances. Yet in this Colony, these incentives, for some centuries at least, cannot on any grounds be expected to get the so-called idler, or even the free working man, to prefer heavy physical work above the easier course of satisfying his own needs over which he, as a free man, is master.

That it would have been desirable that the Colony should have begun without slavery—on this point I am in full agreement with all the philosophers and all reasonable people.

But that is something different—it would change the entire condition of the Colony and of everything in the Colony. One must accept things as they are, and not as they ought to be. Therefore, however one might think about these things, and whatever one has to say about them, in this respect one can do no more than wish. For 125 years the Colony's course has fluctuated with that of slavery. Since then, everything has gained a certain permanence, and to change this now, to bring it back to the condition in which one would have liked the Colony to have been started after so many years, would take a miracle, and be beyond the powers of man. Our paltry efforts towards this end simply could have no other result than the ruin of the Colony—and the demise of all that now exists in it.

Indeed, one might ask which steps would be appropriate for the destruction of slavery in a Colony such as this, or—since this is what it amounts to—to make slavery *unnecessary* for the Colony. To this common sense could never reply: abolition of slavery! Because this would indeed stop slavery, but it would bring about the immediate destruction of the entire colony, and cause misfortune for both free man and slave together. One would also not be able to answer that one should impede the importation of slaves as much as one can, and thus gradually put an end to slavery. This would also have the results mentioned previously—agriculture, and together with agriculture everything else, would fall into decay. . . .

One should accept these matters as they are and not as one might wish them to be, especially in this struggling Colony, and accordingly institute measures for improvement, not with superficial ideas nor by extremes, but with calm consideration and cautious guidance. This will, I believe, at least be sufficient to prevent much harm, and thus to do for the Colony as much good as can reasonably be expected.

Concerning no measure, no aspect of management in the Colony should the Government be uncertain. Such uncertainty would be horrible, as it makes the Government timid, makes it resort to half-measures and thus to miss its aim. There should be a fixed system concerning every important point of administration. For example, slaves should either be imported into the Colony or not. This is to be determined, after mature consideration of the matter; and it is to be determined not *a posteriori*, but *a priori*. One does not first wait to see the results of some system, because then the Colony would have been exposed to it and the consequences will very often be of such a nature that they cannot lightly be undone. Secondary causes may also often lead one's judgement astray as to the real consequences of something, and nothing is more easily conducive to this than a Colony in which everything is still defective. It appears to me that the gradual abolition of the importation of slaves, or the prevention or obstruction of such importation by the imposition of an extraordinary tax, would at present be extremely harmful. . . .

2.6a These are the grounds on which the indenturing of Hottentots was introduced.
—Letter from Landdrost R. J. van der Riet of Stellenbosch to Fiscal J. A. Truter, 1 April 1810. (Translated from the original in the Cape Archives, St. 1/29.)

The practice of indenturing 'apprentices', which was to become such a controversial aspect of the control of indigenous labour in South Africa, first arose in connection with slavery. As formally instituted in 1775 it compelled the children of slave men by Khoikhoi women to serve on the farm where they grew up till they were twenty-five. By the turn of the century many colonists had informally extended this to apply to the children of Khoikhoi in service generally. It is this generalized indenture system that R. J. van der Riet (1758–1828), landdrost of Stellenbosch, defends in the following letter against objections expressed by J. A. Truter (1763–1845), at that time the fiscal of the colony.

It is Your Honour's opinion that the reasons I gave . . . for this nation [i.e. the Hottentots] to serve the inhabitants in whose care they were born and brought up, were not sufficient to explain why they should work for the inhabitants until their twenty-fifth year as compensation for the care and trouble taken in their upbringing. . . .

These objections are very acceptable and would be very applicable, if one were dealing only with Christians. But in my opinion they cannot be applied without adaptation to heathens, and especially not to Hottentots, who are generally accounted to be of the most stupid sort, and who therefore never think, nor can think, as Christians do.

The grounds on which the indenturing of Hottentots was introduced and has been continued from that time until now, Your Honour will find copiously set out in the accompanying extract from the Resolution of the Landdrost and Heemraden taken in 1775 on the authority of Governor Van Plettenberg.

Years of experience have taught me to see quite clearly the utility of such an institution, which is derived from the fact that a Hottentot who is freed from service, and who may therefore come and go as he pleases, is never inclined to work, much less to learning a trade; I have never known a Hottentot who learned a trade. The very prospect is difficult for them to envisage and when effort and time are required, this is a burden to them.

Many Europeans [i.e. visitors] and those who do not know the natives at first-hand, or have never employed them, cannot understand how lazy and stubborn a nation they are. They are by nature untrustworthy, slothful and drowsy, with very few exceptions.

And if the masters can get no work from the children of Hottentots, by obligation, in return for the care and trouble taken in their upbringing, or have no prospect of keeping such Hottentot children in service, . . . then many of the masters will soon perish from concern and worry. They will not be able to make a living anywhere for a Hottentot with children cannot obtain employment. This I have seen so often in the course of my professional duties. The farmers in the interior assert, and do so with right, that the children of this nation are more of a liability than the services of their mothers can be an asset. . . . The trouble and expense is made tolerable [only] by the prospect of the services yet to be received. Should these services be abolished, would not the obligation fall away which motivated the farmer in the interior to bring up the children of this nation? These services having been abolished, the prospect falls away and therefore, this nation, instead of being done a service, would be done a disservice by regarding them as a free people who should enjoy ideal freedom, which would in practice make them unhappy. . . .

I have already dealt with the trades . . . and so I pass on to . . . the way in which the natural freedom which inspires useful conduct might be deadened by a period of 25 years' service. This would certainly be a valid argument, or appear to be, but experience has taught me that, for the greatest part, Hottentots who have grown up outside service wander about and become thieves. As they have never been encouraged to work in their youth, they are completely incompetent and incapable of doing so in their more advanced years, and the idea that they are free is more a burden to them than a real sentiment.

That nobody has the right to force a free people into bondage, as you assert, . . . is correct but superficial, for that flower could bear bitter fruit. What would become of us and of the whole colony if the natives were to feel that they should be free, were to know their power, and then to join together to regain their natural freedom as the original possessors of this country? In effect, nothing but a second St Domingo.[12] Is a policy not therefore required which will ensure that, although this nation is not in effect a nation of slaves, they might still be instilled with a certain sense of service and that the dangerous and idealistic feeling of freedom might be weakened, or at least kept within certain limits?

In my position, it has often been my experience that there are female Hottentots who leave their children, even those who were born among their own nation, and are never even heard to ask after them. What is now to be done with such unfortunate creatures [*schepselen*], who are without a father or mother? Should they beg for food along the road, or should they work? No farmer will take such a child in, except with the assurance that he can demand the labour of the child for a certain number of years. And to prevent such miserable people from perishing from hunger and worry, it has become customary for Landdrosts and Heemraden to bestow such a Hottentot child or children until his twenty-fifth year on one of the inhabitants who takes pity on him. This is done on condition that when the father or mother comes to ask for that child, as often happens once the children are able to work, fair compensation must be made to the inhabitant with whom the child was indentured, according to the judgement of the College [of Heemraden] for the trouble and care which he has taken.

In my experience, it has also often happened that the father and mother of Hottentot children themselves come voluntarily to give their children to the inhabitants until their twenty-fifth year, as they do not think themselves able to support their child or children.

If it were now to be accepted as a rule that nobody should have the right to be made to work without giving his own consent, then all agreements of this sort would come to an end. So would the contracts of parents and guardians of Christian children to the effect that they will work for a certain number of years to learn one or other trade. Such contracts are always considered sacred by the Judge, so that pupils who are subjected to the contracts, without their knowing it at all, are bound to continue their apprenticeship when they have reached the age at which they can serve in the militia, as happened earlier, and have to pay taxes. . . .

2.6b It is to these causes that much of the ill-treatment of the Hottentots must be attributed.

—Letter from Fiscal J. A. Truter to the Colonial Secretary, Colonel Bird, 19 Feb. 1811. (Translated from the original in the Cape Archives, CJ 3447.)

The plight of the Khoikhoi as a more or less involuntary labour force of the colonists was affected by the activities of the missionaries in more ways than one. The mission stations themselves, such as the one at Bethelsdorp in the Eastern Cape, provided an alternative sanctuary to Khoikhoi who did not want to remain in service. And some missionaries, such as Van der Kemp and Read, took up the cause of the many complaints of maltreatment lodged against farmers, and brought these to the attention of the authorities in Britain. The Cape government asked Truter, as fiscal, to investigate and comment on the list of allegations compiled by Van der Kemp and Read.

. . . It is deplorable but true that the Hottentots have not always been treated by the farmers in the way in which successive administrations have desired and prescribed. The lack of civilization and religion in the outlying districts used to be considerable, and it continues still to this day, even if in a lesser degree. This lack always makes men less capable of restraining their passions. And when the curb of the law cannot be effectively employed either, but imposes itself only weakly on the mind because of the remoteness of the administrators of the law, then it is not unnatural that, at the least injury which men think they suffer, a strong inclination should arise to take excessive revenge. It is to this cause, in the first place, that much of the ill-treatment of the Hottentots must be attributed. But a second and no less natural cause is that the Hottentots remain altogether without any civilization and religion, and are also very fond of a wandering life. When employed, they always look forward to change and seldom have such trust in their masters and such devotion to their interests that they come to treat these as their own. On the contrary, their inconstancy often results in their work being indolent and careless. This is to the detriment of their masters and arouses their unrestrained passions. Because of the difficulties accompanying ordinary legal procedures for the outlying farmer, he then often resorts to excessive measures.

These are both natural results of the remoteness of the farmer and the conduct of the Hottentot. But what can the State expect when one takes into account that, as is known, even at Bethelsdorp there is no adequate means to utilize the industry of the Hottentots, and that a large part of them therefore have to spend their time in idleness? Is this condition of idleness not contrary to the rules of the Christian religion and the root of all evil? Being imbued with a deep respect for religion, I refrain from censuring that which might advance religion even nominally. Yet I have been asked in my official capacity to give my opinion in the interests of the country and so no secondary considerations should restrain me from the expression of my real feelings. On these grounds, I cannot conceal from His Excellency that it is indeed to be deplored, and certainly cannot make a good impression on the farmers as far as the Institute is concerned, that the criminal rolls of the Colony include the names of several criminals who were at the Institute and who would surely have had less motive for theft if they had led an industrious life.

Mr Van der Kemp asserts that Governor Janssens summoned him to the Cape 'on his pleading the necessity of the punishment of cruelties committed to the Hottentots'. This I am obliged to contradict directly, as the sole cause of his summons was not the conduct of the farmers, but Mr Van der Kemp's own conduct, which had the obvious effect of going against the spirit of public policy and undoing ordinary social ties. And so far from Governor Janssens letting the cruelty committed to a peaceful Hottentot go by unpunished, he even had a certain Pieter Delsen executed for murder after he had shot dead a Bushman on the frontier. But, above all, what motive can any Government of this settlement have for allowing a poor Hottentot to be treated cruelly in cold blood by a farmer without punishment?

This question applies to all regular Government; and what motive could the present Government then have for tolerating such evil? No, it should be regarded as a matter beyond all doubt that every cruelty, regardless of who perpetrates it and who suffers it, which comes to the attention of the Government, will not be left uninvestigated or, in cases of guilt, go unpunished. This Mr Van der Kemp and Mr Read ought not to doubt, particularly as they themselves admit that they are in no way uncertain as to the good intentions of His Excellency. . . .

2.7a The state of slavery requires a more severe discipline than need be observed among free servants.

—Letter from Fiscal D. Denyssen, to Lt.-Col. T. Reynell, private secretary to Governor Cradock, 27 Feb. 1813. (Translated from the original in the Cape Archives, AG 31.)

After the abolition of the slave trade in the British empire in 1807, the following decades saw a number of attempts to bring about the amelioration of slavery. In particular the virtually uncontrolled powers of punishment by masters of their slaves were increasingly curtailed. Many slave-owners vehemently opposed these reforms and argued that such severe discipline was essential for their own security. Daniël Denyssen (1777–1855) was born in Amsterdam and received a doctorate in law at Leiden before coming to the Cape where he served on the Court of Justice under the Batavian administration. He served as fiscal from 1812 to 1826.

. . . The extent to which these provisions of the law are adequate to prevent the ill-treatment of slaves is a matter which I do not feel able to decide. If it might be permitted, however, I shall advance some arguments for the continuation of the right of masters to punish their slaves domestically. The state of slavery requires a more severe discipline than need be observed among free servants. In countries where there is an abundance of free servants, those who do not carry out their duties properly are discharged and others taken in their place. This is not the case with slaves who, being the property of the masters, cannot be discharged from their services unless a purchaser is found, who will indemnify the master for the loss of his property. From the moment of their birth, slaves are accustomed to the domestic discipline of their masters, and they cannot possibly be kept in good order without it. To this it must be added that they are imperceptibly drawn by the bonds of slavery into secret hostility towards their masters, so that they cannot be brought to do their duty properly by kindness. They must sometimes be compelled to do it by punishment.

These reasons cause me to place a great interest in the preservation of the right of masters to apply domestic discipline. They would lose a great deal of this authority if they were obliged to address the magistrate for every offence or every refusal of their slaves to do their duty and never have the power of punishing them except immediately under his eye. Therefore, as long as slavery is a necessary evil in the Colony and cannot be replaced by the services of free people, for so long, in my opinion, must the unavoidable consequences of that evil persist. And if the slave is ill-treated, he must be satisfied with the right to take refuge with the magistrate, who cannot be too strongly recommended to support the unfortunate slave by an impartial investigation of his complaint and to alleviate the hardness of his lot as far as is possible.

It must at the same time be foreseen that the extravagantly high price of slaves in this Colony at present will contribute to securing them against ill-treatment. For it is a generally allowed observation that when self-interest obliges men to do what is right, it has a much more powerful influence than any other inducement whatsoever.

2.7b It is not the maltreatment of the slaves but their disappointed hopes of freedom that led to these murderous shouts.

—Speech of Fiscal D. Denyssen as public prosecutor at the trial of the Bokkeveld slave insurgents, 18 March 1825. (Translated from the original in the Cape Archives, CJ 633, pp. 1089–1261.)

The nearly two centuries of slavery at the Cape were marked by only two insurrections. The first occurred in 1808 when some 300 slaves from south-western Cape farms attempted to march on Cape Town and proclaim a general emancipation. The revolt was quickly crushed by the British military. The second insurrection occurred early in 1825, two years after the governor at the Cape had issued a proclamation which aimed at the improvement of the condition of the slaves through such means as regulating the hours of slave labour and the permissible forms of punishment. This gave rise to rumours among apprehensive slave-owers as well as slaves, some of whom believed that emancipation itself was at hand and that their masters were keeping the truth from them. In this context the brief but violent revolt of the small band of slaves led by Galant, who murdered his master in the Bokkeveld, excited great public attention, as did their trial. The following document is taken from the speech of Fiscal Denyssen, acting as public prosecutor.

It is a truth that experience has taught that the impression of being oppressed, whether it be based on fact or not, once having entered a man's consciousness and taken root there, can move him to extremes never before conceived.

As long as each is content with his condition, peace prevails in the minds of men, and one need not fear for outbursts arising from a non-existent discontent, or for turbulent feelings, no matter how unequal the condition of one might be as compared to the other. But as soon as a man begins to feel the inequality between his condition and that of others who are in more favourable circumstances than he is, this gives him a cause for dissatisfaction, and he considers himself to be carrying a burden which has been unfairly laid upon him. Then his emotions are swept into turmoil, thoughts of peace no longer prevail—and he will then not neglect to notice opportunities to rid himself of the burdens he bears.

The country in which we live and the times in which we live have given us more than one proof of the truth of this assertion, and may heaven forbid that we have to see further proof of it.

We live in a Colony in which slavery was instituted under the auspices and sanction of the authorities. Can any greater inequality exist than that between the class of free men and that of slaves, where the latter have not freely consented to bind themselves, for their whole lives, to the service of their masters? However, no example is known to me from the history of the Colony up to the period which we entered in 1808, from which it could be deduced that the least discontent existed at all in the minds of the slaves, which might have spurred them on to break the bonds of their slavery with force.

Having been taught, according to the laws of morality of our Christian religion, to be obedient to their masters, they were never disobedient without becoming aware that they had failed in their duties, and the punishment of their disobedience left no other impression in their minds than that they had brought this punishment upon themselves through their own conduct. This impression was essential in order to preserve this country from unrest and commotion.

Here I do not speak in any way as an advocate of slavery in the abstract but I place myself in the circumstances of the Colony as they actually exist: a land which has been cultivated by slave labour, and in which the free inhabitants, or the actual colonists, are permitted by law, and have been encouraged since the first years of the Colony by the example of their magistrates, to invest a very substantial part of their wealth in slaves. In such circumstances, the conception by which the slaves have been impressed with the need for obedience to their masters, has been—and still is—essential for the peace of the country.

In 1808, however, this conception was removed from the minds of many who belonged to the slave-class, by certain ill-intentioned people, whose apparent aim it was to plunge the whole country into extreme confusion and anarchy and thereby to gain great advantage for themselves. These people would have had the slaves believe, by means of a highly criminal distortion of the benevolent intentions of the British Legislature—which did not abolish slavery itself, but only the slave trade—that they were being kept in slavery against the will of our Rulers in Britain, where there are no slaves.

It has not yet been erased from the memories of the colonists how ominous a cloud was gathered over their heads when that mischievous seed of unrest was sown in the minds of the slaves by those evil-doers, nor how easily this seed entered there and took root. I refer to the conspiracy between James Hopper, Louis and others, whose outcome burst upon us on 27th October 1808, and which had no other purpose than that of arousing the slaves to general rebellion, to gather as many of them with their masters' weapons, to march against the capital, to occupy the batteries, open the prisons by force and to propose the general emancipation of the slaves to the Government, or otherwise to fight for their freedom.

To these ends, they brought together a number of between 300 and 400 persons in the short time of less than two days, and these consisted chiefly of slaves and Hottentots, of whom by far the majority knew nothing of this design when they joined and participated in the conspiracy. They robbed the houses of the inhabitants, and, having taken their rifles, powder and ammunition, they captured the owners of the farms, and bound and took with them all who were able to resist. The speedy intervention of the Dragoon Corps, then garrisoned here, checked this undisciplined mob in their advance and, with the exception of a few who escaped, they took them prisoner.

The example which was made of the leaders of these criminals, and the experience which they had had of their ability to execute a similar design, discouraged them, at that time, from renewing such enterprises, although one has reason to doubt whether that spirit of dissatisfaction with their condition, which then began to prevail among them, has been extinguished. From that time, at least, the complaints which slaves have made against their masters have increased not inconsiderably; and, notwithstanding the fact that the Government has done a great deal to relieve the hardships of slavery, it appears that the fire of dissatisfaction, at their disappointed hope of general emancipation, is still smouldering under the ashes, so that only the slightest fuel need be added from outside for the fire to renew itself and burn more fiercely than ever before.

This disappointed hope was the cause of the insurrection of the slaves in 1808, of which we were then the witnesses, although at that time the lives of the Christian inhabitants were spared. It was, only a short while ago, the cause of the disaster which was brought upon one of our South American colonies by the slaves. And now . . . we too have heard for the first time how the murderous shouts arising from the disappointed hope of freedom have been raised by slaves, who soon found support. And had this not been checked in time, then perhaps at the moment at which I speak this country might have been plunged into the deepest sorrow. Not before their rage had claimed three victims were we fortunate enough to check the progress of the murders they had just begun.

But it is necessary that I consider more closely the immediate cause of the offence of which the accused have made themselves guilty; not only because this might be considered to affect the culpability of their actions, but also so that I should not unjustly be considered to have failed in my judgement of this matter.

I begin then with the leader of this plot, the slave Galant. In listening to his version of events, one is easily moved to suppose that he had to suffer instances of maltreatment, the one following after the other; that his child, who could not yet walk, had died from the effects of beatings repeatedly administered by his master, for which his master had no other reason than that he was displeased with his own wife; that he himself had been hauled up by the arms and punished in that way by his master; that, in a similar way, he was constantly maltreated by his master; that he received neither sufficient food nor sufficient clothing from his master.

How unfortunate, is it not, for the sake of impartial investigation of the truth, that the man of whom all these allegations are made has been slain and cannot reply to them; and that his wife, whom the accusations concern equally, although she is still living, suffers too much from the wounds she received to be able to come to the capital. In the meanwhile, one considers it worth doing to put a stop to Galant's foul libel, to which end there are means of proof at hand, which I believe can be employed with good effect. The examination of the accused has also taught me . . . , for as far as it has proceeded, that foul libels form its chief part. Because, in the first place, the death of the child David, whom he says was so recklessly maltreated, did not occur about one year ago, as he would have it, but more than eight years back. . . .

. . . It was not the maltreatment which the slave Galant has alleged which brought him to the step of, as he calls it himself, trying to 'fight himself free'. No, it was his disappointed hope of freedom which led him to that. I let him speak for himself. What did the accused do, when confronted by the witness Betje, when she claimed that he had said to her, before this year began, that he would wait until New Year, and that if he were not then set free, he would resort to murder? What else did he do but admit the truth of her version of events and name the persons from whom he had supposedly heard in the previous year at Tulbagh that, at the immediately approaching New Year, a general emancipation of the slaves would take place?

There you have the actual admission of the leader of the conspiracy; there you have the pivot on which the entire wheel, which was steered by his hand, was supposed to have turned.

Similar false rumours appear to have been circulated in the country for some time—it is impossible to establish for how long—and have been conveyed not only to the slaves but also to the owners of slaves. No wonder that such credulous and misled people among the slave-owners who imagined that their right of property over their slaves, which, next to their right to live, they regard as one of their holiest of rights, was to be disputed, expressed themselves now and then on this matter in language which depicted the bitterness of their innermost feelings. And, in this way, the slaves in whose presence one was careless enough to speak of such subjects, or those who overheard such conversations, or found the opportunity to draw on the children of their masters to tell them the same thing, would equally be embittered by the opposition which they would feel their masters harboured towards their so strongly desired freedom. No wonder that a hostility of proportions never before known came to be felt among the slaves towards their masters; and that this pernicious distrust of their masters, which is exposed so clearly in Galant's evidence, gained ground and led to the extremes to which it inevitably would lead. On this point, I have in mind the same Galant's allegations of the reluctance of the slave-owners, who did not make known to the slaves the news they had read in the newspapers, or the orders concerning their slaves which had been conveyed to them in writing by the Landdrost; also his searching out and eavesdropping upon the conversations he says his master had had with others, and equally the conversations which, Galant says, had consisted of threats against his slaves and all who undertook to declare the freedom of the slaves. For why would one doubt the truth of Galant's testimony that such conversations among credulous and misled owners of slaves, who thought that they might perhaps suddenly be deprived of all their slaves, would border on anger and despair.

It is not my task in these proceedings to trace the author of rumours foretelling such evil; that task belongs to a closer enquiry which I have yet to carry out. It is sufficient for these proceedings if these rumours existed, and are truthfully said by the slave Galant to be the immediate cause of his undertaking. . . .

. . . Many a free servant has heard his master say something similar in a moment of anger, without attaching the least importance to it, because he knows full well that it is not seriously meant. How much less can hasty words said to a slave by the master, whose property he is, and who necessarily stands to lose a part of his capital with the slave, arouse anxiety or fear.

One would not say that experience teaches that the lives of slaves are taken by their masters. This does happen, but there have also been instances of patricide—and of infanticide, and yet where can a child be as safe as in the arms of his father, how can a father be better protected than by the love of his own off-spring? If one were to compare the instances of murders of slaves by their masters and those which other people commit on others, one would soon find that the slave is almost as safe in the protection of his master as the child is in that of his father. And this is especially the case with house-slaves, in which capacity both Galant and Abel served, for whom a natural feeling of love unites itself with self-interest, so that they find true friends and protectors in their masters. . . .

. . . Carrying on to the grounds of my plea concerning the criminality and culpability of the charges listed, I would remark that the highest form of treason consists in the taking up of arms against the State, and that all who unite to fight against the existing order of public affairs by force of arms are considered, in law, to be guilty of this crime. . . . In a country in which slavery exists, a rebellion among the slaves, in order to gain their freedom by fighting for it, is nothing other than a state of war . . . because it could . . . lead to an entire overthrow of the State. One of the accused themselves—I think it was Galant—has described his actions, during the trial, as *making war*.

It is sufficient in law that such an uprising, and the uniting of its instigators to this end, actually be contemplated, in order for a verdict to be brought that the crime of sedition has been committed. . . .

. . . And now, . . . as it has fallen upon me to demand the death penalty for these guilty men, all of whom stand before you, it only remains to say whether I might be able to recommend to the Judge any mitigation of the sentences. . . . The desire to shake off the yoke of slavery, which has never before led to such extremes, cannot now be interpreted in any other way than as a desire to withdraw from the laws and authority of the Government, as a desire for bloodshed, for war and confusion, for disastrous anarchy. The desire for freedom, in these circumstances, is a reason for increasing the penalty. . . .

2.8a The only matter in dispute is the manner in which the amelioration and even the gradual abolition of the state of slavery is to be effected.

—Memorial of the Burgher Senate against the provisions of Ordinance 19, Cape Town, 30 June 1826. (From Theal, *Records of the Cape Colony*, Vol. 27, pp. 69–98.)

Imperial reform aimed at the amelioration of slavery resulted in Ordinance 19, published at the Cape in 1826. This Ordinance, which followed closely the terms of the Trinidad Order-in-Council (1824), allowed a slave to give evidence in criminal cases against his master and decreed that a master convicted of cruel punishment of a slave would forfeit ownership. It also provided a registrar and guardian of slaves. The following documents reflect the reaction of the slave-owning burghers of the Western Cape to this proclamation. Most resentment was expressed against articles 33 to 37, which laid down a procedure for slaves to purchase their own freedom even against their master's will.

To His Honor the Lieutenant-Governor Richard Bourke, C.B., in Council.

The undermentioned President and Members of the Burgher Senate, with reference to their correspondence with Government under dates of the 27th and 28th instant respecting the new Ordinance about to be promulgated relative to the Slaves of this Colony, feel it a sacred and imperative duty which they owe to His Majesty's Government, as well as to the good and loyal Inhabitants of this Town, who have so earnestly called upon them as the only Representatives of the People under the existing form of Government, to lay the following considerations and remarks before Your Honor's and the Council's most serious and favourable attention.

Nothing but urgent necessity and well-grounded fears for the loss of property and of seeing this once peaceful and happy land converted into a scene of misery and despair could have induced the Burgher Senate thus to deviate from the course usually pursued by them, and thus to interfere in the measures of Government.

The undersigned have gathered some confidence however from the well-known liberality of Government on the one hand, and from the conviction which they have on the other hand, that the majority of the well-informed Inhabitants of this Colony are not averse to, but on the contrary anxious to co-operate with, His Majesty's Government in the amelioration and even the gradual abolition of the state of Slavery.

The only matter in dispute therefore is the manner in which this is to be effected.

The proprietors of Slaves and we think every calm and impartial man will have it observed as an inviolable Basis in this operation,

1st. 'That the rights of private property be not in the least encroached upon,' and in the next place it seems to be admitted by every one,

2ndly. 'That the emancipation of the Slaves should not be so sudden and to such an extent as to become a useless Boon to the emancipated, or inconvenient to the Public.'

The first rule, though sometimes lost sight of by hot-headed Zealots, has never been formally called in question by any one, and has repeatedly been admitted and relied upon by the most distinguished Statesmen in both Houses of Parliament, and in His Majesty's Cabinet. It may not be amiss however to state the following facts relative to the acquisition of this species of property in this Colony.

The inhabitants of this Colony have never embarked on any expeditions to obtain Slaves by conquest or barter in other countries, nor has a single individual of the numerous Tribes of Savages by whom we are surrounded and with whom we have often been compelled to wage war, ever been enslaved by us, and even those who still dwell within the confines of our Colony are free and are protected by the existing laws and regulations.

But we inhabit a country of which the population is not and never has been equal to the extent of Territory nor adequate to the proper cultivation thereof. The expedient resorted to by the former Dutch, as well as by the English Governments has been the introduction of Slaves, and many Vessels under the Flags of various European nations have been allowed to import and dispose of their cargoes of Slaves in this Colony.

The acquisition of this species of property was therefore not only allowed but even encouraged by the legal authorities and the Representatives of our supreme Rulers in Europe. . . .

. . . We therefore beg leave humbly to submit that the present Race of Slaves has been acquired by their owners in as legal a manner as any other species of property, by purchase, inheritance, or otherwise, and that this acquisition has not only been sanctioned by the solemn acts of the Legislatures in Europe, but also by the local authorities, who have moreover encouraged it as a measure of expedience, and finally, that this species of property has as much been guaranteed to the owners as any other species of private property, by the Terms of the Capitulation on which this Colony was surrendered in the year 1806, and finally ceded to the British Crown in the year 1814. Under these circumstances, we humbly contend that the right of property of the Owner in his Slaves is as complete and as sacred as any right which His Majesty's subjects may be deemed to possess in their houses, their lands, or any other of their goods.

Any infringement therefore of these rights either by depriving the master of his

Slave altogether or by making the Slave less valuable to him by means of restrictions, impositions, fines, forfeitures or otherwise, without a fair and adequate remuneration to the Master, is an act of injustice, contrary to the fundamental and elementary principles of Civil Society, whose first object is the inviolable safety of private property.

We therefore humbly but with confidence submit that the Regulations contained in the 33, 34, 35, 36 and 37 Articles of the Ordinance about to be promulgated are unjust in principle, and that the great and laudable object of the British Government, 'the amelioration and gradual emancipation of the Slaves', may be obtained by them by other and more equitable means. . . .

We beg leave finally to say that we are humbly but decidedly of the opinion that the good and benevolent intentions of His Majesty's Government as to Slaves in general have already been anticipated in this Colony, as well by many excellent Laws and Regulations of an early date, as by the Proclamation of 1823. That the Slaves here are gradually improving, and that we have only to look at our Slaves to be convinced that they are better treated and superior to the Slaves of every other country. Nothing is therefore wanting to promote their further improvement, but to restore confidence between them and their Masters, by disclaiming all right and intention to interfere with his rights of property, and emancipation will follow as a matter of course, as soon as a sufficient fund can be raised to indemnify the owners.

We now beg leave to conclude. We spoke freely and with singleness of heart and purpose. We felt that we had an important duty to perform towards the public, towards our King, and towards Him who is the King of Kings. You have the same sacred duties to perform. It will be for you to consider whether you will risk the evils which we have predicted, and the injustice which we have shown to proceed from these measures. We have no Constitutional Power to prevent such Laws from being carried into effect, we are weak and without power even as a Worm. But surely the foot cannot be blessed who will sternly refuse to turn aside one inch because it is only a worm which pleads its rights.

May the God of Wisdom and of Mercy direct you in your Councils.

J. van der Poel, President
J. H. Hofmeyr
G. A. Meyer
P. M. Brink
P. Woutersen

2.8b We see already the ascending flames, kindled by a petulant hand in the hopes of freedom, and our houses falling to ruin.

—Memorial to the Burgher Senate signed by 350 citizens of Cape Town, 3 July 1826. (From Theal, *Records of the Cape Colony*, Vol. 27, pp. 98–105.)

To the President and Members of the Burgher Senate of this town.

GENTLEMEN, when on the 24th June last, the good Inhabitants, driven by solicitude and anxiety, called for your interference with the Government of this Colony, on account of then current reports relative to an Ordinance about the Slaves, the most of us thought, and justly expected, that those rumours would be found unfounded and exaggerated.

But since the very Ordinance was inserted in the *Gazette* of Friday last, we have alas seen with the deepest pain and regret that our fears were but too well grounded.

Our right of property, sacred even amongst the barbarous Nations, is attacked most unjustly and violated; a burning flame of distrust and discord is thrown in our Houses, which should be our safe retreat; our domestics are our enemies; bloody scenes are already seen at a distance; in a word, Gentlemen, the anguish and fear for our lives, and that of our Wives and Children, possesses and agitates every bosom. . . .

For we cannot as yet forget those dreadful scenes—scenes which call for vengeance against those who were the cause and instigators thereof—which last year happened in the Bokkeveld.

It is known to the public from the Trial of the Murderers, how by the Proclamation of 18 March 1823 their minds were filled with ideas which incited them to Murder.

That Proclamation was for them of less consequence than the present Ordinance, and will not the same, yea far more dangerous scenes, take place amongst us, as by the Ordinance they will look upon robbery, false evidence and bloodshed, as the means for obtaining their freedom? Will not our own Country, our only retreat and refuge, become unsafe for us Citizens, through the rapacious and murderous attacks of our Slaves and domestics? Will not the Slave, considering his Master as the only impediment to his Freedom, persecute him with the weapon of death, even in his resting-room? Gentlemen, the ideas of foreseen dangers follow the one upon the other; the one terror and fear for the Murder of ouselves and innocent children is chased away by the other.

We see already the ascending flames, kindled by a petulant hand in the hopes of freedom, and our houses falling to ruin! We see already our Streets, although formerly frequented by Peace, Quiet, and Union, full of Streams of Blood of our fellow Citizens, of our Wives, of our Children, slaughtered by the steel of incited heathen Slaves! And we see a Saint Domingo rising out of the pit of our murdered fellow Citizens.

All these foreseen dangers, Gentlemen, have filled our hearts with terror and fear, and there appears to us no other recourse but to you, as the only representative Board in the Colony, to request for your interference with the Colonial Government, and to appeal in our behalf to the benevolent Resolutions adopted on 7 March 1826 by our parental Rulers in England, by the British Parliament.

We take the liberty to annex those Resolutions to this Our Memorial, whereby it will appear to you that the British Parliament expects from us to ameliorate and abolish slavery, when it could be done consistently with the well-being of the Slaves themselves, with the safety of the Colonies, and the fair and equitable adjustment of private property.

We are animated with the same, have one feeling for the Slaves, our fellow Creatures. We also wish to do every thing in Our power for an amelioration of Slavery, and to promote amongst them Religion and Morality.

This our Fathers have done, this we did since many years, and every enquirer must acknowledge that our Slaves in this Colony are better off than the most Servants in Europe, and that a Cape Slave is not to be compared with a Slave in other Colonies. Notwithstanding, we will accept with eagerness every measure which may tend still more to ameliorate their condition. We also wish for their gradual emancipation because we all prefer free Servants far above Slaves, and consider it better for our Country. But this last our legislators the British Parliament expect from us, when it can be done consistently with the well-being of the Slaves, with the safety of this Colony, and without violation of private property.

And this, Gentlemen, as yet does not take place here.

The Slave who thus far attends to his Service, with quiet and peace, living in friendship with his Master, obedient, and under a less discipline than a free European Soldier, by the Ordinance becomes unquiet and uneasy, he refuses obedience to his Master. Not yet endowed with those Religious and moral principles which can guide a man in sudden prosperity, they wish to be free, they see some of their fellow Slaves enjoy the same, they have no money to buy their freedom, they *will* however also have the enjoyment of their freedom. One immoral and criminal feeling is suppressed by another, the good Slave becomes a Criminal, and it is *done* with the peace and well being of the Slave. Can this Colony, already wretched and weeping over her fate, be safe under similar circumstances and with Slaves so restless and incited towards obtaining, yea, usurping of their freedom? . . .

. . . Gentlemen! for the tranquility and peace of this Colony, for the safety of our persons and property, for the well being of the slave itself, we will undergo some sacrifices and co-operate for ameliorating and gradually emancipating Slavery; but we wish this to be effected in a manner less grievous to ourselves and less dangerous for the Colony.

Our intentions for the purpose are well meant and sincere, and we only wish for an opportunity to prove it in fact.

When we must lose our property for the gradual emancipation and final extinction of Slavery, then in the name of God let us co-operate for the same object, but in a manner less grievous to ourselves. . . .

2.9a There was a general desire to ensure for the slaves the freedom of their descendants in so far as this was not contrary to fairness, justice and the peace of the country.

—Minutes of a meeting of Landdrost A. Stockenström and heemraden of Graaff-Reinet, 24 Aug. 1826. (Translated from the original in the Cape Archives, C.O. 2678, no. 83.)

With the prospects of a forced abolition of slavery by the imperial authorities becoming increasingly imminent, some local initiatives for the gradual emancipation of the slaves began to appear. In Cape Town a meeting was held on 22 July 1826 and a committee set up to provide procedures for ameliorating the condition of the slaves and the gradual abolition of slavery, provided Ordinance 19 was first repealed. The colonists' schemes for gradual emancipation tended to take the form of proposals for the freeing of female slave children after a certain date, as appears also in the following resolutions of the Board of Heemraden in Graaff-Reinet. The Graaff-Reinet proposal also reflected the lesser importance of slaves in the eastern Cape, as well as the personal influence of the landdrost, Andries Stockenström.

Heemrade Present: Landdrost A. Stockenström Esquire, as well as the Heemraden H. A. Meintjes, N. G. Greybe and J. Joubert, the Honourable ex-Heemraden H. A. Meintjes, J. H. Greyling, F. Hartzenberg, Jan Minnaar and Schalk Burger.

First the Honourable Landdrost told the members present that they should bear in mind the fact that there was so liberal a sentiment among the inhabitants of that district in respect of the slave question, that they—instead of opposing themselves to the measures which the Government had in mind for bringing about a gradual but complete emancipation—were prepared to go on ahead of the Government and would gladly stipulate a time, or have a time stipulated by law, after which all female children of slaves would be born as free people.

His Honour had therefore, after consulting some of the members, seen fit to request all the Heemraden and former Heemraden whom he could reach to be present, in order to deliberate on the best means for giving the speediest possible effect to this praiseworthy, philanthropic sentiment of the inhabitants.

At which, after the subject had been discussed at length, the members present declared unanimously that, to the extent that the general feeling was known to them, they were firmly convinced that, with few exceptions, there was a general desire among the inhabitants to ensure for the slaves, in so far as this was not contrary to fairness, justice and the peace of the country, the freedom of their descendants.

Experience has taught—regardless of whatever libel and malevolence as well as ignorance, prejudice and self-interest might have tried to attribute to the inhabitants as their fault—that the inhabitants had already done much on their own initiative, long before the Government concerned itself with the spiritual or moral interests of the slaves, or made any financial sacrifices for the promotion of their interests. Thus the inhabitants had done much for their lowlier fellow-men, without needing the threats of the law to urge them on, but from philanthropic sentiment and concern for them. Some have gone to great expense, others have engaged in personal acitivity, in order to do their utmost to make the slaves better members of society, well knowing that their greater degree of civilization would be continued among those people, and that the more they made religious principles their own, the better they would be as servants and the greater the benefits to their owners would be. Once the Government—as far as this Colony was concerned, at least—had begun to think of this salutary work, the inhabitants, rather than opposing it, had contributed to the work of civilization, to promote both moral and religious improvement.

This declaration does not only rely on the expressed feelings of the natives [*inboorlingen*] of this country who make up this Council, but this Council flatters itself that it is able to challenge the libellers or unseeing writers to prove anything to the contrary, as they commit themselves to making the truth of their declaration absolutely clear. In this, they first make their appeal to the institutes and funds still in operation, without receiving any support from higher authority [*hoger hand*], and to the evidence of those who have visited the domestic circles of the older colonists and exercised their judgement, without a determination to censure these older colonists. On these grounds they assert that it is not to be expected that people—whose feelings and actions are not, generally speaking, of this sort—would not be eager to agree to grant freedom to those female-slaves born after a certain time, and by so doing, provide the prospect of no longer having a single slave in the Colony after at least a century.

Yes, even the emancipation of those who have already been born could be brought about in the interests of the country, for the sake of the slaves themselves and for our general good. . . .

2.9b The evils connected with too much power in the hands of the master are inseparable from slavery.

—Letters from A. Stockenström to the colonial secretary, Sir Richard Plasket. (From *The Autobiography of Sir Andries Stockenström*, Vol. I, pp. 261–4.)

(i) *25 August 1826*

I collected all the Heemraden and ex-Heemraden I could find yesterday, and must do them the justice to say that I heard as liberal sentiments as even a Wilberforce or a Buxton would not have been ashamed of. The following expressions, uttered with great warmth, I am sure will please you: 'Yes, emancipate the children as soon as you like. I will even volunteer to give up those already born, under a certain age, but do not deprive me of my paternal authority, under which both my children and slaves are happy, and which is necessary for their and my peace. . . .'

(ii) *29 September 1826*

. . . In the meantime the town is beginning to be crowded with slaveholders already. I am happy the meeting was thought of, for I am certain some dangerous steps would have been taken ere this; the clamour is prodigious; and I have heard of the most extraordinary instances of irritation, which I consider the more necessary to counteract, as its not availing anything against the Government would only make it fall on the defenceless. I hope everything will now subside into a peaceable discussion of the matter. . . .

As for the Ordinance, I understand it is alleged that the slave is left entirely without constraint, and the master at his mercy. A few days now will show, for I am told that a clever fellow living at Cradock has been sent for to reduce their suggestions to writing. He is a very able man, writes Dutch well, and is well capable of giving good advice if he chooses. If I have anything to do with the Committee, which I would rather avoid, I shall certainly do my duty to *Government* and the *People.*

I remain firmly convinced that nothing short of the extermination of slavery can save us from the greatest calamities; without a prospect of it the people and the Government at home will never cease plaguing the masters, and the slaves will torment them to such a pitch that one execution after the other must be the result. If the people are for perpetuating slavery, I am for upholding the Ordinance; if they will let the girls be born free, I declare to God there is not the least shadow of a pretence left for any opprobrious disabilities against the master that I can see; in that case there are regulations both in and out of the Ordinance, the continuation of which I should consider most oppressive, and I think the Ordinance will have done much good in having shown the people the necessity of putting a stop to slavery; this is what I considered its tendency from the first, and I have made it accessory to my argument for emancipation ever since, but I shall not consider myself in honour justified to insist on the sacrificing (which I think so absolutely requisite) without being able to give the people some sort of assurance that what can really be made out to be a grievance in the slave business shall be redressed.

The *Free Labour Clause* is but a drop in the ocean, in comparison to the removal of the rod from the hand of the master *as long as slavery exists*, and that removal has virtually taken place, and the equilibrium in the Ordinance has been effectually destroyed by the introduction of the instrument now used in prisons. Ill-treatment and cruelty must be powerfully checked on the one side, and the most powerful restraints against insubordination, disobedience and idleness, must exist on the other.

The evils connected with too much power in the hands of the master are inseparable from slavery, and this is the principal reason why I wish to have that state extinct in the present, or at least the next generation. If we desire a proof of the lamentable consequences of a want of proper checks on the conduct of our species proportionate to their condition and feelings in society, let us look to the state of the females of that unfortunate race, the Hottentots, since the indiscriminate prohibition against the flogging of females without the substitution of equivalent punishment. Let those who cry against flogging from purely humane motives (the rest I never thought worthy of notice) say how their feelings revolt at the scenes sometimes exhibited by these unbridled wretches. Let us therefore reject all unreasonable demands on the part of the slaveholders, but let us not allow the slaves to get the upper hand, and above all let us not lose the opportunity of freeing posterity from the dilemma in which we are so deeply involved. . . .

2.10a It would not be unfortunate for the Colony if the present distress of the graziers were to throw numbers out of that line of life into more active ones, which we cannot expect to take place as long as a hope of extension of the boundary exists.

—Letter from A. Stockenström to the colonial secretary, Sir Richard Plasket, 1 Dec. 1825. (From the original in the Cape Archives, G.R. 6/15.)

Already in the early 1820s some trekboers were periodically crossing the Orange River in search of better grazing. Due to a series of severe droughts many more sought government permission to go beyond the colonial boundaries in order to save their stock. In the following letter Landdrost Stockenström discusses the major considerations bearing on official policy in allowing this, but only under strict conditions and as an exceptional case.

. . . From the above state of the pasturage causing the cattle and sheep to sink in great numbers under disease and starvation I have been reluctantly compelled to avail myself of the authority granted by your letter of the third of last month towards permitting to the farmers the crossing of the boundary with their flocks in search of subsistence; but so highly injurious do I consider this indulgence, however unavoidable under present circumstances, that I have made the conditions thereof the most strict and severe, as His Excellency the Governor will find them enclosed. . . . The anxiety with which the indulgence was looked for and the keenness with which it was grasped at, were clear prognostics of the difficulties we will meet with in bringing the farmers back and keeping them within the established limits. The doing so will be nevertheless imperious. The argument, 'My few cattle and sheep are perishing *in* the colony while there is abundance of grass before my eyes just beyond it used by nobody,' is irresistible as far as concerns the individual, but every stretch of migration throws the mass of our borderers back in point of improvement, as long as it is not forced by a redundant population, or scarcity of food, which is far from being the case, for the first cause of the present distress next to the temporary visitations of providence is the minute subdivisions of land, which enables so many to set up as petty independent grazing farmers and overstocks the country. It is a curious fact that the complaints of the diminution of stock are accompanied by as loud a one that there is no market whatever for the little which remains, so that however impalatable I know the theory to be to my countrymen, I think it would not be unfortunate for the colony if the present distress of the graziers were to throw numbers out of that line of life into more active ones, which we cannot expect to take place as long as a hope of the extension of the boundary exists.

Another if not a more weighty argument for checking the crossing of the boundary as it is now taking place is the necessity and justice of leaving the open tracts of country lining our northern frontiers to the free enjoyment of that unfortunate race of Bushmen. I am certain that the liberal policy of the Government we have the honor of serving will embrace the employing of every expedient to improve the state of that wretched people and atoning in some measure for what they have in earlier days suffered from the colony.

The territory just mentioned . . . is so situated as to ensure to any establishment there formed our fullest protection without mixing them with, or making them dependent on, those whose local prejudices we can account for and perhaps excuse, but also see the necessity of jealously watching. By moderately wise measures such control may be kept over the Griquas and the Bushmen, that they would serve as a barrier to said establishments on the other side from respect for us, and the Bushmen may have a fair chance; but if the colonists by repetitions of the indulgence we now feel ourselves forced to grant become fairly settled in said territory every spring and pool becomes beset; the game consequently deserts the country, starvation drives the savages to plunder, and the plea of self-defence keeps the system of commandos alive. . . .

2.10b They should have some fixed abode and honest occupation, beyond which they should be left to dispose of their labour as dear as they can, and to whom they please.

—Reply of A. Stockenström to a government proposal to invite labourers from frontier tribes in the colony, 1827. (From *Papers Relative to the Condition and Treatment of the Native Inhabitants of the Cape of Good Hope*, Imperial Blue Book 252, 1 June 1835, II, pp. 13, 14.)

Intercourse between the colony and the Bantu-speaking peoples on its eastern frontier was prohibited by a series of proclamations from 1778 to 1820. In the 1820s the ravages of the Difaqane and population pressure produced a steady stream of black immigrants into the colony. Their entry into the colony and into the service of the colonists was greatly facilitated by Ordinance 49 of 1828, which regularized such admission of people belonging to frontier tribes beyond the border. In the following document we find the comments of Landdrost Stockenström on the proposed ordinance and on the system of labour controls to be adopted.

The policy of inviting the savages into the colony, binding them when they are thus decoyed away, as it were, from a state of at least independence and perfect freedom . . . appears to me in every one of its stages irreconcilable with the character of the natives, and our relations with them, and calculated only to crowd us with worthless subjects, who soon after the completion of the indenture will show their impatience of restraint . . . and leave the master, the indenture, and the colony, after having perhaps learned the use of our arms, being entrusted with these, and knowing the weakness of our frontier.

No emigration into the colony from the interior can be beneficial unless it be the result of redundant population, or the calamities of war among the native tribes, (causes which generally go together). In such circumstances invitation is superfluous, for hunger or the enemy will drive the good and the bad in amongst us, and there is a chance of industry deriving some acquisition; but it were irrational to suppose that as long as the interior is in a state of peace, and space plenty, that the good savage will abandon his liberty for the bondage we 'invite' him to; the bad, the outcast, will make trial of our favours, and reward us as above.

Next we have the point of apprenticeship; to this I have humbly presumed from the first to give in my dissent (always excepting orphans or children who have lost or been forsaken by their parents), and subsequent experience has confirmed my opinion, that it is hard and inhospitable towards the savage driven under our protection by the sword and starvation, and that it will only tend to generate (instead of gratitude for relief in distress) that feeling of rancour and prejudice between the colonists and the apprentices, which pretty nearly the same system has established between the former and the aborigines of the soil. For some time the parties will be happy together; the master, because he is released from part of his own labour; the savage, because he is released from a bloody enemy, and gets once more a sufficient meal; but no sooner will the latter be recovered from the panic caused by the battle-axe of the foe, or the terrors of starvation; no sooner will he have discovered the liberality of some of our laws; that the power of his master is not absolute over him, that some of his countrymen have perhaps better masters, that besides he might as well be his own master, than he will show his aversion to his fetters, become obstinate, the master resents, the apprentice deserts, is retaken and punished; all mutual kind feeling is lost, the magistrate is a couple of hundred miles distant, the apprentice harasses the master by vexatious complaints, and dragging the latter for weeks after him to defend himself at the seat of authority; for want of proof neither party can get satisfaction; the offended master in his turn takes his revenge at home, where he is despotic, and the upshot is, that they try to do each other as much mischief as they can. . . .

. . . The honourable council desires to be informed as to the conduct of the savages already apprenticed. Those which are in this district cannot in general be complained of; to hard labour they have not been accustomed; as herdsmen they are excellent; they are faithful and appear affectionate; but they are very tenacious about the liberty of choosing their masters, and I am sorry again to have to observe, that the impolitic measure of forcing them from those they originally attached themselves to, either because these were slave proprietors, or in order to procure hands for those parts where the restrictions on slave labour were to be enforced, has been the main source of all the trouble we have had with them. The slave proprietors being the most opulent of the inhabitants were best able to provide for them, and they not being able to comprehend the visionary idea of their being enslaved or substituted for slaves, took offence at our over-solicitude in forcing them on poorer masters, began to vagabondize, collect in gangs, and plunder.

Taking, therefore, every bearing of the subject into consideration, I humbly conceive that the best policy we can adopt relative to the said savages is, not to invite them, and when they do come, to admit to apprentice the unprotected children, as is now done, . . . to restrict the adults merely to a most positive rule so that they shall have some fixed abode and honest occupation, on pain of being taken up and severely punished as vagabonds if they go about or collect in gangs without the means of subsistence; beyond which they should be left to dispose of their labour as dear as they can, and to whom they please; they should be left to lay out the fruits of their industry in whatever legal manner they think most to their own advantage; the apprentices, when their indentures are expired, should be put on the same footing. . . . Thus far, His Honour will observe, I would place them on the same footing with the Hottentots, or as there exists difference of opinion as to the spirit of the laws respecting Hottentots, I should more properly say I would place the Hottentots on the footing I have proposed for them. I confess myself equally remote from agreeing with those who maintain that the Hottentots are unfit to enjoy any extent of liberty, as with their opponents who consider them incapable of doing wrong, provided they were emancipated from the restraints which bind the rest of the community. They should be made to work unless they can prove that they can live without, and in this respect they should be closely watched, for in the country where property, particularly large flocks of sheep and cattle, are so much exposed, it is easy to live by theft; but provided they do work, to apprentice them, or their children if they can maintain them, or to say where, with whom, or for how much they shall work, or how apply their earnings, is as impolitic as it is unjust; and upon this principle I would not only propose to deal with the savages, now the subject of consideration, but all free classes who are not above the reach of such scrutiny, from their known avocation, fixed abodes, or respectability of character.

2.10c The difficulties which will arise from the 49th and 50th ordinances will be far greater than are now anticipated.

—Letter from G. D. Joubert to E. Bergh, resident magistrate of Graaff-Reinet, 20 Oct. 1828. (Translated from the original in the Cape Archives, GR 12.4.)

Colonists on the frontier opposed the system of labour contracts required by Ordinance 49. They particularly emphasized the practical problems involved, as appears in the following letter from G. D. Joubert (1795—1858). Joubert, a field-cornet of the district of Colesberg on the north-eastern frontier, was an associate of Landdrost Stockenström and known for his loyalist attitude towards the Colonial government.

. . . I have received [a copy of] the 49th ordinance, concerning the entry [into the Colony] of natives from across the borders, their entering service with the inhabitants under contract, and the granting of passes. If I understand correctly that this ordinance [provides that] nobody may engage any creature or person who comes from across the borders without a contract—which may only be concluded before the justices of the peace—then I must tell Your Honour quite frankly that I see trouble coming. Where we are, the situation concerning employees is at present such that no inhabitant can consider it worth his while to undertake a journey within the Colony for the sake of a contract which is binding for one year. . . . And if the inhabitants are to be obliged by this ordinance to drive off the hundreds [of natives] who are at present with them and not to let them stay, then I must tell Your Honour truthfully that terrible confusion [*een ellendig harwar*] will ensue. This will have no other consequence but that they will congregate within the Colony in numerous kraals and we shall be faced with vagabonding and the thefts, fires and murders which that involves. And to get them all back across the borders will be an impossible task for the field-cornets. . . .

I also wish to tell Your Honour that I have heard of a 50th ordinance, which I have not yet received. . . . If I have heard a true account of [the contents of] that ordinance—that all Hottentots and other natives will be given their freedom and allowed to go about where they like without passes, and that they may not be controlled by corporal punishment—then I must ask Your Honour whether the honourable Government has not taken into account that the inhabitants will be obliged to get rid of all the Hottentots [in their employment] at once, and have nothing further to do with them. And what other consequence can this have but thefts and murders, to which this nation is strongly inclined once they become dissipated. The difficulties which will arise from this will be far greater than are now anticipated. . . .

2.11a We wish that the indigent classes may be compelled, by the law, to lead an industrious life, in order to prevent the necessity they are now under either to steal or perish from want.

—Memorial of the inhabitants of Worcester in support of the Draft Ordinance for the Suppression of Vagrancy, 11 Aug. 1834. (From the translation published in *De Zuid-Afrikaan*, 22 Aug. 1834.)

2.11 Colonial views on the problem of vagrancy 1834–9

Throughout the 1830s colonists were intensely concerned about the dangers of vagrancy. Ordinance 50 of 1825 had removed the formal inequalities of the Khoikhoi, and complaints of stock-theft and vagrancy increased sharply. Slavery came to an end in the Cape Colony on 1 December 1834 by an act of the British Parliament. In 1834 the Cape Legislative Council passed a Vagrant Ordinance which made mere vagrancy punishable without proof having to be produced of any crime actually committed. Headed by Dr Philip the 'philanthropic party' protested sharply and the measure was vetoed by the Imperial Government. Document 11a is a memorial from the inhabitants of Worcester written four months before the emancipation of the slaves, published in De Zuid-Afrikaan *which at this time acted as an apologist for the slave-owners and was a virulent opponent of Dr Philip and the* South African Commercial Advertiser *edited by John Fairbairn.*

To His Excellency Sir Benjamin D'Urban, Knight, Governor of the Cape of Good Hope, and the Legislative Council.

The Memorial of the Undersigned Inhabitants of the District of Worcester Respectfully Showeth:

That Memorialists have read, with peculiar satisfaction in the *Government Gazette*, of the 9th May, 1834, the Draft of an Ordinance for the better suppression of vagrancy in this Colony. That from a local knowledge and experience of the present state of population in the Country Districts, Memorialists are deeply convinced that such a law is of the greatest expediency and utility in order to check idleness, and the repeated robberies of property belonging to the inhabitants. That the losses already sustained by them, and which they still continually suffer, are very heavy, and that the operation of such a law will be a great and lasting benefit to the Country Districts, as good order shall thereby be restored, and every one obliged to support himself by industrious and honest means.

That the state of the indigent classes who have no fixed abodes, are truly wretched, disgusting, and degrading, especially when overcome by liquor; and that there exists no doubt, that by being compelled by the law to adopt a steady and industrious mode of life, their condition will, in every respect, improve.

That Memorialists, in praying that that law may be enforced, are actuated by no wish that any of these Vagrants shall be forced to enter into the service of the inhabitants against their *free will* and choice, or that they shall be laid under any other restraint than that to which all His Majesty's other subjects are subject, but that they may be compelled, by the law, to lead an industrious life, in order to prevent the necessity they are now under, from leading an idle life, either to steal or perish through want.

Memorialists further beg leave to observe, that as the period at which Slavery will cease to exist in this Colony is approaching, no choice will be left to favour one class of labourers above another, but that they shall all be at liberty to enter into competition, and that the highest wages will be given to the most industrious.

That Memorialists are most anxious that the Law against Vagrancy may be put into operation previous to that period, as the present system of permitting wanderers to roam about unpunished may be detrimental to good order, and have a pernicious effect on the minds of the Slaves to be Emancipated.

That Memorialists clearly anticipate, that without the operation of such a law, crimes and offences will be multiplied, property remain insecure, and the lives of His Majesty's subjects be endangered.

That Memorialists are convinced, that through the operation of so salutary a law this Colony will be more civilized; and that its rejection in the present state of things would be a matter of great regret, as the hope and expectations which Memorialists have hitherto entertained to see this Colony on an equal footing with all civilized countries will then altogether vanish.

Submitting all these observations to Your Excellency and the Legislative Council, Memorialists once more pray that the Draft of the Ordinance may be converted into a Law.

2.11b With an anxious feeling for the future prosperity of this promising Colony, I anticipate the fast-approaching moment when thousands of untutored beings are incorporated with Civil Society, without proper laws to check the ungovernable passions inherent to uncivilized beings.

—Letters from A. J. Louw, of Koeberg, in support of a Vagrant Law, to the editor of *De Zuid-Afrikaan.* (From the translations published in *De Zuid-Afrikaan,* 3 Aug. 1838 and 28 Dec. 1838.)

Though slavery came to an end on 1 December 1834 ex-slaves had to continue working for their previous owners for another four years. For practical purposes the impact of emancipation was thus deferred until 1 December 1838, a date awaited with great anxiety by slave-owners. Document 11b is compiled from two letters from A. J. Louw, one of the wealthiest farmers in the Western Cape, who was active in the protest movement of slave-owners during the early 1830s, written shortly before and shortly after slavery was finally ended.

(i) *29 July 1838*

SIR, With an anxious feeling for the future prosperity of this promising Colony, I anticipate the fast-approaching moment when the crops on the fields will be exposed to destruction, and thousands of untutored, mostly immoral beings, are incorporated with Civil Society, without proper laws to check the ungovernable passions inherent to uncivilized beings.

The working of the 50th Ordinance, in many respects inapplicable to this extensive Colony, must have already sufficiently proved to the Government how far the Hottentots and Caffers are behind in civilization, and what mischief they cause by vagrancy. . . .

Their innate rapacity, savage disposition, indolence, and natural propensity towards a wandering life, peculiar inclination to strong liquor, jealous covetousness to the property of their fellow creatures, faithless refractory character, and unfitness to military duty, are unknown to Parliament, and yet so many thousands of them are allowed to enjoy the privileges of that Ordinance.

Those who have stormed the House of Commons with petitions for the freedom of the Negroes, and have placed it into a dilemma, ought previously to have taken care to provide the Colonies with a Vagrant Law, for the purpose of stimulating the Negroes to more industry, befitting them for Christian society, and inducing them to become field laborers.

The farmers, the most useful class in society, the principal contributors towards the payment of pensions, and the luxuries on the tables of the honourables, are the inexhaustable source of trade, abundantly supplying the town folks with the necessaries of life; but how slightly are their interests consulted.

We daily witness the expatriation of our experienced farmers to the deserts of Africa, among which are the most opulent and respectable cattle breeders; the reasons for their adopting such steps will certainly have come to the knowledge of His Excellency.

The Magistrate in Cape Town, and Special Magistrate in the country districts, can testify my good treatment towards my servants and apprentices, notwithstanding which, some have already purchased their freedom, left my place, and roam through the country without any means of support. . . .

(ii) *22 December 1838*

Wheat farming is a pressing work, which must be performed with favourable weather and wind, without the least loss of time; it requires many hands willing to serve the whole year, and none who will only serve by the month; neither may they be engaged as cooks or cattle herds, merely to indulge their laziness. They had not the least reason to leave my service, for they enjoyed daily their usual rest, with abundance of wholesome food and drink, but they did so merely from a desire to lead a lazy and easy life, and to frequent the canteens whenever they think proper; these are the reasons which stimulate them to work by day, even as the Hottentots, who have since the passing of the 50th Ordinance become a pest to the corn farmers.

My good treatment towards them is generally known; they have all left my service, and roam about. . . .

2.11c Protect the Blacks, but protect equally the Whites!

—Editorial in *De Zuid-Afrikaan* requesting a Masters and Servants Law, 3 May 1839. (From the translation published in *De Zuid-Afrikaan.*)

Following the major reforms brought about by Ordinance 50 and the emancipation of the slaves, there was continued pressure from the colonists for a 'proper' Masters and Servants Law which they saw as a means towards restoring some of the labour controls that had been done away with. The Masters and Servants Ordinance adopted in 1841 was, however, shaped more by the principles laid down by Lord Glenelg and Sir John Russell at the Colonial Office in London than by local interests. It largely consolidated the equality before the law granted to the coloured classes by Ordinance 50, though it was no longer felt necessary to include special protective clauses to this end. Colonists would have to wait until the granting of representative government before they could put their own stamp on the Masters and Servants legislation.

Five months have now elapsed since the general determination of the late Slave Apprenticeship, and not a single step has as yet been taken by the Colonial Government to meet the wants under which that system is necessarily suffering.

It is now a fact, which is no longer open to any doubt, that the greatest number of farmers have been deserted by those late apprentices, and are unprovided with hands for agricultural labour. The effect of this scarcity upon the agricultural produce of the Colony must be apparent. Already a good quantity of the crops and fruits of the last season has been allowed to dry and rot on the field, for want of means to collect or thrash. The ploughing season is approaching, and the corn farmers, being inadequately provided with hands (a great part of them hardly with any), contemplate with sorrow and regret the comparatively insignificant quantity they will be able to sow, and the still less quantity produceable for the market and consumption. . . .

Under such circumstances, therefore, it is the duty of every Government to be active and bestir itself, to avoid the calamitous consequences with which the Colony may be visited, to evade the impending storm, and steer the disabled vessel into a safe harbour. Happily our Government *has* the means; and it is to us, and must be to every thinking soul, a matter of surprise, that those means are not employed, which to a very great degree would remove the causes of distress.

The causes have, on all hands, been admitted to be the absence of a *Vagrant Law*, and a Law regulating the *rights and duties between masters and servants.* We are told that the whole Colony, that the Colonial Government itself, admits the necessity of a Vagrant Law. . . . We ask not for Laws infringing on the rights and liberties of inhabitants, or on any part or set of Her Majesty's free subjects; but the whole Colony loudly calls for certain Rules, or Legal Enactments, whereby idle persons, thieves, and vagabonds, are prevented from living upon the hard earnings of the laborious, and are then consequently indirectly compelled to seek for service, and for work, in accordance with the principle of the present *Poor Laws* in England.

The Government at home have very wisely foreseen that at the termination of the Apprenticeship a new system would be thereby introduced in the social communities of the late Slave Colonies, which would require laws and regulations, fixing the rights and duties between the masters and servants. Her Majesty's Ministers have therefore forwarded regulations for that purpose, approved by Her Majesty, to the different Colonies, West and East. In every country in Europe laws of that nature exist, and yet in the Colony of 'the Cape of Good Hope' nothing is done to meet the evils arising from the absence of such laws. If a master has reason to complain here of a European servant, his case is summarily decided before a summary Court; but if it be against a black, the master is held to bring a civil action. With a European servant the master may make a contract before any Notary, or even in private writing; but with Blacks, or, as the Ordinance says, 'free persons of colour', although they are equally held free subjects, yet with them the masters are not allowed to enter into any indenture, or make any contract for a longer period than one year, except before a Justice or Clerk of the Peace! If a European servant leaves the service in the middle of the month, or without any previous notice, he is in a summary manner compelled to finish his time of service, but if a free Black, having entered the service for one month, leaves a few days after, the master is told by the summary Court that he must bring a civil action against the Black. These are only a few samples, and it will naturally be asked how is it possible for the farmers, under such an unsocial system, to secure hands and labourers to themselves for agricultural pursuits?

We hope our Rulers will see the inefficiency of the system as at present existing, and the improper influence it must have on the minds of the servants, and the Blacks in particular. . . . Protect the Blacks, but protect equally the Whites!

2.12 A general law should be enacted prohibiting all Hottentots or other free blacks from moving about without fixed employment.

—Letters to the Natal Volksraad from J. P. Zietsman, landdrost of Pietermaritzburg, 28 Feb. 1840. (Translated from the text published in *Suid-Afrikaanse Argiefstukke, Natal*, no. 1, pp. 340–342.)

In the Republic of Natalia, established after they had defeated the Zulu kingdom in 1838, the Voortrekkers had their first opportunity to institute their own labour laws. In 1839 the Volksraad passed a Squatters' Law in an attempt to control the indigenous population which had re-entered the territory in which the Voortrekkers had settled. On 5 August 1840, some seven months after the letters of Landdrost Zietsman below, it passed legislation which limited farmers to five Zulu families for each farm. This was an attempt to restrict the number of Zulus in the area, distribute the labour supply evenly and control the labour force.

2.12 J. P. Zietsman on the need for pass laws in Natal 1840

(i) Honourable Sirs, It has come to my notice that a large number of Hottentots and other free blacks are to be found roaming about among our community. Or if they are not simply roaming about, then they are living in this area and others without having masters, so that they can work as day-labourers. It seems that they are employed one day, and then spend many days in idleness. This condition is very rare for the Hottentots, and can cause them to fall into the same state of poverty in which we have known them in the British possessions in South Africa. After due consideration, I should like to propose to the honourable Raad that a general law be enacted prohibiting all Hottentots or other free blacks from moving about without fixed employment, but obliging them, according to the Dutch practice, to bind themselves by contract to a master, and to get passes from their masters when they are sent out on errands. Then the farmers will be able to promote their enterprises all the more and the free blacks themselves will benefit. . . .

(ii) Honourable Sirs, Having defeated Dingaan's tribe and having made a peace treaty with the paramount chief Pando [Panda] who now exercises authority over the remaining Zulu tribes, it is also necessary that provision be made for the Bushmen and other kaffirs who live around us. To some it might appear difficult to make such provision, as it will entail the division of tribes. Yet, to my mind, the difficulty would not be as great as the danger to which we should otherwise be exposed if they remain hidden in their present places. As matters now stand, they fall under one or more chiefs who can bring them together at any moment, so that evil consequences can follow unexpectedly at the will of these chiefs. The lands on which they live and which they cultivate are, for the most part, on property registered as farms belonging to burghers [*menschen*]. This would lead many [other] nations to deny them [i.e. the 'Bushmen' and 'kaffirs'] the right to property [of the land they occupy]. To prevent all this, I have applied my humble powers to drawing up a plan which I now put before the Raad for them to approve or amend as they see fit. And the plan is that, as soon as the burghers [*menschen*] settle on their farms, each who chooses to have kaffirs will be allowed to keep a certain number of families on his farm, though not more than five. He will have to allocate a piece of land to them, where they will be able to live together with their families, and where they can grow crops and keep cattle.

He will be allowed to make use of as many servants and cattle-herds from among this group of kaffirs as he needs, and as are dispensable from the tribe. But he will be obliged to reward those who serve him properly, and in the case of adult males this payment must not be less than one cow per year, or the corresponding amount.

None of these kaffirs who have been chosen to live on someone's land may be hindered if after one or more years he prefers to move together with his dependents to live on someone else's land.

The owner of the land on which kaffirs live or have chosen to live will be regarded as master over them and will remain responsible for them. He will also have to know how many of them are residing there.

Once this measure is approved, all kaffir kraals should be notified of the Raad's decision so that all who prefer to do so can choose masters for themselves. The rest will be allocated proportionately, and if there are more than five families to be allocated to each inhabitant, the number will be increased until all are provided with masters. And once our population is increased by new inhabitants, and the kaffirs have already been allocated then with the consent of master and servant the number of families which can be allocated as bondsmen to masters will be reduced to three.

All who refuse to comply with this law and who are found wandering about without masters will be told, on apprehension, to find themselves masters within one month or to remove themselves beyond our borders, while force will be used against the recalcitrant.

Notwithstanding anything contained in the above proposal, it is to be understood that no maltreatment will be meted out to these creatures or anyone else. Free access to the courts will remain for both servant and master. . . .

3 *Law, order and equality 1780–1850*

The peculiar legal and political order of the Cape Colony in the late eighteenth century and its attempted reform during the first decades of British rule, even if the impact of the latter was more evident at the level of symbolic intent than that of actual practice, provided the context and matrix of the earliest Afrikaner thinking about the purpose of the state, the function of law and questions of legal and civic rights.

The two dominant features of the political order at the end of the eighteenth century were (i) a totally inadequate administrative structure for establishing law and order, especially outside the capital, and (ii) a hierarchy of legal status groups reinforcing the economic and racial order of Cape society, though there was a growing measure of vagueness and ambiguity concerning the exact civic status of the various subordinate groups in the colony. The coming of British rule from 1795 did not all at once overthrow this political order. Instead, for more than two decades the new government followed a deliberately conciliatory policy of interfering as little as possible with the existing legal and political institutions. Yet British rule was also marked by certain features which appeared to challenge the existing political order in important respects. On the one hand the British had a more energetic and autocratic view of the government's role in establishing law and order in the interior and on the frontier itself. On the other hand it demonstrated a paternalistic concern with the rights and liberties of all subject peoples. In a series of measures it set out to clarify and reform the legal status of subordinate groups through such acts as Caledon's code of 1809, the attempted ameliorations of slavery through Ordinance 19 of 1823, the proclamation of the legal equality of all free people of colour with Ordinance 50 in 1828, and the eventual emancipation of the slaves in the 1830s. In principle (though less so in practice) these measures could be seen as undermining the essential structures of the earlier political order. Early Afrikaner thinking on law, order and equality had its roots in this earlier historical order, and was a response to the attempts at its reform.

In analyzing and interpreting the texts collected in this section in their historical context the following questions may be kept in mind:

1 Was the inadequate structure of authority of the late eighteenth century seen as a *problem*, and if so, in what sort of terms was this problem conceived?

2 More generally, what was expected of the state? When, and concerning what kinds of issues, were claims made on the state? And on what sort of grounds were these claims based? The answers to these questions would begin to indicate something of the underlying views concerning the nature and function of the state and the law.

3 What were the responses to the British attempts to establish law and order more effectively? What were the reactions to the various measures aimed at clarifying

and reforming the earlier hierarchy of legal status groups? Were the proclamations conferring 'equal protection' and finally complete equality before the law on subordinate groups like the Khoikhoi judged on an *ad hoc* and pragmatic basis, or were they perceived in terms of overall changes in the total political order? And how was the earlier order evaluated in retrospect?

Distinct traditions

From the texts collected in this section it will at once be evident that early Afrikaner thinking on law, order and equality produced two quite different and conflicting viewpoints. By and large this division coincided with that between the educated Afrikaner officials and the rather less sophisticated Afrikaner spokesmen for the rural and frontier society. On the one hand we have the Van Rynevelds, Truters and Stockenströms, who advanced to prominent positions in the colonial government, had close ties with the burgher gentry of the western Cape, and were much involved in the British attempts to establish law and order more effectively. Rather than being 'pro-British', they were in the main 'government men'. During the early decades of British rule, particularly, they had a key role in colonial government: they were given substantial responsibilities in running the existing legal and political institutions, which they had to explain and interpret to the new governors. They were involved in implementing, explaining and justifying the various measures of reform, and on occasion they even had a considerable part in initiating and preparing these measures. In due course they developed a definite set of ideas about the nature and purposes of law and government, which were reflected in their official correspondence and reports. Because they favoured firm government they were largely in sympathy with the general aims of British rule and the reforms of the old order.

The position of the spokesmen for Afrikaner views in the interior and on the frontier was very different and much more elusive. After the turbulence and uprisings connected with the shortlived 'republics' of Graaff-Reinet and Swellendam just before the turn of the century there was little independent political acitivity in any sense. Government measures affected them, if at all, as foreign and imposed interference in their own way of life. The reports of the field-cornets almost invariably dealt with specific incidents and not with more general policy at all. Memorials to the government were concerned with obtaining specific grants or to express particular grievances and needs. Even if reflection on the ways in which the government did or did not affect their lives had led to more general political ideas, no local free press or literature existed in which these could have found expression. *De Zuid-Afrikaan*, the first Dutch newspaper, only came into existence in the 1830s, and then it was based in Cape Town. Even concerning such an event as the Black Circuit of 1812, which according to all accounts made a dramatic political impact throughout the interior, it has not been possible to find any contemporary expressions of Afrikaner views. It is said that Piet Retief kept a diary in which frontiersmen's grievances had been recorded since before the time of the Slachtersnek rebellion, but unfortunately this has been lost.[1] We are thus forced to reconstruct the frontier viewpoint and its largely implicit political ideas from various incidental passages and oblique references. Even if we can do little more than indicate the general drift of the frontier position, the contrast between it and that of the Afrikaner officials is evident enough.

The problem of order

From the texts collected in this chapter, as well as related material in chapter 2, it appears that the inadequate structure of authority in the interior was conceived by burghers and officials alike as a problem (cf. 2.6b, 3.2), but that they differed in interpreting its effects and on what the proper role of the state should be in remedying this situation.

The largely self-sufficient trekboers of the interior turned to the government when they needed recognition of the land they had occupied or when they required protection, or assistance in the form of ammunition, against enemies who threatened their possessions and security of life. The function of the state, to them, was thus to assist with the basic requirements of their own efforts at self-protection, and to give the necessary legitimation to their property and social relations (e.g. marriage) (cf. 3.4b). When the inhabitants of the Camdeboo asked for a landdrost and clergyman in 1778 (3.1), they were probably above all concerned to legitimize their dubious position beyond the colony's proclaimed borders. It is unlikely that they would have welcomed the presence of a vigorous and effective administration in answer to their complaints about the lack of authority and education, if this had meant any interference in the existing social order. For the burghers of the interior the state's function should rather be to buttress that social order, if at all possible. Outside Cape Town, literacy and the Christian religion were regarded as virtually group possessions of the whites, underpinning their sense of political and cultural superiority. As such, they felt obliged, and entitled, to call upon the state to provide schools and services to counteract the cultural degeneration which they claimed was taking place among the burghers of the frontier (3.1).

The officials agreed that it was the function of the state to maintain order and to provide protection, but they conceived of this protective order in a more inclusive sense. An unspoken assumption in the burghers' claims for protection by the state was that it was *due* to them against whoever they considered as their foes, within or outside the colony. The officials, by contrast, considered it the duty of the state to protect equally the colonists and the Khoikhoi who, in the words of Van Ryneveld, are 'equally to be considered as real inhabitants of the country and equally entitled to the protection of the Government'. (3.5) In their view, moreover, the absence of an effective administration in the interior meant the absence of proper law and order, which needed to be imposed on the recalcitrant individuals in their lawless and unenlightened state. The function of the state was to ameliorate the social practices that had been spawned in its absence, to assail the 'arrogance, dissoluteness and other vices, pernicious to social order' (3.5) prevalent among the frontiersmen. At the time the Slachtersnek rebellion, for example, was seen by the officials involved (and apparently supported in this by the more respectable classes of landowners) as primarily a challenge to the administration's attempts to establish effective law and order. Stockenström, who was then landdrost of Graaff-Reinet, wrote in his journal that the chief conspirators would use any favourable opportunity to 'free themselves from the constraint of laws to which they had never submitted except with the greatest reluctance, if they could bring any ground of objection to them'.[2]

The different conceptions of order were of course vested in different contexts and concerns. In the absence of other agencies which could control labour or police vagrants, the burghers of the interior established their personal power over those in their service or on their land. To the burghers on the isolated frontier their authority had to be unquestioned; their power had to be real and immediate, and submission had to be 'unlimited' (3.9a). They looked to the state as an ally in their attempts to compel unwilling labourers to remain in their service (3.4b), and not at all as an impartial arbiter who might intervene on behalf of their servants. If the state interfered with the established relations of subordination it eroded the only visible source of authority; if it did so without effectively assuming the duty to police and control, it in effect subverted order. Consequently, the state should only assist when the burghers were unable to maintain their interests themselves.

The officials at the Cape, in contrast, regarded the unrestrained domination of the burghers and the complete subjection of their labourers as a major moral and political problem. They were much concerned with 'despotic and barbarous treatment' suffered by Khoikhoi workers (2.4), and with their positon of 'slavish subjection' (5.1), which were linked directly to the absence of a strong governmental authority (2.6b). In this they were of course aware of current humanitarian sentiments and responsive to the paternalistic concerns of British imperial policy with the rights and liberties of all its subject peoples. This paternalist concern, which was combined with the idea of equality before the law, is perhaps best expressed in Sir John Cradock's circular letter to the landdrosts in 1812, which may be quoted at some length: 'In thus addressing you, sir, I have only to follow the instructions I have myself received from His Majesty's Government, which are to extend to all classes of persons "equal justice and equal protection". . . . We are ever to bear in view that in the dispensation of justice, no distinction is to be admitted, whether the complaint arise with the man of wealth or the poor man, the master or the slave, the European or the Hottentot. . . . I am desirous to impress that it is not to the greater crimes I so much point your attention (for they but seldom occur, and they from the common sense of danger mostly afford their own remedy), as it is to the lesser description of offences, which from their obscurity and supposed insignificancy escape observation and punishment. . . . It is the uncontrolled severity of the powerful over the weak, so difficult to describe, it is the nameless tyranny of the strong over the defenceless, and the thousand means that the spirit of oppression can employ and which I cannot recount, that fill me with more solicitude, for such persecutions evade the direct interposition of the law, and are alone to be remedied by the energy of an active and enlightened Magistrate, intent to advance the progress of true religion and Christianity.'[3]

Even more important, however, was the officials' conviction that labour oppression was not only wrong but not in the interests of the state. It bred discontent and resistance, 'constantly requiring extraordinary measures, which will not only occasion great expense and trouble, but never effect a lasting peace in the colony'. (3.5) One of the root causes of all the turmoil which the frontier experienced in the 1780s and 1790s was, in fact, in the eyes of the officials, the complete subjection of the labourers to the arbitrary powers of their masters.

It was accordingly one of the state's main tasks that, in the words of Van Ryneveld, it should not only ensure order and tranquillity but also 'administer Justice to everyone in particular'. (3.5) Justice would in fact become the major political concept in the thinking of someone like Stockenström (cf. 3.9a). Justice demanded that the state should protect and sanction the interests of all groups and individuals in society; it was the task of the state to function as an impartial arbiter and 'to regulate and adjust the interest of these contending parties'. (3.5) This was the theory. In practice, however, the necessary administrative apparatus for implementing this vision of the state as an impartial arbiter of justice did not yet exist. Moreover, slavery and the paternalistic world view underpinning it tended to vitiate the conceptual basis of the officials' insistence that arbitrary power be replaced by the reciprocal duties of employer and labourer. The basic assumption, shared by most officials (who were often large slaveholders, as Van Ryneveld was), was that the interest of the master was invariably that of the slave; that masters motivated by a true paternalistic spirit were acting as 'Fathers rather than Judges . . . not only in punishing but also in rewarding.' (3.3) The burghers took this argument further: accepting that masters act in the interests of themselves and their slaves, there is no need for the state to interfere in such a relationship, 'to protect one part of society against the other part'. (3.10) On the frontier burghers would undoubtedly have agreed that these paternalistic assumptions must hold in regulating indigenous labour as much as slavery. Here, as well, one class need not be protected by the state against the other.

The assumptions of reform

To the burghers in the interior, then, the attempts to reform the old order constituted a challenge and a threat. When the magistrates failed to support them in their property claims against blacks on their land, they complained 'that there is no longer any justice for us in this land from our courts'. (3.11b) The officials, however, who were committed to reform the old order, developed quite different views of the relation of the state to society. In fact, the texts collected in this and other chapters allow us to trace the outlines of that development. In the Dutch period the conception of the state as minimal was still dominant: little more is expected or claimed than that it should provide the 'first necessity of an orderly state'. (2.1b) Thus, we find Van Ryneveld as late as 1805 still maintaining that the state cannot do more than provide and enforce the framework of criminal law (2.5). However, from the second decade of the nineteenth century we find officials like Truter beginning to articulate the function of the state in much more ambitious terms. The basic category became that of the founding and progress of *civilization*, and the state acquired an essentially educative function, particularly with regard to those parts of society that were still in a 'backward state of civilization': 'increased civilization is [the legislator's] aim'. (3.6a, cf. 3.9a) The way in which the state was to accomplish this educative and reforming function was not so much by substantial reforms but by establishing a proper legal framework and contractual basis for all labour and civic relations. The relation of masters and servants, for example, could not any longer be based on personal and arbitrary power or on traditional conventions. It had to be seen and arranged as a binding legal *contract*. In Truter's words: 'What then remains for the Government to do, but to prescribe, through legislative provision, to the farmer the limits of his power, to the Hottentot the extent of his obligation, and to the Landdrost the guidelines according to which he should judge between Hottentot and farmer?' (3.6b) What he was in fact proposing was the creation of a liberal state, a *Rechtsstaat* where the law would provide the formal framework for all rights and liberties in society.

An ideology of the rule of law

One of the main components in the developing political thinking of the Afrikaner officials was what can be called, in a general sense, an ideology of the *rule of law*. The use of the concept of the rule of law in this context must be severely qualified and circumscribed. Clearly there can be no question of the precise and technical sense which this term has acquired since Dicey. Given that the substantial introduction of British law into the Cape Colony was not to take place till about 1830,[4] there can also be little question of any direct links with the rule of law ideology as this had emerged from the earlier constitutional struggles and the common law tradition in eighteenth-century Britain.[5] However, within the historical context of the existing status hierarchies the local tradition of Roman–Dutch law at the Cape in the eighteenth century had in certain respects developed similar features.[6] At the beginning of the nineteenth century we find the government official and first Chief Justice Truter developing the general political concept that instead of the rule of men there should be a rule of law, and that law should be basic to the whole social order (3.7).

Authority relations that were not based on the ordering and sanctioning principle of the law are rejected as 'arbitrary power' (3.7); giving someone the right of punishment over his subordinates according to his own discretion 'would open wide the door to arbitrariness and inhumanity' (3.6a). The argument underlying this rejection of discretionary authority was clearly spelled out by Truter in his inaugural address of 1815. We could not rely on the moral virtue or sense of justice of individuals in positions of power and authority to provide the necessary constraints, since self-interest so frequently and pervasively warped our moral judgement. Therefore we required the law, which was supposed to function as an impartial and disinterested arbiter in social conflicts (3.7). As early as 1802, Van Ryneveld had argued that the self-interest of the field-cornet prevented any possiblity that he could administer impartial justice between fellow farmers and their labourers, and on this basis proposed the creation of a Circuit Court (3.5). Similarly we find Truter opposing discretionary powers not just of farmers or field-cornets but of the landdrosts as well (3.6b). No one should be a law unto himself, all should be under the law.

The ideology of the rule of law propounded by Afrikaner officials like Chief Justice Truter or Landdrost Stockenström encountered varying degrees of resistance from the rest of the colonial community. We may differentiate two main types of reaction. On the one hand we find those who could not accept the basic assumptions of the rule of law approach, and who regarded it as in conflict with their notions of authority and order. Thus we find Christoffel Brand (who possessed no less than two doctorates in law) espousing the paternalistic philosophy of the slave-owners: 'Why may *we* not punish our subordinates when they misbehave?' (3.10) Similarly Retief considered it to be incompatible with his concept of the responsibility of someone in a position of authority if he could not exercise his discretionary powers but had to be bound by the law. (3.12c) On the other hand we find those who accepted the general principles of the rule of law approach, but were unhappy with the way in which it was applied in practice. They agreed that it was the task of the state to administer impartial justice between all parties, but contended that in practice this did not happen, and that they were being discriminated against (3.11a, 3.9b, 3.13a, 2.11c). The idea of an impartial legal order thus did find some wider acceptance in the Afrikaner community, even if sometimes the support for the 'benevolent views' of government reform may have been inspired largely by strategic considerations (3.9b).

In the final analysis the difference between the officials and the colonists may seem to amount only to a slight difference in emphasis on the importance of law and order in theory and in practice. The colonists seldom directly opposed the idea of an impartial legal order as such. They tended rather to stress the many practical inconveniences and their own insecurity. It follows that if an effective legal administration could have provided them with easy access to the courts and with security of property, or, as they termed it, with 'such measures as shall protect us in the legal and peaceable possession of our rights as burghers' (3.13a) which to their minds meant above all effective policing against 'vagrants', then their objections might have fallen away. The officials, for their part, also recognized the importance of the practical administration of law enforcement. Thus Stockenström regarded the provision of a local magistrate as removing 'the most important obstacle to good order'. (3.13b) Nevertheless there are profoundly different sets of assumptions involved here. To Stockenström the law appeared as an ideal and as a matter of fundamental moral principle. Once law and justice was recognized as basic to the social order, only the practical task remained of providing 'a fair and impartial administration'. (3.13b) The colonists, such as the Colesberg memorialists of 1837, agreed on the practical problems of inadequate law and order, but had quite different ideas on its underlying causes. They blamed the increase in crime and insubordination not so much on the local magistrate, as on the law itself: 'We attribute it entirely to a multiplicity of contradictory and ineffective laws, which like an old book ought to be revised, corrected and amended.' (3.13c) Evidently they did not conceive the law itself in ideal terms but as an all too human creation. Law and justice are not absolutes, but instrumental to a particular social order. Two different notions of *order* thus confronted each other, if only implicitly. For the colonists, order was defined as the maintenance and proper policing of the prevailing system of labour and property relations, and there was a breakdown of order when their own interests were being threatened instead of upheld. For the officials, on the other hand, order was defined by the rule of law, and the principles of justice and equality might require legal and social reform.

Equality and gelykstelling

The other main component of the new liberal order was the principle of equal rights, in particular equality before the law. It should be stressed that in this context equality did *not* mean political, social or economic equality. The reforms of the old order that culminated in Ordinance 50 did not give political rights to the subordinate groups; it did not produce major redistributions of wealth and power. Though it changed the legal framework, by and large the major structures of the labour order survived intact in practice, and it would still be several decades before social equality would begin to become a controversial issue. What was at issue now was the standing of blacks as contractual parties in labour relations, and their access to the protection of the courts. More generally, however, this involved the question of their legal and civic status in the social and political order. Given the context of the earlier legal status hierarchy, the introduction of equality before the law could not be limited to the immediate practical issues involved. In principle it proposed a new and different political order in which the basis of the old status hierarchy had been done away with.

Though no primary texts could be found for inclusion in this chapter in which this was directly and explicitly expressed, there is ample contemporary evidence that Afrikaners nurtured in the old order had widely held and deeply ingrained beliefs that Khoikhoi should have a completely different—and lower—legal and civic status from their own. The importance of this question of *conceptual* or *categorical* differentiation is well brought out in the report of Landdrost Alberti from Uitenhage in 1805. 'According to the unfortunate notion prevalent here, a heathen is not actually human, but at the same time he cannot really be classed among the animals. He is, therefore, a sort of creature not known elsewhere. His word can in no wise be believed, and only by violent measures can he be brought to do good and shun evil.'[7] As Alberti remarked, this accounts for the profound objections to attempts to give the Khoikhoi equal rights before the law. In principle it brought them within the same legal and civic category as the burghers: equality before the law amounts to *gelykstelling*, a levelling or equalization of the status differentiation central to the old order.

The conflict between the new political thinking associated with the notion of legal equality and the ideas rooted in the old order is dramatically illustrated by two documents in this chapter. In the letter from the Stellenbosch landdrost and heemraden in 1797 (3.4a) we find the heemraden objecting to allowing the Khoikhoi to have recourse to the court because 'it would open a door and give the Hottentots the idea that they are on a footing of equality with the burghers'. The landdrost, on the other hand, asserted that 'true equality' consisted in recognizing that 'before the law all were of equal standing'. If this illustrates a direct clash between different views, the letter from the Cape Court of Justice (3.3), in defence of retaining death by torture for slaves, shows both principles in an ambivalent combination. At first the Court maintained that the severity of punishments is dependent on the nature of the crime: 'these distinctions are observed equally with free persons and slaves', which amounts to a recognition of the principle of legal equality. But then it went on to argue that 'the distinction of persons' was a traditional principle of Roman–Dutch law, and this, of course, was precisely the hierarchical notion that the principle of equality before the law was supplanting (cf. 3.13a).

The partial recognition of the principle of legal equality in the tradition of Roman–Dutch law would obviously be an important point of departure for the Afrikaner officials in developing their rule of law ideology in the following decades. It is significant, however, that they did not restrict the significance of the question of equality before the law to its narrow judicial context, but saw it as crucial to the abolition of a whole system of legal and administrative differentiations leading to domination and oppression. Talking in 1849 of the old order before the introduction of Ordinance 50, the Rev. N. Smit calls it a 'system of oppression'. (3.16) A more elaborate critique of 'this system of "keeping down"' was provided by Stockenström in 1828 (3.9a). The basic premise that the state had to administer justice to all its subjects made it essential that existing legal inequalities and discriminations should be done away with, and that a new legal order be substituted in which the principle of equal rights for all would be basic. Thus we find Stockenström in 1828 recommending 'the enactment of a law placing every free inhabitant in the Colony on a level, in the eye of the law, as to the enjoyment of personal liberty and the security of property' (3.9a), a recommendation that would be instrumental in the introduction of Ordinance 50. In 1836, as the lieutenant-governor, confronted with Retief as spokesman for the disaffected frontiersmen on the point of trekking, Strockenström once again affirmed: 'From the principles to which I have always clung, I shall not deviate one hair's-breadth; every one, therefore, knows what he has to expect. . . . In one word, equal rights to all classes, without distinction.' (3.12.b; cf. 3.13b, e) This pronouncement was not to be without effect in the events leading up to the Great Trek.

However, significant parts of the Afrikaner community, unlike the officials, did not endorse the principle of equal rights, but utterly rejected it. More than other aspects of the rule of law, the notion of equality was a traumatic reversal of the established, white-dominated social order. Whereas Stockenström attempted to reassure the colonists that granting legal equality to the Khoikhoi would not affect their own rights since 'none of the Coloured Classes are authorized to do anything which the law does not permit any [colonist] to do', (3.13b) this was not the way in which the colonists saw it. They profoundly rejected such equality of everyone before the law as amounting to *gelykstelling*, a levelling or equalization of existing status distinctions, and thus a direct threat to their own rights and privileges. The classic expression of the resentment this challenge to the social order provoked is found in the well-known words of Anna Steenkamp in 1843, explaining the Great Trek as not so much due to the emancipation of the slaves, 'as their being placed on an equal footing with Christians, contrary to the laws of God and the natural distinction of race and religion, so that it was intolerable for any decent Christian to bow down beneath such a yoke'.[8] Significantly, the introduction of equality before the law was not perceived as restricted to a legal context only, but was generalized to include religious equality, and even social equality and integration (3.14). Piet Retief even suggested that political supremacy for the blacks was in the offing (3.12a). The Colesberg memorialists (3.13c) complained of 'a system of licentiousness and insubordination' involving nothing less than an inversion of the old social and political order: 'not only [our] servants but the black population in general have a contempt for all just restraint, are not subject to their superiors, not satisfied with equality [but] thirst for . . . unlawful authority'. From the context of this latter case we know that there was no question of political equality at all; the colonists merely found it more difficult to impose their property rights and their notions of a proper labour order. In practice, then, neither social, religious nor political equality turned out to be really seriously at issue; but that they were raised at all is an indication, however, of how radically unacceptable the notion of *gelykstelling* was considered to be.

Justifications: natural liberty versus racial difference

In conclusion, it may be instructive to consider the kinds of justifications that were offered in support of reforming measures or as grounds for rejecting *gelykstelling*. This would provide some indication of to what extent different and perhaps incompatible traditions of political thought were in the process of formation.

In general, we find the Afrikaner officials backing up their support of liberal reforms affecting the position of the subordinate groups by invoking their equal rights as native-born inhabitants of the country (3.5) or their natural liberty. In the words of Truter: 'They are, and remain, people, and free people at that.' (3.6b) Truter, in particular, attempted to introduce the notion of natural freedom as the proper basis of social relations and obligations: 'The legislator cannot place the Hottentot, who is a free person, under an obligation which extends beyond a contract into which he has voluntarily entered.' At the same time, they did not seem to load this concept of 'natural freedom' with any particular theoretical or even metaphysical connotations. It amounted to little more than an extended usage of the legal category of 'freemen' with its attendant rights and obligations. Thus when Stockenström asserted that 'the Hottentots . . . stand *naturally* on a level with the burghers', this was in fact introduced as a quasi-legal argument. They were not slaves but 'natives of the Colony, and consequently . . . born to the right of citizenship, and entitled to hold land'. (3.9a)

The officials were of course aware of the marked ethnic and racial differences involved. Truter referred to the Khoikhoi as being 'close to a state of nature' (3.6b) and in a 'backward state of civilization'. (3.6a) However, these were not insuperable barriers separating them from civilized society; essentially they should be viewed as an imperfect people 'for whom a greater degree of civilization and perfection is attainable'. (3.6a) Racial and ethnic differences could not, therefore, be invoked as a justification for differential status or treatment. On the contrary, it is part of the educative function of the state to improve the condition of these more 'backward' classes in society. Stockenström even argued that the depraved social conditions of the subordinate groups were not so much their 'natural' condition but a *result* of conquest and systematic oppression: 'This system of "keeping down" being strictly acted upon, gradually degraded the moral character of the natives, and generated the plea that they were too miserable and inferior a species, either to appreciate or be benefited by a participation in the liberties and rights enjoyed by their more powerful and fortunate fellow-subjects, to which they had an equal title.' (3.9a) To improve their condition these restrictions had to be removed.

Justifications: natural liberty versus racial difference

The colonists and slaveholders might be expected to have been inclined to invoke these racial and ethnic differences as justifications for the old order. We do find the Court of Justice in 1796 defending the extreme punishments they thought necessary for slaves by stressing that they were 'descended from wild and rude Nations'. (3.3) However, we do not find in these documents any prominent notions of inherent racial inferiority. On the whole, differences in environmental and social conditions were stressed. Thus the slaves as 'men brought up in a different climate, in a barbarous nature and under a rigid government' were contrasted with others, who 'from better education and better habits' have come to adopt more civilized customs. (3.3) Essentially, then, this did not differ much from the way in which the officials tended to think of the colonists in the interior. Thus, Van Ryneveld described the bulk of the inhabitants of the interior as the products of their natural and deprived social environment: 'Men without any idea of education, grown up in idleness, and in the unrestrained indulgence of the wild passions of nature . . . could have no other notions than those of arrogance, dissoluteness and other vices, pernicious to social order.' (3.5) The colonists would undoubtedly have resented this description of themselves, and in all probability held much more rigid views concerning the significance of inherent racial differences which they advanced as justifications for maintaining discriminatory practices. In contrast with officials they did not see the backward and depraved conditons of the non-whites as amenable to improvement, or even as a result of conquest and oppression, but rather as an immutable fact requiring differential legislation and treatment. Thus we find Landdrost Van der Riet objecting to Truter's application of contractual notions based on the premise of natural liberty to the Khoikhoi, 'who are generally accounted to be of the most stupid sort, and who therefore never think, nor can think, as Christians do'. (2.6a)

What we do find are serious objections against the practical consequences of conferring equal liberties to the subordinate groups without taking into account the differences in social and cultural development. Thus the *Zuid-Afrikaan* argued that, as a consequence of Ordinance 50 and the absence of effective vagrancy and pass laws, 'roving and wandering have already again become so natural to them, that they prefer their natural conditon in the midst of our society above our civilized state and regular intercourse'. (3.9c) Similarly a correspondent from the Hantam claimed in 1834 that in practice equal liberties meant to the Khoikhoi 'the liberty of idly roaming at large, the unrestricted liberty of committing all sorts of crime', and that, far from emancipating them, this freedom delivered them into a 'state of misery . . . [of] the most detestable slavery . . . [to] vice, and sloth, and crime'. (3.11a, cf. 3.9b) This was then contrasted with a notion of 'rational liberty' which would include civil obligations as well. In fact, this amounted to an attempt to transplant the notion of 'liberty' into the old idea of hierarchical social order. Thus N. T. van der Walt wrote that 'liberty without subordination produces insecurity, but liberty with submission and due respect is necessary for our existence'. (3.13d) In the case of the Khoikhoi, this meant their being subjected to vagrancy ordinances, though, as the Rev. N. Smit observed in 1849, there are good grounds for believing that 'what would be viewed in a white person as mere travelling, would be considered vagrancy in a native'. (3.16) Even if we do not find any articulations of a specific theory of racial inferiority, there can be little doubt that racial and ethnic perceptions informed even those more liberal and enlightened notions which gained currency amongst the colonists.

Early Afrikaner political thinking on law, order and equality was thus marked by the development of opposing positions. The rule of law ideology articulated by the Afrikaner officials on the one hand, and the rejection of *gelykstelling* by the spokesmen for the Great Trek on the other hand, both contributed to the formation of an ambivalent, complex and varied public opinion somewhere between these two extremes. Neither position can lay claim to be the exclusive Afrikaner tradition, but both were to be of considerable significance in future Afrikaner political thinking.

Justice and (in)equality in the republics

The ambivalent patterns in Afrikaner thinking on law, order and equality, and the different influences which they reflect, can be traced in some of the documents from the early years of the republican states. It is well known that ideas about the 'proper relations between masters and servants' figured prominently in the writings of the leaders of the Trek (5.5a), and that the rejection of *gelykstelling* actually became part of the constitutions of the new republics. The first Transvaal constitution, the Thirty-three Articles of 1844, contained a clause (significantly, in a judicial rather than a political context) excluding 'half-castes, down to the tenth degree' from sitting in their meetings as a member or judge.[9] And the constitution of the Z.A.R. adopted in 1858 stipulated that 'the people desire to permit no equality between coloured people and the white inhabitants, either in Church or State'.[10] However, this did not mean that the republican Afrikaners totally excluded non-whites from access to the courts or denied them all rights before the law. Though there would be little or no question of any political rights or social equality for blacks in the republics, the idea of a basic equality before the law, which had encountered so much resistance when it was introduced in the Cape Colony, would not be altogether absent.

Something of this ambivalence on issues of justice and (in)equality appears in the exchange of Zietsman and Andries Pretorius in Natal in 1841 (3.15). Pretorius left no record of his views in this particular connection, but it is clear that where blacks were concerned he assumed the right to dispense his own brand of rough justice without more ado in a matter in which he was not only the accuser as well as the judge, but also very much an interested party. To Zietsman, and, he claimed, to many others as well, such arbitrary action was a travesty of justice. He insisted that, even for people considered as 'kaffirs', there should be due process of law: they should be tried before the proper courts of landdrost and heemraden. Like other subjects they had rights, such as the right to prove their innocence before an impartial judge, and the laws of the land applied to them in the same way as to anyone else. Zietsman did not for a moment regard the blacks in his service as his equals in any sense. On the contrary, he explicitly set out to defend the rights of 'my subordinate creatures'. (3.15) His action was probably inspired by paternalist notions rather than by any thought of equality before the law. Even so, his idea of justice implied support for a rudimentary rule of law involving a minimum of legal rights to all subjects, and made it impossible for him to accept without protest Pretorius's arbitrary use of his discretionary powers which amounted to a denial of such basic rights.

The two documents (3.17a, b) from the early days of the Orange Free State show a similar tension between the notions of discretionary and arbitrary powers that long prevailed under frontier conditions, and a different idea of law and order being advanced by the agents of the new state. To the frontiersman involved it was indeed the 'immemorial law of the frontier' (3.17a) that entitled him to deal with any threat to his property at his own discretion and without any thought that 'such creatures' could have rights in law that might be backed up by the state. As against this the government secretary implored another frontiersman that 'nobody may take the law into his own hands', and that thieves must be prosecuted 'in an agreed manner in the properly constituted courts'. (3.17b) Characteristically he invoked the notions of justice and fairness in this connection, but even more significantly he pointed out the dangers to public order of such arbitrary conduct.

Even if the rejection of *gelykstelling* had been a prominent theme in Trekker thinking, and racial inequality had become entrenched in the constitutions of the new republics, the ideals of a public order based on the rule of law and of a basic equality of everyone before the law was thus not entirely absent from the Afrikaners' intellectual heritage.

3.1 We beg to express the desires of our troubled hearts with regard to our melancholy condition in these troubled times in consequence of our great distance from the government.

—Letter from 33 inhabitants of the Camdeboo to Governor Van Plettenberg and Council, 24 March 1778. (From the translation in Moodie, *The Record*, Vol. III, pp. 74–75.)

The trekboers' dispersal into the interior during the course of the 18th century took them ever further away from the official seats of authority and from the locations of the few religious and educational establishments in the south-western Cape. By the 1770s the two main streams had converged in the Camdeboo (later Graaff-Reinet) area, much of which was well beyond the official boundary of the time. For such colonists there was always the danger of their cattle being confiscated as well as possible further penalties for transgressing the boundary. Some of the signatories of the petition below, written at the time of Governor Van Plettenberg's personal tour of the interior to determine a new eastern boundary in 1778, were undoubtedly in this position and keen to secure official recognition of their land claims, though perhaps were not otherwise in favour of government interference in their affairs.

We your most obedient servants beg, with all humility and respect, to express, as we deem it right and fitting to do, the desires of our troubled hearts with regard to our melancholy condition in these troubled times, in consequence of our great distance from the Government who hold power by the will of God, and also from God's House and Church; of which we have been hitherto destitute, for there is not to be found among us any building where we can unite in calling upon the name of the Lord.

Having long reflected upon this matter, we have thought fit to lay our desires before you with all humility, as it is perhaps possible that, on consideration of our prayers, you may favour us with a Clergyman and a Landdrost, not that we wish, from any ground of discontent, to separate from Stellenbosch, but solely on account of the great distance of that place; for many are there here in the country who have already departed from the commands of their God, and, to our great injury, become disobedient to Him, and to those who, by His will, are established in authority. As they live so far distant they commit wilful insubordination from which we apprehend serious oppression, unless God, through your means and power, should be mercifully pleased to prevent it.

But alas! it is no great matter of wonder that things go on so ill in some parts of this country; for, as before said, we have been hitherto without teachers and clergy, so that many fine young people are growing up like the ignorant cattle, without any opportunity of learning in their youth the first principles, from which they may not depart when old. Even among the aged people some are found whose errors might be corrected by the censure of the servants of Christ. But as to the good, many a distressed soul longs and sighs to approach the throne of God, and day and night to seek pleasure in His law, and to partake the sacrament appointed by Christ, which he is sometimes denied the opportunity of enjoying. . . .

We therefore again unanimously request, that the obdurate hearts of some may be humbled, and upon the other hand, that the good and just may be encouraged and supported by the appointment of a Clergyman and Landdrost. . . .

Johan Kruger	Adriaan van Jaarsveld
Jan Adriaan Venter	and 30 others

3.2 Want of authority is the chief reason that the Cape was so easily reduced. Everybody would command here, and nobody would obey.

—J. F. Kirsten's *Memorandum on the Condition of the Colony*, September 1795. (From the translation in V. Harlow and F. Madden, *British Colonial Development, 1774–1834, Select Documents*. The full original text is published in C. F. J. Muller, *Johannes Frederik Kirsten oor die toestand van die Kaapkolonie in 1795* (Pretoria, 1960).)

The first British occupation of the Cape occurred only a few months after the rebellious burghers of Graaff-Reinet, which had been created a new district in 1786, coerced the unpopular Landdrost Maynier into leaving the district. The arrival of the British fleet in False Bay coincided with a similar rising in Swellendam and the involuntary retreat from Graaff-Reinet of the Commissioner sent to investigate matters there. J. F. Kirsten (1759–1820) was a senior Company official before he became a free burgher in 1792. He was a rising entrepreneur at the Cape when he presented this memorandum to the new rulers shortly after the occupation in 1795.

One of the first and indispensable duties of man is the love of his country. Animated with that sentiment I take the liberty to lay before Your Excellencies a few hints on the subject of my country. . . .

This colony has for several years been on the decline, and rapidly approaching its annihilation. The intolerable shackles laid on trade, the monopoly, the paper currency, the stamp taxes of all description, and above all the Jacobin mania, are the chief causes; and I may venture to say that nothing less than a revolution could have saved it. The insurrection for instance which took place in the interior parts of the country (at Grave Reinet) is a sufficient proof of my assertion. The insurrection at Grave Reinet seemed to proceed from a dislike to the Dutch Company's monopolies as well as from a ridiculous notion that, like America, they could exist as an independent state. But where are the resources? The population of this colony does not exceed 21,000 inhabitants, the land is barren, and the enemies with which the people are surrounded are numerous. Government had lost its respect and such was the oppression of the inhabitants that every prospect of reconciliation had vanished. It is now two months since the Government sent a deputation to Grave Reinet—and the Commissioners were obliged precipitately to leave the country, under the most imminent danger of losing their lives. Want of authority on the part of our Government is the chief reason that the Cape was so easily reduced. Everybody would command here, and nobody would obey—it is then no longer surprising that we lost a colony, which although unable to secure its Government against the invasion of a superior enemy, might yet have opposed him a more effectual and durable resistance. The Cape is weak by nature, ill fortified, and has been still worse defended. As in the mother country it was sufficient that one proposed for his neighbour to reject; it is thus that they also lost their country. The inhabitants are for the greater part impoverished—this poverty has disposed them for disaffection and revolt as appears again by the example of Grave Reinet. Those unhappy people are dispersed over an expansive surface and live at a considerable distance from each other—on one side they are incessantly harassed by the Bossies Manns (a species of Hottentots) and on the other they are obliged to struggle under the oppressive yoke of their own Government.

The object of all merchants is gain—it was then consistent that they, the Dutch East India Company, should govern the colony more with an eye to their own interest, than to that of the people. . . .

3.3 While there are Slaves, proper measures must be pursued for the maintenance of good order amongst them.

—Letter from the Cape Court of Justice to Major-General Craig, 14 Jan. 1796. (From the translation in Theal, *Records of the Cape Colony*, Vol. I.)

Judicial torture, particularly of slaves, was an established feature of Company rule at the Cape. The new rulers retained the system of Roman-Dutch law, but soon turned their attention to this particular aspect. In January 1796 General Craig enquired from the Court of Justice whether in view of 'the nature of the punishments inflicted on the blacks in capital cases', it might not be possible simply to impose the death penalty and do away with the various forms of torture accompanying it, while bearing in mind 'the necessity of keeping an exact subordination amongst the very numerous body of slaves which exist in the Colony'. Despite the reply of the Court of Justice below, the traditional practice of torture was abolished by Governor Macartney in 1797.

In the first place, the distinctions which exist between Europeans or free Persons and Slaves in this Colony are by no means the cause of the gradations of Severity with which capital punishments are here inflicted upon Slaves. . . .

The degree of Severity with which punishments are inflicted according to our Laws is measured by the atrocity of the Crime, which in proportion to its magnitude demands a more striking Example. . . .

In our Jurisprudence it is usual to punish with greater Severity Housebreaking and Theft, accompanied with Murder, than Theft alone, whether it is committed by free people or Slaves—a wilful and insidious Murder is more severely punished than Murder perpetrated in the heat of passion when provocation has been given. Simple Murder is deemed less culpable than Regicide, Parricide, &c. An Incendiary is punished by Fire, &c., &c.

These distinctions obtain so universally, that they almost amount to a Rule of conduct for the Courts of Judicature over all Europe, and in this Country they are observed equally with free people & Slaves.

Nevertheless we cannot but observe, with regard to Slaves, that the equality of punishment ceases when they commit offences against Europeans or free persons, particularly their Masters: but this distinction is not peculiar to this Country; on the contrary it is grounded upon analogy with the Criminal Law, according to which the distinction of persons is one of the essential points by which the degree of punishment is measured in most civilized Nations, and this distinction is especially founded upon the Imperial Laws or the Roman Law. . . . Slaves were considered by the Romans as Creatures, who from their enured bodies & from their rude and uncultivated habits of thinking were much more difficult to correct and to deter from doing evil, than others, who from better education & better habits measure the degree of punishment by their internal feelings rather then by bodily pain: and this reasoning may be justly applied to our modern Slaves, many of whom are descended from wild and rude Nations, who hardly consider the privation of Life as a punishment, unless accompanied by such cruel circumstances as greatly aggravate their bodily Suffering.

It may also be observed, that in every Family (with a very few exceptions) the number of Slaves is so great, that the safety of the Family depends upon them. This requires the greatest precautions, that they may not make use of their superior force, because such an event would bring the whole Colony to the brink of ruin.

In order to render these precautions essential, they should comprehend sufficient Motives to prevent the Slaves from disturbing the tranquillity of the Family, and at the same time leave in the hands of the Master such power as is necessary for him to exercise in the Direction of his Family. Experience has taught that gentle means are inadequate, even amongst free persons, to maintain good order, and of this the Military State is an instance, where the authority must be vested in one person, or in much the smaller number; consequently, altho' strongly actuated by Motives of humanity, and viewing the Slaves in the most favourable light, it becomes necessary to adopt severe measure to deter them from revolting against their Masters & taking advantage of their superior strength. . . .

. . . Over and above the alleged political reasons for keeping the Slaves in subordination by extraordinary means, they are for the most part not only destitute of those principles which commonly restrain a thinking being from the commission of atrocious crimes, but they have not those relations in society which would induce one to suppose that they really valued the preservation of a life, the greater part of which they must spend for the advantage of those to whom they are subject, and however unwilling to form a bad opinion of our Fellow Creatures, yet it must be owned that the experience of all ages has taught, and daily confirms us in the belief, that a State of Slavery is always accompanied with a certain Enmity against Masters, in so much that it must be looked upon as an extraordinary event to find a Slave who would not rejoice at any mischief that might befall his Master. . . . It rarely happens that when a Slave sees a plot formed against the life or property of his Master, he endeavours to prevent the execution of it.

These inconveniences will never be removed until Slavery, of which they are the natural or at least the inseparable consequences, be abolished: but as the greatest part of the property of the Inhabitants of this Country consists of Slaves, that could not be attempted without being followed by the most ruinous consequences to a number of Families. . . .

It still remains a doubtful point whether the mitigation of punishments would tend to soften the Manners of the Slaves, for this reason, that altho' capital punishments are ordained in order to deter them from the commission of Crimes, yet the source of those very Crimes, as well as the origin of that Enmity which Slaves bear towards free persons, is to be found in circumstances totally unconnected with the punishment of death. We think, under correction, that these causes originate from the consciousness which a Slave has of his condition—from the great improbability of his being able to ameliorate his condition—from the difficulties that prevent him from even using means to effect that end—from the abuse which Masters often make of their authority—from the want of those principles which might direct and comfort them in their unhappy Situation. It could hardly be expected that Men brought up in a different Climate, in a barbarous Nature and under a rigid Government, who retain their own ways of thinking, should change their manners, even if the severity of capital punishments were mitigated: as matters now exist, he will consider these very measures which are taken to lessen the severity of his fate as additional proofs of the duration of his servitude—such will be his idea so long as he continues to depend upon the will & caprice of his Master.

There are not wanting however other means which might answer the purpose of softening the manners of the Slaves, and at the same time save the Legislature from the necessity of seeking after the means of maintaining good order.

The measures we recommend are the following, viz. that Masters should zealously endeavour to conduct themselves as Fathers rather than as Judges in their Families, and act according to the strictest Rules of Virtue and Humanity, not only in punishing but also in rewarding. Altho' the Rights and Equality of Men have been much talked of lately, yet it certainly is true that the detestable system daily gains ground 'that a slave who does well does no more than his duty'. It is but very rarely indeed that a Slave is deservedly rewarded. Upon these principles we would flatter ourselves with the hopes that it is not impossible to inspire the Slaves with affection for their Masters, for it is indisputably true that affection is a reciprocal sentiment, and always increases in proportion to the good actions of him towards whom such Sentiments are exerted.

The answer to the humane question of Your Excellency, whether this would not be worth the experiment? may be easily gathered from what has been said. We could with confidence answer in the affirmative, could we expect that every Master would co-operate to that end, by exercising his power and influence amongst the Slaves, in such a way as to show them that their state of Slavery originated from no cause depending upon him, and also, by softening that state, to lay a good & just claim for their fidelity & obedience.

The consequence of this would be that if not all the Slaves, at least the good part of them, would contribute to the maintenance of good order, instead of seeing it disturbed with pleasure, as it is the case at present; consequently the necessity for inflicting severe punishments would not be greater amongst them than amongst free persons, even of whom there are some who are destitute of those principles which ought to inspire them with zeal for the happiness of that society to which they belong.

But every one whose knowledge of mankind is founded upon Experience, and above all those who are charged with the unpleasant task of governing in the Society, are well aware how little room there is to hope that while men can so freely dispose of their Fellow Creatures, they will be guided by such motives. . . .

There still remains a difficulty which perhaps might not have been dreaded, but which in our opinion would probably ensue as a consequence of mitigating the mode of inflicting capital punishments, should Your Excellency think fit to adopt such a measure. The mitigation of punishments would raise in the minds of many of the Inhabitants great apprehensions for their personal safety, a circumstance from which several inconveniences would arise.

In the first place, malicious persons, considering the mitigation of punishments in a wrong light, would impute what Humanity has dictated, to a desire of lessening the subjection under which Slaves have been kept. In the second place, the persuasion that more lenient treatment of the Slaves would be a necessary consequence of mitigating capital punishments would rouse fears among the good but ignorant Inhabitants, which they would be unable to conceal, which circumstances could not fail to excite discontent in the Colony in proportion to the number of those affected with it.

We must therefore acknowledge that we do foresee an indirect aggravation in the

Severity of domestic punishments, from whence perhaps there might arise a necessity for returning again to that Severity, the abolition of which is so much desired: for while there are Slaves, proper measures must be pursued for the maintenance of good order amongst them. . . .

O. G. de Wet	C. Matthiessen	C. Cruywagen
W. S. van Ryneveld	J. P. Baumgardt	H. A. Truter
Johannes Smuts	Abraham Fleck	H. P. Warnecke

3.4a If a Hottentot were recognized before the law, it would open a door and give them the idea that they are on a footing of equality with burghers.

—Letter from Landdrost R. J. van der Riet and heemraden of Stellenbosch to Governor Macartney, 6 Feb. 1797. (Translated from the original in the Cape Archives, BO 50, no. 33.)

Initially the official policy of the Cape government had been that the Khoikhoi were not subject to the law of the colony but to their own tribal authorities. In the course of the eighteenth century more and more Khoikhoi were incorporated in colonial society as a subordinate class. The British more than the Company proclaimed that the Khoikhoi were also entitled to protection by the courts, but at the turn of the century their de facto *legal position was precarious. In general their evidence in court was regarded only as information and not as proof except where it was confirmed by other circumstances. As the following document indicates it was uncommon for Khoikhoi actually to appear as plaintiffs in civil cases.*

On the occasion of our most recently-held meeting, the case was to have been heard of a certain Hottentot Cobus who sued Maria Elisabeth Theron, widow of the late burgher Jacobus du Preez, for payment of a debt which the aforementioned Hottentot Cobus pretended to have incurred from the aforementioned widow. The undersigned Heemraden objected to having the case heard before their college, as they are ignorant of whether or not a Hottentot has the right to summon a burgher before the College, and of whether, once being allowed, it would open a door and give the Hottentots the idea that they are on a footing of equality with the burghers. The Landdrost was of a contrary opinion, and stated clearly that a Hottentot should be recognised before the law in the same way as himself, and that this constituted true equality, since before the law all were of equal standing. . . .

Thus they take the liberty to request with great respect very humbly of Your Excellency whether Your Excellency would be good enough to go into the matter to provide the College of Heemraden with an order by which they will have to abide in future. At the same time, however, the Heemraden take the liberty of mentioning for the consideration of Your Excellency that, as such practices have never before obtained here, they are of the opinion that, if it should be established that a Hottentot is free to cite any inhabitant before the courts, this College would increasingly be obstructed and hindered with trivial matters—and that such cases would have to be referred to the Cape Court of Justice. . . .

3.4b Permit me to make the Hottentots in service remain with their masters, and also to restrict and control them.

—Petition from J. H. Conradie and inhabitants of Agter Kogmanskloof to Governor Macartney, 1798. (Translated from the original in the Cape Archives, BO 104.)

3.4 *Colonial views on legal equality and forced labour 1797–8*

Though the government held that the Khoikhoi were a free people, many colonists were in practice devising ways and means of compelling the Khoikhoi, who had been forced off the land, to enter and remain in their service. Conradie and his fellow colonists from the fairly isolated area near the present Montagu saw the government as an ally, and turned to it for official sanction of this process of subjugation.

We the undersigned petitioners submit our humble request and our interests to Your Honour the Governor so that we might be permitted to preserve our welfare and so that we can continue to subsist among our fellow-men. . . .

It is my humble request to Your Honour to enact an ordinance prohibiting the Hottentots who are presently in this district from maintaining their kraals here, and expelling them from here. This is necessary as a result of the frequent thefts and rogueries committed by this nation. They steal our cattle and drive them to their kraals.

Thus I request that the Hottentots who have entered service should be put in leg-irons for a time when they steal or desert so that this nation can be tamed a little, as they are extremely devious. Once their conduct has improved sufficiently, the leg-irons might be removed.

I also humbly request Your Honour not to allow these Hottentots to run away from their masters once they have entered their service, as there is much wilfulness among them, and they go from one master to the next. In this way, many [farmers] are left poor and needy as their servants abandon them. This will not be unknown to Your Excellency who will be acquainted with the life-style of that nation. Thus it is my humble request, and the humble request of all of us, that Your Honour permit me, veldwagtmeester Johannes Hendrik Conradie, to make Hottentots remain with their masters, and also to restrict and control them so that such vagabonds do not wander all around committing thefts, as has recently happened in my district. . . .

Thus it is the humble request of myself and of all of us that Your Honour permit these measures, on the promise that I will execute the office entrusted to me, and to which the landdrost and heemraden of Swellendam appointed me, with faith and integrity. I promise also to commit no injustice to anyone, not even to that nation, but to exercise meticulous care to do that which would meet Your Honour's approval, so that we should not [be considered as] rebels but might submit ourselves, as obedient subjects, obeying the laws and exercising the rights granted us by Your Honour. . . .

3.5 The interior police of this settlement is wholly insufficient to preserve good order in general, and to administer justice to every one in particular.

—W. S. van Ryneveld's *A Plan for Amending the Interior Police*, 1801. (From Theal, *Records of the Cape Colony*, Vol. IV.)

The British rulers gave greater priority than did the Company to putting the administration of the colony on a more effective and professional footing. At their request, Van Ryneveld in 1801 submitted a plan for the reform of this administration. Measures such as the 'Hottentot Proclamation' (1809) and the institution of a circuit court (1811) largely owed their origin to this report.

Whosoever should cast but a very slight regard on the interior Police of this Settlement will immediately be aware that it is wholly insufficient to preserve good order in general, and to administer Justice to every one in particular. And those who have travelled in the interior part of the Country and have attentively studied the nature of the Inhabitants, the various relations which they bear to one another, the opposite interests of the peasant and the Hottentot, who are both equally to be considered as real inhabitants of the Country and equally entitled to the protection of Government, such persons must be convinced that this nominal Police can not any longer Subsist, but that essential alterations, and those immediately, ought to be adopted, in order that Justice may be done to every one, and that tranquillity may be restored to the interior parts of the Colony.

The boundary of the Colony has been extended by slow and insensible degrees under the former Government, which with a careless indifference was overlooked and disregarded. This extension indeed of territory has even been sanctioned by Government, not only by its granting Lands, but also in receiving rents for them; at the same time Laws were enacted and strict orders issued against injuring or maltreating the Natives of the Country.

No public notice however has properly been taken of the extortions and depredations of farmers upon the Hottentots, depriving them of their Lands, and afterwards driving them into the interior, or forcing them to become their Servants. . . .

. . . Such was the form of the interior Police in the year 1795, when the present Government took possession of the Colony. It had already been experienced that the same was insufficient to maintain good order, and put in execution the Laws of the Country. Men without any idea of Education, grown up in idleness, and in the unrestrained indulgence of the wild passions of nature, composed at all times the bulk of the inhabitants of the interior parts of this Country, ignorant and being accustomed from their infancy to command over slaves, Hottentots and other tribes of People, whom they considered as inferior to themselves, they could have no other Notions than those of arrogance, dissoluteness and other vices, pernicious to social order.

The Hottentots already reduced by the Peasants to slavery, by the right which the strong will usurp over the weak (a right that such sort of People know very well how to exercise), have often times showed, and recently given convincing proofs, that they are by no means indifferent as to their situation, that they aim at revenge, whenever opportunity may favour their design.

The farmer on the other side perceives very well that the Hottentot is only restrained by awe and a superior power. He is jealous of all such regulations made in favour of the Hottentots, as may tend to increase his means to oppose himself to them—in short both parties, especially in the remote Districts, consider one another in the light of enemies, and in proportion as Government incline to favour the Hottentots and to protect them particularly against oppression, in the same proportion will discontent arise among the farmers, who imagine that the Interests of the Hottentots are preferred to their own, and think themselves thereby aggrieved.

It will therefore be always a difficult task for Government to regulate and adjust the interest of these contending parties, to cause Justice to be done to every one, and good order and tranquillity to be preserved throughout the whole Colony. This end can never be obtained so long as the Police remains in its present form. Peace may perhaps by an armed force be preserved for a short time, but real tranquillity will never be established by these means; discontents among the farmers and Hottentots will constantly require extraordinary measures, which will not only occasion great expense and trouble, but never effect a lasting peace to the Colony.

I therefore deemed it my duty under the present circumstances to turn in my mind some Plan for amending the interior Police and to consider of measures to be adopted to prevent as much as possible inconveniences for the future.

To this end, two material points appear to me most important:—

1st. The Police in general relative to the Hottentots.

2nd. The particular amendment in the interior Police itself, as it regards both the Peasant and Hottentot.

In respect to the *Hottentots*. These for the most part can not at present but be servants to the farmers. They neither possess Cattle, nor have other means of Subsistence, and become dangerous Subjects to Society when suffered to wander about, without being Servants, or having a Livelihood—they skulk in the woods, and, if they can, steal the cattle of the farmers, upon which they live.

There are some who have Cattle and dwell with their families in Huts [*kraalen*], who can very easily remain there unmolested, and ought with all possible care to be protected in that right *coute qu'il coute*.

There exists a Third Class of Hottentots who belong to the *schools* lately established here by the Missionaries—these also merit every support, and indeed nothing appears more material than to encourage these institutions for the instructing and civilizing the Hottentots. They thereby obtain a safe asylum against violence from the Farmers, and can then have no other inducement than good treatment from the farmers to go and serve them.

It will therefore be necessary to direct that no Hottentot is to be suffered to remain within the Boundaries of this Colony, unless belonging to one or other of the following classes, viz.:

1. The Class of Hottentots serving the Farmers.
2. To the licensed kraals or huts.
3. To the schools of the Missionaries. . . .

For the rest, no Hottentot, unless belonging to one of the above legally established classes, shall be permitted to remain within the Boundaries of this Colony; but all wanderers and vagabonds ought immediately to be apprehended and placed either to the public works, or on Robben Island, there to labor for their bread.

To which end every Hottentot in service, or belonging to the kraals, must always be provided with a certificate from the Landdrost of the District, and those belonging to the licensed schools with a certificate from one of the Missionaries, countersigned by the Landdrost, without which certificate, if found, they shall be liable to be considered as vagabonds, and taken up accordingly.

All which certificates are to be renewed annually, in order to prevent abuses.

This appears to me best calculated for the maintenance of good order, as far as regards the Hottentots, but at the same time it is necessary that effectual measures be adopted that Justice be done to those who conform themselves to the Laws, that prompt Justice be administered between Farmer and Hottentot, and thus both will be obliged to fulfil their reciprocal duties.

To this (which brings me to the second point) the present Police of the interior is insufficient. . . .

In proportion as the Country became extended, and the population increased, so the want of due Police having been felt, Government endeavoured gradually to remedy the same, by appointing from time to time Field Cornets, and even Field Commandants, who took upon themselves as a part of this nominal Magistracy, but these people, being all fellow farmers, and consequently having but one and the same interest, could not thus be impartial men betwixt Farmer and Hottentot, and in fact they very seldom interfere with quarrels betwixt them otherwise than to support the Superiority of the farmers over the Hottentots.

Their chief business is to form bodies of armed men (commandos) against Bosjesmen and other Vagabonds, who disturb the Country and rob the farmers of their

Cattle, and to mark the distances of loan places, *all* the rest remaining under the management of the Landdrosts. . . .

Two measures appear to me fit to remedy these defects, viz.

1. The appointing in each district of several Deputy Landdrosts, and

2. The dispatching yearly of a respectable Commission from the Capital, invested with the necessary powers, in order to proceed throughout every district, for the purpose of taking cognizance of all such matters as they may deem worthy of their attention, and also such as persons concerned may lay before them, and summarily to decide the same after due investigation. . . .

3.6a Through the framing of laws a legislator hopes to promote civilization and order, and particularly the improvement of certain classes of people.

—Letter from Fiscal J. A. Truter to Landdrost A. Stockenström (Sr.), 7 April 1810. (Translated from the original in the Cape Archives, G.R. 9/10.)

At first Caledon's 'Hottentot Proclamation' of 1809, which finally brought the Khoikhoi clearly under the law, was unpopular among colonists who feared that it granted to the Khoikhoi substantially more rights and freedom than they had previously enjoyed. In these letters the fiscal, J. A. Truter, responds to the queries of the elder Stockenström (1757–1811), landdrost of Graaff-Reinet 1804–1811.

. . . Now concerning your . . . objections with respect to the state and the service of the Hottentots—

In framing laws, a legislator should bear in mind that he makes prescriptions for imperfect people. This applies to those who, not only in general, as far as their moral standards are concerned, have not achieved the highest degree of perfection; but also, insofar as they are members of a civic community, are imperfect in many respects, and are therefore not always able to do that which might possibly be required for the welfare of society. But a legislator should equally not take as the measure for his laws the incapacity of certain classes of people—for whom a greater degree of civilization and perfection is attainable, and whose increased civilization and perfection is his aim—in such a way that he demands no more of them than they are able to achieve with ease in their backward state of civilization.

In this way civilization retrogresses. And I am therefore of the opinion that, in the framing of laws, through which a legislator hopes to promote civilization and order, and particularly the improvement of certain classes of people in society, he might and should demand as much of the individuals of this class as they are in any way able to achieve; provided that he does not frame laws which cannot be executed. I acknowledge that the execution of the law, when it is not carried out by all, as the sovereign prescribes for their welfare, becomes defective; but are all principles not difficult to apply and liable to faults? This is how matters stand concerning the registration of Hottentots, the difficulty of which I appreciate, but which I yet do not think is impossible. . . .

I cannot understand at all how, through this measure, as Your Honour says, 'the unlimited freedom of the Hottentots will be violated or the inhabitants exposed to the possibility of being left without cattle-herds'. Is a citizen less free for having his name registered? Is a Hottentot less obliged to carry out his duties as a cattle-herd?

As far as travelling without a pass is concerned, freedom is not hindered by this either, but order alone is promoted, and do the Hottentots not have equal status with such Europeans as have no fixed domicile, or even those whose place of domicile changes from one district to another? In the meanwhile, it appears to me that travelling without a pass is a problem which will solve itself, in that the wandering Hottentots must always be delivered up to the field-cornets or landdrosts, who then investigate the matter and act *pro re nata*.

Your Honour's question as to whether Hottentots should be allowed to enter into service for more than one year at a time, I cannot but answer in the affirmative—I add this remark: for the masters to be embarrassed by the Hottentots leaving as soon as their contracts expired—this I consider wrong. Firstly, this is no new law, but was also applied before the proclamation of 1 November. Secondly, a master can, in any case, re-engage a Hottentot, whose service he would have continued, before the expiration of his current contract. Thirdly, how would a Hottentot have more freedom, or be more inclined, to leave his master on the turn than he would have been since 9 May 1803, when the first regulations concerning their contracts were made? And this question, I think, is equally appropriate for your next remark, namely:—

'If a Hottentot wants to leave a farm, then all the others also want to leave. If they leave, without entering anyone else's service, they will continue to wander and will remain idle with their friends at the expense of their masters, under the pretext that they cannot find opportunities for satisfactory employment. Where there are many, more will go; those who have few Hottentots, will lose those as well. Litigation between them and the inhabitants will keep the Landdrosts and Heemraden occupied at all hours.'

Yet why should all this be more important now, than when a Hottentot placed himself under contract before the 1st of November 1809? . . .

. . . Will one not be allowed to punish one's servant? According to anyone the right of punishment over one's servants by an explicit law would open wide the door to arbitrariness and inhumanity. It is obvious that neither the Fiscal nor the Landdrost will consider it an offence for a master to apply moderate correction to a Hottentot who has been negligent or has otherwise erred slightly. The maintenance of good order requires this in respect of children, apprentices, servants of the kind of the Hottentots, and slaves. However, such correction cannot be more than moderate, and if it is to be more strict, then the master of a Hottentot as well as the master of a slave ought to address himself to a magistrate. And that this is the intention of the proclamation is evident from section 6, in terms of which [the Council of Justice or College of Heemraden] are empowered to take note of complaints of *maltreatment*, to which moderate and deserved correction surely does not belong.

3.6b What then remains for the Government to do but to prescribe through legislative provision to the farmer the limits of his power, to the Hottentot the extent of his obligation, and to the Landdrost the guidelines according to which he should judge between Hottentot and farmer?

—Letter from Fiscal J. A. Truter to Landdrost Stockenström (Sr.) 13 March 1811. (Translated from the original in the Cape Archives, G.R. 9/10.)

. . . For the rest, the only comment I have in mind on the passage on the Hottentots is that it would be extremely difficult to remove altogether the difficulties which accompany their employment. They are, and remain, people, and free people at that. To increase the power of the farmers over them, taking into consideration the farmers' lack of civilization, would be irresponsible and cruel. To grant the field-cornets any discretionary powers in this respect would, for the same reason, not be free of the danger that cruelty would ensue. And to grant greater discretion to the Landdrosts in their exercise of authority over the Hottentots would be highly irregular, and could also lead to extremes, because not all Landdrosts make the effort to concern themselves to the same extent with the Hottentots, and to conduct as much discussion with the Hottentots, as I was very glad to see from your letter that you do. What then remains for the Government to do but to prescribe, through legislative provision, to the farmer the limits of his power, to the Hottentot the extent of his obligation, and to the Landdrost the guidelines according to which he should judge between Hottentot and farmer? Drawing up these provisions, the legislator cannot place the Hottentot, who is a free person, under an obligation which extends beyond a contract into which he has voluntarily entered.

The only defect which I find in the above proclamation [of 1809] is that contracts can be concluded before the field-cornets. Many irregularities might arise from this, especially as all the field-cornets, with very few exceptions, if any at all, perpetuate the impression that the Hottentots are compelled to work. For people who are so close to a state of nature, and who are of exceptionally inconstant character, this brings about a distaste for their duties, which makes them incapable of being trusted. All their contracts—and these could also be simpler—should be concluded before the Landdrost, who can then explain both to the farmer and to the Hottentot what their reciprocal rights and duties are, in such a way that no uncertainty remains as to either the service owed to the farmer or the freedom of the Hottentot. The Hottentot, especially, should understand that he was indeed free, but, by entering the contract, he has voluntarily diminished his freedom in favour of the farmer, who, for the period agreed upon has some control over his freedom, and that the law will support him in the reasonable exercise of this. At first this would take a great deal of trouble, but soon it would become a familiar task, after which, without much talking on the part of the Landdrost, the procedure could be completed at once.

. . . Concerning the female-slave of the Secretary Muller, of whom Your Excellency wrote to me in your letter of the 8th December, I must refer Your Excellency to the 69th section of the Ordinance for the Management of Outlying Districts. As far as the distinction between male-slaves and female-slaves is concerned, as the law makes no distinction in this matter, we may not do so either. Nonetheless I believe that the natural distinction will in itself always be deserving of consideration, in the meting out of all forms of punishment, and that, when it is necessary to put a female-slave in chains, the chains ought to be less heavy than those used to chain a male-slave. Furthermore, it appears that not only our present Governor, like Governor Janssens, disapproves of the practice of putting female-slaves [*meiden*] in chains, and when this cannot be avoided, I am quite sure that it is the desire of His Exceleency that no such female [*meid*] should appear in public. This is what I try to do in the city, even with male-slaves, as far as this is within my power. . . .

3.7 It is especially necessary that the administration and application of the law be effected with unbiased judgement and without respect of persons.

—Address of Chief Justice J. A. Truter on the occasion of the first assembly of the court in the new Court House, 19 Jan. 1815. (From *The Cape Town Gazette and African Advertiser*, 28 Jan. 1815.)

When the proceedings of the court were thrown open to the public in 1814 in accordance with British legal traditions, a new court house became necessary. J. A. Truter was appointed Chief Justice in 1812, succeeding W. S. van Ryneveld after the latter's death in mid-career. He acted as chief advisor to successive British governors on such topics as land tenure (1813), tax collection (1814) and criminal procedure (1819). In 1820 he became the first South African to be knighted, as Sir John Truter.

. . . 'Everything is precarious the moment we lose sight of Justice.' This indisputable assertion of the Roman Orator is founded on that experience, which, from the first existence of man, through all his ages to the present day, must have carried conviction to every thinking being, that mankind has never existed any where, or in any shape, without laws; and that by a deviation from justice and the laws, all safety, all regularity, and consequently all true happiness, as inseparable from tranquillity and order, have been lost and destroyed.

This is by no means surprising, when we consider that, however gifted every man may be with a true sense of right and wrong, with a just perception of good from evil, still however self-love, and more especially that species, denominated self-interest, frequently so warps his understanding, and so often smothers in him every sense of virtue, that, deaf to the voice of reason, and blind to the beams of truth, he becomes incapable when self-interest is concerned to do, or to say, that which his conscience tells him is just and right. If, therefore, we were to leave mankind to act from their own feelings of right and wrong, the community would become instantly exposed to the greatest disorder and uncertainty, and which, therefore, rendered it necessary, on the very first formation of men into society, to think of framing laws and regulations, which were not to be subjected to the self-love and self-interest of every individual, but of which the maintenance and preservation should be entrusted to the power and authority of impartial persons, who had not any interest in the application and enforcing of the same.

It is certain that, dangerous as it is, on the one hand, to leave man to the arbitrary direction of each interested individual, equally dangerous is it, on the other, if the laws prescribed on the establishment of society be not kept sacred and inviolate. Then, says Cicero, every thing is uncertain; no citizen is longer safe in his person—his property becomes a prey to avarice and plunder—confidence and tranquillity are banished from his mind—happiness is but a visionary illusion—and, in one word, all is uncertainty.

Such being the case, it needs no demonstration that it may well be considered as an essential privilege in every society, that the system of the laws and usages, which must form the guide in deciding over the life, honour, and property of a member of the community, is so framed and established, that not only a deviation therefrom is difficult, and a reparation easy, but also that every individual carries this conviction in his mind; for in this conviction is to be found true contentment, and consequently the unimpeded progress of every man's welfare and prosperity.

To create this conviction, it is not sufficient that we make good and wholesome laws, but it is besides especially necessary that their administration and application be effected with unbiased judgment, and without respect of persons; so that every individual, of whatever rank and situation, living according to the laws, may be assured in his daily labours, and in the bosom of his family, of the peaceable and undisturbed enjoyment of his respective share in that good which he has a right to expect from society; and that the road to protection against all annoyance, from whatsoever rank it may proceed, stands open for him faithfully guarded, so that no insurmountable, nor even discouraging, obstacles can render his access thereto either impossible or difficult.

These are the principles upon which the administration of justice must rest, to avoid encroachments whereby every thing would be reduced to doubt and uncertainty.

In all civilized societies, those principles are acknowledged. . . . Yet, notwithstanding, the code is not every where regulated in such manner that the actual existence of those principles is perceptible in every community. When I say this, I by no means allude to the general imperfection of human nature, whereby many regulations in society are either imperfect in themselves, or imperfectly carried into effect; no, but I here mean that inconsiderate spirit of ambition, through which, in some states, the legislative power is not kept sufficiently separated from that to which the execution of the laws is entrusted, whereby the latter has not competent liberty to follow the dictates of his conscience in the application of the laws, without fear of injury, or expectations of reward, from those who make them; and whereby a man of worth in vain consults the law, to enable him to judge of the consequences of his acts, and is always in doubt what he ought to do, or what he ought not to do, for the preservation of his interest and his just rights; while a villain or a knave, like a beast of prey seeking whom he may devour, commits his crimes with impunity in the face of justice, through the influence and protection of the hand of power.

Should this state of things not immediately and evidently be productive of doubt and uncertainty, it will nevertheless prove a cancerous wound, which will at last consume the vitals of social order, and, in the mean time, most certainly banish all confidence, prosperity, and happiness from the society of man.

Although this picture does not afford the most pleasing representation of judicial proceeding, it cannot, however, disturb those who, comparing therewith the state of the community in which they live, find that the principles I have above stated are not only acknowledged, but in reality so interwoven in the political system of their government, that human weakness and frailty only leave the possibility of deviation; and that even then such deviation need not be suffered with impunity by any person, however inferior his rank in life may be: and how happy I feel myself in being enabled here to add that this is the state in which I consider we live in South Africa. . . .

All that I have here said is not the result of my particular ideas, or the inferences I have deduced therefrom, as existing only in my own imagination; no, we see that on the part of Government nothing has been left untried to show the high estimation and respect in which it holds the administration of justice, and that all its acts here are in the true spirit of the British Constitution. Where can we have a more lively proof of this, than the very building in which we this day, for the first time, assemble: a Building erected with great expense, and peculiar ingenuity, purposely to give to the administration of justice in this Colony all that external lustre which can tend to place its dignity and freedom in the most exalted point of view; a thing which always makes a favourable and very essential impression on the minds of all those who have, or take any interest in, a regular and impartial maintenance of the laws.

Whatever may be the future lot of this Colony, this Structure will be an everlasting monument of the liberality of the British Government in this Settlement. Be then this Building now dedicated to Righteousness! Let justice never be forsaken within its walls! Then may every member of the community, with awe and respect, but at the same time with the fullest confidence, approach the Temple in which his guardian angel resides, assured that he will never forfeit her protection but by a violation of the laws, and the perpetration of crimes. . . .

3.8 . . . the revolting, and for the inhabitants of a civilized community, shuddering idea that a slave, accusing his master, . . .

—Memorial from Stellenbosch burghers to the Burgher Senate against the provisions of the Ordinance 19, 10 July 1826. (From the translation in Theal, *Records of the Cape Colony*, Vol. 27.)

Ordinance 19 of 1826 sought to bring about the amelioration of slavery and provoked considerable reaction from slave-owners generally, who saw their property rights threatened (2.8a, b). The Ordinance also extended the legal rights of slaves in court proceedings. Article 17 established a procedure whereby a slave-owner could be required to show that alleged maltreatment of his slave was lawful punishment. As the following memorial from the burghers of Stellenbosch show, colonists objected in principle to such provisions.

. . . The extraordinary dangers which surround us, and the uncertainty under which we labour, compel us again to address ourselves jointly to you with this Memorial, as we are convinced that you, Gentlemen, as Fathers of this District, will with eagerness take into your consideration our grievances and the dangers which surround us, and which, as your Children, we now come to lay before you.

Warm and enthusiastic zealots, of an exaggerated philanthropy, and consequently of violent emancipation of Slaves, have depicted and exposed our grievances as groundless, and our foreseen dangers as mere chimeras. But do not facts confirm the grievances laid before you in our former Memorial? . . .

Such were the accusations brought forward by the Slaves against their Masters, when they were by Law obliged to prove an accusation or a Crime, and what will they now do, as according to the Ordinance no obligation rests upon them to prove the Accusation? . . .

Now then, will any one say that our apprehensions for false accusations are unfounded? And will not every Master, on the false accusation of his Slave, according to the 17th Article of the Ordinance, become a Sacrifice? When two Citizens of this Colony, when two Christians appear before the Court, and the one accuses the other, then the Accuser must prove his Statement, and failing in this respect the accused is free. And Gentlemen! it grieves us, it brings our Nerves and Bowels in agitation, on the revolting, and for the Inhabitants of a Civilized Community, shuddering idea, that a Slave, accusing his Master, and shewing merely a wound, the Master, denying the accusation, is notwithstanding to be condemned as a illtreater of Slaves, and to lose his whole credit and reputation, whilst the Slave as a reward of his false accusation, and of his immoral conduct, receives his freedom from His Majesty, according to the 43rd Article of the Ordinance.

The consequences, Gentlemen, of all this are that the Slave enjoys more privileges in this Colony than his Master. And, Gentlemen, must this not be a heartrending idea to an Inhabitant of this District, yea to the whole Colony, that *we*, who pay taxes, even for the Slave himself, *we* who leave our homes to sacrifice our life and property on the Frontier against the Kaffers and our Enemies, for the protection of our Country, without receiving the least reward or thanks for it, while the Slave passes his time here at his ease and leisure, that the word of us, who are educated in morals and religion, will deserve less credit than that of an immoral and heathen Slave?

And where is the benevolent Regent who will still say that we Inhabitants of this District have no reasons to complain, no grievances against that part of the Ordinance? . . .

Your interest, Gentlemen, is ours, our Interest is yours. The black clouds of dangers hover over our heads as well as over yours. The murder from the dagger of the incited Slaves, animated with a spirit of freedom, is aimed at the heart as well of you as of Us!

Not we, not we alone, but you all will weep over the Corpses of murdered Wife and Children. The flames of devastation will not alone destroy our habitations, but will also cause your Houses to fall to ruin! Not alone our Wives and Daughters, but also yours, will in a libidinous manner be prosecuted by our Slaves with rape and defloration, and when, after all this, out of the pit of our murdered fellow Citizens a Saint Domingo has arisen, then may God grant that we be no more amongst the living, but then you yourselves will be compelled by the Slaves who fought themselves free to carry the bones of your Wife and your Child to make a monument of their freedom obtained by fire and murder. . . .

F. R. L. Neethling
and others.

3.9a I recommend a law placing every free inhabitant in the colony on a level, in the eye of the law, as to the enjoyment of personal liberty and the security of property.

—A. Stockenström's *Memorandum submitted to His Honour the Lieutenant-Governor by the Commissioner-General*, 3 April 1828, preceding Ordinance 50. (From *The Autobiography of Sir Andries Stockenström*, Vol. 1, pp. 286–291.)

Ordinance 50 of 1828 removed the legal restrictions on Khoikhoi, 'Bushmen' and other free people of colour and granted them equality before the law with whites. It was largely based on a report by Andries Stockenström, who had recently been appointed commissioner-general for the eastern districts. At the same time the missionary Dr John Philip was also lobbying for the same cause in Britain and succeeded in getting the imperial government to insert a clause which forbade any amendment without its consent.

The distinction made between the several classes of the free inhabitants of the colony by the existing laws appears, in a great measure, calculated to retard the improvement of those which are considered, either through prejudice or on account of their unfortunate condition, as belonging to the lower orders of this community. I allude particularly to the coloured classes; and in as far as the aborigines are concerned, those laws have not only thus retarded their improvement, but they conspired with the said prejudices, which they keep alive, and the humiliation they generate in the minds of these oppressed people themselves, to lower, more and more, the degraded state in which they are at present placed in the scale of society.

The policy of this distinction and these partialities seems to have originated in the necessity, felt by the earliest migrators into the interior, to prevent the possibility of retaliation on the part of the natives for the aggressions and outrages committed against them, by crushing their power altogether and securing their unlimited submission. The impotence of the Government, its ignorance of the true state of affairs in the remote parts of the colony, hardly ever visited by any enlightened individual capable or willing to give the necessary faithful information—and, perhaps, the interest which some of the rulers themselves had in the perpetuation of the oppressions alluded to—caused too ready an ear to be lent to the representations relative to the necessity of using every precaution against the chance of the natives recovering themselves, and becoming again of consequence in their lost country, and dangerous to their conquerors. This system of 'keeping down' being strictly acted upon, gradually degraded the moral character of the natives, and generated the plea that they were too miserable and inferior a species, either to appreciate or be benefited by a participation in the liberties and rights enjoyed by their more powerful and fortunate fellow-subjects, to which they had an equal title. But these laws, kept alive under the same pretences and pleas, have now existed too long not to have convinced us that (if even a more liberal system should do no good) they certainly have not been productive of one single beneficial effect. Thus much is said merely to show that, at any rate, the old system is not worth retaining any longer; but it is confidently hoped (and the writer thinks himself supported by experience, after having weighed all objections and arguments on both sides of the question) that, by doing justice to the said classes, the inconveniences inseparable from the system complained of will disappear, without making place for those apprehended by the advocates of the existing disabilities of the blacks. I, therefore, do not hesitate to recommend the enactment of a law placing every free inhabitant in the colony on a level, in the eye of the law, as to the enjoyment of personal liberty and the security of his property, subject, of course, to those limitations which the local circumstances of individuals may subject them to, upon principles admitted and acted upon under most civilized governments, such as the disqualification of persons not having the right of citizenship to hold landed property, and the like.

Having particularly in view the Hottentots, I shall more minutely refer to that race, though I must again urge the necessity of including the free blacks of all classes in the intended boon, in as far as the same can apply to their condition.

The Hottentots, being natives of the colony, and consequently, in my opinion, born to the right of citizenship, and entitled to hold land (though I have heard this disputed), stand naturally on a level with the burghers, save the drawbacks entailed upon them by the laws which I propose to remove. There are many of these scattered through the enactments from the earliest legislation of the colony—too numerous perhaps, to collect; as, for instance, the prohibition against their possessing firearms; their liability to perform duties to which the whites would not condescend; their obligation to show passes to any person of the latter colour, though in every other respect, perhaps, their inferior; the deprivation and apprenticeship of their children when often they themselves can provide for those children, and, perhaps, better than the master to whom the same are bound. All these, and many such, it would be difficult to repeat by name and date, as some might escape unnoticed; and *therefore*, as also to avoid the odium of denominating particular classes, it would be advisable to frame one comprehensive law, embracing *all free inhabitants without reference to colour or name of the tribe*. . . .

. . . The law I would propose would necessarily enact strict prohibitions against such an abuse of the liberty generally conceded as would endanger the peace of the community. It would become absolutely necessary that a person travelling to any distance from where he is known should be provided with a pass, or be able to satisfy the local authorities that his pursuits are legal; but no one should be bound to account for his proceedings or objects, except to such authority, unless he be taken upon well-founded suspicion of criminality, skulking in secret haunts without apparent means of subsistence, or collecting in gangs, in which cases it would become the duty of every inhabitant to secure such person or persons, immediately delivering them over to the nearest justice of the peace, field-cornet, or constable, and the laws against vagrants would undoubtedly require to be rigorously enforced. As a necessary concomitant of such regulations, the obligation under which the white inhabitants now lie of being registered in some one of the districts, would also rest upon all others, and be insisted on with equal strictness. . . .

3.9b These people have not yet arrived at such a state of self-esteem as to make beneficial use of the wholesome provisions of Ordinance 50.

—Memorial of P. Aucamp and forty-six inhabitants of the field-cornetcy of Rhenosterberg to Sir Lowry Cole, 5 Feb. 1829. (Translated from the original in the Cape Archives, C.O. 2715, no. 38.)

Ordinance 50 provoked widespread opposition from the colonists, who opposed it for a variety of reasons, as the following two documents show. Document 3.9b is a memorial from the north-eastern frontier and attempted to cast its opposition in a diplomatic mould that would be acceptable to the authorities. Document 3.9c was published as an editorial in the Cape Town newspaper De Zuid-Afrikaan *under the heading 'The Hottentot Magna Charta'.*

The memorial of the undersigned inhabitants of the field-cornetcy of Rhenosterberg most respectfully shows:

That the memorialists have long been wholly convinced of the absolute necessity of some provision being made to ameliorate the condition of the Hottentots and other native tribes of the Colony so that they can be brought to that level of civilization where they might become useful members of society.

That the memorialists have also seen with the greatest satisfaction the benevolent views of the Government, as contained in Ordinance 50, by which their earnest wishes have been anticipated.

The memorialists rest assured that the enactments of this Ordinance will have the best effects in improving the state of these unfortunate beings. On their parts they would willingly contribute everything in their power to the welfare of the natives.

But the memorialists have, with regret, learnt from experience that these people have not yet by any means arrived at such a state of self-esteem as to make beneficial use of these wholesome provisions. The memorialists have learnt from experience that some of them, on the sudden change in their condition, have not reformed, but have given themselves up to the most dangerous excesses. As they have given themselves over to licentiousness, frivolity and idleness, they are obliged to support themselves by plunder to the great loss of the memorialists. Soon having consumed what they had earned from the colonists, and being now unwilling to work, they are obliged to steal. Should the herdsmen oppose the theft, their lives are endangered, and herdsmen have already been murdered in this field-cornetcy without the perpetrators being discovered. The memorialists can only conclude that these murders have been committed by the Hottentots who have lately been set free. The memorialists feel assured of this from the general brutality of these people, who have on several occasions been so far guilty of cruelty as to leave alive oxen which they had wounded by cutting pieces of flesh from their legs. Thus the memorialists have judged it necessary to make Your Excellency acquainted with these circumstances not at all with the intention of opposing the provisions of Ordinance 50, to which, on the contrary, as already stated, they attach the greatest value. And they therefore take the liberty of appealing to the testimony of the resident magistrate of Graaff-Reinet and to all the inhabitants of that district in order that Your Excellency may see the injurious influence which the said Ordinance has had upon the Hottentots. It is upon these grounds that the memorialists pray Your Excellency to make such regulations as will at once secure the beneficient intentions of Ordinance 50 and protect their lawful property. The memorialists submit further to Your Excellency's consideration the difficulties under which they labour from the weather and locusts, the high taxes which they are still called upon to pay, and the personal services which they are constantly obliged to render for the maintenance of peace on the frontier, whilst during their absence their families and property are exposed to the ravages of the wandering Hottentots who have scarcely destroyed the stolen cattle before they commit fresh robberies. In this way many of the memorialists have nearly been ruined not only as regards their cattle but also by the breaking open of their houses and stores, as may be seen from the returns of the prison, which is often crowded with offenders of this description.

3.9c We do not envy the Aborigines the freedom which we ourselves possess, but when they with this freedom which they have obtained make use of a greater liberty than all other Colonists, we then believe we are justified in pointing it out.

—Editorial 'The Hottentot Magna Charta' of *De Zuid-Afrikaan* on Ordinance 50, 23 March 1832. (From the translation published in *De Zuid-Afrikaan.*)

Whoever is not a total stranger in our country, and is not unacquainted with our local regulations and institutions, will be obliged to acknowledge that, however much some self-interest seeking persons and enemies to the European Colonists have attempted of late to maintain the contrary by false reports and representations, yet our Government has never lost sight of the real welfare of the Aborigines of our country, and has never failed to take at heart their true interests, and to adopt such measures as, according to circumstances, might be supposed best calculated to promote their real happiness. . . .

Every one must admit that each successive Governor, far from desiring to lower them in the scale of civilization, has had, on the contrary, no other object than to bring them from their wild and savage state to a civilized communion with each other, in order by so doing to afford them an opportunity of becoming capable of social intercourse, and at a *proper time* to become joint Burghers with us of one society, and not only then to fill but also fulfilling the duties of a citizen.

. . . The philanthropists of our times—which we here will more properly designate would-be, or rather, false friends to human nature—who have cried so loudly about the unlawful, inhuman and cruel treatment which they pretended that the Aborigines here are subjected to and harassed with, have, however, in the mean time not scrupled to lay an undeserved and almost indelible blame even on our former lawgivers. . . .

They therefore still dare so shamefully to pride themselves as having been the principal instigators and advisers for the cancelling of all former local laws and institutions relating to and respecting the Hottentots and other free persons of colour, and that Ordinance 50 was created in lieu thereof. It is not our object in this place to investigate and prove whether, or in how far, this Ordinance, which we will readily admit, as all other previous ones, to have been framed with a salutary intention and object, has been beneficial or detrimental in its operation—this we will, perhaps, more fitly treat about on a future occasion. We will only prove in this place that every law, when we take into consideration the circumstances under which it was framed (for instance, the condition of the Aborigines, their natural inclination to rove about and to wander in the deserts, the opportunities which are given them by the thin population and the great distance of the farms of our countrymen from each other, in the neighbourhood of which there are almost everywhere caves, forests, and mountains, in which they may find a hiding-place, to endanger the property and lives of the Colonists), that each law, we say, was framed with a salutary intention and object. . . .

. . . However . . . good and sincere the intentions of all our lawgivers have been towards us, and have wished to secure the prosperity of the Aborigines, as well as all other Colonists, we still from both sides have seen persons appear, among whom certain fortune-hunters, armed and protected by the cloak of religion, as if they were obliged to save a too long oppressed mankind, in a country where peace reigns amongst all classes, who have meditated on all kinds of crafts and snares for the purpose of knocking on the head all old laws founded upon local experience and local necessity, and to raise the Aborigines over and above all other classes. . . .

We, on our part, do not envy the Aborigines the freedom which we ourselves possess, but when they with this freedom which they have obtained make use of a greater liberty than all other Colonists, we then believe we are justified in pointing it out. The Aborigines, for instance, permit themselves not to choose a fixed residence in our country, by whose laws they are protected; they rove about the whole country without accounting for their object in so doing to any one; if any harm is done to them our laws protect them, but if they do anything amiss, and if they escape, then it is to no purpose to look for them in their dwellings, for they have none—they pay no taxes, but when they have furnished themselves with a fixed residence or dwelling; and thus they allow themselves many other liberties which other Colonists would themselves consider irregular and even criminal.

We will in this place not say anything of the prejudicial influence which all this, in the mean time, has upon free labour, which is at present so generally wished for and desired, and the introduction of which, by all possible means, ought to be *encouraged* and made *practicable.* And if the Aborigines cannot perform the usual labor they may be used as herdsmen! For this service thousands of them were hired in former years by the Colonists, whereas at present probably hardly a hundred will be found in the whole Colony who have hired themselves out as such; and even if there be a hundred, yet not fifty will be found who remain six months after another at a stated place, however generously, friendlily, or well they are treated by their masters. The roving and wandering have already again become so natural to them, that they prefer their *natural condition* in the midst of our society above our civilized state and regular intercourse. We will also say nothing about the great influence which all this has on all civil agreements and connexions, into which the other classes of the inhabitants . . . could . . . enter with their fellow-burghers, the Hottentots—for it is difficult to give a proper and speedy effect to a contract when one of the parties has no fixed place of residence.

3.10 Why may we not punish our subordinates when they misbehave?

—Speech by Christoffel Brand at a protest meeting of slaveholders, 17 Sept. 1832. (Translated from the proceedings of the meeting, published as a brochure, Cape Town, 1832.)

In 1831 the Trinidad Ordinance, drawn up for the plantation system of slavery in the West Indies, was imposed on the Cape Colony in its entirety. This ordinance prohibited the flogging of females and stipulated that no slave was to be punished until twenty-four hours after the offence had been committed, and then only in the presence of a free person. It also required that a 'punishment record book' should be kept by every slave proprietor and that it should be submitted twice a year to an official called Protector of the Slaves. This provoked a number of protest meetings in the western Cape. Christoffel Brand (1797–1875) was a young advocate practising in Cape Town and editor of De Zuid-Afrikaan.

. . . When we examine section 14 [of the Slave Ordinance] . . . then we see that nobody may punish his slave for taking ungrounded or false charges to the Protector, except in cases specifically mentioned. These cases are provided for in section 42, and what, my friends, is stipulated there? That no master may punish any slave for making false accusations against his master, unless he has first obtained such a sentence, in the ordinary way, from a competent court, and notified the Protector accordingly. Thus it stands, my friends, that when one wants to punish one's slave for bringing the most groundless and unjust charges against his master, one must first go through the ordinary court procedure before a judge. How many instances do we not encounter every day in this colony of slaves accusing their masters falsely? . . .

. . . Some people accuse us Afrikaners of being vicious oafs. But, my friends, the charge is false. Our children are beaten and punished when they deserve it. Yes, we chastise our own blood, and are the slaves better than that?

. . . Why may we not punish our subordinates when they misbehave? Each one of us, as men and as citizens, must be subordinate to the Governor as our Regent, but is the slave subordinate to nobody? If a child comes back from school, and complains about his teacher, alleging that the teacher has maltreated him, or that he has not been accorded the kind of treatment to which he, in his childish wisdom, would like to lay claim, what do right-minded parents do? Do they then say, 'The teacher has maltreated you, and we shall punish him for that'? No, my friends, they take the child to the teacher and they punish the child for complaining unjustifiably. And then we may not privately punish our slaves, who are our children in our households, when they make false complaints! And when they are punished in terms of section 42, what form does that punishment take? Hard labour? Hard labour, my friends, is a pleasant punishment for a slave, but it is a troubling, grievous punishment for his master. The master loses the service of his slave, and, in return for his false accusations, the slave leads a pleasant life. How many examples do our law courts not produce every day of slaves who deliberately commit offences so as to be placed among the convicts? One sees them along the main road, and in the streets—with irons on their legs, it is true, but one will see one of them standing at his ease smoking a pipe, and two others carrying on a pleasant conversation. This is no deterrent at all, but rather an incentive to be convicted to hard labour. . . . Even the very idea, in a colony in which slaves and free men live, of giving the slaves a Protector or Guardian with such extraordinary powers is itself ridiculous and dangerous, for it creates the idea that one part of society should be protected against the other part; and it provokes the hostility of the one towards the other. We, my friends, we poor free subjects of His Britannic Majesty have no guardian, but we do have an Ordinance which tells us that a Governor can expel any one of us from this country at his own discretion, without any legal procedure or enquiry. Where then is our Guardian? Where is our Protector? The protection which is thus extended to one part of society only is blatantly unjust and most grievous. . . .

3.11a Rational liberty can only exist when impartial justice is done to all, when the interest of the Farmer as well as the Hottentot is consulted.

—Letter from 'An Inhabitant of the Hantam', 29 July 1834. (From the translation published in *De Zuid-Afrikaan*, 15 Aug. 1834.)

Throughout the 1830s many colonists continued to find it difficult to come to terms with the new legal status that had been bestowed on the 'coloured classes' by Ordinance 50. Most of the opposition was centred on the problem of 'vagrancy' (2.11a, b), but as the following two documents show many colonists viewed equal legal rights for the Khoikhoi as an infringement of their own rights and interests. Document 3.11b is of further interest because it suggests a connection between this issue and the origins of the Great Trek.

There is one subject of vast importance to all the frontier inhabitants; I mean the Draft of an Ordinance by His Excellency for the Suppression of Vagrancy. I did indeed conceive this to be a proposition of that self-evident nature, of such manifest utility, that neither the artfulness of sophistry, nor the arguments of malice, could weaken. I conceived that all persons of common sense would unanimously concur in the formation of a law which the experience of ages has proved to be so indispensable to good order in all civilized countries. Much have I been surprised to find oppositionists start up to oppose the measure. After having examined all the rodomontade brought against it, I find it resolves itself into this, that this law would be an infringement of liberty . . . of a liberty to commit murder, robbery, incest and other frightful crimes with impunity. Now liberty can only be esteemed a blessing inasmuch as it promotes the general welfare of mankind; to be this blessing it must be controlled by reason. Now will any man of sane mind maintain that the liberty of idly roaming at large, the unrestricted liberty of committing all sorts of crimes, is to be preferred to that liberty upon which both civil and religious laws impose a salutary discipline? I am indeed a strong advocate for rational liberty, I would risk my life to preserve it; but this liberty can only exist when impartial justice is done to all, when the interest of the Farmer as well as the Hottentot is consulted.

The necessity of a law for the suppression of vagrancy has been long felt in the Interior Districts, and repeatedly expressed; the inhabitants of all colours have felt the injurious effects of letting loose a horde of vagrants upon them, and their flocks and herds have suffered, and still suffer, losses to an almost incredible amount. Let those who oppose this excellent measure leave Cape Town, travel into the Interior, turn aside from the high road into the mountains and ravines, and they will then discover scenes of which they could form no conception—scenes revolting to humanity; creatures bearing a human form congregated in holes and caverns, *totally naked*, almost devoured by vermin, without any visible means of subsistence, or the least knowledge of the Author of their being. Can they be called Philanthropists who are endeavouring to keep these wretched beings in such a state of misery? Or can they be called friends to liberty or the Hottentots who oppose a measure which would deliver them from the most detestable slavery, from the slavery of vice, and sloth, and crime. . . .

. . . It would be cause of deep regret, if His Excellency should be diverted from the measure he has in contemplation by the sophistry of inexperienced theorists—a measure founded on wisdom, justice, and humanity, and which would prove most beneficial to the best interests of the Colony, and produce an amelioration in the state of the most wretched race of beings who are now rapidly advancing to extinction.

3.11b I should wish that the Hottentots be given no rights, because otherwise we shall be obliged to leave. There is no longer any justice for us in this land from our courts.

—Letter from P. J. Swanepoel, Kouka, to Mr Mijntjes, the resident magistrate of Beaufort West, 19 Nov. 1838. (Translated from the original in the Cape Archives.)

I have heard that the case of H. Oosthuijsen and of the impudent Hottentots is to come before Your Excellency. But, Sir, if I were in the place of Your Honour, I should let the case go by. Because if it should happen that Oosthuijsen has to pay a fine or expenses, then we, the inhabitants of Beauford [Beaufort West] will be shown publicly that there is no longer any justice for the burghers, but only for the blacks. I can also tell you the reason why this will be so: the Hottentots called Piet Stuurman, father Piet Stuurman, Kobes Stuurman and Oranje and, even more, *dik* Kobus [fat Kobus] have none of them any right to be on my farm. They have occupied land measured and allotted to me at Whaaikraal. Then I told them before witnesses that they were to leave, but they did not want to, and I then complained to the provisional field-cornet, asking him to remove them, and then Oosthuijsen came to drive them away. But they still did not want to leave, and then I made my bitter complaint to you and made a friendly request for your instructions as to how I should conduct the matter. But then I received no answer from you. Thus we have to note that there is no longer any justice for the burgher, and also that the government do know for what reason the people are leaving as they are. But, Sir, you should reflect that it is due to such cases that we no longer have any rights to our property, that the blacks can do as they please and we must go bowed under this burden as there is no longer any justice for us here. Sir, I should wish that the Hottentots be given no rights, because otherwise we shall be obliged to leave our property and to trek as well. For you do not know how the blacks are dealing with us and how they dominate us. But, Sir, I should not wish Oosthuijsen to be put in the wrong, because many people are waiting to see how the case of H. Oosthuijsen turns out. Sir, the people have hardly settled down again since the Trek, so I should not like to encourage the people to trek any more. For if the case turns out badly, then you can imagine that you will bring the people to trek without end: because then we shall be obliged to let the conditions of the burghers get into the newspaper, [to show] that there is no longer any justice for us in this land from our courts. Sir, I remain, in expectation of good news from you. . . .

3.12a We now have to suffer so that the coloured classes might be richly rewarded.

—Letter from P. Retief to G. Jarvis, 9 June 1836. (Translated from the original in the Cape Archives, MOOB 2/719.)

Piet Retief (1780–1838) was a respected spokesman of the frontier farmers, often arguing their case against the criticisms of missionaries and philanthropists such as Dr John Philip. Retief lost all his possessions during the Sixth Frontier War (1834–5) but did not immediately join the Great Trek then getting under way. Waiting to see whether the government would provide greater security on the frontier, he insisted on strong action against Khoikhoi and Xhosa 'vagrants'. In the following letter to George Jarvis, a personal friend of Retief's, who had been appointed assistant commissioner for the distribution of relief funds following the frontier war, he explains his doubts concerning the value of further petitions or deputations to the imperial government.

. . . We have sent various memorials of the greatest importance to England from this colony. And after all this, we might ask what good this has done us.

We believe that we are viewed so contemptously in England that we now have to suffer so that the coloured classes, after they have deprived us of our belongings and our blood, might be richly rewarded. And we are neither willing nor able to change our colour in contempt of our Creator and for the sake of temporary happiness. And just as little will we resort to the Philippine hypocrisy, as we have been taught that there is no greater crime which we can commit before the Highest Judge than that of an unnatural turning away from God [*onmenslike Godvergetendheijd*] under pretext of spiritual work. And it pains us to have to see that these our co-religionists are not satisfied with our being robbed of belongings and blood, but moreover try, without our giving cause, to destroy our good name altogether.

And what is the most serious, which none of us doubts, is that they will on top of that be considered worthy to be placed over us as masters by the Government in England.

What upright, honest human nature will suffer such treatment in silence? This is our question and we want it answered. If we can be convinced that our feelings have led us astray, we shall be silent. And no matter how completely ruinous our condition now might be, our conviction that we should have a better life will lead us to contribute to the best of our abilities to the Representatives' funds.

Sir, these are the feelings and sentiments of the inhabitants of my division. . . .

3.12b In one word, equal rights to all classes, without distinction.

—Letter from A. Stockenström to P. Retief, 23 Sept. 1836. (From the translation published in J. C. Chase, *The Natal Papers*, Vol. I, pp. 66–67.)

Stockenström was appointed lieutenant-governor of the Eastern Province in February 1836. Even before his arrival a popular campaign of agitation was mounted against him, particularly among the settler community of Grahamstown led by the Grahamstown Journal *and its editor Robert Godlonton, in connection with Stockenström's evidence before the Select Committee on Aborigines in London the previous year. Retief, as spokesman for the Afrikaner community, was apparently more prepared to suspend judgement and allow Stockenström the opportunity to explain his reported criticisms of frontier policy and of the colonists generally. After some delay Retief met Stockenström at the Kat River on September 20, 1836. The meeting, and Stockenström's subsequent letter below, did little to counter Retief's growing disillusionment with the government.*

. . . As I have fully communicated my sentiments to you verbally, you will be easily enabled to make them known to your burghers. They, I believe, all know me. Many years have they been acquainted with my government. From the principles to which I have always clung, I shall not deviate one hair's-breadth; every one, therefore, knows what he has to expect,—my utmost exertions to promote the prosperity, and the protection of the good, peaceable and honest, of whom so many surround us, and the rigid punishment of the laws to those who by deeds of blood and injustice may again place the country in danger. In one word, equal rights to all classes, without distinction. In this I know you and all good men (particularly those who bear the name of 'Christian') will assist me, that we may once more grow and bloom together in peace, and we hope to show that all endeavors to move us from our duty will be fruitless.

With respect to those who intend leaving the colony, I can only say that I cannot prevent them from so doing, and if they could be happier in another country, I would myself advise them to remove; but I place so much interest in the fate of my countrymen, that I consider it my duty at least to advise them fully to weigh what they undertake, and what the consequences may be to them and their posterity, and not to allow themselves to be led away by the cunning and deception of persons who have nothing but their own interest in view. . . .

3.12c It is incomprehensible to us that the Kafirs after they have robbed us of everything can yet have any claim upon us.

—Letter from P. Retief to Captain Armstrong, 16 Oct. 1836. (From the translation published in J. C. Chase, *The Natal Papers*, Vol. I, pp. 66–67.)

On 9 October 1836 Retief had written as frontier commandant to the resident magistrate at Fort Beaufort, Captain Armstrong, that he 'could no longer tolerate that Kafirs, with or without passes, should pass through my ward'. Armstrong replied on October 13, pointing out sympathetically but firmly that Retief remained bound by law: 'I must, in the mean time, beg you will upon no account interrupt Kafirs who have passes.'

SIR, I have to acknowledge your letter of the 13th, by which I learn that I am not to apprehend any Kafirs having passes. Am I then to understand that if I, or my patrols in my ward, find Kafirs with passes for six or eight days, with which they wander about plundering for six months, if we find Kafirs with passes for quite a different ward, and these are occupied in woods and hills in my ward building huts and congregating together, without any other prospect than solely to live by plunder, as I have sent and reported to you, let me then now understand you clearly, am I not to cause such to be apprehended and sent to you? Is this to be the consequence? Then I must tell you plainly that we would do better at once to give up the little we yet have to subsist upon to the robbers spread all over the country, than to trouble ourselves further to remain masters of our property. And then I must ask you, whether we are to lead this barbarous life, or how we are to live? It is quite impossible for us to execute our daily labor, and then to watch against robbers both day and night.

I may also ask, why we are to endure the grief and vexation, that after the Kafirs have despoiled us of kindred and property, they are suffered to come to us, not only to rob us of the little that we yet have to subsist upon, but to taunt us in our impoverished situation; and to pride themselves upon the deeds of murder, fire and plunder committed by them? What father or mother will silently endure this? And what deplorable deeds may not this give rise to? I, therefore, find myself under the necessity to state, that as long as I am to serve as a preserver of the peace and happiness of this ward, I must set myself against this influx; and if I am to suffer it, I shall be compelled to resign, not to burden my conscience with such weighty responsibility to the Almighty.

The indifference is to me incomprehensible, that by giving such passes *our* peace and happiness are not once thought of! It is also incomprehensible to us that there exists such weakness as to believe that the Kafirs, after they have robbed us of every thing, can yet have any claim upon us, and to grant them passes accordingly. From fear that *we* may injure the Kafirs, we are prohibited from personally going to them, to demand the restitution of our plundered property; but there appears to be no fear lest *we* should be injured by the influx of Kafirs into the colony. . . .

I will console myself, and those connected with me, yet for a short period in our dejected situation, in expectation that our Lieutenant-Governor will soon let us see in deeds that which I have understood from His Honour both verbally and in writing; but if it be that we may not experience our long-expected wish of a better life, then I believe that with the greatest regret the abandonment of the colony will be the consequence. . . .

3.13a We call upon your Honour to devise such measures as shall protect us in the legal possession of our Rights as Burghers.

—Memorial of the Inhabitants of Colesberg to Lieutenant-Governor A. Stockenström, June 1837. (From the Cape Archives, G.H. 8/4 No. 297, Enclosure no. 1.)

Relatively few of the stockfarmers on the north-eastern frontier joined the Great Trek. Many trekboers from this region did indeed move across the Orange River, but unlike the Trekkers they tended to remain loyalist in their orientation towards the colonial authorities, though they shared many of the same grievances. In 1837 Gideon Joubert, one of the signatories of the following letter, was entrusted with the mission by the colonial government of investigating whether the Trekkers had taken any freed slaves along against their wishes. The letter was drawn up by Thomas Reid, the Scottish minister of the Dutch Reformed Church at Colesberg, but clearly reflects the views of his parishioners rather than his own.

. . . We approach your Honour with a statement of grievances under which we groan, and which, if not speedily removed, must induce us to seek relief in a foreign land.

Convinced that if the present system of licentiousness and insubordination among the black population is not speedily checked and abolished, it must lead to the commission of those crimes which have already stained the land with blood, and darkened the page of history, we humbly, but firmly, call upon your Honour to devise such measures as shall protect us in the legal and peaceable possession of our Rights as Burghers.

We deem it incompatible with our Rights as British subjects to be prevented from following the depredators of our property beyond the Orange River, when often, by following them to the opposite bank, we could recover our property at no expense or detriment to the execution of the Laws within the Colony.

We have further to assure your Honour that, while we have hitherto hazarded our lives and sacrificed our property at the command of the Government, in the hope that by our loyal and dutiful obedience our interests should be regarded and our grievances redressed, we are now incapable of defending ourselves and families from wanton outrage, far less of yielding the Government the least assistance, should it be required of us.

From the infidelity and insubordination of our servants we are rendered incapable of using the means of grace undisturbed in our families or in the church, and must thereby not only suffer in our temporal but also in our eternal interests.

Being apprehensive that those fearful crimes of former days shall again be committed by those fierce and insolent fellows who infest the country, who will neither work nor want, we earnestly solicit your Honour to appoint such a Law, for all classes of the community, as to prevent the same, and to subject all who wander about without the means of a lawful subsistence to merited punishment.

. . . We deplore that the same causes which have led us to seek redress from your

Honour have already induced so many of our brothers, friends and countrymen to leave their country in quest of a secure and peaceful home in a foreign land, and are assured that effectual measures may yet be devised to prevent thousands from following their unfortunate example, and to cause our land, with the undeserved blessing of the Lord, to prosper. With this hope do we look and rely upon your Honour as earthly Governor, as the Defender of our Rights, and the protector of our Laws, and trust that our hopes and expectations shall not be in vain or disappointed.

Thomas Reid	P. Aucamp, Veldkornet
G. D. Joubert	N. T. van der Walt and others

3.13b As your object is that of equal laws and equal justice for all classes of the community, a fair and impartial administration appears to me all that is requisite to meet your case.

—Reply of Lieutenant-Governor A. Strockenström to the memorialists of Colesberg, 28 June 1837. (From the Cape Archives, G.H. 8/4 No. 297, Enclosure no. 2.)

Stockenström sent the following letter as the official reply to the memorialists of Colesberg. At the same time he wrote to F. Rawstorne, the recently appointed Civil Commissioner of the district, to make enquiries about the actual number of cases of theft or insubordination that had been brought before the court.

. . . It is to me a source of satisfaction that the Memorialists feel themselves convinced of my deep and unalterable interest in their welfare, and I can only assure them that, as they have for a length of years seen that interest exhibited in the extension of equal protection to all classes of His Majesty's subjects and the due enforcement of the laws, they will never justly have reason to complain of any change or diminution of zeal on my part. . . .

. . . You complain of 'the present system of licentiousness and insubordination of the black population', and I must request of you to state wherein that present system exists, by what means it is proposed to remedy the same, whether the laws for the protection of your rights as Burghers are not duly enforced, in what respect they are deficient, whether the establishment of a magistracy in your parish has tended to increase or diminish the licentiousness and insubordination complained of, and in which case any misconduct duly prosecuted and proved has gone unpunished.

. . . Nothing can be more true than that the inhabitants of this Colony have been most prompt and zealous when called upon to defend their lives and property and those of their fellow colonists, nor can anyone be more competent to bear testimony to their loyal and dutiful obedience than an individual who has so amply partaken of their services as myself, and they may rest assured that they will never be called upon to yield the Government any assistance except in their own behalf.

With reference to the infidelity and insubordination of your servants and the fearful crimes which you predict, . . . I was under the impression that when the execution of these laws was facilitated by the residence of a special Justice in your parish, the most important obstacle to good order was removed. At least you are aware that it was beyond my power to do more. You will I trust upon inquiry find that none of the Coloured classes is authorized to do anything which the law does not permit any of the memorialists to do, and that as your object is, as you state it, and as I believe it to be, equal laws and equal justice for all classes of the community, a fair and impartial administration appears to me all that is requisite to meet your case.

I have reserved for the conclusion of this reply to notice that part of your Memorial which states that the non-removal of the grievances under which you believe yourselves to groan must induce you to seek relief in a foreign land. . . . Whilst I can give you the most solemn assurance of the paternal views of His Majesty's Government with reference to yourselves and the Colony in general, and whilst I entertain the most sanguine hopes that under the blessing of divine providence this country will flourish and be happy under the realization of those views, I am equally certain that not a single principle of just and liberal Government will be sacrificed in order to reconcile anyone to a continued sojourn under British jurisdiction, and that no steps have been taken to prevent emigration, except by the exposure of its dangers. I think it but proper to warn those who may take that step that they are not to expect that the British Government will ever acknowledge their right to any land beyond the frontier, or acknowledge any bargain of any sort for such land entered into by any Emigrant British subject without its consent.

Trusting therefore that you will consider and reconsider your measures, and take the advice of one who never flattered the prejudices of his countrymen, but made the promotion of their welfare his most anxious study and fondest boast. . . .

3.13c Not only our servants but the black population in general have a contempt for all just restraint, are not subject to their superiors, not satisfied with equality, but thirst for unlawful authority.

—Reply of the Colesberg memorialists to Lieutenant-Governor Stockenström, July 1837. (From the Cape Archives, G. H. 8/4, No. 297, Enclosure no. 4.)

In his reply Stockenström had intimated that he did not consider it altogether proper for the minister, Reid, to concern himself with matters of this kind. The somewhat sarcastic tone of the following letter may be due to this personal aspect, as well as to the fact that by this time Stockenström's political position had become very controversial indeed, owing to the virulent criticism of his frontier policy and his involvement in a sensational libel case. The substance of the letter, however, again primarily reflects the views of these frontier colonists themselves.

. . . Your memorialists have well considered their 'measures', that is their memorial, and can assure your Honour that their grievances were not diminished nor their fear of approaching danger lessened by your Honour's attempts on this occasion to promote their welfare. They grieve to be compelled to say that you either have not or will not comprehend their requests and that you have so framed your answer as to overlook the burden of their memorial. . . .The explanation which your memorialists have to give you of the system of licentiousness and insubordination complained of, is that not only their servants but the black population in general have a contempt for all just restraint, are not subject to their superiors, not satisfied with an equality, [but] thirst for and in various instances have exercised unlawful authority. Their conduct may therefore justly [be] styled a system of licentiousness and insubordination.

Your memorialists could adduce innumerable proofs to elucidate their explanation, were they not confident that it is unnecessary for one who has had so much intercourse with the black population and is so well acquainted with their characters as yourself. It is well known over the whole colony that the Hottentots go from place to place just as they please; [that they] take up their residence on particular spots of our fields which we had reserved for our oxen or horses; that it is not without difficulty and considerable loss that we can displace them; that our servants, regardless of their agreements with us, leave us without reason or warning whenever they think fit; that the coloured tribes, who have been in our service for months and years, take a malicious pleasure in disturbing us in attempting religious duties in our families; that it is impossible for us to expose our children to imminent danger by sending them after our cattle; that it is also dangerous for ourselves to leave our unprotected families and properties to attend the public ordinances of religion.

You also demand by what means it is proposed to remedy the said grievances. Your memorialists will not hazard an opinion regarding the measures which may be employed by those in power to remedy the said grievances, but they unite in testifying that formerly your Honour was one of the most zealous agents in bringing the coloured tribes from their dens and caves, and in placing them within the means of civilization where till of late they remained in subordination and peace.

In answer to another of your questions, your memorialists have to assure you that since the establishment of a Magistrate in this parish crime has been on the increase. Should you question this statement we are convinced that a reference to the quarterly expenses of this district will place the matter beyond a doubt. You will not however suppose that we attribute this increase of crime to any dereliction of duty on the part of your respected Magistrate. On the contrary, we attribute it entirely to a multiplicity of contradictory and ineffective laws, which like an old book ought to be revised, corrected and amended. . . .

. . . Nothing can be more true than that you are qualified to judge of the services rendered by the colonists in defence of their lives and property, and also of the zeal and dutiful obedience to the call of Government in performing the same. Your memorialists however have already assured you that they are no longer able to show their zeal and obedience to the call of Government or to come to the assistance of their fellow colonists should it be required of them.

. . . Your memorialists have to acquaint you that circumstances have occurred since the date of their memorial, which have deepened their conviction and increased their fears and which render it impossible for them longer to protect their cattle or property without armed force. Not to trouble you too much, your memorialists shall adduce but two out of many examples. . . . Reports of theft and housebreaking reach us almost daily and excite but little wonder, knowing as we do that there are swarms around us who have no means of subsistence—and although they steal from and live on us, while we cannot clearly prove them thieves we must patiently bear our losses. . . .

3.13d Liberty without subordination produces insecurity, but liberty with submission and due respect is necessary to our existence.

—Letter from N. T. van der Walt to Lieutenant-Governor Stockenström, 31 Aug. 1837. (From the translation in the Cape Archives, G.H. 8/4, No. 297, Enclosure 5.)

Some of the signatories of the Colesberg memorial, like Gideon Joubert, knew Stockenström well from his years as landdrost of Graaff-Reinet. Many still held him in high esteem, and Stockenström also attached considerable significance to these long-standing personal relationships with his fellow Afrikaners. The following personal exchange with N. T. van der Walt, another old friend and signatory of the memorial, took place soon after the official reply to the memorial.

I humbly submit to Your Honour a respectful request for your paternal support. Liberty without subordination produces insecurity, but liberty with submission and due respect is necessary to our existence. It is not our intention to subject the Bushman people to slavish bondage, but [rather] not to allow them to remove themselves from society. . . . For many years, at our own expenses, efforts have been made to civilize this people as they now are. . . . I dread conspiracies, and [fear] that they will congregate to commit mischief as in former times. . . . The country is in such a state of excitement as I cannot describe with the pen. We allow that they shall never be bound to serve anyone against their will, but shall always be at liberty to remove with their property from one person to another. Your Honour knows all my manner of life[:] that I never sought to injure anyone, but always [to serve] the best interests of every creature. It is still so. I cannot think or say otherwise but that we have been educated in one house; nothing would hurt me so much as to see that peace destroyed, to establish which I have done so much. . . . I continue daily to provide the living with cattle and provisions. I therefore hope in no other but in Your Honour for some change. The emigration to foreign countries is to me as a dark valley. . . .

3.13e We will never again see the day when different degrees of rights and privileges will exist for different classes of subjects.

—Extracts from the reply of Lieutenant-Governor Stockenström to N. T. van der Walt, 20 Sept. 1837. (From the translation in the Cape Archives, G.H. 8/4, No. 297, Enclosure 6.)

. . . You may rest assured that if all act as you and many others have done and allow to the Bushmen remunerating wages for their services, not according to the will of the master but according to the demand of the servant, as is the case in respect of free labourers throughout the world, there would be no occasion to compel these unfortunate people to remain within the boundary and under the protection of the laws rather than to expose themselves to the oppression of those who acknowledge no rule but their own will.

Let me tell you this—and you may rely upon it, my dear friend. We will never again see the day when under British rule different degrees of rights and privileges will exist for different classes of His Majesty's subjects—and time will show that such an oppressive partiality is not necessary for our safety: on the contrary, we should thereby entail upon us the hatred of the blacks, and be in danger every moment that they would avail themselves of the first opportunity to break their bonds and be revenged upon us. . . .

3.13f I have always maintained that something ought to be done to put an end to vagrancy in the Colony, but what sort of vagrant law is it that all this clamour is about?

—Report by Lieutenant-Governor Stockenström to Governor D'Urban, 27 Sept. 1837. (From the Cape Archives, G.H. 8/4, No. 297.)

Stockenström forwarded copies of the three communications from Colesberg, together with the reply from Civil Commissioner Rawstorne, to the Governor. Stockenström found it politic to suggest, and may have sincerely believed, that the memorial was primarily the doing of Reid, and that the other signatories were ignorant of its contents. On this point, however, he was almost certainly wrong.

As the supreme Government can only judge of the best mode of regulating the affairs of this Country by becoming acquainted with its real conditions and the causes thereof, I never fail to transmit copies of such documents as appear to me to throw light on the subject, and have the honour therefore to enclose a copy of a memorial . . . from the Minister and the inhabitants of the parish of Colesberg, representing several of the most serious grievances under which they consider themselves to 'groan', and stating the alternative to which they would be compelled to resort if the said grievances were not speedily removed.

I am in justice bound to say that . . . the memorialists have been known to mè for a number of years, and taking them in the aggregate I don't believe that there is a more loyal, peaceable and responsible set of men in His Majesty's dominions. From many of them I have for a length of years as their magistrate received the most cordial co-operation in my humble efforts to improve the condition of the aboriginal tribes, and I have known them to make the most considerable sacrifices towards that and many other objects of the Government with the utmost cheerfulness and patience, often under very great privations, and as I had so lately had the strongest proofs of the continuation of those sentiments and had reason to believe that the establishment of a seat of magistracy in the midst of them, immediately after my assumption of this Government, had convinced them that no means would be neglected to promote their interests, I was the more surprised to find their condition depicted in such distressing terms, and that matters should so suddenly have come to such an awful crisis. . . .

That the memorialists understood what they had subscribed I could not for a moment doubt, . . . and as the Civil Commissioner, resident in the midst of the parish, had given me no reason to believe the state of affairs as bad as the memorial represented it, I called for this officer's report, tendering at the same time a reply . . . expressive of my sentiments and strongly pointing out the danger of an emigration which has become an unfailing threat accompanying almost every complaint.

The Civil Commissioner's report is enclosed. . . . It will be seen that since his arrival at Colesberg which was in January last only three instances of people charged of idleness, disobedience or insubordination on the part of Hottentots had come before him, and he is decidedly of the opinion that that class are not generally or flagrantly disobedient or insubordinate.

He also states that throughout the whole of the said period not a single case had been reported to him of cattle having been driven across the Orange River except by their rightful owners. On the eastern borders of his district only twice had cattle been carried off, and of those two cases one remained yet to be redressed, so that as the Civil Commissioner very justly observed the real and only ground of grievance is the idleness and insubordination of the Hottentots and Bastards which are in service, and the wandering and petty depredating habits of those who are not. As a remedy for this the object desired is, of course, tho' not stated, a Vagrant Law, but the Civil Commissioner gives us a clue to solve the question more rationally when he feels himself 'bound to admit that the wages which have been usually granted to Hottentots and Bushmen are greatly too low to operate as a stimulus to industry, or induce them to enter into service with the farmers, varying from three goats to twelve, four shillings and sixpence to eighteen shillings, annually'.

Now, let the Secretary of State compare this report with the memorial. . . . I was in hopes that my reply and warning . . . would have caused a more dispassionate consideration of the subject, until the last post brought me a [second] memorial . . . to which it is almost superfluous to say I have returned no answers, and which would only excite compassion but for the fact that, as I have said before, it is subscribed by some, tho' very few, of the best-disposed men in Her Majesty's dominions. That all did not, if any did, understand what it was that they were induced to put their names to, is evident from . . . a letter from one of the most worthy and respectable of said subscribers [i.e. Van der Walt], which reached me almost together with said [second] memorial.

It was only from this honest farmer's affectionate, tho' simple, letter that I made out . . . that, as the Civil Commissioner also guessed, the real thing wanted was a Vagrant Law.

Here I must observe that I am not one of those who are seized with a chill of horror at the name 'Vagrant Law'. I have always maintained that something ought to be done to put an end to vagrancy in the Colony; but what sort of Vagrant Law is it that all this clamour is about? My unsophisticated friend Van der Walt shows the cloven foot, meaning well all the while. . . . He says, 'The Bushmen are not to be subjected to a slavish bondage, but they are not to remove themselves from society. They shall not be made to leave anyone against their will, but they shall serve some one of us.' The plain English of all this is, the Bushmen shall not be registered and saleable as slaves, but they shall stay in the midst of us, and—as we possess all their land in the Colony, so that they can have no residence of their own—they must be in bondage with someone or other who will treat them worse than ever slaves were treated. In other words they are to have the freedom of being whomsoever's slaves they please, and as the Civil Commissioner has shown that now, whilst liberty is so unbounded, and servants so scarce, a Bushman or Hottentot year's wages amounts to four shillings and sixpence to eighteen shillings, we may calculate what it would come to when the desired Vagrant Laws shall be enacted and shall have glutted the labour market.

[The memorial] is possibly correct in stating that I have been 'one of the most zealous agents in bringing the Coloured tribes from their dens and caves and placing them within the means of civilization', but . . . I never believed Civilization to consist in one man being forced to serve another who had deprived him of his country, his game, his all, under a severe lash for four shillings and sixpence per annum. I know what my countrymen suffer, . . . and I shall to relieve them be ready to make any sacrifice short of that of common justice. . . . Now to compel the unhappy remnants of that race into compulsory unpaid servitude, upon what was once their own land, or to deprive them of the alternative of flying from the scenes which can only remind them of better days and retiring to some yet unusurped part of their country, or to some part which they believe, erroneously or not, in the hands of kinder masters, would not only be the essence of cruelty and oppression but would soon woefully react upon us, through the despair and revenge of the oppressed, and thus renew those very crimes 'which have already stained the land with blood'—and are here expected to spring from liberty. . . .

3.14 In the colony they have no control over their servants, no authority whatever to make them attend to their work.

—Letter from J. N. Boshoff, dated 17 Feb. 1839. (From the translation published in *The Grahamstown Journal* as reprinted in J. C. Chase, *Annals of Natal*, Vol. 1, pp. 511–512.)

J. N. Boshoff (1808–1881) had served as clerk at Graaff-Reinet under Landdrost Stockenström and Civil Commissioner Van Ryneveld from 1824 to 1838. With Gideon Joubert he visited the Natal Voortrekkers in 1838. Dismissed by Stockenström because he had exceeded his leave, he joined them again in 1839. Just before his departure he published this analysis of the causes of the Trek in the Grahamstown Journal. *Further extracts from this important article are included in Chapter Six, Document 6.10a.*

. . . Another reason assigned by the emigrants is that in the colony they have no control over their servants, that is, no authority whatever to make them attend to their work. To turn them away would often be depriving themselves of the only herdsmen on the farm, while they cannot themselves herd the flocks without neglecting their other farming pursuits. Besides, those who may be obtained in their stead are sometimes worse than those discharged. To complain to a fieldcornet is useless: he cannot interfere or exercise any authority in such matters. To complain to a magistrate is such a vexatious proceeding that the farmer finds it more profitable to rest satisfied with the loss of ten, twelve, or twenty sheep, though he should moreover be abused by the herdsman upon [the herdsman's] being upbraided for his negligence, than to take him before a magistrate, at a distance of from twenty to eighty miles, attended by witnesses, and after all have to employ an attorney or agent to conduct his case, he not being himself acquainted with the rules of court, or capable of examining his witnesses according to legal practice, and perhaps have to provide himself with an interpreter, the courts being English, and not bound to understand him. And [he] having complied with all these rules, what is the punishment of his servant? Two or three days' confinement in the gaol, perhaps on spare diet; or otherwise a lecture from the magistrate to behave better in the future.

Now, what is the natural result? The farmer the next time takes the law into his own hands, gives his servant a blow in the face, or perhaps a few lashes with the sjambok: a complaint is lodged against him: and now look at the difference of the legal proceedings. . . .

Her Majesty's prosecutor interferes; the defendant and witnesses, perhaps all the people from the place, are summoned at the public expense; the assault is proved, and, whatever the provocation may have been, the law has been transgressed, and the offender is fined and imprisoned. He returns home, finds himself minus a considerable number of sheep or cattle lost in his absence, and his servants sulkier than before. He either gives up farming or quits the colony.

There are a few other reasons of minor importance sometimes given, but I have upon inquiry invariably found that they have not alone sufficiently influenced to quit. As for instance:

1. An idea that it is the object of the Government to encourage the intermarriage of whites and blacks.

2. That the blacks are encouraged to consider themselves upon an equal footing with the whites in their religious exercises in church, though the former are heathens and no members of such church or community, because they have already been married by the ministers of the reformed congregation, and by the same forms, thereby showing a disrespect for the religious institutions of the people.

3.15 Do you think that it could be possible for me to have my subordinate creatures innocently punished and chastised without the least semblance of a trial, and not to defend their rights? No.

—Letter from P. H. Zietsman to A. W. J. Pretorius, Pietermaritzburg, 23 Aug. 1841. (Translated from the text in H. S. Pretorius *et al.*, *Voortrekker-Argiefstukke*, pp. 134–6.)

3.15 *P. H. Zietsman on the punishment of his black servants 1841*

In 1841 A. W. J. Pretorius (1798–1853) was acting commandant-general of the Voortrekker republic in Natal, a position which entailed special responsibility for enforcing Trekker policy concerning the indigenous peoples in the area. He was also a substantial farmer in his own right. On both counts he was inclined to take a stronger line with regard to the inequality before the law of blacks than did some of his fellow Trekkers, as appears from the following dispute with his neighbour, P. H. Zietsman.

Honourable Sir, However disinclined I might be to involve myself deliberately in such disputes, I am however obliged to do so in this case if I am to act according to my conscience.

It must still be fresh in your memory that on the 12th of this month you [threatened to] capture my kaffirs with a patrol on my farm. You accused them of having unlawfully set fire to the veld, which caused you to suffer much damage. You said to me that you were determined to punish such unlawful action to the utmost, that you would detain them for a while and that I could then take five families for myself, while you would allocate the remaining families to others. To this, of course, I could not offer any reply. I saddled my horse and rode to Umlaas on private business. There I made enquiries about the origin of this fire, . . . but what did I find, to my intense displeasure, on my return here? That when I had hardly been away for half an hour, you tied five of my kaffirs—however innocent—to a wagon, without giving them any trial, without informing yourself properly of the matter, and even without giving them the opportunity to prove their innocence, and gave each of them 25 lashes on their bare bodies, and also made them work here for 10 days.

You yourself must concede to me that these uncivilized creatures were quite simply made to suffer innocently. How is it possible that nine kaffirs could together take one burning brand and set the veld on fire with it? Only one could have been the guilty party, and it was your duty to find out who that was and to punish him alone if the offence was culpable. But put all that aside and suppose that they did actually set the veld alight. Even then they could not have transgressed any law, for you yourself helped to pass a law permitting anyone to burn the veld during the month of August and this fire, according to your words, was supposed to have started on my farm. And do you think, Sir, that it could be possible for me, who professes the Christian belief, to have my subordinate creatures innocently punished and chastised without the least semblance of a trial, and not to defend their rights? No.

Suppose now that some or other person, who abhors your illegal conduct regarding my kaffirs, should make an exact account of the matter and send it to the editor of the *South African Commercial Advertiser*. How would our Afrikaans character not be stigmatized anew as that of barbarous tyrants? And who would be the cause of this? I have heard many people speak emphatically of your illegal conduct. . . . If you consider this matter in retrospect, you will have to admit yourself that my kaffirs should have been tried before the landdrost and heemraden, so that they, like other subjects, could have had the opportunity of proving their innocence. And to prevent this case from becoming more widely known, I want to suggest quite simply that you pay my five kaffirs one cow each, which can more or less compensate them for the pain and suffering they have endured. And if you should refuse to comply with my suggestion, then, for the time being, I must tell you that you will have to bear the detrimental consequences, which you will certainly later come to regret. This is a private letter to you, so that this reprehensible case might be settled amicably. On this then I shall conclude and expect your reply without delay.

3.16 As soon as might takes the place of right, all sympathy between masters and servants will vanish.

—Evidence of the Rev. N. S. Smit of Grahamstown to the Cape Masters and Servants Committee, 21 Nov. 1848. (From *Masters and Servants Blue Book*, Cape (1849), pp. 178–180.)

The Masters and Servants Ordinance of 1841 had consolidated the equality before the law granted to the coloured classes by Ordinance 50, and contained no special racial differentiation of parties to labour contracts. Throughout the 1840s the colonists continued to feel strongly about 'vagrancy', and complaints about the labour shortage increased. In September 1848 a committee of the Legislative Council addressed a questionnaire on the working of the Masters and Servants Ordinance to magistrates, clergymen, justices of the peace, field-cornets and other prominent residents. Their replies were published in a Masters and Servants Blue Book (1849), from which the following evidence of the Rev. N. S. Smit is taken.

. . . In regard to the enactment of a vagrant law, I beg to state that I am decidedly unfavourable, and for the following simple reasons:

The enactment of such a law at this moment I consider unnecessary, for reasons hereunder set forth:

First. No such law is, in my opinion, necessary to secure good servants to all just persons, who are willing to pay liberal wages. The difficulty to obtain good servants is, I have reason to think, in most cases, not greater than it is to obtain good masters. That difficulty (if it exists) no vagrant law, I think, will diminish, but rather increase.

Secondly. No individual acts of theft, which might be committed by a few roaming persons, can, in my humble opinion, justify the enactment of a law which would affect a whole community of honest and industrious persons.

Thirdly. No vagrant law will, in my opinion, prevent, but rather it will induce crime. The enactment of such a law would, I have no doubt, drive all real idlers to the bush, from whence they would be able, I think, to carry on robberies against farmers and others, far more successfully than by an occasional visit from one place to another. Whilst, on the other hand, I think it will be plainly seen, on investigation, that crime in the colony, since the promulgation of the 50th Ordinance, has been rather on the decrease than otherwise.

I beg further to state that I cannot but regard the enactment of a vagrant law as calculated to introduce the same system of oppression against the natives which obtained in the colony before the promulgation of the 50th ordinance.

It might be said that such a law would not be intended for any particular class of persons, but to prevent vagrancy. Yet I cannot but view it as a law which would bear more particularly on the natives.

First. I cannot but regard it as one of the most difficult things so to define vagrancy as to secure individuals against injustice.

Secondly. I have no doubt that among the many who would take every advantage against the natives under the pretext of preventing vagrancy, but few, if any, would be disposed to interfere with a white person, should he even not possess the means of an honest livelihood.

Thirdly. I have reason to believe that, at least in many cases, what would be viewed in a white person as mere travelling, would be considered vagrancy in a native; and thus, that which would often be considered necessary with a white man, would be punished in a native.

Fourthly. A native, far from home, apprehended on a charge of vagrancy, might, I think, also be exposed to not a little unnecessary inconvenience, and have unjustly to suffer imprisonment for a crime of which he is really not guilty. His very distance from home might put it out of his power to rebut the charge; whilst seldom, if ever, would a friend be found to assist him out of his painful dilemma. And should his innocence in every case be even proved at last, his commitment before trial, however short, cannot but be regarded as extremely hard; whilst the degradation of imprisonment, so far from exciting in his mind any real reverence for the law, would in my opinion, only fill his mind with disgust against a Government that could lend itself either to frame or sanction laws which will admit of such cruel treatment.

It might be said that passports would prevent all such inconvenience and suffering. They proved, however, no such preventative in bygone years. How easily, for instance, might a man forget his passport at home, or lose it on the road! Whilst it sometimes happened, before the enactment of the 50th Ordinance, or the system of passports was done away, that passports, after being demanded and produced, were torn to a thousand pieces, and committed to the mercy of the winds, and the poor native, after being thus deprived of his only safeguard, was thrown into prison as a vagrant.

Fifthly. I should conceive that the enactment of a vagrant law would not only affect the native population, but also inflict an injury on the colony at large. For a season, our prisons would, no doubt, be filled, and masters enabled to obtain (as in former years) from the local authorities servants to work for them for a mere trifle; and that that may be the case is, no doubt, the sincere wish of many of those who have petitioned for such a law. But of this I feel persuaded, that as soon as might takes the place of right, and a compulsory system is introduced, all sympathy between masters and servants (a thing so necessary to their mutual comfort) will vanish, old prejudices be awakened in the minds of the natives against the whites, and, as a consequence, the harshest treatment exercised towards many who might have the misfortune to be in service. Many of the natives, too, would fly for safety to the institutions, and should they find no safety there, for ever abandon in disgust the land of their fathers, in quest of a better country; and thus would the colony, in a short time, be stripped of an immense quantity of available labor. . . .

3.17a Fearing that the Kaffir would get away, he shot him. This has been the law of the frontier since time immemorial.

—Letter from J. S. van den Berg to the president of the Orange Free State, M. W. Pretorius, 17 Feb. 1863. (Translated from the original in the State Archives, Bloemfontein, G.S. 292, pp. 16–18.)

The new republics recognized by the Sand River and Bloemfontein Conventions of 1852 and 1854 had little administrative expertise or powers to enforce any centralized control. For a considerable time the discretionary powers of the local field-cornets were the only means of ensuring any kind of law and order. Gradually the executive officers of the new states began to make more serious efforts towards government by law, though this did not always coincide with the views of all its burghers, particularly in frontier zones such as on the Basotho border, as the following two documents make clear.

I, the undersigned, your humble memorialist, an old resident of the frontier, respectfully request Your Honour, if it is possible, to investigate personally the condition of this frontier and the following complaint. My nephew, Christian van den Berg, and I are awaiting trial in the High Court of this state, where we are to face a charge of *murder*. The charge has been brought against us by the public prosecutor, almost certainly acting on the report or statement of the frontier field-cornet. The following is what happened. On these grounds these improper steps are being taken against us. On the fourth of November last year, during the night, the kaffirs stole thirty head of cattle from this farm. The next day Christian van den Berg came suddenly upon a kaffir in the veld, who jumped out in front of him from a bush, and took to his heels. Christian van den Berg called to him several times to stop, but in vain, and fearing that he would get away, as the kaffir was near the stream, he shot and wounded him high up in the thighs. On hearing the shot, I went up to Christian van den Berg, and after I had enquired what he had fired at, I went up to the kaffir and found him lying on the bank of the stream, to all appearances dead. I shot him once more and went back. I have a letter from my field-cornet, the complainant, in which he instructed us to 'put out of the way' any such creatures who do not want to surrender themselves. From our worthy commandant we have the same order, also in writing. Indeed, this has been the law of the frontier since time immemorial. And now, for obeying the law and doing as has been done many times to my knowledge and as every frontier resident does in such cases, we face the accusation of murder. That is intolerable.

Your Honour, this is the first time to my knowledge that I have complained, although I have previously been ruined by the kaffirs. . . . I would not have spoken of the damage I suffered, but it is grievous to me who has worked for the country with sacrifices of blood and belongings then to be prosecuted for it. If this unjust case should ever be heard in court, I feel sure that no conviction could ever be made, but I should still have to pay the expenses. . . .

Your Honour, I know that you have never been able to tolerate persecutions, nor want to allow them, and therefore I solemnly and humbly beg you to visit our frontier on your travels and investigate how, when a thief is shot dead, a frontier field-cornet can complain of this deed to the landdrost in such a way that a charge of murder follows. . . . Our worthy commandant and other of the officers of the militia are of the opinion that I have not in any way acted unlawfully. Why then should so much damage and disgrace be inflicted on me? . . .

3.17b Nobody may take the law into his own hands, as the greatest evil arises from this.

—Letter from the government secretary of the Orange Free State, J. Nielen Marais, to J. P. Botha, 22 March 1864. (Translated from the original in the State Archives, Bloemfontein, G.S. 1527, pp. 160–162.)

It appears from the statement you made on the 26th of August that you took 62 head of cattle and 8 horses from Chief Manchenga as compensation [for the cattle and horses stolen from you and others]. . . . It is of the greatest importance, in all our dealings with the natives, that we avoid and carefully refrain from all actions which bear even a semblance of injustice. For if we do not demonstrate that justice and fairness are the mainsprings of our actions, how can we then expect these people to do what is right?

It has not yet been sufficiently proved that the aforementioned horses and cattle were stolen by Manchenga, and if there are grounds for suspecting him, then one must prosecute the thief in an agreed manner in the properly constituted courts. Our records show that Manchenga lives in this state, and can therefore easily be brought before a competent court if you think that you have grounds for complaint against him. Nobody may take the law into his own hands, as the greatest evil arises from this. Your conduct in this matter, and your capturing of Manchenga's cattle and horses, cannot but have a most detrimental influence not only on Manchenga himself, but must also instil all the surrounding natives and their chiefs with the feeling that an injustice has been done to him. Thus he can be brought to take the cattle of others, so as to recoup his loss, and others might do likewise. For these reasons I wish urgently and seriously to request of you to return as speedily as possible to Manchenga the cattle and horses which you took from him. If you have grounds for complaint, you are to take these in the proper manner to a competent court, and there is no doubt that you will receive satisfaction. . . .

4 *The politics and morality of frontier conflict 1780–1870*

The frontier was not, of course, the scene only of conflict. As has been pointed out by De Kiewiet, 'these men of opposite race were doing more than quarreling with each other'.[1] Recent historians have emphasized the importance in frontier history of interaction through trade and barter, of co-operation in various shifting alliances, and of partial incorporation through labour and tribute.[2] However, the non-conflictual aspects of frontier life did not receive much public attention at the time, or if they did, then it was as part of the more general problems of colonial society, such as the issues arising from labour coercion (see Chapter 2) or the establishment of law and order (see Chapter 3). Though the theme of frontier conflict did not by any means constitute the whole story of the frontier, such conflicts were frequent and disruptive enough to be a central concern of frontier politics. The periodic outbreaks of open hostilities were dramatic focuses of public attention. Each new frontier war would be preceded by an outpouring of memorials appealing for help from the government, and followed by reports providing justification and legitimation for deeds of violence and aggression. Often there would be recriminations for failures of policy or strategy, and sometimes even some attempts to determine the underlying causes and to propose solutions for the endemic conflict. The political ideas and moral arguments put forward by Afrikaners in this connection remain highly relevant to the enduring problems of South Africa's racial politics today.

In analyzing and interpreting these documents it would serve little purpose to become embroiled once again in the rights and wrongs of the many historical disputes to which they relate. In any case these documents themselves hardly provide sufficient evidence concerning the substantive issues which were at stake in the many claims and counterclaims put forward. From the nature of the case these are partisan views of the historical events, and must be treated as such. They do provide us, however, with material for reconstructing the thinking of frontier Afrikaners on the crucial moral and political problems posed by frontier conflict. In doing that, the following questions may be kept in mind:

1 How were frontier conflicts described and perceived?

2 What kinds of issues were involved?

3 What were seen as the causes or objectives of these struggles?

4 How were the adversaries conceived, and what motives or strategies were imputed to them?

5 What were seen as the main options in resolving such conflicts, and on what underlying assumptions were these based?

6 What legitimations were offered for coercive or aggressive measures, and on what kinds of grounds were policy proposals justified?

Care must be taken in relating the answers to these questions to their specific historical contexts. Even if much the same complaints concerning stock-theft or calls for a commando were to be heard again and again, they do not necessarily have the same significance and function at different times and places. The context of frontier conflict between colonists and Xhosa changed in a number of important ways from 1770, when these peoples first came to live in close contact with each other. We have to distinguish:

1 the period of the open frontier from 1770 to 1793 when trekboers and Xhosa jostled each other in the disputed areas of the eastern frontier, but before any major frontier wars had taken place or set patterns of strategy and thinking had evolved;

2 the frontier crisis from 1793 to 1810 when civil authority repeatedly broke down, and colonists and Xhosa, in shifting alliances with the Khoikhoi, increasingly resorted to force in backing up their claims against each other, but when neither of the contending groups was able to establish clear ascendancy;

3 the closing frontier after 1812 when the presence of a permanent British military force had decisively changed the ultimate balance of power on the eastern frontier;[3]

4 the period after 1836 when Afrikaners played an increasingly minor role on the eastern frontier, while those who had participated in the Great Trek had to take on military as well as political responsibility on the new frontiers in the interior.

The texts in this chapter will therefore in the main be analyzed in a chronological order corresponding to the major stages of frontier conflict. The writings of Stockenström will be discussed separately, in view of his exceptional position and the controversial nature of his views and policies.

The ambiguities of conflict on the open frontier

The letter from Landdrost De Wet in 1780 and the report of Commandant Van Jaarsveld in 1781 (4.1a, b) relate to the very earliest period of hostile conflict between colonists and Xhosa. Prior to this a decade and more of bitter wars of extermination had been waged against the 'Bushmen' on the northern frontier. No such lines of conflict had yet been drawn on the eastern frontier in the first decade after 1770 when the migrant trekboers and Xhosa first began to settle in the Zuurveld. Nor were the issues clear-cut even in the sharpening conflicts of 1780–1781.[4] In these two documents, written from the different perspectives of the commandant in the field and of the distant administrator, we can follow how the issues were defined and how the earliest thinking about such frontier hostilities took shape. One should perhaps refrain from speaking too readily of these events as the 'First Frontier War', for this invokes a whole ready-made conceptual framework that was not available to those who had to deal with the events without the benefit of hindsight. At the time it was not such an easy matter to recognize what was happening, and to decide what to do about it. For the first frontiersmen it involved both conceptual problems and political decisions to view these disputes as situations of 'hostility' and of potential 'war', and thus to proceed against the other parties concerned on the basis that they were 'enemies'.

Consider the characteristic features of interaction and strife on the open frontier. This was not the scene of a stable and settled order where developments would be readily recognizable as actions of corporate hostility and aggression. It was inevitable that disputes would arise as more trekboers and Xhosa moved into the same area. They shared it with each other and with the last of the Khoikhoi clans, the latter more often than not being dispossessed in the process. Sometimes they competed for land or water, at others they engaged in mutual trade and barter. In both cases, disputes developed easily (cf. 4.2b). Often the roots of such disputes would be genuinely unclear. Who exactly had priority of occupation in a given area and on what grounds? Did a Khoikhoi or Xhosa labourer voluntarily enter into the service of a trekboer on certain conditions of service, or was he being detained in this way against his will? And later, when stock-theft became more of an issue, were the cattle stolen or simply lost? Such individual disputes might be further complicated by different cultural traditions. The trekboers' conception of *exclusive* occupation of the land, for example, was basically at odds with the Xhosas' notion of *communal* usage of land.[5] In general Xhosa society was prepared to incorporate alien individuals or groups; the trekboers, on the other hand, tended to exclude others from their culture and kinship network, while incorporating them differentially as labourers and subordinates.[6] More specifically, such practices as the 'begging' of the Xhosa had a different social function in trekboer society.

The ambiguities inherent in social exchanges shading off into disputes between such different cultural groups are well caught in a letter (4.9) of Landdrost A. Stockenström (Sr) in 1810, describing the practice of the Xhosas' 'wandering visits' to the farmers. He remarked that they regarded receiving hospitality and food as a 'sign of amity', but 'not satisfied with staying a single day at one farm, they often remain several days, insisting upon having victuals furnished to them, and watching their opportunity to carry off something for their journey into the bargain. It often happens that one of the party makes off with some booty, while the rest remain to prevent suspicion. Sometimes the thieves, when afraid of being discovered, restore the booty themselves, pretending that they have recovered it from others, and demanding ample recompence for their trouble.'[7] With amicable exchanges thus turning into unwelcome impositions or veiled threats and taunts, it was difficult to know when disputes might turn into serious hostilities.

Another kind of ambiguity appears in the conduct of an intermediate figure like Coenraad de Buys, 'an example of a type of character that lawless frontier regions have tended to foster at all times in many parts of the world'.[8] This forceful personality sojourned for appreciable periods in Xhosa territory beyond the colonial boundary, and entered into intimate social and conjugal relations with the Khoikhoi and Xhosa, but also became involved in violent altercations with them to the extent that his conduct was regarded as one of the contributing causes of the frontier war of 1793. It is significant and characteristic that precisely De Buys, who knew that the colonial authorities might regard him as 'a seditious person', and that he might be accused of being 'a friend of the Kaffirs' (*Cafversbroeder*), would call on the government to make an end to his being 'subject to the Kaffirs', who 'lord it over me, my cattle, and servants'. (4.2a)

Most important of all, there was no recognized authority capable of settling such disputes as might develop. The open frontier can best be described as the scene of an authority crisis.[9] There were, of course, various authorities exercising some control on the colonists as well as in the various tribal communities, but none was capable of establishing itself as undisputed authority in the frontier zone, restraining unauthorized actions, or enforcing treaties and settlements on its nominal subjects. In the absence of any common and generally legitimized conventions for conflict regulation, frontiersmen intent on pressing their claims usually had to make do with whatever coercive powers were at their own disposal (cf. 4.2a). This does not mean that life on the frontier constituted some Hobbesian state of nature, a 'war of every man against every man'. The intensity of such disputes as would arise was constrained by the limited powers of coercion available to individuals and groups, as well as by the risks of open conflict. As Van Jaarsveld explained in 1795 in a specific case, 'The people wish to see that the Kaffirs are defeated. . . . The reason why they have not come right out with this is that they fear the consequences. . . . If that populace were not afraid that they were too weak and would require assistance, hostilities against the Kaffirs would long since have commenced. . . .' (4.4c) There must also be borne in mind the advantages of co-operation and, given the low population density, the relative ease with which conflict might be avoided by access to alternative land or water. Still, the frontier was often the scene of 'violence and annoyances' (4.1a). But more than with actual incidents of violence or aggression, the frontier was rife with rumours and threats and taunts.

How and when, in such an ambiguous situation, do the lines of battle come to be drawn between hostile groups? The landdrost was confronted by the report from the field that 'actual hostilities have broken out', and, indeed, by the time eight or nine people had been killed and more wounded, it was clearly no longer simply a question of private disputes (4.1a). But on the frontier itself, and to those directly involved, the situation was much more complex and ambiguous. In the report of Commandant Van Jaarsveld we can follow the thinking of someone with direct responsibility for deciding whether what was happening was just the usual 'violence and annoyances' or whether it constituted something quite different.

The occasion for Van Jaarsveld's mission, according to his report (4.1b), was the fact that the Xhosa had 'again moved in among our people with all their property'. Even if from the colonists' point of view this could be construed as a breach of Governor Van Plettenberg's treaty line, the real question was whether it should be seen as evidence of corporate hostility and aggression, of 'this evidently impending violence'. Van Jaarsveld had to decide whether it should be taken as a threat of war. Accordingly, he conducted further inquiries on the spot into the various messages and rumours, and the 'molestations' and wrongful occupations allegedly committed by the Xhosa. Even from the words of Van Jaarsveld's own report, it is not clear that these did constitute anything beyond the usual 'violence and annoyances'. On the other hand, if they could be taken as potential threats of war, then desperate countermeasures were called for, 'in order, if possible, to beat the unreasonable portion of the Kaffirs into a proper peace' (4.1b).

It should be noted that both the landdrost and the commandant did not assume any inherent superiority of the burghers' cause. If the adversaries were not intimidated by the mere presence of the commando with their horses and guns, then it was by no means certain that the colonists would prevail in open conflict. 'Upon the proceedings of this commando,' wrote Landdrost De Wet in 1780 (4.1a), 'will depend the doubtful question whether the Kafirs are to be forcibly dislodged, or the inhabitants obliged to abandon that country.' And in the next year Commandant Van Jaarsveld, having decided that it might be necessary to resort to force, evidently had equally little confidence in the ability of his commando to impose a coercive order on hostile forces in open combat.

Van Jaarsveld's account (4.1b) of the series of incidents leading to the massacre of almost an entire chieftainship dramatically illustrates the desperate ambiguities of such a situation of 'impending violence'. His initial commands to the chiefs that they and their people should remove and go back to 'their own country' proved quite ineffective. Clearly the Xhosa chiefs neither recognized his authority to give such commands, nor were they intimidated by the physical threat of the assembled commando. Still, this did not prove they were bent on war. Similarly, when some of the Xhosa warriors pushed or pressed in among the commando, asking for tobacco, and kept Van Jaarsveld himself surrounded by ten or twelve men, he at first saw nothing particulary suspicious or threatening about this, but, after receiving some warnings, he later reflected that it might also be consistent with a deliberate and hostile strategy threatening possible attack. While the situation remained essentially ambiguous, the stakes were getting higher and higher. 'I clearly saw that if we allowed the Kafirs to make the first attack, it could not be otherwise than that many must fall on my side.' In a situation of (possible) deadly conflict, where there is no clearly overwhelming superiority of force on your own side, the pre-emptive strike on the unsuspecting adversary must be a powerful temptation. And so he resolved the ambiguities by a stratagem resulting in massacre.[10]

This massacre is an archetypal event of frontier conflict. It had an enormous impact on frontier history, and was still remembered many generations later.[11] It would find its counterpart in a number of strikingly similar events in later frontier conflicts, the most famous of which involved the deaths of the elder Stockenström in 1812, and of Piet Retief in 1838. These tragic events are the obverse of those cases where responsible individuals deliberately ignored the dangers of possibly hostile circumstances and succeeded in defusing confrontations through amicable negotiation.[12] Both the massacre (Van Jaarsveld) of the unsuspecting adversary, and the brave and trusting venture (Stockenström and Retief) to continue discussions in the midst of possibly extreme danger are rooted in the same ambiguities.

A notable feature of both Van Jaarsveld and De Wet's accounts is the unromanticized view they took of these earliest conflicts. We have here no grand designs for aggressive territorial expansion or beliefs in the manifest destinies of one race at the expense of another. The emphasis is on actual or potential injuries and losses; it is recognized that the colonial property rights that are to be defended may well rest on somewhat dubious claims. There is no mention of either heroes or villains. Landdrost De Wet was well aware that among the colonists there were 'mischievous inhabitants . . . who cause disquiet . . . in order to enlarge their own farms', and that there were those who engaged in 'increasing illicit traffic', and he considered it 'by no means improbable that [the Xhosas'] complaints and accusations were more or less founded in fact'. The Xhosa, for their part, were not conceived as especially base or evil in character, nor were unduly sinister motives and intentions imputed to them. 'The natural disposition of the Kafirs, however revengeful it may be . . . is not so cruel as to provoke them to such daring attempts without just cause.' (4.1a)

Van Jaarsveld, persuaded that he had much to fear from the Xhosa, and that he could not trust their designs against him, resorted to force as an unwelcome and uncertain measure against a redoubtable adversary rather than as a justifiable punishment of a base enemy. His qualifications are highly significant: '*Knowing no other means* of preventing the daily threatened violence of the Kafirs and putting an end to the numberless complaints of the inhabitants, than proceeding in order, *if possible,* to beat *the unreasonable portion* of the Kafirs into a proper peace. . . .' (4.1b)

Notable, also, is the relative absence of legitimations or justifications, particularly in view of the serious atrocity committed by Van Jaarsveld's commando. From the outset he was careful to put all his proceedings in the context of implementing Governor Van Plettenberg's treaty, and to involve the Governor's name in his commands to the chiefs, but this can hardly be extended to the massacre itself. Perhaps Van Jaarsveld's earlier experiences on the northern frontier, where the colonial authorities had sanctioned similar actions against the 'Bushmen', influenced him. Certainly, to judge from Landdrost De Wet's letter of the previous year, the colonial authorities' criticism of and annoyance at the behaviour of the colonists on the frontier did not detract from their basic support of the colonists in their disputes with the Xhosa. For this reason also Van Jaarsveld might not have considered it necessary to do more than stress the potential danger to himself and his men in his account of the events leading up to the massacre. His account could hardly have satisfied any serious doubts or challenge from the colonial authorities on the propriety of his actions, but then he was evidently not expecting that sort of challenge. This mutual confidence between frontiersmen and colonial administrators would later be rudely shattered, and would greatly change the thinking of both parties on frontier conflict.

The frontier crisis and the corporate uses of violence

Starting from the early 1790s the character and context of frontier conflict changed markedly. Colonists, Xhosa and even Khoikhoi increasingly sought to redress their grievances, and back up their demands and claims, by turning to force while the representatives of colonial government were more than once sharply challenged. The frontier wars of 1793 and 1799, and the series of revolts against the government of 1795, 1799 and 1801, in conjunction with the Khoikhoi rising of 1799, constituted nothing less than a general breakdown of all civil authority on the frontier (see Chapter 1, p. 14ff).

The corporate uses of violence, its limits and consequences, are problems central to the documents from this period when various groups and factions contended for ascendancy by banding together in unstable and shifting alliances. Commandos were raised, often acting without sanction from the legitimate authorities, and sometimes used directly against the representatives of that authority. For our purposes it is irrelevant to enter into the many heated and longstanding controversies on the causes of these conflicts, or to decide who was more to blame for them. More relevant is the basic question of resorting to corporate violence as a means for settling disputes, a feature so characteristic of this stage of frontier conflict. On this point both the writings of Maynier (4.3a, c, d, 4.5) and the documents from the Graaff-Reinet burghers (4.3b, 4.4a, b, c) provide important material.

There were major differences between the thinking of Landdrost Maynier and that of the unruly colonists of the south-eastern divisions of Graaff-Reinet. Still, we must take some care in defining the precise nature of these disagreements. Despite his belief in the efficacy of 'lenient measures' and of amicably negotiated settlements, Maynier was no pacifist. The letter of early 1793 (4.3a), setting out his views and policy before assuming his duty as landdrost, shows that he was not only aware of the losses and injuries suffered by some colonists at the hands of the Xhosa, but that he also realized that in the circumstances 'gentle means' had been of no avail in persuading the Xhosa to remove beyond the boundary. He consistently approved of the colonists being allowed to pursue and forcibly retaliate against 'rogues and thieves' (4.3c). The allegations by the burghers of Graaff-Reinet that Maynier denied them the right of self-defence (4.4a, b) should obviously not be accepted as literally true. In fact, from their own letter to Commissioner Sluysken (4.4b) it appears that what they were objecting to was that they were 'only permitted to go out with a small force, which neither dares to, nor is able to, take back [their] lawful property from the enemy'. What was at issue, therefore, was not the right to individual self-defence but the use of a *general commando* as the appropriate means to resolve such frontier conflicts. And this turned on different assessments of what such a commando could or should achieve, and on certain basic assumptions on the very nature of frontier conflict itself.

Maynier was not opposed to the use of commandos. He himself led the large combined commando with Landdrost Faure during the war of 1793, but (i) he approved of such commandos for aggressive purposes only in the most extreme circumstances

(4.3d), and (ii) he did not believe that such commandos would be capable of achieving coercive supremacy, given the balance of forces on the frontier: 'It is impossible to oppose [the Xhosa] by force with any hope of success—at least until . . . we find ourselves in a condition to attack them with force and to bring them to obedience. For as experience has alas! more than too well proved, we should run a greater risk of making matters worse, than of improving them.' (4.3c)

On both counts, the frontiersmen tended to disagree. They had other views of the aims and purposes of commandos, and they were also more confident of their prospects for success. They were convinced that a suitably aggressive use of force, which after all was the purpose of a commando, would provide an answer to the problems of frontier conflict. The aim was, to adapt Van Jaarsveld's words, 'to beat the Kafirs into a proper place'. The highflown justifications of the right to self-defence in the letter to Sluysken (4.4b), invoking both the teachings of God and 'the laws of nature', thus turn out to be more in the nature of attempted legitimations for corporate violence. Moreover, they believed that the commandos were, in fact, capable of achieving this goal. 'We on the contrary', replied Commandants Botha, Linden and Van Rooyen to Governor Janssens in 1803, 'are strong enough to recover our belongings at the point of the sword and to provide a peace that would give quiet and security to your Government for years to come.' (4.6)

It was to these aggressive purposes of the commandos that Maynier objected. In his Provisional Justification of 1802 (4.5), Maynier contrasted his own position with that of the frontiersmen, who in his view, 'longed for nothing so much as to attack the Caffres again and to profit by new troubles', and who 'wished for Great Commandos, [desiring] to destroy the Craals where their inoffensive Women and Children dwelt'. These objections were clearly based on humanitarian and moral grounds. But Maynier also objected to such commandos on more pragmatic grounds of policy. So far from the commandos succeeding in imposing the coercive control they sought, he considered that they would merely result in making implacable enemies of the Xhosa and thus bring ruin upon the entire frontier district. Drawing on his experience of the combined commando in 1793 he contended that, owing to the difficulties of the terrain, the commandos were simply not capable of expelling the Xhosa from the Zuurveld. It would therefore be wiser to suffer the vexations and annoyances inherent in frontier co-existence and, until a proper force could be mobilized, not to interfere forcibly with the Xhosa, in view of all the ruinous consequences that that would entail (4.3c). In taking this view, and in pointing out the danger of a combined threat of the 'Bushmen' and Xhosa frontiers, Maynier was, in fact, simply restating the considered policy of the officers of militia of Graaff-Reinet, who represented the interests of the northern frontier as well.[13] And it would appear from the sad fate of the commandos in battles in 1799 and 1802 that this assessment of the balance of forces obtaining on the eastern frontier was indeed more realistic than that of the burghers who believed that the commandos could solve all their frontier problems.[14]

Maynier's characterization of the Xhosa and his assumptions about their nature and strategy also reflected official policy rather than an idiosyncratic view. His typical descriptions of them as 'that otherwise so peaceable nation (4.3d)', and as a people amenable to reason, faithfully repeated the very terminology of the instructions originally drawn up for the frontier commandant by Landdrost De Wet and the heemraden of Stellenbosch in 1780: 'The Kafirs . . . are comparatively capable of being treated with, . . . [they are] in themselves a very peaceable and timid people.'[15] It is quite understandable that Maynier, as someone born and educated in the Western Cape, should have subscribed to these official views about the nature of frontier conflict at the outset of his career as landdrost, and that in 1793 he might still have had reasonable confidence in treaties and negotiations as a means of settling frontier disputes rather than in countering force with force (4.3a). It is more difficult to understand how in 1802, after a full decade of violent turmoil and a number of disastrous wars, he could simply repeat, without any qualification or support, 'I feel the most perfect conviction that Peace may be preserved with these Creatures, by fair means, and with little trouble.' (4.5) This view assumed that there were, in the end, no basic or substantial conflicts of interests involved between the contending parties, a view that might have been credible before 1793, but hardly in 1802. It also ignored the extent to which the violent disputes during this period of frontier crisis were connected with a breakdown of political authority itself. In such circumstances a mere reaffirmation of the claims of authority ignored the central problem of dealing with corporate violence on the frontier. Against this, the burghers of Graaff-Reinet insisted on the violent nature of the prevailing frontier conflict: 'The Kafirs have penetrated with force. . . . They have taken all our cattle by force; taken the lives of citizens and their workers.' (4.4a) Even if they were unrealistic in their assessment of what a commando could achieve given the balance of forces on the frontier, they had a surer grasp of the unnegotiable nature of the conflict.

The same strengths and weaknesses in the thinking of Afrikaner officials about frontier conflict also appear in Van Ryneveld's letter of 1806 (4.7), written on the eve of the second British occupation. Van Ryneveld showed insight into how, in the larger context, the resort to unauthorized corporate force would set off a chain reaction: disturbances among the burghers lead to disturbances among Khoikhoi and Xhosa; these frontier scares lead to commandos which lead to reprisals and counter-raids, drawing the whole interior into a chaotic civil war. But having warned of this, what was his counsel? Simply that each individual should comply with authority and interest himself only in his own affairs, repudiating faction and letting the government deal with all public matters. Thus the Colony's peace and order would be assured. We have here the same assumption that there were no serious conflicts of corporate interest involved in frontier hostilities, and that the problems would disappear if everyone would just mind his own business and let the colonial government get on with its task. Certainly this official view failed to address itself to the major problem of the breakdown of civil authority and the resort to corporate violence instead. Indeed, only the presence of a superior military force would begin to allow civil authority to resolve the frontier crisis itself.

Conflict regulation on the closing frontier

The permanent presence of a British military force on the eastern frontier from 1810 profoundly changed the context and character of frontier conflict. First, it helped to resolve the frontier crisis in colonial society. Secondly, it replaced the commandos as the basic instrument of colonial defence. Thirdly, it changed the basic balance of power in frontier conflict. Whereas the frontier colonists before 1810 could often only with difficulty maintain their position, the presence of superior military forces inaugurated a period of renewed colonial expansion at the expense of the Xhosa (see Chapter One, p. 15ff).

This did not mean that frontier conflict became a one-sided affair in favour of the imperial forces or that the interests of the colonists would henceforth uniformly prevail. The point is rather that increasingly the conduct of frontier affairs was no longer in the colonists' own hands. Their continual complaints about the uses to which the colonial authorities put the forces at its disposal, and more often, of course, their complaints about its failures to use such forces properly in defending the colony and punishing its enemies, all assumed the prior recognition that these decisive forces were at the disposal of the colonial authorities and not of the colonists themselves. In fact, colonial frontier policy was determined by considerations (including fiscal economizing and the influence of the missionaries) other than simply the interests of the frontier colonists.[16] The details of conflict on the eastern frontier, from stock-theft and threats of reprisal to full scale frontier war, increasingly functioned within the wider and more complex framework of expanding British imperialism.

The changed context is already apparent if we compare the memorial of the eleven frontier farmers of Uitenhage in 1810 (4.8b) with the reply given by Commandants Botha, Linden and Van Rooyen to Governor Janssens in 1803 (4.6). In place of the confident assertion that the commandos are strong enough to achieve peace and security at the point of a sword, we find a plaintive description of the grievous and dangerous conditons in which the colonists found themselves, ending in an appeal that the troops be used to drive the Xhosa 'into their own territory'. (4.8b) It is of even greater interest to compare the claims made by Piet Retief in his reports as field-commandant in 1822–3 (4.11a, b, c). Like the three commandants, Retief made substantial claims about what he would be able to achieve with a commando: 'I should certainly have been able to regain the stolen stock.' (4.11a) And again: 'I should surely have been able, with God's help, to bring about peace and quiet.' (4.11c) On closer analysis, however, it will be clear that these claims were very different from those of the commandants in 1803. Retief was not for a moment suggesting that the commandos could be *substituted* for the system of military defence, or that they would be more effective than it. On the contrary, Retief's claims for the commandos were based on the assumption that they now functioned within this military framework and were subject to regulations. His point was that certain of these regulations did not allow him sufficient freedom of discretionary judgement (4.11a). Rather than any general rejection of the way in which the commandos had been brought under the control of the colonial authorities, Retief tended to accept this and to make the matter into a more personal grievance: 'I find, to my most grievous sorrow, that I have been called to an office where I am not trusted.' (4.11c)

Retief's reports may also be compared with despatches of Landdrost Andries Stockenström (Jr) at the beginning of 1819 (4.10). In view of the later confrontation between these two men[17] it is remarkable how similar their approach to frontier problems was at this time. Stockenström, like Retief, assumed that colonial frontier policy now depended on the presence of a superior military force which would at the same time limit the independent options of the colonists themselves. Both knew that, in arguing for changes in the implementation of that policy, account had to be taken not only of the colonists' interests but of other 'well grounded reasons' (4.11b, cf. 4.11c) that might underlie the government's regulations, and both also were aware that their own motives might be regarded as suspect (cf. 4.10, 4.11a). They were also agreed that more vigorous measures might be necessary against the Xhosa: 'I think it absolutely necessary . . . that they be most effectively set down.' (4.10) Surprisingly, Stockenström rather than Retief proposed the view that frontier conflict had now become more polarised in racial and ethnic terms, and that the days of cross-cutting alliances were drawing to an end: 'The general cry is let us meet any number of Kaffirs, but let us meet them as enemies, for our enemies "they are all of them".' (4.10)

However, there were also subtle but nevertheless important differences in their thinking, foreshadowing the later rift. While Retief was essentially arguing for a more active role for the commandos, Stockenström objected to 'those petty Commandos' as onerous burdens on the burghers and as 'inefficient measures whereby nothing can be gained but the revenge of the enemy'. (4.10) When he went on to argue for 'the absolute necessity, if anything at all be done, that a force be employed capable of crushing the Kaffirs most effectually', this meant the deployment of substantial *military* forces with, of course, some support from the commandos. There was also a further difference in their approach to the use of force. Whereas Stockenström was quite frank about the necessity of superior coercive force if the frontier conflicts were to be settled, Retief tended to be rather vague and elusive on this crucial point. Thus we find him claiming that, at the head of a commando, he would 'either address all the chiefs and get back all the stolen stock without violence', or he would pursue the thieves and demand the stolen goods, and then 'there is no doubt that they will cease their activities'. (4.11a, cf. 4.11b) Retief gave no indication why the Xhosa would suddenly be so willing to comply with his requests and demands. If he was counting on the commando as an instrument of coercion, then he was not coming into the open on just how he proposed to use force to settle frontier conflicts. Moreover, there is no indication here that Retief gave any serious thought to what the possible motivation, interests and strategy of the Xhosa reaction to such coercive measures might be. Stockenström, on the other hand, explicitly recognized that the actions even of 'cruel barbarians' were governed by understandable social motivations and economic interests. He also clearly expressed his views on the purposes of, and the limitations to, the use of force. Echoing the opinion of his father a decade earlier,[18] he held that in a situation of open conflict, lenient measures amounted to half measures that stimulated rather than contained further conflict. (4.10) In the final analysis, however, establishing coercive supremacy was not an end in itself, but merely the precondition for the proper functioning of civil and political authority.

This last point is at best implicit in Stockenström's despatch of 1819 (4.10), but it is basic to his whole policy on the northern frontier (4.12c). Against the 'Bushmen', but never against the Xhosa, the colonists had waged and the colonial authorities had sanctioned an actual war of extermination in the 18th century. By the 1820s circumstances had changed and more conciliatory practices were supported by the colonists.[12] As responsible landdrost, Stockenström recognized that against the 'Bushmen' extreme measures might still be 'occasionally necessary'. Above all, however, he was concerned to lay down the rules of justifiable conduct even in such circumstances: 'If in this just attempt they meet with resistance [from the 'Bushmen'], there is no alternative between destroying the robbers and being destroyed. But if on any occasion such as can be seized without risk be wantonly killed, and I find it out, as far as the laws enable me . . . I will use every exertion to put it out of the power of the offender to repeat such excesses of revenge.' (4.12a) Thus even the 'Bushman' frontier was closing as extermination campaigns were subjected to regulations and law. In Stockenström's thinking, however, such effective civil authority in a frontier zone rested on the precondition of deploying coercive power when necessary (cf. 4.12b).

Stockenström and the controversy about frontier politics

Apart from Stockenström, Afrikaners had a relatively minor part in the major controversies about frontier policy that dominated colonial politics from the 1830s. Even before the Great Trek removed the greater part of the Afrikaner community from the eastern frontier, British officials had taken over most of the key administrative positions in the frontier districts. Spokesmen of the British settlers took the lead in defending the colonists' cause against the criticisms of the London Missionary Society and their allies. Thus few Afrikaners remained directly involved in the public conduct of frontier affairs. In its own way the Great Trek was, of course, a response also to the state of frontier affairs. The dramatic impact of the Trek, however, has tended to obscure the extent to which the expression of frontier opinion from the war of 1834–35 on was dominated by the British settlers of Albany and the merchants of Grahamstown. Such Afrikaner reactions as there were tended to be confined to either applauding what was perceived as more immediately favourable developments in government policy, with echoes of the antiphilanthropic sentiments of the *Grahamstown Journal*,[20] or to giving voice to their many grievances and their lack of security.[21] Occasionally a spokesman for the loyalist trekboers on the north-eastern frontier, such as Gideon Joubert, expressed paternalistic concern with the plight of the refugees from the Difaqane as a reason for being given greater discretion to act beyond the colonial boundaries, which may or may not have been linked with the trekboers' interest in new land beyond the Orange (4.14a). What we do not find are any serious attempts to address the major issues and principles of frontier policy. For this we must turn, on the one hand, to the critique of colonial frontier politics documented and propagated above all by Dr Philip, aided locally by John Fairbairn as editor of the *South African Commerical Advertiser*, and in Britain by his influential allies at 'Exeter Hall' and in the imperial government itself. This indictment, first set out in Philip's *Researches in South Africa* and culminating in the hearings of the Aborigines Committee in 1835–36, was countered primarily by the leaders of settler opinion in Grahamstown—above all by Robert Godlonton as editor of the *Grahamstown Journal.*

The only Afrikaner who took a prominent part in these public debates was Andries Stockenström, and he was very much caught in the middle of the furious controversies. His involvement followed from the high office in frontier affairs which he held, rather exceptionally for a colonist in these years. After long experience as landdrost of Graaff-Reinet, he was appointed commissioner-general for the Eastern Province, and following his resignation in 1832 he was called as one of the major witnesses before the Aborigines Committee in London. He was subsequently appointed lieutenant-governor to implement Lord Glenelg's treaty system. During the war of 1846 he again emerged from retirement to become commander of the burgher forces. During this whole period he was involved in a host of complex controversies. The Stockenström documents in this chapter are, in fact, only a partial selection from the mass of his official correspondence and polemical writings. Leaving aside the historical questions raised by his evidence before the Aborigines Committee, and the many allegations concerning the nature of his testimony (which resulted in a sensational libel case), and leaving aside too the acrimonious exchanges and in-fighting accompanying the political manoeuvres that led to the failure of the Glenelg treaty system, we must consider what were the main principles of Stockenström's thinking about frontier politics.

Before 1836 Stockenström confined himself to a critique of the prevailing frontier policy, and did not give more than a general statement of his fundamental principles. From 1836 these principles were then elaborated in terms of the new treaty system that he was to implement as lieutenant-governor. In his criticisms of the existing frontier policy Stockenström emphasized, on the one hand, what he considered to be its fatal inconsistencies, and, on the other hand, the abuses inherent in the prevailing system of reprisal and frontier defence. Taken together these criticisms illuminate different aspects of this particular stage of conflict and policy on the closing frontier.

Stockenström's diagnosis in 1829 of the major defect of the prevailing frontier policy as lying in its inconsistency and vacillation did not yet indicate any substantial disagreement in principle. His charge that the great mistake in the policy of frontier defence consisted in 'the sudden transition from measures of too great severity, and sometimes wanton cruelty, to the opposite extreme . . . of supposed conciliation' (4.13a) may or may not have been justified as a description of the conduct of frontier policy in the preceding years. However, since he himself approved the use of severe coercive force, when necessary, and negotiation and conciliation, when possible, he could hardly quarrel with these aims of official policy. In effect, these same aims were contained in his own recommendation of a 'proper medium' as the basis for future frontier policy. His strictures should therefore be thought of as directed towards the practical implementation of that policy. In effect he was admitting that the frontier was not yet completely closed, and that the colonial government still experienced some difficulty in establishing its undisputed authority and in implementing its policy effectively.

However, Stockenström's critique of the abuses inherent in the system of reprisal and frontier defence assumed that the uncontrolled actions of different individuals and groups in a frontier zone beyond the reach of civil authority had been replaced by established and regularized civilian and military defence. Only in this way can we understand the apparent conflict with his own earlier policy on raids and reprisals. On the relatively open northern frontier, where there were 'Bushmen' communities with little or no institutionalized authority structures, he had favoured allowing the farmers to pursue raiders even beyond the boundary limit, insisting merely on such *post hoc* controls by the legal authorities as the circumstances would permit (4.12c). But the presence of an institutionalized system of defence on the eastern frontier lent itself to a variety of abuses. Stockenström's summary of the abuses inherent in the practice of patrols and reprisals under these conditions given before the Aborigines Committee in 1835 (4.13e) had already been anticipated by his correspondence as commissioner-general in 1829.[22] In each case he was careful to stress that the majority of the colonists were rightfully interested mainly in their own protection and security and did not harbour aggressive or vengeful intentions towards the Xhosa. But there were also some unscrupulous individuals who would take whatever advantages they could get away with. Rather than castigating the colonists, and in particular the Afrikaner frontiersmen, for their supposed brutality and venality, he suggests that it would be better to look to the defects of the whole system of frontier defence: 'Then where lies the blame? Is it not your system which compels them to be butchers today, and would have them submit to be butchered without resistance tomorrow?' (4.13c)

Stockenström's objections (4.13c) to those 'unprincipled men' who availed themselves of the opportunities inherent in this system for enriching themselves at the expense of their weaker (Xhosa) neighbours were clearly of a moral nature. But his objections were equally based on considerations of policy. In his description in 1834 of the reprisal system and its origins he particularly emphasized that it constituted an additional 'obstacle to peace' on the frontier.[23] And in what was more or less his last word on the reprisal system in 1836, he allowed that colonists could protect their property by force, if necessary, but added that this should always be subject to the overriding considerations of order and security on the frontier: 'The reprisal system must be finally put a stop to. The Colonists must be allowed to protect their property and lives against plunderers and murderers, even if it be necessary to shoot the assailants; . . . but no risk of a bloody war ought to be incurred for every cow which strays, or is destroyed by wild beasts, or may even be stolen.' (4.15a, cf. 4.15b)

At times Stockenström extended this critique beyond the reprisal system itself and suggested that certain parties, presumably the merchants of Grahamstown and some career officers in the army, had vested interests in fomenting a crisis atmosphere on the frontier, which would result in large military expenditures and create opportunities for career advancement and the extension of patronage (cf. 4.13c, 4.15b). In doing this he was making a general criticism of the autocratic, military, imperial regime as it impinged on frontier affairs, and no longer confining himself to the more immediate conditions of frontier conflict—thus indicating some recognition of the fact that the old days of limited conflict on the open frontier were over, and that present conflict should be seen in a wider and different context.

What principles did Stockenström advance as basic to a just and effective frontier policy? He obviously set great store on basing himself on the (to him) simple but profound principle of *equal protection*. He regarded this as holding the middle ground in the contending claims of colonists and Xhosa: 'I have, from first to last, acted on one consistent principle of courting neither the white nor the black party.' (4.13c) It also held the middle ground between Dr Philip and the 'philanthropists', and the vigorous apologists for settler interests. Stockenström could thus say: 'Whilst the voice of humanity is justly raised in favour of the long and cruelly oppressed blacks, that of justice and prudence remind us that the whites also have a claim to protection.' (4.13b) But this attempt to give both sides their due meant that Stockenström tended to fall foul of both parties in the controversy.[24] Rather than asking whether Stockenström could in fact achieve any sort of true impartiality in these conflicts between colonists and Xhosa, or attempt to sort out his colonial prejudices from the humanitarian influences on his thinking, it is more instructive for our purposes to consider the assumptions and the implications of his application of the principle of equal protection in this particular context.

Stockenström usually expressed his fundamental principle in the most general and abstract terms: 'I have the cause of truth to serve; I am to call "murder, murder" and "plunder, plunder", whatever be the colour of the perpetrator's skin.' (4.13d) And again: 'Injustice to whites—English or Dutch—, to blacks, Kaffir, Hottentot or Bushmen, I will still consider injustice and deal with it accordingly.' (4.13c) What he was doing here in thus invoking the abstract principles of truth and justice was to transpose to the context of frontier conflict the rule-of-law ideology subscribed to by such as Van Ryneveld and Truter in their activities as officials establishing law and order in colonial society (see Chapter 3, p. 79ff). This could only be done on the assumption that the frontier had in fact closed, and in two respects. First it had to be assumed that the colonial government had established itself as the undisputed authority with the ability to impose the rule of law on its subjects. However, frontier conflicts also involved the Xhosa communities beyond the colonial boundaries, and here there could be no question of the colonial government's being the undisputed authority. How, then, could the frontier be assumed to be—or to be able to be—closed in this second respect? The option could be entertained of making these territories part of the colony through annexation. On his appointment as lieutenant-governor, Stockenström was confronted with precisely this as a result of D'Urban's annexation of the territory up to the Kei River subsequent to the war of 1834–35. Stockenström's response was to state that, rather than resolving the authority crisis on the frontier, this measure would tend to renew it.

In his letter to Lord Glenelg at the beginning of 1836 (4.15a) he explained that he had no objection to the incorporation of people such as the 'Bushmen' who could not be controlled in any other way except through direct administration. But in the case of the Xhosa the imperial government had to deal with communities who were politically and socially 'so far organised and consolidated' that interference in their internal affairs was not advisable. The introduction of English law among the Xhosa was not practicable; the chiefs could not be expected to administer an alien legal system, while any attempt to weaken the authority of the chiefs and the traditional tribal institutions would be counterproductive: 'The prejudices of a nation, however absurd they may appear, are not easily removed or disregarded; violent opposition often strengthens them.' In short, it is only by recognizing and promoting the traditional structures of political authority in the tribal communities that a basis could be gained for a stable resolution of frontier conflict.

The assumption of Stockenström's treaty system was therefore that on the Xhosa side as well the frontier had (or could be) closed, and that frontier conflicts could henceforth be conducted on the model of international politics. How this system was applied can to some extent be followed in his reports of 1836 and 1837 (4.15b). But the ultimate rationale was expressed in a letter of ten years later: 'I am told that it is absurd to apply to our dealings with "savages" the rules which regulate the intercourse between civilized nations, . . . that all that is wanted on the frontier is a man who can "keep down" our troublesome neighbours, and crush them, and exterminate them if necessary. I may be wrong, but I dissent from this view of the subject. I believe the principles of truth and justice to be universal, as well as eternal, . . . with nations, as with individuals.' (4.17b)

Stockenström may indeed have been wrong in his assumption that the frontier had been finally closed; he may have been mistaken, like other colonial administrators before him, in his view of the authority structure of Xhosa society; and he may have underestimated the extent to which the conflicts of interest underlying frontier disputes were non-negotiable. In short, the necessary preconditions for applying the rule-of-law ideology to frontier relations may have been absent. If this were the case, then he insisted that frontier wars reverted to a basic contest to assert coercive supremacy (4.17a, c). They could end only in a thorough-going imperial subjugation requiring military superiority and enormous expense—otherwise the experiment in civil co-existence had to be resumed: 'So much, however, I may tell you, that whenever you abandon "extermination" you will have to deal with the native tribes through their chiefs. . . . You must enact the Hottentot history over again, which with the Kafirs and others will not be so easy a matter, or you must respect those for whom the natives have a natural and even a superstitious veneration.' (4.17c) Stockenström wrote these words in something close to a spirit of despair at the time of the great frontier conflagration of 1851, though he never espoused the view that the nature of the frontier conflict precluded the necessary preconditions for applying his principles. His own views, associated as they were with the much-maligned Glenelg treaty system, were never to be implemented on the eastern frontier, which increasingly went the way of imperial annexation. It is of some significance, however, that this latter tendency was opposed at the time by other Afrikaner spokesmen both in the eastern and in the western Cape (4.18a-d). And surprisingly enough certain parallels with Stockenström's approach appeared in the attempts of the leaders of the Free State to deal with the conflicts on the Basotho frontier in the 1850s.

Frontier issues at mid-century

The Great Trek opened a number of new frontiers in the interior. Some, like the Basotho frontier in the 1850s and 1860s, could be seen as extensions or replications of the Cape eastern frontier. Others varied greatly: in Natal a small and tenuous white settlement bordered on the strong Zulu kingdom; in the Transvaal widely scattered Trekker settlements were interspersed and surrounded by a variety of smaller chiefdoms; in the Trans–Orange, Griquas, loyalist trekboers, rebellious Trekkers and a variety of Sotho–Tswana and 'Bushmen' communities all mingled in the same territory. In each of these frontier zones white frontiersmen and administrators had to meet different demands and contend with different sets of problems. Beyond the colonial boundary the Trekkers obviously had greater freedom to act on their own ideas of the proper way to settle frontier conflicts. Nevertheless for a considerable time they did not succeed in establishing anything like white hegemony, and they were greatly hampered by the scarce resources at their disposal. In addition, the threat of imperial interference remained a factor throughout southern Africa.

What were the main developments in Afrikaner thinking on the politics and morality of frontier conflict in this period? For the duration of the Great Trek itself the situation of the Trekkers was so unstable that definite ideas about frontier policy could hardly be elaborated. Perhaps the closest approach to something of this kind was the letter of Piet Retief to the Griqua captains written in July 1837 (4.14b (ii)). A remarkable feature of this document is its strong religious aspect, which has little parallel in other writings of this period, whether by loyalist colonial Afrikaners or by other Trekker leaders. Retief repeatedly invoked the direct aid of God on the side of the Trekkers in their conflicts with other groups, pointing to the defeat of Mzilikazi's Ndebeles as a sign of divine intervention, and warning the Griqua captains that in a conflict with the Trekkers they would find themselves 'contending with a mighty God'. At the same time Retief did not forget to point out the more mundane facts concerning the Trekkers' relative and growing military strength, and to make it clear that if necessary he was more than prepared to use it. As he explained in his accompanying letter to Sir Benjamin D'Urban, he 'had been taking lessons on your [colonial] frontier for the last twenty-two years', and the one thing he had learnt above all was the danger inherent in 'indecision' and 'a want of promptitude' (4.14b (i)).

Nevertheless he also insisted again and again that the Trekkers had no specific aggressive intentions, and that they would use violence only in self-defence. What he proposed was thus basically a policy of mutual non-interference, with treaties 'of peace and amity' to take care of possible disputes and provide the basis for mutually beneficial co-operation (4.14b (ii)). Without Retief's religious rhetoric this was also the basic conception in a letter of A. H. Potgieter to the Griqua leader Adam Kok some years later. Trekker and Griqua leaders were to retain full authority, each within their own spheres, and the settlement of disputes was to be based on a mutual recognition of this. A notable feature of Potgieter's letter was his emphasis on the footing of equality on which the two parties stood with regard to each other: 'We are emigrants together with you and are regarded as such and regard ourselves as emigrants who together with you dwell in the same strange land, and we desire to be regarded as neither more nor less than your fellow-emigrants, inhabitants of the country, enjoying the same privileges with you.' (4.14c) Something of the same spirit can still be recognized in the letter (4.20a) of J. J. Venter, acting president of the Orange Free State, to Chief Moshweshwe some twenty years later. The Voortrekkers were thus aiming at some kind of 'treaty system', and the political thinking underlying this policy was not radically different from that behind the 'treaty system' of Glenelg and Stockenström. Similarly, to the extent that the leaders of the Orange Free State evolved distinct political conceptions of frontier policy during the long years of negotiation and wrangling on the Basotho frontier, their guiding principle appeared to be a quest to find an effective authority with whom settlements could be made and who could enforce them within his own part of the frontier zone (4.20a). Failing this, the only alternative was military conquest, if that were possible (4.19c, 4.20c).

The belief in a military solution found even stronger support among some Cape Afrikaners at mid-century, but by no means among all. Christoffel Brand, writing in 1846 as editor of *De Zuid-Afrikaan*, expressed deep scepticism concerning any policy based on treaties and negotiations and saw 'complete subjugation' as the only viable option (4.16). This view was taken further by F. W. Reitz (Sr) in 1855, when he claimed in the Cape parliament that what the colonists expected was 'that if ever unfortunately a Kaffir war should break out again, such a number of colonists will be called out, and the war carried on in such a manner, that they would be enabled to crush the power of our barbarous neighbours from one ocean to the other'. (4.18b) Reitz's thinking, perhaps expressing the confidence of a maturing colonial society backed up by the resources of imperial power, was tending towards aggressive and expansionist ideas that had hitherto been unknown in Afrikaner thinking on frontier policy. But other Cape Afrikaners of the time did not share these views and assumptions. In an editorial (4.18c) in *De Zuid-Afrikaan* in 1856, Dr Changuion sought the causes of the recurrent frontier wars not so much in the alleged treachery and savage state of the Xhosa, as in the inconsistencies and vagaries of government policy moving from 'ill-timed leniency' to 'unnecessary interference'. Rather than entertaining any ideal of a civilizing mission justifying military conquest and territorial annexation, Changuion depicted the Xhosa as equal partners in conflict, capable of fending for themselves and entitled to a fair deal. In a speech in the Cape parliament the following year J. H. Wicht in a similar vein raised doubts about the motives and interests underlying military mobilization on the frontier. In his somewhat sardonic view military conquest and territorial annexation only served to provoke Xhosa aggression in retaliation: 'We cannot blame the Kaffir for this. It is the Kaffir's uncivilized way of thinking that he has a right to get back the country he has been deprived of, if he can.' (4.18d) The most comprehensive statement of such critical and more sophisticated views was that given in the speech (4.18a) by J. de Wet on the Burgher Force Bill in 1854. From the distance of the western Cape, and with the help of a longer historical perspective, this was perhaps the best summary of Afrikaner thinking on the politics of frontier conflict and territorial expansion, bringing together themes from the thinking of Stockenström as well as that of more lowly colonists. In the subsequent decades the frontiers in the interior would finally begin to close, and frontier conflict would become past history; but the problems of racial and ethnic conflict would return in other forms, and the 'lessons' of a century of frontier conflict would return to haunt other eras under radically different conditions.

4.1a Upon the proceedings of this commando will depend the doubtful question whether the Kafirs are to be forcibly dislodged, or the inhabitants obliged to abandon that country.

—Letter from Landdrost O. G. de Wet of Stellenbosch to Governor Van Plettenberg and council, 13 March 1780. (From the translation in Moodie, *The Record*, III, pp. 92–93.)

The eastern frontier opened in the 1770s when trekboers and Xhosa began to settle interpersed with each other in the Zuurveld area between the Sundays and Fish Rivers. Open hostilities first broke out in December 1779 amidst reports of a cattle raid by some trekboers (among others the Prinsloos) on the Xhosa beyond the Fish River and complaints by trekboers of cattle-stealing by the Xhosa. At this time the northern section of this disputed area was still part of the Stellenbosch district, with O. G. de Wet (1739–1811) as landdrost. Early in 1780 two commandos took the field against the Xhosa. Responsibility for frontier policy rested with De Wet and the Stellenbosch Krygsraad some 500 miles away, and ultimately with the governor and the Council of Policy in Cape Town.

By the two inclosed letters, which I received the day before yesterday from Josua Joubert, the Field Sergeant beyond the Camdeboo River to De Bruyns Hoogte, it has been first brought to my knowledge that, during the last three months, some actual hostilities have broken out between the Kafirs beyond De Bruyns Hoogte and the inhabitants residing there; that a considerable number of cattle had been stolen from the inhabitants by the Kafirs; that in the reciprocal attack, some of the inhabitants having been wounded by the force collected by the Kafirs, [the Xhosa] had been put to flight, leaving behind them eight or nine killed, while, in order to meet the still threatened violence of the Kafirs, a strong commando was about to take the field. Upon the proceedings of this commando, as it appears to me, will depend the doubtful question whether the Kafirs are to be forcibly dislodged, or the inhabitants obliged to abandon that country. . . .

From the first letter the Council will perceive that these hostilities are chiefly caused by the violence and annoyance committed against the Kafirs by inhabitants, with respect to which they had complained to the Field Sergeant that Willem Prinsloo, sen., had taken possession of some of their cattle, and also of Marthinus Prinsloo, by whom or by some of his companions, during a journey into Kafirland, one of the subjects of Captain Gaggabie had been killed; regarding which complaints, however, these persons had advanced opposite allegations, or the best exculpatory pleas they had to offer.

It is by no means improbable that [the Xhosa's] complaints and accusations are more or less founded in fact, for the natural disposition of the Kafirs, however revengeful it may on the one hand be, is, on the other, not so cruel as to provoke them to such daring attempts without just cause.

The Council must be well aware that any endeavour to ascertain the precise truth by close examination would be rendered nugatory by this great distance.

It is meanwhile certain that most of the family of W. Prinsloo, sen., are mischievous inhabitants of that country, who cause disquiet and will not fail to do all that is possible to have the Kafirs removed thence, in order to enlarge the extent of their own farms. Thus the promise made to your Excellency by the Kafir Captain Koba, to remove beyond Fish river with his people, is already used as a good pretext to justify [the Prinsloos] in forcibly urging the Kafirs to fulfil that promise (although no orders have been as yet given to proceed to these extremities).

I should imagine that the object of your Excellency in those negotiations was not so much to extend the country for the benefit of our inhabitants, as, by their separation from the Kafirs, to prevent, as far as possible, the increasing illicit traffic with that people, by which, as experience has taught, much violence and annoyance to that people on the part of the inhabitants is brought about, which naturally produces the hostilities of those tribes. Probably your Excellency and Council will deem it necessary, before coming to any final determination, to await the report of the result of the last commando of the burghers; but . . . the anticipation that unless proper means be adopted betimes for the purpose of pacifying the Kafirs, further evils may, perhaps, be expected from them, or from the Bushmen, who are, as it is now said, beginning to unite with the Kafirs; all these considerations have urged me, under your indulgence, earnestly to deliberate upon what is the most advisable course in this matter. . . .

4.1b Knowing no other means of preventing the daily threatened violence of the Kafirs than proceeding in order to beat the unreasonable portion into a proper peace, I attacked them.

—Report of Commandant A. van Jaarsveld to the Cape Council of Policy, 20 July 1781. (From the translation in Moodie, *The Record*, III, p. 110.)

Adriaan van Jaarsveld (1745–1801) was appointed commandant of the eastern frontier in October 1780. He had made his name as a cunning and resourceful leader of commandos on the north-eastern frontier in the bitter war of extermination against the 'Bushmen'. Van Jaarsveld was authorized to raise commandos and to use force to drive the Xhosa over the border if peaceful methods proved unsuccessful.

The Kafirs having, subsequently to the treaty, again moved in among our people with all their property [*met all het haren*], it became of the most urgent necessity that resistance should be offered to this evidently impending violence [*daags drygende gewelt*].

I therefore assembled a strong Commando, and began to expel the Kafirs on the 23rd of May last, at the farm of the burger Erasmus Smit. I warned Captain Koba in the most earnest manner to depart with all his people, and also to tell all the other Captains to return to their own country; when he went away, with much reluctance [*met veel tegen*], I prosecuted my journey beyond De Bruyns Hoogte, to the Field Sergeant Cornelis Botma's where, having particularly inquired into all the messages from the Kafirs, as also into the molestation they had committed upon the farms by night, with occupying the farms, and taking away from them by force the faithful servants of the inhabitants, I found that the matter had reached the utmost pitch, and that it was very necessary to stop it, either by gentle means or by force.

On the 1st June, I warned the nearest Captains, Jerambam [Jalamba?], Luca and Bazana, in the presence of the whole Commando, that they must remove, and that we must also have a restoration of the stolen cattle, to which they would not even give any answer, but pressed in among us, every one of them having his weapons in his hands; on which I again, as before ordered them to depart in the name of the Governor, so that friendship might be preserved; and, leaving them peacably, returned to our camp.

On the 2nd, having come to them as before, I found that they had not made the least preparation to depart, and they conducted themselves towards me as before, and said they would not go. On this the interpreter, Karkotie, secretly warned me to be well on my guard, not only because they were a people with whom he was very well acquainted, but also that he had heard them, with his own ears, encouraging each other to push in boldly among us, and pretend to ask for tobacco, when we could do nothing to them lest we should shoot our own men. I reflected upon this, and remarked, with some uneasiness, that the Kafirs kept me surrounded by ten or twelve of their armed men, which I had before thought was that they might listen to what I was saying, when I formed a sudden resolution, and again ordered them, for the last time, to remove within two days, otherwise that on my return they must expect a battle. We then retired from them, and thought that they hounded their dogs after us.

On the 6th, I went to them for the third time; and as we approached them, they were again ready to push in among us with their weapons, but were forbidden by me with sharp threats, and I ordered [my men] to keep in the saddle and retire from them; but the Kafirs, following quickly, again pressed in among our men, on which we halted and drew up the Commando in a line, so that we could fire to the rear as well as in front, and let the men dismount; and as I clearly saw that if we allowed the Kafirs to make the first attack, it could not be otherwise than that many must fall on my side, I hastily collected all the tobacco the men had with them, and having cut it into small bits, I went about twelve paces in front, and threw it to the Kafirs, calling to them to pick it up; they ran out from amongst us and forgot their plan. I then gave the word to fire, when the said three Captains and all their fencible men were overthrown and slain, and part of their cattle, to the number of 800, taken.

Further—knowing no other means of preventing the daily threatened violence of the Kafirs and putting an end to the numberless complaints of the inhabitants, than proceeding in order, if possible, to beat the unreasonable [*onbehoorlyke*] portion of the Kafirs into a proper peace—on the 7th to the 10th I returned to our camp at the place of W. Prinsloo, and went out again, upon and behind the Boschberg, where I found the other portion of the Kafirs, namely the Captains Koba, Magoti, and Thatthoe; attacked them also, took from them 1030 head of cattle, and informed them through the prisoners, that whenever they fulfilled the promise they had made to His Excellency, and had also given up the cattle, theirs should be restored to them, and the peace should be renewed. . . .

4.2a I do not know that I am subject to the Kaffirs, and that they are to lord it over me, my cattle, and servants.

—Letter from Coenraad de Buys to the landdrost of Graaff-Reinet, 6 April 1788. (From the translation in Moodie *Afschriften*, Vol. 5, Cape Archives. The original cannot be found.)

Coenraad de Buys (1761 to after 1825) was a strong and colourful frontier personality, forming closer associations with some non-whites than was the norm among colonists. At the time of the following letter he was living with a 'Coloured' woman, later he formed a liaison with the mother of the Xhosa paramount chief Ngqika and subsequently married a Tembu woman. De Buys was also accused of assaulting Xhosa, and thus provoking the frontier war which broke out in 1793.

[I consider it my duty] to tell you what I have found out and what has happened to me. The Kaffir Captain has gone to live close to my cattle farm and 15 of my cattle are missing which I cannot find. My presumption is that he has stolen them. The same is the case with Wijnand Bezuidenhout who has lost three. I have also caught one of the Hottentots who have been in Caffreland; and I asked him kindly and without compulsion what were the intentions of the Kaffir Captain Langa; and he replied that it was some time since he had been in Caffreland and that he did not know what he intends now, but that when he was in Caffreland Langa and his men meant to attack the Christians, because it was said that one of the Kaffirs, who had been into a sheep kraal in the night, and had stolen sheep, had been shot dead, and I do not know that such things may be, for men are pilfered and robbed, and I do not know that I am subject to the Kaffirs, and that they are to lord it over me, my cattle, and servants. I know not what it means, it seems no longer of any importance that I submit my complaints of what has been done to me by the Kaffirs, but I receive no help and no support, and I do not know for what reason. It would seem as if false odium had been given against my complaint, which I have truly stated, and which I can prove. I hereby sign that if you Sir and the Heemraden think that I have spoken falsely in the complaint which I made, and which I now make, you are welcome to regard me as a seditious person, and I should be deserving of punishment. But were I ever so much a friend of the Kaffirs [*Cafvers broeder*] as I should be if I defended them for their thefts, I would not dare to complain against them. . . .

4.2b It is a hard thing to be oppressed by the heathens on our own loan-farms.

—Letter from Gerrit Scheepers to Landdrost Woeke of Graaff-Reinet, 2 Dec. 1789. (Translated from the original in the Cape Archives, GR 1/9.)

Gerrit Scheepers was a colonist living in the Zuurveld, the disputed area which at various stages was claimed by Khoikhoi and Gqunukhwebe (the earliest settlers) as well as colonists and Xhosa (most of whom moved into the area particularly from 1780). The colonists expected that the government, to whom they paid taxes for their farms, should force the Xhosa to retreat beyond the Fish River, the official boundary proclaimed by Governor Van Plettenberg in 1780.

This letter is written to state my complaint concerning the annoyances which I suffer from the Kaffir chief Langa on my farm, 'Soete Melks Vontijn'. He is now located, with his people and cattle, between Zwaanepoel's farm and mine, and not only lets his cattle graze on the veld and drink up the water there, but also destroys the veld with fires. Not only I, but almost everyone in the vicinity of the Bushman's River is suffering annoyance from the Kaffirs around them. And they are coming in in such large numbers that I fear the land will be taken over before this has been realized or men can be seconded [to prevent it]. I have already been ruined once by the kaffirs, Sir, and I fear for the second time. Thus I am requesting that you, Sir, should still care for us as a father, for it is a hard thing to be oppressed by the heathens on our own loan-farms. Therefore I humbly request a speedy response. . . .

4.3a [Unless these measures against both white and black are taken,] it will be impossible to prevent trade and intercourse between our people and the Kafirs, and thus a certain rupture and war may be expected.

—Letter from Landdrost H. C. D. Maynier to the Political Council of the Cape, March/April 1793. (From the translation in Moodie, *Afschriften*, Vol. 8, Cape Archives.)

H. C. D. Maynier (1760–1831) was appointed landdrost of Graaff-Reinet in 1793, at a time when frontier conflicts were increasing sharply. Maynier had already gained some experience of the frontier as secretary at the drostdy since 1789. Soon after his appointment and before taking up his new position Maynier outlined his proposed frontier policy in the following letter. In substance he adhered to official Company policy, which was to maintain territorial separation and to prevent trade or other intercourse between the Xhosa and the colonists. The directive to persuade the Xhosa by conciliatory measures to retreat beyond the Fish River had first been formulated by the Stellenbosch Krygsraad in 1780, and the strategy of preserving the military resources of the district for battle against the 'Bushmen' on the northern frontier had consistently been adopted by the Graaff-Reinet Krygsraad despite contrary pressures from the colonists in the south-eastern wards.

The undersigned Landdrost of Graaff-Reinet, being about to proceed to his magistracy, cannot avoid bringing it respectfully to your knowledge that, long before his departure from that place, repeated complaints were made by the inhabitants that a great number of Kafirs, who had been defeated in their last internecine wars and thus compelled to fly, had settled jointly in a group on this side of the Great Fish River. Being destitute of the necessities of life, they had constantly given all kinds of trouble to the inhabitants either by stealing their cattle or damaging the crops with the few cattle brought with them. Their mischief and rapacity are frequently attended with the most abominable murders, and all the friendly measures and gentle means devised and employed in order, if possible, to induce these expelled tribes beyond the Great Fish River have not produced the slightest effect.

This has been attended with the consequence that various ill-disposed inhabitants, almost all residing on De Bruins Hoogte, the Great Fish River or in the Zuurveld, seeing that not the slightest consent has been given to their remonstrances [directed to the government] to have these creatures driven off their farms by force, but that, on the contrary, they were earnestly exhorted to treat that otherwise peaceable people with all possible moderation and to take great care not to incur high displeasure and punishment at the hands of their rulers by shedding any of their blood, have, under the pretext of daily fears of attack from the multitude of Kafirs wandering amongst them, endeavoured to evade their sacred obligation of forcibly opposing the wicked and ruinous enterprises of the ever-predatory Bushmen, by means of commandos or otherwise, and under the specious pretext of severe drought have removed with their families and stock beyond the Great Fish River, contrary to the express letter of the *placaat* of 5th April 1774, so frequently and imperatively brought to their notice.

From this it must naturally follow that, unless the culpable conduct of these people is immediately met by adequate measures, obliging them to carry out forthwith the commandos which are so absolutely necessary, and obliging them to reoccupy their farms on this side of the Great Fish River, and unless also the vagrant Kafirs are at the same time forced to settle themselves beyond the Great Fish River, the most fearful consequences and disorders may be expected. For whatever care and watchfulness may be employed, it will be impossible to prevent that trade and intercourse between our people and the Kafirs, so strictly forbidden by law, and thus a certain rupture and war between them and our people may be reasonably and justifiably expected. The first signs of this have already frequently appeared in the hostilities committed upon our inhabitants. As however it is for many reasons inadvisable to oppose force by force, measures should on the contrary be devised and executed to secure constant peace with that nation, to reconcile to each other chiefs now continually at war, to bring back to this side of the Fish River the inhabitants who settled on their own authority beyond the appointed boundaries, and thus to cut off entirely the intercourse between them and the Kafirs. The use of force is especially inadvisable in the unpleasant and lamentable state of Graaff-Reinet with reference to the constantly plundering Bushmen. . . .

4.3b We are in a perilous condition because of the Kafirs.

—Letter from H. J. van Rensburg to Landdrost H. C. D. Maynier, 10 June 1793. (Translated from the original in the Cape Archives, GR 12/2.)

H. J. van Rensburg (1759–1828) was a burgher officer (veldwachtmeester) *in the Zuurveld, and would later play a prominent part in the Graaff-Reinet rising of 1801.*

At this time he was still sympathetic towards Maynier as landdrost, although he was to suffer considerable losses in the frontier war of 1793. The following letter was written soon after open hostilities had broken out in May 1793.

My lord and good friend Maynier.

I inform your Honour that we are in a perilous condition because of the Kaffirs, that my immediate neighbours have all fled and that I am the outermost, and that I see no means of fleeing in consequence of the two wounded men who were brought to me according to your Honour's orders to protect the outermost men. I always thought that your Honour would provide better orders, for I am nearly ruined. . . . I doubt not that your Honour will send us speedy aid, or shall I and my other men allow ourselves to be murdered? For there are so many men dead already, and I also see my death daily before my eyes. Many men have innocently fallen who never had any blame from the Kaffirs. As to all your Honour has written about doing no harm to the Kaffirs, and thus taking the death of the people on your own conscience, I know that the Governor and Council can have given no orders to ruin and murder us. Your Honour may reflect and consider that it is a dangerous situation for all the people in accordance with your Honour's orders that we may not defend ourselves against that nation. . . .

4.3c Try all gentle means of bringing the Kafirs to an amicable agreement, for [at present] it is impossible to oppose them by force with any hope of success.

—Letter from Landdrost H. C. D. Maynier to H. J. van Rensburg, 6 Jan. 1794. (From the translation in Moodie, *Afschriften*, Vol. 8, Cape Archives. The original cannot be found.)

With Landdrost Faure of Swellendam, Maynier had led the combined burgher commandos during the frontier war of 1793. He found it impossible to conquer the Xhosa, and decided to conclude peace before the commando had carried out its instructions to drive all Xhosa from the Zuurveld and retake the cattle they had stolen. As a result he became very unpopular among the colonists, while complaints about Xhosa incursions into the Zuurveld persisted. According to Moodie, when the following letter was brought before the board of heemraden in May 1794, J. G. Tregard said, 'You have satisfied the Government, but have you satisfied the people?' On the same occasion, though, Van Jaarsveld maintained that 'the best way of making a lasting peace with the Kafirs would be to give them back the Zuurveld, as having formerly been their own land'.

I have this day received your letters of the 9th, 18th and 29th of December last, and have learnt from them with the utmost surprise and concern that the Kafirs continue to rob and murder. As it does not however appear to me from your said letters that the whole body of the Kafirs are guilty in this matter, but only some wanderers and rogues (*schelmen*), it seems to me that nothing else can be done for the present by you and the other good inhabitants than abide by the promise I have so solemnly made, to pursue such wandering Kafirs on their traces and shoot them. For you best know that it is the desire of the Captains that all Kafirs guilty of such acts after the conclusion of peace should be pursued and shot—and that we have not to apprehend that we shall thus excite the hatred of that nation.

Besides I am not at present in a condition to comply with your request of sending you the assistance of some men, or of a Commando, as well on account of the horse sickness, and because the Bushmen are more furious than ever in this part of the country, as because everyone is now engaged in trying to harvest the little corn that has survived the recent severe drought. . . .

. . . I again most seriously recommend you to try all gentle means of bringing the Kafirs to an amicable agreement. For the reasons above stated, added to many other unfortunately concurring reasons and circumstances, it is impossible to oppose them by force with any hope of success—at least until Providence makes our hands somewhat more free and we find ourselves in a condition to attack them with force—and to bring them to obedience. For as experience has, alas! more than too well proved, we should run a much greater risk of making matters worse, than of improving them.

For these reasons, you must not only give no assistance to those who have come to you and formed a plan so ruinous for the whole country as to retake from the Kafirs any of their cattle still to be found among them, but you must most earnestly forbid them in my name, and point out to them that, if they disregard my directions, they will bring on themselves the hatred of their fellow burgers, as well as well-deserved displeasure and punishment from the supreme Government. For such persons, whether they obtain their object or not, would in all probability, like other faint-hearted people, abandon the country, and leave their fellow burgers exposed to the fury of the Kafirs. . . .

4.3d The discord with these Kaffirs should at all times be counteracted with the most lenient measures and one should resort to extremes only when it is essential for defence.

—Report of Landdrost H. C. D. Maynier to Commissary A. J. Sluysken on the frontier war of 1793, 31 March 1794. (Translated from the original in the Cape Archives, C106, pp. 178–201.)

Maynier presented his official report on the war of 1793 during his visit to Cape Town early in 1794. Setting out to answer not so much the general question on the causes of the war, but—in accordance with his instructions—the narrower question concerning what had provoked the Xhosa into making war, he found much to blame in the colonists' conduct. From the colonists' side also the disagreement on Maynier's Xhosa policy grew irreconcilable, leading eventually to their expulsion of Maynier from the district in February 1795.

The undersigned, together with the landdrost of Swellendam, the ensign Hans Abue and other burgher officers, produced their provisional report on the result of the expedition on the 27th November last year. This expedition was conducted on Your Excellency's orders, to drive the plundering and murdering Kaffirs from the properties of the Christians, to settle these Christians there again, to provide them with adequate compensation for the thefts committed, and to effect a stable peace with the Kaffirs.

We then had no opportunity to report to Your Excellency on the allocation made among the inhabitants of the cattle taken from the Kaffirs, as well as on the actual reasons and causes to which one could attribute the uprising of this otherwise so peaceable nation, as no complete enquiry into this could then have taken place. . . .

. . . Now concerning the second point, viz. the result of the closer enquiry which I have made into the causes of the theft and destruction brought about by the Kaffirs.

In this respect, I have the honour to remark that in general the following should be regarded as the sources of the discord and unrest—

First, the continual intercourse which the inhabitants of this Colony have had with the Kaffirs for some years past, even to the extent of taking into service considerable numbers of this nation, contrary to the statutorily enacted orders in this respect, and once in service cases of maltreatment occur. . . .

Secondly, various inhabitants have disregarded the express letter of the *placaat*, issued by this government on 19 July 1786, by crossing the Fish River, thus penetrating into Kaffirland, where they have increasingly settled.

This has brought about an irregular trade and barter with that nation, which has at all times been rightly regarded by the government as extremely detrimental for the country and has been strictly forbidden. . . .

. . . I shall now take the liberty of respectfully proposing . . . the measures which, in my opinion, could be suitable for preserving the peace with the Kaffirs or for making it a stable one:

Whoever has even an average knowledge of the disposition of our country and the nature of the Kaffir nation will quickly understand that the discord with them must bring about the most disastrous consequences for the colony and its inhabitants. The colony is already plagued by the vexations of the Bushmen, who have now eventually been reduced to a wild and savage nation, staying alive through theft alone, so that the inhabitants of the colony are hardly able to protect themselves and their possessions against them. And who does not then realize that hostilities with the Kaffirs, who are so powerful a people and of whom—as experience has taught—even a small part can throw the country into tumult, will produce the most fatal consequences for this colony.

I am convinced, Your Excellency, though I speak under respectful correction, that these consequences cannot be countered, nor can peace and quiet be preserved, by any other means than by lenient and moderate measures.

Such measures, as I have often found, can have a great influence on the Kaffir nation, as a people susceptible to reason and jealous of their freedom. Yet these are also measures so alien to the way of thinking of many of our inhabitants that I must add, though it grieves me greatly to do so, that in continuing with these measures I am meeting with the most extreme opposition and have difficulty in keeping some of the inhabitants from violence against this nation. Signs of this have already appeared, as in instances such as Lieutenant Carolus Johannes Tregard's declaring . . . in an insolent manner that the commandos against the Kaffirs were not well-executed, on the grounds that the inhabitants did not get their stolen cattle back, that the Kaffirs had not been sufficiently punished, and that peace had been made only between the landdrost and the Kaffirs. He also asserted that the inhabitants had to go short of cattle because the Hottentots had also received some. . . .

Your Excellency will immediately perceive the unreasonableness of these allegations, when you consider that the Hottentots who served in the commandos were always employed where the fighting was thickest and in the most dangerous places. They consistently did their best with all signs of willingness, and risked their lives, so that no objection was then raised to giving those on this expedition a reward. . . . Moreover, this was done in a way that could never be considered to have been at all to the detriment of the interests of the inhabitants, as most of the Hottentots had to be satisfied with one or two animals, notwithstanding the fact that the number of the Hottentots on most expeditions against the Kaffirs or Bushmen certainly far exceeded that of the Christians, so that caution bids one ensure that these Hottentots are never tempted to leave the Christians and ally themselves with the enemy. . . .

But to continue. . . . I have remarked and I believe that this is in accordance with

Your Excellency's intentions, that the discord with these Kaffirs should at all times be counteracted with the most lenient measures. At the least, one should in no cases resort to extreme measures, but only do so when it is essential as a means of defence, and all other more humane measures have been tried without success.

One consequence of these principles is that it is of the greatest importance for Your Excellency that immediate and effective steps be taken to prevent commandos from being undertaken in any circumstances except those of absolute necessity. . . .

With this I should end my report, were it not that both my duty and good order require that I bring to the attention of Your Excellency the insolence to which some few persons in this district have resorted, for the sole reason that I have not given free rein to their designs and inclinations with respect to the Kaffirs and other natives. . . . And therefore I regard myself as being obliged to beg Your Excellency in the humblest manner to maintain his authority in the face of disobedient persons, in whichever way Your Excellency deems to be most suitable for the preservation of good order in the district of Graaff-Reinet and the maintenance of the authority of this government. If this is done, people in this district will realize that however far they may be from the capital, the capital still is, and continues to be, able to safeguard and protect her legitimate authority against all malevolent designs. . . .

4.4a The Kaffirs have penetrated with force.

—The *Tesamenstemming*, signed by Barend J. Bester and 43 others, 29 Jan. 1795. (Translated from the copy of the original in the Cape Archives, VC 68.)

At a meeting demanded by the rebellious colonists and held on 6 February 1795, the following document, entitled Tesamenstemming *and detailing their grievances, was read aloud. Maynier was ordered to leave the district immediately and some officers who had supported Maynier's peace policy towards the Xhosa were also removed from their posts. The remaining militia officers were threatened with a similar fate if they did not 'take up the sword again' and recover the cattle captured by the Xhosa in 1793.*

. . . The Kaffirs have penetrated with force and have deprived us of a large part of the territory which we, the citizens, inhabit and which was granted to us as a loan by the honourable Company. They have taken all our cattle by force, taken the lives of citizens and their workers, and driven the farmers from the area so that it was left open for the enemy. At this Mr Maynier and his council issued an edict stipulating that every farmer was to return to his farm within one month, and that, if this was not done, he would give the farm to another. At once the threat can be seen! While the farmers are suffering destruction and deprivation enough through the stock-theft and arson of the Kaffirs, Mr Maynier intended to place the farmers in a more difficult position by using his right of eviction. This devastation by the enemy has left us in such dire poverty that the farmers have no means of supporting their wives and children, and it embitters every man because Mr Maynier . . . does not allow us to resist our enemy, but gives instructions for them to be allowed to pass unhindered where they will; yes, passes are even issued to them to go in and out of Kaffirland, and to spy in the country for as long as they like. . . .

4.4b Do our God and the laws of nature not teach us that we may and must meet force with force?

—Letter of complaint to Commissary A. J. Sluysken, signed by Barend J. Bester and 276 others, 16 April 1795. (Translated from the copy of the original in the Cape Archives, VC 68.)

4.4 *The writings of the citizens of Graaff-Reinet 1795*

In April 1795 a commission led by O. G. de Wet arrived in Graaff-Reinet to inquire into the causes of the disturbances. At a meeting on 30 April the following Klagschrift, *emanating from Bruyntjeshoogte, was handed to De Wet. For the most part it consisted of a series of scurrilous allegations against Maynier in particular, and other Graaff-Reinet officials in general. Barend J. Bester was a leading member of the* Volkstem *party. (See Chapter 6, Introduction.)*

. . . We offer for Your Honour's consideration whether it is not a most grievous hardship for a citizen to have to see himself robbed of his cattle, his servants murdered, himself to go in danger of his life; and then not to be allowed to pursue such murderers and arsonists, or to avenge himself upon them, but to be allowed only to go out with a small force, which neither dares to, nor is able to, take back his lawful property from the enemy. We ask with respect whether it were then not better, when the Kaffirs come to attack us, if we were to surrender ourselves to their command and desire, with wife and children, with all we possess, without offering any resistance, than to continue under such a restriction. To subject ourselves to our enemy, who murders, robs and destroys us—we ask under respectful correction—is that a law? Do our God and the laws of nature not teach us that, when another would take my life, or would make himself master of my property, I may and must meet force with force? And now that we meet our enemy in this way, who robs and murders us, who seeks our very souls, is it not then a grievous hardship for us to be placed under such a restriction as not to be able to avenge ourselves with an equal force? No Bushman surrenders without resistance. . . . Oh Great and Honourable Lord, consider it yet, is this not hard and sorrowful for your poor, miserable and suffering citizens? Should they not become despairing and downcast? Had this happened elsewhere, would Maynier not have been ripped apart by every man? Does this not cry out against God and all righteousness? . . .

4.4c If the populace were not afraid that they were too weak and would require assistance, hostilities against the Kaffirs would long since have commenced, for they regard this as the most suitable way of regaining their lost cattle and farms.

—Memorial presented by A. van Jaarsveld and A. P. Burger to O. G. de Wet, 7 May 1795. (Translated from the copy of the original in the Cape Archives, VC 68.)

Adriaan van Jaarsveld was one of the leading figures in the Graaff-Reinet rebellion, but he did not associate himself too closely with the Volkstem. *He preferred to act as an intermediary between the* Volkstem *and the authorities, as in the following memorial which he and Burger presented to De Wet, outlining the wishes of the* Volkstem *as ascertained at a meeting with them.*

In the first place, the people [*het volk*] say that the commando against the Kaffirs was not properly executed by the landdrost and heemraden, but that it was conducted in an arbitrary manner by them to the ruin of the country and the people. This the people give as their first reason for acting against the landdrost and heemraden, as well as the following reasons.

Secondly, that the officers of the militia have allowed the sword to be taken from their hands and the people now demand that the sword be taken up again for their protection. If this does not happen, [the authority of] the militia officers will never again be acknowledged by the people. . . .

Finally . . . it has become clear and certain to the undersigned that the people wish to see that the Kaffirs called the Madankies [Dange] are defeated, and wish to preserve peace only with Zambie [Ndlambe]. The reason why they have not come right out with this is that they fear the consequences, as do we, and therefore they insist that this [fighting] be done on the orders of a higher authority, so that they might retain the right to demand help and assistance at all times in case of need. If that populace [*dat hoop volks*] were not afraid that they were too weak and would require assistance, hostilities against the Kaffirs would long since have commenced. They do not expect to get such help from Camdebo and Zuurbergh without orders to that effect from the Government. For they regard this [commencing hostilities against the Kaffirs] as the most suitable way of regaining their lost cattle and farms. . . .

4.5 The positive orders of Government were not to attack the Caffres; but to promote Peace and Tranquillity between them and the Inhabitants by mild and gentle means; and to protect the Hottentots against the Oppressions and Violence which they continually suffered from the Boors.

—Provisional Justification of H. C. D. Maynier to the Cape Court of Justice, April 1802. (From Theal, *Records of the Cape Colony*, Vol. 4, pp. 283–329.)

Maynier returned to Graaff-Reinet as resident commissioner on the frontier for an equally controversial two years from 1799 to 1801. After his recall an official inquiry was instituted into his conduct as commissioner. The following document is taken from his official defence on this occasion. Having investigated a series of accusations against Maynier, the commission pronounced him entirely innocent of all the charges brought against him.

Being appointed in the Year of 1793 as Landdrost of Graaff-Reinet, the disturbances rose to such a height that Government found itself under the necessity of allowing a numerous *Commando* of both the Districts of Zwellendam and Graaff-Reinet to act against the Caffres. The Landdrost of Zwellendam, Mr Faure, and myself were placed at the head of this Commando. After having defeated the Caffres, and taken a good deal of their Cattle, which were divided by Mr Faure and me among those who had suffered by the invasions of the Caffres, and who had behaved well in the Commando, we made peace with the Caffres, a thing of great importance to this Country.

I then employed all means to convince the Inhabitants of Bruinshoogte that it was their real Interest to live in peace with the Caffres, but in vain, they longed for nothing so much as to attack the Caffres again and to profit by new troubles. . . .

The positive orders of Government were not to attack the Caffres; but to promote Peace and Tranquillity between them and the Inhabitants by mild and gentle means; and to protect the Hottentots against the Oppressions and Violence which they continually suffered from the Boors.

These orders so coincident with my own feelings were of course executed by me with all possible punctuality. But the more I fulfilled in this regard both as a Man and as a Public Officer, the more Enemies and Adversaries I created to myself among those who saw their schemes thereby frustrated. . . .

The Hottentots I always endeavoured to engage to take service with the Boors, and the latter I persuaded that it was their and their Children's interest to treat the Hottentots with kindness; and to impress upon their minds that the idea of extirpating the Hottentots, or to make Slaves of them was but a Chimera, that Nature had placed these Creatures here, that most of them were already robbed of their Land and their Cattle, but that Divine Providence which always provides for its Creatures would certainly not allow the execution of the horrid enterprizes which many among them meditated, and a double punishment would attend such crimes. . . .

This Plan of driving the Caffres and Hottentots beyond the Groote Vis River so much favoured by some, I have always disapproved, and maintain that whoever knows the State of that part of the Country where they live, and the Immense Woods and Dens which offer a safe retreat to them, will look upon such a plan to be unwise, because greatly difficult to be accomplished, and still more so to confine them there, and cruel on account of the hardships which they must consequently suffer. And I feel the most perfect conviction that Peace may be preserved with these Creatures, by fair means, and with little trouble.

I do not say that they should be allowed to proceed unmolested in Stealing the Cattle of the Peasantry. This I have always opposed, and encouraged the Boors to Pursue and fire upon such Vagabond Hottentots and Caffres as they should find Stealing their Cattle; and so that this might be the better effected, I formed small patrols on the Limits of the District, consisting of the Young Peasantry, who on the least alarm rode about and secured the District. But with this they were not satisfied, they wished for *Great Commandos*, they desired to destroy the Craal where their inoffensive Women and Children dwelt. This I always resolutely opposed with all my means. I have ever represented to the Boors that they would by such deeds bring ruin upon themselves, and that I trembled for the consequences, that I should not be astonished if in that case the Caffres and Hottentots should not only commit further depredations but destroy a Great part of the Districts of Graaff-Reinet and Zwellendam, the beginning of which might be easily seen, but the end and consequences thereof would be incalculable. One need only reflect on the Bosjesmen, from which may be learnt that a Continual War with these Creatures for nearly 34 Years has produced no change in them, has had no other effect than to render them the implacable enemies of the Boors.

If therefore the Hottentots and the Caffres should be treated in the same way, what will be the consequence? Should they like the Bosjesmen, who are but a handful of men in comparison of them, become the implacable enemies of the Boors, no Farmer would then be safe.

They may have high notions of the (so called) Commandos; I have attended many of them, and not neglected to make my observations with as much care as possible, and whatever may be said of them to the Contrary, I have always found that when there were not a considerable number of Hottentots with them to be placed in the front, and the first exposed to danger, they never succeeded. . . .

It should not be imagined that the Hottentots who refrain from disturbances are quiet from Love and Attachment to the Boors. Such supposition will prove deceitful. Every circumstance shews that they think themselves to be the weaker party, and it is the fear of this ideal or imaginary superiority of the Boors which keeps them quiet.

To preserve Peace and Tranquillity in the country, it is indispensibly necessary to maintain this prepossession, but tumults, disobedience, and distrust in Government are calculated neither to promote Happiness to the Boors, nor to maintain this prepossession; and these inconsiderate and unnecessary commandos are as little likely to contribute to one or the other. Havock and destruction rather follow their Steps and, like Oil thrown into the Flame, increase the Blaze to Explosion. . . .

4.6 We are strong enough to recover our belongings at the point of the sword and to provide a peace that would give quiet and security for years to come.

—Letter from Commandants Botha, Linden and Van Rooyen of the Sundays River to Governor Janssens, 22 May 1803. (From W. Blommaert and J. A. Wiid (Eds.), *The Journal of Dirk Gysbert van Reenen*, pp. 119–120.)

4.6 *Frontier commandants on the need for a commando 1803*

In hostilities during the period 1799 to 1802 the frontier colonists suffered devastating losses at the hands of the Xhosa. Nearly half of the farms in the eastern districts were plundered, and large numbers of cattle and sheep were lost. Early in 1803 Governor Janssens of the new Batavian administration visited the frontier to investigate the situation.

It is certainly true that Your Honour has been placed over us, as father and commander, to protect and guard this Colony of South Africa; but it is at the same time our duty to assist you in this task. We have no doubt that Your Honour, having this in mind, will not fail to support our good intentions, namely, that we must recover from the savages the territory up to the boundary-line constituted by the Great Fish River, where it was previously fixed.

As regards our cattle, if they cannot be recovered amicably, a peace that safeguards our interests will console us for the loss, but we must insist on the return of our horses, slaves and guns. Undoubtedly Your Honour's main intent is to secure, with respect to the savages, peace and quiet for us; nevertheless we shall consider their victories as robbery which they have accomplished in a feeble and surreptitious way. We on the contrary are strong enough to recover our belongings at the point of the sword and to provide a peace that would give quiet and security to your Government for years to come. This, however, cannot be achieved otherwise than with a good supply of powder and lead, and by obliging our fellow-burgers to take up arms with us. But, in order to see an end to the calamities, we unanimously desire peace, yet without the cession of a foot of ground. It is in this sense that we shall not fail to obey Your Honour. . . .

4.7 The first thing then is for everyone to obey, and to occupy himself with his own affairs, to forget all partisanship, to leave all public affairs to the government, and to cultivate his land and guard his cattle. In this way peace will be preserved in the colony.

—Letter from W. S. van Ryneveld to A. Stockenström (Sr), landdrost of Graaff-Reinet, 23 Jan. 1806. (Translated from the original in the Cape Archives, G.R. 9/10.)

The following letter by Van Ryneveld was written only a few days after the capitulation of the Batavian administration under Governor Janssens and the start of the second British occupation in January 1806. At the outset Van Ryneveld was appointed chief civil magistrate. From the letter it is clear how this official's views were still shaped by the frontier crisis at the time of the first British occupation, when the frontier wars of 1793 and 1799 were compounded by burgher rebellions in 1795, 1799 and 1801 as well as by the Khoikhoi rising in 1799.

. . . It will not be necessary for me to point out to Your Honour the necessity of this, as the experience of this colony has already shown by so many telling examples how bitter are the consequences of unrest and dissension in these circumstances. The first disturbances among the farmers always lead to disturbances among the Hottentots and Kaffirs, who try at once to profit from such circumstances. The farmers, who are widely dispersed, are then filled with fear, they leave their farms, come together, and from fear make unnecessary commandos. On these occasions, the innocent are sacrificed first, and from this arises an internal war between farmers, Kaffirs and Hottentots. The bitterest consequences are always suffered by the farmers whose wives and children are the unfortunate victims of these wars. And thus the entire colony bears the burden arising from [the promotion of unrest] in these circumstances.

The reason why I write to Your Honour is to prevent this *now*, while there is *time*. Since first the capital and then the Governor and General, Janssens, as well as the remaining Batavian troops have surrendered, all idea of hostility has come to an end in the colony, and one should pay sole attention to ensuring peace and order.

To achieve this purpose, it will therefore be necessary for Your Honour, as landdrost, to exhort the inhabitants of your district to remain quiet and peaceful. They are to be informed that if this occurs, they will be treated as friends by the English government, and will enjoy all possible protection. Nothing that might have happened previously will be held against them at all; in this respect, all will be treated as forgotten.

The first thing then is for everyone to obey, and to occupy himself with his own affairs, to forget all partisanship, to leave all public affairs to the government, and to cultivate his land and guard his cattle. In this way peace will be preserved in the colony. If this does not happen, then those who cause disturbances will certainly only have themselves to blame for the bitter consequences which usually result and which could not be avoided now. I ask you, Landdrost, to impress these principles upon the farmers, and to assure them that no account at all is to be taken of what has previously happened in the outlying districts, that nobody at all has anything to fear, that all local arrangements will continue to be based on just principles, just as was the case with the previous government, as long as all preserve the peace, nobody commits any injustice nor gives rise to disorder. . . .

4.8a The commando has done no more than punish the evildoers, and I have never shot dead an innocent man.

—Letters from J. C. Greyling to Landdrost A. Stockenström (Sr), 6 Dec. 1809. (Translated from the originals in the Cape Archives, GR 12/1A.)

Existing regulations prohibited colonists from pursuing or firing on marauders except in self-defence. From internal evidence it appears that Field-Cornet Greyling, the writer of the following letters, was suspected by Landdrost Stockenström of having committed irregularities on an unauthorized commando.

6 December 1809

As the Kaffirs have caused such apprehension among the inhabitants in this part of our district by their constant and incessant plundering, the position of various inhabitants has deteriorated greatly. From time to time this plundering grows worse and causes intolerable difficulties. Thus I have taken the liberty of bringing this to your attention, and I humbly request that if possible such arrangements might be made as would, in your judgement, be useful and necessary. As far as humanitarian treatment is concerned, it will be well known to you that all benevolence which has been exercised towards them has produced no other result than a general mockery of and contempt for the Christians. . . . Another deplorable matter is the ruin of the colonists of Uitenhage. They have been plagued day in and day out by the Kaffirs to such an extent that it has become unbearable for them. Who knows how soon they will have to leave their district—which could have the consequence of causing further disturbances in our district. Once again, I request that you make arrangements or carry out a plan for ensuring a favourable outcome which frees the colonists from plunder, and from the consequence which will follow in its trail, namely murder. . . .

29 December 1809

You write to me, Sir, of the bloodthirstiness of the inhabitants. But it would be hard on you if you were to see your property disappearing every day. And if there was an end to it, then it could be endured. I have done as much as is in my power, and continue to do so daily. Yet I still see no change and it is getting worse by the day, as you will be able to see from my reports. And I think that the murders of Christians committed by this nation, of which you will indeed have heard, have now continued long enough.

You are also very dissatisfied, Sir, with the activities of the commando. But we have done no more than punish the evildoers when we have found the stolen property, as I can testify myself and can prove to them in the case of the stolen horses. . . . Thus I can see how it has come about that the talebearers now no longer sleep and that they are believed and do not stop at that. And if my country should be ruined, then I feel that I shall have to account for the way in which I have abandoned it. Otherwise it would not have been necessary for me to act as field-cornet and things could have remained as they were. I have never shot dead an innocent man, and of this I can testify before my conscience. Yet it is hard for me to have to suffer at the hands of this [?odious] nation. Potgieter and I made peace with a kraal where there was no stolen property and that kraal still remains among our people. Thus we have not killed any who were innocent. . . .

4.8b We now see no further possibility of living in this district any longer unless the Kaffirs are driven into their own territory.

—Memorial of 11 frontier farmers to Landdrost Cuyler of Uitenhage, 19 April 1810. (Translated from the original in the Cape Archives, CO 2572.)

The British administration thought it inadvisable to embark on strong military measures against the Xhosa on the eastern frontier while the Napoleonic wars were still in progress. During the first decade of the century Xhosa strength grew considerably as Ndlambe and a few allied chieftains settled in the Zuurveld. From 1809 cattle thieving by marauding bands greatly increased. Though troops were sent to the frontier, Governor Caledon was not prepared to embark on a frontier war and refused to commit them in a war, or to allow a general commando against the Xhosa.

Honourable Sir! We, the undersigned, have noticed the deterioration of this country with much sorrow. For this reason, we have felt it necessary to canvass the most virtuous of its inhabitants and convey to Your Honour trustworthy testimony of the dangerous conditions facing the inhabitants. For not only have our cattle been stolen, but, which is even more disastrous, we see the murder of slaves and Hottentots. In the month of March 6 men-slaves and 4 Hottentots were murdered by the Kaffirs. Also, at least 500 cattle were stolen.

Honourable Sir! Our most humble request is that, for the general good of the inhabitants, it should please Your Honour to communicate the content of this document, with a suitable address, to His Excellency the Governor and Supreme Commander, as soon as is possible, because it is most grievous for the inhabitants to be robbed each day. And, in these dangerous times, our wish is that it may please Your Honour to view with concern their dangerous and oppressive situation. Having seen convincing testimony of His Excellency's good will, in the dispatching of troops, we offer our heart-felt thanks in anticipation of His Excellency's much-needed further help. We now see no further possibility of living in this district any longer, unless the Kaffirs are driven into their own territory. And we hope that His Excellency will be favourably disposed to permit and effect by ordinance the proscription of the residents of this country, as the dangers are already of such a nature that this is required.

Gabriel Stols, field-commandant
B. J. de Klerk, Heemraad
Willem Nel, field-cornet
Louis Jacobus Nel, field-cornet
and 7 others.

4.9 Neither peace nor friendship can subsist between the inhabitants and the Kaffers while both inhabit the same country.

—Letter from Landdrost Anders Stockenström to Governor Caledon, August 1810. (From the translation in Moodie, *The Record*, V, pp. 57–58.)

Anders Stockenström (1757–1811), father of Sir Andries Stockenström, was landdrost of Graaff-Reinet from 1804 to 1811. In the following letter to Governor Caledon he gives a general description of the nature and causes of frontier conflict, based on his own experience and observation. Stockenström was killed at the start of the frontier war of 1811–1812, in a sudden massacre of a party of colonists while they were attempting to gain a settlement through negotiation.

. . . I trust your Excellency will permit me to submit some general observations upon the frontier districts, which, though they do not apply to the whole of this district, have much connection with some parts of it; and which, when compared by your Excellency with information already obtained, may enable your Excellency to judge of what may be justly said in favour of the inhabitants, and against them, as regards their present state.

When the Kaffers reside on the further side of the Fish River, they have more difficulties to contend with in stealing, as they have to drive the plunder a greater distance, and through more open country, and they are consequently more readily discovered and overtaken; so that there is in that case a possibility of living in a certain kind of amity with them.

In the Zuurveld, the case is different. Neither peace nor friendship can subsist between the inhabitants and the Kaffers while both inhabit the same country; and the residence of the latter in the colony is highly prejudicial to the inhabitants who live on and beyond Bruintjes Hoogte, along the Sunday, the Riet and the Vogel Rivers, and as far as Buffels Hoek.

The causes of this are interwoven in the character of the Kaffer, in that of the Colonist, and in the nature of the country. The Kaffers are naturally insatiable beggars and thieves. All domestic and agricultural labour being performed by the women, and the cattle being herded by the boys, the men have nothing to do but to hunt and to wander about among the colonists.

Not satisfied with staying a single day at one farm, they often remain several days, insisting upon having victuals furnished to them, and watching their opportunity to carry off something for their journey into the bargain. It often happens that one of the party makes off with some booty, while the rest remain to prevent suspicion. Sometimes the thieves, when afraid of being discovered, restore the booty themselves, pretending that they have recovered it from others, and demanding ample recompense for their trouble.

The bushes and thickets generally prevent detection until they have reached one of the kraals; to prevent the traces being followed, they do not leave the booty there, but take it away to some more distant kraal, or to the deep ravines, until they are able to exchange it beyond the Key, or to the Tambookies, and thus entirely conceal it.

The traces are not to be followed by the searchers after they have reached the first kraal, for they are obliterated by those of the cattle belonging to that kraal.

The inhabitants losing their property by these practices, sometimes to the extent of reducing them to poverty, are no longer so liberal in bestowing food; at least, they do not give it in such a friendly way, but often accompanied with bitter reproaches and threats.

The Kaffers, long accustomed to this kind of reception, and remarking that these threats are never carried into execution, treat the farmers with contempt, and often exhibit actual violence; but [?alarm them] chiefly by indirect messages through individual Kaffers, Ghomas, or Hottentots, that in the long nights they will attack the farmers, and commit robbery and murder.

The colonists are credulous and timorous, and have not as yet recovered from the dread produced by former events; and thus they dare not maintain their ground in that rugged country, through the long nights. . . . When all these things are considered, it is really no matter of surprise that at that time of year they take refuge in an open country, where by day every thing may be under the eye, and, if [something is] stolen in the night but not discovered until daybreak, where they have still hopes of overtaking the thieves before they reach the thickets.

In this hope, though often deceived by it, the inhabitants pass their time with less care and anxiety by day, and they value a good night's rest.

The retreat of the inhabitants of the Zuurveld has, however, this year obliged those of the nearer districts to remove also. Thus on Bruintjes Hoogte and beyond it they do not move, as they untruly allege, because they must fly from the Kaffers. It is true that in proportion as the inhabitants retire the Kaffers approach; there is not, however, the least reason to think that the latter intend to commence open hostilities. . . .

Such, my Lord, is a view of the case, drawn, I will presume to say, from the life [*naar vaarheid*]. Matters are so situated, that no change for the better is likely to occur for some months; but unless some precautions are adopted by government, we may expect a change for the worse. . . . Meanwhile it is my opinion that we should not absolutely prohibit their wandering visits [*kuyeren*], as in their opinion this prohibition is the reverse of a sign of amity. Particular kraals that might not discontinue their aggressions [*veel kwaad*] must be subjected to a proportionate correction. But, above all, we must hold out no threats, if we do not intend to execute them, for I consider this the great cause of their boldness, as they fancy us afraid or unable to punish them according to their deserts. . . .

4.10 Believe me the Kaffirs are no more to be trifled with.

—Despatches from Landdrost Andries Stockenström to the colonial government, 12 Feb. 1819 and 18 Feb. 1819. (From *The Autobiography of Sir Andries Stockenström,* Vol. I pp. 142–150.)

After a colonial force had driven the Xhosa from the Zuurveld in 1812, military detachments were stationed at border posts, but these were insufficient to prevent further cattle raids across the border. In 1817 the commando system was replaced by the reprisal system, under which burgher patrols accompanied by a military detachment could cross the border and demand compensation from the kraal to which the spoor of stolen cattle had been traced. The small military force on the frontier was insufficient to intimidate the Xhosa and its feeble attempts to punish kraals only exacerbated hostilities, as the young Andries Stockenström, landdrost of Graaff-Reinet from 1815, pointed out in the following letters. The immediate cause of the frontier war of 1818–1819 was an attempt by the colonial forces to intervene in the conflict between the Xhosa chiefs Ngqika (whom they favoured) and Ndlambe in 1818, leading to reprisal raids into the colony by Ndlambe in December 1818 and January 1819.

. . . I have thus far refrained from entering into any discussion respecting the state of the Eastern Frontier, for fear that my sentiments might have been construed into a wish to reflect upon the conduct of others, or to meddle with affairs not belonging to my line of business; but what I anticipated as the consequences of the last Commando into Kaffirland being in every respect realized, and a strong force from this district being again necessary for opposing the Kaffirs, I think that I would make myself unworthy of your confidence, and lose sight of the interests of the inhabitants entrusted to my superintendence, in a most essential point, were I longer to withhold from you that it is becoming more and more evident to every person knowing the Kaffirs and the state of the interior that the present system upheld with respect to the savages cannot be continued. Excuse me if I speak too clear—consider my motives, and your own zeal for the service will plead for my anxiety in this cause. Total silence would be better than partial candour mixed with the least duplicity, as the former would leave you to act for yourself, and the latter might lead you astray. How many lives have not been lost since the last Commando? What determined and successful attempts upon our armed parties have not lately been made by a race who formerly fled at the sight of a musket? And what else could be expected from a populous tribe driven to desperation by being deprived of all their cattle, their only means of subsistence; left to choose between starvation and retaliation? God forbid that I should plead the cause of cruel barbarians, who have given me too much cause for revenge. On the contrary, I think it absolutely necessary . . . that they be most effectually set down. . . .

. . . You will perhaps ask what would you have us do? If the farmers cannot be taken from their homes, are the Kaffirs not to be punished for the murder of two valuable officers, so many soldiers and others? Are they to triumph in the possession of the fruits of the industry of so many wretches reduced to beggary and nakedness by their depredations? On the contrary, I only object to inefficient measures whereby nothing can be gained but the revenge of the enemy, who, encouraged by partial successes, render the repetition of those petty Commandos necessary, whereby the inhabitants are obliged to be perpetually on the move, called away for instance during the lambing, ploughing or reaping season, as has been the case of late, the corn having been left ripe in many places and having perished on the field before a sickle could be brought to it. . . .

. . . The principal points are, in the first place, the absolute necessity, if anything at all be done, that a force be employed capable of crushing the Kaffirs most effectually, so as to reduce them to the necessity of praying for mercy, laying all your arms they have taken from the unfortunate victims of their cruelty at your feet, and bringing your deserters to your camp, for these are the most dangerous incendiaries among the Barbarians, prone to every thing horrible, and all petty efforts on our side will add fuel to the flame.

In the second place, the danger of allowing any Kaffirs, apparent friends or enemies, to mix with your force; for should they even harbour no treacherous designs for the moment, the inhabitants, for whose conduct I will answer if they be well managed, will be a useless body, perhaps run all risks and abandon the Commando when they shall be surrounded by those against whom they possess a natural and well grounded antipathy and suspicion. The general cry is, let us meet any number of Kaffirs, but let us meet them as enemies, for our enemies 'they are all of them'. . . .

. . . My motives may be considered to proceed from revenge or from imaginary apprehensions, but to refute the former I have only to ask whether false notions of philanthropy are to lead us to waste the blood of those who have a claim to our protection, from a wish to have it to say that we brought about civilization by lenient measures, when those very measures are a stimulus to the most savage barbarity by allowing the greatest cruelties to go unpunished; and as to the latter charge experience will soon enough prove the truth of what I have advanced, were even my own conduct not a sufficient check to such insinuation should it exist. . . .

Believe me the Kaffirs may be brought to their bearing, but they are no more to be trifled with. . . .

4.11a We do not desire the spilling of innocent blood, still less the Kaffirs' stock, but only our own that has been stolen.

—Report of P. Retief to Landdrost Rivers of Uitenhage, 4 Sept. 1822. (Translated from the original published in J. L. M. Franken, *Piet Retief se Lewe in die Kolonie*, pp. 149–150.)

After the frontier war of 1819 Governor Somerset made a verbal treaty with Ngqika that the land between the Fish River and the Keiskamma was to be 'neutral territory', free of both Xhosa and colonists. However, the territory was never effectively cleared. Some Xhosa chiefs stayed on or settled there and grants of land were freely made in the territory to colonists. Retief, who in 1822 was appointed field-commandant of Albany district, received instructions to assemble a commando and help clear the neutral belt of marauding bands who continued to raid farms in the eastern districts. This military force was, however, specifically prohibited to cross the border in search of stolen cattle, something which had previously been permitted under the reprisal system. As the following letters indicate, Retief objected to these restrictions and suspected that they derived from mistrust of him and his men.

. . . I found many tracks of stolen horses and cattle and set off after them in haste, but I could not catch up with them until they were beyond the limit, where I then saw thousands of cattle, from which I should certainly have been able to regain the stolen stock, if the order had not forbidden me, for the second time, from going beyond the limit. The effect of this order is to contribute considerably to the courage of the Kaffirs and to detract considerably from that of the burghers, causing them to complain that they have been given a Commandant and no trust is placed in him.

We do not desire the spilling of innocent blood, still less the Kaffirs' stock, but only our own that has been stolen. I only hope, Sir, that the Government does not think I am indifferent to the spilling of innocent blood or the taking of the Kaffirs' stock. If I were given an order for this reason, I should heartily wish for my discharge.

It is not unknown to Your Excellency, Sir, that I indicated to Your Excellency at the time of my appointment that I did not have sufficient freedom to counter this nation, as I have not been allowed to address all the Chiefs. I do not doubt that if I am allowed to ride in with 300 burghers, I shall either address all the Chiefs and get back all the stolen stock without violence, or if I am allowed to pursue those who steal stock and demand the livestock and the thieves, there is no doubt that they will cease their activities. . . .

4.11b As long as I am not permitted to cross over the border with my troops, no commando will ever be carried out in this district with any success.

—Letter from P. Retief to Governor Somerset, 25 Nov. 1822. (Translated from the original published in J. L. M. Franken, *Piet Retief se Lewe in die Kolonie*, pp. 152–154.)

My Lord, much honoured by my appointment as Field-Commandant, I have tried from the beginning to fulfil the obligations of that office to the best of my knowledge and for the greatest good of the general public. . . .

In the meantime, it came to my notice some time ago that, when both the Landdrost of this district and the commandant of the Frontier judged it essential to call up a commando to counter the all too often repeated plundering of the Kaffirs, I was not permitted to cross over the border with my troops, as I was not trusted.

For my own part, I should acknowledge that well-grounded reasons might exist which might make the order not to cross over the borders essential, but, at the same time, I must assure Your Excellency that as long as this state of affairs continues, or as long as neither the Landdrost nor the Commandant of the Frontier is empowered to change it according to the circumstances, no commando will ever be carried out in this district with any success.

I am also obliged, in my aforementioned office, to let Your Excellency know that the plundering of the Kaffirs has now become so persistent that a number of the inhabitants of the area along the Great Fish River have now been obliged to abandon their farms, whereby that valuable part of our district is left to itself once again.

And I shall add that if no other measures are taken for the defence of the same, their example will be followed by others.

To give Your Excellency an idea of the losses suffered by the inhabitants of this district in the past five years, I have the honour to submit to Your Excellency an account of the number of cattle, horses, sheep, etc., which have been missed over a short period, also with the number of murders committed by the Kaffirs, for which they [the colonists] have received no compensation, in spite of the fact that adequate means and opportunity, in the form of cattle captured from the Kaffirs, have existed for about four or five years now.

It would be useless, my Lord, to trouble Your Excellency by describing all the losses which have been suffered here by the inhabitants. I was of the opinion, however, that I should submit this to Your Excellency as further support for my request, and I trust that it will provide sufficient reason to bring Your Excellency to withdraw the abovementioned order in part, when circumstances make this necessary, and that I might be allowed to go into Kaffirland with a commando of 300 men, in order to ascertain the nature of the Kaffir chief's feelings and also, when any plundering may take place in future, to let chosen commandos or patrols follow the tracks of stolen cattle over the borders, and if they identify the stolen cattle in the Kaffir's kraals to take them back, or to take back a number equal to those originally stolen. . . .

4.11c I find that I have been called to an office where I am not trusted, and where I should surely have been able to bring about peace and quiet.

—Letter from P. Retief to Landdrost Rivers of Uitenhage, 13 Sept. 1823. (Translated from the original published in J. L. M. Franken, *Piet Retief se Lewe in die Kolonie*, pp. 157–158.)

I am once again obliged, in the general interest, to report to Your Excellency that the plundering of the Kaffirs has increased to such an extent that many inhabitants of this district are presently living in danger. Many have, in effect, been robbed of all their cattle, while many do not have enough left for the maintenance of their families, so that the daily complaints have become more than I can bear, and, because of the despair of these people, I can assure Your Excellency that not half of their troubles come to Your Excellency's attention, as they can get no compensation for all their stolen cattle.

I might say, Honourable Sir, that however well-intentioned the present orders might be, they provide the Kaffirs with so much courage to rob the inhabitants of all they have, by forbidding me from following the stolen cattle across the border with my commandos, and demanding them back from the Kaffir chiefs.

If, at my request twelve months ago, I had been given the freedom to go to the Kaffir chiefs, the inhabitants would now be left to live in greater peace; yet I find, to my most grievous sorrow, that I have been called to an office where I am not trusted, and where I should surely have been able, with God's help, to bring about peace and quiet.

Far rather, Honourable Sir, would I wish for my discharge than to continue, untrusted, in this position and see the inhabitants being ruined.

May God believe that it is far from my thoughts to try to spill innocent blood or do this nation an injustice. I request therefore that Your Honour submit this for the consideration of His Excellency.

4.12a We consider those extremities only justifiable on the following principles.

—Letter from Landdrost A. Stockenström to Deputy-Landdrost Harding of Cradock, 20 Sept. 1820. (From *Papers Relative to the Condition and Treatment of the Native Inhabitants of the Cape of Good Hope* (Imperial Blue Book No. 252 of 1835), pp. 62–63.)

On the northern frontier the colonists and the 'Bushmen' had long engaged in a bitter and bloody battle. To repulse the encroachment on their hunting grounds the hunters raided farms, and in retaliation burgher commandos went out to slay as many raiders as possible. During the last quarter of the eighteenth century this war of extermination was officially sanctioned by the colonial authorities, but with the turn of the century a new policy was adopted. It was sought to conciliate the hunters by offering them cattle and other gifts, and some frontier farmers provided them with food in times of drought. Although the policy achieved considerable success, raids continued in some parts until well in the nineteenth century. Commandos were sporadically sent out against such raiders, although, as shown in the following letters from Stockenström, the authorities made more vigorous attempts to control their actions than in former times.

I have been favoured with yours of the 14th instant, enclosing a copy of Commandant Van Wyk's report of the recapture of horses taken by the Bushmen, and the attack of the plundering kraal.

Nothing can be more painful than to see those sanguinary examples, still occasionally necessary, but I feel confident that you will use every exertion to impress upon the minds of those who may be from time to time engaged in the same that we consider those extremities only justifiable on the following principles. It is natural for them to try to recover what is taken from them, and what constitutes the support of their families. If in this just attempt they meet with resistance, there is no alternative between destroying the robbers, and being destroyed. But if on any occasion such as can be seized without risk be wantonly killed, and I find it out, as far as the laws enable me, or my representations to the government can avail, I will use every exertion to put it out of the power of the offender to repeat such excesses of revenge. I do not hereby intend to cast any censure on the Commandant Van Wyk; on the contrary, it appears to me that he must have used great caution, as otherwise in the confusion of a conflict more women and children would have fallen; but I wish that the above sentiments may be on the mind of every commander of similar parties. They must recollect that the Bushmen, possessing no property themselves, are not sensible of the full extent of the crime of stealing, and that often absolute starvation is the only impulse.

Conciliatory measures, whenever they can avail, must be employed; they have contributed vastly to the tranquillity of the northern frontier. Let me beg of you, therefore, to be particularly watchful over the treatment of those which have been taken, and now live amongst the farmers, and cautious to whom you entrust the orphans.

4.12b Experience has taught us that prudence, forbearance and kindness are the best means of keeping the mass of these savages not only on peaceable terms with, but also very useful to us.

—Letter from Landdrost A. Stockenström to the colonial secretary, Lt.-Col. C. Bird, 5 June 1822. (From *Papers Relative to the Condition and Treatment of the Native Inhabitants of the Cape of Good Hope* (Imperial Blue Book No. 252 of 1835), pp. 67–68.)

. . . As to the general principle, however, upon which parties of the above nature are conducted, the taking of prisoners (especially women and children), the manner in which they are disposed of, and the authority upon which such proceedings are based, about which his Excellency is justly solicitous, I beg leave to give you the following information:

Without going back to a remote period of the existence of this colony, in order to find out the origin of Bosjesmen commandos, a review of which would reflect but little credit on those who first rendered those cruel expedients necessary, by being the first aggressors, and thereby exciting the revenge of those savages, we still cannot help allowing that, in the present state of our frontier, the constant depredations of that unfortunate race of people must be occasionally checked by some serious example, to keep our remote districts at all habitable. Experience has taught us that prudence, forbearance and kindness are the best means of keeping the mass of these savages not only on peaceable terms with, but also very useful to us, and every impartial observer will acknowledge that the present generation of colonists (with some exceptions indeed) show by their conduct to the Bosjesmen their conviction of this truth, and of the inhumanity of destroying them on every slight provocation. . . .

Still there can be no doubt that severe alternatives are sometimes unavoidable, as in Van Wyk's case, . . . and in another distressing one, which has just reached me from Beaufort, . . . distressing because it is quite clear that the continued droughts and consequent misery among the Bosjesmen are the principal causes of the accumulated aggressions which have of late taken place, an impression which has made me perhaps too averse to those commandos.

Now, then, when a kraal has been thus attacked and dispersed, the bringing away of such men, women and children as surrender themselves or offer no resistance is a matter of course, or rather of charity. Indeed they will very seldom stay behind; for the desperate characters on whose depredations the kraal depended for subsistence having most generally fallen in the conflict, or escaped into the deserts, the rest would perish unless they did come among the farmers, upon whom they must be a burthen for some time, but who keep and feed them with a view to induce them, by kind treatment, to stay with them as servants; for it is perfectly understood at the present day that they are under no restraint whatever; that when they do not like one master they can go to another; and when they wish to return and join some peaceable kraal of their own tribe, they cannot be prevented. By these means, numbers of them, at last finding an abode that they like, become the most useful herders, assist the farmer in every other business, till at length they are as it were confounded with the Hottentots; often bind themselves involuntarily by contracts, and enjoy the full protection of the laws, which indeed they do from their first coming among the colonists; objects which in my humble opinion are very desirable as the first steps towards their improvement. That the above system once was liable to be much abused I have every reason to believe, and it was against such abuses, among others, that my representation of the 5th May 1817 was levelled; but I am convinced that the proclamation to which that representation gave rise is the most effectual barrier Government can oppose to those abuses.

4.12c It is not with the Bushmen as with the Kaffirs, where there are Chiefs with authority and where the community can be held responsible for the acts of its members.

—Reply of Landdrost A. Stockenström to the commissioners of enquiry, dated 9 Aug. 1826. (From *The Autobiography of Sir Andries Stockenström,* Vol. I, pp. 231–232.)

. . . Another delicate point connected with all the above remains to be touched upon, viz., the pursuit of robbers, and some specific regulations on that head are absolutely necessary. If we say that the Boers are not to follow up murderers and plunderers beyond the Frontier, we lay the firmest foundation for the very thing we are so anxious to prevent, viz., a new frontier petty war; for the order had only to become generally known (which it must, or else it cannot be acted on), and one night will be sufficient for the destruction of half the families on the extreme borders, by those who know that the crossing of a river or a ridge ensures a safe retreat. Before reference can be made to Cape Town, the gang may be beyond the Tropic, and could we then take indiscriminate vengeance on all kraals? It is not there as with the Kaffirs, where there are Chiefs with authority to be found at all times and where the community can be held responsible for the acts of its members; the savages here are divided into hundreds of small independent parties whom, unless you follow them on the spur, you can never find out again; the impunity of one set of depredators will stimulate others, and the flame once kindled, the scenes of blood of earlier days will be acted over again. The best check on these pursuers of marauders which I have been able to adopt was to make every individual employed on such a party, particularly blacks, as soon as they return at the Drostdy give a deposition of all the proceedings, by which it is easily discovered whether the pursuit was wanton, or necessary, or whether any extremities which could be avoided were resorted to. No Boer will inconsiderately run the risk of such enquiry, if his cause be not just; but to check one evil by the substitution of a still greater one, I humbly beg leave to dissent from. . . .

4.13a The great mistake committed in our policy of frontier defence consists in the sudden transition from measures of too great severity to the opposite extreme.

—Letter from A. Stockenström, as commissioner-general of the eastern province, to Governor Cole, 6 Feb. 1829. (From *The Autobiography of Sir Andries Stockenström*, Vol. I, pp. 308–310.)

In 1828 Stockenström was appointed commissioner-general for the eastern province. Although he was supposed to be the senior civilian authority on the frontier, the actual military command was in the hands of his bitter personal rival, Colonel Henry Somerset. Somerset continued to favour the reprisal system even after it had been suspended by Bourke in 1826. Stockenström's friction with the military stationed on the frontier grew after he had become convinced of the futility of the reprisal system and of punitive expeditions against chiefs. He instead issued regulations relating to the guarding of cattle and the conditions under which the immediate pursuit of stolen stock was permissible.

. . . I must take the liberty to repeat what can be found in some of my earlier communications, that the great mistake committed in our policy of frontier defence consisted in the sudden transition from measures of too great severity, and sometimes wanton cruelty, to the opposite extreme of sacrificing the safety of His Majesty's subjects on the borders by paralyzing their efforts, even in defence of their lives and their property; and the vigour with which this sytem of supposed conciliation was enforced generated the idea which caused so much discontent, clamour, and confusion: that it was criminal to resist any attack made by savages. . . .

. . . I should be the last person to exaggerate in the eyes of Government the unfriendly feeling of the Colonists towards the native tribes. I am aware that the ferociousness with which that feeling was given vent to, has, in a great measure, given way to the dictates of that humanity which proceeds hand in hand with the moral improvement of our remote brethren; and I know numbers whose dispositions in regard to those natives does them honour; but, that a most powerful check upon the parties pursuing marauders is absolutely necessary, is equally true. . . .

. . . The basis to be laid down in legislating on this subject is that if, on the one hand, the savages be allowed with impunity to drive off the cattle of the farmers, they will soon add murders and fire to their thefts, as has repeatedly been proved, and the vicinity of the frontier becomes uninhabitable; and, on the other hand, if the Colonists are on every trifling provocation to be permitted to pursue and (as they would call it) punish the offenders, the old system of terror and extermination will be revived with full force.

To hit upon a proper medium, regulated by a humane consideration of the wretched condition of the savages, without losing sight of the right of the Colonists to the protection of Government, will be the difficult but not hopeless task which your Excellency will have to perform. . . .

4.13b Whilst the voice of humanity is justly raised in favour of the long and cruelly oppressed blacks, that of justice and prudence remind us that the whites also have a claim to protection.

—Memoir of A. Stockenström as commissioner-general, London, 31 Dec. 1833. (From *The Autobiography of Sir Andries Stockenström*, Vol. I, pp. 344–347.)

4.13 A. Stockenström's views on frontier policy 1829–35

While strongly opposed to the use of indiscriminate force against the blacks in frontier expeditions, Stockenström was also critical of the philanthropic party led by Dr Philip, which laid all the blame in the frontier conflict on the colonists. Stockenström became increasingly frustrated with his position as commissioner-general and more and more critical of the frontier policy of the administration of which he was part. When a visit to London in an attempt to gain greater independence for the position of commissioner-general proved unsuccessful, he resigned in 1833.

. . . All my experience on the subject of Commandos by the Colonial forces against the native bordering tribes has confirmed me in the position, which I have always maintained, that there is as much danger in the one extreme as in the other. It is impossible to deny that the oppressions of the European colonists, and their descendants, is the cause of the degradation of most of the natives, and the hostile feeling existing between the Colony and its black neighbours. The conviction of this fact alone is sufficient to induce the Government to make those amends, which are still within its power, by protecting those natives against further persecution, and exerting every possible means to improve their condition and civilize them. But I am far from thinking that these desiderata can be obtained by 'turning the tables' as it has been called, and allowing those tribes to murder and plunder with impunity, and by preventing the Colonists from protecting their lives and property against those outrages. Such a system could only end in the extermination of the weaker party, and a mistaken humanity would be found the height of cruelty at last.

Let the sincere philanthropist for a moment contemplate what would be the result of a Government being altogether passive under the excesses, which savages and barbarians are capable of perpetrating, not only against those by whose ancestors they feel themselves to have been wronged, and against whom they harbour a feeling of implacable revenge, but against their own fellow sufferers, who, with themselves, must in the end, if not checked, become the sacrifices of their own indiscriminate and mutual massacres. I have upon this principle always considered it an imperious duty to root out any gang of robbers, murderers and marauders, as soon as they were discovered, before the evil should spread to such an extent as to involve the lives of hundreds. . . .

. . . Whilst the voice of humanity is justly raised in favour of the long and cruelly oppressed blacks, that of justice and prudence remind us that the whites also have a claim to protection; that they have also lives and property and rights to lose, and that the wanton abandonment of these to the ferocity of a few desperate gangs among the native tribes will not benefit and civilize their brethren in the aggregate, but must generate that irritation and despair which ultimately no government can prevent from terminating in the most unrestrained indulgence of revenge. . . .

4.13c I have, from first to last, acted upon one consistent principle of courting neither the white nor the black party.

—Correspondence of A. Stockenström during his European sojourn (1833–1835). (From *The Autobiography of Sir Andries Stockenström*, Vol. II, pp. 8–12.)

While in Europe, Stockenström heard of the outbreak of the disastrous frontier war of 1834–1835, and resolved to settle permanently in Sweden, his father's country of origin. Though no longer in any official position he still maintained an impassioned correspondence on frontier affairs with colonists at the Cape as well as with friends in humanitarian circles in Europe.

. . . The history of my administration of the Graaff-Reinet District would convince any unbiased man that the Colonists generally were not blindly bigoted on the subject [i.e. of the emancipation of the Hottentots]. Though I have been sneeringly numbered amongst Dr Philip's converts (a charge like many others which I have never condescended to refute, nor would I see cause to be ashamed if it were true), every honourable man who knows anything about the matter will admit that I have, from first to last, acted upon one consistent principle of courting neither the white nor the black party. I knew my father's sentiments and tried to adopt them. . . .

In short, if I continue to have anything to do with the public administration, I see no cause to deviate from what my conduct has hitherto been. Injustice to whites—English or Dutch—, to blacks—Kaffir, Hottentot or Bushman—, I will still consider injustice and deal with accordingly. To see the white man persecuted and libelled because it has pleased Providence that he should be a slave-holder or, because he defends his life, family, and property against thieves, robbers, and murderers, when the Government cannot or will not do so—is to me as cruel and abominable as the tearing asunder of man and wife, mother and babe, for filthy lucre's sake, or the extermination of tribes, the plundering of nations. . . .

If these principles can satisfy the Government, the missionaries, or my fellow-colonists of either class, I will be proud to serve them. If not, I can only say that I can dispense with their approbation, however much I value it; I can dispense with office, however poor and ambitious I may be, but I cannot possibly dispense with peace of mind.

After all I do not fear that much difference would be found between any of those parties and myself, if we could but understand each other for ever. On the point I have first alluded to, it is most unjust to charge the colonists *en masse* as cut-throats, and as being averse to the amelioration of, and good understanding with, the aboriginal tribes. It is the fashion to associate everything that is barbarous, brutal and cruel with the idea 'African-Boer'. If my object had been to gain popularity with any one set of men, I would have adopted a more partial course than I did, but as I do not mean to cajole either friend or foe, I neither hesitate to say that if a wise and efficient system had been adopted, so in this respect (as I have formerly said on the slave and Hottentot questions) the majority of colonists, English and Dutch, would have given that their most cordial co-operation. I never found them, in the aggregate, hostile to any plan which would ensure *protection* to themselves, as well as their black neighbours. There is but a small section interested in the disturbances on the Frontier, and the acquisition of the cattle of the natives, but mismanagement makes the good suffer with the bad, and embitters the feelings of all. . . . But how can they help their situations? Then where lies the blame? Is it not your system which compels them to be butchers to-day, and would have them submit to be butchered without resistance to-morrow? I am sick of the business. God grant that this were the last line I ever have to write about it. . . .

4.13d I have the cause of truth to serve in order to apply such remedies as will render the Cape Colony prosperous and happy.

—Reply of A. Stockenström to Spring Rice's queries, 5 Nov. 1834. (From the *Minutes of Evidence before the Select Committee on Aborigines*, p. 123.)

In May 1835 Buxton, a leader of the philanthropic party and a close associate of Dr Philip, succeeded after repeated efforts in having a parliamentary select committee appointed to investigate the treatment of 'aborigines' in all the British colonies. Exten-

sive evidence was heard on frontier matters in South Africa, and Stockenström was called from Stockholm to appear before the committee in August 1835. An earlier reply of November 1834 to a questionnaire from the colonial secretary, Mr Spring Rice, was also included in the minutes of evidence before the select committee.

. . . I know that my views generally, as above stated, are not popular. I am aware that many friends of humanity and civilization think them not sufficiently liberal and enlightened with reference to the blacks, whilst, on the other hand, some of my countrymen charge me with abandoning the cause of the whites. No man can feel more respect than I do for the principles and objects of the former party, amongst whom I have the pleasure of counting some of my most valuable and intimate acquaintances, however much I may differ with them on particular points of expediency; and birth, education, prejudices and ties of affection warmly attach me to the other, who, though thrown by the course of particular events into unhappy circumstances in regard to some of the lower classes in their midst, constitute, nevertheless, under a sound system of policy and just treatment, in the aggregate, the best disposed and easiest managed people in His Majesty's dominions. But I am not called upon here to please either; I have the cause of truth to serve; I am to call 'murder, murder', and 'plunder, plunder', whatever be the colour of the perpetrator's skin, or the power and influence of the man who countenances the same, in order (by stating facts as they are) to enable you (as you are known to have the wish) to apply such remedies as will render the Cape colony what it is capable of being made, one of the most prosperous and happy communities on the face of the globe. . . .

4.13e The great source of misfortune on the frontier was the system of taking Kaffir cattle by our patrols.

—Evidence of A. Stockenström before the Select Committee on Aborigines, 19 Aug. 1835. (From *The Autobiography of Sir Andries Stockenström*, Vol. I, pp. 341–344.)

. . . I had long since made up my mind that the great source of misfortune on the Frontier was the system of taking Kaffir cattle under any circumstances by our patrols; and I shall give my reasons. If Kaffirs steal cattle, very seldom the real perpetrators can be found, unless the man losing the cattle has been on his guard, and sees the robbery actually perpetrated, so that he can immediately collect a force and pursue the plunderers; if the cattle be once out of sight of the plundered party, there is seldom any getting them again: our patrols are then entirely at the mercy of the statements made by the farmers, and they may pretend that they are leading them on the trace of the stolen cattle, which may be the trace of any cattle in the world. On coming up to the first Kaffir kraal, the Kaffir, knowing the purpose for which our patrol comes, immediately drives his cattle out of sight: we then use force and collect those cattle; and take the number said to be stolen, or more. This the Kaffirs naturally, and as it always appeared to me justly, resist; they have nothing else to live on, and if the cows be taken away the calves perish; and it is a miserable condition in which the Kaffir women and children, and the whole party, are left. That resistance is usually construed into hostility, and it is almost impossible then to prevent innocent blood-shed; it also often happens that when the patrol is on the spoor of cattle really stolen, they find some individual head of cattle, which is either knocked up, or purposely left behind by the real perpetrators, near a kraal, and that is taken as a positive proof of the guilt of that kraal, and leads to the injustice which I have just pointed out. . . .

. . . Many farmers, both English settlers and Dutch, have often spoken to me about the injurious tendency of this system. The majority of these farmers wish for nothing but peace, and the protection of themselves and their property; but it is impossible in such an extensive community as ours, living in the state as some of our people do, that there should not be among them unprincipled men, who would be glad to avail themselves of every opportunity of enriching themselves at the expense of their weaker neighbours: and it is cruel that a whole community shall suffer for the crimes of these few, nor is it reasonable to suppose that in a nation of barbarians there should not be numbers addicted to plunder; but then again it is equally cruel to drive a whole nation to desperation for the aggressions of a part. . . .

4.14a It is heartrending to be obliged to hear of the murder and rapine committed on the oppressed Caffers without daring to prosecute the culprits at the other side of the frontiers.

—Memorial of G. D. Joubert to the colonial government, 15 Aug. 1831. (From the translation in the Cape Archives, CO 3951.)

On the north-eastern frontier trekboers steadily expanded towards and sometimes even across the Orange River during the 1820s and early 1830s. At the same time smaller tribes fleeing from the ravages of the Difaqane settled close to or even within the colonial boundaries. Unlike the frontiersmen who would join the Great Trek, these trekboers were anxious to maintain their relations with the colonial government which, for its part, insisted on the traditional frontier policies, not allowing colonists to move beyond the boundary. G. D. Joubert was to become the most prominent leader of these loyalist colonial trekboers.

. . . The Bushmen have no fixed country and it is of little consideration to them whether they live a number of miles nearer to or farther from the Orange River. [Moreover] there are extended uninhabited countries to the east towards the sources of [the] Vaal River, that might be able to provide [for a] hundred times as many Bushmen as inhabit the said tracks. . . .

. . . Single colonists, who have no places [i.e. farms] in the colony, or have been too poor to pay the expenses of surveying, etc., are living beyond the frontiers, dispersed here and there. [They] however in no way wish to separate themselves from the authority of the colonial government, but pay their taxes to the nearest fieldcornets.

Your Excellency's memorialist represents to Your Honour furthermore how heartrending it is to him to be obliged to hear . . . [from] . . . the oppressed Caffers (that solicit his assistance) of [the] murder and rapine committed on them, without daring to prosecute the culpables [i.e. culprits] at the other side of the frontiers over the Orange River and to bring them before the tribunal of the colonial government. . . . Such orders are serving to multiply bad deeds, as appears from the increasing temerity of little robbers [in raiding, for example, the Caffer Captain April]. . . . This kraal, formerly inhabiting other tracks, where they had been spoiled of their property, had expressly taken their residence close to the frontier in order to be safer, supposing that the humanity of the colonists [which is] known amongst them would certainly not refuse them assistance in times of necessity. By their industry in trade with various trinkets with the burghers and by entering the service of the same, also by presents received, these Caffers had collected again a great quantity of goats (the milk of which is their principal food) and sheep, which have [now] all been lost. They have then applied for assistance. . . . However your memorialist does not find himself authorized to apprehend the culpables [i.e. culprits] beyond the frontiers. . . .

Your Excellency's memorialist, when he takes in consideration how the generous British government has always excelled in protecting its feeble friends against powerful oppressors, remarks with astonishment how little this European principle is imitated in respect to the oppressed inhabitants of the opposite sides of the Orange River, that throw themselves in the arms of Government. Without any expenses for government whatsoever, your memorialist would joyfully take upon himself to shed his blood for the right of man and for the defence of the feeble and helpless. If he had the authorization of Your Excellency for it he would, with a few of his burghers, force the Coran[n]a captain Witvoet to give restitution of his spoil, and he would apprehend the robbers of April's Kraal and their bad acts would most likely cease for a long time. He would also bring to authority the Griquas on occasion of future excesses. Your Excellency's memorialist humbly solicits that it might please Your Honor to sanction this, and furthermore allow him to publish to the inhabitants of the opposite side of the Orange River that government will consider the care of the unhappy Caffers its own, because the same are continually appealing to the protection of His Majesty's subjects and of H. M. Government itself. . . .

4.14b Such who may stubbornly refuse to enter into these desirable relations will soon see and feel that they are contending with a mighty God!

—Correspondence of P. Retief, as leader of the Trek of 1837. (From the translations in J. C. Chase, *The Natal Papers*, pp. 112–116.)

In his capacity as 'Governor' of the assembled Trek parties between the Orange and the Vaal Rivers, Retief engaged in correspondence and negotiations with the colonial authorities as well as with various tribal chiefs. His letter to the Griqua captains, who had settled in the Trans-Orange well before either the Trekkers or the trekboers moved into the same area, gave some idea of the notions underlying the frontier policies envisaged by the Voortrekkers.

(i) *To Governor D'Urban, 9 September 1837.*

. . . I am continually receiving reports that I am surrounded by enemies, but I make myself perfectly easy, assured that the Almighty arm will support those who are in the right. . . . I have heard that great apprehensions are entertained in the Colony that we shall treat Matzalikatse too harshly. . . . Rest assured that I can thank God I do not possess a thirst for blood, or an unfeeling heart; but while I take care not to act with undue severity, I shall be equally guarded that I do not by indecision increase the evil. I have seen too much of the disasters which have befallen the Colony from a want of promptitude, not to be wary on that subject. It is enough that I have been taking lessons on your frontier for the last twenty-two years, and know what should be done or left undone. . . .

(ii) *To the Griqua captains, Sand River, 18 July 1837, a copy of which was enclosed with (i).*

Captains, In consequence of several depositions made before me, by some of your Captains, as well as by other individuals, there remains no doubt in my mind that Waterboer has been incited and bribed to induce you all to combine with him in making a treacherous attack upon my several encampments. As a Christian I advise you all first to wait and see the result of Matsellikatse's treachery against us. Rest assured that we shall not attack or interfere with any tribe or people: but on the contrary you may also rely upon it, that whoever interferes with us, will have to rue it for ever after. We have been induced to quit our native land, after sustaining enormous losses, and depend upon it that we have not taken this step to lead a worse, but a better life. On the other hand I have also to inform you that I have not been elected as the chief of this people by my own act, or even by the general voice of the people; but I have sufficient reasons to recognise the hand of God in placing me at the head of my countrymen. Let it, therefore, be sufficient for you to know that I can fearlessly call upon God, and may safely depend upon His mighty arm. Be, therefore, again assured, that as long as it may please Him to allow me to govern over this people, no nation or tribe, of whatever class or colour, will be molested by me or my dependants; and that all who suffer themselves to be misled by designing men, to set themselves against me and my possessions by murder or plunder, will assuredly see that I shall act with inflexibility, and that my coming will be sure and their punishment certain.

I must also call to your recollection the awful visitation of God upon you, after your unlawful, murderous, and plundering attack upon Matsellikatse; when you were assembled in such great strength, and on your side alone so many hundred men, horses, weapons, &c., were lost. In this alone you may see the just reward of those who go out to strife without the aid of the Almighty. On the other hand it will also be well for you, for us, and for the world, to remark how wonderfully God has enabled us, with so weak a force, to stand against the frightful and superior numbers of Matsellikatse. Be, therefore, advised by me, as your sincere friend, to consider the subject well before you take the advice of bad men, that you may not plunge yourselves into acts which you may for ever repent. I may also tell you, that I have never wished unneccessarily to shed the blood of my fellow creatures. . . . My strength increases every day, and I am continually moving further on; it will consequently be well for you to remark, and I mention it to show how little I regard your hostility, that the longer you delay to attack me, the greater the difficulty and danger will become to you. . . .

I have further to inform you all, that on my arrival at Blesberg, I concluded a Treaty of peace and amity with Morocke and Towana, as Chiefs of the Moroles tribe, and that they have from the date thereof . . . convinced me that they and their people will strictly adhere thereto. . . . Morocke has acquainted me that certain Corannas had declared their intention of attacking him, robbing him of his cattle, and burning his village. My answer to him was as follows: Moroko, keep yourself innocent from crimes against all nations and tribes; you know that I have sworn fidelity to you, as you have also sworn to me; adhere to your engagement with me; and let it be sufficient for you that I again say, that whoever injures you, injures me; and that whether I am near to, or far from you, send me word, and you will speedily have your friend to your assistance.

You will perceive from this what advantages such Treaties are calculated to confer upon a people; and may I not, therefore, ask you, why cannot we all, without distinction, unite ourselves in the same bonds of friendship? Again may I ask you, why should this beautiful and fertile country, so bountifully blessed by Providence and which can be so advantageously occupied, be any longer looked upon as an insecure wilderness, abounding in deeds of murder and plunder? It will, therefore, now be your faults if we do not convert it into a peaceful and happy country.

I now finally declare to you with a clear conscience that it is not my wish to lead a single benighted and uncivilized being astray, much less do I desire to see their blood shed while in that state; my sincere wish, on the contrary, is to enlighten them, to lead them from their wicked ways, and to instruct them in the principles of the Christian faith. . . .

Now, Captains, let this be enough to induce you to consider what is the best for you to do. I will in conclusion, in accordance with my duty as a Christian, again offer to you all, without distinction, my real and lasting friendship, the same as I have done to all tribes and shall continue to do. I also conjure you to accept and preserve the same, and with the blessing of God, I trust that it will be to our mutual benefit and happiness. If you determine on rejecting my overtures of peace, you may hereafter repent it. I now fully trust, that with the blessing of God, my sincere and earnest desires, as herein communicated, will be abundantly useful to you, and that I may ere long see that the present race of benighted beings inhabiting this country will be bound together in the bonds of peace and friendship. On the other hand, I am fully convinced that such who may stubbornly refuse to enter into these desirable relations, will soon see and feel that they are contending with a mighty God! If there be any among you who imagine any difficulty in entering into these engagements, let them come to me, and I will endeavour to convince them to the utmost of my power. See and hear now, ye Captains, Field-cornets, and other rulers of your people; I have acquitted myself before God, of my duties to you as a Christian; my last wish is that the day may soon come when I shall see you all united in truth and brotherly love.

4.14c We are emigrants who together with you dwell in the same strange land.

—Letter from A. H. Potgieter to Adam Kok, 1844. (Quoted in a letter by Thomson to Philip, 25 Dec. 1844, as published in Robert Ross, *Adam Kok's Griquas,* p. 56. The original of this letter is in the London Missionary Society Archive, 21/2/A.)

We are emigrants together with you and are regarded as such and regard ourselves as emigrants who together with you dwell in the same strange land, and we desire to be regarded as neither more nor less than your fellow-emigrants, inhabitants of the country, enjoying the same privileges with you.

It is by no means the intention of the Head Commandant and his council to bring any native chief under their laws and authority, but to leave each one to exercise his own authority. But in the case of any crime committed by a white against a native, the native shall complain to the leader of the whites and when a crime is committed by a native against a white, the white shall complain to a ruler of the natives. In case of hired servants of either party absconding they shall be mutually delivered up by both parties.

4.15a Not only sound policy but justice forbids that we should crush the prostrate enemy. Our object ought to be the maintenance of the Kaffir nation as an independent ally.

—Letter from A. Stockenström to Lord Glenelg, 7 Jan. 1836. (From *The Autobiography of Sir Andries Stockenström,* Vol. II, pp. 31–38.)

4.15 A. Stockenström's views on the Treaty System 1836–7

Towards the end of 1835 Lord Glenelg, the minister of colonies, decided to undo the D'Urban settlement, in particular the conquered territories annexed after the frontier war of 1834–1835, and to embark on a new frontier policy based on a system of treaties with the Xhosa chiefdoms. This policy was announced in a long and momentous despatch to Governor D'Urban on December 26, 1835. In the mean time Glenelg had again called Stockenström from Sweden, and after a number of interviews to ascertain the latter's own views and proposals on frontier matters, he appointed Stockenström as lieutenant-governor of the eastern districts in February 1836.

. . . I am by no means opposed to the principle of incorporation, where the people to be disposed of cannot by any other means be rendered harmless to us and acquire the means of their own improvement, whilst I am equally anxious to avoid rendering our own system of administration more complicated and expensive by conquest, or by interference with the internal affairs of 'nations or tribes' who are so far organized and consolidated as to require only our example and justice, our commerce, and the free and friendly communication of those improvements which they would gradually become prepared to cultivate, in order to advance in the path of civilization and peace, as rapidly as under our dominion. . . .

To come to a still more important consideration, I confess I do not see how the introduction of the English laws among the Kaffirs in the manner proposed in the Treaty is at all practicable. The prejudices of a nation, however absurd they may appear, are not easily removed or disregarded; violent opposition often strengthens them, and our magistrates and judges might in the strict performance of their duty raise questions, or provoke acts of resistance, which the executive would be much at a loss how to deal with.

I think, moreover, that every measure tending to lower the importance of the Chiefs is calculated to weaken the hold we have on the people, as it is by means of these Chiefs we will soonest succeed in securing peace and promoting civilization. The supersession of their authority by that of our magistrates, however desirable in many respects, will constantly remind them of their fall from independent power, and keep secretly smouldering in their bosoms, and that of their adherents, a discontent which cannot fail to break forth with destructive violence as soon as it gets vent. I am aware that it is provided that the Chiefs themselves may be appointed magistrates; but the present generation of Kaffir Chiefs cannot administer English law; and if they could, it appears to me they can serve our purpose and their own country better as Chiefs, in a manner I hope to be able to show in the sequel. . . .

Having thus stated the objections and difficulties which appear to me to stand in the way of the execution of the said treaty, I proceed to comply with your Lordship's further commands by humbly submitting a plan which I consider it advisable to adopt in the present emergency. In doing so I must premise that my views are founded upon the (perhaps unpopular) impression that the late attacks of the Kaffirs, though they have caused me more painful reflections than it is necessary to trouble your Lordship with, have not been altogether unprovoked.

My earlier correspondence with your department shows my feelings on this subject. Consequently, not only sound policy but justice forbids that we should crush the prostrate enemy. I think, therefore, that our objects ought to be these. In the first place and above all, the safety of the Colony against future inroads, and the security of His Majesty's subjects in the same. Secondly, the improvement of the Kaffir nation, and its maintenance as an independent ally. To obtain these points we must now for some time keep up an efficient military force, and strengthen our Frontier, which I cannot recommend to be advanced beyond the Keiskamma permanently.

In connection with this as dense a population as possible ought to be settled in villages in the territory between the said boundary and the Kat and Fish Rivers, upon the same principle as the new Hottentot settlements, the advantages of which were fully demonstrated during the late contest, modified according to circumstances; and the people in the ceded Territory west of the Kat River ought to be made to comply with the conditions upon which they accepted their grants, or relinquish them. The burgher force ought to be placed under strict regulations, and its assembling and operations narrowly defined or controlled, so as to keep it efficient for defence and prevent uncalled-for offence. . . .

The reprisal system must be finally put a stop to. The Colonists must be allowed to protect their property and lives against plunderers and murderers, even if it be necessary to shoot the assailants; this in the actual state of things cannot be prevented. The vacillating and contradictory doctrine which has been held forth on this point, rushing from one extreme to another, has been one of the main causes of our misfortunes. For some time to come it will even be dangerous to allow the Kaffirs free access to the Colony, and where they are found armed they can be no other than enemies, and dealt with accordingly. But the inhabitants living near the Frontier come there knowing that they have the Kaffirs in their neighbourhood. Government cannot prevent cattle being kept, but the party keeping them must guard them, and if they be stolen, the thief must be found out if possible, and punished according to law; but no risk of a bloody war ought to be incurred for every cow which strays, or is destroyed by wild beasts, or may even be stolen.

No armed person or force ought to be allowed, except under peculiar clearly-defined circumstances, to enter Kaffirland; and private individuals, including traders, even unarmed, ought only to be allowed to do so upon terms to be agreed upon between the Governor, or other competent authority, and the Kaffir Chiefs. If then, in spite of our care, we be overpowered and plundered or otherwise injured, and can prove the Kaffirs the aggressors, if the Chiefs then refuse redress and satisfaction, there may be just cause for the Government regularly to go to war; but to give every man who has a real or pretended grievance a military force to go and avenge his own cause, is enough to account for everything that has occurred. . . .

4.15b As these treaties secure the tribes against all aggression on the part of the Colonists, the protection of the Colonists against aggression on their part must be as complete before we can hope to see peace maintained.

—Letters from A. Stockenström to Governor D'Urban, 3 Nov. 1836, 3 Feb. 1837 and 18 Dec. 1837. (From *The Autobiography of Sir Andries Stockenström,* Vol. II, pp. 106–107, 117–118, 125–128.)

Even apart from the unsettled conditions on the eastern frontier in the wake of the war of 1834–1835, Stockenström's efforts to implement Glenelg's treaty system met with every kind of political obstruction and opposition. Governor D'Urban, whose own settlement had been overturned, was far from favourably inclined to the new policy; Stockenström's relations with the military commanders on the eastern frontier were beset with longstanding rivalries and acrimonious disputes; and the settler community of Grahamstown, led by Robert Godlonton, staged a virulent campaign against the treaty system even before Stockenström's arrival. Nevertheless Stockenström endeavoured to make the best use of his big chance to implement some of his own ideas in frontier policy, and put a brave face on his actual progress, as the following official despatches show.

3 November 1836

. . . We must either have extermination or conciliation and justice: a middle course is ruin.

I shall not at present trouble Your Excellency with the details of the treaties to be entered into 'with the Chief of every tribe, to which a portion of said territory is to be assigned', . . . beyond stating that reprisals by military force shall not be allowed. Responsible Kaffir authorities to be resident on the Eastern side of the Frontier, as we have our posts on the West. We to obtain redress from their councils, as they would through our courts of Justice. A Colonist to have no more right to cross the boundary eastward without the consent of the Kaffir Chiefs, than a Kaffir has to cross it westward without our consent. Colonists beyond the said boundary to be as fully subject to Kaffir law, as a Kaffir in the Colony would be to ours. A Colonist found there stealing cattle or committing any other crime, if he cannot be otherwise taken, to meet with the same fate which a Kaffir under similar circumstances would meet with in the Colony, viz., death. Our agents to be no longer magistrates, but ministers or consuls. Through them satisfaction to be obtained from us and for us. They will collect the proofs of losses caused by Kaffir depredations, and demand compensation in the proper quarter, as well as watch over the interests of British subjects, permitted by the Kaffirs to be amongst them, and they will also secure redress for Kaffirs injured by Colonists. In short, I do not intend to exact anything from the Kaffirs that I do not believe the Colony prepared to grant reciprocally. . . .

13 February 1837

. . . Having now to the best of my abilities, for so far as the Kaffirs, Tambookies, and Fingoes on our immediate border are concerned, complied with that part of the instructions . . . which directed me to enter into treaties with the native Chiefs on the part of His Majesty, . . . I beg to premise that, as these treaties secure the said tribes against all aggression on the part of the Colonists, the protection of the Colonists against aggression on their part must be as complete, before we can hope to see peace maintained, or claim the credit of having done justice.

The principle upon which I start, therefore, is that which I have always maintained, that no punishment can be too severe for real murderers and plunderers, Kaffir or colonist; and in a community like ours, that principle cannot be too strictly enforced. A feeling of insecurity generates the very outrages which partial laws, whether dictated by mistaken philanthropy or prejudice, vainly strive to repress. Thus the Kaffirs could not leave us at rest as long as they were not safe from our inroads and oppressions; and it will be equally futile to expect that the colonists will permanently remain at peace with them, if *within our territory* life and property be not rendered perfectly safe against their revenge, avarice or any species of encroachment . . .

18 December 1837

. . . These details are tedious, but the question which hinges upon them is important, viz., whether people bordering upon a barbarous nation shall take care of their property, and obtain compensation only when the robbery as well as the robbers are ascertained beyond all doubt; in short, whether the treaties, the Secretary of State's system, the plan now tried for a year, shall be adhered to, or whether we shall convert Her Majesty's troops into cattle herds; harass the whole army when a cow is missing, which a wolf may have destroyed; throw Kaffirland into a commotion when a mare has strayed out of the sight of a careless owner; provoke another war, spend another million or two and ruin two nations. And for what? To enrich a few fishers in troubled waters, a few speculators in confusion, and conciliate the favour of those whose hatred is the surest indication of worth in the hated object. . . .

Thus much for the Kaffirs in our immediate neighbourhood, they are perfectly contented; we have their entire confidence; they are vexed at the occasional petty thieving, which will continue here as in the most civilised countries, though in a less degree; but the country is quiet.

Beyond the Kei the aspect of affairs is equally gratifying, . . .

. . . Then again I say, if what we see is reality, to what cause is such a result to be ascribed? Only to the just principles upon which the Minister's measures are founded. Let them be adhered to; let additional sacrifices be made to instruct the people on both sides of the frontier, and useless expenditure stopped to meet this indispensable one; let timely measures be adopted to check a system of extermination and traffic in human flesh and blood which is organized by British subjects in the interior. We shall then not altogether stop thieving any more than the new police stopped pocket picking, but we have chance of gradually, though slowly, improving—or let us give way to clamour or be cowed by scurrility or perjured cabals, let us give every man permission to help himself; but then let us not leave a black man alive or retreat behind the lines of Cape Town. . . .

4.16 The momentous question is that of passive submission by means of negotiation or severe contest to bring about complete subjugation.

—Editorial by Christoffel Brand on the Frontier War of 1846, *De Zuid-Afrikaan*, 5 Nov. 1846. (From the translation published in *De Zuid-Afrikaan*.)

The treaty system implemented by Stockenström worked fairly well until his resignation as lieutenant-governor in August 1839, and then gradually collapsed. With cattle-thefts increasing again, colonists demanded that the chiefs in the land between the Fish and Kei Rivers (i.e. D'Urban's conquered territories) be subjugated by force, and the territory placed under British authority once more. The 'War of the Axe' broke out in March 1846 and dragged on for 21 months.

The present position of the Kafir War is most important. Within a few days the momentous question will be decided respecting the passive submission of the savage hordes, or a prosecution or rather resumption of the struggle with renewed vigour. The favorable decision of the first involves nothing less than, nay must be inevitably accompanied by, the complete restoration of all the stolen cattle, the delivery of all fire arms in the possession of the enemy, compensation for the devastations committed in his unprovoked incursion, and an entire evacuation of the territories hitherto occupied by him. In case he should however refuse complete submission to these terms, the ends involved will have to be attained by force of arms. All the colonial cattle, wherever to be found, must be traced out and taken; not a single musket must be left in the possession of the enemy; and he for ever driven from a country, the possession of which will produce but a slight recompense for all the atrocities and cruelties by which he has incurred the present war.

This, in our opinion, is a true view of the war question. Passive submission, by means of negotiation, or severe contest, to bring about complete subjugation, with all the details inseparably connected with both these positions. No one will certainly be foolish enough to deny or to dispute the importance of such a state of things; and it cannot therefore be without weight calmly to consider whether there is any likelihood that the end thus strictly to be aimed at will be realized by means of the first measure, the latter being deemed an inevitable consequence of its failure.

It will have been observed from our last number that we are among those who are of opinion that however desirable an opposite result may be, little or nothing will be effected by negotiating with a people whose craftiness and cunning have become proverbial, especially when the advantages are taken into account which they have unfortunately obtained in the present war with the Colony. Those who are no strangers to such matters will no doubt recollect how highly difficult it was in the 1835 war, notwithstanding the defeat sustained by them at almost every point, and amidst the conditions in which they then found themselves placed, to bring them to a voluntary submission. [It will be recollected] how they constantly, during the most well-meant endeavours for the attainment thereof, dictated by mere humanity, harassed the most audacious attempts to retrieve their losses, to recover the booty captured from them, and by retaliating incursions, however desperate often, to lead their pursuers into the belief that their courage had not forsaken them, and [that] they knew of no other subjugation except that brought about by the sword. And if this was the case at a time when they could boast of obstinacy alone and not of advantages achieved, what prospect, we ask, can there exist, at a moment when they are thrown into a stupor, as it were, by the success of their operations, to indulge a well-founded hope that negotiation will effect that which hitherto has been fruitlessly attempted by force of arms? Will it be possible now to convince them by mere policy that by their unprovoked invasion and wickedness they have degraded themselves from the station of allies to that of ungrateful criminals, robbers and murderers; that they deserve to be extirpated, and that it is an act of mere mercy and compassion to show them the favor now, after all their atrocities and base ingratitude; passively to submit to the demands of retaliating revenge without any further chastisement? We apprehend that those who indulge in these suppositions allow themselves to be overpowered by their fancy, and we fear that they will be sadly disappointed!

It is certainly a most easy task, as far as *words and vague promises* are concerned, to induce these innocent children of nature to concede any terms demanded from them. The sad experience of the past ten years, which have been so prolific in similar political jobbing, has fortunately placed this assertion beyond the chance of doubt or dispute. No further experiments are required in that respect. The colonists now require something more substantial. They are wearied of all such wavering. They demand, and have a right to do so, that the curtain be dropped on all such farces, and that the next scene present nothing but manly acts, calculated to put a stop for ever to Kafir audacity and violence. . . .

4.17a Terror should be struck into the Paramount Chief of Kaffraria and the law laid down to himself in person at his very door.

—Report of A. Stockenström, as commander of the burgher forces, to Lt.-Col. Cloete, 14 Nov. 1846. (From *The Autobiography of Sir Andries Stockenström*, Vol. II, pp. 233–239.)

Stockenström came out of retirement to serve as commander of the burgher forces during the war of 1846–47, when the burghers refused to serve under a military commander. The war was characterized by a comprehensive breakdown of trust and co-

operation between the burgher forces and the military command. Stockenström's commando mounted a successful punitive campaign, described in the following report, against Sarili (Kreli), paramount chief of the Xhosa, in August 1846. However, the outcome of the campaign was placed in doubt when officials questioned the validity of the treaty Stockenström had concluded with Sarili, leading to an acrimonious and drawn-out political dispute.

. . . On the 5th August, I encamped on the upper branch of the Kaboosie, after having thoroughly scoured the higher kloofs, forests, and fastnesses of the Keiskamma and Buffalo. The First and Second Divisions were to do the same on a parallel line farther south. We had seen numbers of the enemy; but, with trifling exceptions, we had failed to bring them to a stand anywhere, and it could not be denied that our grand combined movement had proved on the whole a complete failure, through our delays, which, with the exhausted state of the pasturage and the impossibility of obtaining forage, had rendered our horses almost useless. From the numerous spoor of men and cattle leading eastward—from the flight of those whom we saw in the distance—and from the precipitation with which the kraals had recently been abandoned, it was easy to perceive—and the women who were wandering over the country informed us—that the Kaffirs were in a state of great panic, and had lost all hope of retaining possession of Kaffirland since they had been attacked and beaten in their mountain fastnesses. In short, the tables were turned, and the Kaffirs, as they sent to tell the Tambookies, saw 'that Kaffirland was lost, and that the Amakosa had no longer a place of rest'. Still it was clear they were not subdued. They saw that we were more than a match for them in the bush and krantz, as well as in the plain; but they also knew that our force would not long be kept together; that by burning the grass they had helped to disable our cavalry, and by taking refuge among the Galekas beyond the great Kei for a period they could easily escape our present grasp, and return at a time more convenient for retaliation, when their worst enemies should have returned to their homes.

It consequently appeared to me a matter of great importance that Kreli's interest should be separated from that of the Gaikas, the Slambies, and the Gonaquabes, whilst our conflict with these latter tribes lasted; and that with that view terror should be struck into the said Paramount Chief of Kaffraria, by showing him that neither the burning of the grass, the destruction of horses, the fatigues of distance, nor the fear of numbers of the enemy, can stop the progress of a British Force; and by accordingly marching a Commando into his territory under every disadvantage, and laying down the law to himself in person at his very door. From him (Kreli) we had a right to demand satisfaction, as no doubt could remain of his having at some period been implicated in the present war against the Colony. . . .

. . . In short, we did exactly that which we conscientiously believed we were sent to do. We showed him that we could at any time and under every disadvantage come to his door and lay down the law to him, or destroy the country. We made him, in spite of his terrors, appear before us, and submit to our terms. We separated him from our more immediate enemies, whom we thus isolated. We made him promise to restore property, which we cannot now possibly get at. We made him cede territory which he and his council alone can cede, and which we may avail ourselves of or not, as we see fit. And we did all this without binding ourselves to one single act, obligation, or concession, or in the least fettering ourselves, in, when we are able, doing that to compel him (if he should prove faithless) to comply with his engagements, which we are now not able to do. . . .

4.17b With nations as with individuals ultimate retribution follows in strict proportion to the observance or disregard of universal and eternal principles of truth and justice.

—Letter from A. Stockenström to Lieutenant-Governor Young, 22 July 1847. (From *Documents Relative to the Question of a Separate Government for the Eastern Districts of the Cape Colony* (Cape Blue Book, 1857), pp. 251–252.)

. . . The frontier farmers have been taunted with having clamoured for war, and now having got it to their heart's content. I shall not be accused of too strong a leaning towards my fellow-sufferers on the frontier; my bias is suspected of a contrary tendency; but this does not signify. I trust I can feel for them, and serve them without trying to blind them by flattery. We have amongst us foolish and violent men, as in every community, but we have also our due proportion of the rational, honourable, well-disposed; and *I am bound to declare upon personal observation that at the period referred to the fears and complaints were perfectly just.* There was no safety whatever for either person or property; and though I myself was cruelly cut up in the speeches of the complainants, I invariably found the principal inhabitants deprecating war, if a secure peace could be maintained. . . . But soon effect followed cause, as the night the day. We had to recede from a false position, and this could not be done in a very dignified manner. The Kafirs had previously lost all confidence in us; they now lost all respect and fear for us, and an outrage was the result which drove us to the alternative of crushing the so-called 'war-party' in Kafirland, or abandoning the Albany, Somerset, and Uitenhage districts. . . . Our main object seemed to be to swell the ranks of our enemies. Submission to any terms which might satisfy us was offered, but declined. The chief Makomo, who though very much exasperated, had the sense to see the ultimate ruin of war to his nation, and who might have been a powerful lever in our hands, begged and prayed with tears in his eyes to the last moment, to be allowed to remain neutral, and reside in the colony, but was repudiated—driven to join the hostile bands, fought honourably and powerfully against us, and is a brokenhearted maniac in consequence! We commenced operations—the sequel is before us. . . .

I know that I am strongly condemned for 'making the Kafirs of too much importance'. I am told that it is absurd to apply to our dealings with 'savages' the rules which regulate the intercourse between civilized nations; that a Governor has more important matters to attend to, and that all that is wanted on the frontier is a man who can 'keep down' our troublesome neighbours, and crush them, and exterminate them if necessary. I may be wrong, but I dissent from this view of the subject. I believe the principles of truth and justice to be universal, as well as eternal; I believe them to bind the mightiest power, as well as the most insignificant community; that exactly in proportion to the pretension of superiority ought to be the inflexibility of adhesion to those principles; and that with nations, as with individuals, ultimate retribution follows in strict proportion to the observance or disregard of those only safe standards of christian and civilized duty. Nor can the question be got rid of by calling our tormentors a mere banditti; as it would, moreover, not be paying ourselves a very high compliment to admit that with all our vast resources and political refinement we have been beaten in the field, as well as in the cabinet, by a gang of thieves! In short, I consider the salvation of some hundred thousand of fellow-creatures, and the saving of two or three million sterling to the mother country every ten or twelve years, besides other momentous objects, quite important enough for the personal superintendence of a responsible Governor. . . .

4.17c Our peace and safety depend entirely on the maintenance of a prestige of the immutable truth and justice, as well as the irresistible power of the British Government.

—Essay by A. Stockenström on the causes of the 1846–7 war, London, 1 Oct. 1851. (From A. Stockenström, *Brief Notice of the Causes of the Kaffir War* (London, 1851), pp. 1–9.)

After the frontier war of 1846–47 the new governor, Sir Harry Smith, extended the colonial boundaries to the Orange River and in the east to the Keiskamma, and embarked on a more vigorous and aggressive frontier policy, openly repudiating the principles of the treaty system and blaming it for the outbreak of the war. He proclaimed the territory between the Keiskamma and the Kei 'British Kaffraria'. This was to be occupied exclusively by Xhosa chiefs who were compelled to accept British rule. Under Smith the authority of the chiefs was attacked and eroded. When he appointed a white official in 1850 to replace the Xhosa paramount chief, a frontier war again broke out and lasted for two years. Stockenström saw Smith's policies as a disastrous flouting of the principles of sound frontier policy in which he himself still believed. He used every opportunity to voice his criticism and unsuccessfully campaigned for an official inquiry into frontier matters.

. . . On Frontier matters I can only repeat those sentiments which you know me to entertain. Soon after I became more immediately connected with border policy as Commissioner-General, I was satisfied that our peace and safety depended entirely on the maintenance of a prestige of the immutable truth and justice, as well as the irresistible power of the British Government, which *then still* prevailed in the minds of the natives to a very considerable extent. I saw that by strengthening this prestige—by convincing the barbarians of our *moral* superiority, through an undeviating course of honour and honesty—*and by no other means*, should we be able to prevent those collisions, which would at first render our *physical* superiority questionable, then bring our political influence into contempt, and at last draw the many tribes, whose conflicting interests and consequent jealousies had so long kept them asunder, and made us their umpire and dictator, into alliances for the destruction of the white man. . . .

. . . So much for the causes of the war. As to the remedy, I am sorry to say, I must speak with great diffidence, and I fear I shall be found to differ very widely from you and your friends, as I have already given great offence to some excellent philanthropists by my opinion, that whatever be the means by which we have got ourselves into our present predicament, we *dare* not make the slightest concession to our barbarous foe before we shall have convinced him that we are the stronger party. Such is the double evil of injustice that it often makes justice inexpedient if not ruinous. But matters are coming to such a pitch that it may soon be doubtful which side shall dictate the terms of peace! When we had the Kaffirs and Tambookies to deal with separately, and the Bassutos, Griquas and Hottentots all on our side, the question was simple enough, but I defy almost any man to decide *now* what policy ought to be pursued after we shall have subdued our enemies, if we *can* subdue them. All must depend upon *how* you subdue them. Since the mandate of 'Extermination' has gone forth, all parties think that it is better to exterminate than to be exterminated, and it is questionable which side is likely to be most successful at the game. The prospect is most awful, and I confess myself completely stupified. But for our faith in Providence I should begin to consider our case desperate.

So much, however, I may tell you, that *whenever* you abandon *'extermination'* you will have to deal with the native tribes *through their chiefs*. I cannot as matters now stand take upon myself to recommend either the Glenelg system, or the *taking in* more, or *giving back* territory, for, as I have just said, all must depend upon how you terminate the war. You cannot deal with the Kaffirs either as wolves or as lambs. They are neither irreclaimable savages nor mild gentle shepherds. They are fierce warlike barbarians. Vigour is as necessary as justice in your dealings with them, and if you allow them to become masters you must give up the Colony. This much I predict with certainty: *you must go on exterminating, or you must restore the power of the chiefs*. You must enact the Hottentot history over again, which with the Kaffirs and others will not be so easy a matter, or you must respect those for whom the natives have a natural and even a superstitious veneration. You must humanize them by raising them in their own estimation, and in that of their people and your people, but above all by raising *yourself* in *their* estimation: in shewing your moral superiority by strict truth and justice, in giving them a taste for Christianity, by proving the virtue of your faith in your practice, and making them virtually levers in your hands by which you will move their tribes at *your* pleasure, while you leave *them* ostensibly all powerful, until in process of time you may find them dwindling into *your* Magistrates through the conviction of the whole community that a Christian *is* a better man than a heathen, and does not merely *call himself* better, and that British laws, when faithfully administered, are better than Kaffir laws.

This will be called 'chimerical', I know. It is human nature nevertheless. The example of India will be cast in my teeth. But the people of South Africa are not the people of South Asia. 'England can do anything'; but she may send ten thousand troops, and perhaps restore *the system* and apparent lull of 1849 and 50, but let her withdraw one thousand out of the ten and try how long coercion and land sales will prosper. Be sure another decree for 'Extermination' will be the immediate sequel. . . .

4.17d Justice and protection for all classes, of whatever tribe, nation, or colour, cannot be attained without security of life and property.

—Speech by A. Stockenström on the Burger Force Bill, Cape Legislative Council, 12 Sept. 1854. (From *Cape of Good Hope Parliamentary Debates*, 1854, p, 295.)

I need hardly say how entirely I concur in the objects avowed by the hon. mover, knowing them to be sincere, that he aims at justice and protection for all classes, of whatever tribe, nation, or colour, and that these objects cannot be attained without security of life and property—without peace, in fact, which is essential to the enforcement of equal laws, and which can only be maintained by being completely and at all times prepared for war. I believe this doctrine to hold good as applicable to the most civilized state of society. The condition of Europe proves this at the present moment; but it is no less a paramount consideration in your dealings with barbarians. Justice, good faith, humanity, must, as my hon. friend justly observes, be the principles upon which you must base your intercourse with the native tribes on your borders; but he maintains with equal truth that you cannot strictly adhere to justice, nor keep your engagements, nor act upon philanthropic principles towards a people whose interests may in their estimation be opposed to your own, and who see, or think they see, you weak and unprepared to resist their attacks or aggressions. As much as I have always repudiated the idea of our border neighbours being irreclaimable savages, I have no less dissented from those who think that they can be dealt with as doves or as lambs. They are barbarians, they have all the vices of barbarians;

you cannot allow them to get the better of you, without ruin to yourself. They have also the virtues of barbarians. They are men in fact governed by human nature. The laws of human nature teach us that in proportion as we are able to defend our rights, will our opponents respect them, and it is only as long as we are strong that we shall be able to turn the virtues of the barbarians to account. . . .

4.18a Why should we fight for the territory the mother-country has thought proper to take possession of?

—Speech by J. de Wet on the Burgher Force Bill, Cape Legislative Council, 11 April 1855. (From the report of the debate in the Cape Legislative Council in *The South African Commercial Advertiser*, 21 April 1855.)

In 1854 Sir George Grey became governor. He embarked on a policy of transforming Xhosa society in Kaffraria through European institutions which would hasten the process of integration of blacks in European society and so eliminate the frontier. The new Cape parliament in its second session in 1855 passed the Burgher Force Bill, supported by Stockenström, that put the civilian force on an equal footing with the military. The debates on this bill also gave Afrikaner spokesmen, including those of the Western Cape, a rare opportunity to spell out their own ideas on frontier policy. J. de Wet (1794–1875) was an advocate and businessman, and had been a prominent figure in educational and political circles in Cape Town since the 1820s. He was a member of the Cape Legislative Council 1854–68.

Mr de Wet said that . . . the burden of defending the colony should rest upon the mother-country. . . . He would not dispute that trite principle that every member of society is bound to contribute his share to the defence of the country; but, in the first place, this refers to integral parts of a country, or such parts as it is fair to presume to have been conquered by the desire or tacit consent of the whole community. But this is not the relative position of the colonists with the mother-country. The Home Government caused the colony to be continually extended against the will of the inhabitants. They, therefore, cannot be expected to defend these new conquests. . . . He had heard it often spoken of as an example that the American colonists were bound to defend their country, which he admits, but this only strengthened his position. For theirs were chartered colonies, who mostly made wars on their own account, and for their own profit, and of course they were bound to pay the expenses of these wars. They were continually invading and encroaching upon the territories of the Indians; where then was the hardship that they should bear the burden of these wars? The case, however, is different with this colony. Again, it was said that the colonists had no right to object against a principle which had existed since the time of Van Riebeeck, of which there exist proofs in every page of our records. But what was the nature of the duties they then had to perform? Were they called upon to march six or seven hundred miles to fight the Kaffirs? Were they called upon to pass weeks and months away from their wives and relatives, in order to fight the battles of those who had brought on war by continually extending the colony, in spite of all the warnings to the contrary from the inhabitants? The colonial territory was then, comparatively speaking, very limited, and thus the service to be performed quite insignificant. . . .

He admitted that in after times a burgher force was . . . established. . . . The commandoes had to defend [the colony] northwards, against the attacks of Bushmen, and eastwards against the other native tribes. Upon any outbreak, one of the near inhabitants, bearing the title of Commandant, had the right of at once mustering as many people in the neighbourhood as he could collect, he holding authority to that effect from the Government, and within 24 hours or two days, with a comparatively small force, he so unexpectedly fell upon the enemy that all disturbance was soon crushed, and further combinations prevented. It thus not seldom happened that the first messenger who brought tidings of an outbreak was almost immediately followed upon his heels by another messenger bringing tidings of its being checked, and that everything was quiet again. And the same mode of warfare was followed in respect of the Kaffirs when any hostile inroads took place on their part; always such of the inhabitants were only called upon to repel the enemy as lived in their immediate neighbourhood. None of the burghers of the more inland districts was ordered out for such duties. It was only in later years, and especially under the English Government, that the alteration took place. And although the name of commandos was then retained, they were totally different from what they used to be. Nor was there any hardship or injustice in leaving the defence of the particular localities to those who dwelt on the spot, for in going to settle there they knew beforehand that they chose a very precarious existence, and if they went to a place and established themselves there, surrounded by enemies, they could not blame the Government in not coming forward to their defence, for it could not afford it, and the border colonists were perfectly aware of it. Government had this right to expect that they would defend themselves. . . .

It was also perhaps not immaterial to consider for a moment in what way our frontier was extended. . . . In former times it was advanced much against the will of the local Government. Our old Governments always used to look upon the colonial territory as far too large, yet, against its will, in most cases, they were obliged again and again to put the landmarks further off, because after it had fixed new boundaries, immediately there were found colonists, mostly consisting of foreigners or discharged soldiers of the garrison, and so on, who squatted on the lands beyond for the purpose of having more extensive grazing ground, and thus went on peopling those territories; but they being beyond the pale of colonial rule acted as they pleased, having no other law than their own will. After these had collected in sufficient numbers, Government found that great irregularities took place; they could not permit this, and were with great reluctance thus driven to the necessity of extending that boundary, in order to bring those lawless people within the colonial jurisdiction. But then it had this advantage that the frontier, when it was extended, was already peopled, so that there was found within the territory newly taken possession of sufficient strength and force to defend it.

This is not the case when, in our days, the frontiers are extended. Every new Governor, mostly a General in the Army, being upon his arrival pestered with complaints of Kaffir depredations, has some new policy to try. In most cases this leads to war, and those wars are invariably followed by aggrandizing the colonial territory. With a stroke of the Governor's pen thousands of acres of waste land, from which the aborigines are driven away, are annexed to the colony, but also thereby as many inveterate and implacable enemies are created. The colonists, especially the old ones, are neither consulted nor their remonstrance in the matter much heeded or cared for. Everything is done in spite of all their warning and remonstrance to the contrary. There being thus much land for disposal, Mr So-and-so on the frontier gets a good slice of the cake, Mr So-and-so another slice, both having rendered some personal service to the Governor, or having upheld his fancy policy, and so on. These grants are brought to market, and dealt with as is nowadays done with the copper mine shares. There is nothing blameworthy in that. This newly acquired territory may be excellent land, but you have not a sufficient population to defend it from the

Kaffirs, smarting as these do under irreparable injuries in having lost their all, by their patrimony and ancestral dwelling places being taken from them. In this manner the colony has been continually more and more extended, and its enemies in the same proportion multiplied till it has now become quite unmanageable. What right is there, under these circumstances, to call upon the inhabitants to defend it, or now to throw the whole burden upon the colony? . . .

. . . He did not know what means remain to a people, if you take away their country, more especially if they depend for support, as the Kaffirs do, on their flocks, unless perhaps you allow them to steal. But you drive them back one upon another, and the country becomes too small for them. The Kaffirs, a pastoral nation, who require a wide extent of territory, must feel it keenly when you take such large extents of territory away from them. . . . In proportion as you extend your territory you come in contact—not with more friendly but with more hostile tribes. Your enemies are continually increasing. . . . The more you get northward the more you meet with tribes comparatively more civilised in the arts of war, and as they have to fight for their very existence, of course they are more brave. . . .

As England had for purposes of her own placed more of the Eastern Province inhabitants in the places where they now were, it was her duty to defend them, and they had no right to call upon the inhabitants of the Western Districts to defend their country, except as volunteers. . . . It was not only the distance, but other serious grievances as well. . . . If we are to leave our homes, who is to protect our wives and children against the coloured population, formerly our slaves, and who are particularly intermixed with the inhabitants of the Western Districts? Or against the aborigines, entertaining all sorts of wild and extravagant ideas, as to their proprietorship of the land we now possess? The want of manual labor now already presses hard upon us. And were we to march to the frontier, who are then to till our grounds? The absence of a proper Master and Servants' law causes an intolerable spirit of insubordination amongst the field and other agricultural labourers on our farms; how much more will this be manifested when we will be from home? . . .

Why should we fight, say the Burghers, for the territory the mother country has thought proper to take possession of? What do we gain by it? We are not in every respect enjoying the same advantages from the colony as the mother country does. Our wants, our desires are only satisfied as long as England finds it to her own advantage to do so. If there is a collision of interest between the mother country and the colony, does not her interest prevail to our disadvantage? Is not every high station here filled by her sons? Whilst the natives are to content themselves with the crumbs that fall from the rich man's tables. . . .

God forbid that the position he had taken should be construed to be an indifference to the sufferings of the border inhabitants; on the contrary, whether England came to their support or not, a moral and religious obligation rests with the old inhabitants to take a warm interest in the safety and well-being of their brethren in the East. But while he thus considered it as a moral and religious duty, there must be no other compulsory means appealed to than the dictates of morality and religion. . . .

4.18b The people expected that if they once had a Parliament of their own there would soon be an end to all little Kaffir wars, and they would be enabled to crush the power of our barbarous neighbours from one ocean to the other.

—Speech by F. W. Reitz (Sr) on the Burgher Force Bill, Cape Legislative Council, 11 April 1855. (From the report of the debate in the Cape Legislative Council in *The South African Commercial Advertiser*, 21 April 1855.)

4.18 *Cape Afrikaners' views on frontier policy 1855–7*

F. W. Reitz (1810–1881) studied and travelled in Europe before settling in the Swellendam district and becoming one of the most progressive farmers in the colony. He was a member of the Cape parliament 1854–63 and again 1869–73, and one of his sons later became president of the Orange Free State.

Mr Reitz said that . . . when he stated his opinion, it was founded on the principle that every citizen is bound by the most sacred ties to do all he can in defence of his country. . . . Most of the petitions presented to the House seemed to object more to a muster than to the principle of the bill. . . . The older colonists generally, with very few exceptions, approve of the general principle of the bill. And he thought there were very few who hold the opinion that because some of our fellow-colonists have settled on the borders, and by their industry and enterprise have reaped in part the reward for their sacrifices, they should therefore be left to defend themselves single-handed, against the ruthless barbarian, without receiving any assistance from this end of the colony. He had ever hoped that the different national feelings, which must exist in so motley a population as ours, would be replaced by the one strong feeling that we were all fellow-colonists. . . . However some of us may feel a greater sympathy for those of the same origin as ourselves—whether Englishmen or Dutchmen—we must all allow that our duty in this case is clear, and the only question which is to be decided is, how most effectually to protect districts nearest the enemy with least possible injustice to those further removed. . . .

The inhabitants do not wish to deny that it is their duty to serve on commando when the country is in danger. On the contrary, . . . the people expected that if they once had a Parliament of their own there would soon be an end to all little Kaffir wars, which were the causes of tremendous expense to England, and great loss of lives and time, which to us is money, to the colony. They expected that our Governors would no longer be led by a false philanthropy to pursue a vacillating policy which but renders our savage neighbours more insolent, more independent, and which ultimately brings ruin upon themselves, and on the colony greater evils.

They expected that if ever unfortunately a Kaffir war should break out again, such a number of colonists would be called out, and the war carried on in such a manner, that they would be enabled to crush the power of our barbarous neighbours from one ocean to the other, and thus prevent them, for many years at least, from disturbing the safety of the colony; and then will be the time for a Christian people to tame and civilize them. Where a civilized people is placed in juxtaposition with a barbarous people, you can never expect to maintain peace for any length of time by a balance of power. You may, where two civilized nations are contiguous; but where a civilized and a barbarous nation come together, the savage must learn to fear the punishment which will follow upon an act of aggression committed by him.

He did not believe that the colonists had any desire for the lands of the Kaffirs. He believed that they would be satisfied if they could retain what they now had in peace and safety. He believed that they would find it a better plan to endeavour to make two blades of grass grow where one grew before, and this would be the best way to double their number of acres, but in order to obtain such victories as these, we must first have peace and safety.

4.18c Our frontier wars with their endless train of losses, public and private, have been caused by injudicious treatment of the Natives.

—Editorial by Dr Changuion in *De Zuid-Afrikaan*, 30 June 1856. (From the translation published in *De Zuid-Afrikaan*.)

It is well known that our frontier wars, with their endless train of losses, public and private, have been caused by injudicious treatment of the Natives. Our Governors, with few exceptions, have been lamentably deficient in this particular; and their delegates who, with the title of Resident Magistrate, lived in immediate contact with our swarthy neighbours, and consequently had the best opportunities of studying their particularities, have in the majority of instances exhibited the same want of practical wisdom. On some occasions ill-timed leniency, which savages never fail to ascribe to a sense of weakness, has engendered contempt; on others, unnecessary interference with their national customs has exasperated them, or gratuitous outrages committed on those whom they had learned to revere have goaded them on to acts of summary vengeance. Promises that were not fulfilled, and threats that could not be executed, have in turns taught them to despise an enemy, whose most solemn asseverations failed alike of inspiring confidence and of striking terror into the minds of men, whose criterion of good faith and power is not in words but in actions. After the humiliating lessons which British authorities have repeatedly received at the hands of the Kafirs, one would expect more caution in their dealings with people who, however much our inferiors in the arts of civilized life, are perfectly competent to distinguish between power and imbecility, justice and its contrary. . . .

4.18d If the colonists occupy the land of the natives, they cannot expect to sleep upon a bed of roses.

—Speech by J. H. Wicht in the Separation Debate, Cape Legislative Council, 9 May 1857. (From the report in *The Cape Argus*, 16 May 1857.)

From the middle 1850s the issue of a possible separation between the western and eastern provinces of the Cape colony became a dominant issue in Cape politics. The question of frontier policy, which was primarily an Eastern affair, but which from time to time caused colonists from the western districts to do military duty as in the frontier war of 1846, was one of the issues at stake. J. H. Wicht was a prominent Cape Town property-owner, and a member of the Cape Town Municipality as well as of the Legislative Assembly.

. . . When the Eastern Province speaks so loudly of its progress, it may be as well to remind them that they have the expenditure of 10 000 troops. . . . [We are asked to] consider the danger of the Frontier. There may be more danger, but gentlemen seem to amass large fortunes in a very short time up there in spite of the danger. Our sympathies have been appealed to—hon. members have drawn such a dreadful picture of barbarism rushing into the country, and laying everything waste with fire and sword. But in the same breath we are told that the value of farms is increasing at an enormous rate. It is very strange. We submit to Burgher laws, Gunpowder laws, pay large sums of money for the defence of the Frontier, there is a large army on the Frontier, the Kaffirs are completely denuded of their property, they are miserable and starving—then where is [the cause of] the fear? But [we are told that] hon. members are in momentary fear of their lives. If such be the gloomy prospects of the Frontier, what can make farms rise so much in value? But hon. members complain of those barbarian Kaffirs who also wish to come back to the country from which they had been driven, and which those gentlemen have taken possession of. Well, if the colonists occupy the lands of the natives, they cannot expect to sleep upon a bed of roses. If you go near the savages, it is like going near a nest of hornets—they will sting you. But we cannot blame the Kaffirs for this. It is the Kaffir's uncivilized way of thinking that he has a right to get back the country he has been deprived of, if he can. It is a savage idea, and, no doubt, cannot be found in the breast of any civilized person—although, perhaps, if the French were despoiled of a portion of France, they would very likely try to get it back again. There is a sort of principle in human nature that, if possible, a man will recover that of which he has been dispossessed. He hoped, however, that the Kaffirs may see the error of their way, and retire into some distant part, beyond the interference of the white man. . . .

4.19a The best way to secure peace is that friends meet and speak their minds.

—Minutes of a Conference between President J. N. Boshof and Chief Moshweshwe, Governor Grey being present; Smithfield, 5 Oct. 1855. (From *Correspondence between Sir G. Grey and the Secretary of State for the Colonies, of the Affairs of the Cape Colony, Natal, and Adjacent Territories* (presented to the Cape parliament, April, 1857), pp. 26–29.)

During the first two decades after the founding of the new republic of the Orange Free State in 1854, the question of the frontier with the chiefdom of Moshweshwe overshadowed all other political issues. Conflicting land claims and cattle thefts on the eastern border caused continuous friction between the two states. J. N. Boshof, who became president in 1855, believed that the Free State was not strong enough to declare war and tried to reach a peaceful solution through the mediation of Sir George Grey, governor of the Cape Colony.

President. I am very glad to see Moshesh here in the presence of His Excellency Sir G. Grey, on the first official opportunity we have had of meeting in the Free State. I think it well that we should often meet, as personal visits are always much more satisfactory than correspondence by letter. As we meet now personally, we had better speak of business. I have often heard that Moshesh is a man of peace, and is desirous of holding peace with the whites. I am also a man of peace; and now in the presence of his chief men, I wish to show him on what terms we make peace and friendship continue. As the best mode to do so, my view is that as I am chosen on the one side, and Moshesh on the other, to see that peace is not interrupted, we should, in case any disturbances occur, let each other know our minds freely. I shall, therefore, tell him at once that I have, on my arrival, been very sorry to hear of many thefts having been committed within our boundary, by wicked people from the other side. I would be glad to convince him that such things must be put a stop to, or the consequences will be that they will put the country in a blaze, and do great harm to all. . . . He has promised to punish the thieves, and put a stop to the stealing. I have no doubt that he will prove himself a man of his word, and make his chiefs help him to carry out his promises. . . .

Moshesh. Peace is the mother of all. . . . The complaints have not been sufficiently established. If you can show me the cause of dissatisfaction, let me know. . . .

President. I will take him up at the last word. The cause he must know, but the way is this—his people come in and steal. The missionaries have been long enough in the country for them to know that stealing is wrong. I believe that Moshesh has enough good men among his people to help him to put down the wicked men who steal. . . .

. . . Stealing will never cease, unless the thieves are punished. Retaking stolen cattle from the thief is no punishment. He ought also to be fined or receive corporal punishment. If the chief refuses to give up a thief, he makes himself responsible. We put thieves in prison, and punish them when convicted. If he did so we would not have any more stealing. He need not tell me that he has no power to punish those who do wrong, for if they can retake the stolen cattle, they can punish the thief also. . . . I mention these things to show that they give rise to quarrels. My people will not submit to it any longer. Now, as he asked my advice, I say that if his people will not obey him, he must make them. He must take his people against them. Those things that they should not wish us to do, he must not do. He would not be satisfied if I said I could not help such things, if committed by my people. I know that they can do it, because sometimes, for months long, no thefts were committed, so if they could stop the thieving once, they could do so again, and there are other chiefs who never steal. I conclude, therefore, that those chiefs who will exercise their power can stop stealing. . . .

. . . I think the best way to secure peace is that friends meet and speak their minds. I have stated all I had to say, and I want Moshesh to state any grievances he has to speak about. . . .

. . . I shall always be happy to hear from him about anything that is done wrong by my people, as war would only break us all down; but if there is any other thing, as His Excellency is present, of which he feels aggrieved, I would be glad to hear of it. . . .

4.19b I ask you to prove whether you are willing and able to deal out to offending tribes and their chiefs the exemplary punishment they deserve, and to cause compensation to be made to the sufferers.

—Letter from President J. N. Boshof to Chief Moshweshwe, 27 June 1856. (From Theal, *Basutoland Records*, Vol. 2, pp. 205–207.)

In protracted negotiations and diplomatic correspondence the Free State consistently attempted to get Moshweshwe to assume responsibility for the actions of lesser chiefs in the frontier zone. On his part Moshweshwe never relinquished claims on land which the Free State also claimed. Finally the Free State declared war on 19 March 1858.

Great Chief,

You will receive this letter by the hands of two gentlemen, whom I have found it expedient to send as a deputation to you . . . and whom I have instructed to speak with you on a very disagreeable subject, one which I fear may lead to very unpleasant results, viz., the stealing of cattle and horses which has of late been by your people resumed and carried on to such an extent . . . as to be no longer bearable. In addition to which, besides burning down two farmers' houses, the Natives have lately assumed so insolent a tone . . . that my personal presence and influence in this part of the district became absolutely necessary in order to prevent the Boers, goaded as they have been to desperation by rapine and insult, from attacking those tribes to which the marauders have been clearly proved to belong.

I have with difficulty succeeded in restraining these men for the present, and have persuaded them to await the results of the final appeal which I now make to you, thereby to prove whether you be willing and able to deal out to offending tribes and their chiefs the exemplary punishment they deserve, and to cause ample and satisfactory compensation to be made to the sufferers. . . .

Should you not cause compensation to be made . . . and should you fail to punish the chiefs and to take such measures as will for the future assure security and confidence to our border inhabitants, and thus induce them to return to their farms and houses, and live there unmolested in the peaceful possession of their own property, or should you tell me that you have not the means of doing so, I shall then of course not refer again to you on such subjects, but shall take measures as I myself shall feel called upon to avenge the many injuries which for so long a time have been endured by our people, in the fullest assurance that you will neither interfere with their punishment, nor deplore the fate of tribes who have proved themselves to be vagabonds and incorrigible robbers, who in defiance of your authority have hitherto persevered in the perpetration of acts which no longer can admit of our forbearance. Should it, however, be otherwise, and should you constitute yourself the protector of such tribes (a line of conduct of which I cannot and will not believe you capable), in such case I could but deplore the interruption of the friendly relations which, for our mutual advantage, I am anxious to maintain with you, though the men of the Free State will ever find consolation in the consciousness that, for the sake of peace, they submitted to losses and annoyance until past all endurance.

I shall anxiously await your answer, and the result of such active measures as you will now most undoubtedly take to enforce your own authority and cause it to be respected, hoping that they will be such as to strike terror into all evildoers, and convince me that you are ever ready and willing to co-operate with me in maintaining the present good understanding between us. . . .

4.19c A war with the Basutos seems now unavoidable.

—Letter from President J. N. Boshof to Governor Grey, 16 March 1858. (From Theal, *Basutoland Records*, Vol. 2, pp. 320–322.)

. . . I think it right in consideration of the interest which you have on former occasions shown in the welfare of this State, to inform you that I have been obliged to call out the Burghers in defence of the rights of this State, violated by the Basutos, and that we are at this moment on the point of a war with all the tribes that acknowledge Moshesh as their head.

This Chief has, notwithstanding his solemn engagements to compensate for robberies from time to time committed on our frontier farmers, failed to comply therewith. Several hundred horses are not yet given up; the few delivered up by him are miserable Kaffir horses and mares, whilst the best horses stolen from our farmers are still retained and ridden by the natives, even before the eyes of their owners. . . .

Pretending that we occupy a considerable portion of the Basuto country, and wilfully misinterpreting the treaty entered into by Moshesh and myself at Smithfield in October 1855, they have from time to time, in defiance of our laws to the contrary, entered far into the State in numerous armed bands, hunting and riding about, and thereby disturbing the peace of our farmers and their families. . . .

That this Chief encourages them in such proceedings is evident, as no satisfaction can be got from him, and as he has, in fact, informed me that he claims a very considerable part of the Smithfield district, many years ago occupied, built upon, and improved by our people; and is prepared to support his claims, if need be, by support of arms.

Under such circumstances it cannot be wondered at that our borderers, expecting an attack from the Basutos, have gone into laagers. Whilst this was being done and measures were being taken for the security of our whole frontier line, cattle stealing has been carried on by the natives on the borders of the Winburg district. . . .

Moshesh has refused to give us any satisfaction. . . . The Chief pretends that the complaints of our people are frivolous; that they occupy lands which he only lent them; that they are in fact his subjects, and ought to have looked to him for redress if they had any ground of complaint; . . . that his people had a right to settle down on the same farms with our Boers, and that he was even surprised that they, the Boers, should go into laagers on his, Moshesh's, territory. . . .

A war with the Basutos seems now unavoidable, and whether the Griquas and the native tribes over the Vaal will keep out of this quarrel remains to be seen. The Free State has many enemies, and the natives are easily excited and urged on to mischief by villainous white men. God only knows what will be the result of this struggle; but it is clear to me that it cannot be avoided; and I would only beg as a favour of Your Excellency that you will not prevent the colonial farmers from voluntarily coming to our assistance, to prevent the ruin and destruction of their relatives and fellow countrymen, should they be inclined so to act.

4.20a I call upon you to do justice, and help me to do the same, and we and our children shall enjoy sweet peace.

—Letter from Acting President J. J. Venter to Chiefs Moshweshwe and Letsie, 6 Aug. 1863. (From Theal, *Basutoland Records*, Vol. 3A, p. 228.)

During the early 1860s tension again increased on the Free State–Basutoland border despite the treaty signed after the war of 1858. The ageing Moshweshwe found it difficult to control rival Basotho chiefs who desired more land to relieve the congestion of cattle and horses in Basutoland. On the Free State side there was similar pressure for an extension of the border. Cattle-raids conducted from both sides increased friction and tension on the frontier. J. J. Venter (1814–1889) was a leading Free State politician who served several times as acting president. Venter was a typical representative of the ultra-conservative 'Dopper'-trekboers and played a role in the establishment of the Gereformeerde *Church (a break-away group from the Dutch Reformed Church) in 1859.*

Chiefs Moshesh and Letsie,

I greet you both with sincerity as your old and true friend. I am obliged to complain to you, Moshesh and Letsie, about Paul Moperi and Molapo. Old friend Moshesh, when I was with you at your mountain last, you said . . .: 'The white people should not complain to Moperi and Molapo, for they are not Chiefs, they are mischief-makers.' I now find it is so. You did not lie. I and Moshesh try to preserve peace, and the others to stir up war. This I regret. . . . Why do the petty Chiefs brew mischief to get us to fight and shed innocent blood? . . . The criminals flee to Moperi, and he gives them ground in the Free State, as likewise does Molapo.

If the Free State rebukes them they do not show us their teeth, but those of Moshesh. If Moshesh calls them to account, they show him the teeth of the Free State, and say 'We shall take refuge with the Government of the Free State.' I assure you, Moshesh, we shall not receive them or help them. How can we think of punishing the peaceful and the good, and protect the wicked? If Moperi and Molapo would behave like Moshesh and Letsie, our friendship would continue to grow like young grass. What shall we do? I ask Moshesh and Letsie for advice. They increase their strength with rogues in order to wrench the kingdom from Letsie after Moshesh's death, and the Free State must give their men ground. I can eat them up, but I do not like to break the peace between us. I fear them, Molapo and Moperi, as much as a vulture does the carcase of a horse. I only dislike to see innocent blood flow, and no more.

Now Moshesh, I ask you and Letsie, how must our Government look upon you, as friends, or as enemies? I am really your friend, and perhaps Moshesh and Letsie will say the same to me, but our acts must prove our words true. Children also speak good words, and still they take each other's things, and so it is now with Moperi and Molapo. I send you a report of the Inspector of Police, from which you can see how matters are going on. Now, I ask you, Moshesh and Letsie, lay your hands on your hearts, and consider that He who gives us rain and is Great also loves Justice. I call upon you to do Justice, and help me to do the same, and God will bless us, and we and our children shall enjoy sweet peace.

4.20b It is my heart's desire to live with you and your people upon a friendly footing.

—Letter from President J. H. Brand to Chief Moshweshwe, 10 Feb. 1864. (From Theal, *Basutoland Records*, Vol. 3A, pp. 252–253.)

J. H. Brand (1823–1888), the son of Christoffel Brand, studied law in Cape Town and the Netherlands, and practised as a lawyer in London and Cape Town before becoming president of the Orange Free State in 1864. The following letter to Moshweshwe was sent soon after Brand assumed his new office in February 1864.

Great Chief,

It is with pleasure I have to inform you that on the 2nd of this month I was elected State President, and that I have taken the oath of office and commenced the administration of the Government.

It is also with pleasure that I give you my assurance that it is my heart's desire to live with you and your people upon a friendly footing and that on my part all that is possible shall be done which will preserve and promote a good understanding between us. I am convinced that you are thoroughly of the same wishes, and that you will use your powerful influence to awaken and confirm the same feelings amongst your people.

The good ministers of God's word whom you have gathered around you have ever testified that you evince a disposition to adhere to the good principles which religion teaches us. As my great aim shall be to promote justice and equity, and as I shall always be ready and willing to see that right and justice are observed towards your subjects, I think I may cherish a firm hope that you on your side will not tolerate by any of your people an act of injustice committed against any of the inhabitants of the Orange Free State.

If we and our people are faithful to this principle, we may then hope and expect that the Almighty will bless and prosper us. Should it ever occur, which, however, I trust will not happen, that any of your subjects have just reason of complaint against any of the inhabitants of the Free State, be good enough in that case to inform me immediately thereof, and I will see that the complaint is properly investigated, and that justice is done in the matter.

On my part I repose such confidence in your good disposition and willingness to do all you can for the promotion of friendly relations between your country and mine, that I am satisfied you will not permit any of your people to go unpunished who commit an act of injustice towards a subject of this country, but that such a case has only to be brought to your knowledge to ensure a proper investigation, satisfaction to the injured party, and the due punishment of the offender. By so doing, peace will dwell upon our borders, and our people will be satisfied, happy, and prosperous.

With the assurance of my best wishes for your health and welfare, and with the hope that we shall long continue to preserve a good understanding between the countries over which we are placed, . . .

4.20c It is a sad truth that there was and is no other way of securing the blessing of peace with the Basutos but through the means of war.

—Letter from President J. H. Brand to Chief Moshweshwe, 25 Aug. 1865. (From Theal, *Basutoland Records*, Vol. 3A, pp. 446–448.)

In October 1864 Sir Philip Wodehouse, Governor of the Cape Colony, made a 'final' boundary settlement between the Orange Free State and Moshweshwe's Kingdom. When the Basothos did not voluntarily remove from the territory allotted to the Free State, Brand cleared the area with commandos. In reprisal, Lesoana, a lesser chief, attacked the village of Bethlehem and when Moshweshwe was not prepared to act against him, Brand declared war in August 1865.

When I assumed office in February, 1864, I wrote to you that nothing would give me greater pleasure than to see the people of the Free State and the Basutos live in amity with each other. I and my people acted up to our professions, and by deed showed the sincerity of our professions. No act of aggression or other cause of complaint was given by my people. You also professed to be desirous of cultivating amicable relations between us. But what did you do to secure so great a blessing? It was my painful duty to complain, almost in every letter which I wrote to you, of the continual thefts committed by your people, and what redress was given by you? Promises, which were never fulfilled. Your people and chiefs encroached upon the boundary line clearly laid down in the treaty of Aliwal, signed and sealed by you. All this was done under the pretext of a disputed boundary line. . . .

Anxious to avoid an appeal to arms as long as it could be honourably done, I suggested, and you consented, to leave the question of the boundary line to the unqualified decision of His Excellency the Governor. The decision of His Excellency was entirely in our favour. I at once gave notice to you of His Excellency's decision, and what did you do? . . . It was not until the burghers, whom I had called to the front to maintain the line, if necessary, by force, were on their march to the frontier, that you sent me word that you would submit to His Excellency's decision. . . .

To my mind it is now clear from the sad experience which I have gained of the character of the Basutos, that if they had not seen the large force which was ready to maintain our rights, they would still have been squatted on our side of the line, so clearly laid down in the treaty of Aliwal. . . . You now talk of restoring peace. I have always been and still am desirous of peace, but not peace in name, not a peace of professions, whilst the acts of your people are war; but a real and substantial peace, under which our burghers will be able to enjoy the fruits of their labour, and not be constantly subject to the depredations and annoyance which they have endured with so much forbearance for a very long time. Sad experience has, however, shown me that such a peace can only be procured by the sword. For I am convinced that we shall have no peace until the Basutos shall have been taught to respect the property of others, and not to appropriate what does not belong to them.

After failing to procure an amicable settlement of the many causes of complaint, after waiting in vain for the fulfilment of your promises, no other resource was left to our Government than to vindicate our rights by the sword. Trusting in God, we took up arms in defence of our rights. . . . I have brought these facts to your notice to show the true character of the Basutos. It is a sad truth that there was and is no other way of securing the blessing of peace with the Basutos but through the means of war. If your people had abstained from acts of hostility and aggression, and you had given redress for the wrongs committed by them, you might still have enjoyed the blessing of peace; but it is sheer hypocrisy to be constantly talking of peace, and not to employ the means of securing its blessing; but, on the contrary, to allow your sons, your brothers, and your people to rob and plunder, instead of compelling them to earn the fruits of honest labour.

We have only taken up arms to teach the Basutos that their thefts and other acts of hostility will no longer be tolerated. If you wish for peace I am willing to grant it upon the hereunto annexed terms and conditions; you will have three hours to consider. If after that time the required answer and hostages are not given, then the armistice is at an end, and hostilities will be resumed. . . .

5 *Settlement, conquest and trek 1800–1860*

Settler communities may come to need their own 'foundation myths',[1] and they may require such special communal justifications and legitimations in more than one context. On attaining a degree of independent political consciousness the former colonial dependency has to define and justify its new position with respect to the 'mother country'. Also, the settlers' relations with the indigenous peoples are usually based on dispossession, if not on outright conquest, and may require special apology. Both themes may be followed in early Afrikaner political thinking.

The settlers' relation to the mother country was the first to be dealt with explicitly, and their thinking showed a clear line of development. At first they pressed their local claims and rights against the metropolitan power from a perspective which was itself still essentially metropolitan, in which they appeared as mere extensions and instrumentalities of the colonizing power. Thus the Cape Patriots of the eighteenth century did not yet fully view themselves as members of a separate society with its own origins and history. Their history, insofar as it was more than a succession of individual cases of economic grievances and official malpractices, was still perceived as part of the Dutch struggle for liberation from Spanish oppression. Even where Van Riebeeck's first settlement was projected as a lost Golden Age (cf 6.2), this tended to mirror the characteristic Dutch invocations of the Golden Age of the Republic, and it was not yet employed as part of a foundation myth for a separate settlement. However, in the course of the nineteenth century a different historical consciousness and orientation began to appear at the Cape. In the pages of the *Nederduitsch Zuid-Afrikaansch Tijdschrift*, the first local Dutch journal, published from 1824, we find a definite preoccupation with the founding activities of 'Father' Van Riebeeck, and with the local history of the earliest settlements at Cape Town and Stellenbosch. The political significance of this new concern with the *founding* of the settlement is that it provided a different and closer focal point for settler thinking on colonial issues and problems. Such settler thinking no longer necessarily orientated itself to the longer historical vistas and the larger imperial perspectives as these appeared from the metropolitan centre. No doubt the British takeover of the Cape also contributed to this reorientation of settler thinking away from the colonizing power as mother country. Henceforth, under alien rule, the former Dutch burghers at the Cape could only come to see themselves as primarily British subjects after a somewhat difficult process of assimilation, while the cultural links with Holland were also increasingly severed. Still, the progress towards consciousness of a distinctive nationality with its own historical legitimation was very slow and gradual, and would only become significant in the second half of the nineteenth century.

During the first half of the nineteenth century, polemics and apologies were more concerned with the settlers' relation to the indigenous peoples with which they had come to share the emerging plural society at the Cape. Of course in this case, too, conscious attempts to provide any kind of justification or legitimation for the consequences of settlement and conquest came late and largely retrospectively. From the outset it must have been evident that colonization did not take place in uninhabited territories. Clearly the growth of the settlement at the Cape could only take place through a prolonged process of encroachment on the land and dispossession of the property of the original inhabitants. If in the case of the Khoikhoi outright military conquest was relatively seldom necessary, the end result of establishing white domination was no less complete.[2] With the San, an outright war of extermination was fought during the last quarter of the eighteenth century. But none of this seemed to raise serious moral or political problems in the minds of the colonists, nor to call forth any particular attempts at justification. On occasion high officials, both Dutch and British, would voice criticism of the colonists' dealings with the indigenous peoples resulting in their dispossession and subjugation,[3] but the colonists did not find it necessary to provide any general answer or defence. This would change with the advent of the missionary and philanthropic critics of settler society in the early nineteenth century. The thrust of the complaints of Van der Kemp and Read about individual cases of maltreatment of Khoikhoi on the part of the colonists was broadened into a general indictment of settler society as based on the violent conquest and continuing exploitation of the original inhabitants in Dr Philip's *Researches in South Africa*, published in 1828. Philip had influential allies in the colony such as John Fairbairn, editor of the *South African Commercial Advertiser*, he had powerful supporters in London, and an excellent forum in the proceedings of the Select Committee on the Aborigines in the mid-1830s, so that his activities and criticisms constituted a considerable political force. Above all, however, they posed a direct challenge to the very moral and political basis of settler society: they questioned the legitimacy of the settlers' position in relation to the claims and interests of the original inhabitants of the colony. Belatedly some legitimation for settlement and the settlers' right to the land had to be provided. Inevitably this involved the construction of an acceptable version of the origins and growth of the settlement so as to fit these apologetic needs in the controversy about conquest and the right to the land.

It was at the height of this controversy that the Great Trek got under way, a fact which greatly influenced the public statements of the leaders of the Trek. If the Trekkers, unlike the puritans in New England, did not set out with the primary objective of founding a *new* society based on their own political and religious ideas, but rather aimed at conserving important aspects of the earlier social order (cf. Chapter 1, p. 16ff), they also did so in the full consciousness that violent conquest of the indigenous peoples of the interior and dispossession of their land would no longer go unchallenged. As it turned out, they could not avoid settlement disputes and even military engagements with the chiefdoms of the interior, and the survival of a new trekboer society was only possible if the Trekkers could establish control over the local population and gain some degree of political independence from the metropolitan power. The Trek thus involved once again all the main issues of the initial settlement, but in a more acute form and now very much alive in the minds of the leading participants. Not only retrospectively, but in anticipation and concurrently, justifications and legitimations were provided for the Trekkers' actions and objectives. In the process, and from the historical experience of the Trek itself, new notions also began to emerge about the grounds and purpose of this dramatic founding of a new settlement.

In analyzing the documents brought together in this chapter the following questions may be kept in mind:

1 What are the underlying or explicit issues which are being addressed, and within

what kind of assumed moral or political framework are they being discussed?

2 What is the function of the normative views canvassed: do they serve as justifications or legitimations of the *de facto* situation or can they also serve as normative principles for action?

3 To what extent is a specific and external audience being addressed, and to what extent are firmly held personal convictions being articulated?

4 What is the historical context, and what are the possible political consequences envisaged?

The settlers' right to the land

The opening documents of this chapter show clearly the enormous impact of the philanthropic critics, and Dr Philip above all, on colonial thinking at the Cape about the issues of settlement and conquest. The first two documents (the extracts from Egbertus Bergh's Memoir on the Cape of 1802 and from Christoffel Brand's dissertation of 1820) reflect the assumptions of the pre-Philip era. On the other hand, the rather contrived apologetic arguments (5.4a, b) produced by Truter and De Wet in the mid-thirties indicate the urgent efforts to find some moral and intellectual counter to Philip's critique. The position of Stockenström (5.3a, b, 5.9) is as usual more complex, constituting neither a straightforward apology for nor an outright condemnation of settler claims.

So unproblematical were the issues of colonial settlement and conquest to the early settlers that it has not been possible to find any general expression of their right to the land with respect to the indigenous peoples before well into the nineteenth century. Stockenström would later claim that in his experience the older colonists had been well aware of the historical facts of conquest and dispossession: 'It never entered the imagination of the simplest of the Boers to deny the oppression, knowing that he could not take a step without crossing ground of which those he holds in bondage were once the free and contented owners.' (5.9a) In the surviving documents we certainly do find forthright expressions from an early period by spokesmen of the Khoikhoi, and later of the Xhosa as well, of their right to the land and their bitter resentment of dispossession.[4] There is also an occasional indication of some recognition by the colonists of their prior claims to disputed territories, as in Van Jaarsveld's proposal in 1794 to return the Zuurveld to the Xhosa for the sake of peace.[5] In Stockenström's view (5.9b) the lack of any such generalized excuses for or justifications of this aggression argued for less hypocrisy on the part of the Dutch settlers. However this may be, the fact is that at that time they did not put their thinking on the subject in writing.

The other side of this coin is that, when an enlightened Afrikaner official like Egbertus Bergh expressed severely critical views on the subject, he still tended to deal with it as a generalized academic issue rather than as a matter of immediate practical concern or political relevance. Bergh considered the Khoikhoi to be the 'freeborn and rightful possessors of the land in which they are now made subservient'. By implication this questioned and perhaps even denied the settlers' moral right to the land. Bergh was also very outspoken in his description of the Khoikhoi's condition as a 'state of completely slavish subjection', 'suffering the most inconceivable maltreatment', etc. (5.1) However, this amounts to little more than a generalized expression of moral outrage. The implicit assumption in Bergh's moral condemnation of the settlers' dealings with the original inhabitants of the country, much as in Van Ryneveld's views on slavery as a 'necessary evil' (cf. 2.3), is that the process of settlement, conquest and dispossession is an irreversible historical process. It is the inevitable fate of the Khoikhoi to disperse further, and eventually to die out. At best, we can sympathize with such 'sorry individuals'. But if this is indeed the case, then the political force of Bergh's critique of the basis of settler society is far from clear. If the course and consequences of colonial settlement have some sort of historical inevitability then these expressions of moral outrage are of little consequence. In short, Bergh does not yet address the basic political problems of settlement and the right to the land in any serious sense.

Much the same holds for the way in which Christoffel Brand (5.2) took a different and more favourable position concerning the settlers' right to the land in 1820. The formal topic of this section of his dissertation is nothing less than the question of the manner in which, and the extent to which, colonists can rightfully gain control of vacant or already inhabited territories. But clearly Brand rehearsed the traditional distinctions and arguments in this regard as a mere academic exercise, and his application of these doctrines to the settlers of the Cape was very perfunctory indeed. Brand readily admitted that the claim that the earliest settlers at the Cape rightfully acquired the territory through a compact with the original inhabitants at best amounted to their observing 'the form of a purchase and sale'. However, in his mind this did not raise any serious problems; rather he made it the occasion for some moralistic observations on the foibles of mankind, with analogies from Herodotus. In short, Brand, who proudly identified himself with the Cape settler community, saw no reason to provide any particular justification or legitimation for the settlers' claim to the land. Two other aspects of Brand's position should be noted. First, the purported transaction by which the earliest settlers 'purchased' the territory from the Khoikhoi is clearly regarded as some kind of 'founding' action that did not apply merely to specific individuals at a given time and place but somehow to the entire history and growth of the settlement. Secondly, though Brand claimed that the settlers' right to the land was based on compact rather than on war or violent conquest, he would have had little difficulty in shifting his ground to the latter claim. Acquiring a territory through force or conquest is held to be an 'imperfect means' that leads only to an 'imperfect right', but it is not clear that these distinctions held any particular moral or practical force.

In contrast, Chief Justice Truter and Advocate De Wet, a little more than a decade later, but following the publication of Philip's *Researches in South Africa*, very deliberately set out to provide a defence, on behalf of the Cape settlers, to the charges against them 'about the supposed injustice done to the original inhabitants by allegedly dispossessing them of this country by force'. (De Wet, 5.4b) They also shifted the ground of their defence. It was no longer adequate to base the settlers' right to the land on either conquest or compact, presumably because both had in the mean time become morally and historically suspect. Instead they chose the higher ground of arguing that in the relevant sense the land was not yet occupied at the settlers' coming. Thus Van Riebeeck, according to Truter, 'made himself master of the land not by right of conquest, nor by right of purchase, but by right of occupation, as he did not then find that any nation or individual either occupied the land or claimed ownership of it'. (Truter, 5.4a) (Again this is seen as a primary founding action whose validity is carried over into the later progression and growth of the settlement.) In effect they are claiming that the Khoikhoi, as a primitive and nomadic people, did not yet recognize or enforce any system of exclusive property rights among themselves. Since the original inhabitants did not at that time have a Western-style system of property rights it could be concluded that 'the accusation that our forefathers violated those rights is without any grounds'. (De Wet, 5.4b)

The Euro-centric assumptions which thus made the settlers' right to the land a foregone conclusion were not, of course, new or exclusive to these apologists for the Cape colonists. The Swiss jurist Emer de Vattel, for example, said to be the most influential of all eighteenth century authorities on international law,[6] had specifically denied any right of sovereignty to 'wandering tribes' of hunters and gatherers. De Vattel introduced the human obligation to cultivate the earth as a necessary condition for the natural right of every man or nation to land and property, thus providing a general legitimation for European imperial expansion.[7] De Wet and Truter were more specifically concerned with the history of settlement rights at the Cape itself, but the upshot of their quasi-legalistic arguments was also to provide an ideological picture in which the historical facts of the conquest and dispossession of the indigenous peoples had simply been made to disappear. Though well aware of the historical and indeed continuing presence of the Khoikhoi and other indigenous peoples at the Cape, De Wet could thus claim that 'our forefathers did no more than dispose of barren, uninhabited and uncultivated land and make this their property, which . . . was what was intended at the establishment of this settlement'. (5.4b)

As against this glossing over of the issues, the central feature in the thinking of Stockenström is his frank recognition of the historical realities of conquest and dispossession entailed by colonial settlement (5.3a, b, 5.9a, c). Nor could he conceive of the accompanying injustices, cruelty and bloodshed as mere excesses or somehow unnecessary; these, like the commando system, are indeed natural consequences 'grown out of the principle of colonization'. (5.3b) Stockenström was careful not to make this into a onesided indictment of the white settlers only: the Xhosa also, in their dealings with the original inhabitants, are alleged to have forcefully dispossessed them and imposed their own rule 'with equal injustice and cruelty towards the original proprietors of the soil'. (5.3b) The conflict on the eastern frontier he thus viewed as a confrontation between 'these two conquering parties [who] found themselves in contact upon ground to which both had obtained a title by the same means, unjust violence'. (5.3b) Stockenström did not attempt to provide any ideological justification or legitimation of the settlers' claim to the land. But neither did he conclude that the unjust and violent means by which it had been obtained therefore invalidated all settler claims and rights. In the historical context of conquest and dispossession the situation of a settler community constituted a moral and practical dilemma that allowed no easy solutions. Certainly, in Stockenström's view, the present generation of colonists could not be held accountable, as they did not find themselves in this 'scrape' through any doing of their own but rather on account of the actions of their ancestors and the colonial authorities. They, as well as the oppressed indigenous people, had legitimate interests and rights. Stockenström was not prepared to deny the moral basis of the entire settler society. According to his political thinking only a strict adherence to the rule of law, to the impartial standards of truth and justice, could in practice resolve the conflicting claims and rights of settlers as well as indigenous peoples (5.9c). Whatever the virtues of this position might have been in practice, however, it cannot be said that at a theoretical level Stockenström had satisfactorily resolved the moral problems posed by the settlers' occupation of the land.

In defence of the Trek

The earliest public statements connected with the Trek are of a peculiarly defensive character. It has to be borne in mind that almost all the documents in this section were directed either at the colonial authorities or at the general public remaining behind in the colony, and that they attempted to explain and defend the Trek to these external and sometimes hostile audiences. The more positive propaganda, aimed at potential participants, concerned the Trek as leading to a proposed new settlement, and was largely restricted to favourable reports about the climate and territory of Natal. If there were more constructive proposals as to what it might achieve in terms of the extension of European civilization, then this was not reflected in any contemporary documents of the 1830s. Certainly there was no question of any notion of the 'manifest destiny' of the Afrikaners as a colonizing power justifying the territorial expansion and the founding of new settlements, as was the case with the westward expansion in the United States.[8] Even given the external audience at which it was aimed, the notions concerning the nature and purposes of the Trek which these earliest writings do contain are surprisingly negative. Only gradually, in the course of the historical experience of the Trek itself and of the actual founding of new settlements, did a different and more positive orientation emerge among the Trekkers themselves.

The Trekkers' essentially negative self-conception and orientation towards their enterprise was reflected in the contemporary terminology. The heroic and honorific nomenclature fixing the central significance in South African history of the *Great Trek* and the *Voortrekkers* is of very much later origin.[9] At the time the participants conceived of and described themselves as 'emigrants' and 'expatriates' (*uitgewekenen*). Rather than emphasizing any pioneering role these terms reflect a continuing orientation towards the established settlements as the social and political centre of gravity. Moreover the colonial society from which they were emigrating was conceived in the most affectionate and positive terms. It is 'the fruitful land of our birth' (Retief's Manifesto of 1837, 5.5a); the 'motherland' (Pretorius 1839, 5.5d); the 'paternal home' and the 'beloved country' (Natal Volksraad 1839, 5.6a). If in later times analogies would be drawn between the Trek and the departure of Israel from Egypt, it was certainly not true that at the outset the Trek was conceived in terms of a long wished for emancipation or inspired by political visions of the promised land. Instead we find it constantly emphasized by Trekker spokesmen that the emigration had been forced on them by circumstances beyond their control, and that it was a painful and disturbing experience: 'We left our motherland behind with concern and sorrow' (Pretorius 1839, 5.5d); 'Compelled to leave their beloved country and dearest beloved friends and relations' (Natal Volksraad 1839, Doc. 5.6a); 'Having torn ourselves loose from the British Government and departed from our motherland' (Ohrigstad Volksraad 1845, 5.7). The relative balance at the outset of the Trek between the Trekkers' positive attachment to the settled society from which they were departing and their apprehensive visions of what might be awaiting them is perhaps best caught in these words from Retief's Manifesto (5.5a): 'We are now quitting the fruitful land of our birth . . . and are entering a wild and dangerous territory.'

Apart from their own apprehensions concerning the outcome of the Trek, its leaders were also very much aware that such an enterprise of founding a new settlement in the interior would call forth serious objections and criticisms, in particular from the influential philanthropic and humanitarian circles. The time was past when it was possible for the colonists to found extensive new settlements at the expense of territory claimed by the indigenous peoples without meeting serious moral and political challenges from sources close to the colonial authorities. From the beginning, therefore, deliberate attempts were made to disarm such criticisms. In the words of the Ohrigstad Volksraad some years later: 'We have to anticipate the blame and the accusations of scandalous deeds that will be levelled against the Afrikaners by their enemies, and to convince them entirely of the contrary.' (5.7) And thus Retief in his Manifesto (5.5a) primarily set out to counter the 'numerous reports [that have been] circulated', and to prevent the 'unjustifiable odium' that had been cast on the frontiersmen being attached to the Trek. Such a defence was obviously necessary for pragmatic and strategic reasons: if the criticisms of the Trek and its purposes were not refuted they might become threats to the success of the enterprise itself. But it would also appear that the Trekkers, in the 1830s and early 1840s, had to some extent come to share the moral basis of this humanitarian critique itself. Though the documents show a constant refrain of complaints about 'our false libellers' (Pretorius, 5.5d) and their 'continual accusations' (Natal Volksraad, 5.6b), there is, somewhat surprisingly, no attempt to dispute the basic argument that it would be unjust to found new settlements through violent dispossession of the rightful territory of the indigenous peoples. To this extent then, Retief's claim that 'we desire to stand high in the estimation of our brethren' (5.5a) can be taken as indicating an attempt to provide not merely a pragmatic defence of the Trek and its purposes, but a justification in terms of moral principles shared with the 'philanthropic' critics.

The apologists of the Trek thus found it necessary to argue on two fronts at once. On the one hand leaving the established settlement had to be justified: they had to provide 'the most sufficient reasons' for 'severing that sacred tie which binds a Christian to his native soil' (Retief's Manifesto, 5.5a). On the other hand the project of founding a new settlement also required special legitimation. In particular it was necessary to demonstrate that they did not have aggressive intentions towards the indigenous inhabitants of the interior. Over and over again it is affirmed that 'we did not go out . . . with aggressive purposes' (Pretorius, 5.5d); 'we will not molest any people, nor deprive them of the smallest property' (Retief's Manifesto, 5.5a). Similarly we find repeated protestations that it was the desire of the Trekkers to live in 'peace and amity' with the peoples of the interior (5.5b). Where it is acknowledged that they are prepared to and might have to use force on occasion, it is also at once conceded that this would only be justifiable in self-defence (5.5a, b, d). On occasion, though rarely, the Trekkers even cast themselves in the role of instruments in God's hands 'for the promotion of Christian civilization among many thousands who, until now, have been left in deepest darkness'. (5.6b) Whether or not all these statements also expressed the deepest convictions and independently-held views on these subjects of the Trekkers themselves, they clearly set out to present the Trek in terms which would be acceptable to their humanitarian critics. Inevitably this brought about serious tensions with what actually happened in practice. Thus in Potgieter's account (5.5c) of the sequence of events since 'the bloodthirsty tyrant Musilicaats fell on us', the actual punitive expedition that caused him to have 'fled so far away that we do not know where he is' is somehow and conveniently never explicitly mentioned. Presumably the punitive expedition itself is played down in view of possible humanitarian objections against such a military feat, though in Potgieter's own mind it must certainly have been fully justified.

It was only after the traumatic experience of 1838 in Natal that the Trekkers began to give a different kind of justification for their right to the land, and one that was perhaps a more direct product of their own experiences and emergent political thinking. They now no longer claimed only that they had bought, or bartered, or had otherwise obtained by treaty, territory from the indigenous peoples (cf. 5.5c, 5.6a, 5.8). Henceforth they also asserted that it had been paid for by their sacrifice and blood. Thus Pretorius in 1839: 'We have a right to Natal, which was acquired not only by means of free purchase, but for which we had to pay the price of suffering indescribable cruelty, and not with the blood of men alone.' (5.5d) And similarly Potgieter, two years later, writes of 'our country which has been bought with human blood'. (5.5e) Superficially these metaphors might seem to be an extension of the more traditional legalistic notions of obtaining a right to the land by a commercial transaction or by means of a treaty, though now one 'ratified by blood'. (5.6a) However, the analogy does not hold, since there could clearly be no question of any exchange of lives and blood for the land. In fact, we are confronted here with an existential, even a quasi-religious notion: 'The gathered, bleached bones of . . . the . . . innocently and treacherously murdered will remain a lasting evidence and as a visible beacon of right on that land.' (Natal Volksraad 1839, 5.6a) In a sense it is almost an inversion of the customary idea of a right obtained by conquest: it is the sacrifices that were made and the losses that were suffered rather than the military victories which were gained that gave them a right to the land. Of course, successful conquest remained a necessary condition for establishing any new settlement at all, but if it was preceded and accompanied by sacrifices and losses then it was no longer a question of the brute force and might of the stronger giving him any rights. With their own blood the Trekkers had earned the moral right to the land. Henceforth there would be a 'sacred tie' binding them to the soil of the new settlement.

The right to a new settlement

The Trekkers did not set out to found a new society or create an independent state. In fact, they did not have clear and set ideas about the nature and status of the new settlement that would result from their venture. At the outset and during the early stages of the Trek this was not a matter of great importance to them, compared with the many grievances against the colonial authorities and the quest for greater economic and material security. Only in the course of the Trek itself did they come to hold, and sometimes give up again, definite views about their right to establish a new and independent settlement. The frequent references to 'freedom' and 'independence' which occur in Trekker documents in this and other chapters should always be carefully analyzed in their specific historical context: they do not stand for one ideal of political independence but tend to carry different and varying political connotations.

Thus when Retief in his Manifesto (5.5a) asserted that 'we will uphold the just principles of liberty', this did not so much refer to the political basis on which a new settlement was to be founded, but concerned, rather, Retief's views on the labour order. While accepting that 'no one shall be held in slavery', he at the same time maintained that the labour order should be such as would 'preserve proper relations between master and servant'. In effect this tells us more about Retief's position concerning the changes that were taking place in the traditional labour order of colonial society through the emancipation of the slaves and the granting of legal equality to the Khoikhoi than anything about the proposed new settlement.

Retief's Manifesto also announced that the Trekkers proposed to frame their own code of law, but again this was something less than a claim to full political sovereignty. As the Natal Volksraad would later say, subsequent to the British annexation of Natal, it could be taken as simply a necessary but limited exercise in local government, enforcing some minimal degree of law and order: 'We were obliged, as emigrants, who had to govern and protect ourselves, and who would not lead the life of wanderers, . . . to establish a government amongst ourselves . . . without which no civilized community could exist.' (5.6d) Similarly the claim to be a 'free and independent people' (Retief, 5.5b) was, in the first instance, aimed at warding off unwanted interference by the colonial authorities. Rather than expressing any positive conviction about the right to establish an independent settlement, this amounted to the hope 'now not to be troubled nor to be opposed by anyone' (Pretorius, 5.5d). In fact it expresses the frontiersmen's determination to resist the imposition of institutional control, not an ambition to create new and independent political institutions of their own.

On what grounds did the Trekkers base their claim that they should not be interfered with? Again we find that a notion of freedom was involved, though one that is less clear than it might appear at first sight. Thus we find Potgieter claiming (5.5c) that 'We regard ourselves as free citizens who might go where we please without acting to the detriment of any other, as all nations are free and go where they like.' Similarly Pretorius argued that 'We know that all proclaim that every man should be free and we know very well that we are a freeborn people.' (5.5d) But rather than any claim of a right to some prospective national independence these arguments in fact appealed to the legal and civic rights of the Trekkers as erstwhile colonial citizens. They were free citizens, not slaves or bondsmen, who as such had a right to freedom of movement. In fact, as they reminded the colonial authorities, these rights had lately been extended to other subjects, such as the Khoikhoi, as well, and could therefore certainly not be denied them. But to claim such a right to freedom of movement as free citizens certainly did not yet amount to staking any claim to national independence or sovereignty.

Still, in the course of the Trek itself and of its sequel, more ambitious notions were to emerge, and the concept of being a 'free and independent people' gained a more definite political content. Undoubtedly the historical experience of venturing on the Trek and having to found new settlements from scratch played a formative role in the emerging political thinking of the Trekkers. The impact of these dramatic experiences was, in fact, increasingly articulated in social and political terms. Thus we find the Natal Volksraad in 1839 still summarizing their recent history in existential rather than political terms, and as a series of privations rather than creative actions: 'We have been wandering about for three years, in regions to us unknown, without compass, without guide, without experience, exposed to all obstacles which nature put into our way, by insurmountable mountains reaching the clouds, exposed to serious wants and disappointments, surrounded and pursued by innumerable beasts of prey, with whom we daily had to struggle for the purpose of obtaining food, and without any government and laws. . . .' (5.6a)

By 1842 this same history is recounted much more positively and in political rather than in personal terms as the story of the creative founding of a new and independent settlement: 'Immediately after our departure we declared our independence; we established a Government of our own, prosecuted wars that came upon us unexpectedly and made peace, took possession of uninhabited tracts of country which we purchased by friendly treaties as well as with our blood and treasure. . . .' (5.6c) In the meantime, the Trekkers had increasingly come to regard themselves not merely as a group who as free citizens had a right to freedom of movement, but as together constituting a new settler society with its own political claims and obligations. This was implicit in the terminology of 'our whole united society of burghers' (*vereenigde burgerlyke maatschappy*) (cf. 5.5e) which gradually became current. It was also expressed in the Natal Volksraad's desire in 1841 no longer merely that the British Government should not interfere with the Trekkers, but now that it 'would be pleased to recognize our settlement here as a free and independent state'. (5.6b)

These claims to political sovereignty and independence became particularly urgent in the face of the threat that the British Government might once again incorporate the new settlement through the annexation of Natal. In this sense 'freedom' was now discovered as a threatened value and projected as an abstract political principle that must retrospectively explain the purposes of the Trek itself.[10] Looking back to both the Trek and the loss of Natal as history, Pretorius would thus exclaim in 1848 that from the outset it had been inspired by the ideal of freedom: 'For liberty we sacrificed all!' (5.8) Similarly the Ohrigstad Volksraad in 1845 described the history of the Trek as aimed at independence: 'We were once again obliged to set out into the world to look for a piece of land . . . so that we might achieve independence.' (5.7) Moreover for the first time they now also produced an actual argument for the *right* to establish such a new and independent settlement: 'There is a law recognized by all nations, that when a certain group of people leave its government and this group of people settle in a region which is independent of any government, then they have the right to live under and make their own laws.' (5.7)

But if such notions finally emerged in the aftermath of the Trek, they certainly were not present from the beginning. And in the meantime many Trekkers, including some of the leading figures such as Pretorius and Boshof, had decided, sometimes on more than one occasion, first in Natal and then in the Orange River Sovereignty, *not* to give an overriding priority to such claims for the right of independent settlement, while the trekboers had consistently emphasized their colonial orientation and loyalties.[11]

The rationale of colonialism

In comparison with the earlier documents, the defence produced by the executive of the Republic of Lydenburg in 1860 (5.10) will at once be seen not to be characteristic of the mainstream of earlier settler and Trekker writings on these themes. The letter, which is evidently the product of a relatively educated and sophisticated mind, was in fact largely the work of the Dutch-born H. T. Bührmann. Unlike earlier apologists for the settlers, he was inclined to take a somewhat sceptical, not to say cynical, view of the norms proposed for rightful settlement by missionaries and humanitarian critics. Similarly he was not afraid to propose 'rightfully waged wars' next to lawful purchase as an acceptable ground for the settlers' right to the land.

At first sight the strategy of this polemical rebuttal seems to be directed mainly at turning the tables on the colonial clergymen who had questioned the rightful claims of the Republics in the interior. Not just the Republics, but the entire colonial settlement, it is argued, were based on the dispossession of the original inhabitants. Rather surprisingly, however, the argument proceeds beyond this *ad hominem* attack and turns into a general theological justification of colonialism. The logic of the humanitarian position, it is claimed, amounts to a denial of any right gained by conquest: 'If it should be as you say, . . . then no just war has ever been waged, nor any land rightfully acquired.' But this, the argument proceeds, is equivalent to an attack on the moral basis of the entire process of European colonization: 'The original inhabitants of Asia, Africa, America and Australia never first invited the European to come to their countries. . . . These countries were originally sought out by the Europeans with the fixed intention of establishing their paramountcy there, and when this was resisted, they have taken possession of these countries by aggressive means. . . . Thus you and all of us who are of European origin and are outside Europe, occupy land unlawfully there.' And this conclusion is held to be intolerable since it is in conflict with God's sovereignty in history: 'Do you mean to say that God has ceased to rule? That the acquisition of Asia, Africa, America and Australia took place without

God's will and consent, but occurred even against His will?' If we accept that God rules in history then, it is claimed, this provides a justification for the spread of European dominion in the various colonial territories.

Bührmann thus produced a theological justification for European colonialism in general, basing this on the sovereignty of God in history and on the idea, important in Calvinism, that 'the lord has created the earth to be lived upon and cultivated'. On both counts he imported essentially European notions and perspectives and attempted to use these in defence of the local settler community whose own perspective was much more limited and less ambitious, and whose attempts to jusfify their right of settlement and right to the land had typically, and particularly at the early stages, been much more defensive and tentative.

5.1 The Hottentots and other original inhabitants of this country were brought to a state of completely slavish subjection; these people, freeborn and rightful possessors of the land, do not now own even an inch of land as their property.

—Memoir of Egbertus Bergh, 1802. (Translated from the text *Memorie over de Kaap de Goede Hoop*, in Theal, *Belangrijke Historische Dokumenten*, Vol. 3. In the original the whole of this passage is part of a single sentence.)

With the spread of enlightenment and humanitarian ideas, towards the end of the eighteenth century some officials at the Cape became concerned with the plight of the Khoikhoi and other indigenous inhabitants of the colony, though by this time the process of colonial conquest and encroachment on their original lands was almost completed. Egbertus Bergh (1758–1827) was born at the Cape and advanced through the ranks of the Company to become a member of the Council of Policy in 1795. He wrote the 'Memorie' *while living in Europe, as a critical evaluation of the Company's policies at the Cape with a view to the imminent transfer of the colony to the Batavian Republic in 1803. A further extract from his memoir appears as Document 6.6.*

. . . The Hottentots and other original inhabitants of this country were also brought to such extreme poverty and misery, indeed to a state of completely slavish subjection —with less bloodshed, it can be said, but not less cruelly, than were the Mexicans and Peruvians by the Spaniards—that, deprived of all enjoyments, oppressed and maltreated, they, instead of being able to increase their numbers, are gradually being reduced and must eventually die out. That this was actually the case will be easily understood when it is said that these people, free-born and rightful possessors of the land in which they are now made subservient, do not own even an inch of land as their property. Yes, they are not even tolerated, unless it be for them to keep their wives and children on a piece of land situated in some remote corner where they had erected a miserable hut, while they themselves, for a trivial wage, suffering the most inconceivable maltreatment, are obliged to do the most difficult and despicable work as serfs [*lijfeigenen*] of the farmers and other inhabitants. This also made it necessary for the wives to seek work on the same basis, often in a region completely removed from the place where their husbands were. This practice always has the cruel consequence for the children, who are born into such conditions of servitude that the farmer, on whose farm such a child has the misfortune to come into the world, registers him, keeps and treats him as his serf [*lijfeigene*], if not for the entire life-span of such a sorry individual, then at least for his first twenty years. Neither do they have permission, as the farmers do, to let their cattle graze for payment of a specific fee on a certain piece of veld in their own land, that they had never forfeited or relinquished except for a very small part. Consequently, they are so poor, oppressed, and persecuted, that no other alternatives remain for them but to disperse themselves, sacrificing the most precious gifts that nature has given them, putting themselves at the discretion of their overlords and oppressors, among whom there are some proper tyrants. . . .

5.2 Territory which belongs to another may be acquired either by compact, free concession or war.

—Christoffel Brand, 'Concerning the method and law of acquiring colonies', 1820. (Translated from the Latin text of *Dissertatio Politica-Juridica de Jure Coloniarum*, Leyden, 1820.)

Christoffel Brand (1797–1875) studied at the university of Leyden in Holland following his schooling at the Cape. In 1820 he received two doctorates from this university, one in law with the Latin dissertation from which the following extract is taken. On his return to the Cape in 1821 he practised as an advocate and soon became a leading figure in the Afrikaner community.

In general, things are either subject to someone or they are not. Applying this distinction here, we would say that colonies are founded in territories or regions which either belong to someone or belong to no one. By the expression 'belonging to no one' we indicate a territory which is subject to no man's authority or power, or which is not held in dominion by anybody, and which is deserted, not being populated or tenanted by any inhabitants. . . . For clarity, we may add another qualification, and thus define the territory belonging to no one as that territory which 'is held subject to no man's power' at the time when the colonists arrive. But when the colonists gain control of such a land or region, they hold it either by right of perfect acquisition or by right of imperfect acquisition.

A territory is acquired *perfectly* if it has never up to that time been inhabited or occupied by others and is now discovered for the first time.

A territory is acquired *imperfectly*, on the other hand, when it has been deserted by its inhabitants. Such desertion must be distinguished from desertion caused by the might of a stronger enemy or expulsion. . . .

From these two methods of acquiring territory arise two kinds of rights. Who can doubt that a perfect right derives from perfect acquisition? What lawmaker would create a precedent for disallowing a perfect right of dominion to whoever exercises the right of discovery? If a thing has been acquired by discovery, shall it be surrendered to any intruder? This point has been sufficiently considered by the Roman lawgivers.

But we may not say that imperfect acquisition leads to an imperfect right. In this case there is rather a full right and a less full right. Colonists have a full right when they take a land which the inhabitants have left and which they no longer want to be theirs. However, when the inhabitants have been forced through scarcity, hunger, poverty and other misfortunes of this kind to leave their homeland with the intention of returning again when the problem ceases, then a colony established in a region abandoned in this way has a less full right.

We turn now to the case of land which belongs to someone. Upon examination, it will be apparent that this too is of two kinds. For since land belongs to someone when it is occupied or held as the possession of someone, it follows that it can be under the dominion of either the same state that is preparing to establish a colony or that of another. In the former case no one will deny that the state is able to establish a colony, and this practice is called populating a region or an island with colonists.

But when a colony is established in a territory which is subject to someone else, it is clear that this person holds some sort of right to the land. Territory which belongs to another may be acquired either by compact, the free concession of the ruler, or war.

The right which is obtained to land conceded by compact is either *proprium* or *commune.*

By rights held *proprium* we mean a case in which a place is conceded to someone in order to found a colony, but on the condition that the mother city retains the right to send a colony there. . . . But a different system has been contrived by the founders and settlers of the Cape of Good Hope, my fatherland. They did not arrange to pay the Hottentots, from whom they procured a tract of land, an annual rent for the land but, as they say, they purchased the territory from them for a small sum of money. (Although there are some who deny that my fatherland was purchased from the Hottentot inhabitants, . . . nevertheless this is affirmed by A. B. T. Raynal. . . . However, we should add that . . . the form of a purchase and sale was observed. But who will maintain that men drunk with wine . . . cannot be seduced into selling very cheaply something that is of very great value, since we have it from Herodotus that the Marsegetae, after they had become drunk on the jars of wine set out for them, to all intents and purposes handed their lives over to Cyrus. This deed of Cyrus's does not really differ from that of the founders of the Cape. For how subtle is the persuasion and eloquence of money.) However this may be, it is sufficient at this stage to note that the land was acquired by the settlers by purchase and sale, i.e. by *compact.*

By rights held *commune* we mean a case in which a ruler concedes to someone the right to lead a colony into his own territory, the place or city which he designates being then already populated by its own inhabitants. Here the intention is not that the law of the colonials should apply to the original inhabitants, but that the colonials may nevertheless have certain privileges. . . .

Now as for the right which someone holds over land acquired by war, we define this also in two kinds. Such rights are either *perfect* or *imperfect.*

A *perfect right* is acquired when the inhabitants or possessors of a territory are expelled from their dwelling-place. . . . Thus the Phoenicians, for example, expelled the inhabitants of Rhodes and founded a colony there.

Imperfect acquisition occurs when the inhabitants, reduced by slaughter, compelled by the extremities of war, or even by defeat, accept the victors or their colonials as common inhabitants of their land, . . . that is, when the inhabitants are not completely expelled but still live in the town or place concerned together with the victor's colonists. An example of this kind of acquisition is the community which existed in very early times between the Romans and the Sabines at Rome.

Yet we should not be reproached for having distinguished the right held *commune* and the *imperfect right* (acquired by war). Indeed at first sight they seem to be one and the same, but close examination and comparison will show, I am sure, that they differ. In both cases the colonists and the inhabitants share a community. They have this much in common, to be sure, but they are different nevertheless.

First, the colonies established by *right commune* do not retain the rights of their own mother city or state but lose these and become subject to the laws of the region in which they live. But where acquisition is by *imperfect right* it is not the victor's colonists, but the inhabitants who lose their rights.

Secondly, a colony created by *imperfect right* is a part of the mother city of the victors, but one created by rights held *commune* remains a colony of the mother city.

Thirdly, the two also differ in the manner in which they are acquired. The right held *commune* is acquired by free compact or grant; the *imperfect right* by force or war. . . . The *imperfect right* also obtains for both the original inhabitants and the new colonists. For the victors, although they have won, do not enjoy all the rights of victory; and the inhabitants, although vanquished, do not suffer all the misfortunes and deprivations of rights of conquered people.

From this observation it becomes clear that the former do not acquire *perfect rights* and the latter do not lose them.

5.3a The encroachments on the Aborigines began at Cape Town, and never ceased to extend by degrees until the colonists had got to where they are now.

—Reply of A. Stockenström to the commissioners of enquiry, 9 Aug. 1826. (From *The Autobiography of Sir Andries Stockenström*, Vol. I, pp. 224–225.)

As landdrost of Graaff-Reinet, Stockenström in 1822 fixed the northern boundary of the colony. Dr Philip, who had already clashed with Stockenström about his dealings with the missionary stations, alleged to the British commissioners of enquiry into conditions at the Cape, Bigge and Coalbrooke, that Stockenström's boundary was a new encroachment on the territories of the San. In the course of 1826 Dr Philip visited Stockenström at Graaff-Reinet and discovered that they shared some common ground despite major differences in approach.

. . . He who dates the excesses committed against the Bosjesmen, their reciprocal atrocities, and the encroachments on their territories, from the crossing of the old boundary, is either totally ignorant of the history of the Colony, or desirous of stigmatising the present generation, or has some other deceitful object in view. The encroachments on the Aborigines began at Cape Town, and never ceased to extend by degrees until the colonists had got to where they are now; as the leading adventurers advanced, their countrymen followed, and as a tract of country became what they called full, the more enterprising again set forward and were followed as before. If the Government had had sufficient knowledge of the interior and sufficient authority in it, when the first settlers came to the chain of the Sneeuw and Newveld bergen, and there had fixed the boundary, and there checked migrations inland, the Bosjesmen might have remained in peaceable possession of the country beyond; but when the farmers of those days, with their immense flocks, were once permitted to gain possession of the high lands just mentioned, no one with the least idea of the life of a grazier in a country like this would have maintained the possibility of keeping them out of the farmer tracts beyond, and of maintaining a boundary of imaginary lines drawn zig-zag over an open country of almost boundless extent.

5.3b This is a system which has as a natural consequence grown out of the principle of colonization which has prevailed in South Africa since its earliest history.

—Reply of A. Stockenström to the questionnaire of the colonial secretary, Mr Spring Rice, Stockholm, 5 Nov. 1834. (From the *Minutes of Evidence before the Select Committee on Aborigines*, pp. 117–119.)

Philip's Researches in South Africa *appeared in England in 1828 and his account of the indigenous population's conquest and oppression by the colonists in South Africa made a great impact on public opinion. Philip's critique of the colonists was further corroborated by such works as Saxe-Bannister's* Humane Policy or Justice to the Aborigines *(1830) and Thomas Pringle's* Narrative of a Residence in South Africa, *published as part of his* African Sketches *(1834). Stockenström's views on the historical process of colonization in the following letter, written during his stay in Europe, are to a considerable extent meant as a commentary on these philanthropic critiques.*

Question 2: What, so far as your observation and experience extend, has been the system of policy pursued by the colonial government in regard to the native tribes or hordes beyond that frontier?

Answer: In order to give an intelligible answer to this question, it is necessary to point out the position of the border tribes, and refer to the causes of our troubles with them. A volume might be written on this subject, which has often been handled by persons more competent to do it justice. It will however suffice for the present purpose to state that the white colonists having from the first commencement of the settlement gradually encroached on the territory of the natives, whose ejectment (as is too well known) was accompanied with great injustice, cruelty and bloodshed, the most hostile feelings were entertained by the weaker party towards those whom they considered as their oppressors. The Aborigines who did not become domesticated (as it was called) like the Hottentots, seeing no chance of retaining or recovering their country, withdrew into the interior as the whites advanced, and being driven to depredations by the diminution of the game, which constituted their principal means of subsistence, and which gradually disappeared when more constantly hunted, and as the waters became permanently occupied by the new comers, they often made desperate attacks on the latter, and in their turn were guilty of great atrocities. Some of the rulers of the colony in those days were no doubt favourable to measures of conciliation, but the evil soon got beyond their power of control. In proportion as the pastoral population increased, more and more land was taken possession of, and more desperate and bloody became the deeds of revenge on both sides, until the extermination of the enemy appeared even to the Government the only safe alternative; at least it became its avowed object, as the encouragement given to the hostile expeditions, the rewards of the successful commanders of the same, and many documents still extant clearly demonstrate. The contest being beyond comparison unequal, the colonial limits widened with great rapidity. A thin white population soon spread even over the great chains of the Suven [Sneeuw] and Newveld mountains, whilst the hordes, who preferred a precarious and often starving independence to servitude, were forced into the deserts and fastnesses bordering on the frontier.

It will be at once perceived that I am here alluding to a period of the colonial history not long previous to the close of the last century, and that the Aborigines spoken of are the Bushmen and some tribes of Hottentots, for our relations with the Caffres and others are somewhat of a different nature, as I will show in the sequel. Thus the isolated position of most of the intruders afforded the strongest temptation to the savages occasionally to wreak their vengeance. The numerous herds of our peasantry grazing on the usurped lands proved too seductive a bait for the hungry fugitives, who saw the pasturage of their flocks (the game) thus occupied; but their partial success against individual families was generally dearly bought by the additional loss of life and land in the long run.

An attempt was made to check these enormities, and generally to control the population in these remote parts by the establishment of a seat of magistracy at Graaf Reinet: but the disturbances which soon followed, and the inability of the Government to restore order, as well as the rapid changes of Dutch and English dominion, caused the interior to be left in a great measure in a state of anarchy, and mutual depredation had full scope. In the meantime, whilst this was the course of events in the northern and north-eastern directions, the colonists of the eastern frontier, being no more under restraint than their brethren in other parts, continued to migrate eastward as the Caffres did towards the west, with equal injustice and cruelty towards the original proprietors of the soil; and here let me observe, that a late writer on the Cape colony (Mr. T. Pringle) is decidedly mistaken, when in his *African Sketches,* page 415, he gives the impression that the conquests of the Caffres over the Hottentots were more merciful than those of the whites. It is but a poor comfort to us that we have not been more ferocious than Caffres, but that consolation cannot be denied us, and historical truth forbids the suppression of the fact. However, the several tribes of Hottentots having been dispossessed by their Christian and Pagan enemies, these two conquering parties found themselves in contact upon ground to which both had obtained a title by the same means, unjust violence; jealousies, of course, forthwith sprang up between the dividers of the spoil. We were unfortunately again the first aggressors, but the Caffres being a better organized, more warlike, and more numerous people than the Hottentots, did not so easily give way. . . .

The frontier is at least 800 miles in extent, along one-tenth of which (viz. as far as Caffreland extends) there are military posts established. In these circumstances the field-cornets were vested with the power, in cases of sudden irruptions or depredations, to collect a force, repel the attacks, and pursue the plunderers with a view to taking them prisoners and delivering them into the hands of justice, as well as recovering the property they may have carried off. It is needless to say that with the mutual hereditary hatred and prejudices of the parties, as well as the wrongs mutually done, acts of the most bloody revenge were inseparable from these contentions, as the pursued party would not easily surrender, and the least resistance would be considered by an unscrupulous leader as a justification for proceeding to extremities, and too often the innocent suffer for the guilty. When these emergencies were not acted upon, a regular commando could be sent out, where I think the danger of mistakes still greater, as the real perpetrators would take care to be out of the way, and an excuse could easily be found for slaughtering all those who came in the way by provoking them to defend themselves. This is a system which has as a natural consequence grown out of the principle of colonization which has prevailed in South Africa from its earliest history, and which has brought matters to such a pitch that it must puzzle the best disposed Government to know how to avoid extremes, either of which would be fatal to all parties concerned.

5.4a This is then the way in which possession was first acquired of the land on which the Colony was established.

—Lecture entitled 'The Origins and Development of the Laws of the Colony', 1836. (Translated from the text published in *Het Nederduitsch Zuid-Afrikaansch Tijdschrift*, 1836, pp. 125–126, 306.)

Philip's allegations against the colonists in his Researches *provoked a furious outcry at the Cape. Throughout the 1830s newspapers like* De Zuid-Afrikaan *and* The Grahamstown Journal *conducted a sustained campaign against what they called 'the Philipian party', setting out to disprove the historical accuracy of many of his assertions. Colonists apparently felt that their rights of settlement itself were being disputed, and at the meetings of cultural societies in Cape Town lecturers attempted to give gen-*

eral and historical vindications of these. The following extract is taken from a lecture that was probably given by Sir John Truter, chief justice of the Cape from 1812 to 1828, and at this time a respected elder statesman of the Afrikaner community in Cape Town.

. . . On their arrival here, they [the first colonists] met with no resistance in choosing a piece of land for themselves on which they could plant the Dutch flag.

The Hottentots, who were divided into tribal groups, possessed no other land than that on which they had established their kraals and allowed their cattle to graze. They led a wandering life, continually moving from one place to another, and left the unoccupied land to the first claimant. They had never united into a nation, nor as such claimed possession for themselves of the entire extent of the land at this outpost. The Hottentots just as little thought of disputing the appropriation by the Dutch of the land on which they wished to build their fort, as the Dutch thought of settling on another's land. We read nowhere in any authentic documents that Jan van Riebeeck intended, or was obliged, to enter into negotiations about the land with its previous occupiers. Still less was he required to make himself master of the land by force.

On the contrary, we read in the first *placaat* which was issued by Jan van Riebeeck in his capacity as Commander, on the 9th April, 1652, . . . that all the people, sailors and soldiers, were to work with diligence at the building of the fort, but that nobody would be allowed to cause the least inconvenience to the natives of the country. And could any inconvenience have been greater than that of arbitrarily appropriating a piece of land, however small, which the natives regarded as their own property? But in that *placaat* it is explicitly stipulated that anyone who caused harm to any of the natives would be punished in their presence, so as to convince them in this way that the intention of the Commander was, in accordance with his instructions, to deal with them in peace and friendship. Thus ownership by right of occupation was vested in Jan van Riebeeck, on behalf of his principles—i.e. of the States-General of the United Netherlands and the Dutch East India Company as represented by its directors—of the whole extent of the land on which he initially built a fort, and later a castle, and on which he established his garden for the refreshment of the ships, and of the previously uninhabited Robben Island, where he sent his first sheep to graze. And his principals consequently acquired both the rights of sovereignty, or of *dominium eminens*, and of landed property, or of *dominium utile*, so that the Dutch state became in this way master of the land occupied by them and acquired the indisputable right to govern it by its own laws.

The first possession of the colony, considered from this point of view, excluded all notion of the laws of the colony accommodating any institutions or customary practices of the natives, even if they had possessed the land, which I doubt. This was because, at the first establishment of the colony, the natives remained separate from the colonists, subsisting on their own, and although they gradually came to mix with the colonists, this was far more in the nature of a voluntary subordination to the colonial government, or one made necessary by circumstances, than it was a constitutional union with the colonists, involving the retention of their own laws. . . .

. . . This is then the way in which, in my opinion, possession was first acquired of the land on which the colony was established. The land was taken into possession by Van Riebeeck, on behalf of the then Dutch East India Company, and under the supreme authority of the States-General of the United Netherlands of that time. He made himself master of it not by right of conquest, nor by right of purchase, but by right of occupation, as he did not then find that any nation or individual either occupied the land or claimed ownership of it. In the land where he settled himself, that supreme leader did not encounter the authority of any other, who was placed above him, nor any laws to which he had to subject himself. Thus he did not see any objection to governing his subordinates according to his own laws, i.e. according to the instructions which were given him by his principals in the Netherlands, in accordance with which he had also managed the men on the ships which had brought them here. . . .

5.4b No real property rights to the land existed among its original inhabitants, and thus the accusation that our forefathers violated those rights is without any grounds.

—Lecture by Advocate J. de Wet, entitled 'Something about the so-called earlier right of ownership to this country of the Hottentots', 1838. (Translated from the text published in *Het Nederduitsch Zuid-Afrikaansch Tijdschrift*, 1838.)

Like his contemporary Christoffel Brand, J. de Wet (1794–1875) studied law at the university of Leyden in Holland, receiving a doctorate in 1821. From 1823 he practised law in Cape Town. The lecture below was given at a committee meeting of the Maatschappy ter Uitbreiding van Beschaving en Letterkunde *(Association for the Promotion of Civilization and Literature).*

In these days much is written about the supposed injustice done to the original inhabitants by allegedly dispossessing them of this country by force, and driving them out of it, partly at the establishment of this settlement and partly in subsequent times. Thus it must be of interest to every Cape colonist to consider whether there are sufficient grounds for casting this odium on our forefathers, or whether it is altogether a figment of the imagination. To decide this question, one has to enquire whether or not the Hottentots were once the rightful [*wettige*] owners of this country, which is now in the possession of the colonists. . . .

According to the earliest accounts which we have of the Hottentots or natives of this country, they were divided into a number of small tribes, each of which bore a particular name, and these were in turn made up of a certain number of families, or 'kraals' as the colonists described them, usually living at short distances from each other. . . .

Each family or kraal was therefore independent of the others, and their assemblage into tribes resembled more closely that of the fishes and the birds of the air than that of a society of men held together by common ties. . . .

These various tribes wandered with their cattle over an area of more than 120,000 English square miles. . . . They used these pastures in such a way that each tribe remained in the same place for a short time only. . . . Nor did the Hottentots recognize the right of possession among each other. Rather, possession depended on whether those who arrived later thought themselves able, and were indeed strong enough, to drive off those who had settled earlier, and thus immediately took up weapons to this end. Thus bloody battles arose continually among them—a true *bellum omnium contra omnes* [war of all against all]—accompanied by all the atrocities by which barbarous peoples so sorrowfully distinguish themselves from those who are civilized. . . .

. . . Such was the general state of the natives who occupied this country at the establishment of our settlement. . . .

When Van Riebeeck landed no buying or selling of land could thus take place between parties able to enter such a transaction, nor was there any such transaction.

Before the Dutch came, no such title was essential for rightful ownership of the land. For this, nothing more than ordinary occupation of the land was required, and it was by this means that our forefathers acquired possession. And we maintain that the Dutch had every right to do this, because, although the Hottentots, as indicated above, intermittently occupied the land with their cattle, one cannot infer from this, by generally accepted and indisputable principles, that they had any right of ownership, in the sense in which someone exercises exclusive and discretionary control over the material things of this world, without anyone else being able to lay claim to them. . . .

If the conduct of our forefathers is tested by these principles, the question which naturally arises is whether or not Van Riebeeck, when he and those with him settled here and established their fort in this country, found the land occupied by the Hottentots, either as individuals or as tribes. If he did find the land occupied, the question is whether the Hottentots made it clear by their conduct that they wished to make exclusive use of the land. We speak of the Hottentots as individuals or tribes [*horde*] and do not consider them as a nation or people because, although we admit that the various tribes jointly occupied the land and wandered about there, one cannot say that they were therefore to be regarded as a nation who had taken possession of it. As for their being a nation, there existed no common ties or agreement among them, as has already been shown.

The earliest accounts which we have of the Hottentots, their customs, life-styles and activities, show us that no individuals nor any tribes among them had taken as property any fixed permanent place in the whole vastness of the settlement. . . .

Taken at its best, the Hottentots followed this rule among themselves: 'Whoever comes and finds any piece of land unoccupied, and can keep it by force of weapons, he takes possession of it, if he so chooses, and once he leaves in his turn, the same tacit conditions apply to any other.' This was indeed a barbarous principle which gave rise to the most sorrowful consequences.

I believe that one should already be able to see, even from the brief survey which has been given, that no real property rights to the land existed among its original inhabitants, and thus also that the accusation that our forefathers violated those rights is without any grounds. They did no more than dispose of barren, uninhabited and uncultivated land and make this their property, which, as I have already remarked, was what was intended at the establishment of this settlement. . . .

5.5a We are now quitting the fruitful land of our birth and are entering a wild and dangerous territory.

—Manifesto of P. Retief, 2 Feb. 1837. (From the translation published in *The Grahamstown Journal*, 2 Feb. 1837.)

The manifesto of Piet Retief, published in The Grahamstown Journal *on the eve of his departure from the Colony, is one of the best known documents in South African history. Whereas some other Voortrekker leaders who had preceded him had been careful to hide their intentions from the authorities, Retief publicized his reasons for deciding to trek. The Manifesto is not so much an account of the causes of the Great Trek as an attempt towards a defence and justification directed at the general public remaining behind in the colony and at the colonial authorities.*

Numerous reports having been circulated throughout the colony, evidently with the intention of exciting in the minds of our countrymen a feeling of prejudice against those who have resolved to emigrate from a colony where they have experienced, for so many years past, a series of the most vexatious and severe losses; and, as we desire to stand high in the estimation of our brethren, and are anxious that they and the world at large should believe us incapable of severing that sacred tie which binds a Christian to his native soil, without the most sufficient reasons; we are induced to record the following summary of our motives for taking so important a step, and also our intentions respecting our proceedings towards the native tribes which we may meet with beyond the boundary:

1 We despair of saving the colony from those evils which threaten it by the turbulent and dishonest conduct of vagrants, who are allowed to infest the country in every part; nor do we see any prospect of peace or happiness for our children in any country thus distracted by internal commotions.

2 We complain of the severe losses which we have been forced to sustain by the emancipation of our slaves, and the vexatious laws which have been enacted respecting them.

3 We complain of the continual system of plunder which we have ever endured from the Caffres and other coloured classes, and particularly by the last invasion of the colony, which has desolated the frontier districts and ruined most of the inhabitants.

4 We complain of the unjustifiable odium which has been cast upon us by interested and dishonest persons, under the cloak of religion, whose testimony is believed in England, to the exclusion of all evidence in our favour; and we can foresee, as the result of this prejudice, nothing but the total ruin of the country.

5 We are resolved, wherever we go, that we will uphold the just principle of liberty; but, whilst we will take care that no one shall be held in a state of slavery, it is our determination to maintain such regulations as may suppress crime, and preserve proper relations between master and servant.

6 We solemnly declare that we quit this colony with a desire to lead a more quiet life than we have heretofore done. We will not molest any people, nor deprive them of the smallest property; but, if attacked, we shall consider ourselves fully justified in defending our persons and effects, to the utmost of our ability, against every enemy.

7 We make known that when we shall have framed a code of laws for our future guidance, copies shall be forwarded to the colony for general information; but we take this opportunity of stating that it is our firm resolve to make provision for the summary punishment of any traitors who may be found amongst us.

8 We propose, in the course of our journey, and on arriving at the country in which we shall permanently reside, to make known to the native tribes our intentions, and our desire to live in peace and friendly intercourse with them.

9 We quit this colony under the full assurance that the English Government has nothing more to require of us, and will allow us to govern ourselves without its interference in future.

10 We are now quitting the fruitful land of our birth, in which we have suffered enormous losses and continual vexation, and are entering a wild and dangerous territory; but we go with a firm reliance on an all-seeing, just, and merciful Being, whom it will be our endeavour to fear and humbly to obey.

By authority of the farmers who have quitted the Colony, . . .

5.5b We desire to be considered as a free and independent people.

—Letter from P. Retief to Governor D'Urban, 21 July 1837. (From the translation in Theal, *The D'Urban Papers*, South African Public Library, Cape Town.)

On joining the other main Trek parties in the present northern Orange Free State, Retief assumed the offices of 'Governor' and Head Commandant of the Trekkers assembled in the region. He also acted as their main spokesman in their relations with the colonial authorities in Cape Town. A letter similar to the following one to Governor D'Urban had earlier been sent in the names of both Retief and Maritz.

The undersigned Pieter Retief, as Conductor in Chief of the United Encampments, most humbly sheweth, that we, as subjects of the British Government, during our distressed circumstances, submitted our grievances to His Majesty the King; but all our endeavours proved fruitless, we have ultimately found ourselves compelled to quit the land of our birth, in order that we might not become guilty of opposition or rebellion against our Government.

That this abandonment of our native country has occasioned us enormous and incalculable losses, but that, notwithstanding this, we, on our side, will not show any emnity towards the British nation.

That, consequently, all trade and commerce between us and the British Merchants will, on our part, be free and uninterrupted, as with all other nations, with this understanding, that we desire to be considered as a free and independent people.

That we have learnt with grief that almost all the native tribes, by whom we are now surrounded, have been instigated to attack us; but although we feel ourselves fully able to resist all our enemies, we would however beg of your Excellency to prevent, as far as lies in your power, such hostilities, so that we may not be compelled to spill human blood, which has already been the case with Matsilikatzi.

That we will prove to the world, by our conduct, that it never has been our intention unlawfully to molest any nation or people; but that, on the contrary, we have no greater satisfaction than in the general peace and amity of all mankind.

That, finally, we confidently trust that the British Government will allow us to receive the amount of all the just claims and demands which we still have within the colony. . . .

5.5c We regard ourselves as free citizens who might go where we please without acting to the detriment of any other, as all nations are free and go where they like.

—Letter from A. H. Potgieter, Sand River, to Governor D'Urban, 3 Dec. 1838. (Translated from the text published in H. S. Pretorius *et al., Voortrekker-Argiefstukke*, pp. 29–41.)

Andries Hendrik Potgieter (1792–1852) had led the first large party of Trekkers from the colony towards the end of 1835. In the course of 1836 Potgieter's party came into conflict with Mzilikazi's Ndebeles and succeeded in defeating them at Vegkop. Unlike other Trekker leaders and because of his desire to settle as far as possible from British jurisdiction and interference, Potgieter preferred the highveld to Natal as an area of settlement, and consequently gave priority to breaking the power of the Ndebele conquest state in this region. Early in 1837 a combined commando with Maritz succeeded in sacking Mosega, though not Mzilikazi's capital Kapain. When the Ndebeles removed to north of the Limpopo, Potgieter regarded the area as his by right of conquest. Potgieter's letter should also be seen as a response to the Cape of Good Hope Punishment Act, published by the British government in 1836, making British subjects south of the 25° South latitude liable to punishment in the Cape courts.

We remind His Excellency that in words that were published some years ago it was proclaimed that in his judgement any Colonists who refused to submit to his laws should leave the Colony. And so we emigrants have seen fit, for the security of our families, to leave the Colony, and not only in view of His Excellency's laws, but mainly because we were not able to maintain our wives and children.

. . . Since we have left the Colony in peace and have had no ill intentions of doing anything illegal, we regard ourselves as free citizens who might go where we please without acting to the detriment of any other, as all nations are free and go where they like. And we cannot understand why we should be accused of such an unforgiveable crime from which, in terms of section 5 of your proclamation, not even time can absolve us. It is our desire to live in peace with His Excellency and with all nations, as will become evident.

[We concluded peace treaties with the different chiefs that we encountered, Danser, Maroka, Pieter Davieds, Sikonjala and Makwana.]

Our objective was to reach a country where there were no other peoples, and while on our journey in the upper reaches of the Vaal river in Makwana's country the bloodthirsty tyrant Musilicaats fell on us, and murdered some of our families in a bloodthirsty way and took away many cattle. Upon this we retreated to Doorenkop at the Renoster River, where he fell on us a second time with a countless horde, and again killed two people and took away our last cattle so that we were to starve to death. Maroka, Pieter Davieds and Mr Archbell assisted us to get to Maroka, whereupon we went on patrol, with a little help from Maroka, Pieter Davieds and Sikonjala, with a view to getting back our cattle. In this way we got back some of our cattle, and later on a second patrol we again regained a few. Many of us are still destitute because of this bloodthirsty tyrant Musilicaats.

From Makwana, who had also been ruined by Musilicaats, we bought a part of the country, since we do not want to do anything to the disadvantage of the nations that are here. But we are definitely occupying [Musilicaats's] country until he returns our cattle to us, though he has fled so far away that we do not know where he is. We do not believe that this is an unjust cause that we are now representing to you.

And so we ask Your Excellency on what grounds we are to be regarded as bloodthirsty enemies, to such an extent that even time will not protect us from punishment. . . .

. . . We did not ask for the assistance given us by Maroka and Sikonjala. They did it from their own free will because they had also been cruelly and bloodthirstily devastated by the same Musilicaats. Many of them who had survived would have starved to death, and not only that but great parts of the country were depopulated and devastated by the same tyrant Musilicaats and are still lying empty. Because of us the nations that are still here can live in peace. . . .

5.5d We know very well that we are a freeborn people, and that we have a right to Natal for which we had to pay the price of suffering indescribable cruelty.

—Letter (unsigned) from A. W. J. Pretorius to Governor D'Urban, Sand River, 24 Feb. 1839. (Translated from the text in H. S. Pretorius *et al., Voortrekker-Argiefstukke*, pp. 50–1.)

In contrast to Potgieter most Trekkers favoured Natal as an area of settlement. In 1838 they suffered heavy losses here at the hands of the Zulus until a commando under Andries Pretorius (1798–1853) crushed a Zulu army at Blood River in December 1838. Pretorius, who had been a leading farmer in Graaff-Reinet, assumed leadership of the Natal Trekkers when he arrived there in November 1838, following the deaths of Retief, Uys and Maritz, and the return of Potgieter to the highveld.

. . . Once again I am sending Your Honour the sworn treaty [*den eed*] which I also found with the remains of the late Mr Retief in order to make our false libellers see that we did not go out, as their false tongues allege, with aggressive purpose, but had sworn by the living God to do no harm to the cruel Dingaan, nor to his people. This is how we have acted towards all people. But if they first harm us by such gruesome murders, then we will defend ourselves as brave Afrikaners. We also notice that the government threatens us much, yet in the first place we know that all proclaim that every man should be free . . . and we know very well that we are a freeborn people, and that we have a right to Natal, which was acquired not only by means of free purchase, but for which we had to pay the price of suffering indescribable cruelty, and not with the blood of men alone. . . .

. . . But on the other hand, we shall never surrender our weapons and subject ourselves to the law. But we do not wish to enlarge on this, but just as quietly and calmly as we left our motherland behind with concern and sorrow, so we hope now not to be troubled nor to be opposed by anyone. It is vain to nurse the hope that we shall return again, all would rather die than that. . . .

5.5e I do not want to subject myself to any Briton, and I am no Briton nor, I hope and trust, will I ever become one.

—Letter from A. H. Potgieter to Commandant-General A. W. J. Pretorius, Potchefstroom, 28 Aug. 1841. (Translated from the text published in H. S. Pretorius *et al.*, *Voortrekker-Argiefstukke*, pp. 136–7.)

On behalf of the Natal Volksraad, Pretorius had entered into negotiations with Potgieter in October 1840, leading to an act of unification between the Trekker community centred at Potchefstroom and the republic of Natal. With the threat of British intervention in Natal, Potgieter became increasingly concerned that a too close association might implicate the settlement on the highveld in possible British action against Natal. The following extract comes from a letter in which Potgieter set out his reasons for not rallying to the cause of the Natal republic.

. . . I do not want to subject myself to any Briton, nor in justice to any other power in the world; and I am no Briton, nor, I hope and trust, will I ever become one, and I pray to the Almighty for this, not only for me, but for our whole united society of burghers [*vereenigde burgerlyke maatschappy*], and I would rather go ten steps forward than one backward.

Concerning our country, which has been bought with human blood, I hope and trust that not only I, but all who reside here as burghers of our united society, will come to feel that not only this country, but all the land that has been bought with the blood of our citizens, should be defended and championed, and that not even an inch of land should be lost, but, in justice, more should be sought after, in the interest of our society. . . .

5.6a The gathered, bleached bones of the innocently and treacherously murdered will remain a lasting evidence and as a visible beacon of right on that land.

—Declaration and Protest of the Volksraad of Natal, 11 Nov. 1839. (From the translation published in Bird, *The Annals of Natal*, Vol. I, pp. 544–546.)

In Natal the Trekkers were under constant pressure from the British government. In terms of the Cape of Good Hope Punishment Act they were still considered British subjects and in 1839 a detachment of British troops was stationed at Port Natal. Though for financial reasons the British were unwilling to annex Natal as British territory, such annexation remained a real possibility. When reports reached the Trekkers towards the end of 1839 of proposals for the settlement and colonization of Natal from Britain, they protested sharply and insisted on their own right of settlement, as shown in the following official declaration of the Natal Volksraad.

. . . The Cape emigrants, finding their rights and privileges daily violated and trampled upon, themselves incessantly insulted, ridiculed, and degraded in their honour and reputation, their right of property violated, and protection of life and property refused, have been compelled to leave their beloved country and their dearest, beloved friends and relations.

This emigration has taken place publicly under the eye of the Colonial Government, and after due payment of their taxes, for which they have sacrificed their valuable farms. They have been wandering about for three years, in regions to them unknown, without compass, without guide, without experience, exposed to all obstacles which nature put in their way, by insurmountable mountains reaching the clouds, exposed to serious wants and disappointments, surrounded and pursued by innumerable beasts of prey, with whom they daily had to struggle for the purpose of obtaining food, and without any government and laws, other than such as were deeply engrafted in their hearts by the mighty finger of the Lord, notwithstanding which, during their prolonged wanderings, no crime has taken place which could affect their character in any way.

All this, however, was not able to discourage them: driven away like bastard children from their paternal homes by strangers, they felt it as a painful grievance, and were pained at their very hearts by deep sorrow. Religion and the conviction of the justice of their case relieved them in surmounting all those difficulties. . . . On approaching Dingaan's kingdom, an agreement was entered into with that chief for obtaining a piece of land under certain conditions, which were strictly fulfilled by our brave, honest, and unsuspecting predecessor, P. Retief, and which was afterwards ratified by his blood and that of seventy more of our bravest men, shed by the treacherous murderer, Dingaan; whilst the gathered, bleached bones of the additional 370, innocently and treacherously murdered relations and friends at Boschjesman's River, will remain a lasting evidence and as a visible beacon of right on that land, until another beacon of similar materials shall overshadow ours. Thus guided by the same mighty Hand, which in former days saved our ancestors on the fearful St Bartholomew's night, we approached the long-wished-for seashore. . . . But now that we may expect every moment the arrival on our shores of thousands of poor deluded strangers with the view of driving us from our dearly-purchased and lawfully-acquired new country, the Assembly have, for the maintenance of our indisputable right to this land, obtained by virtue of treaties with the chief Dingaan, and afterwards ratified by the chief Panda, as well as for the maintenance of our independence, honour, and safety, come to the following resolutions. . . .

5.6b Far from bringing destruction or corruption to the heathen peoples in these parts, we are instruments of God's will for the promotion of Christian civilization.

—Letter from the Volksraad of Natal to Governor Napier, 14 Jan. 1841. (Translated from the text in H. S. Pretorius *et al.*, *Voortrekker-Argiefstukke*, pp. 117–20.)

5.6 *The correspondence of the Volksraad of Natal 1839–43*

The British troops occupying Port Natal were withdrawn at the end of 1839, removing the most direct threat of British annexation of Natal and encouraging Trekker hopes for eventual recognition of the settlement. On 4 September 1840 the Volksraad wrote to the Cape Governor, Sir George Napier, offering friendly co-operation with their 'beloved mothercountry' and requesting recognition as 'a free and independent people'. Napier replied on 2 November 1840 that it was not clear to him how people striving for political independence could also desire 'to share in the advantages enjoyed by those who have the happiness to live under the Queen of England's Government', and that negotiations would be premature until the basis of the Trekkers' proposals were clarified. The following letter was the Volksraad's attempt to provide such a basis for negotiations and recognition.

Thus, after careful deliberation, we have decided to submit to Your Excellency that we, as representatives of all the Dutch emigrants from the Colony of the Cape of Good Hope who reside at present within our boundaries, are ready and willing to conclude a long-lasting alliance with the Government of Her Majesty the Queen of England, on the following principles:

1st That the honoured Government of Her Majesty the Queen of England would be pleased to recognize our settlement here as a free and independent state with the name of the Republic of Natal and adjoining lands, the boundaries of which can be stipulated later. . . .

8th That this Republic promises never to make any hostile movements against any natives or inland tribes who might reside between the borders of the said Republic and those of the Colony of the Cape of Good Hope, without first having given notice of this intention to the representative of that Government here or to the Governor of the Colony. . . .

9th That we further bind ourselves not to extend our borders any further, where this is detrimental to any of the surrounding tribes, nor to make any hostile movements against them, unless such tribes should give us reason to do so through any hostile action, so that we shall be compelled, for the maintenance of our rights and the security of our property, to take up arms against such tribes.

10th That this Republic promises to give every encouragement to the spreading of the Gospel and to the civilization of the heathen people who surround us or live under our government. . . .

12th That this Republic undertakes, and binds itself, never to conduct any trade in slaves, nor to encourage or co-operate with such trade, nor to allow any ship or vessel used for this trade to enter our port or provide it with any refreshments. . . .

. . . It will be apparent to Your Excellency from the preceding that we are very desirous of remaining, at all times, on the best and friendliest terms with the British Government, and, if possible, to continue living in peace with the peoples who surround us, and only wish to protect and govern ourselves on our lawfully acquired territory, without ever causing harm either to your Government or to the nations which surround us, if they are desirous of living in peace with us. . . . Notwithstanding the continual accusations, groundless and completely devoid of truth, which are repeatedly pressed upon Her Majesty's Government in England from certain sources, we do not hesitate to say that we hope to convince the world that, far from bringing destruction or corruption to the heathen peoples in these parts, we are instruments of God's will [*een middel zyn in Gods hand*] for the countering of theft, murder and violence among them, for the greater safety of the Cape Colony, and for the promotion of Christian civilization among many thousands who, until now, have been left in the deepest darkness, as is already recognizable from the cases of those heathen tribes who are living under our protection and from others with whom we have concluded peace agreements. . . .

5.6c May we not ask where there is a Colony or conquered possession of Great Britain to which a stronger claim or right can be asserted?

—Letter from the Volksraad of Natal to Governor Napier, 21 Feb. 1842. (From the translation published in G. Eybers, *Select Constitutional Documents Illustrating South African History*, 1795–1910, pp. 167–174.)

Throughout 1841 pressure increased for the annexation of Natal by the British Government. Apart from strategic and economic considerations, the Trekkers' punitive campaign in December 1840 against Ncaphayi, a Bhaca chief in the south of Natal, and the proposals for the removal of blacks to separate settlements adopted by the Volksraad in August 1841, added weight to the demands from missionaries and philanthropists that the British government should intervene on humanitarian grounds to prevent ill-treatment of the indigenous peoples. After a protracted correspondence with the Volksraad, Governor Napier issued a proclamation on 2 December 1841 declaring that the Trekkers had no right or claim to be recognized as an independent people or state, and that he had been authorized to send a military force to Natal. The following letter of the Volksraad, drafted by J. N. Boshof, was a final attempt to prevent annexation by refuting allegations against the Trekkers and validating their own claims.

. . . Immediately after our departure we declared our independence; we established a Government of our own, prosecuted wars that came upon us unexpectedly and made peace, took possession of uninhabited tracts of country which we acquired by friendly treaties as well as . . . with our blood and treasure. . . .

. . . We are able to convince every true philanthropist that our views in making arrangements respecting the removal of the Kafirs . . . are furnished in a true love of humanity, in as much as we have thereby sought to obviate or to prevent the probability of hostility and bloodshed, which would otherwise inevitably result if we permitted Zoolahs and other Natives to leave their former abodes and settle themselves in thousands amongst us, as is at present the case, first to be protected by us against their enemies, and, when they shall have strengthened themselves, to be placed in the best opportunity possible to root us out solely to obtain possession of our cattle; or, their design being detected, they would compel us to attack and expel them without delay. Our measures are thus framed to provide in time, as far as practicable, against the probability of such occurrences, and not to allow the evil to increase too much or first to become irremediable and then show a disposition to be active.

. . . May we not ask where there is a Colony or conquered possession of Great Britain, or any other Power, to which a stronger claim or right can be asserted? We are convinced that there is not. . . .

. . . The surrounding warlike Zoolahs have been checked in their constant hostile attacks, so that from a fear for us they very seldom and only stealthily take up arms against us. Two missionaries under our protection are already labouring amongst them, and we have the best prospects that the civilization of that people will be sooner promoted than that of the Kaffirs on the Colonial frontiers. And all this has been accomplished whilst we are only beginning to get out of our difficulties. . . .

5.6d It may be maintained that we cannot have a lawful claim to these lands, that the grants as well as the sales made by us amount to nothing more than a loose speculation.

—Letter from the Volksraad of Natal to Commissioner Cloete, 4 Sept. 1843. (From the translation published in Bird, *The Annals of Natal*, Vol. II, pp. 277–280.)

The Volksraad of Natal continued to function subsequent to the subjugation of the area to British rule on 15 July 1842. After a final meeting to protest against British rule in August 1843 in Pietermaritzburg, many Trekkers departed once more for the highveld. Others stayed on, and to them recognition of their land claims was a crucial issue. Napier's proclamation of 12 May 1843 apparently implied that land rights would only be recognized on property that had actually been occupied. If enforced by Commissioner Henry Cloete, this would have invalidated the claims of many Trekkers.

We believe that we ought not to proceed to the statement of any particulars for your recommendation respecting the possession of land, without saying at the same time that this is a subject concerning which a deep and general interest is felt; and we may not conceal from you that it is our positive opinion that on the final decision of this question will depend the contentment or dissatisfaction of the people, as far as the country is inhabited. . . .

Not only those who possess occupied lands consider themselves to have a fair and reasonable claim to the same, but also all those who have obtained their lands on the same authority, who have suffered and done as much in and for the country, and who have only been prevented from occupying their farms by the unsafe condition of the settlement which has hitherto existed. . . . Should all such persons not be admitted as entitled to a grant of land, as well as those who had the good fortune to occupy theirs, the greater part will be deprived of it; and having been reduced to poverty by the great losses which they have sustained, and consequently unable to purchase from the Government, it would be expecting too much were it thought that the utmost dissatisfaction would not proceed from such a decision, and that such persons could be induced to remain in a country, and to co-operate in its common prosperity, or be willing to join in sustaining its burdens, after they shall have been excluded from all interest in the same, so as to have no prospect of procuring for themselves and their families a place of rest. . . .

It may be maintained that we cannot have a lawful claim to these lands, the grants not having been lawfully made; that we are British subjects, and could have no such authority, except by permission of the British Government; and that the grants as well as the sales made by us amount to nothing more than a loose speculation.

But it will be difficult to convince even a small portion of the inhabitants of the justice, equity, and usefulness of this reasoning. We were obliged, as emigrants, who had to govern and protect ourselves, and who would not lead the life of wanderers (although we may not have thought that we had a good claim to independence), to establish a government amongst ourselves, whose authority we were bound to honour and acknowledge, and we were therefore not only entitled to frame laws for our guidance, but also to dispose of land, so that every man might have his own, without which no civilized community could exist.

Our government or highest authority then consisted of a Volksraad. . . . The Raad framed a law in respect of these grants, of which we take the liberty to subjoin a copy. And sales of land having also been made lawful, many have made purchases to a considerable amount, and others have invested all their ready money in fixed property. . . . When no notice shall be taken of all this, those sellers, who have for the greater part left the country, will be the best off, inasmuch as in some instances they have received the full value of their property; . . . and the purchasers of such land would not only be greatly disappointed, but in many instances they would be impoverished, if not brought down to bankruptcy; and this although they ought to be classed among those who have done much for the welfare and occupation of the settlement. . . .

We feel convinced that Government may confirm the grants made by the Raad without prejudice to the requisite revenues of the country; and much will depend on this to cause general peace, submission, and contentment. . . .

5.7 We were once again obliged to set out into the world to look for a piece of land and to discover where one might find peace and achieve independence.

—Memorial of the Volksraad of Ohrigstad, 7 Oct. 1845. (Translated from the text in H. S. Pretorius *et al.*, *Voortrekker-Argiefstukke*, pp. 162–4.)

The Voortrekkers founded a number of separate settlements north of the Vaal. In 1845 Potgieter, whose party until then had mainly settled in the western Transvaal around Potchefstroom, established the Andries Ohrigstad settlement in the eastern Transvaal. The new move was part of his strategy to reduce the risk of British intervention by moving beyond what he and his trek thought was the limit set by the Cape of Good Hope Punishment Act. They were joined by Trekkers from Natal, but the settlement proved shortlived, owing to the unhealthy climate.

. . . Having torn ourselves loose from the British Government and departed from our motherland, where we had been libelled, pestered and humiliated, we made our way through the wilderness with our wives and children to settle on a piece of land which was quite untamed. Here we thought the air of independence might be breathed, and thought that it would certainly prosper. But, after we had sacrificed everything, and not just possessions but blood as well, so that even now widows and orphans suffer from the absence of the necessities of life, only after all this had been sacrificed did we have to find that our patience and all our sacrifices had been quite fruitless. In these circumstances we were once again obliged to set out into the world to look for a piece of land and to discover where, for once, one might find the peace which is no longer to be found under our ancestral roofs, trusting henceforth in God alone for the protection which we are obliged, as men and as Christians, to maintain so that we might achieve independence. We even have to try actively to find the opportunity where, when required, we are able to demonstrate that independence.

And not only that, but we have to anticipate the blame and the accusations of scandalous deeds that will be levelled against the Afrikaners by their enemies, and to convince them entirely of the contrary. For we Afrikaners have never been defended [against such accusations] in other countries, but all the infamous lies have even been endorsed in print. . . . It has been stated in print that 'Each place where that rebellious scum has settled can be recognized by the numerous bones of stolen cattle, and still they are spreading themselves more and more all the time as the terror of every region through which they are trekking.' . . .

On the other hand, again, there is a law recognized by all nations, that when a certain group of people leave its government and this group of people settle in a region which is independent of any government, then they have the right to live under and make their own laws. And so, although we consider ourselves to be independent, we have to be active in maintaining this independence, in order not to give the jealous British government any opportunity which might come about through ignorant delays. . . .

5.8 We wish to entreat you to leave us unmolested and without further interference on those grounds which we have justly obtained.

—Manifesto of A. W. J. Pretorius to Governor Smith, Bloemfontein, 18 July 1848. (From *Correspondence Relative to the Establishment of the Settlement of Natal*, Imperial Blue Book, pp. 24–25.)

Pretorius had stayed on in Natal after the British annexation, but became increasingly disaffected with the British government, which had imposed legal equality between black and white, and which was not prepared to take the measures against blacks which Pretorius demanded in order to provide proper security of property. After appeals to Lieutenant-Governor West of Natal and Governor Pottinger of the Cape Colony had proved unsuccessful, his hopes were revived by a meeting in 1848 with Sir Harry Smith on the latter's whirlwind tour of South Africa. Smith, the new British Governor and High Commissioner, had immediately embarked on an expansionist policy but he gave Pretorius to understand that he would not annex the highveld territory until the Voortrekker leader had sounded out Afrikaner opinion and reported back to him. Pretorius used the opportunity to mobilize anti-British sentiment at meetings both north and south of the Vaal. However, in 1848 Smith proclaimed British sovereignty over all inhabitants between the Orange and the Vaal, and Pretorius responded with the following manifesto, signed by himself and about nine hundred others.

We all, the undersigned Commandants and Field Cornets of different districts here assembled, hereby acquaint Your Excellency that we perceive, in a manifesto, that you threaten us with a war of military power; which appears to us very unjust to constrain us on lands which we have justly bartered from the natives—to them having been allowed self-government and all privileges of liberty; and we whites must be governed by laws which come from another place (or country).

One might ask, are we then worse, are we more contemptible than the coloured population? To them are acknowledged and secured the lands they have inherited; to them are allowed the privileges of self-government and their own laws; but as soon as we whites are on the same lands, which we have justly obtained from them, these privileges are immediately taken from us, so that we may justly say that we do not even share equally with the coloured tribes; but that now, though all other creatures enjoy rights and liberties, we are constantly constrained to be in fetters. . . .

Now, we state to Your Excellency, and we state it to the world, yes, we state it as men with clear hearts and much experience, that we white cattle farmers cannot, with any feeling of security, under Her Majesty's jurisdiction, reside in a country inhabited by so many coloured people, especially as they are left to their own laws, and we are placed under other laws. We repeat again, as well to Your Excellency as to the world, that had we perchance been coloured, it might perhaps be possible, but now we find it impossible, because we are white African Boers. We speak not loosely; we speak not in hatred; because we were oppressed by the British authority (of which oppressions we will not even make mention, for these no newspaper could contain, it would certainly comprise a whole volume): but we will briefly make mention of only two instances by way of supporting our complaints.

How many years have not the inhabitants of the old colony (where blacks are) remained in a state of insecurity, and how many irrecoverable losses and hardships have they not suffered under British rule? When we were all youths and children then there was Kafir war; now we are men with gray hairs, and there is still Kafir war; and we ask whether the inhabitants there have recovered their losses sustained through a war caused under British rule, as well in the year 1835, as in 1847 and 1848? . . . And now do we arrive at the great Mirror of Natal. . . . How did we obtain possession of that country—unjustly or easily? No; we obtained it justly from a Sovereign power; and subsequently it cost us the blood of dearest wives and children, and we will never refrain from exclaiming it before the great Creator and the world. And where is the country now? Still in possession of the owners? Have these same proprietors been enabled to reside there in greater security since the British power has taken possession of it?

And now comes the great and weighty question! Did Government take possession of the country upon the majority and at the desire of the proprietors of the said country, or because it was right to do so? Oh, no! . . . It took place with power alone. But where is the word of right? Can any one call that right which first deprived us of our liberty and country whilst we were living in peace and quietness; and, afterwards, through insecurity, not only our places but also our corn and our sheaves and houses full of property? With tearful eyes are we obliged to look back on our churches, and dearly-bought land. . . .

Where are then the former proprietors of the land? Here they are wandering in the wilderness of South Africa. Your Excellency asks me if we are richer or better? No, we have sacrificed all for the country which the British authority has taken from us. . . . If you continue to oppress and drive us away, how shall we then be enabled to establish a church and house of God amongst us? Behold our church standing at Natal as a testimony to the world that we have not so far forsaken God and become so unbridled as we have been represented. . . . Thus Your Excellency's question whether we have become better? Who can expect it after all the hardships which we have been obliged to undergo; but we are justified in saying, that after all this, and previous to the taking possession, we enjoyed security. But should you now drive us deeper into the wilderness, will you thereby make us better? As we have undergone so many examples and such experience, who would be so very perverse as to speak of security of life and property and churches and schools in a country of so many coloured tribes under British sovereignty, especially since such inequality is decided upon—that the barbarians may exercise their own, and we whites to be brought under the laws of the Cape. If we may make so free as to ask, in allusion to that part of the old colony, where the coloured are, whether Her Majesty's subjects residing there are rich and contented, or are they plundered by the coloured or barbarians? And what hope is there for us who now reside on the boundary? Will not the thousands of coloured people in the midst of whom we are living [and have always considered ourselves secure] immediately become our enemies? . . .

Oh, these hardships you will never eradicate from the heart of an African Boer, neither with promises nor with threats; you will cause a further flight and dissatisfaction, but never a silent submission. And thus we have severely suffered; we have silently left our motherland under all these hardships; for liberty we sacrificed all! We will not say that all the people who are with us have left for liberty; we see every day that fortune-hunters and all misleaders who are treacherous towards us likewise constantly remain with us, and cause much strife amongst us; and it is greatly owing to Your Excellency's interference that such evade the well-deserved punishment amongst us; so that when we can only obtain the privileges of the coloured people, we will soon convince the world that crime will be punished by us, and that we will then use our best endeavours to introduce churches and schools; yes, even the Holy Sacrament amongst us.

Oh, we could mention a volume of hardships and support them with many testimonies of truth; however, we will pass it all by. But we wish to entreat Your Excellency to leave us unmolested and without further interference, on those grounds which we have justly obtained from the legal proprietors, and thus we shall exclaim to the world and our Creator, (who we know looks down upon us from on high, and to Him alone we owe all gratitude and reverence), that we have not yet been totally extirpated.

5.9 It never entered the imagination of the simplest of the Boers to deny the oppression, knowing that he could not take a step without crossing ground of which those he holds in bondage were once the free and contented owners.

—A. Stockenström's autobiographical notes, c. 1856. (From *The Autobiography of Sir Andries Stockenström*, Vol. I, pp. 78–79, 124–5, 243–5.)

Sir Andries Stockenström retired from public life in South Africa in March 1856 and proceeded to Europe, where he died in London in 1864. In retirement, he prepared large parts of his Autobiography, *which consisted largely of contemporary documents, but also of retrospective comments on the events and issues of his earlier life, as in the following extracts.*

(a) [On his first appointment, as deputy landdrost of Graaff-Reinet in 1813]

. . . It is true that strong prejudices existed against Lord Caledon's Proclamation of 1809 concerning the Hottentots, which it became my duty to enforce, and it is equally true that this often brought me into collision with some very good people; but I always found myself supported by the sense and equity of the influential classes, with whom I often discussed the point for hours, not only in the office, but in their own houses, for my duties always kept me on the move amongst them, and they were easily made to see and admit what the aboriginal tribes had lost through our progress, and how much it became our duty to mitigate their sufferings. Without this support I could not have gone on a single month.

The theory which makes the blacks irreclaimable savages, fit only to be exterminated, like the wolves, was not of Boer origin. We had possessed ourselves of their lands; we wanted more of their land, together with their services. Oppression had been going on for a century and a half; but we did not oppress for mere oppression's sake. The refinement of our system was due to what Mr Commissioner Bigge long after truly called 'your pupils, who were such apt scholars, that they soon became your masters'. It never entered the imagination of the simplest of the Boers to deny the oppression, knowing that he could not take a step without crossing ground of which those he holds in bondage were once the free and contented owners. The reflecting part (that is many) of the old population regretted the evil, but could not see a remedy. It remained for their 'pupil-masters', by the most barefaced impostures, to fish for their favour and their money by teaching them to look upon those as their enemies and libellers who dared admit the notorious historical fact of the extermination of a comparatively defenceless race. . . .

(b) [On the 1818 war]

. . . Having alluded to the relations of my so-called 'Cape Dutch' countrymen with the native tribes, I think this the proper place to admit that nothing can be more shocking to any philanthropic, philosophic mind than the extermination of the Bushmen and Hottentots and the seizure of their lands by the self-styled followers of the divine apostle of love, peace, truth, and justice! But let us be impartial, and remember that the *Christian* work was originally begun by the *Government*, and had gradually become a matter of course, and of supposed necessity and self-defence. But, pray, what have these Cape Dutch done that we *Anglo-Saxons* and *Anglo-Normans* have not perpetrated on a much more extensive cruel scale in Ireland, America, in Kaffirland, in India, in China, as we will do in Japan? . . .

The Cape Dutch at least did wrong with less hypocrisy, for I never once heard our aggressions attempted to be excused or justified by the pretence of spreading the Bible or civilization; whilst, on the contrary, many of the elder members, who had fortunately come in contact with right-minded Christians, or had otherwise obtained an insight into the principles of the sacred volume, would sit up whole nights relating to me and lamenting over the scenes of injustice and cruelty which they had witnessed, or heard of in earlier days. . . .

(c) [on his discussions with Pringle and Philip in 1825]

. . . To have denied the extermination of the Hottentots and Bushmen, the possession of their country by ourselves, the cruelties with which their expulsion and just resistance had been accompanied, the hardships with which the laws were still pressing upon their remnants, the continuation of the same system against the Kaffirs, or the iniquity of the aggressions and murders then lately perpetrated upon the latter race, would have been ridiculous, as well as dishonest, as there was not in the Colony, even among the Boers, one single being of the slightest decency or respectability, who did not see the facts before his eyes and lament them. . . .

There was consequently little to be disputed between my guests and myself as to the past; but they certainly tried my temper by the virulence with which they persisted in denouncing the present generation of the Colonists and refused to make any allowance for their actual position, which rendered self-defence often absolutely necessary for the preservation of both parties, invariably cutting the Gordian knot by the maxim, which no people on earth have ever violated one hundredth part as much as the English themselves, viz., 'You have no business here at all.'

In talking of *systems*, I happened to say, 'My system is to do my best to get the white man hanged who murders a black; but I also do my best to root out any gang of robbers and murderers among the blacks, who cannot be otherwise reclaimed.' This was met by an exclamation, 'An awful necessity into which you have forced yourselves!' Granted; or rather, our ancestors and the Government have forced us into it, and being in the scrape, we must either run away, sit still and have our throats cut, or defend what we have. Neither of the two former alternatives will benefit the blacks—either must ultimately ruin both them and ourselves; whereas the third persisted in with firmness, strict justice and moderation may in a country like this enable both parties to live in peace and plenty. My opponents were disposed to find some reason in this argument, but remained sceptical as to the existence of the soil on which the justice and moderation were to be cultivated. . . .

5.10 Which country is in more rightful possession of the descendants of Europeans than our country?

—Letter from the Executive of the Republic of Lydenburg, published in the *Oude Emigrant*, 3 April 1860. (Translated from the copy in the State Archives, Pretoria, L 18.)

5.10 The Lydenburg Republic Executive's rationale of colonialism 1860

One of the main settlements north of the Vaal was at Lydenburg in the eastern Transvaal. For a brief period from 1857 to 1860 it formed a separate republic. The following letter was written in response to an open letter of 13 April 1859 from the Committee of the Evangelical Association (Committee van het Evangelie-verbond) *at Port Elizabeth, signed by the Revs A. Smith of the Reformed Church and W. A. Robinson of the Anglican Church. The response was drafted by H. T. Bührmann (1822–1890), who had arrived in 1848 from Holland and settled in the eastern Transvaal. He played a prominent part in the politics of Lydenburg and the Transvaal, throughout the 1850s and later.*

. . . We are a group who form part of that people whom you so misjudge . . . and to whom you have addressed your open letter. . . . We all belong to that people whom you have attacked and held in contempt. This people have sacrificed all their possessions and set out with apprehension and concern in order to acquire and establish their own country and their own form of government, just as was done by your forefathers and ours and all European nations before us. In this way we hoped, and still do, to free ourselves from all the laws and customs of other nations which are contrary to our consciences and our national sentiments and appear to us improper. . . .

You refer to our departure from the colony and our withdrawal from civilized life. You say that you would have rejoiced in this and thanked God without cease, if we had done this with the purpose of bringing Christ's gospel to an ignorant people in the wilderness. Truly, brothers, to hear such language from learned people is incomprehensible to us. Where, in the history of the world, have you heard of a people that left its fatherland, its own happiness, sacrificing peace and property, with the sole purpose of all becoming missionaries, and of forcing a savage people to accept civilization and a religion which they do not desire? We are aware, and we thank God for it, that exceptional people are often aroused to devote themselves to the cause of the gospel, but if whole nations were to do this, they would probably fail in the purpose for which God has called them. You place on our shoulders burdens which are too heavy to bear. . . . In any case, in what sense can we be said to have withdrawn from civilized life? The civilized life of each nation consists precisely of their own activity, and as a body of many hundred people we could be regarded as having taken with us our part in that civilization which we shared with you and had in common with you. That this is so will be known and recognized by everyone who does not condemn us, and has intercourse with us. . . .

You ask whether the Almighty said to our Commandant-General, 'Arise and take possession of the land!' . . . We answer that He did not, but that the largest part of this country north of the Vaal river, as well as a large part of what is now the British colony of Natal, and the Orange Free State, was lawfully purchased by the Dutch emigrants from its earlier owners—the Kaffir tribes who lived there—and a part was acquired by rightfully waged wars, caused by the unwarranted attacks of the natives of that country. Thus we have in our opinion acquired the land by right and in accordance with the tenets of God's word. . . .

You ask whether God has given South Africa to us through any promise and to whom it has been given.

On both these two questions we must ask for further clarification since you treat these national matters as theological issues, and you well know that we are not theologians. . . . But we would also . . . direct a few questions to you. Did God give the Cape Colony first to the Dutch government and then to the British government? Was it said to you, while you were still in Europe, arise and take possession of

Uitenhage and Port Elizabeth, and encourage those who are already living there, and who are the descendants of those Europeans who had taken possession of that country, to cultivate assiduously the land taken from the natives, so that you all may live, and that the salaries might be paid of those ministers who, just as much as we, are involved in dispossession? Have you, our brothers and fellow-possessors of different parts of that same land, not reminded each other, in the course of your writing, to ask the question first of yourselves? Why do you ask it of us? Is it perhaps because you do not dare to ask and reprimand other governments which are stronger, more highly regarded and more feared than we are? And that you regard yourselves as above us and more entitled to the occupation of South Africa? Have you raised up your voice and asked why Natal, and earlier the Orange Free State and now British Kaffirland have been taken into possession?

If you have not yet done this, then do it. And when you are answered, make sure that every inch of land which was not rightfully acquired from the previous owners by you and all other Europeans, is returned again to its original owners—the Hottentots, Kaffirs and Bushmen. And even then, if we were to follow your example, we would demonstrate conclusively that very little of the emigrant's land need be returned.

We cannot in any way at all comprehend Your Excellencies' feelings about the Lord's word and the history of the world. . . .

If it should be as you say, if your opinion were true, then we should have to believe that since the Israelites' empire ceased to exist, no just war has ever been waged, nor any land rightfully acquired. Then we must also believe that God's judgement has never yet in all this time been brought to bear on any nation or people, and thus that it was only the Israelites' promised land which was given by the Lord in accordance with His will. Do you mean to say that God has ceased to rule? That the acquisition of Asia, Africa, America and Australia took place without God's will and consent, but occurred even against His will? Has the Lord God allowed the world and its management and changings to be taken out of His hands, so that man now obeys his own will alone, in all that he does, and is no longer an instrument in God's hand, to bring into being His judgements and wise decisions, as were the Jews and other nations before the birth of Christ? You call wars which involve aggression, such as those which we conduct, 'theft and murder'. . . .

According to this statement of yours all countries which are acquired by means of aggression are not acquired in accordance with God's wise counsel and His will, but by unlawful theft and murder. Thus you and all of us who are of European origin and are outside Europe, occupy land unlawfully there, as the original inhabitants of Asia, Africa, America and Australia never first invited the European to come to their countries. And although there was no divine judgement, and although no miracles occurred, these countries were originally sought out by the Europeans with the fixed intention of establishing their paramountcy there, and when this was resisted, they have taken possession of these countries by aggressive means. Was this beyond God's omnipotence? Would you call all these occupations theft and murder? Do you have the right to say that this is what they are? Dare you say, and can you prove, that all this has taken place without God's will, without His wisdom and world sovereignty? That all this has been done by man, contrary to God's will, through their greed alone? If this is so, then woe betide you and us, because you and we enjoy and treat as our own the unlawful fruits of the murders and thefts of our fathers and of our own generation. . . .

In this our faith or our understanding of the Lord's word does not correspond to yours. We believe that the same God of the Old Testament still rules, and, just as He did then, He executes His wise plans and decisions for the government of the world, the establishment and destruction of kingdoms, states, peoples and countries, and uses man as his instrument in this. . . . Our belief in these matters (the occupation of the four continents) is, therefore, that the Almighty in His wisdom, having decided to spread His word and His law over the whole earth, is using the European peoples for this and has therefore given them the intelligence and power not only to discover these countries but also to occupy and possess them.

Our belief is also that the same God, knowing, in His profound wisdom, that Europe is not able to feed its own population and give them land on which to live, and wanting to provide for this need, opened these outlets for Europe, and that this was not the work of man. We believe further that the Lord has created the earth to be lived upon and cultivated, and will not allow it to be left uncultivated and unoccupied, and that it is thus through His will that the unoccupied land is increasingly becoming occupied. . . .

According to your writings, our occupation of this land took place by theft and murder. How will you prove this? . . . As far as we are concerned, we want to know in what respect this can be said. We ask, which country is in more rightful possession of the descendants of Europeans than our country? . . .

6 *Colonial grievances, civil liberties and self-government 1778–1854*

The early political history of the Afrikaners has often been represented in terms of the classic model of decolonization. Like that of the American colonies before them and the Afro–Asian peoples much later, the basic historical pattern is held to consist in a long tradition of colonial grievances, ever-growing demands for self-government, and finally the achievement of representative institutions and political independence. However, it is only at the most general and superficial level that this account fits the development leading from the first protests of the Cape Patriots in the 1780s to the eventual granting of a new constitutional dispensation to the Cape Colony, as well as to the creation of the two northern republics in the early 1850s. In fact, throughout this period public expressions of grievances and agitations for more self-government occurred only sporadically. When they did occur, the striving for political rights and self-government was rarely the main issue. More often demands of this nature were made as by-products of movements concerned with what was conceived as the more pressing problems of the time: official malpractices and monopolies in the 1780s, the threatened rights of slaveholders in the 1820s and early 1830s. Even the Great Trek was not primarily motivated by any quest for self-rule or political independence (see Chapter 1), though these goals did come to be valued more highly as a consequence of the Trek. Only towards the late 1840s did a strong movement aimed at self-government emerge, in the colony as well as in the interior. However, its main objectives were granted almost at once, and there was no sustained and general movement pressing for the further extension of representative institutions. Thus during this period there was no strong, continuous tradition of political thinking on the general themes of colonial oppression, the significance of civil liberties or the value of national independence.

The texts collected in this chapter contain some of the most important writing dealing in one way or another with these themes. In view of the foregoing, it is clear that particular care should be taken to analyze and interpret them within their respective historical contexts. Questions like the following may be kept in mind:

1 What were the intellectual origins of the central political concepts like *the general welfare* or *the voice of the people*, and to what purposes were they being used in specific colonial contexts?

2 What were the functions of the claims to have more *self-government* and *political representation* in the specific historical circumstances in which these were made?

3 Were there continuities in the ways in which similar sets of political concepts were used throughout this period, or did these similarities cover underlying differences and discontinuities in political orientation?

4 Is there any indication of a broad and general development of political thinking on these themes, or do we find a number of divergent and sporadic expressions of different political positions?

Citizenship and the general welfare

Constitutional politics and political theory were not the major concerns of the Cape Patriots. The larger part of the Burgher petition of 1779, for example, consisted simply of a long catalogue of particular grievances concerning the various malpractices of specific officials. On a more general level the Patriots were concerned with the 'constitution' of the colony in the sense of the underlying structure of its political economy (see Chapter 2). But their writings also show the impact of a number of general political ideas and theories coming into currency in the Western world at the time, such as the idea of 'the general welfare' and the claim to rights of citizenship, though these were put to somewhat different uses in the distant colonial context of the Cape.

In a global perspective the Cape Patriots appear as a distant part of a general revolutionary movement which swept the Western world during the last quarter of the eighteenth century, and of which the American and French Revolutions were only the most dramatic manifestations.[1] Certainly the colonists at the Cape were very much aware of the American precedent and its implications, and they had close contacts with members of the Patriot Movement which got under way in Holland at about the same time.[2] The Dutch Patriots, in turn, had been influenced by such political theorists as Price, Hutcheson and Locke. The reception of such political ideas at the Cape, however, was not only mediated in this way; it was also highly selective and partial.

This can be demonstrated from some of the earliest writings of the Cape Patriots. In 1778 two pamphlets were distributed anonymously at the Cape. The more substantial of the two, entitled 'The Power and Liberties of a Civil Society' *(De Magt en Vrijheeden eerner Burgerlijke Maatschappije)*, was in fact an almost verbatim transcription of portions of a pamphlet produced in 1754 in Holland by Elie Luzac.[3] The second and more modest pamphlet (6.1a) was the Cape Patriots' own work. By comparing the two it is possible to trace the way in which contemporary European political theory influenced political thinking at the Cape.

Luzac's pamphlet dealt with some of the central theoretical problems in the relations between subjects and governments, and did this very much in the way of the modern natural rights tradition. Quoting authorities such as Locke, Grotius and Pufendorff, it presented the theory of popular sovereignty. The welfare of the people—conceived in terms of their individual and collective interests—was the supreme law, and all authority consisted essentially in maintaining the rights of subjects. Government was necessary for the purpose of coordinating the multiplicity of particular interests into a general will aimed at the common good of society. As such the function of government was to provide both the internal administrative framework of law as well as the means of protection against external threats. In this way it ensured the freedom of the individual to pursue his own interests in so far as this did not conflict with others, thus reconciling the obligation towards the general welfare with the pursuit of particular interests. But it also followed that subjects retained the right to resistance against their rulers, if and when the latter should fail in their duty or endanger the welfare of the people. The natural right to individual survival was inalienable, and it was even an obligation for subjects to intervene in the conduct of public affairs when it became clear that the government was failing in its essential tasks.

It cannot be assumed that the Cape Patriots appropriated this entire body of theory.[4] There is no indication that they were at all interested in the theoretical issues of popular sovereignty as the basis of government, or with the problem of reconciling the general welfare with the pursuit of particular interests. In fact, concerning the most controversial and central argument of Luzac's pamphlet, that of the citizens' inalienable right to resistance, the Cape Patriots took a notably cautious approach. At the conclusion, in one of the few additions to the original text of Luzac, they denied that they wanted to provoke popular agitation against their rulers. In the circumstances, of course, they could hardly have been expected to broadcast any revolutionary aims, had they held these, but it is significant that even at a strictly theoretical level they shrank back from the argument for a right to resistance. Their aim, it was claimed, was solely to justify their intention of handing a petition to the government, and to convince their fellow burghers who thought otherwise that they did not owe an *absolute* obedience to the government.[5]

In their own pamphlet (6.1a) the Cape Patriots adopted, from this whole range of concepts and arguments, only Luzac's opening statement of the two fundamental laws of all duties. According to the first law every man 'must promote his own welfare, together with that of his fellows, and in particular that of his fellow citizens', while the second law, following from this, demanded that 'every man should contribute . . . to the welfare of the general community, and in particular to the welfare of the citizenry of which he is a member'. The Patriots thus wished to base their political thinking on the notion of *the general welfare*; but applied in a colonial situation, and taken out of the total context of a democratic theory grounded on natural rights, these precepts lost much of their universalistic significance. They now served essentially to legitimize the claims and interests of that section of the colonial community constituted by the 'free citizenry' *(burgerstaat)*. They wished to justify the claim that this 'citizenry' did have legitimate interests. But they did not venture beyond this point on the path of democratic theory. In the colonial context of the Cape they were clearly acting on behalf of sectional interests and not of the local community as a whole: the 'citizenry' did not include the numerous minor Company servants or lowly whites in the employ of others. Slaves and Khoikhoi obviously did not count as *burghers*, and even free blacks did not do so as a rule. The Patriots also did not assert the claims of popular sovereignty with respect to the government. It could hardly be maintained that Company rule at the Cape did, or could, exist for the sake of the general welfare of colonial society. On the contrary, it was obvious that the interests of the Company itself and of the local officials as a section of the colonial community were both in conflict with that of the 'citizenry'. The Patriots could not in any way dispute the basic rights and interests of the colonizing power. They merely insisted that the local citizenry *also* had rightful interests, and could legitimately pursue their own general welfare. The appeal to the two fundamental laws of all duties thus served to provide a general moral backing to this pursuit of their sectional interests, given this colonial setting, and it is in this sense that their central concept of the general welfare should be understood.

More specifically the Cape Patriots based their claims not so much on any universal conception of natural rights—despite occasional use of natural rights terminology[6]—but on the rights and privileges granted to them by the Company itself and historically pertaining to free citizens of the Netherlands: 'Most worthy citizens, consider whether you at present possess the privileges which the Company has granted you. . . . We have allowed our laws and privileges to be assailed and have forgotten to be free citizens of a colony of the free United Netherlands.' (6.1) Basically they were concerned with the question of their *citizenship*, and with securing the rights and privileges which they thought inherent in this status. In the Burgher petition of 1779 a central pre-occupation is to document what they considered the arbitrary and tyrannical way in which the Cape officials, from the Independent Fiscal, W. C. Boers, down, abused and flouted their presumed rights as free citizens. A number of their own proposals and recommendations were aimed at securing these rights and privileges, above all the right to free trade, and measures for greater legal security (6.1b). Their proposals also included demands for a greater measure of representation in various institutions of government, but these were clearly seen as instrumental to the main purpose of securing their rights as citizens, and there were no general demands for self-rule or popular government. It was also entirely consistent with the sectional nature of the citizenry, and with the promotion of its general welfare, that a number of other proposals called for greater powers over their slaves, and for the exclusion of alien groups from these rights and privileges (6.1b).

In the course of the next few years more elaborate expositions of the Cape Patriots' political thinking were produced. The most comprehensive of these, the pamphlet *Nederlandsch Afrika* (6.2), dealt extensively with the political situation at the Cape, sketched its historical origins, analyzed the current condition of the main political institutions, and proposed a number of reforms.

In *Nederlandsch Afrika*, as well as in the letter from the Cape correspondent in 1786 (6.3), the political situation at the Cape was once more portrayed in terms of oppression by arbitrary and despotic rulers. In both cases the history of the colony is sketched in terms of the consistent abuse and denial of the burghers' civil liberties and privileges by a succession of tyrannical governors and officials. As in the earlier petitions the main political objective was the restitution of these rights and privileges, above all of legal security and the right to free enterprise, in recognition and confirmation of the burghers' proper status as free citizens. To this end it was also proposed that some measure of representation in the various political institutions be granted (6.2).

On what grounds were these claims to civil liberties and political rights based? In these writings no attempts were made to derive such claims from any doctrine of universal natural rights. Nor do we find any stress on the growing autonomy and independence of the colonial society as against the metropolitan centre. Instead the political links with the mother country were emphasized: the Cape burghers based their claims on the common citizenship they shared with the free citizens of the Netherlands. The settlers who came to the Cape, it is argued, retained their civil status, (i.e. the rights and liberties which they had enjoyed in the mother country), and they should be governed on the same footing as their fellow citizens in the Netherlands (6.2).[7] The views of the Independent Fiscal, W. C. Boers, who denied their status as citizens and maintained that the Company could dispose of them as its servants, were vehemently refuted. In support of their own claims they advanced, above all, some highly charged versions of Cape history and of the historical link with the mother country, adopting the same kind of quasi-historical argument that was current in much of contemporary Dutch oppositional literature in its appeals for the restoration of the 'original Batavian liberties'. Thus the writer of *Nederlandsch Afrika* stressed the *original* rights and privileges of the first settlers at the Cape. It is suggested that colonial society was based on a kind of original social contract between the first settlers and the colonizing power in which the civil liberties of the settlers had been guaranteed (6.2).

The rule of the founding governor, Van Riebeeck, was described in idealized terms as an original—and lost—Golden Age. It exemplified the exact contrary to the Patriots' own situation of arbitrary rule and abuse of their rights of citizenship. After Van Riebeeck the subsequent governors and colonial administrations had, however, departed more and more from the proper foundations of 'justice, humanity and social virtues' on which he had originally founded the settlement, and which should now be restored (6.2). Taking a slightly different line the Cape correspondent writing to Holland in 1786 (6.3) stressed not so much the rights of the original settlers in Van Riebeeck's Golden Age but the history of heroic struggle against tyrannical rulers of the colony such as the Van der Stels. By means of the rhetorical language which the writer employed, and the values he invoked, an explicit parallel was drawn between this colonial conflict and the heroic history of Dutch struggle against Spanish oppression during the Eighty Years' War. In this way Cape history was identified with that of the mother country: it was essentially part of the *same* historical struggle for liberty against tyranny. This is brought out clearly by the conclusion in which 'the brave Afrikaners . . . say to the free Netherlands that we love freedom just as much as they do, that we have been born of their stock and feel the same free blood in our veins. For just as it was fair for them to defend themselves against oppression after fruitless pleading, so it is fair and just that we deal with [oppression] as they did with Philip the Tyrant!' (6.3)

If the Cape Patriots thus sought to base their claims on a purported common citizenship and shared struggle with the citizenry of the distant mother country, there was no question of any common ground with the local colonial rulers. The governor and the other major officials of the Company, it was claimed, had particular interests that were in direct conflict with the interests of the colonists. There could be no question of these officials being their representatives in the various institutions of government. On the contrary, they were the colonists' 'adversaries' and 'personal enemies'; these rulers were 'in a sense an alien people' (6.2, cf. 6.3). Though they did not dispute the sovereign rights of the Company itself as the colonizing power, they were fervently opposed to the unfair rivalry resulting from the private interests of the officials.

The Cape Patriots' grievances were rooted, then, in their colonial condition, but their political thinking tended towards (re-)claiming citizenship of the mother country. There was no question of asserting the independence of the local community and severing the political ties with the metropolitan centre. Political salvation was expected to come not so much from democratic self-government of the Cape society, (which was in fact inconceivable, given the fundamental conflict of interests between officials and colonists), but rather from intervention and recognition by the metropolitan power in Holland.

Two documents from later periods, the extracts from Christoffel Brand and Egbertus Bergh, in which some of the central notions of the Cape Patriots recurred in somewhat different contexts, may help to put these notions into clearer perspective. Christoffel Brand, writing his dissertation of 1820 (6.7), at a time when the bond between colonial citizens at the Cape and the Dutch mother country was no longer a burning question but had already become a matter of history, explicitly articulated what had been the Cape Patriots' underlying views on the nature of 'the bond and the rights which should exist between a colony and the mother city'. According to Brand the relation between the colonial settlement and the colonizing metropolis could either be one of subjection through coercive force, or it could be a 'natural' bond, a paternal and filial union of ethnically similar citizens with equal rights. It is not disputed that the mother country should have some authority in the administration of the colony, but the colonists should retain the rights which they had had as citizens of the mother city. 'As the colonists and the citizens of the mother city are descended from the same tribe and people, use the same language and are formed by the same customs, it is necessary that they enjoy the same rights of citizenship, the same laws, institutions and privileges . . . so that the colony should be one people with the mother city, speaking the same language and enjoying the same rights, but divided, as it were, into two cities.' On this view it naturally followed that the colony should have a measure of self-government, but not with any view to political independence or, in Brand's words, not so as to make the colony 'altogether free of the mother country'.

Whereas the young Christoffel Brand could reproduce the main ideas of the Cape Patriots in the changed circumstances of 40 years later, indicating some continuity in the political stance and thinking of an important section of the colonists, the extracts from Egbertus Bergh's Memorial on the Cape of 1802 (6.6), despite superficial similarities, in fact represented a different position altogether. Bergh, like the Patriots, used the concept of the general welfare as a central motif, and he repeated many of the same complaints about oppressive policies, arbitrary and self-interested rule by local officials, lack of effective representation for the colonists, etc. But Bergh's basic political perspective was different. Unlike the Patriots, he was not concerned with advancing and justifying the sectional interests of the colonial citizenry. His stance was that of the relatively enlightened official judging the condition of colonial society as a whole in the light of universal norms for civilized progress drawn from contemporary Enlightenment thinking. Thus, for example, he was as much concerned with instances of religious intolerance and with the interference of the official church in matters of education as with the Company's restrictions of the colonists' freedom to trade. No doubt this was to some extent due to his own position as a Lutheran in the face of the reigning Calvinist orthodoxy, but his comments on administration, law, education, the library and even defence were throughout informed by a consistent attempt to view these matters as concerns of 'the whole public'. In other parts of his Memorial he extended his discussion to deal with such sections of colonial society as the Khoikhoi in the same perspective (cf. 5.1).

In Bergh's political thinking, then, the central concept of the general welfare must be taken in the universal sense which it had in the contemporary political theory of Enlightenment thinkers. In this he differed sharply from the Cape Patriots, who put this same concept to merely sectional use. On the other hand, unlike the Patriots, Bergh's thinking was not rooted in an organized political movement. His views were those of the dispassionate individual critic with experience of local affairs and concern for the general improvement of the colony's condition, but without a clear political base in colonial society itself. In some ways his views were similar to those of such officials as Van Ryneveld and Truter who did achieve positions of power and influence in colonial government. Taken together these enlightened Afrikaner officials constitute a different political tradition from that of the Patriots. In some ways they were opposed in their political thinking, in other respects they could find common ground. Characteristically, the most important social and intellectual institution originating at the Cape at the beginning of the nineteenth century bore the title of 'Society for the General Welfare' *(Maatschappij Tot Nut van't Algemeen).* It is easy to see that this could reflect both the more sectional and the more universal notions of the general welfare held in these two traditions.

The right to make representations

There are a number of different grounds on which the 'citizenry' could have based their claims for democratic rights. The Cape Patriots' writings, as we have seen, were often cast in the quasi-historical mode of arguments appealing to a heritage of civil rights which they were supposed to share as Dutch citizens. No doubt in practice their specific and economic interests as producers, who had to compete with powerful high officials favoured by monopolistic policies for a small and fluctuating market, were of more immediate significance. Moreover the burghers could with some reason consider themselves rather than the Company or its officials as the colonizing pioneers. In addition the burghers, with few exceptions, were all whites or 'Christians'. In theory, therefore, they could have based their claims to representative rights not only on (i) their historical status as Dutch citizens, but also on (ii) their legitimate interests as producers and (iii) as the colonizing pioneers, or on (iv) the racial grounds that they were whites, and not slaves or Khoikhoi. It is of some significance that we find no explicit mention of this last category of racial argument. In part this may have been due to the fact that their principal rivals, the high officials, were also all whites. If they had been threatened by a rising class of free black entrepreneurs the position may have been different. We also find no explicit appeal to their prior claims as colonizing pioneers, though this may well have been an implicit consideration in their arguments. What we do find is a strong emphasis on their *interests* as producers and colonists. In fact, it was on a defence of the legitimacy of the interests of the citizenry that the Patriots' claims to have a right to make representations were primarily based.

Interests and representation were closely linked in the Patriots' thinking as well as their practice. It was the threats to their interests by the Company's monopolistic policies and the malpractices of its officials that first gave rise to organized attempts to make representations to the directors of the Company and, when this proved to be of little avail, to the States General in the Netherlands. Prominent among their own proposals were demands for a greater measure of representation in various institutions of government at the Cape. Thus the Burgher petition of 1779 requested that 7 burgher councillors should participate in the decisions of the Political Council in matters affecting the citizenry, and that the Council of Justice should consist of an equal number of burgher councillors and Company officials (6.1b (9, 11)). These demands proved to be largely unsuccessful, but it did have the consequence that the whole issue of the *right* of the burgher councillors to make representations on behalf of the citizens began to be challenged.

Ever since their inception in 1657 burgher councillors had acted as intermediaries between the government and the citizenry in a variety of matters. It was ironically at a time when the burghers were extending their claims for representative rights in the 1780s that the officials countered by disputing this very right. Whether it was the result of personal animosities or an indication of sharper conflicts of interest in the prevailing economic conditions, the fact was that officials went out of their way to deny that the burgher councillors could have any representative function other than their judicial function on the Council of Justice, or that they could act as an independent body in their own right. Upholding this view, the Political Council decided in 1789 that if any representations were to be made to the government on behalf of the citizenry, then it was to be done by the *combined* college of commissaries, drawn from the Council of Justice and consisting of both company officials and burgher councillors, that had been instituted in 1785. This amounted to a denial of the right of the burgher councillors to make separate representations on behalf of the citizenry. At the same time the government, probably in reaction to the actions of the Patriots, tended to insist on its right to appoint new burgher councillors without the customary regard to the nominations by the outgoing burgher councillors. Thus in 1790 strong protests were evoked in Cape Town when the governor appointed the retired official

Abraham Fleck as burgher councillor in this manner, while in the same year Adriaan van Jaarsveld was not reappointed as heemraad in Graaff-Reinet, although he had been nominated.

The colonists responded by taking up the battle for the right to make representations. In a number of memorials to the Political Council from 1790, and subsequently to the Commissaries Nederburgh and Frykenius, the burgher councillors sought official recognition for their existence as an independent institution with the right to make representations on behalf of the citizens (cf. 6.4c), and to nominate their own representatives (6.4a). And in Graaff-Reinet the board of landdrost and heemraden in 1791 adopted a petition presented by Adriaan van Jaarsveld arguing their right to make representations (6.4b).

With what kind of arguments did the colonists back up their claimed right to make representations? The letter from the burgher councillors to Nederburgh and Frykenius of June 1792 (6.4c) did not contain any appeals to natural rights or to the necessity of obtaining the consent of the governed, or even such slogans as 'no taxation without representation' on the American model. Ostensibly they set out to provide a historical and legalist justification. Citing precedents from the earliest beginnings of the colony as well as its more recent history, they attempted to demonstrate that the right to make representations was vested by the Company in the office of burger councillor (even though it may never have recognized it officially as an independent institution) (6.4c). But it is clear that the substantial argument was based on a number of claims concerning the *interests* of the citizenry. These claims were, first, that the citizenry as producers possessed a specific and distinct common interest; secondly, that this interest of the citizenry was in conflict with the interest of the Company and of its officials; and thirdly, that only someone who shared common interests could be trusted to attend to such interests 'with sufficient diligence' (6.4c). It followed that officials could not be entrusted with the care of the interests of the citizenry. And, assuming that the citizens' interests were legitimate, it also followed that they had the right to make representations to the government where their own interests were concerned.

It should be noted that in pressing for effective protection of their own interests these spokesmen of the citizenry did not dispute the legitimacy, and indeed the paramountcy, of the Company's interests as colonizing power. 'It is by no means our intention,' wrote the burgher councillors in 1790, 'to imply anything in conflict with [our] state of dependency, along with the whole citizenry and indeed the entire colony, under the rule of the . . . Company.' (6.4a) Given the conflict of interest between Company and citizenry, it followed that the interests of the citizenry, though legitimate, were also recognized as sectional. It also followed that any right to representation in government derived from this sectional interest could only be limited and partial. In fact, the burgher councillors only argued for their right to make representations *to* the government on behalf of the citizenry, and not for representative government as such.

The contemporaneous document (6.4b) from the frontier district of Graaff-Reinet shows some instructive similarity and difference in its thinking and assumptions. Van Jaarsveld's petition also set out to argue for the right to make representations: 'We proceed to present our own notions . . . of whether we are still not competent to represent the pressing needs of the people . . . and to request alleviation of their burdens.' Like the burgher councillors, Van Jaarsveld found it necessary to defend and justify this as a right. But there were also significant differences. On the one hand we find an appeal to some notion of natural rights: 'For the law of nature teaches that the inherent right to do this [i.e. to represent the needs of the people] belongs to the people since ancient times.' However, as this was only a single and passing reference, it is not clear how much weight should be given to it. More important are the subtle differences in the implicit assumptions concerning the relations between 'the people' and 'the government'. Here we find no indication of any perception of a basic underlying conflict of interests between them. In fact, it does not seem that the government was perceived at all as an alien colonizing power with independent interests of its own. On the contrary, it was simply assumed that when the 'true interests' and the 'pressing needs' of the people were represented to the government, then it both should and would attend to such 'lawful and necessary demands'.

It is not entirely clear *why* the petitioners found it necessary to justify their right to make representations. It may have been due to some conception that they were calling for an adjustment in the relations between the heemraden and the government, involving the traditional prerogatives of the government. Or it may have been a side-effect of Van Jaarsveld's nomination being pointedly ignored in the appointment of heemraden. What is clear is that in their minds the justification for the right to make representations was provided by the overriding consideration of the 'pressing needs' of the people. In the final analysis, it was simply a question of whether or not such representations on their behalf were practicable and 'well grounded and absolutely necessary'. It followed that 'in all cases of unjustified refusals [by the government] to accede to the requests of the people, or where [the government] does not adjust to their lawful and necessary demands, . . . the people have the right to press respectfully once more for satisfaction of their demands'. Unlike the writings of the Cape burghers, this petition from the spokesmen for a frontier community thus contained at least the germs for a conception of the government itself as representative, instead of merely seeking to secure the right to make representations on behalf of sectional interests.

The Volkstem and popular representation

The Patriot movement at the Cape and the burgher rebellions in the frontier districts of Graaff-Reinet and Swellendam saw some of the earliest Afrikaner demands for and experiments in some form of popular representation in government. Some historians have claimed to find here the sources of a distinctive Afrikaner tradition of democratic and 'republican' political thinking.[8] However, the precise significance in the historical context of the various demands for representation of 'the people' or for 'free elections' is problematic, and it is far from clear in what sense such expressions as the 'voice of the people' *(volkstem)*, 'representatives *(representanten)* of the *volkstem*' and the like were intended at the time. It is tempting to understand this terminology today in the sense which has become familiar in the context of modern representative democracy. But that would be wholly anachronistic. The representative institutions of the time, at the Cape and in the mother country, were not based on popular election and the majority principle, but were exclusive bodies reproduced by various forms of nomination and co-optation. In fact, the very concept of popular representation or *volksverteenwoordiging* only began to acquire its modern democratic connotation in the course of the late eighteenth century democratic movements, particularly in Holland and France. It is true that the notion of *volksverteenwoordiging*, of a sovereign representative institution of the people, was not unknown in Dutch political history. Indeed it was central to the famed *Deduction* of 1587 by F. Vranck, who argued that the colleges of magistrates and councillors of the cities *(Vroedschappen)*, together with the nobility, 'undoubtedly represent the entire state and the whole body of the inhabitants'.[9] However, this did not mean that these colleges 'represented' the people in the modern sense that they consisted of the (elected) deputies of the people. In fact, as the *Deduction* also made clear, these colleges themselves were rather supposed to elect deputies to possible national assemblies. Thus the colleges 'represented' the people in the sense that, strictly speaking, the magistrates, regents and nobles together *were* the sovereign people. Other members of the community, including the majority of ordinary inhabitants, simply did not count as part of 'the people'.[10] The Dutch Patriot movement in the 1780s was instrumental in widening this exclusive conception to one of the political community encompassing the whole citizenry, the *volk*. Thus the Utrecht *Deductie van het Volk van Nederland* of 1786 proclaimed the sovereignty of the (burgher) people as against the *Deductie* of 1587, which effectively had maintained the sovereignty of the regents and the nobles. At the same time the Patriots introduced the modern notion of a smaller body of *delegates* 'representing' this sovereign people. The transition from the older feudal concept of representation to the modern democratic one did not, of course, take place at once. Even in the early 1780s the notion of popular representative government *(regeering bij representatie des volks)* sometimes still occurred in an ambivalent sense, combining elements of the new democratic thinking with older feudal views.[11]

The new language of popular representation coming into currency at the end of the eighteenth century therefore requires careful interpretation in its rapidly changing historical context if it is not to give rise to serious misunderstandings and confusions. In the case of the Cape Patriots and the Graaff-Reinet burghers the problem is particularly urgent since we have hardly any systematic elaboration of their views at all, and most of the evidence consists in the occasional usage of a few phrases and terms. It cannot simply be assumed that these phrases and terms carried the meanings a modern reader might tend to associate with them—which were then only beginning to gain currency in Europe. We have already seen that the Cape Patriots tended to have a sectional rather than an inclusive notion of citizenship. This alone should raise some doubts about what exactly they had in mind in referring to 'the people'. And the same applies to the other notions of popular representation which they invoked.

In a critical interpretation of the terminology of popular representation used by the Cape Patriots and the Graaff-Reinet burghers we may keep in mind the following questions:

1 When claims were made by individuals that they represented 'the voice of the people', did they simply proclaim that they belonged to that group which *constituted* 'the people', or were they claiming to be the delegates of a wider and inclusive political community?

2 Were the 'representatives of the people' determined by some form of popular election on the majority principle, or were they an exclusive body extending membership by nomination and co-optation?

3 Did requests for 'free elections' ask that the wider political community be given the opportunity to choose delegates, or did it refer to the way in which the members of the representative colleges themselves could nominate and co-opt new members?

4 Did demands for 'representation' mean (i) the right to make representations *to* the government, or (ii) the right to have popular representatives who participate *in* the decision-making of the government, or (iii) the notion that all government should be based on the consent of the governed?

5 Were the claims for popular representation based on some concep-

tion of the sovereignty of the people, and if so, in what sense of 'the people'?

Only a particular combination of answers to all these questions constitutes the touchstones of modern representative democracy: an inclusive political community, itself the locus of political sovereignty, electing its delegated representatives in government in free popular elections on the majority principle in accordance with the ideal that all government should be based on the consent of the governed. It is questionable whether anything like this combination of views can be found in the writings of the Cape Patriots or of the citizens of Graaff-Reinet. Thus the requests of the Burgher petition of 1779 for a measure of representation in the various political institutions, and for 'free elections in all civil councils' (6.1b (9, 13)), clearly do not amount to a demand for popular elections. They only ask that the Company allow some burghers to participate in the decisions of such bodies as the Council of Justice and the Council of Policy, and that the members of such civil councils may freely nominate their successors. The Patriots themselves on 11 October 1784 formed a permanent body of popular representatives *('s Volks Representanten)*, and these were claimed to have been appointed 'through the participation of the voice of the people' *(door de deelneemende Volksstemme)*. However, these 'representatives' were not elected at some general meeting. The actual procedure appears to have been that they were appointed at a house-meeting of some leading Patriots, and that subsequently the general populace was given the opportunity to express their approval by signing prepared lists.[12] In this connection it is not clear whether the expression 'the voice of the people' refers to the smaller group who took the lead in selecting the representatives, or to the approval by the signatories from the wider community, or to some combination of both.

The earliest general statement of views on popular representation from the circles of the Cape Patriots occurs in B. J. Artoys's *Nederlandsch Afrika* of 1783 (6.2): 'Any people which does not consist of slaves must have a visible representative acting for it with the supreme rulers. . . . All peoples have as their representatives those among their own numbers whom they appoint to guard over the interests of the people.' It will be noted that this was not a plea for representative government *tout court*, but only for the limited role of popular representatives 'acting with the supreme rulers'. Again, in dealing with the way in which 'the people' appointed their representatives, Artoys used very ambiguous language: 'These deputies are usually chosen from among the most intelligent and prominent members of the whole body of the citizenry. The deputies usually empower a small number from among them selves . . . [to represent them] in all matters which concern the rights and privileges of the inhabitants.' There was no explicit reference to any form of popular election, and the passage can bear the interpretation of a small group of leading citizens simply taking it upon themselves to act on behalf of 'the people' and to appoint its representatives. What is clear from *Nederlandsch Afrika*, however, is that such popular representatives could not simply be appointed by the ruling powers. 'It is true that the Cape settlement does have burgher councillors,' wrote Artoys, but continued, 'yet they are without real authority and are not nominated by the citizens. . . . Thus they cannot represent the citizenry in any way except extremely inadequately and uselessly.' He accordingly proceeded to recommend that the Company should allow the citizenry 'an annual nomination of burgher councillors'. He may or may not have had in mind the same procedure as that proposed by the burgher councillors in their request of 1790 (6.4a): 'It has been the practice among all nations since ancient times that when they are granted representation on certain bodies in some matter in which they have an interest, they are also given the freedom of nominating the representatives themselves. . . . Therefore it is requested that the nomination of burgher councillors . . . might in future be undertaken *by burgher councillors alone* [our italics].' What these claims to the right to nomination or to free elections probably meant was that the burghers councillors, and not the government, should have the right to appoint other burgher councillors. It did not mean that burgher councillors should be chosen by popular election. Still, as an exclusive body based on co-optation, the burgher councillors would no doubt have claimed the right to speak and act as representatives of 'the people'.

Rather different notions of popular representation prevailed among the Graaff-Reinet rebels, who were not prepared to accept the heemraden in these terms. When the rebels, led by Marthinus Prinsloo, ordered Landdrost Maynier to leave the district in February 1795, they also removed two heemraden and a militia officer from their posts. In the *Te Samenstemming* outlining their grievances, the rebels made scathing references to the heemraden as a 'degenerate cabal'. Though Bresler (6.5b) would later attempt to persuade the heemraden that they 'in the proper sense ought to be considered as the true Representatives and Promoters of the general welfare', the Graaff-Reinet heemraden were clearly not recognized in this way as popular representatives. They were associated with the government rather than with 'the people', who acted through other representatives.

The notion of the 'voice of the people' *(volkstem)* appeared prominently in the politics and writings of the Graaff-Reinet rebels. The first such reference to the *volkstem* occurred in the *Te Samenstemming* when the rebels declared that they 'will never again obey such bastard laws, but will again demand and reinstate conformity [with right principles] through the general voice of the people'. Again in June 1795 O. G. de Wet, head of the commission of inquiry, was likewise ordered in the name of the *volkstem* to leave the district. From the next month 'Representatives of the People' *(Representanten des Volks)* participated in the meetings of the boards of heemraden and of militia, where they played an increasingly prominent role. The selfstyled *Representanten* acted as a separate group distinct from the heemraden: they were seated at a separate table, and also signed the minutes separately. They, and not the heemraden, were the popular representatives. The *Representanten* explicitly claimed to derive this position from the 'voice of the people'. In their letter to General Craig of October 1795, the Graaff-Reinet burghers thus wrote that 'it has been judged expedient by the general Voice of the People to choose Representatives to maintain the Rights and Interests of the Burghers before the respective Colleges'. There is no indication, however, that the *Representanten* were actually chosen through popular elections. From the available evidence it would appear that the *Representanten* proclaimed themselves as such, or adopted some form of co-optation with subsequent opportunity for popular acclamation.[13] For this purpose any larger gathering of ordinary burghers in Graaff-Reinet would simply constitute the 'voice of the people'.

There are a number of ambiguous features in the attitudes of the burghers to the *volkstem* and the *representanten*. Thus a burgher leader like Adriaan van Jaarsveld did not associate himself too closely to the *volkstem*, and preferred to act as an intermediary between the *volkstem* and the authorities. Though the *heemraden*, unlike the *representanten*, were not recognized as popular representatives, there was no attempt to do away with them and they continued to function alongside each other. The *representanten*, on their part, apparently derived some legitimacy in the eyes of the burghers from the events of 1 May 1795 when Commissary De Wet had proposed to a gathering that they elect representatives for the purposes of consultation (cf. 6.5b).

As for the *volkstem*, rebel leaders often made statements in its name without apparently canvassing burgher opinion in any way, and on one occasion some rebel leaders requested the authorities that they themselves be recognized as the *volkstem*.[14] There are indications that the *volkstem* was manipulated by a particular section of the burghers, those of the south-eastern wards, to promote their sectional interests.[15] Again, in Bresler's words, the *representanten* tended to invoke the *volkstem* as 'a sort of politicks' (6.5b), through which they could disclaim personal responsibility for a specific view or decision, while the people often remained in the dark about what was being done in its name.

These ambiguities may in part be ascribed simply to confused and loose thinking, to be expected in such frontier conditions. They also indicate that the views of the Graaff-Reinet burghers on popular representation, though in some ways more radical than those which had been entertained by the Cape Patriots, were also of a limited and transitional nature. There may have been vestiges of the predemocratic notion of *volksverteenwoordiging* in the way in which a group of burghers could simply claim to *be* 'the voice of the nation'. Certainly neither the notion of the *volk* as the inclusive political community nor the concept of popularly elected delegates was yet fully developed. The Graaff-Reinet burghers did not yet demand representative government as such, but at most wished that the *representanten* would have some recognized say in local government. At no time were claims to sovereignty made on behalf of the *volkstem*, and the rebels maintained that they had throughout been prepared to pay tribute to a lawful government, and had wished to be under the sovereignty of the States General in the Netherlands. The development of some recognizably democratic notion of popular representation and self-government would only come about four decades later in the course of the Great Trek.

Trekker self-government

It is more than a little problematic to what extent the Trekkers' earliest experiments in self-government from 1836 on can be ascribed to the influence of distinctive ideas of popular representation. They certainly did not set out on the Trek with well-defined ideas about founding a representative democracy. Uppermost in their minds were the many particular *grievances* against the colonial government, perceptively summarized by J. N. Boshof in 1839 under the main rubrics of a pervasive 'insecurity of life and property', and a general 'distrust in the . . . government' (6.10a). In Boshof's comprehensive survey of such grievances there was no mention of any constitutional issues or of the lack of representative institutions. Once outside the colonial boundaries, however, provision had of necessity to be made for the orderly conduct of the affairs of the main Trekker parties. At various general meetings held in December 1836, and in April and June 1837, leaders were appointed and a rudimentary form of self-government instituted. This was the first opportunity for these Afrikaners to implement any ideas of their own concerning political institutions. On the other hand, it could hardly be expected that they would have elaborate ideas or strong feelings on this score: very few of them had any intimate knowledge of the conduct of public administration, and they were almost wholly lacking in any legal and constitutional expertise. Moreover, under the circumstances the practical imperatives of an organized migration had to have precedence. Nevertheless the kind of arrangements that were made, and the texts (6.9a, b) of the earliest Trekker 'constitutions' recording them, showed some notions of popular representation at work that were at once seminal and ambiguous, containing the germs of later constitutional developments as well as political tensions.

The Trekker leaders, first Potgieter and Maritz, and then Retief, were appointed at general meetings of the main Trek parties. In the corresponding documents the 'voice of the people' was invoked. To what extent can this be taken as an indication of a definite underlying belief in the free and popular election of representative leaders? This question cannot be answered on the basis of an analysis of the rather fragmentary and cryptic documents only, but must be considered in context. There were a number of different factors bearing on the nature of Trekker leadership, and on the significance of the procedures adopted and the expressions used. None of the Trekkers could lay claim in his own right to any recognized high office or leading position in civil government. Trekboer society, too, had neither an hereditary nobility nor an established social hierarchy that secured recognized leadership, beyond the range of their own family groups, to specific individuals. The leaders of the various Trek parties, like the heemraden and field-cornets generally, were from the wealthier and better educated classes. However, given the largely self-sufficient lifestyle on the open frontier of even the poorer trekboers, leaders could hardly gain extensive economic controls over others so as to ensure their support in a power struggle with rivals. Nor was there any tradition of armed conflict as a means of deciding contending claims between whites. Therefore any claims to general political leadership could not have been legitimized on traditionalist grounds, or decided through a direct power struggle.

In practice, leadership was largely a question of the patriarchal family structure combined with the military reputation of experienced frontier commandants. Typically the nucleus of a Trek party was formed by a group of families recognizing the patriarchal authority of the Trek leader, whose primary task was that of military organizer. (With the exception of Maritz, all the main Trekker leaders had made names for themselves in the frontier wars.) Given this, it is still quite conceivable that the Trek could have taken the form of a loose association of a number of distinct Trekking parties each proceeding towards its own settlement, and requiring no form of general political leadership. To some extent this did in fact happen. However, *to the extent* that the Trekkers began to view themselves as part of a more inclusive community, encompassing the various Trek parties each with its own leader, the question of general or overall leadership also became more significant. It is precisely on occasions where attempts were made to settle the general leadership that we also find expressions like 'our united community' (*onze vereenigde Maatschappy*, 6.9b). Still, it did not necessarily follow that the leadership of the 'united community' would take the form of chosen representatives of the sovereign people held responsible to them. After all, patriarchal authority was neither elective nor representative in nature, and military command generally required an autocratic rather than a democratic form of organization. Accordingly leadership could well have taken the form of some senior patriarchal leader taking on the position of supreme commander of the Trekker community, vesting political authority in his own sovereign position. In fact, the arrangments and writings of the Trekkers showed both kinds of tendencies, towards representative leadership and towards autocratic leadership, and an implicit tension between them.

At the meeting at Thaba Nchu on 2 December 1836 a notion of popular representation appears to have been dominant in the procedures adopted to determine a first rudimentary form of government. A governing body of seven members, with Maritz as civilian 'president' and Potgieter as military commander, was chosen by secret vote at a general meeting.[16] Popular election had taken the place of the traditional procedures of co-optation and nomination. When the resolutions recorded that the 'judges' were chosen 'by the general voice of the people' (6.9a), this now definitely referred to the inclusive (Trekker) community rather than to any section styling itself as such—as used to be the case at the time of the Graaff-Reinet rebellions. The resolutions in fact explicitly articulated this wider notion of 'the people' when it referred to 'the common people who make up the *volk*'. An intriguing feature of these brief resolutions was the reciprocal relations which were apparently envisaged between the people and their newly elected representatives. The 'government' *(regeeringsvorm)*, which was to combine in itself executive, judicial and legislative functions, would not be sovereign but would 'at all times adhere carefully to such laws and regulations as made by the general assembly', where the latter referred to popular meetings of the wider Trekker community. To this end the chosen representatives had to subject themselves solemnly under oath, but the people, for their part, 'also promised under oath to subject themselves loyally and peacefully to the judgements and orders of the leaders' (6.9a). We might see in this a notion of some kind of social contract underlying the institutions of representative government. It could also be taken as indicating that sovereignty was ambiguously located both in the people themselves and in their chosen representatives.[17]

The nine resolutions (6.9b) adopted under Retief at Vet River on 5 June 1837 do not appear to have had quite the same purport. Retief had been chosen unanimously as 'Governor' of the Trekkers, combining the civilian and military command, at a popular meeting on April 17, and there are indications that he saw this position not so much as that of being the delegated representative of the people but rather as involving supreme responsibilities before God. 'I have not been elected as the chief of this people by my own act,' he wrote a few months later (4.14b), '*or even by the general voice of the people*; but I have sufficient reasons to recognize the hand of God in placing me at the head of my countrymen [our italics].' The nine resolutions did not directly express his own views. They were presented to Retief as 'supreme commander of our united community' in order that, with his approbation, they might be sanctioned at a popular meeting. The resolutions were not concerned to emphasize the sovereignty of the people or the representative nature of the leadership. Instead they set out, in a series of sometimes rather enigmatic clauses, to describe and enforce the obligations of the members of the political community to the leadership. They had to undertake to sever any allegiance to other outside institutions (article 1); they had to take an oath to honour and obey the elected or appointed leadership on pain of punishment (2); those who were not prepared to subscribe to these resolutions would be expelled from the community (3), and would not be allowed to settle in its eventual territory (4) or to share in any spoils or advantages gained by commandos (8). Absentees at the initial meeting and newcomers would also have to take these oaths of allegiance (5, 9), and it was made clear that abstention or non-compliance would be considered as active opposition (6). No doubt these measures were also intended to promote the general political cohesion of the emergent Trekker community, but they set out to do this primarily by bolstering the authority of the leadership. As such they may be said to reflect a tendency to patriarchal and autocratic leadership rather than any notions of popular representation.

Significantly, Retief's leadership and the nine resolutions soon encountered criticism from other Trekker leaders on just these grounds. Undoubtedly these differences were very much informed by personal rivalry and by conflicts on other issues related to the practical conduct of the Trek. To some extent, however, the criticism of Retief's leadership was also based on certain divergent political ideas. Though Maritz was party to the general meeting at Vet River, he was unhappy with some aspects of the oaths of allegiance, and differed sharply with Retief about this at another meeting soon afterwards.[18] The Uys party, who had not been at the meeting at Vet River, went so far as to adopt a set of counter-resolutions in which they declared that they unanimously disapproved of the structure of authority that had been instituted under Retief: 'We have resolved once for all not to submit to any laws which might have been enacted by a few individuals.' (6.9c) Maritz, in a letter circulated some months later in Natal, likewise objected to the proceedings under Retief at Vet River as constituting 'an improper oath': 'On the basis of this oath, he has appropriated for himself unprecedented power and dominion, and it is certain that if we were to subject ourselves to his rule and power, we can never become a happy people.' (6.9d) Maritz went on to warn in general against the dangers of authorities with 'overbearing power', and to extol, instead, the virtues of a government based on 'fraternity and equality', adding a clear statement of the sovereignty of the people: 'The voice of the people will be the supreme power and government.' Uys, in his earlier resolutions (6.9c), had also indicated that the new settlement was to be based 'on the same principles of liberty as those adopted by the United States of America', and he likewise envisaged a popular election of the leaders by 'all our countrymen assembled together'. In their fears concerning the potential dangers of autocratic leadership and in their preference for some form of popular representation, the two documents of Uys and Maritz were indications of an emergent tradition committed to certain general notions of popular sovereignty and to a collegial rather than an autocratic type of government.

The constitutional arrangements of the Trekkers in Natal, after the death of Retief (soon to be followed by the deaths of Maritz and Uys as well), were largely influenced by notions such as these. From 1838 an elected Council of Representatives *(Raad van Representanten)*, which quickly became known as the *Volksraad*, began to function on a more regular basis. With the help of J. N. Boshof two sets of regulations, one providing a kind of constitution for the *Volksraad* and the other governing the judicial offices, were drawn up. In these Trekker arrangements there was thus a first differentiation between the legislative and judicial institutions of government, but a striking feature was the absence of any definite or strong executive branch. Even when a strong leader appeared in the person of Andries Pretorius, his powers were largely confined to the military duties of the commandant-general in times of war. Efforts were made to prevent the position of commandant-general from becoming a permanent office, and to limit his role in the Volksraad. Pretorius had certain executive duties and functions, but the Volksraad insisted that these were to be carried out on their instructions and not on his own authority. Here we find the beginnings of the *Volksraad*-'party' as a definite political position among the Trekkers, strongly opposed to any possibility of individual autocracy and committed to a collegial form of government as a representative embodiment of popular sovereignty. Significantly, when the Volksraad in its letter of February 1842 to Governor Napier (6.10b) once again enumerated the familiar list of grievances against the colonial government, it now connected this with the issue of representation: 'All these evils we attribute to a single cause, namely, the want of a representative government.' This should be taken not so much as an accurate description of the earlier motivations that had led to the Trek, than as an expression of political convictions taking shape in its aftermath. Even so, the new *Volksraad*-'party' were not democrats in any general sense; they probably continued to hold patriarchal views of social authority and their notions of popular representation applied only to a section of Trekker society. Blacks, both coloured servants and *agterryers* who had come along on the

Trek and members of the surrounding tribes entering service as labourers or living on the land they claimed as their property, were excluded from even the most inclusive notion of the political community as a matter of course. So, for that matter, were women. Given these restrictions on what counted as 'the people', the *Volksraad*-'party' believed in popularly elected representative leadership.

Nevertheless, patriarchal and autocratic views of leadership remained influential. The Potgieter party, which had settled on the highveld rather than remaining in Natal, tended to accept Potgieter's patriarchal leadership, and the Potchefstroom *Raad* was of very limited significance. On 6 May 1845, in a characteristic decision, Potgieter was confirmed as permanent supreme commandant with an entrenched say in the council chosen to assist him, while all other commandants who might come from elsewhere would have to subject themselves to this leadership.[19] When many of the Natal Trekkers removed to the highveld after the British annexation of Natal in 1843, political conflicts developed between the adherents of the *Volksraad*-'party', led by the former Secretary of the Natal Volksraad, J. J. Burger, and the Potgieter party, particularly in the shortlived republics of Ohrigstad and Lydenburg.[20] After he left Natal for the highveld in 1848 Pretorius also established himself as a strong and autocratic patriarchal leader. And the leaders who succeeded Potgieter and Pretorius were decided upon more in terms of patriarchal succession than by popular election. In the various Trekker communities on the highveld the *Volksraad*-'party' had become a limited and sectional position, only one of the various influences that were to shape the constitutional development of the new republics in the second half of the nineteenth century.

Colonial Afrikaners and representative government

Those Afrikaners who did not emigrate to the interior were members of a more developed colonial society with established churches and schools, a professional judiciary, and qualified magistrates and civil commissioners in local government. But whereas the Trekkers were steadily experimenting with rudimentary forms of self-government these colonial Afrikaners were to remain without representative government for a further two decades. The Western Cape had been the centre of the Patriot movement as early as 1780, and at first sight it may seem somewhat surprising that an organized movement pressing for popular institutions and self-government did not emerge there. The belated movement towards representative government from as late as 1850 will become more intelligible if we briefly consider the nature and context of the earlier agitations for representative institutions which did take place.

In the years between 1826 and 1834 Cape Afrikaners participated in the signing of petitions calling on the imperial authorities to grant representative government to the Cape, and Afrikaner spokesmen took a prominent part in a number of public meetings and protest gatherings ostensibly connected with this issue. However, the actual political aims of these actions, and the thrust of the political thinking expressed in the documents from this period (6.8a-e), were quite different from, on the one hand, the concern of the Cape Patriots with the protection of their civil liberties and with their right to make representations, and, on the other hand, from the political aims of the later movement for representative government. Primarily this was due to the great difference in the respective political contexts. In the 1780s the Patriots had been the confident spokesmen for a 'citizenry' intent on challenging the arbitrary powers and monopolistic practices of Company officials, where these conflicted with or frustrated their own interests. In doing so they could invoke their historic rights and privileges as Dutch citizens. In the mid-1820s, however, the colonial Afrikaners had involuntarily become British subjects and their traditional representative institutions, such as the Burgher Senate and the boards of landdrost and heemraden, were in the process of finally being dismantled. Their economic condition was unsettled and the prospects depressing, particularly in the Western Cape: the boom in wine exports to Britain came to an end with the withdrawal of imperial preference in 1825, the price of slaves—the colonists' largest capital investment—was dropping steadily in anticipation of emancipation, and the conversion to sterling with the subsequent revaluation of the rixdollar forced painful accommodations and retrenchments. Politically the initiative was seized by the British Settlers who were in the vanguard of protests against the autocratic regime of Governor Somerset and who took the lead in the struggle to establish the freedom of the press, confident in their rights as British subjects. Above all, imperial reforms such as Ordinance 50 and the new slave regulations assailed the very basis of the privileged position of the Afrikaner in the traditional legal status order.

In short, the Cape Afrikaners were increasingly forced into the position of a minority group who saw their interests and traditional rights and privileges threatened and curtailed on every side.

In this context the participation of Cape Afrikaners in petitions calling for representative government in the years following 1826 could hardly be considered as support for a progressive movement aimed at genuinely democratic reforms and popular government. Rather it was a defensive and reactionary political strategy aimed primarily at upholding the property rights of slaveholders and shoring up their traditional privileged position in the social order. The threat to their interests and traditional privileges by imperial Orders-in-Council brought home to the colonists the importance of having a greater measure of local control over their own affairs. Conversely, opposition to the imperial slave ordinances quite logically took the indirect form of seeking first of all the *means* to obtain such a greater measure of local control, and thus arose the requests for a representative assembly. 'Consider from how many evils and grievances we would have been freed had a Legislative Representative Body existed in this Colony,' wrote *De Zuid-Afrikaan* in response to the imposition of the Trinidad Ordinance on the Cape in 1831. 'There can hardly exist a doubt but that through such a Representative Body we would have had an opportunity of timely preventing the evil, or of diminishing its effects.' (6.8b) Of course the aim of obstructing and diverting these imperial reforms could not be avowed in too blunt and direct a fashion. The strategy therefore was to express their agreement with the general aims of the amelioration and eventual abolition of slavery, but to insist on the granting of representative government as a precondition for any active support in bringing this about. In this spirit a large protest-meeting of slaveholders passed the following motion in support of representative government in September 1832: 'This meeting is convinced that a representative Legislative body is alone capable of issuing such laws for this settlement in such a way as to ensure the peace and welfare of this settlement, and that the owners of slaves here, in this case, would co-operate to fulfil the intention and desire of the Government to improve the conditions of slavery and eventually to bring it to an end.' (6.8e) Speaking in support of the motion, Christoffel Brand rhetorically suggested that the desire to emancipate the slaves was one that was universally shared, even among slaveholders. But he indicated something of the underlying political thinking when he went on to say not only that the immediate objective remained the safeguarding of the interests of the slaveholders, but also that the interests of the slaves were best served by leaving them in the hands of their paternal guardians: 'The owners of slaves pay attention to the interests of themselves, as well as the interests of the slaves.' (6.8e) Self-government for slaveholders was perceived as the most effective means of safeguarding the interests of the slaveholders in the face of the imminent and perhaps inevitable prospect of the emancipation of the slaves.

These ulterior motives (of safeguarding their interests as slaveholders) in their quest for representative government were apparent to the imperial authorities in London, and not only strengthened the latter in their resolve to withhold the granting of such local powers for the time being, but also led to the increasing political isolation of the Afrikaners in the Colony itself. At first there had not been any serious conflicts between the older Afrikaner community and the newly arrived British Settlers. In their struggle for the recognition of the freedom of the press, Greig, Pringle and Fairbairn received some assistance from important Afrikaner spokesmen such as Christoffel Brand and Faure. Once this goal had been reached, *De Zuid-Afrikaan*, together with the *South African Commercial Advertiser* edited by Fairbairn, took the lead in guiding colonial opinion on public issues of the day. Until 1831 the issue of representative government was a common cause. Fairbairn, however, supported representative government on essentially liberal grounds as a further extension of the freedom of speech and of the press in the struggle against arbitrary despotism. When it became clear that *De Zuid-Afrikaan* was really acting as an apologist for the slaveholders, and that it was pressing for representative government to secure their interests, Fairbairn broke with these Afrikaner allies and criticized them roundly. The correspondence columns of the two newspapers and the speeches at public meetings reflected a considerable rise in ethnic animosity from 1832 on.

The uncertain base of the Cape Afrikaners in their defensive strategy was reflected in some confusion about the kind of argument that should be harnessed in support of their request for representative government. Attempts were made to list the many benefits to be expected from a local representative assembly (6.8b), and to point out the defects of a mere advisory council (6.8c). However, these arguments had a somewhat perfunctory quality, lacking political urgency. Other moves were more revealing of developments in the Cape Afrikaners' political thinking. On the one hand they tended to fall back on the familiar grounds of their historical heritage as Dutch citizens, with references to time-honoured representative institutions such as the boards of landdrost and heemraden or the Burgher Senate (6.8b, c), and with invocations of the heroic struggles against governor Van der Stel and the Fiscal Boers (6.8d). This was the kind of quasi-historical argument which the Cape Patriots could still press with some force under Dutch rule, but a British government who had just recently abolished these very institutions could hardly be expected to be swayed by such an approach at all. If anything, these references now only served to arouse a sense of grievance in the Afrikaners as a minority group, but this was done more in the nature of a plaintive protest than as a serious attempt at ethnic mobilization to gain political power. There were also recurrent attempts to appeal to the *British* tradition of civil rights: as British subjects, it was claimed, they could expect to be granted representative institutions as 'that privilege which every Englishman considers his birth-right' (6.8b). However these appeals did not appear to carry a great deal of commitment to the liberal values of free and representative institutions. They were intended rather as *ad hominem* arguments: since the British nation prided itself on being '*free, enlightened* and *liberal*' (6.8b), and standing 'pre-eminent for liberal and free institutions' (6.8d), she could with some justice be expected to extend these political rights to her colonial subjects.

However, the slaveowning Afrikaners of the Western Cape definitely did not want such political rights to be extended to *all* colonial subjects. The emancipation of the slaves and the lifting of legal inequalities and restraints from the Khoikhoi were precisely the kind of imperial reforms which they were attempting to counter. What their appeals amounted to was the somewhat paradoxical argument that in terms of its own liberal heritage the British government should grant the Cape *slaveholders* control of their own affairs—and of their slaves and servants. It was on this point that someone like Fairbairn, who stood more squarely in the liberal tradition of British politics, found that he could not go along with this particular agitation for representative government. In the end the only arguments which really rang true were the direct defences of the slaveholders' interests: 'Can we be silent when the safety of our property and our dwellings is destroyed, when the security of our peace and the safety of our lives are made uncertain? . . . The slaves are our property, and whoever takes our property from us takes from us our lives. Expropriation of property destroys the bonds of society.' (6.8e) The rights of slaveholders, not the liberal values of free institutions or democratic notions of popular government, provided the central political motivation for the Cape Afrikaners' agitation for representative government around 1830.

A number of subtle but crucial differences appear in the arguments used during the next resurgence of public agitation for representative government a decade later (6.11). The political context, of course, was quite different. By this time both the emancipation of the slaves and the proclamation of legal equality for all were historical facts. The public meeting of August 1841 was addressed by leading spokesmen of both the English section and the Cape Afrikaners, who were now much more concerned with the virtues and advantages of representative government in its own right. Where points substantially similar to those of 10 years before were made—for example, in the emphasis on the difference between a nominated council with advisory functions only and a responsible representative assembly (Wicht, 6.11, cf. Cloete, 6.8c), or in the denial of the allegation that the Colony was 'not yet ripe' for representative institutions (Cloete, 6.11, cf. Cloete, 6.8c)—these were now more central to the whole argument. Even more important, they now appeared in a different political and historical perspective. Gone are the futile appeals harking back to the historical rights of Dutch citizens and their dismantled representative institutions. Instead we find the Cape Afrikaners accepting British rule, positively identifying themselves with the norms of British political history and taking their stand on their rights as British subjects. Thus Wicht simply assumed 'the inherent, unquestioned right of every British subject to be represented in the Councils of the State' (6.11) as his point of departure. This political tradition is acknowledged as historically alien, but also as a tradition with which they now wanted to identify. As Cloete, himself one of the earliest leading Afrikaners to become anglicized, explained, 'The influx of British Colonists spread abroad that spirit of freedom which we are all anxious to acquire but often do not know how to attain.' (6.11) In this perspective representative government now appeared not as a way to protect the rights of slaveholders, but as an extension of the struggle for a free press and as the alternative to arbitrary despotism and autocratic government (Wicht, 6.11). It was no longer seen as a means for warding off threats to existing privileges, but as an evolutionary development, which had been prepared by such earlier institutions as the legislative council and the establishment of municipalities, and which was needed for the development of the colony's agricultural and commercial resources. In Cloete's words, the present stage of the colony's constitutional and political development should be seen as 'a stepping stone to a still further advance in political freedom, and as a dawn of those brighter and (politically speaking) happier days, when the public shall find themselves more efficiently and directly represented in their interests.' (6.11)

The next stage in this progress towards representative government came a decade later in the wake of the successful anti-convict agitation. Compared with the earlier requests for constitutional reform the documents from this period reflect a decisive change of gear in the mode of political action and thinking (6.12, 13). No longer do we have respectful petitions addressed to distant authorities or careful public speeches elaborately setting out the case for representative government to fitfully interested and lukewarm supporters. These writings simply report the demands of an aroused public opinion. 'The people . . . do not choose longer to have others rule them. They will not that the heel of power shall longer be upon their necks. They now demand that there shall be established in their country, forthwith, a free and liberal constitution.' (Watermeyer, 6.12a) Rather than setting out to mobilize popular support, such support was assumed and it could even be necessary to warn against the dangers of direct action and violence (Stockenström, 6.13b). These documents were the products of a popular political movement such as the Cape had not yet seen.

A full analysis of this movement in its historical context and of the details of the constitutional struggle from 1850 to 1853 cannot be given here.[21] In the next volume we will deal with the question of *the franchise*, which constituted one of the central issues. Here we will only briefly indicate some of the main features of the political thinking expressed in these documents bearing on the general question of representative government.

In the first place we find that the Cape Afrikaners increasingly tended to adopt British political history, rather than any notions of their own historical rights as Dutch citizens, as their frame of reference. Thus the *Zuid-Afrikaan* defined the colonists' goal as 'that real liberty . . . which every Briton justly considers his birthright' (6.12b). In accordance with what they still considered as these 'English principles', representative government was viewed as the logical and historical culmination of the earlier struggles wrought mainly by the British settlers for such 'liberal institutions' as a free press (Wicht, 6.13c). Even in asserting their demands for self-government against the imperial power of Britain, the Cape Afrikaners were thus appropriating its historically alien political tradition as their own. The popular movement for colonial self-government was no awakening of (Afrikaner) *nationalism*; rather it sought to bring about an extension of the political institutions of the mother country. 'The general cry of the Colonists', wrote the *Zuid-Afrikaan*, 'is that they are no slaves, and that the colonies, as integral portions of the parent state, claim the same noble institutions of which the mother country so justly boasts.' (6.12b)

This lack of insistence on the Afrikaners' own distinctive political history facilitated the formation of a coalition across traditional ethnic boundaries in a movement which brought together Fairbairn, the liberal editor and son-in-law of Dr Philip, and Stockenström, the controversial author of the Glenelg Treaty System, with Christoffel Brand, erstwhile champion of the slaveholders, and Reitz, a rural Afrikaner landowner. This unlikely combination was the elected leadership of the popular movement for representative government. In the words of their spokesmen, 'the people' stood united against the despotic colonial government. In speaking thus liberally of the demands and wishes of 'the people', these spokesmen obviously had mainly the whites in mind. Nevertheless it was an inclusive rather than a sectional or exclusive concept. Acknowledging traditional ethnic rivalries and differences between Afrikaners and colonists of British descent the emphasis was on a common cause and on shared interests (Stockenström, 6.13b; Wicht, 6.13c). Even more significantly, blacks and former slaves were on occasion specifically included; and attempts to create divisions along these lines were held up as attacks on the very basis of the popular movement. While acknowledging the history of mutual 'prejudices' of masters and slaves, this was deemed to belong to the past and the goal of the movement for representative government was stated as 'the social, political and moral elevation of all classes' (Wicht, 6.13c). The political test for these sentiments was of course the question of a low and popular franchise that would extend political rights to blacks and former slaves as well. It is a remarkable fact of the constitutional struggle of the early 1850s that the Cape Afrikaners emerged as the committed champions of such a low franchise. No less remarkable were the changes in their views of the meaning and function of political representation and self-government. In the space of 20 years they had shifted from seeking self-government for slaveholders as a means of staving off threats to their property rights and traditional privileges, to support for a popular movement for representative government that would include the extension of political rights to subordinates and former slaves.

In other respects the political thinking of the Cape Afrikaners at this time also showed signs of radicalization. Instead of careful statements that the colonists too have political rights, even if these are limited, we now begin to find confident assertions of popular sovereignty. Thus Watermeyer, consciously drawing analogies with the 1848 revolution in Europe, proposed that 'the people were of right the holders of all authority in the country which they occupied', and hence that 'their object is not to *pray* for a dissolution of the Legislative Council; but as a people, possessing a people's power, and desirous of enforcing a people's authority, they resolve upon its instant destruction.' (6.12a) Christoffel Brand, too, held that his legitimacy as a representative did not derive from his formal appointment to the legislative council by the governor, but from the implied and basic contract with the people who had elected him as their representative (6.13a). Such notions contained the germs of a popular and even revolutionary democratic ideology. However, they only surfaced occasionally and were not developed into more coherent political theories of any kind. Despite the aura of quasi-revolutionary excitement which surrounded the popular movement during the brief constitutional struggle of the early 1850s, its impact on the development of Afrikaner political thinking proved to be slight and superficial. 'The people' briefly confronted 'the government', but apart from Stockenström's rather personal critique of the colonial 'system' of patronage and despotism (6.13b), no substantial political analysis was developed either of the current regime or of any proposed alternatives.

Unsurprisingly the popular movement quickly subsided when its main objectives were granted with the new constitution of 1853, leaving little trace in the political history of the Afrikaner of the Cape. It is interesting to speculate, however, on the possible consequences had the granting of representative government been postponed, and had a long and arduous constitutional struggle forged durable political alliances and brought about a further radicalization and clarification of political views. It may be argued that whereas the abolition of slavery had made it possible for the Cape Afrikaners to support a popular movement for representative government, the early success of this movement prevented the consolidation of a popular and democratic tradition in Afrikaner political thought.

6.1a We have allowed our laws and privileges to be assailed and have forgotten to be free citizens.

—Anonymous pamphlet distributed in Cape Town, 1778. (Translated from the text published in C. Beyers, *Die Kaapse Patriotte*, pp. 310–312.)

The distribution of two anonymous pamphlets in Cape Town during the first half of 1778 was the earliest indication of the Cape Patriot movement. The more substantial pamphlet, entitled 'The Power and Liberties of a Civil Society' (De Magt en Vrijheeden eener Burgerlijke Maatschappije) *was a transcription of a pamphlet produced in Holland some 25 years earlier. The other pamphlet was the colonists' own work and set out their grievances against the commercial policy of the Company. The Company had prior claim to the colonists' cattle, wheat and wine; its needs had to be met before these products could be sold to passing ships. In general, large-scale trade was in the hands of a small entrenched merchant class which had the necessary capital and contacts with officials.*

To our brothers, fellow-citizens of this Colony of the Cape of Good Hope, these words are dedicated, and recommended for their consideration.

We have found for ourselves that there is nothing truer, nothing which reason or the Holy Scriptures teach more firmly, than that the Almighty has laid down this law for every man, whoever he may be, wherever he may live, as the first law of all duties.

Namely, that he must promote his own welfare, together with that of his fellows, and in particular that of his fellow-citizens, as far as this lies within his powers, and do this according to the best of his knowledge and skill.

From this general and basic duty which the Almighty Creator lays down for each man follows this second law, which is that every man should contribute, according to the condition in which he finds himself, to the welfare of the general community, and in particular to the welfare of the citizenry of which he is a member, as far as this lies within his powers.

These two laws of morality oblige us, then, to harness all our powers for the task of bringing to your attention, our most true citizens, the miserable condition of our commerce, our trades, etc., and the condition to which these might be brought, with directions as to the lawful and proper means by which we should be able to gain possession of these.

The largest number of the inhabitants of the colony, especially those who are here in the city, find their sustenance and occupation in commerce, which consists in their dealings with Dutch ships and those of foreign nations which put in here for refreshment. These ships carry European and Indian goods, and use these to buy the produce of this country. This source of our existence is permitted by the East India Company only to the free burghers and to those in the city, with the proviso that none of the company's servants at all will occupy themselves with commerce, skilled crafts, etc., or own any lands, but will have to be satisfied with their emoluments, as is instructed in the letters of the same Company, written in 1706 to the Honourable Louis van Assenberg, at that time Governor and Counsellor. Now, most worthy citizens, consider whether you at present possess the privileges which the company has granted you. Are the greatest merchants not company servants, or what are Staring, H. Mulder, Cruywagen and company, as they call themselves? And are Schelder, Sandenberg and others not all company servants? When a ship comes to port and trade can be done, no burgher can go on board, sometimes for three or four days, without being hindered by the bailiff, until such time as the bloodsucker Staring has had the opportunity to corner all the trade which can bring him any advantage. . . . All the currency of foreign countries must go to Cruywagen and company, all wage-accounts go through their hands, and this allows them to stay in control of trade. Ask who are the largest transport contractors—are they not Van Outshoorens and Van Oorde, both equally well known to you? Do not even Messrs Bergh and Schelder sell vegetables from their farms? Does all this not run directly counter to the will of the Company, and to the privileges granted to us?

Consider now your position, and that of your fellow-citizens. It is true that this colony appears to have grown, but once its real condition is considered, should one not be surprised to learn how many families can still survive, if one knows that they have little or no income? The situation is certainly miserable, for does one not see each day how those families which are not well off are brought to poverty, and how widows and orphans are obliged to seek support from the Church? Are our commerce and our trades not languishing from moment to moment? . . . If we persist any longer in this indifference, will our wives and children not have every reason to complain about us, even to call us cowards and say we are frightened, for the reason that we have allowed our laws and privileges to be assailed and have forgotten to be free citizens of a colony of the free united Netherlands, which owes its very existence and its renown to its heroic citizens, . . . who have thought it an honour to sacrifice their property and blood in the general interest? Who is there who does not agree with us completely that it is our duty, according to the two afore-mentioned laws of morality, to employ our abilities for the single purpose of promoting the general interest, and to use all the means to that end which God and nature have given us as free citizens of the united Netherlands, which won its freedom in battle?

All who have the inclination to promote the general interest are therefore requested, as true citizens, to sign a petition with us, to be presented to the Honourable the Governor—a gentleman known to all of us to be considerate and friendly. This step will surely give us satisfaction, according to his duty, and, if it does not, there will always be a door open to us, to take our complaints directly to the most powerful Lords of the States-General of the united Netherlands, whom we recognize, with God, as our sole sovereign, and in particular to His Almighty Highness who, according to his laws, will not neglect to do us justice and to take us into his protection as members of the body of which he is the head.

6.1b Now you can see the fair and well-grounded complaints of the burghers against these officials.

—Second and concluding parts of the Burgher Petition of 9 Oct 1779. (Translated from *Kaapsche Geschillen* (Amsterdam, 1785) in the Cape Archives, C 742.)

In 1779 the Cape Patriots bypassed the local government and sent four delegates (Jacobus van Reenen, Barend Jacob Artoys, Tieleman Roos and Nicolaas Godfried Heyns) to the Netherlands to present a lengthy petition to the directors of the Company. Extracts from the first section of this Burgher Petition of 1779 are included as Document 2.1a. The second and most substantial part of the petition consisted of an exhaustive catalogue of allegations against various local Company officials and their associates, starting with the Independent Fiscal Boers, and giving instances of malpractices, corruption and abuses of power. The final section proposed a number of reforms.

. . . This languishing condition of the Cape citizenry and colonists . . . is largely caused, and further aggravated, by the oppression under whose burden the entire citizenry [*burgerstaat*] must groan, and the unauthorized private trade conducted by several of Your Honour's officials here against which we and our fellow-citizens direct our legitimate objections and just complaints . . . which will now be made clear in the second part of this memorial. . . .

The first and most prominent official of the honourable Company who has been guilty of improper conduct towards our fellow-citizens at the Cape is the fiscal, Mr Willem Cornelis Boers.

This official has conducted himself in the execution of his duties towards the burghers and colonists of the Cape with such arbitrary tyranny, oppression and irresponsibility, that all those who have even the least feeling of freedom left cannot contemplate this without being deeply moved. . . .

The aforementioned fiscal not only imposes the heaviest and most unprecedented fines on the people at his own discretion, but also confiscates their goods. This happens even when the offences are very minor, or are committed only out of stupidity or ignorance of the law, of which most burghers often have no knowledge nor any means of acquiring such knowledge. . . .

Notwithstanding this hard manner of governing the burghers, His Honour is, however, not as strict, but much more lenient, in the correction and punishment of slaves (when nothing is to be gained from it). His Honour sometimes sees fit to let the slave boys go unpunished, even when requested by their masters to punish them for their obstinacy and dereliction of duty. . . . He does this even though it can obviously lead to dire consequences if the wantonness of the slaves is left unpunished. . . . [Similar complaints against other officials are detailed in 16 further clauses.]

Now you can see, honorable gentlemen! We have accurately depicted not only the present languishing and truly pitiable condition and circumstances in which the Cape burghers and free colonists find themselves, much to their sorrow and grief, but also the most important causes of these, namely their oppression and maltreatment at the hands of various of Your Honour's officials, and in particular the unlawful trading of these officials which is openly conducted in contravention of Your Honour's express orders. [We have also depicted] the fair and well-grounded complaints and objections of these burghers against them. . . . It is fully apparent that the citizenry has addressed itself more than once—indeed, several times—to the honourable Governor and Political Council with various specific requests for redress and for the maintenance of the same civic privileges [which have been abrogated] by various of the abuses and underhand practices, which have already been mentioned and sufficiently described, and which contribute to our oppression and do us harm. All these requests have not had the least effect, nor any beneficial consequences. . . .

. . . [Therefore] we now request Your Honours to give favorable attention and consideration to the following specific requests for redress, with which we conclude this memorial.

1 In the first place, then, Your Honours are most earnestly requested on behalf of the citizens and inhabitants of the Cape . . . to ensure that no official discharged with pension nor anyone who is still in service at the Cape, from the highest to the lowest, with no exceptions whatsoever, may carry on any trade or commerce, directly or indirectly for themselves or for others. . . .

2 Secondly, Your Honours are respectfully requested to issue the necessary instructions so that a citizen might in future have the freedom to sell and deliver his produce, once the honourable Company has been adequately provided for, to foreign ships, without having to pay any duty on it to the fiscal. . . .

4 [Your Honours are requested] to see that the fiscal is instructed, on pain of the

heaviest penalties, not to have any burgher apprehended by soldiers [?] [*met geweldiger*] and Kaffirs, to have him imprisoned, or to have him arrested on a criminal charge, except in such criminal cases where the offender has been apprehended *in flagrante delicto*. Still less are they to remove any burgher by these means from his house. On the contrary, [Your Honours are requested] to decree that a burgher may not be arrested in any way except by other burghers, and will be kept imprisoned or detained in the burgher guardhouse in terms of the civil law [*uit kragte van het Burgerregt*]. . . .

5 Furthermore [Your Honours are requested] to prohibit anyone born at the Cape or any free burgher who has faithfully served out his contract with the honourable Company from being pressed into the service of the honourable Company once again, or being sent as a sailor from the Cape to Batavia, as this is in conflict with the civil law [*Burgerregt*], and those who have gained their freedom have had to pay a considerable sum for this. But [it is requested] that a citizen who has earned this [deportation] in terms of the law should be sent directly to the fatherland though only after notice has been given, proper enquiries have been made, and permission has been obtained from the burgher councils.

6 [Your Honours are requested] also to allow the burghers to punish their slaves themselves, although they should not be allowed to tyrannize them. . . .

7 Furthermore Your Honours are requested with great urgency to determine according to exactly which general laws those at the Cape are in future to be governed, whether according to the written statutes of India or according to the *Placaat* of the honourable States-General of these countries [i.e. the Netherlands]. [Your Honours are requested] also to see that Burgher councils and heemraden are given instructions in terms of which they can act and that authentic copies be made available to them of all individual *placaats*, or statutes and resolutions which are effective in the Cape and concern the burghers . . . so that neither the fiscal nor the landdrost will in future be able to demand arbitrary fines from the burghers, and the inhabitants in this way might no longer be kept in ignorance as to the laws of the country and the respective orders of the honourable Company. . . .

9 [It is hoped] that, in order to place the affairs of the citizenry on a better footing in the course of time, Your Honours might see fit to appoint seven men to the burgher council . . . and also [allow] these seven to take part in the proceedings of the honourable Political Council when matters are to be considered there which affect the citizenry and the common good of the Cape Colony. No one should be eligible for election to any council of burghers [*Burger Collegie*] before he has been a burgher for five or six years and gives adequate proof of his good conduct. . . .

11 [It is requested] also that the honourable Council of Justice might consist of an equal number of members of burgher councils as of Company officials, and the most senior burgher councillor might serve as vice-president. . . .

13 [It is requested] that in all civil councils [*burgerlijke Collegien*] free elections might be held. . . .

6.2 The settlers had real cause to complain, and request that they might enjoy their civil liberties, the benefits of their constitution, the freedom of lawfully permitted trade, and the freedom to dispose over the fruit of their labour.

—*Dutch Africa; or an Historical and Political Description of the Original Condition of the Settlement at the Cape of Good Hope, compared with the Present Condition of this Settlement*, 1783. (Translated and edited from *Nederlandsch Afrika; of historisch en staatkundig Tafereel van den oorsprongelyken Staat der Volksplantinge aan den Kaap de Goede Hoop, vergeleeken met den Tegenwoordigen Staat dier Volksplantinge* (Leyden, 1783).)

This anonymous publication did not appear at the Cape, but was published in Leyden in 1783, originally in French. M. A. Bergh, a member of the second group of Cape delegates which arrived in Holland in 1784, publicly alleged that it was a secondary and misleading fabrication. He was repudiated by his fellow delegates, who subsequently broke with him on this issue. In all probability Nederlandsch Afrika *was the work of Barend Jacob Artoys, one of the original four delegates who had come from the Cape in 1779, in collaboration with Francis Bernard, a publicist of French origin active in Dutch Patriot circles. No doubt Artoys's sojourn in Holland and his collaboration with Bernard influenced his thinking, but this pamphlet remains the most comprehensive statement of the Cape Patriots' political ideas, and shows sufficient similarity with other writings emanating from the Cape itself at the time.*

Europe has almost no arbitrary despots any longer, as almost all its peoples have gradually been enlightened as to the rights which they are granted by nature.

Arbitrary despotism does however have such attractions for rulers that, not longer being able to exercise these powers unhindered in one part of the earth, they continue to exercise them to an even greater extent in remote parts, where men degenerate almost wholly from their noble origins, let themselves be managed as beasts of burden, dare not murmur about their enslavement, and even kiss the hand of the cruel tyrannous despot who keeps them in chains. Natural feelings seem to be blunted in those wild regions inhabited by beings created to be *reasonable*, but who resemble us only in their animal bodies which we all have in common.

One forgives the tyrannous despots of the East for ruling their peoples with an iron rod. . . . But can one forgive the rulers of Europe for tyrannizing those of their subjects who have left their fatherland and settled in remote countries, distant from their sovereignty? This arbitrary despotism is all the less excusable as these countries were first settled and built up for the benefit of those same rulers, who pluck the most precious fruits of the sweat and diligence of the settlers.

But it is only too true, however, that almost all the settlers in Asia, Africa and America are oppressed, vexed and mistreated. It is only too certain that these victims of arbitrary rule complain most bitterly of the oppression under which they suffer. . . .

The settlers in America provide us with an example worthy of consideration. The English have found to their detriment how impolitic it is to oppress their subjects and no longer to consider them as brothers all of the same motherland. . . . The example of the English Americans can be followed by the settlers of both Indies [the East and West Indies]. This example can become infectious. . . . The terrible arbitrary despotism which England wielded over her settlers before their rebellion must teach those powers which have colonial possessions to moderate their rule . . . and to treat their settlers on the same footing as their European subjects. . . .

This is particularly and most obviously the case with the valuable settlement of the

Cape of Good Hope. The officials of the Dutch East India Company have for many years permitted themselves conduct which has become intolerable, and it is with confidence that I dare to say that the settlers at the Cape . . . deserve the care, the respect, the affection and the especial protection of the mother country. . . .

In order to deal with this grave matter in a clear and orderly fashion, I shall indicate in the first chapter the nature of the settlement at the Cape, what the original privileges of the settlers were, and what their original obligations were with respect to the Company. In short, I shall try to set out *the original social contract* entered into by the Company and the first settlers it sent to this fruitful part of Africa. In the second chapter I shall try in broad outline to depict the hideously bad and pernicious government of this settlement—a government which must sooner or later force the ruined settlers to some or other act of violence and despair and which must eventually pull the Company over the precipice on whose edge it has for many years been poised. In the third chapter, I shall take the liberty of indicating briefly the first measures which the Company, or rather the supreme authority, should take to correct the excessive abuses and also, as far as is possible, to prevent the discontent of the settlers from bursting out—as is now ready to happen—against the faithless officials who have become their oppressors. . . .

Chapter I. The original condition of the civil and internal government of the Cape of Good Hope.

. . . In the first years of this settlement, when it gave rise to nothing but well-grounded expectations of a fortunate outcome, [Van] Riebeeck was able singlehandedly to maintain good order, peace, unity and harmony. . . . Under his rule, one had nothing to fear from the officials of the Company. These officials, who would become bloodsuckers under Riebeeck's successors, kept within the limits of their offices. Under Riebeeck's rule, the settlers and inhabitants of the capital could sleep peacefully in their beds, without fear of being taken away by violence, or being unexpectedly removed from the heart of their families and sent, as they are today, to Batavia or any other possession of the Company in the East Indies. They did not need to fear, as they do today, that they would be charged as wrongdoers and as such brought into the service of the Company to work for it for the lowly wage of a slave and end their days in misery. . . . Riebeeck never permitted himself to resort to force against the settlers whom he knew to have come to the Cape under the stipulation that they would enjoy proper civil liberties. . . .

In the time of Riebeeck, although still in the first years of its establishment, the settlement found itself in conditions of abundance, because the settlers enjoyed proper, natural and fitting freedom. At present the settlement does not any longer have life or vitality, as its welfare has been cloistered. In the time of Riebeeck the settlement was attached to the interests of the Company, as the settlers were treated well by it. At present they curse the Company and long for the moment at which they will be released, at whatever cost, from the unbearable burden it has placed on them, or which it at least obstinately refuses to lighten.

The short period in which justice and fairness reigned at the Cape, during the government of Riebeeck, can be called the *golden age* of the settlement. . . . If one were to judge from the present condition of the settlement, one would be inclined to believe that this golden age of the Cape settlement is just as chimerical as that which poets have celebrated with respect to the entire world. Yet one would mislead oneself, because it is certain that Riebeeck laid the foundations of the settlement on the cornerstones of justice, humanity and the social virtues. . . .

Riebeeck's successors destroyed the whole of his accomplishment almost at once, overthrowing the pure order which he had established. . . .

Chapter II. The present state of civil government at the Cape of Good Hope.
It is remarkable that the settlement of a commonwealth . . . whose form of government is almost that of a popular government [*volksregeering*] . . . should fall under the rule of a government which is more than tyrannous. . . . This contradiction is all the more strange while the settlers are not subjects of the commonwealth by conquest. . . .

Let us look briefly at the way in which the eight councils [which constitute the civil government] deal with the matters falling under their jurisdiction. We shall easily be persuaded that the Company, the settler and the citizen could place their most precious interests in better hands. This superficial investigation will, however, be adequate to show that the complaints of the citizens and the settlers at the Cape are only too well grounded and that the officials of the Company, from the highest official down to the lowest, have abused the authority entrusted to them by the Company to an unusual extent, according to their ability to do so and the opportunities which have arisen. They regard their offices only as means to make a fortune without worrying themselves about whether the citizen and the settler suffer thereby or not.

1 The High Council, commonly called the Council of Policy: . . . The High Council consists of members who are devoted to the Company and in its power, and whose particular interests are always directly opposed to the particular interests of the citizens and settlers. This High Council is composed of members who, far from representing the people, are at all times, whether taken individually or as a group, manifestly in opposition to the settlers and citizens. On the basis of the extortion of which they are guilty with respect to the citizens I could say, without deviating far from the truth, that the members who constitute the High Council are always personal enemies of the settlers and citizens. . . .

. . . The *placaats* which are issued [by the Council] all tend to making heavier the yoke of the citizens and settlers, under the pretext of maintaining good order. . . .

2 The High Court of Justice: The cases which are heard before this Court are either civil or criminal. In both cases, the ruling burgher councillors are called in. They occupy the remaining places [in the Court] and vote only after the other councillors, who are all officials of the Company, have voted. As far as this [procedure] is concerned, it can easily be seen that the burgher councillors, who are called in in both cases under the pretext of protecting the property of their fellow citizens, are of no use at all. They cannot prevent this property from being taken and dealt with according to the discretion of the judges, who are officials of the Company. This is because when the burgher councillors are asked for their views, the matter has already been settled by the majority of the votes of the judges, who are officials of the Company. The burgher councillors are only called into this Council to act as witnesses of the unjust sentences usually given against the settlers. . . .

. . . The Independent Fiscal, who sits as a judge in civil cases, acts for the public interest only in criminal cases. But as he is an official of the Company, he cannot be regarded as the protector of the accused. Thus the accused has no one in the Court to plead for him or even to intercede for him, and he is left entirely to the mercy of his judges. What does he not have to fear from these judges, who constitute in a certain sense a people alien to him, a society firmly and powerfully set against the citizenry of the Cape? In this particular case, one could say that the settlers no longer have the original characteristic of inhabitants of a free state. . . .

7 The Burgher Council: Here the abuses are many and unusually excessive, especially in the capital. I have already said that any people which does not consist of slaves must have a visible representative acting for it with the supreme rulers. The citizens and settlers of the Cape would seek such a representative in vain; he is not to be found. All peoples have as their representatives those among their own number whom they appoint to guard over the interests of the people. These deputies [*gemagtigdes*] are usually chosen from among the most intelligent and prominent members of the whole body of the citizenry. The deputies usually empower a small number from among themselves, for a certain time or for their lifetimes, [to represent them] in all matters which concern the rights and privileges of the inhabitants, considered both as private members of civil society and as the body of the people. . . . It is true that the Cape settlement does have burgher councillors. Yet they are without real authority and are not nominated by the citizens. . . . Thus they cannot represent the citizenry in any way except extremely inadequately and uselessly. They are simply silent attendants and as such of no use to their fellow citizens. . . . The reader can well imagine that none of the burgher councillors would be incautious enough to object to [the procedures for appointing new councillors]. One does not usually offer futile resistance to something which one cannot prevent. Still less does one resist when one has good reason to fear the displeasure of an arbitrary despot, and when one might incur the terrible consequences of his unbridled displeasure. . . .

8 The Militia Council: . . . It appears natural that, while the government has sufficient trust in the citizens and settlers to allow them to arm themselves and do weapon drill, it should place complete trust in them by allowing them to choose a [military] commander from among themselves, to act as chairman of the Militia Council. . . . But the arbitrary despot must always govern with an iron rod and make this felt at more or less every opportunity. There, without doubt, you have the only reason which the government can give for the lack of trust they place in a military people, who alone are able to defend the possession of the Cape from a hostile invasion. . . .

. . . The Civil Militia at the Cape are not in the pay of the Company. Pure love of their fatherland leads them to arm themselves, and the same love of fatherland leads them to serve without reward. Theirs is a voluntary service, and one must allow it to retain at least the trappings of freedom. [The Militia] is of direct use to the Company and the Company must treat it with all the respect that is due to a body of volunteers who have armed themselves for the general good of the settlement. . . .

That then is the general picture of the present government of the Cape of Good Hope . . . as far as its civil administration is concerned.

Chapter III. Measures which the supreme Authorities must take to prevent abuses.

. . . What then was the beneficial purpose which the good Riebeeck, father of the separate settlement of the Cape and founder of the whole settlement in general, could have had in mind with the establishment of the Burgher Councils? . . . In a word, that which shows most clearly the aim of Riebeeck in establishing the Burgher Councils is that he founded the settlement on the same footing of freedom which the people living in the seven united provinces [i.e. the Netherlands] enjoyed. The supreme authority and the Company itself have always acknowledged that the citizens at the Cape have these freedoms, and they acknowledge this still. . . .

The Fiscal . . . has tried to defend himself by means of a childish yet despicable distinction which is most insulting to the settlers and citizens. He admits that they are *free* only insofar as they are *not officials of the Company*, i.e. because they obviously draw no wage from the Company, as the officials and the servants of the Company do. There, according to him, you have the sole way in which the epithet of *freemen* should be understood. But, according to him, this epithet of freemen should not be taken in the same way as it is understood with respect to the inhabitants of the seven provinces. . . .

I shall not repeat what I said at the beginning of this work in order to prove that the first men who left Europe to live at the settlement at the Cape, left with the assurance that they would enjoy the benefits of freedom which they had enjoyed in the commonwealth, and that their descendants would naturally be the heirs to this condition of freedom granted to their fathers when they left the fatherland. Here the Fiscal is deliberately confusing the Cape citizens who are descended from the first settlers sent to the Cape by the supreme authority, with the Cape citizens who were officials of the Company and acquired their citizenship at the Cape after they had served the Company as soldiers and sailors. He asserts that these are only provisionally citizens and that the Company tacitly retains the right to treat them as subjects after selling or giving them their freedom. This assertion is absurd. It cannot be disputed that every soldier who has served his time or has bought himself out before his contract expires regains all the rights of freedom which he had before he bound himself. Thus every soldier at the Cape who is no longer in the service of the Company and who has acquired citizenship here has all the rights and all the privileges which are enjoyed by those citizens who have never been in the service of the Company. Together they constitute one body [of citizens]. There is no distinction between them as far as the privileges of citizenship are concerned. . . . Mr [Fiscal] Boers appears to have forgotten that . . . not only the inhabitants of the large cities of our [Dutch] Commonwealth are privileged, free inhabitants, but that even the poorest farmer who lives in the smallest country village of the commonwealth is as much a free privileged person as the most powerful burgher councillor of the largest city of our Commonwealth can be. . . .

We acknowledge that at this moment, i.e. since the beginning of this war or more precisely since the French military came to the Cape, the settlement is no longer as oppressed as it was in time of peace. We acknowledge that the settlers are relatively free to conduct trade, that they have been somewhat enriched by the higher prices for which they are able to sell their goods, and, in a word, that their condition is at present beneficial and fairly prosperous. But this prosperity is only coincidental; it is only temporary. When the war is over, oppression will once again take its old course, and misery will be more intensely felt than ever. This has consistently been true of all previous wars. The settlers do not complain about their present economic condition. They complained when they had real cause to do so, and they persist in requesting the Company to introduce the most vigorous measures so as to ensure at all times, in peace and war, that the citizens and settlers might enjoy their civil liberties, the benefits of their constitution, the freedom of lawfully permitted trade, and the freedom to dispose over the fruit of their labour. . . . In a word, [they request] complete security in their homes for as long as they conduct themselves as respectable men. . . .

. . . The following are the means which should be adopted for the general welfare of the settlers, i.e. to ensure their freedom, their property and their welfare, to regain their trust, affection and good disposition and, in a word, to make them happy.

1 The civil liberty of all citizens and settlers must be guaranteed. To this end, I think, the Company ought to allow the citizenry of the capital to hold meetings at the town hall [*Stadhuis*] to discuss matters which directly concern the community of citi-

zens and settlers in the vicinity of the Cape. [The Company should allow the citizenry] an annual nomination of burgher councillors. . . . At all these meetings of the citizenry of the capital, the senior burgher councillor in office must act as chairman. . . . What I say here with respect to the particular settlement of the Cape [i.e. Cape Town] must also apply to the other settlements. They must also be free to meet and elect their heemraden who must represent the settlers in the outlying regions remote from the capital, just as the burgher councillors must represent the citizens and settlers at the Cape.

2 The Council of Justice, the lower Court, the Orphan Chamber, etc. must consist half of officials of the Company and half of burgher councillors, with even a few ordinary burghers. These bodies must, however, always have a prominent official of the Company as chairman and the vice-chairman must always be chosen from among the burgher councillors. . . .

3 The Commander [*Bevelhebber*] must be expressly forbidden by the company from pressing into service any burgher or settler, either as a soldier or as a sailor, whatever the reason for such obligatory service might be. The government itself should have no power to expel a settler or citizen without a formal charge previously being laid and his having been sentenced to exile by the judgement of the Council of Justice. The Fiscal must be forbidden from having any citizen or settler arrested by the Bailiff accompanied by the black constabulary [*kaffers*] in his house or on the street or anywhere else. A citizen or settler should not be arrested at the capital by anyone except the sheriffs of the court, and in the outlying settlements by the policemen [*gerechtsboden*] of those settlements. The black constabulary must serve only to assist the executioner in carrying out sentences.

4 The Company should absolutely forbid the government from taking upon itself the right of forcing the citizens and settlers to provide slaves or money for the Company's works. The Commander should be forbidden from obliging the Civil Militia to do forced service for himself, and from making them guard the coast when a foreign ship appears to be approaching the Cape or when any ship has been wrecked on the coast, etc. . . .

After provision has been made for the civil freedom of the settlers, the security of their property must still be provided for. For this purpose the Company must take vigorous steps to curb the greed of its senior officials. In particular, the excessive and arbitrary fines which the Fiscal imposes on the settlers and citizens under trivial pretexts must be resisted. . . .

To enable the settler and the citizen to subsist decently, one must in the first place make it easy for him to pay his taxes and his annual returns. In the second place, one should allow him proper freedom to make transactions. He cannot prosper without trade; without trade, he languishes, neglects to cultivate his lands and makes no use of his abilities. Without trade, in a word, he is lifeless, and without initiative becomes lazy, falls prey to licentiousness, neglects the virtues and turns to crime. He does more; he becomes restless and promotes cliques because he is discontented. And if he finds no way of conducting illicit trade, which is always detrimental to the supreme authority and the state, then the idleness in which he lives eventually serves to make him rebellious. . . .

6.3 The brave Afrikaners say to the free Netherlands that we love freedom just as much as they do, that we have been born of their stock and feel the same free blood in our veins.

—Letter in *De Post van de Neder Rhijn*, 1787. (Translated from the original in *De Post van de Neder Rhijn*, Vol. XI (No. 522), pp. 502–514.)

When the largely unfavourable response of the Company to their various petitions became known at the Cape, in the course of 1784 preparations were made for an appeal to the highest political authority, the States-General of the Netherlands. In August 1784 'a most emphatic proposition' was circulated among burghers, and on 11 October 1784 a permanent body entitled 'Representatives of the People' ('s Volks Representaten) *was appointed. In November a further committee of 'delegated representatives'* (Gecommiteerde Representaten) *was formed as an executive organ. From this resulted the new petition of 14 December 1784 to be presented to the States General in the Netherlands. In his letter of a few years later the Cape correspondent of* De Post van de Neder Rhijn, *one of the mouthpieces of the Dutch Patriots, a copy of the 'most emphatic proposition' was included as indication of the views of the Cape Patriots.*

. . . Even superficially considered, the sorry state of the Cape settlement must be apparent to anyone who is at all knowledgeable and who is not prejudiced or wilfully blind to the facts. Indeed, as various remnants of the history of the settlement remind us, even in the year 1668, after the Colony had only been established for about 16 years, regulations had to be made by the then commanders to curb the ambition and greed of their officials here. [The documents also show,] however, that these regulations could often be violated without punishment, as their implementation depended too much on the discretion of the supreme government in the Indies and the Cape government itself. . . .

Even at the establishment, then, or in the earliest infancy of the settlement, the oppression was already begun! Soon we were to see *particular interests vying with the common good*. This continued for about 50 years, but then widespread discontent burst out, making memorable the end of the previous century and the beginning of this one, especially the years 1705 and 1706. At that time an accumulation of malpractices stained the governments of two commanders, father and son, Simon and Adriaan van der Stel, and made the citizenry groan under cruelty and corruption similar to that suffered under an Alvares of Toledo. In particular, the latter Van der Stel excelled in the abuse of power at the expense of the citizens and at enriching himself.

I shall try here to sketch the excellent characters of two citizens who were at that time the most notable victims of an unrestrainedly violent government, but whose incomparable courage can serve as an example to all who love their fatherland more than they love themselves.

These objects of exalted civic virtue bore the names Jacob van der Heijden and Adam Tas. . . . Both were endowed with sense and sound judgement. But with all their abilities they would still have been useless to the burgher community, if these had not been combined in them with a love of man and a burning desire to serve their fellow citizens above all. . . . Their great spirits, breathing nothing but the air of freedom, became impatient of the tyranny under which the citizenry then groaned; and, wanting to have justice done to humanity, they resisted the cruel extortion of their tyrannizers along with many prominent citizens—at first with propriety and submission. When their complaints were not heeded by the governor, they undertook to draw up a petition and sent it, signed by many citizens, to the supreme authorities and to the high council of the Indies at Batavia. . . .

. . . The tyrant proposed to make his wrath felt by these lovers of their fatherland, Van der Heijden and Tas, and he carried out this godless intention. [An extensive description of their sufferings at the hands of the government follows. . . .]

. . . One could ask why these men were so severely dealt with? And the answer is, because they were complaining citizens, that was their only crime! . . .

Although some degree of satisfaction has been granted for the complaints made at that time, the arrangements made to prevent further disorder were so much subject to the discretion of the new commander and his successors that their consequences could not be other than renewed discord and confusion. . . .

. . . This gave rise to the most far-reaching oppression, which eventually led to a dangerous rebellion in the district of Zwartland about 50 years ago. This was led by a certain Barbier who died a shameful death as a rebel, although he might have been crowned with fame and honour if he had triumphed over his enemies. . . .

Thus it will be very easy to understand that such violent means were often resorted to in order to smother the discontent, that this discontent had to grow greater as time passed and that eventually such repugnance would be felt for a government consisting solely of Company officials that it would be understood that the leaders of these parties were nothing but the complete enemies of the citizenry, and that it was therefore unnatural to be governed any longer by a few embittered and vengeful enemies! . . .

I could recount to Your Honour a whole series of similar instances of maltreatment. . . . But . . . I shall save these and carry on with the way in which all these complaints were treated with scorn by the authorities!

Feelings about this humiliating treatment have assumed such proportions that they have given rise to a remarkable affirmation [*verbintenis*]. The cruelly persecuted burgher, isolated from the political [centre of] Europe, can come to no other conclusion, on the grounds of the responses made to his complaints, than that *he has been condemned to slavery*! This affirmation I append in the form of a proposition. It is of utmost gravity and expresses the language of the heart, or rather the feelings of the downtrodden and persecuted Afrikaner [*Africaan*]. . . .

A most emphatic proposition, made to all true patriots, supporters of right and justice, and freedom-loving citizens at the Cape of Good Hope:

Beloved compatriots and fellow-citizens! It is more than sufficiently well-known to you how, in the year 1779, we delegated four persons from the number of our distinguished body to demonstrate to the rulers of these East Indian lands with convincing proofs the extent of the wicked tyranny, the unauthorized conduct and abuses of power of their officials here in these parts, and to request them most humbly to improve the deteriorating condition of our civil liberties. These demonstrations and requests were so humbly made and were so thorougly based on justice, that one could not expect anything but the legitimate redress of our complaints, which had been ringing in the ears of most of the peoples of Europe.

Then, beloved citizens! Who of you does not know that the decision on this grave matter was delayed for five years? If this had been caused by the nature of the consideration, and if the result had been at all favourable for our esteemed citizenry, we should have been silent. But then the pretence was stripped away and we were shown the depth of the ruin for which we were destined. We were shown that we and our children were in future to be managed as slaves, as beasts of burden!

But, dear citizens, our blood is far too noble for us to bend immediately under the yoke of slavery, before we have attempted all honest and virtuous means to ensure our salvation. . . .

Thus . . . we have considered it necessary to arrange a meeting among us . . . in order [to preserve] ourselves and our descendants, as far as this is within our powers, from the shameful slavery with which we are presently threatened. . . . For what would the consequence have been of such disgraceful forbearance, if we had resigned ourselves to the no less disgraceful decision? Dear citizens, it would have been a disgraceful condition of slavery, defiling human nature. And in order to resist this, as far as is possible, we have assembled together.

And the safest of the means, beloved citizens, by which we can bring these matters to a conclusion and preserve ourselves from vengeance and persecution is for us once again . . . to send two or three competent men from among our number to the fatherland in order to present our just cause to our supreme and lawful sovereign, the States-General of the United Netherlands! . . .

By these means, i.e. through the courageous decision rather to risk everything than subject ourselves slavishly, . . . you, dear citizens, will fulfil the duties of man, as God commands you, according to the noble capacities of your souls, and will defend yourselves against tyranny and suppression. That noble ability God has even given to unreasoning animals, and should we be less? Should we scorn the inspiration of the Creator of all things? No, this statement is blasphemy!

Therefore, beloved citizens, give your assent to our grave proposition.

. . . And so the brave Afrikaners . . . say to the free Netherlands that we love freedom just as much as they do, that we have been born of their stock and feel the same free blood in our veins. For just as it was fair for them to defend themselves against oppression after fruitless pleading, so it is fair and just that we deal with [oppression] as they did with Philip the tyrant!

But things have not come to such a dangerous extremity yet! We are hoping for an adequate and favourable redress of our complaints from our benevolent sovereign, for whom we are at all times ready to shed our blood! And once redress has been obtained, how passionate will the gratitude of the relieved Afrikaner then not be. And this goodwill, based on grateful feelings to such a fatherly sovereign, will be passed on from generation to generation. And so the free name of the Netherlands will be perpetuated in Africa! . . .

6.4a We beg that the nomination of burgher councillors [representing us on the Court of Justice] might in future be undertaken by burgher councillors only.

—Memorial of burgher councillors to the Cape Council of Policy, 12 April 1790. (Translated from the original in the Cape Archives, C 88.)

One of the concessions which the Cape Patriots did succeed in winning from the Company was an increase in the number of burghers on the Court of Justice, giving them equal representation with the officials. (The request that burghers serve on the Council of Policy was refused.) In addition, a commission of the Council of Justice, consisting of three burghers and three Company servants, was given certain responsibilities in the field of local government and the determination of prices for local produce. The Company retained the right to appoint burgher councillors from the list of nominations it received. In 1790 the Governor appointed a retired Company official, Abraham Fleck, as burgher representative on the Court of Justice, without the custom-

ary regard for the nominations of the burgher councillors themselves, giving rise to the following protest.

. . . Memorialists take the liberty of bringing to Your Honours' attention that it has been the practice among all nations since ancient times that when they are granted representation on certain bodies in some matter in which they have an interest, they are also given the freedom of nominating the representatives themselves. It is by no means the intention of the memorialists to imply anything in conflict with their state of dependency, along with the whole citizenry and indeed the entire colony, under the rule of the honourable Dutch East India Company. No, Your Honours, they know as well, and are always aware with grateful hearts, what benefactions this colony has enjoyed under the favourable rule and protection of the Dutch East India Company, and the extent to which our lords and masters, who find themselves in control of this Company, have regarded and taken to heart the prosperity and well-being of this colony with loving and fatherly care. But as it has pleased these our lords and masters in their goodness to allow the Cape citizenry, in a matter of the greatest gravity and importance, viz. the administration of justice, to have six burgher councillors from their midst serve on this council with an equal number of members who are Company officials, . . . the memorialists think it fair to beg, on their behalf and on behalf of the citizenry, that the nomination of these burgher councillors . . . might in future be undertaken by burgher councillors alone. . . .

J. Smuts — H. T. de Wet
G. H. Meijer — etc

6.4b Therefore we proceed to present our own notions of whether we are still not competent to represent the pressing needs of the people.

—Petition from A. van Jaarsveld and others to the Cape Council of Policy, 12 July 1791. (Translated from the original in the Cape Archives, G.R. 1/1.)

Adriaan van Jaarsveld, who had been appointed as commandant of the eastern frontier in 1780, played a leading role in the establishment of the new district of Graaff-Reinet in 1786. In 1790 Van Jaarsveld was not reappointed as heemraad in spite of his being nominated. This may have been one of the reasons for Van Jaarsveld's introduction, for approval, of the following memorial before the board of landdrost and heemraden of Graaff-Reinet in 1791.

If we are to acquaint Your Honours with the lamentable condition of the colonists, as it has been from time to time and has now come to a pitch, with their pressing needs and with the main causes [thereof], then Your Honours should know, in the first place, how fearful we are at present of [the idea] becoming current among many of our colonists, as it has done in the past, that they have to abandon their farms and fields. They believe that in the whole world they cannot suffer more damage, or be more insecure, by fleeing and wandering than [by staying] where they are now. Formerly some farmers did indeed [abandon their farms], causing further depredations by the robbers, which are still continuing at the present moment. [The imminent danger of a mass abandoning of the farms cannot be averted] unless we [re-]present the body of the people like true guardians, in order to bring about some alleviation of their burdens in this way. Thus the undersigned humbly approach the paternal guardian of the country to represent, to the best of our abilities, the true interests of the people, and to request alleviation of their burdens.

We humbly submit

1 That peace and quiet is a most precious matter when the inhabitants of a country can enjoy this in quiet obedience under the protection of their government, [but] that this has apparently not been possible [in this district] until now. . . .

6 Therefore we proceed to present our own notions, which Your Honour in his wise judgement may consider, of whether we are still not competent to represent the pressing needs of the people in such cases and to request alleviation of their burdens. For the law of nature teaches that the inherent right to do this belongs to the people since ancient times.

7 It is understood that it may well happen that the people request the improvement or abolition of some weighty and well-grounded burden at a time when such improvement or abolition is not practicable. In such a case one should instruct the people concerning their lack of knowledge in these respects. At least it should not diminish the appreciation due to them for their zeal, nor the respect which their representatives ought to receive according to their rights and dignity.

8 It is also understood that it may happen that the people can make requests which they truly consider to be well-grounded and absolutely necessary, while that is not so. In that case one should point out their error to them, and it is their duty to see to it that they are more careful in future. And in case a deceived and obstinate multitude might attempt to compel their government to concede what is evidently unjust, then it is also understood that, in accordance with our oath and duty, we are obliged to assist the government to make a proper use of all the means which the law has put in their hands to counter such an imposition.

9 It is also understood, on the other hand, that in all cases of unjustified refusals to accede to the requests of the people, or where [the government] does not adjust to their lawful and necessary demands, or at least provide adequate replies, the people have the right to press respectfully once more for satisfaction of their demands. . . .

12 Finally, we, who can see the calamities suffered by the people on their faces, also understand very well that a small number of signatories to a well-grounded, truthful and urgently necessary request is sufficient in all cases where it does not concern a total change of the constitution, or a change of great significance to the whole country. For truth and fairness have their value of themselves. They are not measured by the yard nor weighed on the scales. The motive causing a thousand people to request an unfair and injurious matter cannot be compared with the motive causing ten people to request something fair and necessary.

13 If then the matters requested and presented in the present address in this case constitute an urgent necessity, then we do not doubt that in fairness our government will receive it gratefully and hasten to supply the groaning memorialists with consolation. . . .

A. van Jaarsveld — Joshua Joubert
A. P. Burger — etc

6.4c It appears beyond doubt that someone with interests will have greater trust in a guardian of those interests when he shares these.

—Memorial of the burgher councillors to Commissioners Nederburgh and Frykenius, 25 June 1792. (Translated from the original in the Cape Archives, C 692, pp. 353–359.)

6.4 Colonial views on the right to representation 1790–2

With the Company close to bankruptcy in the early 1790s two commissioners-general, S. C. Nederburgh and S. H. Frykenius, were appointed to bring about overdue reforms and general retrenchment in the Company's possession at the Cape and in the East Indies. They arrived at the Cape on 18 June 1792, and already on 9 July they were presented with the following memorial from the burgher councillors. At first Nederburgh and Frykenius refused to grant the burgher councillors their request to be recognized as an independent representative body in its own right, but following further representations they did recommend this in their report in 1793. Thus statutory recognition was granted to the Burgher Senate, as this body came to be known during the British Occupation from 1795.

The undersigned burgher councillors take the liberty, with all due respect, to submit to Your Honours, according to the information we have received from time to time, how the inhabitants both in the capital and the outlying districts have felt burdened by a number of matters concerning the civil government of the colony. They earnestly desire that the necessary reforms be made in this regard. They consider it their ineluctable duty to benefit by the presence of Your Honours in these remote parts by making representations in their capacities [as burgher councillors] concerning the complaints which are known to them and which they consider most suitable for rectification so as to prevent all individual dissent, which leads not seldom to disorder.

They have had to discover to their regret that the government persists in the idea that the undersigned burgher councillors are as such not capable of making any representations of whatever nature on behalf of the inhabitants to the rulers of the colony without at least the concurrence of the company officials who constitute the Council of Justice together with them. Consequently they have considered it to be of the greatest importance to start by bringing to Your Honour's attention, with due submission, the reasons and motives which convince them, in all good faith, that their position as burgher councillors brings with it the undeniable right jointly to address themselves in a suitable way to either the Chamber of Seventeen or the local government on behalf of the citizenry, without the concurrence of the remaining members of the Council of Justice. In order to do this as briefly as possible and also convincingly the undersigned will argue:

First, that this [*right*] *is in accordance with the constitution of this colony, and the intentions of the Chamber of Seventeen.*

Second, that they have been given this right by the local government.

Concerning the first, it is not unknown to Your Honours that, at the establishment of this colony or settlement, provision was soon made for giving those inhabitants who were not in the service of the Dutch East India Company the privilege of having the most capable of their number acting as members of the court, when judicial matters which concerned them had to be decided. This can be seen from the Memoirs of the first governor of the colony, Jan van Riebeeck, for the date 15 May 1662. . . .

From this it is natural to deduce that even from the earliest times a diversity of interests prevailed between the officials of the Company and the burgher inhabitants. This diversity [of interests], which was recognized by Van Riebeeck, could not but gradually increase as the colony expanded, and the interests of the inhabitants became increasingly independent of those of the officials. Although this did not necessarily have as a consequence that the regents neglected the interests of the burgher inhabitants in favour of the Company, it still appears beyond doubt that someone with interests will have greater trust in a guardian of those interests when he shares these, than when he either has differing interests or has absolutely no interest in what concerns the interested party. This point we consider, under respectful correction, to be of great importance, as it follows that when all the members of the Council of Justice are to be considered as a body representing the citizenry, distrust will not seldom arise. [People will fear] that the officials of the honourable Company, as members of such a College, will not attend to their interests with sufficient diligence or impartiality, either because they have no interest in that which concerns the burghers, or out of fear of those on whom they are dependent. This is particularly so because the complaints of the burghers could well be directed against some arrangement of the government which is prejudicial to them. And such distrust could also very easily lead to irregularities: it could lead the citizenry to make representations, either on their own account or through other unauthorized bodies, which must inevitably have detrimental consequences both for the Company and the inhabitants themselves, as precedents are in such cases usually taken as grounds for [claims to] competence.

Therefore the supreme commanders were wise, when deciding which matters were to be allocated to the College of Commissaries of the Council of Justice, to make no mention of any representative function, enabling it to address the [local] government or the supreme commanders on behalf of the citizenry. In constituting that college [i.e. the Council of Justice] it is clear that their only aim was to relieve the Council of Policy of some matters of lesser import. At the same time certain other matters belonging exclusively to the functions of the burgher councillors, but which did not presuppose any representative function, were also delegated to this College of Commissaries, of which the burgher councillors were an essential part, without its being anywhere stipulated however that the College of burgher councillors had become defunct through the founding of the College of Commissaries [of the Council of Justice]. On the contrary, it appears from the letter to the local government of 28 July 1785, on the reforms decided on concerning the complaints of the citizens, that a College of burgher councillors certainly had to exist at that time. Otherwise it would not have been appropiate for the government to have been instructed to give copies and extracts of the *Placaäten* and resolutions to the burgher councillors when these concerned the citizenry. [From this] it is evident that the supreme commanders certainly do consider the burgher councillors as a separate college and attribute to them the competence to keep in their custody everything resolved or proclaimed which concerns the citizenry, so that they might inform the burgher inhabitants about what has been prescribed to them when this is necessary. In this respect, the burgher councillors are certainly considered in a different capacity, and in closer connection with the citizenry, than is the College of the Council of Justice.

Having thus demonstrated our first point, we will now in the second place show Your Honours that the competence to which we are laying claims in this repect has been recognized by the local government itself on more than one occasion. We will not embark on a laborious listing of everything that has been done and executed by our predecessors in their capacities as burgher councillors since the founding of this colony. We will restrict ourselves to a few cases that took place since the establishment of the College of Commissaries [of the Council of Justice] even though for some time now it has been maintained that this College should replace that of the burgher councillors. From this it will be evident that there must be some particular reasons why the government has gradually conceived the notion of denying the undersigned that which the supreme commanders have seen fit to award to them. . . .

J. Smuts	H. T. de Wet
G. H. Meijer	etc

6.5 It has been unanimously decided and resolved that representatives be elected for the maintenance of the state and the constitution.

—The *Proposition to the Honourable Mr. Bresler* of the Graaff-Reinet burghers, 22 March 1796. (Translated from the text published in C. Beyers, *Die Kaapse Patriotte*, pp. 263–266.)

Some months after the start of the first British occupation the rebellious burghers of Graaff-Reinet wrote to General Craig on 27 October 1795 in a conciliatory spirit, requesting that 'proper magistrates' be appointed for the district. In reply Craig sent F. R. Bresler as landdrost to Graaff-Reinet, but on his arrival early in 1796 he encountered resistance and defiance from burghers, who hauled down the British flag and refused to take the oath of allegiance. At a meeting on 22 March 1796 Martinus Prinsloo and fourteen other representatives of the people presented him with the following document outlining their grievances and explaining why they thought they should not take the oath of allegiance.

It is considered sufficiently well-known that the citizenry of this remote district have had to fight the indigenous enemy for twenty-eight years until now with terrible loss of blood and belongings. At one time it was universally assumed that the establishment of the drostdy and Church would be able to effect a change, and the inhabitants have contributed a great deal of money to build up their proverty-stricken state without any noticeable improvements being made to the district or the colony. But it can immediately be shown that district officials appointed by the Company, through maladministration of accounts and by other means, have pilfered the district coffers. Thus it has been unanimously decided and resolved:

1 To have a landdrost of the district who is a burgher, so that such underhand conduct—about which the colonial officials are unconcerned and indifferent—might in the course of time be prevented.

2 That representatives might be elected for the maintenance of the state and the constitution, according to fixed stipulations. . . .

3 That the powder and lead, which is necessary for the preservation of this state, be provided on payment as before.

4 That the rulers of the country will be pleased to ensure that restitution is made to those who have been robbed by the kaffirs or driven off their property either through peaceful means or by force of arms.

5 That the refusal to take the oath [of allegiance] is not in any way motivated by the desire to resist His Britannic Majesty or His Majesty's officials, for which the citizenry are too few in number . . . but solely in accordance with the true and simple aim [of ensuring] that the oath of allegiance is taken to and for the best interests of the country so that it can be adhered to regardless of revolutions. . . .

6 That in all this it might, in some slight measure, be presumed that this idea might accord with the wish of our Supreme Ruler, who has promised freedom to all who believe and trust in Him. This was so when he led Israel from the land of the Pharaoh and the people desired a king to reign over them. He lamented that His people had turned from the living fountain to the broken cup that held no water and said to His prophet Samuel: They have not rejected thee, but me, who is their true King.

7 As the Lord God later released His people from the monstrous tyranny of the Spanish yoke of iron and led them to freedom after eighty years of bloody war, we, who are aware of the precedent of that time, would sin twice as grievously as the unsuspecting people did then, as one finds no word in the New Testament to the effect that a people who have taken the Messiah as their king need a temporal king as well.

8 If one could be exonerated from this great difficulty, then one would swear to serve the temporal king in faith next to that which is owed to God.

9 The citizenry of this oppressed . . . corner of the colony . . . have to complain greatly concerning the unconsidered conduct of the honourable Mr Bresler, . . . which is no more than arbitrary tyranny and serves only to bring about discontent among those citizens who had previously been calm, hoping for improvements. This has always had the further effect, in the circumstances of the district, of provoking the citizens by any excuse, so that the citizens might be vilified by accusations of improper conduct. . . .

10 It is certain that the laws promulgated by [General Craig] are far better suited to ensuring good order in the country than are the aristocratic rulers such as De Wet and Maynier, etc., etc., and others who by their conduct are enemies of the citizens. The general Voice of the People requests that such disturbers of the peace . . . may never again be placed in any official position. . . .

As representatives of the people.

Marthinus Prinsloo	Hendrik Klopper	Jan Durand
A. H. Krugel	B. J. Bester	and ten others

6.5b I know of no representatives, and would fain wish to know what creatures those representatives were.

—Letters from F. R. Bresler to General Craig, 2 March 1796 and 26 May 1796. (From the originals in the Cape Archives, BO 68.)

When Bresler could not get the rebellious burghers of Graaff-Reinet to submit themselves to British authority he returned to Cape Town in April 1796. Throughout his stay he had been in correspondence with Craig, and on his return submitted a full report. Bresler was of course an interested party in these proceedings, but his accounts appear to be a fairly objective and perceptive summary of the discussions between himself and the spokesmen for the Graaff-Reinet burghers.

2 March 1796

. . . [The Heemraden Andries van der Walt and Schalk Burger] replied—while Capt. Van Jaarsveld entered—that the people would never allow that a meeting be held without the Representatives, and those Representatives were excluded from the direction of the letter [from Craig]. Whereupon the undersigned [i.e. Bresler] declared that they, as members of a College which ought to have previous notice of his Commission, then must not take it amiss, when he now should pass them by and lay open his Commission immediately to the community—and that he knew of no Representatives but only of Heemraden and Krygsraden—and fain would wish to know what creatures those Representatives were—that these persons were entirely unknown to him and did not exist in the other Colonies, nor ought they of course to exist here—and moreover that he was not authorized to introduce new Constitutions . . . nor could he comprehend that they did not perceive how prejudiciable this Institution of Representatives was to their character, as they, in the proper sense, ought to be considered as the true Representatives and Promoters of the general welfare, who were to assist the undersigned with their advices, in case he through ignorance of the internal situation of the country, might in some or other matter be mistaken.

The said Capt. Burger said, that he was with me of the same sentiment in that respect, but the others declared unanimously that the Representatives were chosen by Mr De Wet and that the community had approved of them for their security. Whereupon the undersigned replied that it was not well possible, that Mr De Wet should have chosen them on such a footing as they showed themselves at present, viz. to take their seats at a separate table in the meetings of the Landdrost, Heemraden and Krygsraden, and to look into all the secrecies which from time to time may come from the Chief Commander or Governor; that this only belonged to the Heemraden, for so far it may concern them, and to nobody else—that it was easy to be believed and very probable that the said Mr De Wet has chosen these Representatives only to be at that time the speakers in the name of the Multitude, as it is impossible to give ear unto 20 or 30 persons at once—that they ought not from thence [to] conclude that such Representatives were to be permanent—but that they may be chosen occasionally in order to represent in a decent manner the grievances of the Community—and that this had been the intention of Mr De Wet, so as it has appeared afterwards. Whereupon Capt. Van Jaarsveld declared that the people had already conceived a suspicion against the undersigned and did consider him as a person who intended to mislead or betray them, expressing himself with these words: 'They are raging, and say that they no longer believe any miracle, and that they already are misled and deceived sufficiently.'

26 May 1796

. . . [Capt. Van Jaarsveld intimated] that not he, the said Van Jaarsveld, but that the underwritten gave occasion of the uproar among the people—which pretence is not only by the said Van Jaarsveld but also by the other principal Instigators used as a sort of Politicks. All their wicked Actions they put to the account of another—altho' the people or the unenlightened People remain ignorant of the Proceedings of the Representatives. Everything is however done in this manner—when the Representatives in an erroneous notion are contradicted by the one or other of the Heemraden who understand the business better, then they exclaim immediately: 'The People! The general Vote of the People!' Never do they use the expressions of 'I' or 'We will it so', but always 'They, they force us, they, the silly People!' Under the name of the People they remain then at liberty to do all that they please. . . .

6.6 The conditions that prevailed in the Colony were those of decline and decay, caused by oppressive policies.

—Memoir of Egbertus Bergh, 1802. (Translated from the text *Memorie over de Kaap de Goede Hoop*, in Theal, *Belangrijke Historische Dokumenten*, Vol. 3.)

Egbertus Bergh's Lutheran affiliations may have contributed to his critical views of Company rule at the Cape. Until late in the eighteenth century Lutherans had suffered some discrimination in the political and social life at the Cape. Church and school were rigidly controlled by the state, while the Dutch Reformed clergy avidly protected their pre-eminence in spiritual matters. A further extract from his memoir appears as document 5.1.

Before the surrender to the British, the following conditions prevailed in the Colony:

In general, there was decline and decay, caused by the oppressive policies of the Dutch East India Company, which did not allow the population to increase in accordance with what was required for the proper cultivation of the land, nor the inhabitants to dispose freely of the fruits of their labour, much less to enjoy all the benefits which could have been gained from the bountiful land on which they lived.

The reins of government were in incompetent hands. A supreme commander, who knew neither the land nor its inhabitants, who was domineering, base and false as well, had as members of his council either men who were, for the most part, intriguing and self-interested and were always sacrificing public welfare to their individual interests, or ignorant, weak men who, aware of the superficiality of their knowledge, did not have sufficient firmness to maintain their standing and make a proper contribution to the furtherance of the common good. The number of meritorious men was, at the same time, too small for them to put a stop to this mischief with any vigour.

The administration of justice was equally deficient. Even if there was some capable member [of the court], yet ignorance, bias and passion sat in judgement, under the chairmanship of malice incarnate, so that blatant injustice was promoted and the innocent were oppressed.

The citizens saw the furtherance of their interests delegated to men who had not their affection, nor their respect, nor yet their trust, and these people became their representatives not through free elections but by the direct appointment of the Governor. As his dependants, he could often use them as instruments of injustice, and supports for illegitimate authority or abuses of power. Thus they were, curiously, more often called the persecutors and oppressors of the citizenry than their champions. . . .

. . . Rank disparity prevailed in the payment of the civil servants. A few could put a little aside, others had an adequate income to survive, yet by far the most, including the most industrious class, were not paid half as much as was required for a frugal subsistence.

Religious intolerance, in a place where one might come across almost all the religions in the world, was, as already stated, so highly exaggerated that fairness, sound policy and the interests of the Colony, as well as those of the metropolis [*majores*], were offered up to it. After half a century of pleading, the Lutherans had indeed gained the freedom to practise their religion, but this honey was mixed with gall by providing in addition that members of these churches could no longer be promoted to the ranks of highest status. The lot of the Roman Catholics was even less pleasant. Excluded from all church services [of the Reformed Church], they were not allowed to have any church or building in which to pay homage to the Supreme Being. And as far as the Orientals were concerned, who professed the Mohammedan faith, they were watched with such scrutiny that I often saw them being violently dispersed by the officers of the law, acting on orders from above, when they were honouring their God in their customary way or burying their dead, far from the city or in the mountains without causing annoyance or giving any offence.

Because of these stipulations in regard to matters of religion, many very capable men often had to make way for the less capable in official positions for which they possessed all the necessary qualifications, solely because they did not belong to the dominant church.

The arrogance and pride of churchmen had reached such a point of shamelessness that any reasonable person had to be incensed by it. I know of cases in which they have rudely entered the houses of private individuals where children were being taught foreign languages and other sciences by private tutors, in order to make completely unauthorized surprise investigations as to whether anything concerning religion was being taught as well. They also constantly interfere, on all sorts of pretexts, in matters which concern the political authorities alone. But just as they were overly zealous in maintaining their deleterious influence, which had been usurped from the temporal powers, through one means or another, so, on the other hand, were they completely indifferent to other matters which they have also claimed as their own preserve, although these concern all denominations, and even the whole public. This is demonstrated by what has already been said of the condition of complete stagnation in which the public school remains, while it is in their control, [although this school] was intended to provide improved education for the youth. This is made no less clear by their conduct as superintendents of the public library which, although it consists of thousands of volumes in all languages and on all subjects, has contributed absolutely nothing, in the half-century during which it has fallen under their administration, to the amusement, benefit or enlightenment of the public.

The military defences, as has already been indicated, were in themselves good, but the cowardice, the untrustworthiness and the treachery of the leaders, taken together with the lack of necessary policy and ability among the lesser officers, brought about a basic fear and suspicion that all these means of defence would prove inadequate.

No wonder then that at the coming of the English there was general discontent among all classes of the inhabitants, contempt for the government, scorn and distrust of the law and a hearty desire for deliverance. In these circumstances, one would have expected the inhabitants, on receiving a call to arms, to show an immediate inclination to have the Colony surrendered, rather than that they would be prepared to help defend it.

That they did actually achieve sufficient unanimity to decide on the latter course, in spite of their grievances against the Dutch government, when it became known that the enemy threatening them was English and not French, makes it clear that they were even less well-disposed towards the liberties and privileges offered by this nation than they were towards the burdensome rule of the Dutch East India Company. Consequently, if proper use had been made of the means available and of those who came to volunteer their services, then considering the negligible extent of the enemy's forces, the attack could well have been repelled, and the English compelled, if not to surrender, at least to take to their ships again and leave the Colony. But this was not the plan nor intention of the supreme Commander or the head of the armed forces and their clique, to whom large rewards were offered if they facilitated surrender. And thus it was contrived that the Cape should come into the hands of the English, which is what took place.

6.7 It is necessary that colonists enjoy the same rights of citizenship, the same laws, institutions and privileges as the citizens of the mother city.

—Christoffel Brand, 'Concerning the bonds of law between the mother city and the colony', 1820. (Translated from the Latin text of *Dissertatio Politica-Juridica de Jure Coloniarum*, Leyden, 1820.)

Christoffel Brand's thesis presented at the university of Leyden in 1820 dealt with the rights of colonies. Colonel C. C. Bird, the Cape Colonial Secretary, was perturbed about the political implications of Brand's arguments for colonial citizenship rights. However the fact that Brand's dissertation had been written in Latin persuaded him that it was unlikely to have much popular influence.

It now remains to say a few words about the bond and the rights which should exist between a colony and the mother city. With almost every ancient nation a paternal and filial relation united the two, in an honourable manner. Some, however, such as the Carthaginians, repudiated all paternal ties and kept their colonies in subjection by force and military might, which was a most shameful procedure. Yet as the colonists and the citizens of the mother city are descended from the same tribe and people, use the same language and are formed by the same customs, it is necessary that they enjoy the same rights of citizenship, the same laws, institutions and privileges. And this should be done, as was justly asserted by Plato, so that the colony should be one people with the mother city, speaking the same language and enjoying the same rights, but divided, as it were, into two cities.

Colonists, moreover, do not emigrate so that they can be slaves and serve the whims of the mother city, but in order to live a free and happy life. How beautifully this reasoning is presented in the speech of the ambassadors to Epidaurus in which they said that 'Colonists emigrate not to be slaves but to enjoy the same rights as those whom they have left behind. And it is well-known that when a colony is well-treated it honours the mother city, but when they are unjustly treated they are altogether alienated from it.' Being myself a colonist and glorying in that name taken from the African Cape where I was born, it is with the greatest assurance, relying upon history and schooled through experience of her, that I contend that 'the colony should have its own legislative power'. For even the Phoenicians and the Greek colonists defended this view (and we shall say more of this later). And now too North America, having achieved its independence, is of greater benefit to Great Britain than it was when it was still technically a colony.

We do not propose, however, that this legislative power should make the colony altogether free of the mother country. For although boys leave their parents' homes, their parents nevertheless retain a measure of authority over them. Therefore the mother country should have some authority in the administration of the colony. And this authority should be based on a sort of equality of powers arising from the natural bond between them. Therefore, such authority does not entitle the mother country to prohibit the colonists from instructing their children in the arts and sciences, or to order the colonists to burn their crops and not replant them on penalty of death. Nor should we hear quarrelsome individuals screaming furiously (as has happened previously) that 'the mother country has ordered that the land of the colony may not be cultivated nor may industry be practised, lest the colonists become wealthy and strong and free'. (These were the words of a certain official of the East India Company, which he proclaimed in my fatherland. One can see how humane and upright his civil and judicial administration was by reading and comparing the complaints which the inhabitants of the Cape made to the Chamber of Seventeen through their ambassadors, showing that his administration had been arbitrary, tyrannical and oppressive. How justly he was accused of tyranny when he had ordered a citizen of the colony, who was entitled to full rights of citizenship and had committed no crime at all, to be seized without a charge being made, dragged from his house, and had expelled him from the fatherland on his own responsibility! The victim's cries that 'I am a citizen of the Cape' availed him nothing. Yet whatever the case may be, we have two letters which the Chamber of Seventeen wrote to the officials in my fatherland. Here they wrote, if I may quote this much, 'We have conducted a thorough investigation in special session of your domestic administration, but we have found it to be so corrupt and dishonest and to contain such unbridled wantonness, that it could not but invite our disgust and arouse our indignation.' Thus the Chamber of Seventeen. But enough of this. I beg pardon for having said so much on the topic; yet I am a citizen for whom allowance might be made for being expansive in the defence of his fatherland and in freeing it from calumnies.) This speech would be appropriate in a place oppressed by force of arms, but in a freely administered colony, if someone should utter these words, everyone would shout in loud unison: 'Away, Oh away with you blasphemers,' or 'Having seen this, my friends, can you contain your laughter?'

6.8a A public election of the members of the Burgher Senate would tend to constitute mutual confidence and would co-operate to amalgamate the British subjects and the Cape inhabitants.

—Petition from citizens of Cape Town to Lieutenant-Governor Richard Bourke, 15 July 1826. (From the text published in V. Harlow and F. Madden, *British Colonial Developments, 1774–1834: Select Documents*, pp. 114–115. The original is in the Cape Archives, C.O. 48/82.)

The institution of burgher councillors stemmed from the early days of Company rule at the Cape. As the Burgher Senate it continued to function under the British administration, combining a limited representative role with aspects of the municipal administration of Cape Town. Increasingly the Burgher Senate did not satisfy the needs and aspirations of the colonists, and particularly from the mid 1820s they began to press for more local representation and control in the colonial government.

The Burgher Senate refused to publish the Slave Ordinance of 1826, and when they were put under pressure by Lieutenant-Governor Bourke three of its members resigned. Their resignation prompted the following petition, signed by 242 citizens, for the future election of Burgher senators.

May it please your Honour in Council, we the undersigned citizens and freeholders of Cape Town,

Having been informed that by the resignation of the President and some members of the Burgher Senate all the seats except one have become vacant in the said Burgher Senate,

And considering that a public election of the members of the Burgher Senate from amongst and by the freeholders and citizens of this town would tend to constitute mutual confidence between the Burgher Senate and the citizens,

That it would, far more than any other means as yet resorted to, co-operate to amalgamate His Majesty's natural born subjects and the Cape inhabitants when both meeting as brothers of one community, and electing from amongst both, will have the same common interest and one common object in view, viz. the welfare of both,

And also considering that in all other colonies under the dominion of Great Britain the inhabitants and citizens are duly represented by a body of men elected by the public, without any such body existing in this colony,

We therefore humbly beg that it may please your Honour in Council to grant us and other freeholders, citizens of this town, the privilege to appear on a certain requisition at the Town House, and there publicly to elect by majority of votes such person or persons, being freeholders and citizens, as we may think fit and qualified to be our representatives in the town administration.

6.8b Consider from how many evils and grievances we would have been freed had a legislative representative body existed in this Colony.

—Editorials in *De Zuid-Afrikaan*, 1831. (From the translations published in the *Zuid-Afrikaan*, 20 May 1831 and 3 June 1831.)

6.8 Cape writings on the need for representative government 1826–32

Whereas the Nineteenth Ordinance of 1826, which sought to bring about the amelioration of slavery, had aroused the indignation and fears of colonists (see 3.10; 2.8a, b), the imposition of the Trinidad Ordinance on the Cape in 1831 sparked even sharper opposition among slaveholders in the Western Cape. An organized campaign of civil disobedience was mounted against the provision to submit punishment record books to the Protector of the Slaves. A number of protest meetings were held, and the newly founded newspaper De Zuid-Afrikaan *championed the cause of the slave-owners. A common theme in the speeches and editorials was the need for representative government which would prevent such imperial interference in the affairs of the colonists.*

20 May 1831

. . . Consider from how many evils and grievances we would have been freed had a *Legislative Representative Body* existed in this Colony, through which we should at least have had an opportunity of making timely remonstrances *before* a law was made or promulgated. When we consider that such a Representative Body is composed of men, elected by the people, without whose consent no law can be made, or taxes be imposed—which jointly with the Governor and his Council administers the affairs of the Colony, and through whom the people have not alone the opportunity of acquainting the Government in a legal way with their interest and the prosperity of the country, but who also, for some part, have the power of making the necessary provisions themselves. There can hardly exist a doubt but that through such a Representative Body we would have had an opportunity of timely preventing the evil, or of diminishing its effects. Why then should we not all join in a prayer to His Majesty for a *Charter* constituting such a Legislative Representative Body, similar to that which exists in the West Indian Colonies, Canada and Jamaica? Why should we not, as British subjects, enjoy the same privileges as the other British Colonies?

No, this we may not expect from the *free, enlightened*, and *liberal* British nation; we should rather presume that the nation itself will go hand in hand with us to obtain for us that privilege which every Englishman considers his *birth-right*, namely to tax himself and to make his own laws. Yes, we may feel convinced of this, more particularly when the English nation shall have gone through the calendar of our grievances.

Has not the *Burgher Senate*, that body which has existed ever since the foundation of the Colony, been abolished, and the whole administration of the town been placed in the hands of a stranger, who had just arrived in the Colony, and who, consequently, could have no local knowledge? Has not the *Board of Landdrost and Heemraden*, that Body so useful and important for the wants of the Farmers, been abolished and annulled in the same way? And what have we obtained in its place? A *Council*. True, but what are the rights of its members? This is a secret to us; we only know that, notwithstanding the majority of the Council refused the adoption of a certain article requesting the disposal of the *Private Fund of the Orphan Chamber*, that article became a law! What good, therefore, can such a council do? It is only a *Legislative Representative Body* to which the inhabitants must look for bettering the state of the affairs of this Colony.

Had such a body existed, the law giving to a *solitary Magistrate* the power of inflicting *75 lashes*, upon the body of a Burgher, without any appeal, would probably not have passed; the *Public Library*, procured from the tax paid by the Wine-farmers for every leaguer of wine, would not now be under the direction and for the particular use *exclusively* of some individuals who have at first joined in a *Circulating Library*; the *Town House*, that old civic building, created out of the private purses of the Burghers, and by their subscription, and the so called *granary*, etc., etc., would, probably, have been used differently; the *Bible and School Commission* would now, probably, be constituted upon a more equitable footing, and a more national use [would have] been made of the funds for the extension of education and enlightening. The *Latin School fund*, raised by the Dutch inhabitants in 1792, for the erection of a Latin and French seminary, would probably long ago, but more particularly now, have been used in compliance with the original object. The inhabitants of Albany would probably already have the *Municipal Body* for which they so earnestly applied, and which, if anywhere, is so essentially useful and necessary in such a remote district. Probably, when the Hottentots were exempted from civic duties, the farmers would have been freed also from the obligation of giving voorspan, of carrying mails etc., etc., under which they are still suffering; the praiseworthy and truly parental endeavours of our Governor for the amelioration of the roads, etc., would not have been thwarted, but would rather have been supported upon a more extended scale; our *representations to the Government at home* would probably have had more influence, as those about the duties on Cape wines, Cape spirits, etc., etc; while from the recent papers we find that, notwithstanding our having during the last two years forwarded Petitions one after the other for diminishing those duties, that it was proposed by the Chancellor of the Exchequer to add to the amount of duties. . . .

The proposed measure, we presume, must only be ascribed to an entire ignorance of our local and Colonial circumstances. Our representations to Government would probably have occasioned that we had also jointly with the other English colonies been allowed to trade with North America, and that we had consequently been included in the recent Commercial Treaty. We would then, having the direction of our finances, no longer go back under the pressure of taxes, which now more than ever may truly be said to earn in the 'Sweat of our face'. . . .

May it therefore please His Majesty, upon our repeated prayers, to grant us a Charter for that object: we will then have an opportunity not only to redress the evils that have already occurred, or to lessen their effects, but we will also be liable for the future to make such regulations, and to adopt such measures, which will occasion prosperity, peace, and happiness to re-occupy their seats in our habitations, agriculture and commerce to raise their heads, education and enlightening to extend themselves more widely, and will increase the fidelity and attachment of the inhabitants to the British nation more than ever, while amalgamation and fraternization will proceed with gigantic steps. . . .

3 June 1831

. . . A Legislative Representative Body will soon put things to right, of which the public will now again see the imperative necessity.

If we had a Legislative Representative Body in this Colony we would not hear so much complained of the state of freedom which the Convicts enjoy, and the comfortable life which they lead. What punishment does the slave or Hottentot undergo, when, as a convict, he can lead such a life, and enjoy the pleasing effects of liquors? . . .

Has it been considered already what will be the effect, detrimental to the peace and safety of the Inhabitants, if the convicts, who by law have been declared to be bad men, are allowed to enjoy such a degree of Liberty? We have already, frequently through our paper, called the attention of the proper quarters to this subject, and we have even in this town not yet seen any good results therefrom. What, therefore, can assist or help us? A Legislative Representative Body! Let us, then, continually pray His Majesty for it, until we obtain it.

6.8c We are not ripe and not amalgamated because we are without a free assembly where the people could meet and soon understand each other's interests.

—Speech by H. Cloete at a public meeting in Cape Town, July 1831. (From the report published in the *South African Commercial Advertiser*, 20 July 1831.)

The Burgher Senate was abolished in 1827 on the recommendation of the Commissioners of Inquiry, Bigge and Coalbrooke, as was the other main representative institution, the boards of landdrost and heemraden. In their places, two burghers were appointed on the Advisory Council, but they were retired officials and appointed from London. In the minds of the imperial authorities, such as the Colonial Secretary Sir George Murray, major considerations counting against the granting of representative government was the fact that the Cape was still a slave colony and the danger of ethnic conflict between the two white groups. Hendrik Cloete (1792–1870) came from one of the wealthiest and best-known families at the Cape, which was also among the first to become anglicized.

Mr Cloete said that the Colony had in fact retrograded, instead of having advanced. Under the Dutch Government, the Council controlled public affairs. In prosecutions, civil and criminal, the Court of Justice was assisted by two Burghers, who acted as a Jury for the accused. The Burgher Senate was appointed as a check upon the Government. The Board of Heemraden was chosen from among the people; and the influence of the Principle which it recognized spread to the furthest extremities of these shores. This germ of political freedom ceased in 1806, at the Capture. The Council was abolished; the Governor became pre-eminent and making the President of the Burgher Senate a Stipendiary Magistrate completely destroyed the independence of that body. Government from that time had swallowed up everything: the Judicial, Commercial, and Religious branches of the country were all in their control. This naturally excited disgust. It was a dreadful spectacle, but a true one. . . .

He stated frankly that he did not accuse the persons, but the System: with their almost omnipotent power, it was miraculous that so much good had been done. . . .

In 1815 we all became British Subjects, and matters were a little different. Our complaints could no longer be stifled; and at length Commissioners of Inquiry were sent here to investigate. But their labours appeared so dilatory or unsatisfactory that Government found it necessary to do something to appease us: and a Council was appointed; but he must confess that, after a careful inquiry, the only fact we knew respecting this body was that His Majesty declared they were 'all honorable men'. (Hear! and laughter.) The Public, he repeated, knew nothing more of their competency or jurisdiction.

Now he had reason to believe that not one iota of power had been given to the Council. . . . The members, it was true, were 'all honorable men': but then, unfortunately for themselves and the country, they were mere pageants in the Show of State: or rather, to use a more lofty illustration, they more resembled well-trained Race-horses, that were brought out in their fine trappings to exhibit their paces at the will and pleasure of their lord, and then led back again. He expressed himself thus boldly, because he felt assured that all those gentlemen must feel with him and the Meeting. Most of them were Colonists, and ready—nay anxious—to promote the welfare of their country, but they lacked the power or liberty to do so.

. . . Still the cry is, 'You are not ripe.' It is said there is not yet a sufficient amalgamation of the several Classes, and that a Representative Assembly would be productive of only discord and anarchy. At this time of day he was surprised and disgusted with such shallow subterfuges. Not ripe! And not amalgamated together! Why, in sooth? He would tell these objectors: because we are without a Free Assembly, where the people would meet, and soon understand each other's interests. The Colonists should be cautioned; these objections came from the Advocates of the System so long and banefully followed here: 'Divide et impera.'

The Cape Dutch were essentially English. Their habits, their intermarriage, their general improvements, all exhibit and prove this fact. And it was rank folly to consider their interests as disunited. Was there an Englishman present who would not feel ashamed of not competing with a Dutchman? In short, nobody now-a-days could be misled by such objections. . . .

But another objection had been alleged. The possession of Slave Property was said to stand in the way of our obtaining a Legislative Assembly. Was it objected to Washington, when he became President of the United States of America, that he was a large Slave Proprietor; indeed it was, he believed, an historical fact that he was a very severe master.

Were not the Members of Congress chosen indiscriminately from among the people, without their possession of Slaves being any bar? Had any discord on this head arisen in America? It was, he said, a triumphant answer to the objection. But what if it were a good objection? He was proud of being one of those who had voluntarily come forward, to lay the cornerstone of the Liberty of the Colony, by proposing to the British Government to emancipate all Female Slave Children from the moment a Representative form of Government should be extended to this Colony.

As to the last shift—of their not being 'ripe'. He did not speak of himself: but he did venture to opine that in this Colony some thirty or forty good sound heads could be found to administer our affairs. If it were wished for a Canning or a Brougham, or some 'Heaven-born Minister' to arise, who shall say that there are not such men among us; but they are not called forth. . . .

6.8d The only remedy for our present political malady is a Legislative Assembly.

—Editorial in *De Zuid-Afrikaan*, 22 June 1832. (From the translation published in *De Zuid-Afrikaan*.)

The Cape was granted freedom of the press in 1827, but this was not at first accompanied by freedom of assembly. Permission to hold public meetings had to be obtained from the governor. A revised and even more stringent Order in Council with further slave regulations issued in November 1831 caused a renewed public outcry. De Zuid-Afrikaan *wrote threateningly of 'the rights of Dutch burghers and the length of Boer rifles' on 25 May 1832, and its stand was applauded at a meeting of farmers in Koeberg. The governor, Sir Lowry Cole, reacted by issuing an ordinance in June 1832 tightening the restrictions on public meetings even further, and a proclamation threatening banishment for agitators. The ordinance occasioned the following editorial in* De Zuid-Afrikaan.

Our Readers will have read the Ordinance respecting *meetings*, together with the Proclamation of the Governor in our former Number. It will be seen that any meeting (without the approbation of the Governor, or, in the remoter Districts, without a written consent of the Civil Commissioners) is forbidden to be held for the purpose of passing any resolution, or considering any petition to His Majesty's government, under a penalty of imprisonment of from four to twelve months; and that any person publishing any report or proceedings of such a meeting, *or which are said to be of such a meeting*, shall be punished in like manner. While the Governor, by Proclamation, has made known that He will remove or send out of the Colony any person who to Him shall seem dangerous for the peace of the Colony.

We are sorry that so severe a measure should have been taken, which must tend to frustrate the Colonists in representing their grievances freely and uncontrolled; while the power of removing from the Colony is one beyond that which the King of England himself has over his subjects. We remember when Lord Castlereagh proposed his famous *Alien Bill*, granting the power to Ministers to remove any *alien* or *foreigner* who should to them appear dangerous to the peace of the empire, a very great number of Members of the House of Commons and Lords objected to place such an uncontrolled power in the hands of Ministers. We know not by whom that power was given to the Governor, but we must deeply regret that it should have been given over any of His Majesty's subjects, or Burghers of the Colony, to one single individual, who, however high he may stand in respectability and justness of character, may be subject to the impulse of any human passion, and fall the victim of any private influence or misrepresentation, by which frequently acts of the grossest injustice have been committed.

We need not refer to the history of other nations; our own affords sufficient proof. Who does not remember the case of Mr Buitendag, who was removed from the Colony by a similar power, about 1770, because he did not with proper speed and haste (as it was by the mighty of the day considered) attend at the office of the independent Fiscal Mr Boers. We have only to name the days of Fiscal Boers and Governor Van der Stel to call to our recollection more than one act of a similar nature, and to know what such power means. That immense power was at that time given by a Company of Merchants, Jan Compagnie, who paid more regard to their speculations, interest, and commerce, and their consequent profit and loss, than to the welfare of the people; but surely we are not prepared at this time, while England stands pre-eminent for liberal and free institutions, where tyranny and absolute power lies prostrate at the footstool of civil liberty, to see the same extraordinary power placed in the hands of one single individual. What is good law in Turkey is not always good law in a civilized country.

In how far, however, the Supreme Court, the present and indeed only, we say so advisedly, the only bulwark of our civil liberty, and protector or our rights, will allow such a power of removing without trial, and on the arbitrary opinion of one man, to be executed against any one of His Majesty's subjects in this Colony; or in how far they will protect them by the Habeas Corpus law, remains to be seen. It will be for them to consider and decide in how far that extraordinary power has been conferred by the Legislature, or in how far any instruction can have the effect or force of a law. We are, however, convinced that our confidence in the Supreme Court for the protection of our rights and liberties is just and well founded.

Our astonishment is further increased by finding from the Ordinance that we are forbidden to hold any meetings for the purpose of considering about petitioning even Parliament on the subject of a law already existing, or even about to be made, without the previous sanction or approbation of the Governor. . . .

Our countrymen will therefore see that the only remedy for our present political malady is a Legislative Assembly, in which we may be sure that every law which may be considered to infringe upon our rights and liberties will be maturely weighed, and which will be a control to absolute power and to absolute sway. We cannot therefore refrain from again recommending our fellow Colonists to Memorial the Governor for permission to hold a Meeting, in order to petition Parliament for a Legislative Assembly, not as a boon, but as something which is due to us by right, which had since the establishment of the Colony existed in another shape but which was abolished without any cause in 1828.

6.8e A representative legislative body is alone capable of issuing such laws for this settlement in such a way as to ensure the peace and welfare of this settlement.

—Speech by Christoffel Brand at a protest meeting of slaveholders, 17 Sept. 1832. (Translated from the report published in *Verslag der gehoudene bijeenkomst*, South African Bound Pamphlets, S.A. Library, Cape Town.)

Despite the official efforts to discourage the holding of public meetings, a large meeting of slaveholders, attended by almost two thousand persons, took place on 17 Sept. 1832. Speakers included Christoffel Brand, editor of De Zuid-Afrikaan, *and a motion calling for representative government was proposed by A. J. Louw, one of the wealthiest farmers in the Western Cape.*

. . . A recently promulgated order from the King in Council has brought us together here; an order which was drawn up by people to whom the interests and needs of this Colony are unknown. Has this been done so as to promote simultaneously the interests of master and slave? Or to strengthen the ties of love and solidarity between them? Or to improve the slave, or grant him his freedom? No, my friends! If this should be your impression, you are misled. . . .

. . . It paves the way by which our property, the slaves, [bought] with the pounds of the slave-owners, will be taken away from us. The question, then, my friends, is whether we shall now be silent, and take the yoke upon our necks that we can neither carry nor tolerate? Can we be silent when laws are imposed upon us which, contrary to all fundamental principles of social obligation, force us to become our own accusers, and to act as witnesses against ourselves? Can we be silent when the safety of our property and our dwellings is destroyed, when the security of our peace and the safety of our lives are made uncertain, and when we stand exposed by night and day, so that we might be maliciously and arbitrarily imposed upon in our own homes (which the law calls our inviolable sanctuaries) by Protectors and Assistant Protectors? Can we be silent when we foresee, as a result of all this, through this diabolical proposal, how we unfortunate slave-owners are exposed to the murdering steel of our household? Are these the laws which must guard and care for our peace and security? Better to have no laws than these; they do not exist in Great Britain! It is not even countenanced in Turkey, where tyranny and cruelty have taken up the place of right and justice!

Mr A. J. Louw of Koeberg then moved the following resolution, which was seconded by Advocate Brand, Mr Cloete and Mr De Wet:

That this public meeting is convinced, and take this Order of the King in Council as clear proof of this, that it is impossible for His Majesty's Ministers to issue any laws or regulations concerning our possessions.

That this meeting is convinced that a representative Legislative body is alone capable of issuing such laws for this settlement in such a way as to ensure the peace and welfare of this settlement, and that the owners of slaves here, in this case, would co-operate to fulfil the intention and desire of the Government to improve the conditions of slavery and eventually to bring it to an end.

Advocate Brand said: We hear continual talk of the improvement of the [conditions of the] slave-class, but of no improvements for ourselves. We are driven into the chains of slavery, and our slaves become free. There is no answer to our questions, no decision is taken in our favour; and when we do get answers, these only make a mockery of us. . . .

The [?existence of a] slave-class keeps us from attaining this goal [of representative government]. Our intention is to reduce the occurrence of slavery—this is what the Afrikaners want—and should we be given a Legislative body, this will have the desired results. Eventually, my friends, who is there who would not like to see all men free? But the slaves are our property and whoever takes our property from us takes from us our lives. Expropriation of property destroys the fabric of society, and we do not want to depart from a principle which is, in itself, a wrong one. The owners of slaves pay attention to the interests of themselves, as well as the interests of the slaves, and who, my friends, would not like to make his contribution to the slave-class? Where is that stranger who dares to say otherwise? Who does not want an end put to slavery? Which man who is knowledgeable and capable does not want this?

6.9a Those chosen as leaders and the common people who make up the volk have solemnly subjected themselves under oath.

—Resolutions adopted at the meeting of the Trekker leaders, including A. H. Potgieter and G. Maritz, Thaba Nchu, 2 Dec. 1836. (Translated from the text published in H. S. Pretorius *et al., Voortrekker-Argiefstukke.)*

At a combined meeting of Trekkers from the first main Trek parties at Thaba Nchu on 2 December 1836, a governing body of seven members was chosen by secret vote. Maritz was elected as civilian 'president' and Potgieter as military commander. The governing body was to act at once as judiciary, legislature and council of war, though subject to the decisions of general meetings of the assembled people.

On this day, the 2nd December 1836, a general meeting was held, with the intention of choosing judges by the general voice of the people, who will be responsible for the general good and for guarding the peace, and who will at the same time constitute a legislative body. . . . Those chosen by all the undersigned to form a government will at all times adhere carefully to such laws and regulations as might be made by a general assembly.

For this purpose their Honours have solemnly subjected themselves under oath to the promise to administer and promote nothing but the purest form of justice, impartially and to the best of their abilities. This standard of justice must be applied both in civil and in criminal cases, and also in all other matters concerning warfare. At the same time, the common people who make up the *volk* also promised under oath to subject themselves loyally and peacefully to the judgements and orders of the aforementioned leaders. . . .

6.9b All judges and officers who have been elected by the voice of the people will be honoured and obeyed on pain of punishment.

—Resolutions adopted by Trekkers under P. Retief, Vet River, 6 June 1837. (Translated and edited from a copy in the Voortrekker Museum, Pietermaritzburg, and the translation published in the *South African Commercial Advertiser, 29 July 1837.* The text published in *Voortrekker-Argiefstukke* is obscure and problematic.)

Piet Retief was the senior of the other main Trek leaders and had attained consider-

able prominence as commandant on the eastern frontier. When he joined the earlier parties beyond the Orange he was unanimously elected as 'Governor' of the Trekkers at a popular meeting on 17 April 1837. At a further general meeting the following nine resolutions were presented to him in order that with his approbation they might be adopted by the meeting. It is possible that the resolutions had their origin outside the elected representatives; they were presented in the name of the 'voice of the people'.

To the Honourable Mr P. Retief, Supreme Commander of our united community and of these laagers.

Honourable Sir, Your Honour's memorialists respectfully request that these nine resolutions, which we have subscribed with our own hands, may, with Your Honour's approbation, be sanctioned by the meeting of today. . . .

The following resolutions are to be obeyed and observed by the whole council of the community of these united laagers, and confirmed by solemn oath.

1 We, as members of the Reformed congregation, want each and every member of this party, without any exceptions, to sever all ties with England and publicly to repudiate any further such ties.

2 That all judges and officers who have been elected or appointed to either spiritual or temporal office by the voice of the people, and all others occupying any official position, will be honoured and obeyed while exercising their offices, on pain of punishment as decreed by the governor and council.

3 That all who resist these resolutions will have to be expelled from the community of these united laagers.

4 Further, that no person opposing these enacted resolutions will be allowed to settle within the boundaries of the land which these united laagers intends to occupy or to hunt or do anything else there, on pain of such punishment as will be determined.

5 Further, that those who could not attend the meeting held today must be present tomorrow so that they can confirm these resolutions by oath.

6 All those who neglect to do this without giving any reason will be considered as having voted against the resolutions, unless he is able to prove that he was prevented from doing so by sickness or other circumstances.

7 And further, that those who separate themselves from these united laagers must be content to bear the losses they may thus sustain through their unlawful conduct, according to our laws.

8 And that those who do not subject themselves to the first and second resolutions will not be entitled to share in any cattle, wagons, etc. which may be retaken, or to enjoy any advantages which may be gained by the next commando which will be taken against Maselekatze.

9 And further, that all persons who follow our united laagers in order to join our community will immediately have to take the prescribed oaths, and those who wish to separate themselves from us will be compelled, within twice twenty-four hours, to pay all their debts or their property will be sequestrated and sold so that these debts and other expenses can be paid.

6.9c We propose to establish our settlement on the same principles of liberty as those adopted by the United States of America.

—Resolutions adopted by the party of emigrants under the leadership of P. L. Uys, 14 Aug. 1837. (Translated from the text published in *De Zuid-Afrikaan*, 27 Oct. 1837).

Piet Uys (1798—1838) had been the leader of a scouting expedition to Natal in 1834 in advance of the Trek. He was an individualist, and even before the Uys trek joined the Voortrekkers under Retief and Maritz in the present Orange Free State in the latter half of 1837, Uys indicated that he was not prepared to accept the resolutions of June 6. His relations with his fellow Trekker leaders continued to be marked by rivalry, and it was only at the beginning of 1838 that Uys agreed to take the oath of allegiance as formulated at Sand river.

Resolutions adopted by us, the undersigned travellers and emigrants from the Colony of the Cape of Good Hope. . . .

3 . . . We have placed ourselves under the leadership of certain chiefs, acting as our field commandants and our protectors, who must investigate and redress all grievances which may arise during our journey.

4 We place our trust in the All-wise ruler of heaven and earth, and are resolved to adhere to the sure foundation of our reformed Christian faith, in the hope that we shall live better and safer lives when we reach the place of our destination.

5 As regards the establishment and administration of the judicial authority which is exercised by some of our compatriots, we declare unanimously that we disapprove of it entirely. While in this wild country, we shall conduct ourselves solely in accordance with the old burgher-regulations and the duties they impose, and all disputes which might arise among us will be settled in accordance with these regulations.

6 We have resolved once for all not to submit to any laws which might have been enacted by a few individuals, and which we regard as having the effect of changing our state of exile into a state of slavery.

7 When once we have attained our object, and have arrived at our place of destination, we hope to have all our countrymen assembled together, and then to hold an election of our leaders by general vote, and to proceed with the framing of proper laws and the consideration, in general, of what will benefit both the country and the people.

8 The judicial appointment and the enactment of laws, as these exist at present, will not be recognized at all by us, but will be regarded as null and void.

9 We trust that all will share these sentiments, in order to achieve the condition of free citizens.

10 We propose to establish our settlement on the same principles of liberty as those adopted by the United States of America, carrying into effect, as far as practicable, our burgher laws. . . .

6.9d Fraternity and equality will prevail here among us, and the voice of the people will be the supreme power and government.

—Letter from G. Maritz to the Voortrekkers travelling to Port Natal, 1 Feb. 1838. (Translated from the text published in *Ons Tijdschrift,* 1898—1899, p. 118.)

There was considerable bickering among the rival leaders of the Trek, none of whom was keen to submit to the authority of others. They differed on a number of issues, such as whether Natal should be preferred as area of settlement, whether Erasmus Smit should be recognized as religious minister to the Trekkers, etc. Maritz had been elected with Retief as member of the governing body in April 1837 (when Potgieter was overlooked), but there are indications that shortly after the resolutions of June 6 were adopted he disagreed with Retief on the taking of these oaths of allegiance.

It is not clear whether he merely held that he, as the 'magistrate', rather than Retief should conduct the taking of the oaths, or whether he objected to the autocratic powers granted to Retief in the resolutions. Maritz distributed the following critical letter in Natal when Retief had left on his mission to Dingane.

My worthy men, I consider it my duty to bring [this matter] to your attention, and to advice all of you no longer to take any oaths which Mr P. Retief might demand of you, as it is not his duty, but that of a judge, to administer oaths.

The oath which the aforementioned Mr Retief administered to the people at the Vet River is an improper oath. And it has become completely apparent from his conduct and actions that, on the basis of this oath, he has appropriated for himself unprecedented power and dominion, and it is certain that if we were to subject ourselves to his rule and power, we can never become a happy people. Therefore, my worthy men, watch and pray, so that you are not led into temptation. For if you do not do this, we shall soon all end up in the same miserable condition which obliged us to leave the land of our birth.

Pride was the first sin that spoiled men and made them unhappy. Yes, it is still each day the root of all evil. I tell you: watch and pray! Greed and self-interest perverts what is right—this God's word teaches us, as does experience. So my worthy men, be on your guard! The overbearing power of the authorities drove us from our fatherland, and therefore I shall never allow such dominion to be gained over us. Instead, fraternity and equality will prevail here among us. The judges among us who will govern from time to time will only have to ensure that the strongest man will not lord it over the weak. And for the rest the voice of the people will be the supreme power and government. Thus I expect that you will set about appointing an assembly of the people without delay so as to prevent any disorder and confusion, and so to remove the grounds for my objections. . . .

6.10a The grievances which have caused the majority of emigrants to quit are distrust in the government and insecurity of life and property.

—Letter from J. Boshof published in *The Grahamstown Journal*, 17 Feb. 1839. (From the translation published in Bird, *The Annals of Natal*, Vol. I, pp. 504–513.)

This is a further extract from Boshof's summary of the Trekkers' grievances, based on his visit to Natal in 1838, which appeared in The Grahamstown Journal *early in 1839. The previous extract appeared as Document 3.14.*

. . . The various grievances which I know to have caused the majority of the emigrants to quit may be classed under the following main causes:

I. Distrust in the Colonial, but more particularly the Home, Government; and under this head may be enumerated:

1 The reduction of the value of colonial currency; and though this has not been felt by the farmers, yet the impression remained that Government, acting faithlessly, in an arbitrary mannner seized upon part of our property, which in justice ought not to have been done.

2 The emancipation of the slaves, or, rather, the manner in which it has been effected. . . . The amount awarded to each proprietor was not in consideration of the individual value of his slaves, but indiscriminately according to certain general classifications. . . . The greater part of the slave owners saw themselves declared

entitled to no more than a third or a fourth part of the real value of their slaves. Add to this the vexatious and expensive method of receiving the sums due to them from England. . . . The people considered themselves defrauded and robbed of their lawful property, and openly accused the Government and the Parliament of having done so.

3 . . . The several laws forced upon the colony from time to time, chiefly upon slave owners, some of which were actually so vexatious that they in a body refused obedience to some of their provisions. The colonists clearly saw that the Government in England acted either upon gross misrepresentation, or intentionally to oppress the white inhabitants, as every new law or ordinance in which the black population was concerned betrayed the most tender and paternal care for them, and a disregard of the interests of the whites. Some of the magistrates, or perhaps a single one of them, ventured slightly to punish vagrancy, but the others actually refused to do so. Property became more and more unsafe, murders increased, the peaceable farmers on the frontiers found themselves robbed by Kafirs, Bushmen, Korannas, etc., and were not allowed, even under the orders of the fieldcornet, to pursue the thieves over the borders, or there to recapture their cattle: the use of firearms was declared unlawful, except in the most undoubted cases of self-defence. . . .

4 . . . The inattention shown by the Government to the complaints against thefts committed on the frontiers, and the inefficiency of the military force to protect the frontiers; and that therefore Government found itself unprepared and taken by surprise at the Kafir invasion of 1834. But when this took place, it was believed that now the eyes of the Government here, as well as in England, would certainly be opened: the sufferings of the people had now reached the extreme point of human endurance or forbearance; but Sir Benjamin D'Urban's conduct reanimated them, and inspired them with hopes of at least a better protection in future, whilst they were at the same time made to believe that they would receive compensation for their losses. Again, however, they found their confidence ill-placed. . . . When the despatch of Lord Glenelg to Sir Benjamin was made public, in which they saw the cause of the Kafirs pleaded in the most false and erroneous assertions, and themselves accused of having, as it were, deserved their sufferings, by provoking the Kafirs to take such a step, which was only a just retaliation, the eyes of the people were then opened, and they at once concluded that to live or exist longer in this colony under such paternal care and protection would be an utter impossibility. Bitter were the complaints of many of the emigrants at Natal on this head; and some of them expressed themselves to me in the following manner: 'What confidence could we longer have in such a Government? Our consciences acquitted us of the charges brought against us by Lord Glenelg. The commandoes on which we were ordered out for the protection of this country, upon pain of fine or imprisonment, at our own expense, not to mention bodily sufferings from cold, rain, hunger, fatigue, as also losses there and at home in our absence, were put to our account as our own voluntary acts, with the view of enriching ourselves by Kafir cattle and territory! Even in the last Kafir war, we were not allowed to protect our small remnant of property which the invader had left us, but under promises of full compensation we were ordered, destitute as we were, again to march out in defence of our territory, and to re-capture what had been taken from us. We complied with this sacred duty (as we thought), took our last horses, left our families and remaining property unprotected behind; several then lost what had yet been left them, and the result was, that what was recovered from the Kafirs, of our own property which we identified and could swear to, was laid hold of by Government and disposed of, we know not how. Peace

was made: the Kafirs agreed to give up an immense number of cattle, horses, guns, etc., taken from the colony. They never complied, and we, the sufferers, remained destitute, impoverished, neglected; and at the end we were calumniated and insulted. What human feeling can stand this, and why are we blamed for leaving a country where such a Government existed?' . . .

II. As a second main cause assigned by several who have quitted the colony, and by many who still speak of intending to do so, I can confidently assert the insecurity of life and property, owing to the prospect that the colony will be more and more infested by robbers and vagabonds, and that in the event of another Kafir invasion the defence of the colony must entirely depend upon the military.

These conclusions they have come to for the following reasons:

1 Very few farmers have at present, as formerly, servants to whom they can entrust any part of their property in their absence; and the frequent changes of such servants, in consequence of which their characters are seldom thoroughly known, make it dangerous for the farmer to leave his place and family for any length of time in time of peace, and still more so in time of war.

2 The facility with which vagrants can roam about the country unmolested, and provide themselves with what they can easily subsist upon, the difficulty of apprehending or convicting thieves, unless they are taken in the act or found in possession of stolen property, causes nine out of ten to escape the hands of justice, by which the farmers sustain losses of which the Government can have no idea, because it does not take the trouble to ascertain. . . . Should such returns be furnished to Government of cattle, horses, and sheep that have been stolen, it would then be found a matter of utter astonishment that the farmers could bear such losses from time to time with so much patience.

3 . . . The punishments inflicted upon offenders of the above description are by no means calculated to deter them or others from the commission of crime. . . . Crime is therefore on the increase, though convictions may be less in number, and with the emancipation of the slaves it is apprehended the evil will grow worse: appearances already begin to justify such apprehensions; and the farmers are too often, from want of servants or other assistance, and owing to the difficulty of detecting thieves, compelled to abstain from pursuing them, although the last ox or cow may have been stolen.

. . . I have thus endeavoured shortly to point out to you the real causes of emigration. . . . If I had any influence with the Government, I would advise them, even at the eleventh hour, to take some decisive steps towards restoring, if possible, its long-lost confidence with the people. Thus further emigration would not continue to such an extent as to be injurious to the colony. . . .

6.10b All these evils we attribute to a single cause, namely, the want of a representative government.

—Letter from the president and members of the Natal Volksraad to Governor Napier, 21 Feb. 1842. (From the translation published in Eybers, *Select Constitutional Documents Illustrating South African History, 1795–1910*, pp. 167–174.)

The Natal Volksraad's response (drafted by J. N. Boshof) to Sir George Napier's proclamation of 2 December 1841 announcing the imminent annexation of Natal, arguing its case for independence, has been called one of the key documents of Afrikaner political thinking in the nineteenth century. A further extract appears as Document 5.6c.

. . . We shall not deny, however, that the decisions taken and the laws enacted from time to time by the English government in our regard were the only causes for which we left the country of our birth and our kindred and took ourselves, as it were, to the barrenness of the wilderness to be free of the rule of that government.

To give some examples, who was it that forced upon us the increasingly detrimental consequences of slavery? Who was it that assured us of our right of property in slaves? Was it not the same government which later deprived us of this right, and did so without giving us any say as to the best and most suitable way in which this could be done? Who was it that promised us full compensation for our slaves? Was it not the same government that gave us only a third of the actual value of our property, and then left us prey to avaricious and profit-seeking agents who enriched themselves at our expense? Who was it that employed us, without remuneration and at our own expense, for the defence of the borders of the colony against the hostile and war-loving and plunderous kaffirs? Was it not the same government which later denied to us all claim to compensation, using the misrepresentation that we had provoked their rightful revenge by stealing from them? Who was it that deprived us of the best governor we had ever had because, like a man with a conscience, he defended the unjustly treated Cape colonists and sought their real safety and protection by punishing their destructive enemy? Who then sent us political speculators, bound hand and foot, whose frontier systems exposed us to unceasing and unpunished thefts and threats from the kaffirs, which were accompanied by heavy expenses to the farmers which eventually had to be retrieved from the pockets of the ruined farmers? Was it not the same government that left the country open to roaming vagabonds who led a wild and idle life, living off the herds and other property of the already sufficiently burdened farmer, so that he was deprived of labourers, or, if he still had them, of the necessary authority over them (a grievance under which the colonists still suffer)? All this led to the farmer losing heart, so that when he saw that his repeated remonstrations and petitions were unanswered or ignored, he was faced with the darkest prospects. All these evils we attribute to a single cause, namely, the want of a representative government which has been refused us by the executive government of the same people who regard this very right as one of the most sacred of their civil rights, and one for which every true Briton is prepared to lay down his life. . . .

6.11 Contrast the dignified position of a Representative freely elected by the people with the irresponsible Member of Council called into existence by the mere breath of the executive.

—Speeches of H. Cloete, J. H. Wicht and M. van Breda at a public meeting in Cape Town, 24 Aug. 1841. (From the report published in *The Cape Town Mail*, 26 Aug. 1841.)

Following the passage of the Reform Bill in 1832 in Britain the governor of the Cape was instructed to set up a Legislative Council consisting of five officials and five to seven unofficial members in 1834. Though a step toward representative government, the Legislative Council proved unsatisfactory in practice. A great deal of discretionary power was left in the hands of the governor; a number of important topics were placed outside the competence of the legislature; and the unofficial members, nominated by the Governor, were easily dominated by the powerful executive. In the early 1840s pressures began to mount again for representative government, and on 24 August 1841 a large public meeting was held in Cape Town in support of a petition asking for this. Apart from Cloete and Wicht, the Afrikaans speakers included Michiel van Breda

(1775–1847), who was a substantial and progressive farmer and merchant, member and president of the Burgher Senate, and a nominated member of the Legislative Council from 1834 to his death in 1847.

The Hon. Mr Cloete said, The present system of our local government is ill adapted to the wants and condition of this Colony. A representative system would be likely to develop its commercial and agricultural resources; and tend more efficiently to appropriate the revenue to the improvement of our public works and roads. It may not be altogether improper to take a cursory retrospective view of the political condition of our Colony and contrast it with the present. Although not yet an old man, I recollect the time, when, on my return to this my native land, I found it prostrate under a system of the most grinding despotism. The Governor and his two Secretaries appeared omnipotent in almost every civil, judicial or political transaction. . . .

After this Colony, however, became an integral part of the British Empire, and the influx of British Colonists spread abroad that spirit of freedom which we all are anxious to acquire but often do not know how to attain, legitimate endeavours have unceasingly been made by Petitions to the Sovereign and the Parliament to grant to this Colony the enjoyment of the essential characteristic of Liberty, which almost every part of her Majesty's possessions possesses. We were, however, uniformly met with the answer that we were not ripe; and at some period of time it certainly appeared probable that we would rot before we became ripe for such liberal institutions. (Hear! and laughter.)

Still these applications were not altogether unheeded, or not without some success. An Executive Council was appointed to assist, and there was somewhat to check the Government in any act of wanton oppression or illegality; and in some trying circumstances (which may be in the recollection of some here present), the Members of that Government proved themselves not unworthy. The renewed applications led, after some time, to the establishment of an Executive and Legislative Council; and having had the honor of a seat in the latter, I can only declare that I never ceased to view that institution as a stepping stone to a still further advance in political freedom, and as a dawn of those brighter and (politically speaking) happier days, when the public shall find themselves more efficiently and directly represented in their interests, than they can expect to be in the Legislative Council. Placed there, in an impassable minority, the unofficial Members can only assert a right to enjoy perfect freedom in debate, in any question submitted to their consideration; . . . yet they can never claim, as of right, to look into every act of the Executive Government; and if they should happen, on any question affecting the Executive Government, to be unanimous, (and experience has shown that they are not frequently so), and should they attempt to demand inquiries into acts not belonging to their Legislative province, the Governor has but to bring in his phalanx of officials, to check any such interference and prove that the Executive Government is above any such control.

At the present moment, however, . . . I believe I may venture to assert that, from the Governor down to the lowest of the Governed, there is no voice raised to deny the abstract justice of the present steps we are about to take, or to assert that there exists anything in our social or political condition which should justify this boon being any longer deferred.

Mr H. Wicht said, . . . Gentlemen, I will not waste your time by discussing the inherent, unquestioned right of every British subject to be represented in the Councils of the State, nor will I trespass upon your patience in contrasting the dignified position of a Representative freely elected by the people with the irresponsible Member of Council, called into existence by the mere breath of the executive; but I shall solicit your attention to the consideration of the fact that a Representative Legislative Assembly is the best and most effectual means of improving the condition and raising the character of the inhabitants.

Gentlemen, we have been gravely told, on several occasions, that we were precluded from obtaining, or could not expect, any liberal institutions to be conceded to us, because we were not properly qualified—'we were not ripe'—and this cuckoo note, set up by the men in office to stop the spirit of inquiry and drown the voice of the people, was reiterated loud and long, until its absurdity has become apparent to all. A similar cry was raised to debar us from enjoying the benefit of a free press, and was uttered with the sole view of keeping the minds of the people in perpetual thraldom. If the inhabitants of this Colony were less enlightened than other subjects in Europe, whose fault was it that they appeared to be in such a deplorable condition? Did not a spirit of coercion and intimidation prevail, calculated only to break down the spirit of the people, and make them submissive to the arbitrary mandates of the men in authority? Were not all channels for instructing the mass of the people carefully watched by a lynx-eyed Government, and the rod of power extended to strike terror and dismay into the heart of that individual who should dare to open the eyes of his fellow Colonists? Who does not recollect that even a Chief Justice of this Colony was prohibited to join in forming a literary association? And woe to that man who should have questioned the legality of such tyrannical measures! (Cheers.)

Gentlemen, I will only ask you this question, would such a state of things have been tolerated, if the inhabitants had a share in the management of their own affairs? . . . Gentlemen, it would be superfluous to enumerate all the instances in which a Representative Legislative Assembly will prove of inestimable advantage to this Colony. Even our rulers are convinced that such a form of government is the only one adapted to the spirit of the age, and to promote the best interests of the inhabitants. Shall we then remain inactive, or by party dissensions and petty jealousies allow this opportunity to pass without improving our condition? By no means!

Mr Van Breda said, . . . That form of Government in which the representatives of the people have some share and responsibility, is the most just and beneficial to the country. Now, we all know that, by the nature of our present Government, however willing those who have to administer it may be to discharge their duty faithfully, it is impossible for them to satisfy the wants of the whole Colony. I would ask, how is it possible for a Governor, on his arrival here, to ascertain at once the fitness of gentlemen he never saw before, to act as his councillors? Yet, I can state that, before I received my appointment as a Member of Council, I had never seen the Governor but once, and that was—at Government House, on his arrival, and had never spoken a word to him in my life. But now, if the request of this Meeting be granted, the Districts will join hand in hand in choosing men in whom they have confidence. Difficulties will doubtless be found in the beginning, for where do we find a beginning without difficulties? We know that on the first establishment of the Municipality, the householders could hardly be got to come forward, but now they are striving who shall be appointed Wardmasters, for they find the advantage of free discussion on their own affairs. . . . It has been objected that we shall not find that a number of gentlemen from different parts of the Colony can be found to agree in the management of affairs; but I have no doubt we shall find some twenty or even fifty among us quite as likely to act together as the gentlemen who have to meet and make laws for England, Ireland, and Scotland, and nineteen Colonies besides.

6.12a Be it known that the revolutionary genius of the age has reached even unto the Cape.

—Editorial 'A Quiet Revolution', by F. S. Watermeyer, in *The Cape of Good Hope Observer*, 17 July 1849. (From *The Cape of Good Hope Observer.*)

The anti-convict agitation of 1849 provided the catalyst for a fervent popular movement aimed at greater colonial self-determination at the Cape. In order to prevent the implementation of the decision by the imperial government in Britain to settle convicts at the Cape, colonists organized a boycott against the nominated members of the Legislative Council who were suspected of collaboration. Pariticipants took a formal pledge not to deliver supplies to the ships transporting the convicts, and forceful action was taken against those who ventured to do this. Against the background of the 1848 revolutions in Europe, the colonists' defiance and resistance appeared in a semi-revolutionary light.

F. S. Watermeyer (1828–1864) was a brilliant young law student who founded and edited The Cape of Good Hope Observer *to give support to the anti-convict movement. He became the son-in-law of Fairbairn, the editor of* The South African Commercial Advertiser, *and was also closely associated with Sir Andries Stockenström. Watermeyer supported the 'popular' party in the constitutional struggle from 1850.*

Be it known that the revolutionary genius of the age has reached even unto the Cape: and that we are now in a state of war with the government, not a whit less earnest than that which in France transformed Louis Philippe into the Comte de Neuilly, or elsewhere compelled the blessed Pope Pius to date his Bulls from Gaeta, instead of his venerable seat in the Eternal City.

And be it known further that, without entering into the question whether the French people had just reasons for their conduct, or whether the Romans acted properly in turning out their Pope, we are prepared to aver that we certainly and truly are in the right in *our* present contest, and that great as our success has hitherto been, it has not been greater than we might have hoped that Providence would accord to the justice of our cause.

The convict question has *roused* the people. They do not choose longer to have others rule them. They will not that the heel of power shall longer be upon their necks. They have been made to understand that the security in which they thought that they rested from injustice is naught, and they have learned to be thankful to God that what they have sometimes deemed to be a paternal government has done no *more* mischief to their best interests than during a long course of years it has thought fit to effect. The people of this country have learned from late events to be ashamed of their listless confidence in their government, and of their apathetic neglect of their duty to their country; and they now demand that there shall be established in their country, forthwith, a free and liberal constitution.

And then, laying the axe at the root of the mischief, they insist that the Representative Legislature which has been so long promised them shall be withheld no longer; but not again with prayers or petitions do they approach the government. They are, as we have said, by reason of the convict question, in open antagonism with the government. Why, then, waste time in prayer, or entreaty, or protest? Their object is not to *pray* for a dissolution of the Legislative Council; but as a people, possessing a people's power, and desirous of enforcing a people's authority, they resolve upon its instant destruction. . . .

In most amiable contrast to the European revolutions of last year stands ours at the Cape. The people wished in Europe to teach their rulers that for them they ruled, not for themselves: that they, the people, were of right the holders of all authority in the country which they occupied, that they were of right their own governors, that none else could claim of right, either rule over them, or service from them. This lesson, this principle of human society we, too, have to teach the Home Government and their local representatives. We demand that the sentiment 'I rule the people, through the people' be no longer a mere boast, made to earn a few cheers or an empty 'huzza'. . . .

The pledge, if fully carried out, is such as no man can resist for a week. It was not even fully carried out against the three members, who yet resigned their seats almost immediately. It has not been fully directed against those who have not yet yielded, but it seems impossible that these can resist for a day beyond its actual enforcement. If the government does not seek a speedy reconciliation with the people, if the people are driven to further offensive warfare, this mighty weapon will be put in motion *against others also*; and what will it avail to resist such a proceeding with bayonets or cannon balls?

6.12b The colonies as integral portions of the parent state claim the same noble institutions of which the mother country so justly boasts.

—Editorial in *De Zuid-Afrikaan*, 21 Feb. 1850. (From the translation published in the *Zuid-Afrikaan*.)

News of the imperial decision to give way before the concerted Cape opposition to the settlement of convicts in the colony reached Cape Town in February 1850. The victory of the anti-convict agitation gave a powerful boost to the movement for representative government among the colonists. It had brought together Afrikaner and English colonists in a strong coalition, unified in their resentment of the despotic and arbitrary rule of imperial officials, and thus created the setting in which a popular movement could emerge.

However great may be the victory just achieved, not less so is the duty resting upon the Colonists to profit by it, and to exert themselves at once for the obtainment of those higher immunities of which, as the subjects of a free and enlightened Government, they have been too long deprived.

It would indeed be of little avail were they to view the averting of the moral stain as the consummation of all their wishes, and now to evince any indifference with respect to the momentous subjects, the want of which—especially during the excitement—was so seriously felt, as solely calculated to protect them against the abuse of power, and to secure them the full enjoyment of that real liberty, without which life possesses no real value, and which every Briton therefore justly considers his birthright.

England's extensive Colonial Empire is just beginning to insist on this right, and the general cry of the Colonists is that they are no slaves, and that the Colonies, as integral portions of the parent state, claim the same noble institutions of which the mother country so justly boasts.

. . . The Cape Colonists have joined in the cry. . . . They lack everything. They are nominally free people—compelled to kiss the rod by which they are occasionally unmercifully chastised. Hitherto they have had no voice in the Government—their hard-earned money, contributed in the shape of severe taxes, has been wasted and the treasury exhausted. Confidence in their Courts of Justice has been shaken, whilst at many places there is an absolute want of the same. . . .

Their present position is really no enviable one, and if they do not extricate themselves from it, they will erelong perceive to their injury and shame that however great and glorious may have been the late victory, they would act very imprudently in laying down their arms so soon, instead of availing themselves of the advantages obtained, and remaining in the field until they have obtained their complete liberation. . . .

6.13a We do now what the Barons of England did when they produced the Bill of Rights.

—Speech by Christoffel Brand in the Legislative Council, 20 Sept. 1850. (From the report in *The Cape Town Mail*, 28 Sept. 1850.)

A sharp constitutional struggle was waged at the Cape from 1850. Already in 1848 the governor, Sir Harry Smith, with the support of his Executive Council, had recommended the granting of representative government as suggested by Earl Grey, the Colonial Secretary, and the groundwork for the new constitution had been done in a long memorandum by the Attorney-General, William Porter. However, the unofficial members of the Legislative Council had been forced to resign during the anti-convict agitation. Unofficial elections were held in the municipal and road boards, and four of the popular members who headed the polls for the Legislative Council, Christoffel Brand, Andries Stockenström, F. W. Reitz and John Fairbairn were appointed. However, instead of the fifth popular favourite, J. H. Wicht, the Governor preferred Robert Godlonton, spokesman for the settler community around Grahamstown. This led to a sharp confrontation, further compounded when the popular members insisted that they were not prepared to participate in the ordinary business of the Council, but only in the preparations for the new constitution.

. . . We do now, sir, what the Barons of England did when they produced the Bill of Rights—what my forefathers did when the Barons, headed by Prince William the First, also presented their Bill of Rights, laying aside and discarding all other points except the only great one, that of obtaining their rights and vindicating their liberties. Her Majesty has spoken the word—the Royal faith is pledged—that this colony shall have a free representative legislature. The British people and the British Government have declared that the boon we have so long sought shall no longer be withheld. Why, then, should we hear all this declamation about the danger of the course we are now pursuing? Why should we be threatened with the vengeance of Lord John Russell? Is it likely that that nobleman would look with anything but approval upon a people struggling to acquire those rights and privileges which he and his illustrious ancestors have done so much to secure to the people of England? Will it ever enter into the mind of the Queen to withdraw her gracious promise, and withhold from this colony a free constitution, because we take this means of showing the earnestness of our desire to attain it? . . . I will consider the subject, first, in a moral point of view; next, as to its expediency: and, lastly, as to its constitutional merits.

. . . You charged us with an implied contract. I admit a contract, but with whom? With the Government? No. My contract was with the people, who sent me here; with the municipalities and road boards throughout the colony, who elected me. I repeat, my contract was with the people. The act of the Governor in appointing me was only the means of legalizing that contract. Now, sir, before I accepted a seat here, when I was asked by the municipality of Swellendam whether I would accept the appointment I wrote back at once, saying that if it was for the ordinary business of the Council I would refuse, but as it was only for framing a constitution, I could not withdraw myself from that civil duty. I have since ascertained that it is the public voice that we should confine ourselves to the performance of that duty. The municipality of Cape Town have declared this through their Commissioners, by an unanimous resolution, and we have had the public voice expressed to the same effect in the public papers. . . . It is said—are you going to leave it in the hands of the Governor to spend your money? Certainly that is a strong expression; but I ask, under what authority has the Governor expended the public money since 1849? . . . Now, let me ask, what is the use of forcing us to approve of the expenditure? Why should we take out of the hands of the future Parliament the power of scrutinizing the past or future expenditure, and approving of it themselves? And with regard to the Estimates for the present year, our passing them would merely be giving our sanction and consent to matters which have been begun and carried on without our knowledge. There can be no reason why we should be in a hurry about this. . . .

In deciding on the form of government, the delay of a few months in carrying the change into effect is not material. Some delay is unavoidable. . . . No, gentlemen, let us take the course pursued by the barons of old in securing the Bill of Rights, and like the barons of my former mother country in obtaining those rights they were entitled to.

6.13b The whole fabric of our colonial system is leprous to the marrow from patronage and favouritism, which are at the root of every one of our diseases.

—Letter from Sir Andries Stockenström to the Cape Town Municipality, London 13 Sept. 1851. (From *The Autobiography of Sir Andries Stockenström,* Vol. II, pp. 337–348.)

The popular members resigned from the Legislative Council at the end of 1850 and formed themselves into an opposition pressure group in association with the Cape Town municipality. They prepared their own set of constitutional proposals and Stockenström and Fairbairn were sent as delegates to London. In the semi-revolutionary climate, compounded by the frontier war of 1850 and the Kat River rebellion, the popular members tended to see sinister reactionary motives behind the opposing views on constitutional proposals by such officials as the Secretary of State, John Montagu. The following letter to the Cape Town Municipality was written by Stockenström from London.

. . . The awful derelictions of principle which are revealed by the Blue Books . . . are not without utility, as they unmask to the Colony the system, the character whereof was heretofore only partially understood, though of late it became by degrees so strongly developed. . . .

The most satisfactory part of your communication is . . . the assurance . . . that our fellow-Colonists will confine themselves strictly to legal and constitutional weapons in the struggle against a system which their enemies . . . have at last laid bare. . . . Violence, now particularly, would be utter ruin.

Your Council was smashed on the 20th September, for fear of the elective upper chamber and other liberal provisions . . . becoming the law of the land before there should be time for Conservative reaction (Conservatism at the Cape meaning: 1st. Patronage in the Colonial Office; 2nd. A nominee or aristocratic House of Lords; 3rd. A perpetual Civil List), and if you afford such Conservatives the appearance even of a proof that you do not understand the power of orderly and peaceable resistance to arbitrary abuse of power, it will soon be attempted to impose on this nation that . . . dragoon spurs . . . are the only furniture with which you are fit to be ridden. . . .

Allow me to repeat *violence may ruin all the fruits of your victory*. The Hottentots have proved this. Their best friends cannot sympathize with the rebellious portion in their present proceedings, and whatever may be the nature of their cause, utter destruction must ultimately be their lot. On the other hand, let there be no slackening of vigilance, no false security, and, above all, no giving way to intimidation. . . .

The hour has come when it must be decided whether we are to be ruled as a free people under a constitutional system, or as Russian serfs under a pure despotism, or what is worse, a tyranny under the mask of mock checks. . . . The hour has come when it must be decided whether the reign of patronage and favouritism shall continue, or the reign of truth and justice be substituted. Long before public duty compelled me to declare it openly, those who know my private sentiments were aware that I considered the whole fabric of our colonial system leprous to the marrow from patronage and favouritism, which are at the root of every one of our diseases. It pervades the whole body, beginning at the head.

A Crown Minister takes a fancy to a pet functionary who may have answered some special purpose in some distant land. At once the functionary becomes the beloved pet of the great man, who, instead of bestowing upon his favourite a share of his private property, as he had a right to do, finds it more convenient to make him a present of one of the Colonies, for him as a football to amuse himself and his friends with, or rather as a sponge-cake to slice off amongst his sons and hangers-on. From that instant the devoted Colony becomes, as it were, a private estate; a belt of sycophants, flatterers, and dependants is soon formed round the great centre of bounty; some rags of favour emitted by the great luminary reflect from hundreds of satellites which become foci of lesser vortices of corruption, the disappointed become discontented, murmurs are reported and exaggerated, a system of espionage creeps in, fear seizes upon the weak, its progeny, falsehood and slander, tears society into factions, and secret and underhand correspondence keeps up at headquarters the prestige of the prowess of the mighty conjurer. . . .

If any man who dares say what he thinks will tell me that the above is not a true picture of one branch of colonial administration, let him look to our own poor, helpless community, to the relative positions of our Christian characters, to the road boards and their taxes and their jobs, to the premature waste of our public resources, to a Colonial office, strong and costly enough to do the work of the whole North American union, look to the distribution of the patronage therein, to the patronage and nepotism everywhere in fact. . . .

Let us turn to another branch and ask, Did not the settlers of 1820 show to the commissioners of Enquiry, more than a quarter of a century since, . . . how patronage and favouritism could contrive the treacherous seizure of the Kaffir King by military force in the dead of the night, in a time of profound peace, without even a pretext of provocation, in order to create cause for a demonstration, when fields of glory were scarce and promotion was slack? And yet we pretend to be groping for the causes of Kaffir wars amongst missionaries, anti-convict associations, demagogues, and republicans. . . . Show me one single benefit that has resulted from any Kaffir war to any one man beyond the patronised and favoured few! The best and bravest troops in the world are harassed to death, knowing and seeing that they can do nothing; but Despatches and orders record glories innumerable to which the bystanders were blind, and promotions follow as if every cow taken has cost us a Waterloo; but these advantages limit the benefit except to those who can get a finger in the pie, that is, in the hundreds of thousands which the British Exchequer is fleeced of.

In the meantime the enemy is ruined, and the Colonists are ruined, and, after saving the Colony, are insulted, maltreated, and slandered. . . . Such, then, is the actual position of the Colony of the Cape of Good Hope. Morally and politically never was there a country before in such a state, and how long shall this be allowed to last? Are we *bona fide* the private property, the plaything of some half-dozen, to be given and taken, kicked and cuffed at pleasure? And when we complain that it hurts us, to be told that we are impudent, impertinent, mutinous, rebellious, traitorous, for not liking the gentle strokes of such kind masters. Now the truth must out! This sort of kindness will no longer do! The whole system must be got rid of, root and branch! We are not the property of these men. . . . We will and shall be emancipated. . . .

We ask nothing more than justice and shall have it. . . .

Setting aside the miserable faction and its hangers-on, who are few though noisy, we, the remainder, English and Dutch, do in reality not hate, though we sometimes misunderstand each other. We, the great body, know that we are the same people with the same interests, and we shall yet, I hope, with God's help, all conspire, first to establish liberty and order by means of one Parliament, and then agree to 'separate' in love and concord, or to remain united, as the majority shall deem best for the happiness of the whole.

6.13c In the event of a Parliament being established, the bonds of good fellowship and brotherhood will be drawn more closely together.

—Speech by Mr J. H. Wicht at a public meeting in Cape Town on the new constitution, 1 March 1852. (From the report in *The Cape Town Mail*, 9 March 1852.)

Towards the end of 1851 the draft constitution, mainly based on Porter's proposals, was forwarded to the Cape. In a contentious atmosphere the Legislative Council started discussing the draft constitution on 11 February 1852, but both before and while they were engaged in this the popular members who had resigned made their own views plain at various public meetings in Cape Town.

. . . Gentlemen, I believe you will have observed that no means have been left untried which could possibly cause a division in order to overcome a divided community with greater facility. The East has been endeavoured to be arrayed against the West, English against Dutch, blacks against whites, masters against their former slaves, and *vice versa*; a system of intrigue, espionage, and other blameable practices has been set on foot, copied from the most arbitrary governments, disgusting to the inhabitants and of such a nature that we should neglect the duty we owe to ourselves and our children if we were to refrain from speaking in plain terms, and deprecating such measures as they deserve. . . . In the event of a Parliament being established, the bonds of good fellowship and brotherhood will be more closely drawn together. The social, political and moral elevation of all classes may be confidently looked to. The public mind, in being roused and a proper direction given to it, will then have full scope to devote itself to improvements; and the Cape colony will no doubt progress at a rate commensurate with the impulse given. For we have noticed what remarkable results followed from a reformed legislature in England. . . .

. . . It has been attempted to revive prejudices of the master against slave and *vice versa*; as if the people of this colony were so narrow-minded as not to appreciate merit in any individual, however humble might have been his origin. I have known well-behaved slaves of high moral worth, attached to their masters, faithful and trustworthy, and in the humble station an example to many who boast of a more exalted lineage. Prejudice against these classes, if it did formerly exist, is fast wearing away, or perhaps altogether exploded; and with regard to differences or dissensions between English and Dutch colonists, I hope they may scarcely or ever arise, for we have to thank our friends of Anglo-Saxon descent for many of the liberal institutions in this colony. On them fell the brunt of fighting the battles against despotism, whether arrayed against the press or other institutions dear to them; and we will never forget the obligations we are under to them. A great part of the present population was born under the British flag, reared in English schools, and directed to shape their course by the bright examples, the soul-stirring words and highly moral sentiments of her heroes, poets, philanthropists, philosophers and statesmen. . . . In this colony, therefore, I hope that English principles and ideas, being engrafted on such a stock as the Attorney-General has very appropriately described the inhabitants to be, will produce not only blossoms but fruit in every way worthy of their ancestors.

6.14 The boards of Landdrost and Heemraden constituted a species of representation admirably adapted as a substitute for popular Government until this latter should be conceded.

—Speech by Sir Andries Stockenström on the system of landdrost and heemraden, in the Cape Town House of Assembly, 1854. (From the text published in the Cape of Good Hope Parliamentary Debates 1854, pp. 284–285).

The Cape constitution was confirmed by Order-in-Council in March 1853, and the first session of the new Cape Parliament took place in 1854. Sir Andries Stockenström reviewed the significance of the old system of landdrost and heemraden, and its place in the history of representative institutions at the Cape, in an important speech in the House of Assembly.

. . . My sentiments on the abolition of the boards of Landdrost and Heemraden were openly declared when the mistake was made, and I now repeat that no greater political injury could have been inflicted upon a settlement in the circumstances in which South Africa was then placed. I, perhaps, had peculiar reasons for being wedded to the system thus destroyed, because I had derived individual benefit from it; but my own case, however insignificant, proves to some extent in how far the good of the community was involved in this precipitate change.

It is well known that I was little more than a mere youth with the information which the colonial schools of those days could impart, when I was placed at the head of a district comprising about one-fourth of the whole colony, bordering on several native tribes, with whom we had various relations, and sometimes were in conflict: and the complicated duties and responsibilities which were then centred in the office of Landdrost may be imagined by those who consider the many departments which now conduct the same business. I should indeed be ungrateful as well as presumptuous if I were to pretend that, with so little knowledge and experience, it would have been possible for me to succeed, even to the limited extent to which I did succeed, without the influence of my colleagues of the board throughout the district.

With that influence it was only necessary for the Landdrost as the organ or agent of Government to be actuated by a sincere determination to promote the public interests of those whose affairs were intrusted to his superintendence, and the blunders which he, with such objects, might fall into, as to mere routine or technicalities, could not easily be of an irremediable character.

The radical evil of the system was that the whole board consisted of Government nominees, but even with that defect it could but seldom happen that the Heemraden would not be such men as were generally approved of by the mass of the population, and they would make up for the want of legal knowledge and literary acquirements, to the extent which might be indispensable in a community in an advanced state of civilization, by a thorough acquaintance with the wants, habits, interests and desires of their fellow-subjects. The field-cornets were of the same class, likewise selected on account of their character, ability, and influence.

It is thus clear that if such men were headed by a chief magistrate who was able and willing to render himself trusted by the Government by faithfully informing it of the true state of affairs, and urging such measures as the welfare of the people should dictate, there would exist a chain of links between the rulers and the ruled which would constitute a species of representation admirably adapted as a substitute for popular Government until this latter should be conceded. These links operating with such tendencies gave the Government the means, through their Landdrosts, of influencing the whole community, and inspiring confidence where it was due by explaining the motives, the policy and the justice of its proceedings, by removing in time what was deservedly obnoxious, and by affording redress where real injury had been done.

Such are the links which were cut asunder by the abolition of the system of administration by Landdrosts and Heemraden, and the substitution of one which, notwithstanding the abilities and worth of many of the functionaries who have been employed under it, has failed to produce the counter-balancing advantages which were expected from it; and it may be safely asserted that from the moment of that abolition all confidence between the Government and the masses ceased, and many of the evils which have retarded our advancement and disturbed our peace may be traced to misunderstandings which the executive had not the means nor the channels of clearing up, and to grievances which it could not become rightly acquainted with, and consequently could not duly redress.

That abuses crept into the system which I advocate cannot be denied. It was susceptible of being rendered instrumental in turning the board of Heemraden into a mere official clique or family compact; and such a body being once constituted, would naturally, by the power of self-election, perpetuate the corruption which had created such a corporation. These, indeed, were the considerations which influenced the Commissioners of Inquiry of 1824, with whom I had much discussion on this subject, when they doubted the possibility of reform, and therefore recommended destruction root and branch. Now, this I considered injudicious and short-sighted. So much so, that I declined accepting the office created in lieu of that of Landdrost, for it struck me as perfectly clear that all the abuses complained of could at once be reformed by making the Heemraden popularly elective, whereby the Colony would moreover be gradually prepared for the representative system.

The question then asked was, 'Where is your constituency?' That question has now at least been answered. The existence of slavery was also considered an obstacle. I could not see why. Slavery was an evil we all know, but it could not be aggravated by liberalizing the administration of public affairs. However down went the system, the Heemraden were scattered to the winds, and the field-cornets, till then the most useful auxiliaries to the Executive, and the most influential pleaders or agents between the people on the one side, and the boards and higher authorities on the other, were deprived of their power, lost their importance, and found themselves little better than nonentities, so that Government could only approach the subject through the tax-gatherer, the public prosecutor, the lash of the law, and the Gazette, which never reached one out of a thousand. The fatal consequences I have already alluded to: deception, preying on ignorance, generating misunderstanding on both sides, then disaffection, then emigration; at last rebellion. My hon. friend's bill is intended to lay the foundation upon which the boards of Landdrost and Heemraden may be reconstructed, with the improvements which experience and the altered times suggest. . . .

Notes

INTRODUCTION

1. Political histories of Afrikaner nationalism include: F. A. van Jaarsveld, *The Awakening of Afrikaner Nationalism, 1868–81* (Cape Town, 1961); D. W. Krüger, *The Age of the Generals* (Johannesburg, 1958); G. D. Scholtz, *Die Ontwikkeling van die Politieke Denke van die Afrikaner, 1652–1939* (7 vols.) (Johannesburg, 1967–79); W. H. Vatcher, *White Laager* (New York, 1965). Among more popular surveys are: Sheila Patterson, *The Last Trek* (London, 1957); Douglas Brown, *Against the World* (London, 1966); Edwin S. Munger, *Afrikaner and African Nationalism* (Oxford, 1967); W. A. de Klerk, *The Puritans in Africa* (London 1975). Major biographical studies include: D. W. Krüger, *Paul Kruger* (2 vols.) (Johannesburg, 1961, 1963); C. M. van den Heever, *General J. B. M. Hertzog* (Johannesburg, 1946); J. H. Hofmeyr, *The Life of Jan Hendrik Hofmeyr (Onze Jan)* (Cape Town, 1913). Among institutional histories by professional historians are: T. R. H. Davenport, *The Afrikaner Bond: the History of a South African Political Party (1880–1911)* (Cape Town, 1966); O. Geyser, and A. H. Marais (eds.), *Die Nasionale Party: Agtergrond, Stigting en Konsolidasie,* vol. 1 (Pretoria, 1975).
2. T. Dunbar Moodie, *The Rise of Afrikanerdom: Power, Apartheid and the Afrikaner Civil Religion* (Berkeley, 1975).
3. Irving Hexham, *The Irony of Apartheid* (New York, 1981); ——, 'Dutch Calvinism and the Development of Afrikaner Nationalism', unpublished paper, University of York, Centre for Southern African Studies, 1974.
4. F. A. van Jaarsveld, *The Afrikaner's Interpretation of South African History* (Cape Town, 1964).
5. See, e.g., I. D. MacCrone, *Race Attitudes in South Africa* (Johannesburg, 1957); Sheila Patterson, *The Last Trek*; the chapter by Leonard Thompson in Louis Hartz (ed.), *The Founding of New Societies* (New York, 1964). For a recent statement on 'primitive Calvinism' and South African race relations see Sheila Patterson, 'Some Speculation on the Status and Role of the Free People of Colour in the Western Cape' in M. Fortes and S. Patterson (eds.), *Studies in African Social Anthropology* (London, 1975), pp. 160–205. For a thoroughgoing critique see André du Toit, *No Chosen People: The History and Significance of the Myth of the Calvinist Origins of Afrikaner Nationalism* (forthcoming).
6. For the 'frontier tradition' in South African historiography see, e.g., C. W. de Kiewiet, *A History of South Africa: Social and Economic* (Oxford, 1941); Eric Walker, *The Frontier Tradition in South Africa* (Oxford, 1930); ——, *The Great Trek* (5th edition, London, 1965); W. M. MacMillan, *The Cape Colour Question* (London, 1927). Martin Legassick's seminal critique of this tradition, 'The Frontier Tradition in South African Historiography' originally appeared in *The Societies of Southern Africa in the 19th and 20th Centuries,* vol. 2, pp. 1–33 (University of London, Institute of Commonwealth Studies, 1971), and is reprinted in Shula Marks and Anthony Atmore (eds.), *Economy and Society in Pre-industrial South Africa* (London, 1980).
7. Edgar H. Brookes, *Apartheid: a Documentary Study of Modern South Africa* (London, 1968).
8. D. W. Krüger, *South African Parties and Policies, 1910–1960* (Cape Town, 1960).
9. G. W. Eybers (ed.), *Select Constitutional Documents Illustrating South African History, 1795–1910* (London, 1918).
10. G. D. Scholtz, op. cit.
11. Quentin Skinner, 'Meaning and Understanding in the History of Ideas', *History and Theory* (1969), vol. 8.
12. Van Jaarsveld, op. cit.
13. Bernard Crick, *In Defence of Politics* (London, 1962), pp. 20, 40, 186ff. See also H. Pitkin, *Wittgenstein and Justice* (Berkeley, 1972), p. 208ff.
14. See the writings of, in particular, J. G. A. Pocock, Quentin Skinner and John Dunne. A number of Pocock's essays have been collected in *Politics, Language and Time* (London, 1971).
15. Cape Archives C.O. 2763. The letter has been published in J. L. M. Franken, *Piet Retief se Lewe in die Kolonie* (Cape Town, 1949), pp. 455–8.
16. See chapter 5, documents **5a** and **6d** and chapter 3, document **14.**
17. J. L. M. Franken, op. cit., p. 429 and note 21.
18. See chapter 3, document **9a.**
19. See chapter 3, document **9b.**
20. See Hermann Giliomee, 'The Development of the Afrikaner's Self-concept' in H. W. van der Merwe (ed.) *Looking at the Afrikaner Today* (Cape Town, 1975).

21. J. A. Heese, *Die Herkoms van die Afrikaner, 1657–1867* (Cape Town, 1971).
22. See, e.g., *The Autobiography of Sir Andries Stockenström* (Cape Town, 1887), vol. 1, p. 129 etc; P. J. van der Merwe, *Die Noordwaartse Beweging van die Boere voor die Groot Trek (1770–1842)* (The Hague, 1937), p. 373.
23. See chapter 6, document **3.**
24. J. L. M. Franken, 'Hendrik Bibault of die Opkoms van 'n Volk', in *Die Huisgenoot* 21 Sept. 1928.

CHAPTER 1: THE HISTORICAL CONTEXT

1. A. J. Böeseken, *Jan van Riebeeck en sy Gesin* (Cape Town, 1974), p. 58.
2. For a recent exhaustive study of European settlement see Leonard Guelke, 'The Expansion of White Settlement' in Richard Elphick and Hermann Giliomee (eds.), *The Shaping of South African Society* (Cape Town, 1979); also see Leonard Guelke and Robert Shell, 'Land and Wealth in the Early Cape Colony' (unpublished paper).
3. See Allen Isaacman and Barbara Isaacman, 'The Prazeros as Transfrontiersmen: a Study in Society and Cultural Change' in *The International Journal of African Historical Studies*, vol. 8, no. 1 (1978), pp. 1–37.
4. In 1774, for example, a number of colonists petitioned the government that the person holding the general wine lease and who bought most of the producers' wine should not also be a wine farmer. In the preceding two years this person had produced so much wine himself that he had bought nothing from the other producers. See G. J. Jooste, *Die Geskiedenis van Wynbou en Wynhandel in die Kaapkolonie, 1753–95* (M.A. dissertation, University of Stellenbosch, 1973), p. 40.
5. For a reinterpretation of the role of the Cape Patriots see Gerrit Schutte, 'Company and Colonists at the Cape' in Elphick and Giliomee, op. cit.
6. For a fuller discussion see Richard Elphick and Hermann Giliomee 'The Structure of European Domination at the Cape, 1652–1820' in Elphick and Giliomee, op. cit.
7. As the frontier closed, marked disparities in wealth among colonists began to appear. Only 26 per cent of the burghers of Graaff-Reinet who completed the census returns *(Opgaaf)* in 1798 held farms. This 26 per cent owned 75 per cent of the slaves and more than half of the cattle and sheep.
8. Robert Ross, 'The "White" Population of South Africa in the Eighteenth Century' in *Population Studies*, vol. 29, no. 2 (1975), pp. 217–30.
9. Cited in Eugene Genovese, *In Red and Black: Marxian Explorations in Southern and Afro-American History* (New York, 1971), p. 45.
10. The following figures give an indication of the growth of the slave population:

Year	*European Freeburghers*	*Burghers' Slaves*
1690	788	381
1770	7 736	8 220
1798	c. 20 350	25 754
1820	42 975	31 779

11. Cited by James Armstrong in 'The Slaves, 1652–1795' in Elphick and Giliomee, op. cit.
12. *The Reports of Chavonnes and his Council and of Van Imhoff on the Cape* (Van Riebeeck Society, no. 1), Cape Town, 1918.
13. See chapter 3, document **5.**
14. See Richard Elphick and Hermann Giliomee, 'The Structure of European Domination at the Cape, 1652–1820' in Elphick and Giliomee, op. cit.
15. G. M. Theal (ed.) *Belangrijke Historische Dokumenten over Zuid-Afrika*, vol. 3 (London, 1911), p. 219.
16. See Helen T. Manning, *British Colonial Government after the American Revolution, 1782–1820* (Hamden, 1966), pp. 293–6; John Manning Ward, *Colonial Self-Government, the British Experience, 1759–1856* (London, 1976), pp. 8ff and 82ff.
17. See C. W. de Kiewiet, *A History of South Africa, Social and Economic* (Oxford, 1941), pp. 31 and 42.
18. See K. E. Knorr, *British Colonial Theories 1570–1850* (Toronto, 1944), pp. 246ff and 376ff.
19. Edmund Burke, 'Speech on Mr. Fox's East India Bill', 1 December 1783, quoted in P. J. Marshall (ed.), *Problems of Empire: Britain and India, 1757–1813* (London, 1968), p. 21.
20. See J. S. Marais, *The Cape Coloured People 1652–1937* (Johannesburg, 1957), p. 118.
21. L. C. Duly, 'A Revisit with the Cape's Hottentot Ordinance of 1828' in Marcelle Kooy (ed.), *Studies in Economics and Economic History* (London, 1972).
22. See D. B. Davis, *The Problem of Slavery in the Age of Revolution* (Ithaca, 1975), especially pp. 454–68. For a discussion of the 'unfreedom' of workers in Britain, see E. P. Thompson, *The Rise of the English Working Class* (London, 1968).
23. G. M. Theal, *Records of the Cape Colony* (London, 1900), vol. 7, p. 211.
24. D. J. van Zyl, 'Die Slaaf in die Ekonomiese Lewe van die Westelike Distrikte van die Kaapkolonie, 1795–1834', in *South African Historical Journal* (November, 1978), no. 10, pp. 3–25.
25. We are using this term in the way that white historians have conveniently employed it to indicate the area between the Sundays and the Kei Rivers.
26. For an elaboration of the frontier concept see Martin Legassick, *The Griqua, the Sotho-Tswana, and the missionaries, 1780–1840: The Politics of a Frontier Zone* (Ph.D. dissertation, U.C.L.A. 1969), pp. 6–30.
27. I. D. MacCrone, *Race Attitudes in South Africa* (Johannesburg, 1957), p. 108; cf. also J. S. Marais, *Maynier and the First Boer Republic* (Cape Town, 1944), pp. 35, 69 etc.
28. Under the traditional commando system the landdrost could authorize armed expeditions across the border to recapture stolen stock. Under the reprisal system, adopted in 1817, burgher patrols accompanied

by a military detachment could cross the border and demand compensation from the kraal to which the spoor of stolen cattle had been traced, whether or not the stolen stock was actually found there, leaving it to the kraal to reclaim the cattle from the guilty.

29. C. F. J. Muller, *Die Britse Owerheid en die Groot Trek* (Pretoria, 1969); J. S. Galbraith, *Reluctant Empire: British Policy on the South African Frontier, 1834–54* (Berkeley, 1963).
30. J. S. Marais, op. cit., p. 183.
31. C. F. J. Muller, *Die Oorsprong van die Groot Trek* (Cape Town, 1974), p. 187.
32. L. C. Duly, *British Land Policy at the Cape 1795–1844* (Durham, 1968).
33. Letter from Sterrenberg Spruit, dated 4 Dec. 1837, in Gustav Preller (ed.), *Voortrekkermense* (Cape Town, 1938), vol. 6, pp. 3–5.
34. Cf. 'The Boers moved inland not to found a new society and to win new wealth. Their society was rebellious, but it was not revolutionary. . . . Although the emigrant farmers opened the hinterland and made a great contribution to the development and enrichment of later South Africa, theirs was not the aggressive movement of a people braving the wilderness for the profit that it would bring their purses, or the education that it would give their children.' De Kiewiet, op. cit., pp. 58–59.
35. P. J. van der Merwe, *Die Noordwaartse Beweging van die Boere voor die Groot Trek: 1770–1842* (The Hague, 1937), pp. 328–31; C. F. J. Muller, *Die Oorsprong van die Groot Trek*, pp. 183–5.
36. W. S. van Ryneveld, cf. chapter 2, document **3**.
37. See Stockenström to Plasket, 1 Dec. 1825 (chapter 1, document **10a**). For a discussion of this phenomenon in a wider theoretical perspective, see Tara Shulka, *Transforming Traditional Agriculture* (New Haven, 1964).
38. The Great Trek could perhaps, in one sense, be regarded as a first concerted attempt to deal with the poor white problem. The removal of some 9 per cent of the total white population of approximately 65 000 by 1840 considerably alleviated the pressure on land and created new opportunities for those who trekked.
39. See Monica Wilson, 'The Nguni People' and 'The Sotho, Venda, and Tsonga' in Leonard Thompson and Monica Wilson (eds.), *A History of South Africa to 1870* (Cape Town, 1982).
40. C. W. de Kiewiet, op. cit., p. 53ff.
41. J. D. Omer-Cooper, *The Zulu Aftermath: Nineteenth Century Revolution in Bantu Africa* (London, 1966).
42. Leonard Thompson, 'Co-operation and Conflict: The High Veld' in Thompson and Wilson, op. cit.
43. J. S. Galbraith, op. cit.; C. W. de Kiewiet, *British Colonial Policy and the South African Republics, 1848–72* (London, 1929).
44. For the distinction between the process of white settlement in the interior and the gaining of hegemony, see Martin Legassick, op. cit., pp. 15–18.
45. Cf. F. A. van Jaarsveld, *Die Afrikaner en Sy Geskiedenis* (Cape Town, 1959), p. 66ff.
46. P. J. van der Merwe, op. cit.; M. C. E. van Schoor, *Politieke Groeperinge in die Transgariep*, Archives Yearbook for South African History (Pretoria, 1950/2).
47. A. N. Pelzer, *Geskiedenis van die Suid-Afrikaanse Republiek, vol. 1: Wordingsjare* (Cape Town, 1950).
48. F. A. van Jaarsveld, *Die Veldkornet en sy Aandeel in die Opbou van die Suid-Afrikaanse Republiek tot 1870*, Archives Year Book for South African History (Pretoria, 1950/2).
49. T. R. H. Davenport, 'The Consolidation of a New Society: the Cape Colony' in Thompson and Wilson, op. cit., p. 284.
50. W. M. Freund, 'The Temporary Occupations', in Elphick and Giliomee, op. cit.
51. H. B. Thom, *Die Geskiedenis van Skaapboerdery in Suid-Afrika* (Amsterdam, 1936) pp. 198–9.
52. Albie Sachs, *Justice in South Africa* (Berkeley, 1973), ch. 2.
53. B. J. Liebenberg, *Die Vrystelling van die Slawe in die Kaapkolonie en die Implikasies Daarvan* (M.A. dissertation, University of the Orange Free State, 1959).
54. For a discussion of the effects of emancipation, see J. S. Marais, op. cit., pp. 186–208.
55. L. Duly, op. cit.
56. Cf. J. du P. Scholtz, *Die Afrikaner en sy Taal, 1806–75* (Cape Town, 1964).
57. Cf. the chapter on 'Language and Nationality, 1825–75' in vol. 2 of this work (forthcoming).
58. C. W. de Kiewiet, *A History of South Africa, Social and Economic* (Oxford, 1941), p. 35; cf. pp. 36 and 43.
59. Isobel Edwards, *Towards Emancipation: A Study in South African Slavery* (Cardiff, 1942), p. 162ff.; cf. p. 120ff.
60. T. R. H. Davenport, op cit., p. 320.

Chapter 2: The Colonial Crisis, Labour and Slavery

1. See chapter 1, section 3, *Structural constraints on colonial development*.
2. See Gerrit Schutte, *De Nederlandse Patriotten en de Koloniën* (Utrecht, 1974), p. 65, note 22.
3. Coenraad Beyers, *Die Kaapse Patriotte* (Pretoria, 1967), p. 149 and p. 67, note 1.
4. Cf. De Kiewiet's argument that the reversion of the *trekboers* to a kind of subsistence economy contrary to the supposedly 'natural' sequence of economic progression was in fact a rational response to the prevailing economic conditions of the colony, in *A History of South Africa, Social and Economic* (Oxford, 1941), pp. 10–13.
5. George M. Fredrickson, *The Black Image in the White Mind* (New York, 1971), p. 3ff, p. 43ff.
6. See chapter 1, section 7, *Slavery and the labour order*.

7. Cf. Stockenström's summary of this position in 1837, chapter 3, document **13f**.
8. Cf. W. J. Burchell, *Travels into the Interior of South Africa* (London, 1953), p. 68.
9. Eugene D. Genovese, *Roll Jordan Roll: The World the Slaves Made* (New York, 1972), pp. 4, 5, 144.
10. Margo Russell, 'Slaves or Workers? Relations between Bushmen, Tswana and Boers in the Kalahari' in *The Journal of Southern African Studies*, vol. 2, no. 3 (1976), pp. 178–97.
11. Cf. Fiscal Denyssen on the effects of the essentially coercive basis of slavery (document **2.7a**): 'The slaves are imperceptibly drawn by the bonds of slavery into secret hostility towards their masters.' In this connection it is illuminating to compare the discussion of paternalist views on the 'ingratitude' of their slaves, in Genovese, op. cit., pp. 144–7.
12. The black slaves of the West Indian island of St Domingo massacred their French masters in a rising of August 1791.

CHAPTER 3: LAW, ORDER AND EQUALITY

1. J. L. M. Franken, *Piet Retief se Lewe in die Kolonie* (Cape Town, 1949), p. 429 and note 21.
2. Quoted by Hermann Giliomee, 'The Burgher Rebellions on the Eastern Frontier, 1795–1815' in Richard Elphick and Hermann Giliomee (eds.), *The Shaping of South African Society* (Cape Town, 1978).
3. Circular letter by Governor Cradock, 20 April 1812, cited in *The Autobiography of Sir Andries Stockenström* (Cape Town, 1887), vol. 1, pp. 75–7.
4. Cf. Albie Sachs, *Justice in South Africa* (Berkeley, 1973), p. 38ff.
5. For recent discussions of the ideological functions of the 'Rule of Law' tradition in this context, cf. D. Hay, 'Property, Authority and the Criminal Law' in D. Hay *et al.* (eds.), *Albion's Fatal Tree* (New York, 1975), p. 32ff.; E. P. Thompson, *Whigs and Hunters* (New York, 1975), p. 258ff.
6. Cf. R. Ross, 'The Rule of Law at the Cape of Good Hope in the Eighteenth Century' (unpublished paper).
7. Landdrost Alberti to Governor Janssens, 12 June 1805 (B.R. 68, pp. 280–1, Cape Archives), quoted by J. S. Marais, *Maynier and the First Boer Republic* (Cape Town, 1944), p. 73, note 61.
8. J. Bird, *Annals of Natal* vol. 1, p. 459.
9. G. W. Eybers, *Select Constitutional Documents Illustrating South African History: 1795–1910* (London, 1918), p. 350.
10. Ibid., p. 364.

CHAPTER 4: THE POLITICS AND MORALITY OF FRONTIER CONFLICT

1. C. W. de Kiewiet, *A History of South Africa: Social and Economic* (Oxford, 1941), p. 49.
2. See, for example, Martin Legassick, 'The Frontier Tradition in South African Historiography' in Shula Marks and Anthony Atmore (eds.), *Economy and Society in Pre-industrial South Africa* (London, 1980); Monica Wilson, 'Co-operation and Conflict: the Eastern Cape Frontier' in Leonard Thompson and Monica Wilson (eds.), *A History of South Africa to 1870* (Cape Town, 1982), pp. 233–71.
3. In the Zuurveld, the main area of contention for the previous four decades, the frontier had closed by 1812, but it had not yet done so in the larger frontier zone east of the Fish River.
4. See P. J. van der Merwe, *Die Trekboer in die Geskiedenis van die Kaapkolonie* (Cape Town, 1938), ch. 7.
5. See W. M. MacMillan, *Bantu, Boer and Briton* (London, 1929), pp. 44, 73–4.
6. For a discussion of the openness of Xhosa society see O. F. Raum, 'A Topological Analysis of Xhosa Society', in H. J. Greschat and H. Jungraithmay (eds.), *Wort und Religion: Kalima Na Dini* (Stuttgart, 1969), pp. 321–32.
7. See also H. Lichtenstein, *Travels in Southern Africa* (Cape Town, 1928), vol. 1, pp. 268–9.
8. J. S. Marais, *Maynier and the First Boer Republic* (Cape Town, 1944), p. 29.
9. Hermann Giliomee, 'The South African Frontier: Processes in Development' in Leonard Thompson and Howard Lamar (eds.), *The Frontier in Comparative Perspective: The United States and South Africa* (New Haven, 1981).
10. J. S. Marais (op. cit., p. 9) suggested that Van Jaarsveld's account of the unpremeditated nature of the execution of the eventual stratagem might be misleading. Even so, this would not be inconsistent with the above analysis.
11. J. H. Soga, *The South-Eastern Bantu* (Johannesburg, 1930), pp. 137–8.
12. For a moving evocation of this aspect of frontier history, see Anthony Delius, *Border* (Cape Town, 1976).
13. Minutes of the Graaff-Reinet Krygsraad, 3 July 1792 (G.R. 1/9, Cape Archives); cf. P. J. van der Merwe, *Die Kafferoorlog van 1793* (Cape Town, 1940), pp. 13–14; J. S. Marais, op. cit., p. 28.
14. Hermann Giliomee, 'The Eastern Frontier, 1770–1812' in Richard Elphick and Hermann Giliomee (eds.), *The Shaping of South African Society* (Cape Town, 1979).
15. D. Moodie, *The Record,* vol. 3, p. 100. Maynier's controversial report on the origins of the war of 1793 (document **43c**) should be seen, as J. S. Marais has argued (op. cit., p. 56), not so much as a (biased) account of which party had *caused* the war, but rather as an attempt to answer the narrower question posed by his instructions: if, as the official policy held, the Xhosa were a peaceable nation averse to war, why had they nevertheless come to make it?
16. See C. F. J. Muller, *Die Britse Owerheid en die Groot Trek* (Pretoria, 1969); J. S. Galbraith, *Reluctant Empire: British Policy on the South African Frontier 1834–54* (Berkeley, 1963).
17. The correspondence between Retief and Stockenström in 1836 was published in *The Grahamstown Jour-*

nal, 17 November 1836 and in J. Chase, *The Natal Papers* (Grahamstown, 1834), p. 5ff; see also J. L. M. Franken, *Piet Retief se Lewe in die Kolonie* (Cape Town, 1949), chs. 25 and 26.

18. Document **4.9**.
19. Cf. P. J. van der Merwe, *Die Noordwaartse Beweging van die Boere voor die Groot Trek: 1770—1842* (The Hague, 1937), chs. 2 and 3.
20. Address from the burghers of Graaff-Reinet to Sir Benjamin D'Urban, 1835, signed by G. C. Ochse and 216 others, including A. W. J. Pretorius, in *Correspondence Relative to the late Caffre War* (British Parliamentary Papers, A & P, 1837), vol. 43, pp. 191–2.
21. Letter from Piet Retief to Campbell, 11 April 1836, published in J. L. M. Franken, op. cit., pp. 455–8.
22. Cf. Commissioner-General Stockenström to the Colonial Secretary, 5 May 1829, in *The Autobiography of Sir Andries Stockenström* (Cape Town, 1887), vol. I, pp. 321–3.
23. Stockenström to Spring Rice, 5 Nov. 1834, *Minutes of Evidence before the Select Committee on Aborigines,* p. 119.
24. Cf. document **4.13d** and A. H. Duminy, *The Role of Sir Andries Stockenström in Cape Politics, 1848–56*, Archives Yearbook for South African History (Pretoria, 1960/2).

Chapter 5: Settlement, Conquest and Trek

1. Cf. Henry Tudor, *Political Myth* (London, 1972), p. 91ff., also 65, 131.
2. Shula Marks, 'Khoisan Resistance to the Dutch in the 17th and 18th centuries', *Journal of African History* vol. 8 (1972), pp. 55–80.
3. Cf. e.g. J. A. Baron van Plettenberg to H. Swellengrebel, 12 May 1780 (to be published in G. J. Schutte (ed.), *De Swellengrebel Papieren*); Earl Macartney, Proclamation of 14 July 1798, *Kaapse Plakkaatboek*, vol. 5 (Cape Town, 1950), pp. 138–9.
4. Cf. Van Riebeeck's Journal, 4 April 1660, in D. Moodie, *The Record*, p. 205; landdrost of Stellenbosch to governor, 19 December 1728, Cape Archives C 441, pp. 773–5; J. Barrow, *An Account of Travels into the Interior of Southern Africa* (London, 1806), vol. 1, pp. 392–3.
5. Minutes of a combined meeting of landdrost, *heemraden* and militia officers, 26 May 1794, in Cape Archives, G.R. 1/9A.
6. P. D. Curtin (ed.), *Imperialism* (London, 1972), p. 42.
7. Emer de Vattel, *The Law of Nations* (1758), ch. 8, as reprinted in P. D. Curtin, op. cit., pp. 43–5. De Vattel departed from an older tradition, including the Spanish jurists of the 16th century as well as Grotius and Pufendorff, who did recognize the sovereignty of 'backward' peoples, and for whom imperial expansion was thus a question of the right of conquest, but not of occupation. Cf. M. F. Lindley, *The Acquisition and Government of Backward Territory in International Law* (London, 1926), pp. 12–17, 26–8, 43. For similar views applied to North America, cf. J. Story, *Commentaries on the Constitution of the United States* (Boston, 1873), p. 152, quoted in Lindley, op. cit., p. 29.
8. Albert K. Weinberg, *Manifest Destiny: A Study of Nationalist Expansionism in American History* (Baltimore, 1935).
9. F. A. van Jaarsveld, 'Die ontstaangeskiedenis van die begrippe *Voortrekker* en *Groot Trek*', *Lewende Verlede* (Johannesburg, 1961), pp. 173–201.
10. F. A. van Jaarsveld, *Die Afrikaner en sy Geskiedenis* (Johannesburg, 1959), pp. 69, 73.
11. P. J. van der Merwe, *Die Noordwaardse Beweging van die Boere voor die Groot Trek: 1770–1842* (The Hague, 1937), ch. 12; M. C. E. van Schoor, *Politieke Groeperinge in Transgariep*, Archives Year Book for South African History (Pretoria, 1950/2).

Chapter 6: Colonial Grievances, Civil Liberties and Self-government

1. R. R. Palmer, *The Age of Democratic Revolution* (Princeton, 1959), p. 7 and *passim*. On the Cape, see vol. 2, pp. 204–7.
2. Gerrit Schutte, *De Nederlandse Patriotten en de Koloniën* (Utrecht, 1974), ch. 4.
3. Coenraad Beyers, *Die Kaapse Patriotte* (Pretoria, 1967), p. 182. The text is reproduced in Beyers as Appendix A, pp. 299–309. Luzac was an enlightenend and moderate Orangist who sought to prove from natural law and Dutch history that the restoration of Stadhouderly government in 1748 had been justified. In its propensity to use ahistorical natural law arguments on the model of Locke, his writing was atypical of Dutch political thinking of this period. Cf. I. L. Loeb, *The Ideological Origins of the Batavian Revolution* (The Hague, 1973), pp. 68–75.
4. *Contra* Beyers, op. cit.; G. D. Scholtz, *Die Ontwikkeling van die Politieke Denke van die Afrikaner* (Johannesburg, 1967), vol. 1, p. 262.
5. Beyers, op. cit., Appendix A, pp. 308–9.
6. Cf. ibid., p. 186ff. The characteristic mode of argument of oppositional politics in eighteenth-century Holland, including the early works of the Dutch Patriots, also tended to invoke historical precedents rather than Enlightenment principles (cf. S. Schama, *Patriots and Liberators* (New York, 1977), p. 66ff). It was only with the 'Leiden Draft' of 1785 that we find a decisive shift 'away from the historical justification of liberty towards the more confident affirmation of self-evident natural rights' (ibid., p. 95).
7. In doing this the Cape Patriots were in fact employing a type of argument often used for the same purposes in the Netherlands itself. The 'inheritance of liberty' derived from the 'free Bataves', and the claims for restoration of burgher rights which had fallen into disuse were stock arguments of Dutch oppositional politics taken up and carried further by the Dutch Patriots. Cf. Schama, op. cit., pp. 67 and 77ff.

8. Cf. e.g. F. A. van Jaarsveld, *Van Van Riebeeck tot Verwoerd, 1652–1966* (Johannesburg, 1971), p. 58; C. F. J. Muller, *Die Oorsprong van die Groot Trek* (Cape Town, 1974) pp. 42–3.
9. F. Vranck, 'Deductie ofte Corte Vertooninghe', reprinted as an Appendix in I. L. Loeb, op. cit., p. 286.
10. C. H. E. de Wit, *De Nederlandse Revolutie van de Achttiende Eeuw, 1780–7* (Oirsbeck, 1974), pp. 12 and 63; cf. also P. W. A. Immink, 'Beschouwingen over de ontwikkeling van de begrippen volk en vertegenwoordiging', in *Publiekrechtelijke Opstellen* (*Festschrift* for C. W. van der Pot) (Zwolle, 1950), pp. 114–141.
11. De Wit, op. cit., p. 61; cf. p. 67.
12. Beyers, op. cit., p. 85; Scholtz, op. cit., vol. 1, p. 276ff.
13. G.R. 1/2, minutes of Graaff-Reinet landdrost and *heemraden*, 27 Aug 1795; cf. J. S. Marais, *Maynier and the First Boer Republic* (Cape Town, 1944), p. 83. Cf. also Hermann Giliomee, 'Democracy and the Frontier', *South African Historical Journal* (November, 1974), no. 6, p. 38ff.
14. V.C. 68 *Brieven en Bylagen*, Report of De Wet, 20 Aug 1795, pp. 13–14.
15. Giliomee, op. cit.; also Hermann Giliomee 'The Burgher Rebellions on the Eastern Frontier, 1775–1815' in Richard Elphick and Hermann Giliomee (eds.), *The Shaping of South African Society* (Cape Town, 1979).
16. H. B. Thom, *Die Lewe van Gert Maritz* (Cape Town, 1947), p. 106.
17. Eric Walker, *The Great Trek* (London, 1934), p. 127.
18. Diary of Erasmus Smit 28 June 1837, in Gustav Preller (ed.), *Voortrekkermense* (Cape Town, 1938), vol. 2, pp. 112–13.
19. H. S. Pretorius *et al.* (eds.), *Voortrekker-Argiefstukke 1829–49* (Pretoria, 1937), pp. 182–4.
20. Cf. Scholtz, op. cit., vol. 2, pp. 469–83.
21. Cf. A. H. Duminy, *The Role of Sir Andries Stockenström in Cape Politics, 1848–56*, Archives Year Book for South African History (Pretoria, 1960/2); T. E. Kirk, *Self-government and Self-defence in South Africa: the Interaction between British and Cape Politics, 1846–54* (D.Phil. dissertation, University of Oxford, 1972).

List of published sources

PRINTED BOOKS

Beyers, C. *Die Kaapse Patriotte gedurende die laaste kwart van die agtiende eeu en die voortlewing van hul denkbeelde* (Pretoria, 1967).

Bird, J. (ed.) *The Annals of Natal: 1495 to 1845,* 2 vols. (Pietermaritzburg, 1888).

Blommaert, W. and Wiid, J. A. (eds.) *The Journal of Dirk Gysbert van Reenen* (Cape Town, 1937).

Brand, C. *Dissertatio Politica-Juridica de Jure Coloniarum* (Leyden, 1820).

Breytenbach, J. H. (ed.) *Notule van die Natalse Volksraad volledig met alle bylae daarby 1838–1845* (Suid-Afrikaanse Argiefstukke, Natal no. 1).

Chase, J. C. (ed.) *The Natal Papers,* 2 vols. (Grahamstown, 1843).

Eybers, G. W. (ed.) *Select Constitutional Documents Illustrating South African History 1795–1910* (London, 1918).

Franken, J. L. M. *Piet Retief se Lewe in die Kolonie* (Cape Town, 1949).

Harlow, V. and Madden, F. (eds.) *British Colonial Development 1774–1834, Select Documents* (Oxford, 1953).

Moodie, D. *The Record, or a Series of Official Papers Relative to the Condition and Treatment of the Native Tribes of South Africa,* 3 vols. (Cape Town, 1838–1842).

Muller, C. F. J. *Johannes Frederik Kirsten oor die toestand van die Kaapkolonie in 1795: 'n Kritiese Studie* (Pretoria, 1960).

Nederlandsch Afrika; of historisch en staatkundig Tafereel van den oorsprongelijken Staat der Volksplantinge aan den Kaap de Goede Hoop, vergeleeken met den Tegenwoordigen Staat dier Volksplantinge (Leyden, 1783).

Pretorius, H. S. and Krüger, D. W. (eds.) *Voortrekker-Argiefstukke 1829–49* (Pretoria, 1937).

Ross, R. *Adam Kok's Griquas* (Cambridge, 1976).

Stockenström, A. *Autobiography of Sir Andries Stockenström,* edited by C. W. Hutton, 2 vols. (Cape Town, 1887).

Theal, G. M. (ed.) *Basutuland Records,* 3 vols. (Cape Town, 1883).

Theal G. M. (ed.) *Belangrijke historische Dokumenten verzameld in de Kaap Kolonie en Elders,* 3 vols. (Cape Town, 1896–1911).

Theal, G. M. (ed.) *Records of the Cape Colony,* 36 vols. (London, 1897–1905).

GOVERNMENT PUBLICATIONS

Cape of Good Hope, *Parliamentary Debates, 1854* (Cape Town, 1854).

Cape of Good Hope, *Correspondence between Sir George Grey and the Secretary of State for the Colonies, 1855–7* (Cape Town, 1857).

Cape of Good Hope, *Documents Relative to the Question of a Separate Government for the Eastern Districts of the Cape Colony,* Cape Blue Book of 1857 (Cape Town, 1857).

Cape of Good Hope, *Masters and Servants Blue Book* (Cape Town, 1849).

Great Britain, House of Commons, Parliamentary Papers, *Minutes of Evidence before the Select Committee on Aborigines* (London, 1835).

Great Britain, House of Commons, Parliamentary Papers, *Papers Relative to the Condition and Treatment of the Native Inhabitants of the Cape of Good Hope,* Imperial Blue Book 252 of 1835 (London, 1835).

Netherlands, States General, *Kaapsche Geschillen* (Amsterdam, 1785).

JOURNALS AND NEWSPAPERS

The Argus.

The Cape of Good Hope Observer.

The Cape Town Gazette and African Advertiser.

The Cape Town Mail.

The Grahamstown Journal.

The Journal of Secondary Education.

Het Nederduitsch Zuid-Afrikaansche Tijdschrift.

Ons Tijdschrift.

De Post van de Neder Rhijn.

The South African Commercial Advertiser.

De Zuid-Afrikaan.

Index to the documents

Artoys, B. J.; *Burgher Petition;* 9 Oct. 1779; **2.1a, 6.1b**
—— (possibly); *Dutch Africa;* 1783; **6.2**
Aucamp, P. and others; memorial on Ordinance 50; 5 Feb. 1829; **3.9b**
——; memorial of Colesberg inhabitants; June 1837; **3.13a**
Bergh, E.; Memoir on the Cape of Good Hope; 1802; **5.1, 6.6**
Bester, B. and others; *Tesamenstemming;* 29 Jan. 1795; **4.4a**
——; letter of complaint to Commissary Sluysken; 16 April 1795; **4.4b**
Boshof, J. N.; letter in *The Grahamstown Journal;* 17 Feb. 1839; **3.14, 6.10a**
——; letter from the Natal Volksraad to Governor Napier; 21 Feb. 1842; **5.6c, 6.10b**
——; minutes of conference with Chief Moshweshwe; 5 Oct. 1855; **4.19a**
——; letter to Chief Moshweshwe; 27 June 1856; **4.19b**
——; letter to Sir George Grey; 16 March 1859; **4.19c**
Botha, Commandant and others; letter to Governor Janssens; 22 May 1803; **4.6**
Brand, C.; *De Jure Coloniarum;* 1820; **5.2, 6.7**
——; speech at a meeting of slaveholders; 17 Sept. 1832; **3.10, 6.8e**
—— (probably); editorial in *De Zuid-Afrikaan;* 3 May 1839; **2.11c**
——; editorial; 5 Nov. 1846; **4.16**
——; speech in the Legislative Council; 21 Sept. 1850; **6.13a**
Brand, J. H.; letter to Chief Moshweshwe; 10 Feb. 1864; **4.20b**
——; letter to Chief Moshweshwe; 25 Aug. 1865; **4.20c**
Bresler, F. R.; letters to General Craig; 2 March and 26 May 1796; **6.5b**
Bresler, F. R.; court pleading; 28 May 1801; **2.4**
Bührmann, H. T.; letter from the Lydenburg Executive; 3 April 1860; **5.10**
Burger, A. P. and others; petition of Graaff-Reinet landdrost and heemraden; 12 July 1791; **6.4b**
—— and A. van Jaarsveld; memorial; 7 May 1795; **4.4c**
Burgher Councillors; letters to Commissaries Nederburgh and Frykenius; 25 June 1792; **6.4c**
Burgher Senate; memorial on Ordinance 19; 30 June 1826; **2.8a**
Camdeboo, inhabitants of; letter to Governor van Plettenberg; 24 March 1778; **3.1**
Cape Court of Justice; letter to General Craig; 14 Jan. 1796; **3.3**
Cape Patriots; anonymous pamphlet; 1778; **6.1a**
——; *Burgher Petition*; 9 Oct. 1779; **2.1a, 6.1b**
——; petition to the Governor; 17 Feb. 1784; **2.1b**
——; letter; 1787; **6.3**
Cape Town, citizens of; memorial to the Burgher Senate on Ordinance 19; 3 July 1826; **2.8b**
——; petition; 15 July 1826; **6.8a**
Changuion, Dr A. N. E.; editorial; 30 June 1856; **4.18c**
Cloete, H.; speech at a public meeting; July 1831; **6.8c**
——; speech at a public meeting; 24 Aug. 1841; **6.11**
Colesberg, inhabitants of; memorial to A. Stockenström; June 1837; **3.13a**
——; letter; July 1837; **3.13c**
Conradie, J. H. and others; petition; 1798; **3.4b**
De Buys, C.; letter to the landdrost of Graaff-Reinet; 6 April 1798; **4.2a**
Denyssen, D.; letter to Colonel Reynell; 27 Feb. 1813; **2.7a**
——; speech as public prosecutor; 18 March 1823; **2.7b**
De Wet, J.; lecture; 1838; **5.4b**
——; speech on the Burgher Force Bill; 11 April 1855; **4.18a**
De Wet, O. G.; letter to Governor van Plettenberg; 13 March 1780; **4.1a**
——; landdrost's minutes; 7 Aug. 1780; **2.2**
——; letter from Cape Court of Justice to General Craig; 14 Jan. 1796; **3.3**
De Zuid-Afrikaan; editorial; 20 May 1831; **6.8b**
——; editorial; 3 June 1831; **6.8b**
——; editorial on Ordinance 50; 23 March 1832; **3.9c**
——; editorial; 22 June 1832; **6.8d**